Bridge of Light

Bridge of Light

YIDDISH FILM BETWEEN TWO WORLDS

J. Hoberman

THE MUSEUM OF MODERN ART
New York
SCHOCKEN BOOKS
New York

Copyright © 1991 The Museum of Modern Art, New York
Text copyright © 1991 J. Hoberman

All rights reserved under International and Pan-American Copyright Conventions. Published in the United States by Schocken Books Inc., New York, and simultaneously in Canada by Random House of Canada Limited, Toronto. Distributed by Pantheon Books, a division of Random House, Inc., New York.

Library of Congress Cataloging-in-Publication Data

Hoberman, J.
    Bridge of Light: Yiddish Film Between Two Worlds/
J. Hoberman.
        p.   cm.
    ISBN 0-8052-4107-8
    1. Motion pictures, Yiddish—History.   I. Title.
PN1995.9.Y54H6   1991
791.43'089'924—dc20   91-7609

Illustrations copyright © The National Center for Jewish Film are listed individually in the Photograph Credits, page 381.

Book design by Binns & Lubin/Betty Binns
MANUFACTURED IN THE UNITED STATES OF AMERICA

Published on the occasion of the exhibition "Yiddish Film Between Two Worlds," organized jointly by The Museum of Modern Art, New York, and The National Center for Jewish Film, Brandeis University, Waltham, Massachusetts; shown at The Museum of Modern Art, New York, November 14, 1991–January 11, 1992.

Grateful acknowledgment is made to the following for permission to reprint previously published material:

Crown Publishers Inc.: Excerpt from "Dreyfus in Kasrilevke" from *The Old Country* by Sholom Aleichem. Copyright © 1946, 1974 by Crown Publishers Inc. Reprinted by permission.

Andrew R. MacAndrew: Excerpts from "The Rabbi's Son" and "Zamostye" from *Lyubka the Cossack* by Isaac Babel, translated by Andrew R. MacAndrew and published by New American Library in 1963. Reprinted by permission of the translator.

University of California Press: Excerpt from "Goodnight World" by Jacob Glatstein from *American Yiddish Poetry*, edited by Benjamin and Barbara Harshaw. Copyright © 1986 by The Regents of the University of California. Reprinted by permission.

Contents

Acknowledgments

This book owes its existence to two institutions: The National Center for Jewish Film (NCJF) at Brandeis University, Waltham, Massachusetts, which provided me with unprecedented access to their films, files, and photographic materials, and The Museum of Modern Art, New York. A generous grant to the Museum from the John D. and Catherine T. MacArthur Foundation supported my research and this publication. Additionally, The Nathan Cummings Foundation assisted with support for curatorial research and the presentation of the exhibition "Yiddish Film Between Two Worlds," which this book accompanies.

Sharon Rivo and Mimi Krant, who have made the NCJF the world's major repository for Yiddish films, gave unstintingly of their time, energy, and encouragement, as did Adrienne Mancia, film curator at The Museum of Modern Art, who first suggested this book and served as co-curator, with Sharon Rivo and myself, of the accompanying program. Mary Lea Bandy, Director of the Department of Film at The Museum of Modern Art, has provided consistent support, without which this project would not have been possible. Thanks are also due her Museum colleagues Harriet S. Bee, Managing Editor in the Department of Publications, and Eileen Bowser, Mary Corliss, Anne Morra, and Charles Silver, all of the Department of Film. Marek Web and Roberta

Newman greatly assisted my research at the YIVO Institute; Lia van Leer and Paula Weiman-Kelman made working at the Jerusalem Cinémathèque a pleasure; Marilyn Koolik and Hillel Tryster were most forthcoming in allowing me access to material at the Steven Spielberg Jewish Film Archive.

Hagit Gal-Ed of the Klav Library of the Hebrew Union College; David Bartholomew at the Billy Rose Theatre Collection, New York Public Library; Denise Gluck at the American Joint Distribution Committee; Andrij Makuch of the Department of Slavic Languages and Literatures, University of Toronto; and Bob Burger of the Slavic Reference Service, University of Illinois, were particularly helpful. The late Mark Strotchkov of Gosfilmofond, Kati Vajda at Hungarofilm, Waldemar Piatek of the Filmoteka Polska; and Stefan Hvezdoslan of Ceskoslovensky Filmovy Ustav were instrumental in furnishing rare films and stills. Francine Keery and Jennifer Cotter provided superb frame enlargements and copy photographs. The history of Yiddish film is written not just in Yiddish and English but in Hebrew, Polish, Russian, Ukrainian, German, French, and Spanish. Thus, I owe a singular debt to my translators—Nina Warnke, Daniel Kazimierski, and Virlana Tkacz, as well as Sarah Bachmuth, Vital Drezdner, Joseph Gordon, Rita Karin, Ellen Kellman, Rita Klein, Françoise Mouly, Ann Nelson, Paula Parsky, Annamaria Rona, and Eve Sicular.

It is my hope that *Bridge of Light* will itself mediate between two worlds, facilitating the integration of Yiddish films (individually and collectively) into the history of world cinema, while suggesting a fertile field of study for Yiddishists. I count myself fortunate to have received assistance from colleagues in a half-dozen countries working in at least as many disciplines. This book would have been considerably depleted were it not for the generosity of Kevin Brownlow, Paul Buhl, Ian Christie, Lucjan Dobroszycki, Eva Forgas, Sylvia Fuks Fried, Natan Gross, Tom Gunning, Miriam Hansen, Barbara Kirshenblatt-Gimblett, Naum Kleiman, Richard Koszarski, Edith Kramer, the late Jay Leyda, David Marc, Boleslaw Michalek, Hankus Netsky, Henry Saposnik, Ella Shohat, Michael Steinlauf, Joseph Skvorecky, Richard Taylor, Slava Tsukerman, and Mel Gordon, who contributed to this project in too many ways to enumerate. The book owes much of its strength to them; its deficiencies are, of course, my own.

Ken Jacobs first alerted me to the existence of Yiddish movies (as to much else) in 1969; Richard Goldstein encouraged me to write about them for the *Village Voice* in 1976; Omus Hirshbein made it possible for me to program Yiddish films at the Ninety-second Street YM-YWHA for three seasons from 1977 through 1980. Special gratitude is due Sara Bershtel, who painstakingly edited an unwieldy manuscript through two drafts. My thanks to Fred Jordan, who took over the job and saw it to completion, to Osa Brown for providing a title, to Ed Cohen for his wryly exacting copy editing, and to Jessica Altholz for expert editorial assistance. A timely fellowship from the John Simon Guggenheim Foundation allowed me to focus my attention and bring the project to completion. And thanks to Shelley and to Mara and Anna, for whom five summers were synonymous with Dad's Yiddish book.

J. HOBERMAN
New York, June 1991

Author's Note

With the exception of proper names and those words which have entered the English language, all Yiddish transliterations follow the YIVO system. Films are initially identified in the language of their original release, followed by an English translation in parentheses. If the translation is the same as the American release title, it is italicized; if not, it is in roman type. Films with Yiddish titles are referred to subsequently by their Yiddish titles; non-Yiddish foreign films, by the English translations of their titles, italicized. Endnotes follow each chapter; bibliographic references, arranged by chapter, follow the entire text.

Bridge of Light

INTRODUCTION

A Brivele der Mamen

I N THE YEARS before the First World War, a new sort of performer joined the itinerant organ-grinders and folksingers who crisscrossed the Russian Empire, traveling from town to town, entertaining villagers with topical songs and sentimental laments. These were practitioners of what in Russian was called *kino-deklamatsye* (film recitation): they projected movies, mainly travelogues and brief dramas, that spoke—thanks to the accompaniment of a gramophone or a live actor concealed behind a curtain.

Introduced at the 1900 Paris World's Fair and popularized in Germany several years later, this primitive form of talking pictures proved particularly resilient in Russia, where the indigenous cinema's languorous narrative rhythms and "poetic" moods encouraged the use of external sound accompaniment. A. M. Smolensky's "singing" troupe was one of many *kino-deklamatsye* companies that toured the Russian provinces, but it was the first, apparently, to specifically address the huge Jewish audience concentrated in—and confined to—that area of western Russia known as the Pale of Settlement, a tract extending from the Baltic to the Black Sea, encompassing the Ukraine, Belorussia, Lithuania, and Congress Poland.

Smolensky "performs in Yiddish," the Russian trade journal *Cine-Phono* reported. "He plays the leading role, illustrating comic and dramatic scenes from Jewish life." In September 1911, Smolensky

A movie house in Belorussia, 1914. The poster advertises the film *Twin Sisters.*

premiered *A Brivele der Mamen* (A Little Letter to Mother) at the Modern Electric Theater in Minsk. The presentation was named for and included a rendition of the phenomenally popular ballad by Solomon Smulevits in which an Old World mother pleads for news from her absent, emigrant child. The song's articulation of maternal longing had already taken New York's Lower East Side by storm. The Pale followed: in 1912, Smolensky was reported performing *A Brivele der Mamen* in the southeast Ukrainian city Yekaterinoslav, while a thousand miles away a teenage boy, the future Soviet-Yiddish writer Mark Naumovich Daniel, saw the same *kino-deklamatsye* in his Latvian hometown. "They are showing a Yiddish film, *A Brivele der Mamen,* in the cinema. A real-life artiste has come all the way from Warsaw [*sic*]. For the entire show, he stands behind the screen on which the silent people move. He sings but we cannot see him."

The territory Smolensky toured was a vast pressure cooker in which collective impoverishment pushed against political and economic constraints. Throughout the nineteenth century, restless Jews circulated within its borders, their numbers increasing fourfold between 1800 and 1880. The next third of a century, bracketed by the assassination of Tsar Alexander II in 1881 and the outbreak of the World War in 1914, saw a Jewish exodus unequaled since the expulsion from Spain—a migration that received additional impetus from the pogroms that preceded and followed the failed revolution of 1905. Fully one-third of Russia's Jews abandoned their homes, venturing westward to Poland and beyond.

New York's Lower East Side was the greatest of immigrant Jewish settlements. In 1910, this clamorous city within a city reached its maximum density —more than half a million souls crammed into a few square miles of vermin-infested tenements.

There, as in the immigrant Jewish neighborhoods of other American cities, storefront theaters featured movies with Yiddish intertitles or Yiddish-speaking lecturers, concessions to the audience that persisted, at least on the East Side, up until the First World War. The movie star Paul Muni (born Muni Weisenfreund to a family of Yiddish actors) made his first stage appearance at one such nickelodeon, playing the violin while his brothers sang Yiddish ballads and the management projected appropriate magic-lantern slides. These were a form of Yiddish cinema too, though neither as polished nor as well publicized as *A Brivele der Mamen.*

Smolensky's performance of the American lament was not only Mark Daniel's "First Time at the Movies" but the paradigmatic example of a Yiddish film. At once modern and nostalgic, insular and cosmopolitan, *A Brivele der Mamen* heralded a peripatetic cinema produced at various times in a half dozen countries by a unique mixture of naïve businessmen and opportunistic idealists who, balancing an intimate involvement with their public against a dialectical relationship to larger film industries, drew upon a popular culture that transcended national boundaries no less than cinema itself.[1]

The Yiddish cinema, which came to supplement and in some places supplant the Yiddish stage, is today a relic, but, like all cinemas, it was once a novelty of the marketplace. Indeed, save for a brief period on the eve of World War II, when new Yiddish-language talkies appeared in New York movie houses virtually every month, the Yiddish cinema was a perpetual novelty. The flow of Yiddish movies was rarely sustained; each release was something of an event. As Natan Gross, one of the last practitioners of the form, noted in his history of Jewish film in Poland, "Yiddish film was *tsholnt* [sabbath stew], never bread."

Novel for its audience, that broad, shifting spectrum of Jewish life between orthodoxy and assimilation, the Yiddish cinema is also novel in the history of cinema. Drawing upon an established dramatic and literary tradition, yet employing a language virtually unknown to the Gentile world and considered by many of its users to be only a "jargon," this was not just a national cinema without a nation-state, but a national cinema that, with every presentation, created its own ephemeral nation-state. A language charged with ideology, Yiddish was most important for those nationalists who rejected religion but resisted the Zionist insistence on a reconstructed homeland. For the Yiddishists gathered in conference in the Galician city of Czernowitz during the summer of 1908, Yiddish was not just a language and a folk culture but an entire Jewish world, a *"Yidishland."*

The reflection of national aspirations and victim of nationalist passions, *Yidishland*'s cinema lasted scarcely more than a quarter of a century. The Yiddish word *yidish* (Jewish) identifies a people as well as a language and, in this sense, a Yiddish cinema—made by Jews for a presumably Jewish audience —predates the invention of talking pictures. Like the Yiddish sound cinema, its silent precursor drew on familiar themes in East European and immigrant Jewish culture, adapted works of Yiddish literature, and employed the personnel of the Yiddish stage.

The development of Yiddish cinema has five distinct phases: the first, beginning in 1911 and ending during the World War, coincides with the development of movies as a mass medium and marks the discovery of a Jewish film audience in the tsarist empire and, to a lesser degree, in the United States. Although Warsaw, then a Russian city, was the first center of Jewish film production, the New York Yiddish stage provided much of its material. Most movies were taken from American Yiddish plays, mainly those by Jacob Gordin and his followers, which had only recently been introduced in Eastern Europe. Although scores of such films were produced, virtually none survive.

A second phase of Yiddish film production, presaged by developments in the United States on the eve of the World War, begins with the fall of the tsar in 1917 and extends a dozen years, through the end of the silent period. This period is characterized

An Old Testament fantasy: the fated lovers Yankev (Henryk Tarło) and Rokhl (Ida Kaminska) double as the Biblical Jacob and Rachel in Zygmunt Turkow's *Tkies Kaf* (Poland, 1924).

by sporadic but ambitious attempts to make specifically Jewish movies within the industries of three "new" states—Austria, Poland, and the Soviet Union. Less dependent than earlier films upon the Yiddish stage, these efforts drew upon the work of Yiddish and Jewish novelists—most importantly Sholom Aleichem, but also Isaac Babel, Joseph Opatoshu, and Harry Seckler. (The writings of I. L. Peretz and Sh. An-sky provided further models even though none were adapted.) In general, the Yiddish films of the late silent era were progressive, youth-oriented, and controversial, exhibiting the influence of various vanguard tendencies—Symbolism, expressionism, Futurism, communism—even when concerned with the Jewish past. A half dozen major examples exist, albeit some only in fragmentary form.

Basically a European development, this second phase was weakest in the United States (where Jewish movies competed with assimilationist "melting-pot" films) and strongest in the Soviet Union—at least up until the Stalinist consolidation of 1928. The third phase of Yiddish cinema, that of the early sound period, was, however, an almost entirely American phenomenon. The first synchronous Yiddish talkie was made in 1929 in New York City, eighteen months after *The Jazz Singer* broke the sound barrier with its own particular representation of the Jewish dilemma. Over the next five years, some twenty features and as many short subjects appeared in the context of independent ethnic production and foreign film distribution. Inherently less universal than their silent precursors, these were "exploitation" films that attempted to attract the Jewish audience with everything from canned vaudeville acts and displays of cantorial virtuosity to Biblical pageants,

Mother and sons: Lucy German, Irving Bruner, and Itskhok Grudberg (left) in Joseph Green's *A Brivele der Mamen* (Poland, 1939).

dubbed silent films, and political documentaries. Despite technical and economic difficulties, the period is characterized by two major accomplishments: *Uncle Moses* and the lone Soviet-Yiddish talkie *Nosn Beker Fort Aheym (The Return of Nathan Becker)*, both 1932.

The fourth, and best-known, phase of Yiddish film production began with the rejuvenation of the Polish movie industry in 1935. The first Polish-Yiddish talkies stimulated American producers and initiated a dialogue between Warsaw and New York that continued up until the severing of the Yiddish markets with World War II. This so-called Golden Age coincides with the period of the Popular Front against fascism, and is characterized by several inter-national hits, notably *Yidl mitn Fidl (Yiddle with His Fiddle;* Poland, 1936), *Grine Felder (Green Fields;* U.S.A., 1937), and *Der Dibek (The Dybbuk;* Poland, 1937). Yiddish cinema reached its zenith during the eighteen months between Germany's annexation of Austria in 1937 and the Nazi-Soviet invasion of Poland. During this period, twenty-three films opened in New York—one-third made in Warsaw, and all but seven set in Eastern Europe—and then made their way to Jewish enclaves throughout North and South America. The last Polish-Yiddish feature to open in New York, another version of *A Brivele der Mamen*, was released in September 1939. Within two years, American production had ceased as well.

A fifth phase of Yiddish film production is concentrated in the immediate post–World War II period (1945–50) but, in a general sense, may be said to continue up until the present. It is characterized by a modest and unsuccessful attempt to revive Yiddish cinema in Poland, the United States, and, belatedly, Israel; it returns Yiddish cinema to filmed theater, and retrospectively transmutes every scrap of Yiddish footage into a precious artifact.

Of course, for East European Jews, the preservationist impulse was itself modern. At precisely the moment that Smolensky and other itinerant showmen brought the new recording technology to the *shtetl* (Jewish market town) as entertainment, others used that same technology to document the *shtetl*'s folkways. Between 1911 and 1914, Sh. An-sky headed an expedition for the Jewish Historic-Ethnographic Society of St. Petersburg. Armed with cameras and recording equipment, An-sky and his associates plumbed the tiny hamlets of Belorussia and the Ukraine, transcribing Jewish legends, noting spells and remedies, collecting songs and proverbs, photographing old synagogues and cemeteries, and purchasing ceremonial objects, jewelry, and clothing. This material became the core of the Jewish Ethnographic Museum established in Petrograd in 1916.

The fruits of An-sky's research also include *Der Dibek,* the Symbolist drama of possession and exorcism which, written originally in Russian and first performed in Yiddish as *Tsvishn Tsvey Veltn* (Between Two Worlds), became at once the epitome of Yiddish modernism and the most celebrated single work in the Yiddish theatrical canon. One can imagine the An-sky expedition and the Smolensky troupe crossing paths in some *farvorfn vinkl* (secluded nook). Showmen and scientists, reverse images of each other, both trafficked in miraculously disembodied voices and faraway visions. One (but which?) came to record the twilight; the other to announce the dawn.

Despite a tendency toward nostalgia and the additional pathos with which we cannot help but invest it, the Yiddish cinema was initially contemporary and secular. It was, at least initially, a world of the sons. The men who made Yiddish movies were mainly in their thirties and some were a good deal younger. Cinema is "the art of our era," proclaimed the Polish-Jewish journalist S. L. Shneiderman— then barely out of his teens—in the first issue of *Film Velt* (Film World), a short-lived Warsaw magazine published at the end of the silent period, entirely in Yiddish. For Shneiderman and his equally youthful colleagues, it was imperative that Jewish film production take its place beside other Jewish cultural activities and among other national film industries. Motion pictures could elevate Yiddish culture to new dignity; the "new Jewish man" would be the subject rather than simply the object of cinema (and history). As both Zionism and the Jewish labor movement attempted to instill new pride in East European Jews, Shneiderman's rhetoric echoed prevalent assertions that the Jews were a nation like any other.

This new Yiddish culture was at home neither with the Jewish past nor the Gentile present. As Yiddish artists and intellectuals embraced secular ideologies and opened themselves to their surroundings, they risked the loss of tribal identity; similarly, because the movies were a public sphere, even the creation of a specifically Jewish cinema jeopardized Jewish insularity. For the image-conscious, any representation of Jewish life might provoke anti-Semitism. Looking over their shoulders as well as at the screen, Jews imagined seeing themselves through Gentile eyes. In fact, this was also a projection. Although Shneiderman subscribed to the progressive notion of film as a universal language ("Cinema bridges culture. . . . Through film we can acquaint the world with our literature and with our cultural characteristics"), this was not to be. Yiddish was an international language but, with few exceptions, the audience for Yiddish films was entirely Jewish and predominantly lower-class.

In most countries, only the first movie public was the urban proletariat; in *Yidishland,* it would largely remain so. The American audience for Yiddish films was frozen in a pre–World War configuration—an audience of immigrants and workers. This, perhaps, was inherent in the language itself. Yiddish is imbued with the perspective of the *proster Yid* (common Jew), and, from eighteenth-century Chasidism through twentieth-century socialism, it was the vehicle for those movements that drew strength from below. Earthy, expressive, marked by the experience of dispersion and marginality, and lacking the scriptural authority of Hebrew, Yiddish is neither entirely respectful nor altogether respectable. For religious Jews, it is the language of the secular world; for the "enlightened," the signifier of Jewish insularity.

If Jewish modernizers were antagonistic or indifferent to Yiddish, political expediency dictated its use. The same was true of filmmakers, a number of whom were assimilated Russian, Polish, and Austrian Jews who learned (or relearned) Yiddish in order to make Yiddish movies.

The appeal of Yiddish and the thematics of a Yiddish cinema are inscribed in the very phrase *"a brivele der mamen"* and the ballad of the abandoned Old Country mother. That Yiddish is known to itself as *mame-loshn* (mother tongue) only doubles the urgency of her cry; that "A Brivele der Mamen" was a song written and first popularized in New York underscores the constructed quality of Yiddish mass culture.

Eternally Janus-faced, Yiddish cinema addressed the dislocation between the Old Country and the New World, parent and child, folk community and industrial society, worker and *allrightnik,* that existed within each member of the audience. If individual films often precipitated a conflict between tradition and modernity, the Yiddish cinema in toto can be seen as something of an extended family quarrel. The titles of the movies, like those of Yiddish plays

Theatrical agent's office shown in Joseph Seiden's *Mayn Zundele* (U.S.A., 1939). On the wall are photographs of leading Yiddish stage personalities, including Molly Picon and Ludwig Satz.

Joseph Green's *A Brivele der Mamen* at the
Clinton Theater, a Lower East Side movie
house specializing in Yiddish film and
variety, autumn 1939. The sign above the
marquee reads "Vaudeville."

and novels, invoke blood ties and household relations.

Soviet-Jewish movies most often detailed the misery of the tsarist oppression; Polish films, more fa-
talistic and fanciful, characteristically drew on
Chasidic folklore. However tendentious or sensation-
alizing, both evinced a preservationist impulse that
transcended ideology. The most persistent strain in
American-Yiddish cinema, however, was the family
melodrama: with their images of psychic and domestic disintegration, of unhappy upward mobility, of
Americanized children rejecting, abandoning, or otherwise being lost to the parents who have suffered
and sacrificed for them, such films dramatized the
anxieties of recent immigrants, the disruptive effect
that the New World had on traditional values.

There is a stark, aggressively unmodulated quality
to their tear-jerking that suggests an entirely different tradition than that of the more genteel Hollywood weepies—still, however grimly, these films
share the optimistic trajectory that characterizes
most American mass culture. Indeed, in the 1930s,
the drama critic A. Mukdoyni complained that New
York's Yiddish stage seemed "limited by a coterie of
five librettists with a lesser number of plots [all] re-
volving around the need for a grand wedding scene."
The wedding, of course, is the source of much traditional Jewish music and dance. It is the milieu of
those *shtetl* entertainers, the *klezmer* and the *badkhn*
(a combination bard, master-of-ceremonies, and
stand-up comedian). The wedding, likewise ubiquitous in Yiddish film, also signifies the perpetuation
of the Jewish people according to the customs of the
tribe.

Joyous or pathetic, comic or macabre, the wedding
is the favored set piece of the Yiddish cinema. But
this implicit emphasis on cultural continuity scarcely
papers over the profound uneasiness that haunts
many Yiddish movies. While pogroms, steerage,
poverty, anti-Semitism, and other dismal facts of
contemporary Jewish life are downplayed, Yiddish
cinema is hardly escapist. Rather, it is a site where
historical and cultural forces converged to find often
nightmarish representation—a celluloid commentary on the sixty-seven years (not quite the Biblical
three score and ten) from the assassination of the
tsar to the birth of Israel that may be the most cata-
clysmic period in Jewish history.

If, as Oskar Negt and Alexander Kluge argue in their theory of the public sphere, forms of "proletarian publicity" emerge only during "rifts in the movement of history" (economic crisis, war, revolution, counterrevolution), the Yiddish cinema was born mid-earthquake. Taken as a single utterance, it is a sustained response to the destruction of the East European *heym* (home) which began in the nineteenth century and, increasingly violent, climaxed with the annihilation of East European Jewry during the Second World War. Unlike that of the Yiddish stage or Yiddish literature, the historical memory of Yiddish cinema extends back no further than the mid-nineteenth century, the childhood of its eldest spectators. Its story is the passage from *shtetl* to city, from Old Country to New World; this saga may be dramatized as unwilling expulsion or necessary abandonment, but it is the representation of loss just the same.

Like all secular Yiddish culture, a burning bridge suspended between traditional Jewishness and the civilization of the West, a Yiddish cinema was inherently unstable. The films themselves are often self-contradictory. Images of successful assimilation compete with yearning for the irretrievable simplicity of *shtetl* life; ancient folkways are savored alongside emblems of Jewish progress beyond super-stition. Implicit in these discrepancies, however, is the urge for totality, the desire for a complete and self-contained Jewish world. No matter how debased or clichéd, disjointed or incoherent, each Yiddish movie offered the imaginary fulfillment of a new *Yidishland*.

In its evocation of realms where Jewish peasants tilled the soil and even police or party officials might address the spectator in *mame-loshn*, Yiddish cinema shares that utopian component common to all popular entertainment. But, given the necessity for East European Jews to escape their concrete circumstances and the failure of many to do so, it is a utopia shadowed by history—a utopia rendered desperate, complex, and poignant by a uniquely Jewish struggle for equilibrium in the epochal shift between two worlds.

NOTE

1. Yiddish is the vernacular of the Ashkenazim (from *Ashkenaz*, the medieval Hebrew name for Germany) and, like English, a fusion tongue. An amalgam of High Middle German, Hebrew, Aramaic, and various Slavic languages, Yiddish is one of two European Jewish languages that evolved during the Middle Ages. (The other is Ladino, derived largely from Spanish and spoken by the Sephardim.)

Overleaf: **"In Kino" (At the Movies), a Jewish New Year's card, printed in Warsaw, circa 1910.**

1

Wandering Stars

ON DECEMBER 28, 1895, when the Lumière brothers rented a basement room in a Paris café to exhibit their new *"cinématographe"* to the public, there were some eleven million Jews in the world. Nearly half lived in tsarist Russia, in the Pale of Settlement, and there a Jewish movie audience first announced itself during the summer of 1898—two years after the *cinématographe* was introduced in Odessa—when Francis Doublier, a teenaged employee of the Lumières, toured the cities of the southern Pale with a program of short documentary *"actualités."*

Doublier arrived at the height of the Dreyfus affair, shortly after Emile Zola's second conviction and the sensational suicide of confessed forger Major Hubert-Joseph Henry had further stimulated an already intense interest among Russian Jews. Not surprisingly, the Jews of Kishinev wondered about the absence of Dreyfus material in Doublier's presentation. The young showman didn't have to be asked twice. By the time he reached Zhitomir, his program included an extra attraction. Anticipating the montage experiments of Lev Kuleshov, Doublier assembled a new movie, splicing together four shots—a French military parade, a Paris street scene with an imposing building, a Finnish tugboat meeting a barge, and a panorama of the Nile delta. These, he informed spectators, presented Dreyfus before his arrest, the

Palais de Justice where Dreyfus was court-martialed, the boat that took him to Devil's Island, and finally Devil's Island itself.

"Thus some unsuspecting French soldier became the screen's first recorded Jew," Patricia Erens writes in her study of Jews in American movies. Thus too, a Jewish audience demanded and received recognition. "The customers shed tears," Doublier would later recall, and the willingness with which his audiences believed they were witnessing the events of 1894—a year before the *cinématographe* was even invented!—should tell us something about the importance of representation in the mass media and the significance of shared fantasy in communal life. The Jewish audience was starved for images of itself. It was as Sholom Aleichem wrote of one impresario in his 1913 novel *Blondzhende Shtern* (Wandering Stars), a compressed, satirical history of the Yiddish stage: "Whatever he chose to give them, they would lick their fingers and come back for more."[1]

The first Russian movie houses appeared around 1904. In the heavily Jewish city of Dvinsk, according to one Yiddish memoirist, the "new wonder" was unveiled at a hall with the imposing name of Grand Electro: "How my heart palpitated as I entered this strange emporium for the first time . . . and what a melange could be seen there—murderers, weddings, markets, horses, cattle." Admission was twice that for the local Yiddish theater. Introduced in the cities, the movies proliferated throughout the Pale. In March 1911, a correspondent for *Cine-Phono* observed that "soon in Volhynia you won't be able to find a single more or less decent-sized *shtetl* with a population of five to seven thousand where, during the evenings, there will not flicker the alluring lights of illusion."

As in America, many of Russia's early movie exhibitors and distributors were Jews. Still, Sam Silverstein—who, between 1909 and 1914, operated the Illusion movie theater on the main street of Balta, a railroad junction in the southern Ukraine—maintains that Jewish subject matter would have been considered subversive. (This was scarcely unique: in addition to banning movies dealing with the French Revolution and Mary Stuart, tsarist censorship forbade orchestral accompaniment and filmed farces, at least in the Ukraine.) Nevertheless, some Jewish material did circulate. *L'khaym* (To Life), a bucolic tragedy of *shtetl* life, played by a non-Jewish cast despite its Hebrew title, was released in early 1911 by Pathé Frères's Moscow studio, and proved a considerable hit.

Directed by Kai Hansen from Alexander Arkatov's scenario, *L'khaym* leavened a conventional story of an unhappy marriage with a few authentic details (a *shabes* meal and a traditional Jewish wedding). *Cine-Phono* reported the attention this four-reel "picture of unprecedented content" received in one Belorussian city:

The whole of Mogilev has become interested in this cinematographic pearl and considers it necessary to see it. Everyone, old and young, flocked towards the beckoning lights of the Charm electric theater. . . . All were captivated by this original picture. [*L'khaym*] was screened for seven days with exceptionally colossal success and generated great takings.

L'khaym's popularity was not confined to the Russian Pale. The film played throughout Western Europe, reaching New York in May 1911.

The bucolic *shtetl*: Pathé Frères's popular *L'khaym,* (Russia, 1911), reported in the Russian trade press as "a picture of unprecedented content"; frame enlargement.

The same year, which also saw Smolensky's *A Brivele der Mamen,* Ya'acov Davidon, Tel Aviv's pioneer exhibitor, toured the Pale with a documentary on life in the Yishev (the Jewish settlement in Palestine): "Tears of happiness gleamed in the eyes of Jewish audiences, thirsty for redemption." Such travelogues were eagerly received. Another long-touring sensation—distributed in 1913 by the Odessa firm Mizrakhi, whose Zionist orientation is implicit in its name (Hebrew for "east")—was an *actualité* contrasting Jewish life in Palestine with that in Russia, Western Europe, and America.

For a time, the Pale provided an avid audience for French-made Biblical films. Silverstein recalled that

his greatest financial success was a movie based on the story of Abraham and Isaac. "People came from all over and every grandson brought his grandfather." In mid-1911, Gaumont distributed a film that anticipated Cecil B. De Mille's *Ten Commandments* in drawing from the Book of Exodus; its advertisements seem written to attract a Jewish audience, promising such "majestic scenes" as "the first Jewish Passover, the slaying of the Egyptian first-born, [and] the exodus of the Hebrews from Egypt." Parallels to the tsarist empire could scarcely have been ignored. Soon after, Biblical adaptations were banned.

In Warsaw, which had supplanted Odessa as the

European center of Yiddish culture (and would now rival the Ukrainian city as a film producer), the first Jewish movies were part of a general revival of the Yiddish stage. In 1905, Tsar Nicholas II rescinded his father's twenty-two-year ban on Yiddish performances. (While Yiddish theater had been thriving in the immigrant neighborhoods of London and New York, those itinerant actors who remained in the Pale often posed as German companies, using the artificial, German-inflected Yiddish known as *Daytshmerish* and bribing local officials to let them perform in inns or barns.) Soon, the Polish impresario Avrom Yitskhok Kaminsky introduced European audiences to an innovation they had missed, the plays of Jacob Gordin.

Kheyder scene from Sfinks's *Meir Ezofewicz* (Poland, 1911), the story of an idealistic young Jew who revolts against clerical constraints to join the struggle for Polish freedom; frame enlargement.

Bridling the obstreperous American-Yiddish stage with a measure of artistic aspiration, Gordin employed Russian-style naturalism and borrowed European themes, reworking *King Lear, A Doll's House,* and *Faust* as Yiddish family dramas, Kaminsky had similar universalist ambitions. In 1907, together with his wife Esther-Rokhl Kaminska and the young playwright-director Mark Arnshteyn, he organized the Literarishe Trupe (Literary Troupe) which toured the Pale—and even St. Petersburg—with Yiddish versions of Shakespeare and Gorky. (At the same time, the playwright Peretz Hirschbein and the actor Jacob Ben-Ami headed another self-consciously literary, and equally influential, theater in Odessa.)

Yiddish performances were again outlawed in 1910, and if the ban appears to have been ignored in the larger cities, it may have stimulated promoters to present Yiddish productions by other means. By 1911, it was possible to speak of a Polish movie industry. Following the vogue for filmed theater established a few years earlier by Paris-based Film d'Art, Kooperatywa Artystow made a series of films with Warsaw's Teatr Rosmaitosci. Simultaneously, the Siła firm, owned by Warsaw exhibitor Mordka Towbin, hired Arnshteyn to direct a film version of the Kaminsky staging of New York writer Zalmen Libin's naturalistic melodrama *Der Vilder Foter* (The Savage Father).

Towbin, a Russian Jew who operated a cinema on Warsaw's grand boulevard Marszalkowska Street, had already produced what may have been the first feature-length Polish movie—a series of scenes of Polish life in the then-German city of Poznan. Siła's initial efforts were likely primitive *actualités* and *Der Vilder Foter* was scarcely more elaborate: photographer Stanisław Sebel, who would be the most important Polish cinematographer of the silent period, simply set up his camera in Kaminsky's theater and documented a run-through of the play.

However crude, *Der Vilder Foter* was evidently a success. Herman Sieracki, the leading actor, was soon approached by Pathé Frères with an offer to direct other Jewish films. Sieracki turned the offer down, later telling the historian David Matis that he had refused not only on his own behalf but on that of the entire company, who had stated their preference for performing before a live audience. The audience, nevertheless, was ready for movies. Aleksander Hertz—the Jewish producer who left Pathé in 1910 to found Poland's first indigenous production company, Sfinks—adapted Eliza Orzeszkowa's 1878 novel *Meir Ezofewicz,* in which an idealistic young Jew revolts against clerical constraints to join the struggle for Polish freedom. Two months later, in December 1911, Kooperatywa Artystow released their own "Jewish" film *Sad Bozy* (God's Orchard), a version of Stanisław Wyspiański's play *Sedziów* (The Judges).[2]

Meanwhile, Arnshteyn directed two more Jewish movies for Siła, including a version of Jacob Gordin's *Di Shtifmuter* (The Stepmother). The following year in Vilna, Arnshteyn filmed *Khasye di Yesoyme* (Khasye the Orphan), a Gordin play that had already served as the basis for a movie made in Dvinsk with Naum Lipovsky's Yiddish theater. Arnshteyn shot his *Khasye* mornings during the course of the play's run at the Vilna Circus Theater and, according to actor Israel Arko, insisted on the cast speaking their lines as though to an audience. There was, however, one purely cinematic touch. After *Khasye* closed in Vilna, the troupe left for Odessa, where they filmed a spectacular ending: in the play, Gordin's tragic

heroine took poison; in Arnshteyn's movie, she ended her life by walking slowly into the Black Sea.

Yiddish cinema would gain much in terms of technical proficiency from the widespread presence of Jews at all levels of the film industry (both in Europe and the United States). Still, it was less the cousin of world cinema than the child of the Yiddish stage. The first Yiddish movies recorded the Yiddish theater; well over half the Yiddish films released during the 1930s were also adaptations, while most of the remainder employed the stars, writers, and conventions of the Yiddish stage.

In Europe, the Yiddish stage had been the province of the young and the modern. Traditional Jews kept away, and also prohibited their children from attending. Thus, the theater was attended mainly by students and the new Jewish proletariat, including young women who had left their villages to work in the cities. In America, the audience was more universal. There, the Yiddish stage was not just entertainment but an antidote for homesickness and a source of collective identity. The Yiddish theater was the mass culture of the Lower East Side, its audience half congregation, half extended family. In brazen competition with religious orthodoxy, theaters were packed on Friday evenings and Saturday afternoons.

It is indicative of Jacob Gordin's preeminence that of the two dozen Yiddish plays filmed in various cities of the Russian Empire between 1911 and 1916, half were either taken from his oeuvre or, as in the case of *Der Vilder Foter,* falsely attributed to him. (At the same time, in Prague, Franz Kafka was fascinated by the Gordin plays he saw performed, absorbing their themes—as well as the extravagant gestures of the Yiddish performers—into his own work.)

Gordin, the author of over seventy plays, epitomized Yiddish theater during the period of its greatest popularity. A generation of performers made their reputations as actors in parts he wrote for them. Jacob P. Adler, who in 1892 overwhelmed the Lower East Side as the "Jewish King Lear," extolled Gordin as his "messiah"; it was mainly for her interpretation of Gordin heroines that Esther-Rokhl Kaminska became known in Poland as the "Jewish Duse" and, after her legendary Mirele Efros, the "mother of Yiddish theater." Nevertheless, like more than one Yiddish artist, Gordin had to learn the language with which he addressed the Jewish masses.

The son of a wealthy merchant, the playwright was born in the Ukrainian town of Ubigovrod, and was at least as Russian as he was Jewish. He came of age during the period of political agitation that followed Alexander II's emancipation of the serfs in 1866, and, initially active in the Ukrainian independence movement, founded his own Tolstoyan "brotherhood"—a cult that superimposed Jewish and Christian beliefs. This synthesis fell victim to the anti-Jewish violence that followed Alexander's assassination. (Like many Gentile radicals, Gordin blamed Jews for the pogroms, believing anti-Semitism a justified response to Jewish insularity.) For three years, Gordin lived as a farmer but, harvesting no disciples and harassed by the tsarist police, left for America in 1891 with his wife and eight children.

Since Yiddish theater had been banned in Russia, Gordin discovered it in New York. Not surprisingly, he hated what he saw: "Everything," he maintained, "was far from real Jewish life. All was vulgar, immoderate, false, and coarse. I wrote my first play the way a pious man, a scribe, copies out of a Torah scroll." Actually, Gordin worshipped at the temple of European culture—still, he had arrived at a propitious moment. By the century's end, a number of kindred spirits had made their way to the Lower East Side and there formed an intellectual vanguard. Yiddish was not their preferred language, nor Yidishkayt their primary concern. However, more pious Jews were less apt to immigrate to America, and, in the absence of traditional authority, these Russified radicals became the ghetto's teachers. Gordin's theater was an extension of the night schools and lectures to which immigrant workers flocked. His "naturalistic" dramas eclipsed the unpretentious, fanciful operettas written by the pioneer Avrom Goldfadn, establishing a new solemn tone for the Yiddish stage—and, hence, for the Yiddish screen.[3]

Gordin brought the world into the Jewish family, and vice versa. *Der Yidisher Kenig Lir* (The Jewish King Lear) and *Mirele Efros,* both filmed in America during the 1930s, were the first plays to explore the gap between traditional parents and modern children that was to preoccupy the later Yiddish stage and even the American-Jewish theater. At his best, Gordin was able to transform his source material into authentic Jewish passion plays, crafting culture myths with the weight and authority of stone tablets. But this heaviness had its price. Although Goldfadn was rediscovered by the Yiddish avant-garde of the 1920s, the Yiddish cinema never quite reestablished contact with its musical roots, even after the development of sound. *Yidl mitn Fidl,* made in Poland in 1936, is a happy exception. In America, particularly, Yiddish filmmakers continued to rework Gordin's now shopworn legacy of star-oriented, domestic melodramas. Siła's recordings of Gordin plays set the agenda for subsequent Yiddish cinema. Indeed, Gordin virtually brackets Yiddish film. Adaptations of his *On a Heym* (*Without a Home*) and *Got, Mentsh, un Tayvl* (*God, Man, and Devil*) were the last Yiddish features released, respectively, in pre-Holocaust Poland and post–World War II America.

The development of a public Yiddish culture in the Russian Empire coincided with a heightened anti-Semitism. From spring 1911 on, the sensational and widely publicized Mendel Beilis case—in which the Jewish superintendent of a Kiev brick kiln was framed for the killing of a Russian child—gave the blood libel official credence.[4]

In Poland, a post-1905 upsurge in anti-Jewish agitation peaked in 1912. The targets were recent immigrants from Lithuania and Belorussia, accused of simultaneously Russifying Poland and maneuvering for a Jewish nation-state. (During the elections of 1912, Warsaw's Jewish voters—roughly half the city's electorate—helped defeat the right-wing National Democratic Party, which retaliated by organizing a boycott of Jewish businesses.) Nevertheless, between 1911 and 1913, approximately one-third of all Polish films were taken from Yiddish plays.[5]

Although Siła folded in late 1912, rival companies to the east picked up the slack. When the Kaminskys appeared in Riga, where the first Latvian film had been produced two years earlier, the Semen Mintus

Semen Mintus's *Yom Hakhupa* (Russia, 1912), based on the play by American Yiddish writer Joseph Lateiner; frame enlargement.

Company made a two-reel recording of their "Jewish" version of Tolstoy's *Khozyain i Robotnik* (The Landlord and the Worker). Mintus released at least four more productions made with other Yiddish troupes—including Joseph Lateiner's *Yom Hakhupa* (The Wedding Day); Isidore Zolatarefsky's "Jewish *Hamlet*," *Der Yeshive Bokher* (The Yeshiva Student); Arnshteyn's *Dos Eybike Lid* (The Eternal Song); and the popular Thomashefsky and Zeifert operetta, *Dos Pintele Yid* (The Jewish Essence).

Mintus's cameraman, Yevgeny Slavinsky, recalled these efforts as less *films d'art* than quasi-documentaries. In his memoirs, he describes meeting an itinerant Yiddish troupe in a small town near the Vistula and there filming their theatrical performances: "We had no proper director, and our productions were the result of collective effort. Despite our inexperience and amateurishness, [the movies] were good and enjoyed great success." As only fragments survive, it is not known whether these films employed Yiddish or Polish intertitles. (That the Polish press seems to have ignored them suggests the former.) There were, however, at least two Yiddish plays filmed with Russian titles. Indeed, the Yiddish *film d'art* may be said to have arrived when Pathé Frères Moscow adapted the most notorious Yiddish play of its time, Sholem Asch's *Got fun Nekome* (God of Vengeance), starring Israel Arko as the superstitious brothel-owner Yekl Shabshevitz.

Because Asch's lurid drama of innocence corrupted was considered too offensive for Warsaw—after hearing a reading of the script, I. L. Peretz is said to have advised his former disciple to burn it—the play had its world premiere in Berlin in 1907 at Max Reinhardt's theater, where it was closed down after eighteen performances. (This was only the beginning of a scandalous career: the 1923 New York production was raided by the police, and its star, Rudolf Schildkraut, spent the night in jail. Asch eventually refused to have it produced anywhere.) Pathé's version of *Got fun Nekome* was likely more cinematic, if less Jewish, than the filmed plays produced by Siła and Mintus. Arko and Misha Fishzon, two Lithuanian Jews, both of whom had acted with Kaminsky, headed a mainly Gentile cast. The production was adapted and directed by Pathé's twenty-three-year-old Jewish specialist Alexander Arkatov (who had earlier written *L'khaym*). The three-reel film was released in November 1912. Soon after, Pathé's rival, Moscow Gaumont, produced a three-reel, all-Russian *Mirele Efros*.[6]

Meanwhile, Towbin's erstwhile partner, Samuel Ginzberg, formed Kosmofilm with film-lab owner Henryk Finkelstein. The firm produced a new series of films with Kaminsky, drawing on hits of the New York Yiddish stage—Zalmen Libin's 1903 *Di Tsebrokhene Hertser* (The Broken Hearts), later to be filmed by Maurice Schwartz in New York; an 1899 comedy by the Galician playwright Moshe Rikhter; and two more Gordin plays, *Gots Shtrof* (God's Punishment) and *Der Unbekanter* (Stranger), the latter a Yiddishization of Tennyson's "Enoch Arden." All were released in 1913 and starred Regina Kaminska, who died later that year.

Like Siła, but with greater success, Kosmofilm also made movies featuring performers from Warsaw's Polish theaters—including a version of the opera *Halka*, exhibited with musical accompaniment by a live choir. Releasing twenty movies in its two years of existence (melodramas, farces, crime films, and travelogues, as well as Yiddish stage plays), the firm was Poland's most important production company before the war. Still, lacking the international connections of Pathé or Gaumont, neither Finkelstein nor any other Polish producer was able to market their movies beyond the Russian Empire.

The one exception was *Di Shkhite (The Slaughter)*, a four-reel adaptation of a particularly savage Gordin tragedy in which a sensitive girl is symbolically murdered by her impoverished parents, who force her marriage to a wealthy brute. (Hutchins Hapgood, a young Gentile reporter chronicling New York's ghetto at the turn of the century, saw an early production of the play and noted that it ends in "indescribable violence and abuse. . . . The wife finally kills her husband, in a scene where realism riots into burlesque, as it frequently does on the Yiddish stage.") Released in Warsaw in early 1914, *Di Shkhite* was offered to American distributors in May as *The Slaughter*—"the Dramatic Sensation of the Jewish Stage in Motion Pictures," with Mme. H. Kaminskaia [*sic*] and a cast of "Russian Jewish" actors.

There is no further record of *The Slaughter* in the American trades, but if the first Yiddish movies failed to reach the New World, it was not for want of an audience. The same issue of *Moving Picture World* that announced *The Slaughter* proclaimed Sidney M. Goldin's five-reel version of the play *Uriel Acosta*. Written originally in German and first performed in 1846, Karl Gutzkow's tragedy became the most popular Yiddish "art" play before *Der Dibek;* it is the story of a seventeenth-century *marano* (forceably converted Jew) who, torn between his universalist desires and the traditional ties that bind him to his family, flees Portugal for the scarcely more tolerant Jewish community of New Amsterdam.

Uriel Acosta had been a warhorse for the famous

Esther-Rokhl Kaminska, the "Jewish Duse," circa 1910.

Jacob P. Adler on stage. Goldin's film adaptation, criticized in the trades as overlong and amateurish, starred Ben Adler, a Rumanian non-relation and former child performer, identified in the advertising by his last name only as an "eminent dramatic actor." (This ploy notwithstanding, Adler was excoriated in one review as "a man who had no conception whatever of the character he was called on to portray, and whose histrionic ability fell far below that of the average performer in amateur theatricals.") Whatever Ben Adler's capacity, Goldin—a key figure in the development of the Yiddish cinema—was attempting to attract the Jewish audience with known figures from the Yiddish stage. Adler's costar, twenty-three-year-old Rosetta Conn, had acted as a child with the divas Keni Liptzin and Berta Kalish and appeared in the celebrated production of Gordin's *Got, Mentsh, un Tayvl* with which David Kessler inaugurated his new Second Avenue Theater in late 1911.

Jacob P. Adler himself made a well-publicized film appearance in June 1914 in Sigmund Lubin's five-reel spectacular *Michael Strogoff, Courier to the Czar,* from the novel by Jules Verne. This elaborate production, which was shot in Philadelphia and involved setting fire to the Schuylkill River to represent Strogoff's dramatic escape from Moscow, was praised by W. Stephen Bush in *Moving Picture World,* who noted the presence of a "well-known Jewish actor . . . said to have been very successful on the so-called Yiddish stage." Bush acknowledged Adler's commanding presence but thought him "plainly hampered by a lack of camera experience. He talks too much and too vehemently. . . . Emphatic elocution before the camera is worse than wasted."

Because a brief prologue offered Adler in several of his best-known roles—including Acosta, Shylock, and (hair plastered down, face contorted in a Harpo Marx grimace) Gordin's Wild Man, it's possible that *Michael Strogoff* was intended for a Polish audience as well. As Yiddish theater was an international phenomenon, the same potential existed for Yiddish cinema. In August, however, war broke out in Europe and ties between the Old Country and the New World were abruptly severed.

NOTES

1. The significance of the Dreyfus affair, which first inspired the cry "Death to the Jews" and inspired former assimilationist Theodor Herzl to found the Zionist movement, was hardly confined to Western Europe. Sholom Aleichem's "Dreyfus in Kasrilevke" is a parable in which Russian Jews learn of their persecuted coreligionist from the one man in town who subscribes to a newspaper, and thus absorb Dreyfus into their daily routine:

As the case went on, [the Jews of Kasrilevke] got tired of waiting for Zaydl to appear in the synagogue with the news; they began to go to his house. Then they could not wait that long, and they began to go along with him to the post office for his paper. There they read, digested the news, discussed, shouted, gesticulated, all together and in their loudest voices. More than once the postmaster had to let them know in gentle terms that the post office was not the synagogue. "This is not your synagogue, you Jews. This is not your community hall."

The Diary of the Dreyfus Trial, a reconstruction by either Méliès or the Lumières' successor, Pathé Frères, was among the first films exhibited in Jerusalem, in 1900, at the Europa Hotel.

2. Neither Sfinks nor Kooperatywa Artystow employed Yiddish actors, and neither film has a particularly Jewish point of view. Nevertheless, Orzeszkowa's novel was notable for its "liberal" view of the Jewish Question, and even *Sedziów,* which concerns the murder of a Gentile maid by the Jewish innkeeper who employs her, had been translated into Yiddish and became part of the Yiddish repertoire.

3. The ardor of the Jewish theater audience has been often described in religious terms. When the German historian Karl Lamprecht attended a 1904 performance of *Di Kraft fun Libe* (*The Power of Love*) at the Grand Street Theater on New York's Lower East Side, he was astonished by the spectators' "rapt" and "solemn" faces, their "serious attentive mood."

When the last curtain descends after midnight—the play, I seem to remember, started at 8 P.M.—I know at last the meaning of the tremendous applause that followed each act. Here in the Yiddish theater there still prevails a mood of piety, of devotion and edification that has disappeared everywhere in the modern theater. Here audience, actor, and playwright share an ethos unaffected by critical distinctions between moral or religious and purely theatrical problems and their resolutions. Here the drama has remained a divine service.

"In this externally not particularly attractive, badly ventilated hall," Lamprecht came to realize "what Greek drama meant while it retained its religious significance."

4. Beilis spent over two years in prison. His trial, which lasted from September 25 through October 28, 1913, and featured Russian clergy offering spurious testimony on the Jewish practice of ritual murder, proved a setback for the anti-Semitic and reactionary Union of Russian People (also known as the Black Hundreds) which tirelessly and cynically continued to propagate Beilis's guilt even though the jury had acquitted him after deliberating only a few hours.

5. When, in 1912, Kaminsky opened Warsaw's first permanent Yiddish theater—built, contrary to popular wisdom, in an affluent central district populated mainly by Poles and assimilated Jews—the inaugural production was *Mirele Efros.* Siła released a canned version shortly after, as well as a two-reel version of *Got, Mentsh, un Tayvl.* Later that spring, the company made a bid for a wider audience with *Wojewoda* (The Governor), a drama of the eighteenth-century Polish aristocracy featuring well-

known stars of the Warsaw stage. This expansion presaged disaster. Towbin had more than once been compelled to pawn his equipment to cover his debts; three months after *Wojewoda's* premiere, Siła declared bankruptcy.

6. Mintus's final productions included two more movies with the Kaminsky troupe and the widely distributed *kino-deklamatsye, Vu Iz Emes?* (Where Is Truth?). This latter was the first of several film versions of Abraham Schomer's 1911 melodrama *Afn Yam un "Ellis Island"* (At Sea and Ellis Island) in which a Jewish girl is forced to register as a prostitute in order to attend university outside the Pale. The same film, under the Russian title *Tragediya Yevreiskoi Kursistki* (Tragedy of a Jewish Student), is also attributed to an Odessa-based studio run by M. Grossman, thus raising the possibility that Mintus's Yiddish *kino-deklamatsye* involved the appropriation of an earlier movie. If so, *Vu Iz Emes?* is an early example of spoken Yiddish used to render an existing film "more Jewish"—a practice common in the 1930s, when a variety of silent movies were given Yiddish soundtracks and, in effect, remade for Jewish audiences.

Overleaf: Willet St. Theater, a Brooklyn nickelodeon with posters in Yiddish and English, 1913. Joseph Seiden, seated at left, would become an early producer of Yiddish talkies.

2

Romance in the Ghetto

FIVE YEARS into the American century, the urban working class discovered a new form of entertainment: a half-hour moving picture show that cost five cents and changed each day. *Variety* first reported the proliferation of these 199-seat storefront theaters in March 1906; within eighteen months, the "nickelodeons" were a bona fide social phenomenon. "This is the boom time in the motion picture business," Chicago journalist Joseph Medill Patterson told the readers of the *Saturday Evening Post.*

Everybody is making money—manufacturers, renters, jobbers, exhibitors. . . . The nickelodeon is tapping an entirely new stratum of people, is developing into theatergoers a section of population that formerly knew and cared little about the

drama as a fact in life. That is why "this line is a Klondike" just at present.

Incredible as it may seem, over two million on the average attend the nickelodeons *every day of the year,* and a third of these are children.

By the time Patterson's article appeared in November 1907, legitimate theaters, burlesque palaces, and even opera houses had been converted to show photoplays exclusively, or, more frequently, a mixture of movies and vaudeville. In New York, the pace was set by Jewish exhibitors Marcus Loew and William Fox, both emerging from the slums where they grew up to seek that audience which Patterson had addressed in the *Saturday Evening Post.* In a bid to overcome middle-class distaste for popular amusements, the burgeoning Fox and Loew circuits offered plush surroundings as well as lengthy programs at popular prices—augmenting motion pictures with a half-dozen sing-alongs, illustrated lectures, and variety acts.

Nevertheless, it was in the ghetto where movies made their most dramatic impact. On the Lower East Side, nickelodeons wiped out the primitive Yiddish variety shows found in the back rooms of Bowery saloons. (Later, the two forms would learn to coexist. By the summer of 1913, Jacob P. Adler's former theater was showing the latest photoplays with eight acts of Yiddish vaudeville.) The five-cent theaters seemed impervious to economic downturns. In May 1908, in the midst of a depression, the *Forverts* reported that although "most musical halls have shut down, Yiddish theaters are badly hurt, and candy stores have lost customers," people were still lining up for the nickelodeons: "There are now about a hundred movie houses in New York, many of them in the Jewish quarter." In fact, nearly a fourth of Manhattan's 123 movie theaters were located amid Lower East Side tenements, with another thirteen squeezed among the Bowery's Yiddish theaters and music halls, and seven more clustered in the somewhat tonier entertainment zone to the north, at Union Square.[1]

The nickel movie house was the most dynamic instance of that new public sphere that developed in America around the turn of the century and which included inexpensive variety shows, dime museums, penny arcades, and amusement parks. For the immigrant and working-class audience, nickelodeons were cheap entertainment, and perhaps something more. As Miriam Hansen has observed in her study of silent-movie spectatorship, "the neighborhood

character of many nickelodeons—the egalitarian seating, continuous admission and variety format, nonfilmic activities like illustrated songs, live acts, and occasional amateur nights—fostered a casual, sociable, if not boisterous atmosphere and made moviegoing an interactive rather than merely passive type of experience."

For civic leaders and crusading reformers, however, these dark, unsanitary holes where unsavory men, unchaperoned women, and unsupervised children partook of unlicensed enjoyment—much of it imported from France—were a potential vice problem. The Patterson article had ended on a cautionary note: "Those who are 'interested in the poor' are wondering whether the five-cent theater is a good influence, and asking themselves gravely whether it should be encouraged or checked (with the help of the police)." In New York, the Children's Society began a campaign against the nickelodeons that resulted in the arraignment of a First Avenue theater owner for permitting minors to attend a documentary reenactment of the Stanford White murder featuring scenes with White's mistress, Evelyn Nesbit Thaw. Erratic attempts at censorship climaxed on Christmas Day 1908 when—soon after the collapse of a balcony guardrail in a Rivington Street nickelodeon that killed one and injured fifteen (including several children)—the New York Police padlocked the city's 550 five-cent theaters.

Following the Christmas closings, the embattled nickelodeon proprietors banded together to counterattack. The *New York Tribune* characterized this meeting in ethnic terms, almost as if describing Biograph's 1907 farce *The Fights of Nations*. The paper noted that of the assembled Irishmen, Hungarians, Italians, Greeks, Germans, and "Jewish Americans," the "greater portion" were the latter. Indeed, it was Fox and Loew who led the exhibitors in their successful struggle to reopen their theaters. To regain their licenses, the nickelodeon managers pledged to refrain from Sunday performances and to bar films that offended community morals. Not for the last time, the movies would have to clean up their act.

The year 1909 marked a general period of regulation. The Edison, Biograph, Vitagraph, Lubin, Selig, Essanay, and Kalem companies—which had only a few weeks earlier joined together with the two leading French firms, Pathé Frères and Méliès, to create the Motion Pictures Patent Company, a would-be monopoly over all aspects of the movie business— agreed to submit their productions to an outside agency (the future National Board of Review). For the next few years the movies shifted their emphasis from scattershot sensationalism to sentimental social realism. So far as Jews were concerned, vaudeville stereotypes were counterbalanced by a cycle of sympathetic ghetto melodramas—a trend anticipated by D. W. Griffith and Biograph.

Two 1908 Biograph films, *Old Isaacs the Pawnbroker,* from a script by Griffith, and *Romance of a Jewess,* which Griffith directed as well as wrote, portrayed Jews as honest members of an urban underclass. Lubin's 1909 *The Yiddish Boy,* a tale of a ghetto lad who "returns good for ill," is another early example. (As the first American-Jewish film producer, Philadelphia-based Sigmund "Pop" Lubin presaged the younger immigrants who would come to dominate the movie industry. Although Lubin's output included all genres, he was particularly sensitive to Jewish concerns. In May 1908, he released *The House Next Door,* a film dramatizing the work of the Federation of Jewish Charities; the same year,

his company also produced the first American movie to deal with the persecution of Jews in tsarist Russia.)

Biograph promoted *Old Isaacs* as a corrective to current ethnic stereotypes, announcing in the March 28, 1908, issue of the *Mutoscope and Biograph Co. Bulletin* that the portrayal of the eponymous pawnbroker's charity "dissipates the calumnies launched at the Hebrew race." Still, Griffith's genius for appropriating and developing popular forms is more apparent in *Romance of a Jewess.* Here, a pawnbroker's daughter refuses the match arranged by a *shadkhn* and marries for love, only to be disowned by her traditional father. The film—one of sixty Griffith would direct in 1908—is notable not only for its Lower East Side locations, but for its representation of the broken families and generational combat that were already obsessive themes of the Yiddish theater. Replete with a deathbed reconciliation, this one-reel weepie featured Biograph's first star, Florence Lawrence, and proved to be Griffith's biggest box-office hit up until that time. The following month's *Song of the Shirt* sympathetically portrayed the plight of the Lower East Side's Jewish and Italian seamstresses.

Immigrant subjects were still rare but Griffith's innovations were part of a larger consolidation. Dialogue titles and multiple-reel dramas grew increasingly common and, as movie houses began to open in affluent areas of Boston, New York, Chicago, and Philadelphia, the trade papers called for better films and more luxurious theaters. Although French pictures continued to dominate the American market, the Biographs were recognized by industry observers as the dramatic equal of Pathé's *"films d'art."* Moreover, they were indigenous in tone—and characterized by a measure of "progressive" social concern.

By 1910, when the Lower East Side reached its maximum density, with 540,000 inhabitants, the term *ghetto* was something of a buzzword—as if the movies were now obliged to represent their first partisans (perhaps for the touristic delectation of the middle class). The year brought Yankee's *The Ghetto Seamstress,* New Rochelle–based Thanhouser's *The Girls of the Ghetto,* and Griffith's one-reel *A Child of the Ghetto.* (Here, Griffith anticipated the assimilationist mood of the American films that would follow World War I: his wronged Jewish heroine escapes squalid Rivington Street for the wholesome countryside, to be regenerated by the pure love of a, presumably, Gentile farmer.) Such topical reportage was not restricted to the struggle of Jewish immigrants and working girls. In addition to their presence in ethnic comedies and ghetto tearjerkers, Jews were also the subjects of movies set in the Russian Empire. Indeed, most of these were exposés of anti-Semitic violence which, not coincidentally, portrayed America as offering Jews a refuge.

With a branch in Moscow, Pathé Frères (then the world's largest movie producer) would have been perfectly positioned to exploit this genre, were it not for tsarist censorship. Thus, Pathé's first pogrom film wasn't even shot in Russia. In 1905, Ferdinand Zecca made *Anti-Semitic Atrocities* in a French studio. Thereafter, Pathé produced a few innocuous melodramas which could be sold abroad as representations of Jewish life under tsarist oppression, most notably *L'khaym,* which, released in early 1911, was successful enough to warrant a sequel, written by the scenarist Alexander Arkatov, who this time directed.

The earliest of U.S. "pogrom films," as Patricia Erens has classified them, was Lubin's *The Hebrew Fugitive* (1908); it was followed two years later by Kalem's *Rachel,* Defender's *Russia, the Land of Oppression* (for which director Edwin S. Porter staged a Passover-eve pogrom on Staten Island), and Yankee's *In the Czar's Name.* In the last, a Russian nobleman elopes with a rabbi's daughter. The angry father is framed for antigovernment agitation and, although he miraculously escapes death during a pogrom, is exiled to Siberia. The couple manages to rescue him, as well as the rest of the family, and all ends happily in the United States, where the refugees are welcomed by no less an eminence than President Taft.

Later, the Beilis case inspired several films. The first, a three-reeler released by Lewis J. Rubinstein's Manhattan-based Ruby Features barely a month after Beilis's acquittal on October 28, 1913, was *The Black 107,* directed by thirty-three-year-old Odessa-born Sidney M. Goldin. In this early docudrama—or *tsaytbild,* as the sensationalized topical plays of the Yiddish theater were known—Beilis is framed by an apostate Jew, who has become a vengeful priest as well as spiritual adviser to the anti-Semitic Black Hundreds.

Variety's intrepid reviewer caught Ruby's "homemade Beilis" at the Waco Theatre "in the thick of the movie-mad section of Rivington Street" and was more impressed by the audience (not to mention the Waco's failure to jack up prices for this attraction) than by the film: "Go to Rivington Street, just east of the Bowery any Sunday after luncheon when there's a racial film on the circuit, if you want to know what a human gorge is," he advised his readers.

About the only sympathetic note [of *The Black 107*] is in the personality of the player selected to impersonate the much advertised Beilis. A small body, a gaunt, care-lined face, and an expression of unchanging and genuine apprehension, make one follow him through the theatric situations in which he is placed. . . .

Variety credits the part of Beilis to one "Jacob Adler" but it could hardly have been *the* Jacob P. Adler who, then close to sixty, was tall, solidly built, and preternaturally expressive. The name is given without comment, although the filmed presence of Yiddish theater's most august presence by itself would have guaranteed high excitement at the Waco.

On the Lower East Side, *The Black 107* was but one Beilis *tsaytbild* among many. Within four days of Beilis's acquittal, topical plays opened at the Grand Music Hall on Orchard Street and the nearby Kramer's Comedy Theater. By mid-November, Jacob P. Adler and David Kessler were starring in rival productions. Adler's enjoyed the longer run, although Boris Thomashefsky got the last word when he subsequently imported the actual Beilis. Meanwhile, the Italian American Film Corporation advertised George K. Roland's *The Terrors of Russia* (filmed on a Jewish agricultural colony in Carmel, New Jersey): "The persecution and freedom of the Russian Jew— 500 People in the cast—An entire village in riot." *The Black 107*, considered so inflammatory that it was impounded by the police in Chicago and briefly banned in London, was followed, a year later, by the German-made *Mystery of the Mendel Beilis Case.*[2]

For three years, the Beilis case dominated immigrant Jewish interest. What's striking about Goldin's *The Black 107* is that, unlike *Romance of a Jewess,* it was an insider's film—made from a Jewish point of view, primarily for a Jewish audience. In this it re-flects a shift in the American movie industry. Thanks, in part, to the challenge mounted against the Motion Picture Patents Company by exhibitors-turned-producers like Carl Laemmle, Adolph Zukor, and William Fox, immigrant Jews had become active moviemakers.

Among the techniques these self-described "independents" employed to outflank the trust were lengthier films and the use of stage stars in prestigious adaptations. (By 1913, these ploys were helping American producers capture the lion's share of the American market, as well as the patronage of the American middle class.) In a general sense, however, the independents contributed to a reaction against the Anglo-Saxon gentility of the Griffith Biographs —not to mention authority in general. American movies were rowdier and more sensational, a development that culminated with Mack Sennett's anarchic Keystone comedies and the worldwide Charlie Chaplin craze. Jewish characters, mainly comic, were increasingly apparent after 1912, particularly at Lubin and Keystone; Max Davidson and George Sidney would soon establish reputations as distinctively Jewish comedians, and Chaplin was widely and persistently believed to be Jewish as well.

Apparently, the fascination with Chaplin's racial heritage began with his arrival in the United States in 1915. When a reporter asked him if he was, as everyone imagined, Jewish, Chaplin gracefully replied, "I have not that good fortune." The assumption of Chaplin's Jewishness suggests a popular perception of a new "Jewish" style identified with an urban or immigrant underclass. Despite Chaplin's denials, the association stuck. (With the growth of anti-Semitism in the 1920s, Chaplin was an early target for Nazi propagandists. By this time, according to biographer David Robinson, "he was adamant in his refusal ever to contradict any statement that he was a Jew.")

Although Jewish themes were but a small aspect of overall movie production, the ascendent Jewish producers presented such films with an evident pride and flare. One of Fox's first productions was the six-reel spectacular *Bar Kochba—The Hero of a Nation* (Supreme, 1913), in which courageous Hebrews rebel against Roman domination. Indeed, when Goldin directed *The Black 107* that same year, he was already a specialist in Jewish subject matter. To a large degree, Goldin had mapped out the terrain. In alternating settings between Russian *shtetl* and New York ghetto, in moving from sweatshop melodrama to semidocumentary fund-raiser, in drawing on both historical legend and Yiddish stage "classics," while orchestrating all manner of fatal conversions, spectacular pogroms, dramatic seders, and heartwrench-

Sidney M. Goldin, circa 1920. Born in Odessa, Goldin was hailed by *Teater un Moving Pikshurs* as America's "first and foremost producer of Jewish moving pictures."

ing family separations, his pre–World War output was virtually the entire Yiddish cinema in embryo.

Goldin seems to have been equally at home in Yiddish and American popular culture. His family had emigrated from Russia when he was a child; like many Jewish-American entertainers, he grew up on the street, selling newspapers, hanging around stage doors. According to the historian Zalmen Zylberzweig, the future director made his Yiddish stage debut at fifteen in Baltimore. The extent of his subsequent involvement with Yiddish theater is unclear. He did, however, serve an American show business apprenticeship with Lincoln J. Carter, the Chicago-based producer-writer of *The Fast Mail* and *The Heart of Chicago,* the 1890s stage melodramas that popularized such stirring devices as the heroine bound to the railroad track. Goldin then spent two years at Essanay, a Chicago studio run by Bronco Billy Anderson (born Max Aronson), best-known for its westerns and comedies.

Moving to New York in 1912, Goldin directed a pair of popular crime films before going to work for Laemmle. Evidently he was something of a wunderkind. An enthusiastic profile in Universal's house organ *Universal Weekly* termed him "practically the first independent director of motion pictures in this country," citing his *Adventures of Lieutenant Petrosino* (a topical film about an Italian-American police detective murdered by the Mafia) and *New York Society Life in the Underworld* as having "made more money for the owners and exhibitors than any two pictures last season." In 1913, Goldin directed five films with Jewish themes for Laemmle's various companies, three of them produced by Independent Motion Picture (Imp) supervisor Mark M. Dintenfass.

A forty-one-year-old former "salesman of salt herring," the colorful Dintenfass had left the family appetizer business to run a Philadelphia nickelodeon. As an outlaw producer, he experimented with a primitive sound system called Actophone, dodging the trust in the New Jersey woods, before joining forces with Laemmle and his fractious partners. Indeed, it was Dintenfass who sold Laemmle the shares to become Universal's majority stockholder. (Dintenfass also played a key role in the destiny of the Warner brothers, producing their first success, the jingoistic *My Four Years in Germany,* released in 1918. Later he ran for governor of New Jersey on the single-tax ticket.)

Goldin's first two efforts for the Laemmle consortium, both shot at Dintenfass's studio in Coytesville, New Jersey, elaborated on the pogrom films of 1910. *The Sorrows of Israel,* a three-reel "special" released by Imp in June 1913, was a fantastic melodrama in which a Jewish convert and the Russian princess who loves him escape to America with the help of "nihilist" revolutionaries. The film appears to have been a success. "At present *The Sorrows of Israel* is the talk among the exhibitors, and has, to this early date, been as big a seller as any picture released by the Universal Film Company," the *Universal Weekly* burbled. Goldin, the paper revealed, was known as "Happy-go-Sid, and no amount of work can perturb his complacent geniality." Goldin was so relaxed, according to a cameraman who worked with him during this period, that he would doze off on the set: "He'd sit down and start directing a scene and right in the middle he'd fall over and snore—sound asleep."

This apparent narcolepsy seems not to have hampered Goldin's productivity. The two-reel *Nihilist Vengeance,* which Victor opened a month after *The*

Irene Wallace, 1914. Wallace was the first female star of Jewish film— despite, or perhaps because of, her well-publicized Scotch-Irish background.

Sorrows of Israel, inverted the latter's formula, casting former vaudeville "Dresden Doll" Irene Wallace as a Jewish banker's daughter romantically involved with a Russian nobleman. Goldin then shifted gears, with a naturalistic two-reel dramatic comedy of ghetto life. *The Heart of a Jewess,* released by Universal in August, reflects the romantic betrayals and domestic abandonment that plagued immigrant families.

The Heart of a Jewess deployed a stock situation of Yiddish theater (and movies—sixty years later, Joan Micklin Silver dramatized the same premise in *Hester Street*): Goldin's heroine (again Irene Wallace) toils in a Lower East Side sweatshop, supporting her father even as she saves to pay for her fiancé Jake's passage to America—and then to put him through medical school. After Jake graduates, he ditches her for a wealthier prospect. The heroine's father is made ill; she herself is struck by the car speeding

Sidney Goldin's *The Heart of a Jewess* (U.S.A., 1913). *Universal Weekly* called the scenes depicting the life of the Lower East Side "the acme of realism."

Domestic confrontation: *The Heart of a Jewess.*

Jake to the synagogue where he will be married. In the end, the wronged seamstress finds happiness with the sweatshop foreman who has loved her all along, while the ungrateful doctor is dumped by his new fiancée. (Having learned of her would-be husband's heartlessness, the bride tears off her veil, and the wedding guests each take a turn kicking Jake in the pants.)

According to *Universal Weekly,* Goldin had "assembled a company that comprised some of the best Jewish actors available in America, and the scenes depicting the life of the people of the East Side [were] the acme of realism." These include the tumultuous wedding, a Hester Street sewing factory, a Baxter Street secondhand clothing store, and a scene set in a New York hospital ward.

In its own coverage of *The Heart of a Jewess, Moving Picture World* was convinced of the film's authenticity:

A touch of pathos, a great deal of humor, fidelity of characterization and some unsparingly accurate views of modern Jewish customs in New York City all help in this interesting story. It is a pleasure to see Jewish people play Hebrew roles of comedy and sympathy, especially after so many sickening caricatures have affronted vaudeville audiences for years. . . . All of the early scenes give the impression of being taken from actual living conditions. The sweatshop is such a perfect simulation of reality that it has a Dickens-like intensity and humor.

The reviewer singled out the father as "an actor of rare ability" and called the perfidious fiancé "a type never presented on the stage, though he is visible enough in actual life to those who keep their eyes open."[3]

As striking as Goldin's concern for verisimilitude is his promotion of his star: Irene Wallace seems to have been the first female "Jewish" movie star despite, or perhaps because of, her well-publicized Scotch-Irish background. According to a profile that appeared in *Moving Picture World*, Wallace's work as a Jewish heroine in *Nihilist Vengeance* "stood out so well that it was a surprise to the management." As the lead in *The Heart of a Jewess*—"in which she rose to the occasion beyond all expectations"—the actress

is now looked upon as a star in this particular line and will probably make it a specialty. Miss Wallace has just finished the lead in another big Jewish production entitled *Bleeding Hearts, or Jewish Freedom Granted by King Casimir of Poland*. . . . In due course of time she will no doubt be considered as the leading exponent of Hebraic parts.

Goldin's three-reel *Bleeding Hearts*, released by Imp in the fall of 1913, was less universally acclaimed than *The Heart of a Jewess*, but more steeped in Jewish folk tradition—and even exhibited with Yiddish intertitles. Drawing upon the story of Esterke, legendary Jewish consort to Casimir the Great, the film is essentially a transposition of the Purim story to fourteenth-century Poland, chronicling the interreligious romance of a Polish monarch and a rabbi's daughter (Wallace).

Although no contemporary records of such a relationship are known to exist (the first account appears a century later), the Casimir-Esterke tradition was a staple of early Polish anti-Semitic literature, purporting to explain the Jews' supposedly privileged position in terms of Casimir's weakness for a "foreign" mistress. When the motif was revived in the nineteenth century, Esterke became an enlightened

social ideal, a symbol of Jewish-Polish reconciliation—which, in a limited sense, she was. Stanisław Gabriel Kozłowski's 1887 *Esterka* offered the first Jewish heroine portrayed upon the Polish stage and was the first Polish play translated into Yiddish. Esterke was the protagonist of an 1890 Yiddish play and also the subject of *Purimshpiln*, recorded around the turn of the century in Kazimierz (where Casimir was thought to have built his consort a castle).

Jewish versions of the Esterke story have a markedly different bias than Polish ones. Jews saw the relationship as a marriage—rather than a liaison—made by a self-sacrificing Jewish daughter to better her people's condition. As Chone Shmeruke points out in his study of the theme, Esterke was thus emblematic both of Jewish success and of unhappy assimilation. More romantic and less urgent than European variants, the *Bleeding Hearts* version suggests an implicit analogy between medieval Poland and present-day America as havens from persecution. The film stresses that the heroine's people are in flight from Western pogroms; significantly, the film's villain is not the Catholic priest—shown as sympathetic to the Jewish immigrants—but a duplicitous and pathologically anti-Semitic nobleman.

In a review that criticized the film's excessive violence (and presaged a response Yiddish talkies would evoke in the English-language press), the *New York Dramatic Mirror* scored *Bleeding Hearts* as "unpleasant." Such "academic reproductions of history's dark pages, at best, are morbid and gloomy themes and should remain in the dust of the past." Conversely, one Philadelphia film-exchange owner, in a letter to the *Universal Weekly*, wrote that *Bleeding Hearts* "is one of the most beautiful pictures that I have ever had the pleasure to look at and when I say this, I am

Irene Wallace as Esther in Sidney Goldin's *Bleeding Hearts* (U.S.A., 1913). This transposition of the Purim story to fourteenth-century Poland chronicles an interreligious romance between the Polish monarch and a rabbi's daughter.

Irene Wallace as Esther in *Bleeding Hearts. Teater un Moving Pikshurs* declared the film "a masterpiece in every sense of the word."

only echoing the general opinion of our exhibitors who have used it." And the first issue of *Teater un Moving Pikshurs* (Theater and Moving Pictures), a Yiddish trade journal that had a brief run in late 1913, declared Goldin's drama "a masterpiece in every sense of the word."

Judging from their publicity, Universal treated *Bleeding Hearts* as a major release. A profile of Irene Wallace published in the December 1913 issue of *Photo Play* terms *Bleeding Hearts* "one of the most artistic and therefore the most successful photoplays in the history of the Imp studios." A 1915 clipping on Wallace cites *Bleeding Hearts* as "one of her first hits." By that time her career had gone into a tailspin brought about by an article—perhaps ghostwritten—appearing in the December 1914 issue of *Green Book* in which the actress details the ways in which unscrupulous producers prey upon innocent starlets. Although Wallace stressed that she was describing a prevalent situation rather than her own experience, a contemporary newspaper clipping calls her essay "one of the most daring articles of the year."[4]

Goldin's use of the Esterke theme is indicative of his unusual immersion in Jewish subject matter. There were other Jewish-theme films released during this period. Warners told the story of a poor Jewish immigrant in their three-reel *The Struggle for Wealth*, and Universal dramatized family conflict in *The Third Generation*. But Goldin seems to have been the original specialist, if not the only one.[5]

Teater un Moving Pikshurs, which either reviewed or reported on a Goldin opus in nearly every one of its nine issues, declared him "the first and foremost producer of Jewish moving pictures." His treatment of the Beilis case opened in December 1913; later that month, Imp previewed one more Goldin production—*How the Jews Care for Their Poor,* an "educational" film made for the Brooklyn Federation of Jewish Charities. In this relentlessly downbeat two-reeler, a young widow emigrates to America, where she is met by a representative of the Council of Jewish Women; she dies immediately thereafter, leaving two small sons in the care of her consumptive brother. After he is admitted to Brooklyn Jewish Hospital, the boys are placed in the Hebrew Orphan Asylum. The *New York Times* attributed the film's script to the federation's president and secretary—both evidently conversant with the conventions of the "naturalistic," post-Gordin Yiddish theater.

How the Jews Care for Their Poor introduced progressive social values into what *Variety* termed the "racial film." Later, another institution, the Hebrew Orphan Asylum sponsored *Not a Lamb Shall Stray,* a one-reeler released by Universal's affiliate Victor in September 1915, with Curtis Benton and Sydell Dowling as a childless couple who tour the asylum and finally adopt a baby. Another Jewish social agency, the Bureau of Education for the Jewish Community, was involved in the production of *A Passover Miracle,* released to coincide with the 1914 Passover holiday by New York–based Kalem, a firm whose greatest success had been the six-reel religious spectacular *From the Manger to the Cross* (1913).

Written by Benjamin Barondess, *A Passover Miracle* featured two prominent Jewish actors, Henri Leone and Samuel Lowett, in a familiar tale of an ambitious immigrant dropping the devoted sweetheart who put him through medical school. Like *The Heart of a Jewess* and *How the Jews Care for Their Poor,* this two-reel film anticipates the Yiddish talkies

of twenty years later: Sam throws Lena over for a glamorous stenographer (who, in turn, chucks *him* for a salesman). Disgraced and contrite, he reappears at the climactic moment of the family seder (given a full reel), materializing when Lena opens the door for the symbolic welcome of the prophet Elijah. Like *Bleeding Hearts, A Passover Miracle* was released with both English and Yiddish titles.

Leaving the Universal stable, Goldin made another two Jewish films in 1914, *Escaped from Siberia* and *Uriel Acosta,* both five-reel features released by Great Players. The former, on which Goldin is credited as writer as well as director, is an expanded version of the anti-tsarist thrillers *The Sorrows of Israel* and *Nihilist Vengeance,* and features a star-crossed romance between a persecuted Jew and an aristocratic Gentile. Released a month before *Uriel Acosta, Escaped from Siberia* seems to have had the benefit of a more lavish budget—its scenes include a burning palace and an embassy ball that climaxes in the assassination of the tsar's minister. "Plenty of action," *Moving Picture World* observed, while praising the film's photography as "better than average."

Goldin's last film for Universal was *Traffickers on Soles* (1914), a takeoff on the studio's enormously profitable "sociological photodrama," *Traffic in Souls,* released in late 1913, with Irene Wallace in a supporting role. The Goldin version has a group of Irish police led by a Jewish inspector join forces with a group of Jewish cops headed by an Irishman to break up the white slavery ring. (In the end, Inspector Levy is rewarded with a ham while Inspector McGuiness receives a turkey.) Goldin's five-reel *Last of the Mafia,* a sequel to his *Lieutenant Petrosino,* appeared in February 1915. That same year the trades announced that the director had joined forces with Yiddish superstar Boris Thomashefsky to direct three films, *The Jewish Crown, The Period of the Jew,* and *Hear Ye, Israel.* That Thomashefsky was less than pleased with the result is suggested by his son's account of an outdoor screening at the family's twenty-acre estate in Ulster County, New York: "There were plenty of rocks on the ground and [Father] pelted his image with stones. Then he had [the movie] run again and threw more things until the screen was in shreds."

Goldin was not the only American filmmaker drawing talent from the Yiddish stage. Lubin cast Jacob P. Adler as Michael Strogoff; Sarah Adler, Jacob P.'s first wife, appeared in at least one movie, *Sins of the Parents,* released in late 1914. Jewish producers continued to celebrate their coreligionists even after the outbreak of the World War. In early 1915, Universal announced plans to produce a film based on Bruno Lessing's popular stories of ghetto life, while Fox brought out *The Children of the Ghetto,* a five-reel family melodrama directed by Frank Powell from the stage version of Israel Zangwill's novel. (Meanwhile, enough Yiddish had passed into street English that, also in 1915, Vitagraph could release a comedy called *Cupid Puts One Over on the Shadchen.*)

The Anglo-Jewish Zangwill, whose satiric accounts of London's Jewish community and sentimental tribute to Americanization popularized the terms "ghetto" and "melting pot," was regarded as a West European Sholom Aleichem. *Children of the Ghetto* had been a hit on Broadway in 1908, and Thomashefsky had recently staged a Yiddish version, starring Adler's daughter Celia. For the film, Wilton Lackey repeated his stage role as the immigrant rabbi abandoned by his children. The project anticipates the mood of heroic nostalgia that characterizes the ghetto melodramas of the 1920s: although Jews now constituted 28 percent of New York's population, only a quarter of them remained on the Lower East Side.

Clearly, *Children of the Ghetto* was made with a Jewish public in mind. Noting the film's use of Hebrew (for a title emphasizing the fifth commandment) and Yiddish (in a closeup of a wedding invitation), a reviewer from *Motion Picture News* suggested addressing all the film's intertitles to its "large prospective Hebrew audience." Still, Zangwill notwithstanding, Fox had an even greater success earlier that year with another child (or grandchild) of the ghetto—the Cincinnati-born daughter of a Jewish tailor, twenty-five-year-old Theodosia Goodman, whom he unleashed as the vamp Theda Bara in *A Fool There Was,* also directed by Frank Powell.

The year 1915 saw the term "movie mogul" come into vogue to describe men like William Fox. It was also the year the American film industry came of age: Chaplinitis swept the English-speaking world, *echt* Americans Douglas Fairbanks and Mary Pickford reigned supreme at home, Griffith released *The Birth of a Nation.* The outbreak of war in Europe and the ensuing decline in imported movies created the opportunity for the film factories of Hollywood to consolidate their markets, even as it gave the newly anointed moguls a chance—and the motivation—to demonstrate their Americanism. Several New York theaters on the Lower East Side and in Harlem continued to combine movies with Yiddish vaudeville, but there were no further films with Yiddish intertitles.[6]

NOTES

1. Despite their popularity with immigrant audiences, those primitive movies which represented the urban crowd were casually nativist in their approach. The first recognizably Jewish characters were unscrupulous merchants in mildly anti-Semitic, vaudeville-derived comedies such as *Cohen's Advertising Scheme* (1904) and *Cohen's Fire Sale* (1907), both from Edison.

2. Lenin wrote of seeing another film on the Beilis case, *Tainy Kieva* (Secrets of Kiev), in Krakow in 1913—the revolutionary leader's single recorded visit to a movie theater. Although *Secrets of Kiev* was evidently made in Petersburg, it was banned in Russia. There, no movie on the subject could be shown until after the tsar's fall when the Kiev-based Joseph Soifer directed *Delo Beilisa* (The Beilis Case), a six-reel epic that used authentic locations, including Beilis's house and the factory that had employed him. (The movie was released in April 1917, but was never distributed in the United States.)

3. No credits are given. When Universal remade *The Heart of a Jewess* eight years later as *Cheated Love* the original script was attributed to Lucien Hubbard and Doris Schroeder. Changes for the remake, which was directed by King Baggot, reflect the epic quality the ghetto film assumed after World War I: instead of working in a sweatshop, the heroine (played by Carmel Myers, the glamorous daughter of a San Francisco rabbi) goes on the Yiddish stage; the sympathetic foreman becomes a settlement worker; and faithless Jake is already a doctor before he emigrates from Odessa.

4. Fired from Universal, Wallace went to work for Selig Polyscope in Chicago. The actress drops from the record at this point but she left a more durable memory than did her director. In a meditation on "The Jew as Movie Subject," published in the February 1930 issue of *Close-Up*, Harry Alan Potamkin attributes the treatment of *Bleeding Hearts* to Dintenfass and the scenario to Wallace. Goldin is not mentioned, although, ironically, the essay opens with a paragraph on his *Ad Mosay*, one of the first Yiddish talkies.

5. According to Kevin Brownlow, George K. Rolands—a *landsman* of Goldin's, having also been born in Odessa—was involved in the production of *Sorrows of Israel* and *Bleeding Hearts*, before directing his own films on the Beilis and Leo Frank cases.

6. Nineteen-fifteen was also the year that Leo Frank, a homegrown Beilis, was lynched in Georgia. Several films were produced on the subject, including one by William Randolph Hearst. George K. Rolands's five-reel reenactment *The Frank Case*, released while Frank appealed his conviction (and erroneously predicting that he would be acquitted), was banned in New York City during the spring of 1915. That summer, soon after Frank's throat was slashed by a fellow convict and less than a month before he was dragged from his sickbed and hanged, the Loew circuit exhibited a one-reel documentary under the auspices of the Humanitarian Society.

Overleaf: **Sholom Aleichem (fourth from left) on a tour in Baranovichi, 1908. He is posed with a group of Jewish journalists and writers.**

3

"The Face of the Earth Will Change"

I T IS A perverse tribute to the power of art that the fin-de-siècle flux of *Yidishland* appears to us as static and embodied in a single, often misunderstood oeuvre. Sholom Aleichem, born Sholom Rabinowitz in the Ukrainian *shtetl* of Pereyaslav, produced a number of Jewish archetypes at once emblematic of tribal wholeness and suggestive of social upheaval. In story-cycles composed over a period of years, he developed a gallery of imaginary creatures so vivid they seemed more tangible to his audience than did their actual neighbors—the homespun, long-suffering dairyman Tevye, the feckless *luftmentsh* Menakhem Mendl, the irrepressible orphan Motl Peyse, not to mention the entire town of Kasrilevke.

This uncanny naturalism was a measure of Sholom Aleichem's sophistication, for the "folk writer," to use his self-description, was in fact a citizen of the post-*shtetl* world, and his startlingly accurate re-creations of the Jewish vernacular required more than a measure of critical distance. Sholom Rabinowitz was Russian as well as Jewish. It was in Russian, not Yiddish, that he addressed his children and corresponded with his wife. "Unlike Tevye," Ruth Wisse has observed, "Sholom Aleichem encouraged his children's Russification"; when, along with thousands of other Russian Jews, the Rabinowitz family emigrated west after the failed 1905 revolution, Russian tutors were engaged to insure the children's education. (In a sense, this loyalty proved mutual: Sholom Aleichem occupies a unique position in Soviet culture, the single Jewish artist to continuously enjoy official approval, even during the most virulent anti-Semitic campaigns.)

Nevertheless, Sholom Aleichem—whose pseudonym is the standard Yiddish greeting—did more than any other Jewish writer to present his community to itself, and, ultimately, to the world. As befits so popular an artist, he was famous for his public readings; his work appeared regularly in the Yiddish press and he strove strenuously, albeit with only posthumous success, to write for New York's Yiddish stage. His cinematic ambitions met a similar fate. Although more movies have been drawn from Sholom Aleichem than from any other Yiddish author save Jacob Gordin, none were produced during his lifetime.

Son-in-law I. D. Berkowitz, who collaborated with Sholom Aleichem on the play *Shver Tsu Zayn a Yid* (Hard to Be a Jew), taken from the author's novel *Der Blutiker Shpas* (The Bloody Joke), and who later dramatized *Tevye der Milkhiker,* maintains that even before the World War, the writer had "picturized" *Der Blutiker Shpas,* as well as several episodes from the Tevye cycle and the story "The Enchanted Tailor." (All of these were subsequently filmed in one fashion or another, though not from Sholom Aleichem's scripts, which have never been published.) Others recall that he worked on screen adaptations of his play *Dos Groyse Gevins* (The Big Win) and novel *Stempenyu,* and even an original Yiddish scenario—a Chanukah fantasy entitled *Di Velt Geyt Tsurik* (The World Goes Backwards).

As his early fame spread westward from Russia, Sholom Aleichem had contact with film producers in Berlin and New York. Indeed, *Dos Groyse Gevins* features a pair of rogues who fleece the play's hero, Shimele Soroker, out of the 200,000 rubles he wins in the lottery by persuading the simple tailor to invest in the movies: "What is the idea behind the cinematograph?" one con man asks the other. His comrade replies, "The bottom line: there isn't any idea." Shimele and his wife are regular patrons of the local *"Lusione"* and the tricksters' comic explanation of the mechanics of movie exhibition takes up much of the play's second act.

In the spring of 1915 Sholom Aleichem was, his daughter writes, approached by "an American Menakhem Mendl" to write a scenario based on the Motl Peyse stories. In a 1927 memorial volume, then–Columbia student B. Z. Goldberg describes visiting Sholom Aleichem at Lakewood, New Jersey, to help prepare an English-language script.

He dictated a scenario of every story of Motl in great detail, as though he were telling me of an actual movie he had seen. I saw him now in the great combination of his talents, acting the roles of his characters, as though he was performing it before the lights in the studio, and yet being the observer of it, enjoying it all immensely. . . .

We both roared repeatedly as he improvised the action on the silent screen. He laughed fully, freely, heartily. I have never seen him laugh so much and so boisterously. I have never laughed so much on one occasion in my life. If a stranger saw us then he would think we were touched in the head. Two men sitting and bursting into laughter, like two kids at a Charlie Chaplin movie.

Nothing came of this effort directly, but the cycle's penultimate story, evidently written the same year, acknowledges the power of the new medium. Motl (now "Max") visits a Lower East Side nickelodeon to see the world's greatest movie star: "All the way to the picture house, we talk about Charlie Chaplin. What a great man he is, how much he must make, and the fact"—erroneous, as we know—"that he's a Jew." Motl did not reach the screen for another dozen years; the first adaptation from Sholom Aleichem appeared in Odessa in 1917, one year after the writer's death. By then, the World War—as well as the death of I. L. Peretz in 1915, and of Mendele Mokher Sforim in 1917—effectively brought an era in Yiddish literature to a close.

Khavah (1919), taken from the Tevye story of the same name, was the first American adaptation from Sholom Aleichem. "The question is, how can you present a Russian *shtetl* if you are in America and not Russia?" reporter Ray Ruskin asked in an enthusiastic story run by Sholom Aleichem's erstwhile American newspaper *Der Tog* (The Day) in April 1919. The answer, it turned out, was to build the *shtetl* in Leonia, New Jersey ("past the moving picture studios of William Fox, Paramount Films, and others"). Fascinated by this paradox, Ruskin visited this "real Russian *shtetl*" no less than three times: the actual world of Sholom Aleichem's characters overlaps the birth of twentieth-century mass culture, but it would be filmed only in the past tense.

Although its horrors have been eclipsed by the Holocaust, the war that broke out in August 1914 was catastrophic for East European Jews—as it was, indeed, for all of Eastern Europe. War accelerated the dissolution of traditional Jewish life, driving hundreds of thousands from the countryside to the

S. J. Silberman as Sholom Aleichem's Motl Peyse in the Soviet film *Through Tears* (1928).

cities, subjecting those who remained to hunger and degradation.

The World War was, in large measure, the struggle of kaiser and emperor against tsar for control of territory then home to half the world's Jews. Unlike the static western front, the eastern lines shifted back and forth across the heart of *Yidishland,* wreaking havoc on Jewish *shtetlekh.* By the end of 1915, the Germans controlled much of the Pale. As one military defeat followed another and casualties assumed mountainous proportions, Russian resolve crumbled. By autumn, there were 80,000 Jewish refugees in Warsaw; after the Russians invaded Galicia, there would be nearly as many in Vienna.

If the German occupation of Warsaw and Vilna in some ways liberated the local Jews, the Russian conquest of Galicia was an unmitigated disaster. Jews were driven from their villages and their property set to torch—the elaborate Chasidic courts subject to particular animus. Sh. An-sky, who organized a relief mission, wrote a four-volume account, baldly entitled *Khurbm Galitsye* (The Destruction of Galicia). While Jewish soldiers fought on both sides, Jewish civilians were chief among the "traitors" the tsarist regime blamed for its losses—subject to forced evacuations and pogroms, court-martials and executions on trumped-up charges of aiding the enemy.

A nightmare for Russian Jews, war was a boon for the Russian movie industry, which, for the first time free of foreign competition and called upon to do its patriotic chore, greatly increased production. Subsequent military reversals scarcely affected the public demand for cheap entertainment. An American journalist found the commercial center of Minsk dominated in equal measure by "moving-picture shows, photographers' windows full of officers' pictures, and the officers themselves." In his novel *The Secret City,* former British foreign-agent Hugh Walpole describes a "cheerful scene" of "soldiers, sailors, peasants, women, and children crowded together on the narrow benches" of a Petrograd movie house—the theater reeking of "boots and bad cigarettes and urine" as children and dogs wandered about and a military band accompanied the feature.

The war also brought a handful of Yiddish films. In 1914, the Odessa-based Mizrakhi studio produced *Milkhome un Yidn* (War and the Jews), a four-reel "tragedy" from a scenario by Isaac Teneromo. The following summer, the film was rereleased as a *kino-deklamatsye,* advertised in Kiev as depicting "the heroic act" of Agent Khaym Sheyndlman. It is unlikely, however, that either Agent Sheyndlman, or the subjects of the 1915 *Yidishe Frayviliker* (Jewish Volun-

teers) received much exposure. By the spring of 1915, wartime censorship was in full swing. In *Kino,* Jay Leyda writes that any Russian film

that spoke of Jews was confiscated or cut—*God of Vengeance, Civic Duty of Jews, The Beilis Case.* From *The Life of Wagner* the Jewish cantor scene was cut and the rest was allowed as *The Life of a Composer.* This was carried to its logically ridiculous extreme: all Biblical films were forbidden—*David and Goliath,* etc. ("Very dangerous to see so many Jews on the screen").

On the eve of the war, the Kaminsky troupe had left Warsaw for Odessa. When the actors returned home in late 1914, they found the Yiddish theaters closed and Jewish neighborhoods swamped with destitute refugees. The tsarist commander had decreed that, as potential German spies, all Jews were to be driven from regions behind the front, and for months the roads to Warsaw were clogged with displaced Jews. Often, entire villages, their belongings heaped high on carts, were in flight from their own army. By 1918, the city's population would be 45 percent Jewish.

As the Russian military situation deteriorated, so did living conditions in Warsaw. Although the war inflicted little physical damage on the city, food, fuel, medicine, and housing were all in short supply. By 1915, the economy had collapsed. That summer, the German army arrived—along with an epidemic of typhus. Isaac Bashevis Singer, then an eleven-year-old boy living in the heart of Warsaw's Jewish quarter, the Nalewki, recalls that "between 1915 and 1917, hundreds of people died" on his street:

I saw women shake their fists at the sky and in their rage call God a murderer and a villain. I

saw Chasidim at the Radzymin study house . . .
grow swollen from malnutrition. At home we ate
frozen potatoes that had a sweetish, nauseating
taste. The Germans kept scoring victories, but
those who foretold that the war wouldn't last
longer than six weeks had to admit their error.
Millions of people had already perished, but Mal-
thus's God still hadn't had enough.

The stores were empty. Meanwhile, as "German
marks now mingled with Russian money," the Yiddish daily *Moment* "left off praising the Allies and
began to vilify them . . . [prophesying] the German
occupation of St. Petersburg." Some thought Warsaw would be incorporated into Germany. Meanwhile, the German presence stimulated Yiddish
theater, more comprehensible to the occupiers than
the Polish stage. Within weeks of the German occupation, theaters, vaudeville houses, and cabarets
sprang up everywhere.

According to Ida Kaminska, there were now four
or five Yiddish theaters, with posters printed in German as well as Yiddish. In general, the occupation
authorities were well-disposed toward Jewish cultural
nationalism. There are even accounts of German officers rising, helmet in hand, at a play's end for the
ritual singing of the Zionist anthem Hatikvah. German Jewish officers in particular supported the Vilna
Troupe, which had taken over an old circus building
in Vilna and were performing plays by Gordin, Asch,
and Hirschbein.

As the Yiddish theater briefly thrived, the Polish
film industry—now opened to the German market
—achieved a temporary international stature. Having founded Poland's first indigenous production
company, Aleksander Hertz discovered Poland's first
indigenous movie star in the person of teenage

dancer Pola Negri (born Barbara Apollonia Chalu-
piec). Beginning with the highly successful *Niewol-
nica Zmyslow* (Slave of Sin; 1914), the sultry Negri
starred in seven features for Sfinks—as well as the
anti-tsarist, philo-Semitic *Der Gelber Schein* (The
Yellow Passport; 1918), directed by Victor Janson for
a German firm during the occupation.

Here Negri played a Jewish girl who uses the yellow card of a prostitute to leave the Pale for Petersburg. Studying medicine by day, working in a brothel
by night, she is ultimately rescued by a professor
who turns out to be her long-lost father. (Mintus's
1911 version of this story, *Vu Iz Emes?*, was a popular Yiddish *kino-deklamatsye;* more recently, two
American variants had been filmed, one crediting
Abraham Schomer's 1911 melodrama *Afn Yam un
"Ellis Island"* (At Sea and Ellis Island), the other
taken from *The Yellow Ticket,* Michael Morton's un-
authorized English-language version of Schomer's
play.)

As Jewish Warsaw stood in for Russia, *The Yellow
Passport* included sequences shot in the crowded
streets of the Nalewki. "I had never been in that
strange city within a city, and its alien ways were
enthralling," Negri recalls in her memoirs. "The
bearded and bewigged population could easily have
stepped out of drawings of life made there two
hundred years ago." The movie was Negri's last before departing Warsaw for Berlin and eventually
Hollywood, and, for her, had a special significance:
"We were all inspired in making *The Yellow Passport.*
Its sympathetic portrait of Jews might displease
some of the population but a vast majority would be
very moved by it. It might even help to spread a
little tolerance and understanding." (According to
Negri, her performance as a Russian Jew created a

problem for her when she returned to Germany to resume her career fifteen years later.)[1]

Hertz lost his star but bought out his rival. Kosmofilm was absorbed by Sfinks, which released two more recorded plays during the German occupation —*Di Farshtoysene Tokhter* (The Repudiated Daughter), attributed to Avrom Golfadn, in 1915, and a remake of American playwright Hyman Mysell's *Zayn Vaybs Man* (His Wife's Husband), the following year. These would be the last Polish films to draw on the Yiddish stage for nearly a decade. Pola Negri was not the only movie star to abandon Warsaw. In 1916, with the economic situation again in crisis and Russia on the verge of revolution, the Kaminskys left on an extended tour of the Austrian-occupied provinces—which, in Ida's case, would take her as far west as refugee-swollen Vienna.

In neutral America, the extent of the Jewish catastrophe was not lost on immigrants who, if not in contact with European family and friends, learned of wartime atrocities through reports in the Yiddish press and productions on the Yiddish stage.

Jews were scarcely the only American ethnic group to see the war as a struggle between German civilization and Russian despotism, but no segment of the population experienced greater joy at the tsar's fall in March 1917. JEWISH TROUBLES AT AN END, FULL RIGHTS FOR ALL OPPRESSED NATIONALITIES, NEW LIGHT RISES OVER RUSSIA, the *Forverts*'s headline proclaimed. MAZEL TOV TO OUR JEWISH PEOPLE; MAZEL TOV TO THE ENTIRE WORLD. Yiddish theaters wasted no time in mounting *tsaytbilder* on the Russian Revolution. Nor were filmmakers idle. A large advertisement in the April 11 issue of *Der Tog* announced a new film, *In Darkest Russia: The Last Days of the Romanoffs* at the Wintergarden Theater on Houston Street and Second Avenue: "If you are a Jew and especially a Russian Jew—you will tremble with excitement, you will cry."

In September, the immigrant Jewish producer Lewis J. Selznick released his lavish *Fall of the Romanoffs*. Selznick had been a jewelry salesman until 1912 when his friend Mark Dintenfass, then at Universal, told him of the schisms dividing that firm. According to the legend, Selznick took advantage of the situation to make himself Universal's general manager by simply installing himself in an empty office and circulating a memo that announced his appointment. Each faction assumed one of the others had hired him. Selznick's chutzpah is similarly celebrated in a perhaps apocryphal telegram:

> NIKOLAI ROMANOV
> PETROGRAD RUSSIA
>
> WHEN I WAS A POOR BOY IN KIEV SOME OF YOUR POLICEMEN WERE NOT KIND TO ME AND MY PEOPLE STOP I CAME TO AMERICA AND PROSPERED STOP NOW HEAR WITH REGRET YOU ARE OUT OF A JOB OVER THERE STOP FEEL NO ILL-WILL WHAT YOUR POLICEMAN DID SO IF YOU WILL COME NEW YORK CAN GIVE YOU FINE POSITION ACTING IN PICTURES STOP SALARY NO OBJECT STOP REPLY MY EXPENSE STOP REGARDS YOU AND FAMILY
>
> SELZNICK, NEW YORK

A street in the Nalewki,
"that strange city within a
city": Pola Negri and
Victor Janson in Janson's
The Yellow Passport (1918),
a German production
filmed in occupied Warsaw;
frame enlargement.

Perhaps because the European market was lost to them, perhaps because they sensed a new nativism, perhaps because the American middle class was now attending the movies in ever greater numbers, Jewish producers had abandoned ghetto melodramas after 1915, although anti-tsarist "pogrom films" were released through 1916. In this respect too, the moguls' instincts proved sound: American entry into the World War on April 6, 1917, brought a series of legal measures directed against pro-Germans, pacifists, and radicals—all easily imagined as immigrants. Almost immediately, the *Forverts* was

threatened with the loss of its second-class mailing privileges and advertisers were frightened off for years afterwards. (For his first American job, newly arrived Nathaniel Buchwald—later to become a leading Communist theater critic—was hired by the State Department to furnish daily summaries of the *Forverts* and other Yiddish dailies.)

Assimilated Jews feared being tarred by the immigrant brush. Following the Bolshevik seizure of power in October, the *American Israelite* editorialized in favor of suppressing Yiddish journalism entirely, while the National Security League called for a ban on all foreign-language newspapers with special mention given to "the great Yiddish press."

For Russian Jews, the year 1917 concluded with a series of world-historic events. Not only did the tsar abdicate and his empire withdraw from the war, but in a letter sent to Lord Rothschild in November, British foreign secretary Arthur James Balfour pledged his help in establishing a Jewish homeland in the then Ottoman province of Palestine.

The period between the February and October revolutions saw the rise of a Yiddish cultural vanguard. In Kiev, where Jews made up one-quarter of the population, the writers David Bergelson, Moyshe Litvakov, and Nakhman Mayzel founded a Kultur Lige (Culture League) to encourage modernist Yiddish literature and avant-garde Jewish art. Odessa, which had been successively occupied by a variety of foreign armies throughout much of the Civil War, remained a center for privately owned film companies. There, Alexander Arkatov—who six-and-a-half years earlier had written *L'khaym*—directed a quartet of Jewish-theme films for the same Mizrakhi firm that produced Teneromo's *Milkhome un Yidn.*

Russian movie theaters were ordered closed in February. When they reopened in the spring, no longer subject to tsarist censorship, there was a small flood of Jewish-theme pictures. The most ambitious were Josef Soifer's dramatic reconstruction of the Beilis case; the Era Studio's five-reel *V Ikh Krovi My Nepovinny* (We Are Not Guilty of Their Blood), an adaptation of Yevgeni Chirikov's play *Yevrei* (Jews), which portrayed Jewish revolutionaries, democrats, and Zionists (as well as what one trade paper termed

a "truthfully terrifying" pogrom scene); and Arkatov's four films.

Arkatov's first, *Kantonisti* (Cantonists), was a five-reel historic drama about the forced conscription of Jewish youth during the reign of Nicholas I, based on the story "The Captured Recruit" by nineteenth-century Russian-Jewish novelist G. I. Bogrov. For his follow-up, the twenty-nine-year-old director adapted a more recent work of Yiddish literature: *Der Blutiker Shpas,* shot during the summer of 1917, was taken from Sholom Aleichem's 1912–13 serial novel. This precursor of the 1947 Hollywood movie *Gentleman's Agreement,* an apparent farce, in which a Jewish student trades places with his Russian friend for a year, is darkened for being set during the period of the Beilis case—it ends with the Jew being arrested for his part in the deception.

The Bolsheviks seized power in October 1917 and gave Jewish nationality legal status in January. Later that year, the Communist Party founded the Yiddish-language daily *Der Emes* (The Truth) and established a Yevsektsia (Jewish Section) to implement policy and orchestrate propaganda on the "Jewish street." For the first time in its history, Yiddish became the language of an official culture. The combination of Red blandishments, White atrocities, and the vacuum left by the departed Russian intelligentsia created unprecedented opportunities for Jews in the new Soviet order. The aesthetic vanguard supported its political equivalent. In Vitebsk, the thirty-one-year-old Marc Chagall was appointed commissar of art; in Petrograd, where twenty-nine-year-old Natan Altman was the commissar of art, the even younger Alexander Granovsky had been given the mandate to form a revolutionary Yiddish theater.

In 1918, Arkatov directed *Orupgeloste Oygn*

(Downcast Eyes), a five-reel adaptation from a short story by I. L. Peretz. Yiddish writer Khaym Margolis-Davidson saw the film in Odessa at the newly established State Culture Auditorium, where it was accompanied by a Russian-speaking lecturer. The film—known in Russian variously as *Suditye, Ludi* (Judge, People) and *Rozbitye Skrizchali* (Broken Commandments)—recounted the tragedy of two sisters, the daughters of a Jewish innkeeper. The younger, in love with the son of the local count, is hastily married off to a *yeshive-bokher* in another city. As a result, the count terminates the lease on the inn, the family is ruined, and the parents die. The saintly older daughter is then abducted by another nobleman and compelled to become his mistress. Both women are equally unhappy, but when the younger one dies, she is given a splendid funeral, while the older is buried in an unmarked grave.

Arkatov's last Jewish film was the three-reel *Ven Ikh Bin Rotshild* (*If I Were Rothschild*), taken from one of Sholom Aleichem's best-known monologues —indeed, one which he had recorded for Victor Records in New York in September 1915. Only a few pages long, the story presents the musings of a Kasrilevke *melamed* (teacher) whose wife is nagging him for Sabbath money he doesn't have. To escape this unpleasant reality, he lapses into a daydream of infinite wealth and power. From his first law (that a wife must always have a three-ruble piece in her possession), the narrator imagines new charitable societies for his town, then vast philanthropies for all Jews. In the end, he proposes to do away with war, nationality, and money itself—which brings him back to earth. Even if there was no money, he'd still have the problem of preparing for Sabbath.

The movie has been lost, but however Arkatov embroidered the original, *Ven Ikh Bin Rotshild* articulated a fantasy appropriate to the desperate yet millennial situation of Russian Jews: "No more envy, no more hatred, no Turks, no Englishmen, no Frenchmen, no Gypsies, and no Jews," Sholom Aleichem's narrator exults. "The face of the earth will change. As it is written: 'Deliverance will come.' The Messiah will have arrived."

NOTES

1. Negri's subsequent *Die Augen der Mumie Ma* (The Mummy's Eyes), released in 1918, was the first dramatic feature directed by twenty-six-year-old Ernst Lubitsch, who had broken into movies by appearing as an enterprising yet bungling Jewish apprentice or clerk in a series of short comedies. (One of these, *Die Firma Heiratet* [The Firm Marries], was released in the United States in late 1914 as *The Perfect Thirty-Six,* with intertitles by Jewish dialect specialist Montague Glass, author of *Potash and Perlmutter.*)

Overleaf: **Tevye's daughter. Alice Hastings in the title role of Charles Davenport's *Khavah* (U.S.A., 1919), the first American film adaptation from Sholom Aleichem.**

4

Nineteen-Nineteen

NINETEEN-NINETEEN has been called the first year of the twentieth century. The war's end, together with the Russian Revolution, inspired universal euphoria and unrest. ("Everywhere 'Extras!' fall from above and squash my watery head," wrote Yiddish poet Jacob Glatstein in his "1919.") The Hapsburg, Romanov, and Ottoman empires disintegrated; colonies as far-flung as India, Ireland, and Korea were in rebellion.

Lincoln Steffens returned from Moscow to proclaim that he'd "seen the future and it worked." In Berlin, where Fritz Lang and F. W. Murnau were directing first films and *Das Cabinet des Dr. Caligari* (*The Cabinet of Dr. Caligari*) would soon go into production, the local Dadaists turned revolutionary; the new year had barely arrived when the Spartacist Party held the city for six days. Three months later, in Munich, a motley collective of avant-garde poets staged a coup and declared a Bavarian Soviet. By then, Béla Kun had established a Communist regime in Hungary, and the Allies, still negotiating the Treaty of Versailles, feared that the Red tide would next engulf Austria—Karl Kraus's "laboratory for the end of the world."

Vienna had lost first its imperial grandeur, then its empire, and finally the trappings of civilization. Fuel was scarce; parks were stripped of benches and trees; few pets were to be found in the Austrian capital. For Americans, the summer brought Prohibition, and saw the most profitable theatrical season in New York history interrupted by a strike; that fall, the American Federation of Labor led 250,000 steelworkers out of the factories. Their strike was broken in November, the same month Attorney General Palmer raided "Bolshevik headquarters" in eleven American cities.

Everywhere, demobilized intellectuals and fiery young artists launched journals and founded movements. André Breton started *Littérature,* Bertolt Brecht completed his first plays, Franz Kafka published *In the Penal Colony.* In Hollywood, which, recovering from the slump of 1918, had succeeded Paris as the world capital of film production, a quartet of disgruntled employees—D. W. Griffith, Charlie Chaplin, Douglas Fairbanks, and Mary Pickford —banded together as United Artists.

In 1919 as well, ambitious new Yiddish art theaters were formed in New York and Petrograd. Where the tsar banned the Yiddish theater, the Soviets would subsidize it. For years, intellectuals like I. L. Peretz and Peretz Hirschbein had called for the destruction and reconsecration of the Yiddish stage. The Russian Revolution fulfilled this dream mainly through the endeavors of Alexander Granovsky, founder and first director of the Jewish Academic People's Theater of Moscow (GOSET), who, in order to revolutionize the Yiddish theater, would first have to learn Yiddish.

Born Abraham Azarkh in Moscow in 1890, less than a year before the Jewish community was expelled and his family resettled in Riga, Granovsky was a product of Russia's small, assimilated Jewish bourgeoisie. He attended art school in St. Petersburg, then studied at the Reinhardt Academy in Munich. Returning to Riga before the World War, Granovsky served in the Russian army until the tsar's fall. After a brief sojourn in neutral Sweden, where he worked in the movie industry (then one of the most advanced in Europe), the winter of 1918 found him active in the theatrical life of Red Petrograd—a jittery city suffering queues, cholera, and rule by the Community for Public Safety (Cheka).

Responding to the urgency of the times, Granovsky staged productions for the new Theater of Tragedy, an institution designed to bring classic drama to the masses, and, after directing an amateur Yiddish performance, was recruited by the Yevsektsia to create a new Soviet Jewish theater. (The same month, June 1918, Alexander Arkatov was in Moscow directing the first Soviet film, the two-reel *Signal,* for the revolutionary Mos-Kino-Committee; Eduard Tissé, Sergei Eisenstein's future collaborator, was one of his cameramen.)

Even more than Jacob Gordin, Granovsky was an "enlightened" Jew (albeit Germanized, rather than Russified). Unlike Gordin, however, Granovsky was a modernist. For his new Yiddish theater, he sought applications from young people uncontaminated by professional experience. Among them was a fellow Latvian, a squat, homely twenty-eight-year-old law student from Dvinsk, who had changed his name from Solomon Vovsi to Solomon Mikhoels. Although Mikhoels was exactly the same age as Granovsky and far more steeped in *Yidishkayt,* he surrendered himself completely to the director—the theater was his new religion. (In a sense, Mikhoels and Granovsky taught each other. That both attended the German-language Riga Realschule—a private gymnasium that owed its overwhelmingly Jewish student body to the tsarist *numerus clausus*— raises the possibility of a previous acquaintanceship.)

Although Granovsky's strategy would change when his theater moved from Petrograd to Moscow, his initial aspirations were universalist: "[This] is first of all a theatre, a temple of shining art, of joyous creation, where prayer is sung in the Yiddish language," he would proclaim on the occasion of his studio's first public performance in July 1919. "The functions of this theatre are those of a world theatre and only in its language does it differ from other theatres." A new wind was blowing; in essence, Granovsky had seconded some of the assumptions of the Vilna Troupe and Maurice Schwartz's Yiddish Art Theater, a New York company launched in the fall of 1918.

Schwartz, the Ukrainian-born actor-impresario, was not yet thirty when he joined forces with David Kessler's rebellious stepson Max Wilner and assumed the lease of a former German theater on East Fourteenth Street. With impressive acumen, Schwartz hired a dazzling assemblage of current and future stars—Jacob Ben-Ami, Ludwig Satz, Celia Adler, Lazar Freed, Berta Gersten, Anna Appel—and announced the company's existence with a manifesto in the *Forverts:*

I want the public to have a theater where the actors give themselves to their art with their whole hearts, where the management and the beautiful comfortable theater and everything can work toward one goal: to elevate the Yiddish theater from sensational "punches" and fifteen curtain calls. . . . The theater must be a sort of holy place, where a festive and artistic atmosphere will always reign.

During the 1918–19 season, the Yiddish Art Theater staged plays by Shaw, Schiller, Ibsen, Strindberg, Schnitzler, and Wilde—plus four productions by Jacob Gordin, and two each by Yiddish naturalists Ossip Dymow and David Pinski. In October, Ben-Ami, who had been part of Hirschbein's Odessa troupe, persuaded Schwartz to present Hirschbein's

Soviet director Alexander Granovsky, circa 1925. An assimilated Jew, Granovsky was instrumental in the development of Yiddish modernism.

Farvorfn Vinkl (A Secluded Nook). Ecstatically greeted by critics and intellectuals, as it had been in Vilna when the Vilna Troupe staged it in 1916, this production conventionally designates the birth of a Yiddish art theater in New York.

If Russian Jews experienced the tsar's collapse as a miraculous deliverance from bondage, their relief was short-lived. The evacuation of the Central Powers and the ensuing Civil War brought further misery, including a savage wave of pogroms and massacres. In newly reconstituted Poland no less than the contested territories of Galicia, Lithuania, and the Ukraine, Jews were caught between competing nationalisms. Warsaw was now home to a million Jewish refugees. (The Nalewki, one transient wrote, "was unbelievably crowded, with ear-shattering noises and an assortment of smells. The cat and rat population seemed as large as that of the milling human inhabitants. . . . Each courtyard was a city unto itself.")

The Ukraine, which declared its independence in January 1919, and where there was a complete breakdown of order by the end of February, was the bloodiest of all. Even as Granovsky rehearsed his theater, the newly established Mos-Kino-Committee released *Tovarishch Abram* (Comrade Abraham). Directed and photographed by Alexander Razumni (a pre-October Bolshevik, as well as director of a previous Jewish-theme film), *Comrade Abraham* was one of thirteen single-reel *agitki* (little agitation pieces) made to be shown at Red Army screenings. "These were posters in an urgent advertising campaign," Jay

A Jewish family shelters a Russian soldier: Alexander Razumni's 1919 *agitka, Comrade Abraham;* frame enlargement. This two-reel film was among the first produced by the revolutionary regime.

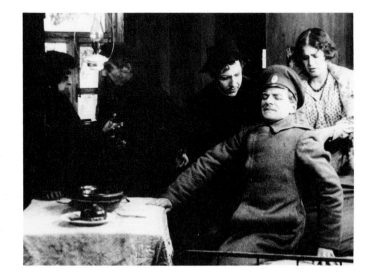

Leyda writes in *Kino.* "Their subjects were drawn from one year of Civil War."

Agitka protagonists were typically marginals—a circus clown, a White general's daughter, a Red prisoner's father—each of whom makes a revolutionary conversion. As its title suggests, *Comrade Abraham* has a Jewish hero and, over the course of a bare fifteen minutes, the film addresses itself to a number of anti-Semitic stereotypes. While Jews are unfairly accused of giving information to the German army, we see that the pious Hersh family have risked their safety to shelter a Russian scout. (The real spy is, in fact, a bourgeois Mata Hari.) A degenerate Orthodox priest plies the Black Hundreds with vodka and, when young Abram Hersh returns home, he learns that his entire family has been massacred. Abram leaves for Moscow where he finds a job in a factory and his calling as a political agitator: "Comrades, all workers are brothers. I suffered doubly—as a worker and as a Jew." With the Civil War, Abram joins the Red Army and, after fearlessly leading a charge to retake a captured city, is made a commissar.[1]

Early 1920 also saw the release of Alexander Arkatov's last and most lavish Russian film, the half-a-million-ruble feature known in English as *Between Two Flags.* Shot in Odessa from an autobiographical scenario by the Russian-born American banker-turned-socialist-and-now-movie-star Jacob Rubin, who had returned to revolutionary Russia in 1919 to offer his help, *Between Two Flags* was a graphic account of the White atrocities—including pogroms —that had been committed in the Ukraine. According to Rubin, the film received a tumultuous reception when premiered in Odessa at the confiscated villa of a former sugar magnate: "There was such a demonstration of enthusiasm as I have never witnessed in America outside of a political convention."

Between Two Flags was less warmly received in Moscow, however, and Rubin, after some difficulties, returned to the United States. He was followed by Arkatov, who arrived in Hollywood in 1920, presenting himself as the director of *The Cabinet of Dr. Caligari.* (The ploy failed. Arkatov spent the rest of his life in California working variously as a photographer, a director of army training films, and a manufacturer of filmstrip adaptations from the Bible.)

If Arkatov was unable to crack Hollywood, he was nonetheless prudent to repress his "red" past. In post–World War I America, a Comrade Abraham Hersh would have been the devil incarnate, the 1919 equivalent of an Arab terrorist. For the United States, too, was experiencing a restive proletariat. Even as *Comrade Abraham* received its first screenings in Moscow, the International Workers of the World called a general strike in Seattle. Wartime xenophobia actually increased after the Armistice. As returning doughboys marched up Fifth Avenue, New York's mayor attempted to prohibit non-English-language public meetings; six months later, his police commissioner proscribed the use of foreign languages in all street gatherings, political or other.

Although Attorney General Palmer asked the movie industry to aid in the anti-Bolshevik crusade, producers were already attuned to the current mood. Not long after soldiers scuffled with socialists during New York's May Day celebration, Lewis J. Selznick released the Mayflower Films production *Bolshevism on Trial,* a sensational account of a "free love" commune in Florida, based on a 1909 novel by Thomas Dixon. The following week, Joseph Schenk presented *The New Moon,* whose "big punch," according to *Variety,* was the dramatization of a Soviet edict "nationalizing all the women of Russia between seventeen and thirty-two." That summer, while the *New York Times* reported Soviet plans for "world rule," *The Volcano* posited a Bolshevik spy ring operating on the Lower East Side. Pressure from the Yiddish press and New York governor Al Smith compelled the producers to dilute the film's anti-Semitism with new titles. Thus, the hero was renamed "Captain Nathan Levison" and the hook-nosed villain given the line, "I am not a Jew; I am a Bolshevik."

The Burning Question, released not to theaters but to a network of some 17,000 Roman Catholic churches, warned against the Bolshevik threat in the form of foreign-born political agitators. Universal's scarcely more reasoned *Right to Happiness* featured one such operative, a girl separated from her parents during a pogrom, brought up by a family of Jewish Communists, and sent to America to organize the factory belonging to her long-lost father. Here, the Jewish generational conflict received its most extreme representation, but it was played out in other films as well: *Khavah,* also known as *Broken Barriers,* was adapted from Sholom Aleichem's Tevye cycle and first released in late April 1919; it predates Maurice Schwartz's stage production of *Tevye der Milkhiker* [Tevye the Dairyman] by several months. The film was directed by Charles Davenport for New York–based Zion Films. The cast featured several Yiddish actors, including onetime opera singer Giacomo Masuroff and Elihu (here "Alex") Tenenholz, an original member of the Schwartz company.

In adapting the story of the same name (and adding to it from the later tale "Get Thee Out"), *Khavah* dramatized the core beliefs of the popular Yiddish theater. When Khavah (Alice Hastings), the "modern" daughter of the dairyman Tobias (Masuroff), marries the Gentile boy Fedka (Tenenholz), son of the village sheriff, her parents mourn her as dead. Secure in her universalist beliefs, Khavah moves in with Fedka's family. The peasants treat her badly; Fedka fails to appreciate her sacrifice; and after Khavah learns her parents are being forced to move to the Pale of Settlement, she renounces her vows and pleads with her father to take her back. The movie ends with their expulsion from the village.

Khavah was the first American movie to be set in *Yidishland* and evoke a lost Jewish folk community. Writing in *Moving Picture World,* William J. Reilly found the ambiance overly authentic, complaining that "too much attention has been paid to the domestic duties and the womanly cares of the household." This, as well as "the many appearances of Khavah's father in an old Russian cart," he wrote, "drag the picture." Deeming the film "melodramatic, losing no opportunity for heavy acting," Reilly targeted the potential audience as those about whom Sholom Aleichem wrote. Indeed, in visiting the set, *Der Tog*'s reporter had been extremely impressed with *Khavah*'s attention to detail: "If not for the yellow trolley car that unexpectedly cuts through this *farvorfn vinkl,* you might think you saw an actual Ukrainian landscape before you."

None of Sidney Goldin's prewar films had been this bluntly insular—or this elegiac. By contrast with the ghetto melodramas that preceded and followed it, *Khavah* was among the few American movies to represent intermarriage as a failure. The suggested sell-line—"Love of Parents Triumphs over Love for Husband in Jewish Story"—has an exotic quality that seems not quite American. Despite a "happy ending," *Khavah* lacks the optimistic thrust of the melting-pot movies epitomized by Frank Borzage's *Humoresque,* the following spring's

surprise hit. Adapted from a story by Fannie Hurst, this early blockbuster from William Randolph Hearst's Cosmopolitan studio mixed colorful ethnicity with patriotic Americanism: encouraged by his mother (Yiddish actress Vera Gordon), a Jewish boy from the Lower East Side rises from the slums to become a famous concert violinist. Although temporarily incapacitated by a wound suffered in the World War, he regains his powers and marries the girl next door.[2]

In this sense, *Khavah*'s victory for parental wisdom was anachronistic—if any single theme characterizes the silent Yiddish films that would be produced in Vienna, Warsaw, and New York over the next half dozen years, it is the defeat of orthodox traditionalists and the successful revolt of the younger generation. There is an irony that the most conservative of early Yiddish films would be produced in the most modern of nations. But then, for its American audience, *Khavah* was a pastoral dream —the actual Ukraine was a landscape of disaster and death.

By the end of 1919, the Bolsheviks reigned victorious over an exhausted land. Meanwhile, the new state of Poland successively or simultaneously waged war against five of its neighbors—Germany, Lithuania, the Ukraine, Czechoslovakia, and the Soviet Union. A visiting American was struck by the "ragged conscripts being marched through the streets" of Warsaw, past boarded-up stores, hordes of beggars, and "flaming posters" exhorting Poles to meet the Russian threat.

On April 25, 1920, Poland's leader Józef Piłsudski invaded the Ukraine. Marching east, the Polish army, which routinely identified local Jews with Bolshevism, added to the mountain of civilian casualties. The campaign, however, was brief. By June, the Poles were driven from Kiev. As the Red Army advanced toward Warsaw, hoping to cross Poland and link up with the German proletariat, Jews were once again in flight.

Isaac Babel's story "Zamostye"—named for I. L. Peretz's native village, which was the site of the Polish counterattack—captures the apocalyptic mood of the Polish-Russian front. Standing guard duty, the narrator peers over the rooftops of the village and, in the company of a Ukrainian peasant, studies "the stealthy lights in the hovels of its ghetto."

The raw dawn trickled down on us like waves of chloroform. Green flares soared over the Polish lines. They hovered in the air, scattered like rose petals in the moonlight, and went out.

And in the quiet, I heard the faint vibrations of a moan. The smoke of secret killing roved around us.

"They're killing someone," I said. "Who can it be?"

"The Pole is scared," the peasant answered. "The Pole is slaughtering the Jews."

"Everyone blames the Jew," Babel's narrator is told. "Our lot and your lot too. There'll be hardly any of them left after this war."

Piłsudski's surprise counterattack split the Reds and saved the capital. After this "Miracle on the Vistula," the Soviets sued for peace. Warsaw was bedecked with flags—although the patriotic display made by the "poverty-stricken, harassed" Jewish quarter reminded Yiddish novelist Samuel Lewin "of a holiday among the inmates of a prison." After six years of war, there was a resurgence of nightlife.

A Lower East Side mother, played by Yiddish stage actress Vera Gordon, encourages her son in the first of the postwar "melting-pot" films, Frank Borzage's *Humoresque* (U.S.A., 1920).

Warsaw was to receive an infusion of post-Bolshevik Yiddish culture. Nakhman Mayzel arrived from Kiev and set up a new Kultur Lige; he was soon joined by his young *landsman* Peretz Markish. Together they would found the influential weekly *Literarishe Bleter* (Literary Pages). Markish was then the epitome of radical modernism. "When [he] came to Poland and thundered, many shrugged their shoulders," recalled critic Shlomo Belis, then a teenager. "It was a drunken dance of the word." Young people, however, "felt with every fibre that this was their poet, that he was singing their confusion, their bewilderment, their eagerness. . . ."

Sh. An-sky, who had also departed the Soviet Union, died in Warsaw that autumn, and *Der Dibek*, never produced during his lifetime, was performed

Sh. An-sky at the Russian-Austrian front, 1916.

by the Vilna Troupe as a memorial on December 9, 1920. Although originally intended only for a short run, the play proved so astonishingly popular that it became the mainstay of the troupe's repertoire. Contemporary accounts report that trolley conductors approaching the Elizeum Theater on Karowa Street in central Warsaw would call out "An-sky!" or "Dibek stop!"

Markish held particular appeal for Jewish youth, but *Der Dibek* was universal. The actress Luba Kadison, born in Kovno and raised in Vilna, remembers being startled by the number of Chasidim when she arrived in Warsaw. She imagined that, for this reason, *Der Dibek* would have special significance in the Polish capital. It did—but not because Chasidim flocked to the production. This romantic folk pageant, at once lyrical and grotesque, mysterious and nostalgic, established a self-conscious Yiddish stage. "With *Der Dibek*, a new era in Yiddish theater begins," another member of the troupe wrote. "One began to play for Gentiles"—and, also, assimilated Jews. The production ran for two seasons, played 300 performances and subsequently toured Europe.

In aestheticizing Chasidic folklore, *Der Dibek* epitomized a new Jewish art. "Our first imprimatur is our modernism, our leftism, and our youth," the Russian-Jewish critic Abram Efros had proclaimed in a 1918 essay on the An-sky Expedition. "Our second imprimatur is our orientation towards the people, our traditions, and our [antiquity]." For Efros, this dual principle was exemplified by the painters Chagall, Altman, and Robert Falk, all of whom reworked Jewish folk motifs in the light of European modernism. It would have its most extravagant expression when, encouraged by Efros, Granovsky moved his theater to Moscow.[3]

In a historical sense, *Der Dibek* belongs with those long-germinating, postwar masterpieces that make up the high modernist canon: *Ulysses* (1921), *Six Characters in Search of an Author* (1921), *The Castle* (1922), *The Waste Land* (1922), *The Duino Elegies* (1923), *The Magic Mountain* (1924). In another context, it can be bracketed with *The Cabinet of Dr. Caligari,* which opened in Berlin in February 1920, as an example of popular expressionism. Maurice Schwartz introduced *Der Dibek* to New York in September 1921. Four months later, Habima gave the play its Hebrew premiere in Moscow. By the mid-twenties, *Der Dibek* was synonymous with Yiddish art theater—David Vardi directed an English version in New York, Max Reinhardt staged a German one in Berlin, Mark Arnshteyn presented a Polish production in Warsaw; the play was subsequently translated into French, Czech, Bulgarian, Ukrainian, Swedish, Serbian, and Japanese.

As *Der Dibek* provided the vehicle by which the Yiddish theater would make its entrance on the world stage, so there were those who sought to introduce the world repertoire into Yiddish theater. The ambitious young actor Zygmunt Turkow returned to Warsaw during the winter of *Der Dibek,* convinced—like Granovsky and Schwartz—that "Yiddish theater must free itself from the *kapote* [long coat traditionally worn by Chasidim], leave the Jewish street where it's been stuck since Goldfadn's time, and rise to the broad highway of a 'world repertoire.' "

Turkow, twenty-five, began as an amateur actor in a workers' theater. Later, he studied at the Polish State Drama Academy, appearing on the Polish and Russian-language stage. In 1918 he married the nineteen-year-old Ida Kaminska and, with her mother's troupe, spent two and a half years touring the war zone, traveling from the German-controlled Ukraine into the Soviet sphere. This ensemble, which included his younger brother Jonas, a veteran of occupied Warsaw's German-language stage, and Jonas's wife, became the Varshiver Yidisher Kunst Teater (Warsaw Jewish Art Theater), better known by its acronym VYKT. In opposition to the parochial old Yiddish stage, the VYKT developed a repertoire of classic and contemporary European plays (favoring those with leftish politics).

If Turkow was a man of 1919, so in his way was *Der Tog's* Ray Ruskin, whose account of *Khavah* is striking for the close attention it pays to the mechanics of filmmaking. Deliberately setting out to demystify the illusion, Ruskin explains the process of editing, describes the specific nature of screen acting, insists on the centrality of the director. Despite its

conservative bias, *Khavah* suggested a radical advance beyond the Yiddish stage. For youthful modernizers, the movies were an inevitable next step. The cinema, sometimes called "the theater of the future," was included in the program of virtually every European vanguard movement, from Futurism to Bolshevism. By the end of 1925, Granovsky, Schwartz, and Turkow would each direct a Yiddish film—and each film, in its way, would be self-consciously modern.

NOTES

1. At least two more *agitki* featured Jewish protagonists. In late 1919, B. Svetlov (who had directed the Petrograd Kino Committee's first offering, *The Victory of May*) made *Fighters for the Glorious State of the Third International,* with Razumni in the cast, from a script written for a competition to explain the counterrevolutionary nature of anti-Semitism. In the spring of 1920, the newly established All-Russian Cinema-Photo Section released *The Masters Attack,* an anti-Polish agitprop most likely intended for distribution in the Ukraine. One of the heroic partisans is explicitly Jewish.

2. The same month that *Humoresque* opened, Henry Ford's *Dearborn Independent* gave the continuing nativist hysteria a particular anti-Semitic focus when it began publishing its own version of the spurious *Protocols of the Elders of Zion.* Nevertheless, *Humoresque* inspired a new cycle of ghetto melodramas, notably Universal's 1921 *Cheated Love* (a remake of Sidney Goldin's 1913 *Heart of a Jewess*) and Samuel Goldwyn's 1922 adaptation of immigrant writer Anzia Yezierska's *Hungry Hearts.*

3. Efros's association of modernism and the past echoed that of the Russian *budetlyane* ("men of the future") who argued that an authentically modern Russian culture could only be developed by using old Russian myths, folk art, and icons as its source. "The future is behind us," declared the painters Mikhail Larionov and Natalia Goncharova in their 1913 Rayonist-Futurist Manifesto.

Overleaf: **East meets West. A traditional Jew (Saul Nathan) and his American niece (Molly Picon) attempt to restrain her father (Sidney Goldin) from attacking her admirer (Jacob Kalich) in Goldin's comedy East and West (Austria, 1923).**

5

Out of Galicia

IN FRANZ KAFKA'S "A Report to an Academy," a talking ape gives an account of his former life as a dumb brute and describes the circumstances under which, captured and imprisoned, he learned to speak German: "There was no attraction for me in imitating human beings; I imitated them because I needed a way out, and for no other reason." It was this story, published in the November 1917 issue of Martin Buber's journal *Der Jude,* that inspired Max Brod to observe that Kafka addressed "the sufferings of his own unhappy people . . . as no one else has ever done . . . without the word 'Jew' appearing in any one of his books."

For a thousand years, Jews had been Europe's internal Other. Although throughout the nineteenth century the trend in Central Europe was toward a rapid Jewish assimilation into German culture, this was accompanied by a rise in political anti-Semitism. The sense of Jews as aliens received new impetus from the World War, which, for the first time, brought ordinary Germans into intimate contact with the Slavic and, especially, *ostjüdisch* (Eastern Jewish) masses. In one sense, the German image of the *Ostjude* had corresponded to such traditional negative stereotypes of the aggressive alien interloper as the Polish (and Polish-Jewish) view of the Russian-Jewish "Litvak." In another, the *Ostjude* was the embodiment of cultural inferiority, whose imperfect adaptation to German civilization was epitomized in the use of Yiddish or Yiddishized German. To these were now added the sense of *Ostjuden* as an uncanny, impoverished, ineluctably foreign mass. All three notions of *Ostjude*—along with the association of Jews and Bolshevism—fueled the right-wing nationalism and radical racial ideologies of the post–World War I period, undermining the position of even those successfully German-identified Jews.

In the aftermath of the war, the German and Austrian movie industries produced a small flurry of films with Jewish characters and themes. Paul Wegener's *Der Golem* (The Golem; 1920) and Henrik Galeen's *Judith Trachtenberg* (1920) were fairly straightforward in their presentation of Jews as exotic, if not uncanny, Others—living in medieval ghettos, apart from Christian society. Carl Dreyer's belated pogrom film *Die Gezeichneten* (The Stigma-

Mysteries of the ghetto: the golem (Paul Wegener) prepares to abduct the rabbi's daughter (Lída Salmanová) in Wegener's *The Golem* (Germany, 1920).

tized Ones; 1921), Manfred Noa's adaptation of Lessing's *Nathan Der Weis* (Nathan the Wise; 1922) —which was banned in Munich after it occasioned anti-Semitic riots—and E. A. Dupont's *Das Alte Gesetz* (*The Ancient Law*; 1923) were more sympathetic, but still defined Jews in terms of their relation to the Gentile world.

The most stylized of these was undoubtedly *The Golem*, a precursor to the American movie *Frankenstein*, set in seventeenth-century Prague. Wegener, who pioneered the supernatural strain in German cinema, had already made the link between Jews and the *unheimlich* in his 1913 *Der Student von Prag* (*The Student of Prague*), which set a crucial scene in a facsimile of Prague's old Jewish cemetery—the very place where, according to the anti-Semitic forgery *The Protocols of the Elders of Zion,* Jewish leaders met once every century to plot their machinations. (Refused permission to film in the graveyard by the Jewish community, Wegener fashioned outsized, Hebrew-inscribed tombstones and shot the sequence in a nearby forest.)

The director had a marked predilection for this material: *The Golem* was his third use of the story— a 1914 version, shot in Prague, used a contemporary setting and was followed by a 1917 comedy about the making of the earlier movie entitled *Der Golem und die Tanzerin* (The Golem and the Dancing Girl). The 1920 *Golem* is, however, the most spectacular, the atmosphere of impending disaster made apparent from the very first title: "The learned Rabbi Loew reads in the stars that misfortune threatens the Jews." An astrologer and magician as well as a Cabbalist, the rabbi creates a man of clay, a golem, when the Hapsburg emperor threatens to expel the Jews from Prague (for allegedly using black magic). Although the golem is intended to protect the Jews, he becomes their destroyer—the film reaches its climax with the creature running amok and the ghetto on fire.[1]

Wegener's *Golem* includes a subplot in which the rabbi's daughter Miriam falls in love with a Christian knight—as in the American ghetto melodrama, intermarriage was an issue in most European Jewish films. The same year as Wegener's hit, Henrik Galeen, who had cowritten and codirected the 1914 version of *The Golem,* made *Judith Trachtenberg* from the novel by Karl Emil Franzos, in which a Jewish maiden marries a Galician count and is ostracized by the entire ghetto. Again, the image of a Jewish cemetery looms large: Judith's pious parents go so far as to bury her in absentia. Later, having come to visit their graves, Judith discovers her own tombstone and swoons upon it.

Galeen subsequently provided the script for F. W. Murnau's 1922 "symphony of horror," *Nosferatu*—a film, which, although not specifically concerned with the Jews, is highly suggestive of anti-Semitic paranoia. The vampire Nosferatu is a threat to German-Christian virtue. He embodies a deadly plague from Eastern Europe; he and his obsequious cohort, both played by Jewish actors (Max Schreck and Alexander Granach, a crossover from the Yiddish stage) whose features have been exaggerated by makeup, communicate in bizarre hieroglyphs. (The epidemic was, of course, a projection: three months after *Nosferatu's* release, the Weimar Republic's most important Jewish politician, Foreign Minister Walter Rathenau, was murdered by a band of fanatical young nationalists.)

Dreyer's *Die Gezeichneten*—given the English title *Love One Another*—which was adapted from the novel by Aage Madelung and made in Berlin with a mainly Russian refugee cast, employed essentially

A street in the Prague ghetto: *The Golem.*

the same elements as the pogrom films Sidney Goldin had directed in New York before the war. Hannah Liebe falls in love with a Gentile and, to avoid an arranged marriage, follows him to St. Petersburg, the home of an older brother who has already converted to Christianity. Hannah and her lover become revolutionaries, but when her Jewishness is discovered she is deported from the capital. Her brother is similarly exposed and is killed in a pogrom. The film ends with the strikes that herald the revolution of 1905.

Only one film showed a Jew making a successful adaptation to the modern world. Dupont's *The Ancient Law*—released during the acme of hyperinflation, sexual acting-out, and political unrest—echoes the American ethos. The hero is a rabbi's son who leaves the ghetto and becomes the star of Vienna's Burgtheater. Anticipating *The Jazz Singer* by four

years, the film dramatizes the movement toward secularism and universal culture in terms of a young
Jew's revolt against the "ancient law" of his orthodox
father (played by Avrom Morevsky, who had come
to Vienna with the Vilna Troupe). Like *The Jazz
Singer* as well, *The Ancient Law* is ambiguous in its
sympathies; Dupont, an assimilated German Jew,
took particular care in his representation of religious
ritual.

This insider's view notwithstanding, *The Ancient
Law* is still primarily an attempt to make Jewish
psychology intelligible to the Gentile world—it is
sympathetic ethnography. The first European movies made by Jews for Jews, from a distinctively Jewish
perspective, were produced in postwar Vienna—
where political tensions were such that Jews were
compelled to shift from passive stereotype to active
self-representation.

From the late nineteenth century on, imperial Vienna had drawn Yiddish-speaking Jews from the
Austrian provinces, as well as Russia. When the
World War broke out, the city's 175,000 Jews were
Europe's third-largest Jewish community, after Warsaw and Budapest, and perhaps its most distinguished. Their numbers swelled dramatically and
their identity underwent a crisis with the Russian
occupation of Galicia.

Correctly anticipating the worst, hundreds of
thousands of Galician Jews abandoned their homes
and fled west with the retreating Austrian army.
Over 75,000 of these destitute *Ostjuden* made their
way to Vienna, increasing the capital's Jewish population by nearly 50 percent virtually overnight. Most
of the refugees were taken in by relatives; the average

density in the Jewish neighborhoods of the Leopoldstadt, a working-class quarter between the Danube
and the Danube canal, rose to six per room. The
Viennese called this district—a colorful world of
peddlers and beggars, tailors and sages, gamblers,
hustlers, and even a smattering of Sephardic rug
merchants—*"Die Mazzesinsel,"* Matzo Island.

While the cafés of the Taborstrasse catered to
Jewish chess players and assorted wheeler-dealers,
the Praterstrasse, Leopoldstadt's other main thor-
oughfare (ending in the Prater amusement park), was
Vienna's major entertainment zone. Before the war,
the Budapester Orpheum—where cabaret was performed in a German-Hungarian-Yiddish patois that,
according to the novelist Friedrich Torborg, was "as
far from the Yiddish spoken in the eastern part of
the empire as it was from proper German"—was
known as "the home of Jewish humor." Such Yiddish
theater as existed was primitive. When Ida Kaminska passed through Vienna in 1917, she was
appalled:

Here was a dirty hall without even a separation
between buffet and stage, and people sat at the
buffet, speaking loudly during the performance.
One could hear the continuing spritz of soda
water from the siphons. The stage was a small
one, and behind the curtain one could see the
prompter, who, poor man, spoke louder than the
actors.

After the Galician influx and throughout the
twenties, however, the Leopoldstadt supported three
or four Yiddish theaters, along with a full range of
Jewish cultural activity. The Vilna Troupe arrived
with *Der Dibek,* in the autumn of 1922—even as
another member of the Yiddish internationale, revo-

lutionary poet Peretz Markish, was sponsored by the Labor-Zionist Poale Zion to deliver a series of readings.

A new Jewish nationalism was further embodied by the Zionist soccer team Hakoakh (the Force) and the Polish-Jewish strongman Zishe Breitbart, who appeared in Vienna several times during the early twenties. The son of a Lodz blacksmith, Breitbart was the idol of Central Europe's urban Jewish masses —he hammered nails with his fists, supported carriages on his chest, balanced anvils on his head, wrapped iron bars around his arm as if they were *tfilin*. A modern Bar Kokhba, if not a one-man Israel before the fact, Breitbart wore a Roman toga with a prominent Mogen David medallion and, as part of his performance, pledged to protect the honor of the Jewish people. Breitbart and the telepathist Eric Jan Hanussen (born Steinschneider), another habitué of the Artists' Café on Praterstrasse, were the subject of a one-reel parody, *Schmalbart als Kann'utzen,* released in Vienna in early 1923; later that year, Breitbart appeared in an Austrian crime melodrama *Der Eisenkönig* (The Ice King) and made an American tour, appearing in New York at the Palace Theater. He died in Berlin of blood poisoning—brought low, according to legend, by a rusty nail.

If the Galician influx contributed to the vitality of Viennese Jewish life, strengthening the Orthodox, Zionist, and Yiddishist camps, it provoked mixed feelings among the city's assimilated Jews. The pejorative term *Ostjude* did not pass into popular usage until after the turn of the century, but the negative stereotype was well established. (Long before the Galician exodus, Vienna had a tradition of political anti-Semitism. Richard Lueger, the city's popular prewar mayor, was only one politician who made anti-Semitic rhetoric part of his stock-in-trade. It was in Lueger's Vienna that the young Adolf Hitler first encountered East European Jews, imbibing the racist vilification that, mixed with pan-Germanism and occult teachings, streamed from the popular press.) Sigmund Freud's *Jokes and Their Relation to the Unconscious,* first published in 1905, is replete with examples of Viennese humor based upon the alleged "dirtiness" of Galician Jews—featuring such stock Eastern types as the *shadkhn* and *shnorrer.* Indeed, Freud's analysis was something of a late development, drawing its material from popular collections like Manuel Schnitzler's *Book of Jewish Jokes,* published for "modern" Jews to enjoy their forefathers' foibles.

For these Germanized Jews, their Polish coreligionists embodied a primitive past whose tangential relation to Western culture was epitomized by their irrational customs and especially the pidgin German of their "jargon." Intellectuals like Martin Buber might idealize the Yiddish language and Chasidic mysticism, but, however ambivalently, other German-speaking Jews, who shared the larger culture's need to designate a linguistically inferior subgroup, perceived the *Ostjuden* as a threat to their own precarious status. "Those who came ten years ago are not pleased to see those who come now," the novelist Joseph Roth wrote in the mid-twenties. "Their cousins and coreligionists who sit in the newspaper offices of the first district are already '*schön*' Viennese, and they don't want to be related to the *Ostjuden,* let alone mistaken for them."

While the tension between established German Jews and immigrant Eastern Jews was felt in urban America, the more heterogeneous New World allowed for the projection of group anxiety onto other

Others. By contrast, describing the Galician exodus in his *History of the Jews of Vienna,* community leader Dr. Max Grunwald identifies with the Austrian majority.

One can readily imagine the feelings of the suffering and downcast Christian population, which had known of Polish Jews for the most part through anti-Jewish nursery tales, when they saw these poor victims of the war occupying the streets and squares of Vienna. Most of them, in order to find some means of livelihood, had to be constantly on the move. In view of the fact that official support scarcely supplied the utmost necessities, they speculated in money and indulged in other reprehensible practices to ward off starvation.

In effect, the Austrian government did its share in criminalizing these refugees. The rigid insistence on proper registration compelled many Galicians—their towns destroyed, birth records lost—to forge documents and find ways to circumvent the authorities. "Everyone marvels at the ability of the Jews to make false statements. No one marvels at the naïve questions of the police," Roth points out, adding that "there is no more difficult fate than being a foreign *Ostjude* in Vienna."[2]

In 1917, the year Ida Kaminska arrived in Vienna vainly looking for work in the Austrian movie industry, only thirty-eight films were made. From 1918 to 1922, however, the industry boomed; in the peak year of 1920, 142 movies were produced. This resurgence included a number of important "Jewish" films.

In 1918, Wiener Kunstfilm released a filmed version of Eugène Scribe's play *Die Jüdin* (The Jewess). The next year, the actor Otto Kreisler—who had previously written and directed an adaptation of Ibsen's *Ghosts* for Wiener Kunstfilm—made a five-reel version of Franz Grillparzer's play *Die Jüdin von Toledo* (The Jewess of Toledo) and followed up with the seven-reel epic, *Theodor Herzl, Der Bannerträger des Jüdischen Volkes* (Theodor Herzl, Champion of the Jewish People), written by Heinrich Glücksmann. Despite its title, the film is not biographical; the protagonist, played by Rudolf Schildkraut, is an Eastern every-Jew—a refugee from Russian pogroms who escapes to Vienna. An actor who himself crossed over from Yiddish to German-language theater (and back), Schildkraut had played Jewish characters—including the "Shylock of Krakow"—in several wartime Austrian films. (His son, Joseph, was also cast in *Theodor Herzl.*)

Herzl, who died in 1904, had once been the epitome of the assimilated European Jew. Born in Budapest, he became a leading journalist in Vienna, and regarded the Jewish Question as peripheral until—radicalized by the Dreyfus affair and the simultaneous rise of political anti-Semitism in Vienna—he became the leading advocate of a Jewish state in Palestine. Kreisler's film was designed to dramatize Herzl's evolution. Militant and ambitious, the movie opens by invoking the Beilis case and its Hungarian equivalent, the Tiszaeszlar blood libel, as evidence of Europe's incorrigible anti-Semitism. There was ample evidence of this while the film was in production. Jews were beaten in the streets during the 1920 elections; the victorious Christian Socials ran a campaign equating corruption with *Ostjuden* (one poster depicts the Austrian eagle choked by a monstrous serpent with *payes*), *Ostjuden* with assimilated Jews, and assimilated Jews with the Social Democrats—

who, after their loss, immediately attacked the converted Jews among the ruling party.

Kreisler's *Herzl,* which appeared even as Zionists organized Jewish self-defense groups, was advertised as "a film that every Jew must see." Termed a *"historischer Monumentalfilm,"* it suggests a Zionist *Intolerance,* which substitutes the leitmotif of a spinning globe for Griffith's "cradle, endlessly rocking," and telescopes all of Jewish history into one dramatic pageant. The action flashes back from Herzl's childhood to King David's palace and King Solomon's temple, then jumps ahead to the fifteenth-century expulsion of the Sephardim from Spain and the tsar's persecution of Galician Jews, to climax in the image of a future, densely skyscrapered Jerusalem.[3]

Theodor Herzl had its premiere on February 11, 1921—opening at a Taborstrasse movie house, where it was held over an extra week before moving to a theater on the Praterstrasse. Altogether, *Herzl* played three Leopoldstadt theaters that month and was subsequently revived. (In September, a special Sunday morning screening was held in Vienna's largest cinema, the 2,000-seat Zirkus Busch-Kino, to benefit victims of the Ukrainian pogroms.) The *Forverts*'s Viennese correspondent, who began his lengthy review of the film by reproaching the Zionist leadership as hopelessly bourgeois, reported that a mixed audience of Jews and Gentiles responded to *Herzl* with "heart-rending cries." Schildkraut "is not one person, he is a *million* people, because he *suffers* for millions. . . ." The suffering of Schildkraut's character ends when, having opened a bookstore, he meets Dr. Herzl, and is granted a pastoral vision of Zion. "With this image the entire audience sighed with relief," the *Forverts* observed.

There was great joy and happiness. Jews and
Gentiles shook each others' hands. . . . And so it

happened that I also embraced the neighbors in my row—two beautiful Viennese *shikslekh* [Gentile girls]. We kissed and hugged each other with great enthusiasm.

Apparently that is how God made good on the tears I had just shed.

That same year, Kreisler celebrated another sort of Jewish champion with *Das Judenmädel* (The Jewish Girl), a one-reel vehicle for the twenty-two-year-old American comedienne Molly Picon, whose vehicle *Yankele* captivated Jewish Vienna, running for some 108 performances in the spring of 1921 before touring Poland, Czechoslovakia, Hungary, and Rumania. In her memoirs, Picon explains that, although already a youthful veteran of Yiddish theater and vaudeville, she was then "a Yiddish illiterate," the Yiddish she spoke was "completely bastardized." Thus, her husband and manager, Jacob Kalich, shrewdly organized a lengthy European engagement in order for her to shed her Lower East Side mannerisms, learn European Yiddish, and then return a star. (As the daughter of a wardrobe mistress, she was too familiar to be taken seriously by the producers of the American Yiddish theater.)

Vienna served as Picon's base and she augmented her stage work with occasional movie roles. (Even before Picon left Boston, where she and Kalich had been the reigning Yiddish stars, the young actress received an offer from the International Film Company. When the couple left for Europe, Kalich told one reporter that he planned to establish a motion picture studio in Palestine "which will deal with the production of Biblical plays only.") The Austrian film industry of the early twenties provided work for refugees not only from Budapest and Berlin (most famously, the exotic dancer Anita Berber) but from Hollywood as well. The acrobat Eddie Polo, once a rival to Douglas Fairbanks, relocated to Europe and made *Der Fluch der Habgier* (The Curse of Greed; 1922). Also in Vienna was the peripatetic Sidney Goldin who had left New York to form his own company. Goldin-Film's initial productions were a pair of luridly titled, five-reel melodramas—*Ihre Vergangenheit* (Her Past; 1921) and *Führe Uns nicht in Versuchung* (Lead Us Not into Temptation; 1922), the latter starring Russian actor Paul (later Ben-Zvi) Baratoff, who had recently learned Yiddish to perform in Vienna's semiprofessional Fray Yidishe Folksbine (Free Jewish People's Stage). In April 1922, Picon was featured in Goldin's lighter *Hütet eure Töchter* (Protect Your Daughters); he subsequently directed her in the six-reel comedy *Ost und West* (East and West; 1923).

Made in an atmosphere of escalating anti-Semitism and described as the "adventures of an American girl in Poland," *East and West* was a film which, no less than *Theodor Herzl*, spoke directly to the situation of Viennese Jewry. By March 1923, pro-monarchist, anti-Jewish rallies and demonstrations —some directed at Yiddish theaters—were an almost daily occurrence in Vienna, with future Nazi propagandist Julius Streicher among the speakers. (A report published in the August 1923 issue of *Menorah Journal* calls Vienna "a center of rampant anti-Semitic agitation, plastered with anti-Jewish slogans and populated by *Hakenkreuz-* [swastika-] wearing students.") Nor were such activities restricted to Austria. Picon and Kalich had that month returned from Bucharest to Vienna, compelled to cut short their engagement when the Rumanian government revoked the license for Yiddish performances.

East and West, which takes its title from a German-Jewish magazine whose particular mission it was to mediate the world of the *Ostjuden,* shoulders the task of explaining East to West and making East seem more comprehensible. To this end, the movie features a number of didactic tableaux that "document" various Jewish rituals—a *shabes* meal, the Yom Kippur service, a traditional wedding—with suitable dignity. (Nevertheless, in deeming the picture suitable only for Jewish audiences, the critic for the Austrian trade paper, *Paimann's Filmlisten,* found its representation of Jewish customs to be beyond comprehension.)

At the same time, the film's breezy, irreverent tone seems particularly American. This quality is accentuated in the surviving print by the Yiddish-inflected English titles added for the movie's 1924 American release—they joke that noodle soup is "a luxury which is music to the ears," tease *yeshive* students as freeloaders, and make topical references to the American quota on immigration. Of course, nothing in the movie is more American than its star. Picon's extraordinary appeal exemplifies the dynamic cultural relationship between the New World and the Old Country. While Kalich brought his wife to Vienna and Warsaw to establish her Old World credentials, it was precisely her New World energy and insouciance which endeared Picon to young Jewish audiences, particularly in Poland.

Written by Goldin and Eugen Preis, *East and West* features the director himself, mugging shamelessly in the role of Mr. Robert Brown, an exuberantly vulgar New York businessman who returns to Europe for a family wedding. Robert brings his daughter Molly (Picon) back to his Galician birthplace, where, as a press announcement explains, "the unfamiliar customs prompt the vivacious girl to some silly pranks." If the *allrightnik* Robert (or Morris, as he is called in the film's American version) can't even read Hebrew—"That's a prayer book, not a checkbook," someone gibes him—his daughter's antics place her far beyond the pale. Molly not only conceals a dime novel inside her *sider* during the Yom Kippur service, she sneaks off to the kitchen and stuffs herself with sacrilegious abandon.

"Ach! That American *shikse!* She ate it up!" moans the cook on discovering that the provisions with which the family planned to break its fast have been impiously devoured. After Molly dons boxing gloves and a newsboy cap and attacks the squealer, her irate father has no recourse but to take her over his knee and spank her. The pugnacious Americans are always ready to use their fists, and more—as the essence of modernity, a modified jazz baby with bobbed hair and bee-stung lips, Picon makes a stunning impact on *shtetl* life. Not long after the Yom Kippur scandal, the irrepressible "American *shikse*" is seen teaching the *yeshive* boys how to shimmy. The smitten students dance around her golden calves as she prances on a tabletop: "Look, an American waltz!"

Anticipating Clara Bow by three years, Picon's hyperactive flapper is almost a force of nature. She crashes her cousin's wedding dressed as a boy (a Picon trademark; in *Yankele* she plays a comic *yeshive-bokher*), then, hopping frantically about in her pajamas, demands a mock marriage of her own. The enraptured youths are eager to oblige, egging her on as she drags one particularly timid student, Ruben (Kalich), under the wedding canopy. The joke turns out to be on Molly, however. When Ruben puts the ring on her forefinger in the presence of two male witnesses, he effectively legitimates the marriage.

Under intense community pressure, Ruben consents to a *get* (religious divorce)—but only following a five-year period of separation. Defying the rabbi's injunction to divorce Molly immediately, Ruben is

Three generations: father (Sidney Goldin, in top hat) looks on as daughter (Molly Picon) strikes a pose with grandmother (Laura Glucksman), in Goldin's *East and West* (Austria, 1923).

The toast of Galicia: an American visitor (Molly Picon) is fêted by the local *bokhurim* in *East and West.*

no less rebellious than the American flapper, and far more a martyr to love. After Brown and daughter return to New York, Ruben also leaves the *shtetl*—for Vienna. He writes to his wealthy uncle and moves to that "wonderful city," where he wanders haplessly about in Chasidic kneepants and *payes* until his uncle, pointing out the discreet Mogen David that adorns his house, persuades him to cut his beard and go European. "Nearing perfection," reads the title as the clean-shaven Ruben leaves the barbershop resembling no one so much as Harold Lloyd.

Five years later, Ruben has become a distinguished orientalist (!), the stylishly attired author of the best-selling, reflexively titled *Ost und West*—his "Report to the Academy," as it were. There's a soirée in his honor at which, providentially visiting Vienna, Molly turns up. She instantly falls in love with the handsome writer but, as a good Jewish wife, must remain faithful to her absent husband. The happy discovery that celebrity and husband are identical is delayed one gag longer. Ruben playfully regresses, disguising himself as an *Ostjude* before revealing his identity for the final clinch.

East and West was unlike any previous Jewish film. E. G. Fried, a Viennese (and presumably Jewish) newspaperman, began his favorable review by confessing that he ordinarily went out of his way to avoid those "badly costumed, ridiculously sentimental" Jewish-subject films which, most likely produced by Otto Kreisler, were "permeated with pogroms, Sabbath tales, and all manner of poorly acted nonsense." But *East and West,* to which Fried was drawn solely on the basis of Picon's reputation, was something else. This film "breathes true Jewish character," even though "it does not satisfy—one might say, thank God—high literary expectation."

In addition to extolling Picon's "natural grace" and "humor," Fried cites the authenticity of the musical accompaniment, which drew on Jewish folk motifs; he also praises the actors, many recruited from the Fray Yidishe Folksbiene, for eschewing "exaggerated pathos" and "cloying sentimentality." Revealingly, he compliments the movie for conveying "true sentiments" rather than Jewish militance. *East and West* is hardly a Zionist statement. By arguing for adaptation as well as understanding, it suggests that beneath the *Ostjude*'s beard and *kapote* is a modern European waiting to be liberated.

Goldin addresses only one of the two stereotypes that dominated Viennese anti-Semitic tracts, namely the "dogmatic," "superstitious" traditional Jew. The film does not feature that "rootless," "amoral" manipulator, the *luftmentsh;* rather, it displaces his imperfect adaptation to Western civilization onto the jovial and confident figure of the American *allrightnik*. Thus, not simply a vehicle tailored to Picon's talents—as well as a playful elaboration on her European tour (and Goldin's own intervention into Austrian cinema)—*East and West* provided a satisfying fantasy for Vienna's beleaguered Jewish community by presenting the successfully Germanized Jew as a golden mean between the primitive *Ostjude* and the crass American.

Despite the inflation, which by the spring of 1923 drove the cost of a movie ticket up to that of a month's worth of food in 1919, *East and West* seems to have been a popular success. The movie opened late in the summer of 1923 and, according to Picon, enjoyed a longer run than even *The Kid,* Charlie Chaplin's most ambitious film to that time. That *East and West* is not cited in any of the standard Austrian histories of the period, however, suggests that Picon may have mistaken Leopoldstadt for Vienna. *East and West* was also a hit in Jewish Warsaw and subsequently played throughout Europe—released in Rumania and appearing in Paris in early 1924 under the title *Metamorphoses* (with *Cinémagazine* hailing Goldin as *"le grand artiste israélite"*). By then, Kalich and Picon had brought *Yankele* to Second Avenue, the star billed as "The Greatest Sensation from Europe."

Although the couple planned to return to Vienna to make a second movie, this projected follow-up was abandoned in the wake of their American success. Over the next five years, Picon would star in an unprecedented string of hit operettas; within two years of her return she had her own theater and was the highest-paid Yiddish stage performer in the world.

Goldin, however, made one subsequent Jewish film in Vienna, again drawing upon visiting American talent. When Maurice Schwartz's Yiddish Art Theater arrived in Austria on the final leg of their spring 1924 European tour, Goldin directed the company for the one-shot Jüdische-Kunstfilm in an eight-reel adaptation of Harry Seckler's *Yisker* (Prayer of Remembrance), first staged by Schwartz the previous season in New York.

A fairly elaborate period piece, *Yisker* is set in eighteenth-century Volhynia and, like many of Seckler's writings, concerns a Jewish martyr. In a published edition of the play, the author gives a legend collected by the An-sky Expedition as his source of inspiration. In the original tale, a nobleman's daughter is smitten by a handsome Jewish youth, tries repeatedly to seduce him, and finally dies "burned in her own hellish fire," after which the duke has the youth buried alive. (Seckler was attracted to the story, he says, because the martyr was beautiful rather than learned.)

The film *Yisker* opens with a procession of mourners passing through a dappled woods on their way to recite Kaddish by the martyr's grave. There, the rabbi (Lazar Freed, an old associate of Goldin as well as of Schwartz) relates the story which, in its account of Jewish-Gentile romance, reverses such early Goldin works as *The Sorrows of Israel* and *Nihilist Vengeance*. The hero Leybke (Schwartz) is a lusty young Jewish forester who attracts the attention of the local count (Austrian star Oskar Beregi, who had played the cruel pharaoh in *Die Sklavenkönigin* [*Moon of Israel*] the previous year) and is taken into his service as a guardsman. Leybke, engaged to be married to a Jewish girl, the innkeeper's daughter Kreyndl, spurns the advances of the count's daughter (Austrian actress Dagny Servaes). As in the Biblical story of Jo-

An Austrian countess (Dagny Servaes) longs for her Jewish guardsman (Maurice Schwartz) in Sidney Goldin's *Yisker* (Austria, 1924); frame enlargement. The film featured the Yiddish Art Theater and was adapted from a play by Harry Seckler.

seph and Potiphar's wife, the countess then falsely accuses him of attacking her.

Arrested on the eve of his wedding, Leybke escapes by scaling the castle wall. He marries Kreyndl but after they flee the entire Jewish community is held hostage. Surrounding the synagogue, the count's soldiers threaten to arrest ten Jewish men if Leybke doesn't surrender. The forester gives himself up and, in one of the film's more exotic set pieces, is subjected to the humiliation of the "Ukrainian bear dance"—compelled to cavort in a bear's skin.[4] Following this amusement, Leybke is buried alive, while, suitably contrite, the treacherous countess commits suicide.

Yisker is a solemn, albeit colorful, tribute to Jewish heroism (and noncompliance) in the face of irrational Gentile behavior. Like *Theodor Herzl,* the film dignifies Jewish history, though less elaborately. Special attention is given to the sabbath meal, to the wedding preparations, and particularly to the ritual in which the Jews, who appear among the count's subjects as a separate group, present their lord with bread and salt. (By way of acceptance, he kisses the Torah.) The movie also alters the stage play by making Leybke an orphan who is raised as a Jew by his non-Jewish adoptive family. Thus, the Jews appear not only as romantic figures but as a nation among nations—an aspiration denied them under the polyglot Hapsburg Empire.

Unlike *The Golem,* or even *The Ancient Law, Yisker* presents Jewish life evolving in dialectical relation to the Gentile world—a point of particular relevance for a city as simultaneously characterized by political anti-Semitism and Jewish cultural achievement as postwar Vienna. In the August 1924 issue of *Menorah Journal,* one correspondent was sufficiently re-

laxed to concentrate on the Jewish contribution to Viennese art, music, and theater: "If a chauvinist of Jewish culture is looking for one of the world's greatest centers to prove his favorite theory of Semitic domination and influence, Vienna is the place for him."

Despite "occasional meetings for the local *Hakenkreuzler* (mild offspring of the fire-breathing parent organization in Bavaria)," the same correspondent concluded, "the twenty districts radiating from the Stephanskirche will seem little less than a German-speaking version of Jerusalem Regained." Indeed, a few months before *Yisker* had its premiere in late 1924, the film *Die Stadt ohne Juden (The City Without Jews),* directed by H. K. Breslauer from the satirical best-selling novel by Hugo Bettauer, offered an anti-anti-Semitic fantasy in which a future chancellor expels Austria's Jews only to watch the nation's economy sputter, courts and hospitals collapse, and cultural life grind to a halt. Chastened, the chancellor must finally beg the Jews to return. In May 1925, a few months after the film's release, Bettauer was murdered by a twenty-year-old Nazi sympathizer.[5] To judge from the extravagantly expressionistic sets shown in a surviving still, *The City Without Jews*—which featured the popular comedian Hans Moser as an alcohol-sodden, anti-Semitic politician—was an example of domestic *Caligarismus.* Not just a forecast of Nazi rhetoric and racial laws, the movie also proved prophetic of the Austrian film industry, although the steep decline in production after 1923 undoubtedly helped account for the disappearance of Jewish theme films.

Austria's currency was stabilized but the tax on cinemas was so crippling that, by early 1926 (when only nineteen Austrian films were released), many movie houses had been forced to close. Even as the memory of imperial Vienna was being fetishized in a mid-twenties spate of Austrian, German, and American productions, including Erich von Stroheim's *The Wedding March*, Berlin-based UFA came to dominate the German-speaking market. Goldin departed Vienna, which had only recently been touted as "the Hollywood of Europe," to resurface as an actor three years later in a pair of *real* Hollywood movies—Frank S. Mattison's *Better Days* (in which he plays a character named "Ten Per Cent" Baumstein, "a great *credit* to the community . . . nearly everybody owes him") and Tenny Wright's western *The Fightin' Comeback.* By the end of the decade he had returned to New York to direct the first Yiddish talkies.

NOTES

1. The film, which opened in New York in 1921—the same year H. Leivick published his Yiddish verse drama *Der Goylem*—appears to have inspired at least one Yiddish operetta. In 1922, Max Gabel staged a musical version of the story at his 116th Street Theater. Jennie Goldstein played Miriam and Gabel appeared as the golem, his costume, as one reviewer pointed out, modeled after that in the movie. Leivick's drama was not produced in New York for another decade.

2. Austria's first postwar election was characterized by sporadic anti-Jewish riots and street assaults. Anti-Semites claimed that Vienna had been overrun by 400,000 Jewish refugees (over ten times the number who actually remained when the election was held in 1918). The Christian Social party issued a manifesto calling upon the Austrian people to "defend themselves as strenuously as possible against the Jewish peril." Nor were the Social Democrats, who feared being labeled a "Jewish party," above demanding the expulsion of the allegedly Jewish kingpins of the black market.

The forced repatriation of Jewish refugees continued after 1920, most deported to newly reconstituted Poland. Although the 1919 Treaty of Saint-Germain guaranteed the rights of the Jewish minority, anti-Semitic politicians enacted a system of *numerus clausus* limiting Jewish enrollment in gymnasia and universities. (In a memoir of the period, Richard Berczeller, then a medical student, recalls the demonstrations where nationalist students attempted to prevent Jews from registering for classes as "a kind of carnival watched by hundreds of Viennese.") Indeed, the very year *The Ancient Law* portrayed a rabbi's son as a star of the Burgtheater, the actual Burg staged Egon Friedell's fantastic *Tragedy of Judas*, with Judas, according to theater historian M. J. Landa, "presented as a Jewish Imperialist" and Herod speaking his lines with "a Yiddish accent."

3. The relatively lavish Biblical settings anticipate the Old Testament spectaculars—*Sodom und Gomorrah, Samson und Delilah,* and *Die Sklavenkönigin*, released in America as *Moon of Israel*—which, also influenced by *Intolerance,* were produced in Vienna between 1922 and 1924 by Hungarian Jewish emigrés Sándor (Alexander) Korda and Mihály Kertész (later the Hollywood director Michael Curtiz). Kreisler and Glücksmann were more *"schön* Viennese." After *Herzl,* Kreisler directed *Mozart's Leben, Lieben, und Leiden* and a movie taken from Heine, while Glücksmann adapted Schiller's *Don Carlos, Infant of Spain.* Kreisler's last film was the 1922 *Ludwig II,* although he served as artistic adviser on *Ein Walzer von Strauss,* released three years later.

4. In *The Manor,* Isaac Bashevis Singer makes reference to balls in eighteenth-century Poland at which "the court Jew was forced to disguise himself as a bear to entertain the guests."

5. Although Bettauer's novel was published in the United States in 1926, the state of New York refused to license the film version for distribution two years later—its satire was apparently regarded as anti-Semitic.

Overleaf: **Mother and daughter. Esther-Rokhl Kaminska and Ida Kaminska in the Vilna cemetery.** *Tkies Kaf* **(Poland, 1924).**

6

Miracles on the Vistula

POLAND'S BORDERS were not settled until 1923; the nation's internal politics were scarcely more stable. A dozen ruling coalitions rose and fell between the autumn of 1918 and the spring of 1926 when Marshal Józef Piłsudski finally seized power in a coup d'état.

Heirs to a century-long struggle for independence, the Polish leadership, understandably, wanted a Polish state. Ethnic Poles, however, constituted only two-thirds of the total population—the eastern borderlands were predominantly Ukrainian and Belorussian, while Jews and Germans were dispersed throughout the country. Thus, political discourse was dominated by a strident nationalism: attacked in

the right-wing press as a tool of the minorities, the nation's first president, Gabriel Narutowicz, was assassinated in December 1922 after five days in office.

By that time, Poland was already teetering at the brink of economic ruin. Raging inflation made foreign trade impossible. Food prices in Warsaw rose 1,200 percent in the course of a single year. Businesses failed daily. A wave of industrial strikes further paralyzed the nation. At the time of the Narutowicz assassination, one American dollar brought 18,000 Polish marks. Twelve months later, the dollar was worth two million Polish marks.

The fledgling Polish film industry barely managed to survive the war. In 1919, the British correspondent Huntley Carter wrote that his first encounter with Polish movie houses sent him "hot-foot to the nearest disinfecting station"—every establishment was uniformly "dirty, dark, and dilapidated." Despite the absence of a functioning Warsaw studio, some twenty-two features were produced in the euphoric first full year of Polish independence. Still, even this modest level proved beyond the means of Poland's struggling filmmakers. Output stabilized at about a dozen films a year as first Austrian, then German, and finally American movies dominated the market, while a ticket tax of 100 percent effectively doubled the cost of viewing a movie. (As attendance declined and theaters closed, exhibitors were driven to organize their own strike, shutting down movie houses in March 1923 to protest government policy. The ploy failed.)

Poland's postwar cinema was limited in themes as well as means. From 1919 through 1923, the industry produced little save nationalist spectacles and "grudge movies" settling scores with tsarist Russia and, occasionally, Germany. Even those literary works adapted for the screen were selected for their patriotic fervor. Not until peace and the short-lived recovery of 1923–24 did producers significantly augment this militarist fare with farces and melodramas. By then, Aleksander Hertz's resilient Sfinks had been joined by two new film companies, Falanga and Meteor (later Leofilm)—the latter established by Leo Forbert, an assimilated Jew and owner of Warsaw's premier photography studio.

Forbert's first efforts were a pair of luridly titled, German-influenced crime films, *Ludzie Mroku* (People in Darkness) and *Syn Szatana* (Son of Satan), both six reels in length. Between 1924 and 1929, however, Forbert would produce three Jewish mov-

ies—all from scripts by his sometime employee, the photographer Henryk (originally Yekhiel) Bojm, a worldly habitué of Warsaw's Yiddish literary circles and an artist whose personal history encapsulated the struggle for a modern Jewish identity.

Born in the late 1890s, the son of a wealthy grain merchant, the screenwriter grew up in a Chasidic household in Sochaczew, a Jewish suburb of Warsaw. The town was the site of a famed *yeshive*, and Bojm was a promising student there when, at age sixteen, he discovered secular thought in the form of I. L. Peretz. Unable to reconcile his father to his new aspirations, Bojm escaped to Warsaw, and after a half-starved existence in the city, traveled from *shtetl* to *shtetl*, earning his living as an intinerant portrait painter. Bojm eventually learned photography, and in partnership with his brother-in-law Oyzer Varshavsky, opened a studio in Amshinov (Mszczonow), another Jewish suburb of Warsaw.

Still in their teens during the German occupation, Bojm and Varshavsky became smugglers—a career that not only supplied Warsaw with contraband food but also provided Varshavsky with material for a stunning literary debut. His novel *Shmuglares* (Smugglers) showed the wartime *shtetl* as the province of thieves, whores, and moonshiners, a place where Talmud scholars turned paid informants and pious fathers offered their daughters as bribes to the German authorities. Published in 1920, and subsequently translated into Russian and Hebrew, this vivid account of moral collapse created a sensation in Yiddish literary circles—the novel was widely regarded as the epitome of a new naturalism and its twenty-two-year-old author hailed as a major talent. (Varshavsky left Poland for Berlin in 1924, then moved on to Paris, frequenting Montparnasse in the company of Peretz Markish and Ilya Ehrenburg. While they soon returned east, he remained in France—never to repeat his precocious triumph.)

Bojm also tried his hand at fiction, without apparent success. While working for Forbert, he began writing scenarios on Jewish themes, finally persuading his employer to undertake one. Although the popular success of *East and West* was doubtless a factor, Forbert may also have agreed because, as his cameraman Seweryn Steinwurzel later recalled, neither of Leofilm's first two productions had made much money.[1]

Cast and crew of *Tkies Kaf:* at far left is producer Leo Forbert; in front of him is director Zygmunt Turkow. To the right are stars Esther-Rokhl Kaminska and Ida Kaminska. At far right is cameraman Seweryn Steinwurzel; beside him (standing) is scenarist Henryk Bojm.

Tkies Kaf (The Handshake), the first and most successful of Forbert and Bojm's Yiddish films, starred Esther-Rokhl Kaminska and her daughter Ida; it was shot by Forbert's cousin and business partner Seweryn Steinwurzel, and directed by Zygmunt Turkow, the guiding spirit behind the Warsaw Jewish Art Theater, VYKT.

In the early 1920s, stage actors were the most professional element of the anemic Polish film industry, and Bojm had written *Tkies Kaf* with the Kaminskas and Turkow in mind. During the winter of 1924, Forbert engaged Turkow; the project was then financed by advances from theater owners on the basis of the VYKT's participation. While the expressionist set designer Bruno Bredschneider had directed Meteor's prior output, Bojm insisted on a Jewish director for *Tkies Kaf.* In the same spirit, perhaps, with which Lenin invited D. W. Griffith to head the fledgling Soviet film industry, Forbert attempted to import the "celebrated" Sidney Goldin, famous in Warsaw for *East and West,* to reinaugurate Polish-Yiddish film production.

In his memoirs, Turkow emphasizes that his agreement to participate in *Tkies Kaf* was contingent on the engagement of a competent foreign director to supervise the film. On the first day of shooting, however, no such director was in evidence. Although an accomplished cameraman, Steinwurzel lacked the personality to handle actors, and ultimately, at the cast's request, the twenty-eight-year-old Turkow, who was to play the eight manifestations of the prophet Elijah, took on a ninth role and assumed the responsibility himself:

My work producing this film was record-breaking. From early morning until evening I was in the studio and from there, often without having eaten, I would travel to the Central to play the strenuous role of Shabbtai Zvi. After the performance I spent several hours with the film-crew planning the next day's work. At the same time I prepared my new role, Tevye the Dairy-man.

If Turkow was further daunted at directing his wife, mother-in-law, brother, sister-in-law, and daughter, as well as himself, he doesn't say.

Turkow termed *Tkies Kaf* "a naïve *emese mayse* [literally "true story," i.e., folktale] with a Jewish moral." The scenario included "holidays and customs, legends and superstitions . . . in a word, everything necessary to make a gripping, thoroughly

Khaym Kronenberg (Adam Domb, left) and Borekh Mandel (Moyshe Lipman, right) pledge the marriage of their unborn children; a disguised Prophet Elijah (Zygmunt Turkow, in background) looks on. *Tkies Kaf.*

Jewish film of educational character and positive effect." More specifically, Bojm had introduced a strain of Chasidic imagery that would remain characteristic of the Polish Yiddish cinema. Nevertheless, his scenario appropriated something of its premise, as well as its title—the term for the handshake that seals a marriage contract—from a 1907 play by Peretz Hirschbein, itself a ghostly anticipation of *Der Dibek.*[2]

Where Hirschbein's *Tkies Kaf* was an attack on arranged marriages and religious superstition, Bojm's was considerably more ambivalent. Opening in the late nineteenth century, the film strikes an appropriately supernatural note with the prophet Elijah, wide-eyed and hirsute, on the road toward Vilna. Elijah was the most popular figure in *shtetl* lore. Typically a traveler disguised (often as a pauper or a Gentile peasant), he was at once the personification of divine intervention and an instrument of social justice, the protector of the poor. Here, transforming himself into a Chasid, the prophet visits a rabbinical court and witnesses two students, Khaym Kronenberg (Adam Domb) and Borekh Mandel (Moyshe Lipman) making a sacred pledge to unite their unborn children in marriage.

In the nineteenth-century *shtetl,* arranged marriages were the rule, particularly among the wealthier *sheyne Yidn* (pious Jews). Popular belief had it that such matches were preordained. As one intertitle in *Tkies Kaf* explains: "Forty days before a child is born, there appears a sign between that child and another." In some instances, a betrothal was arranged while the parties were still children; in other cases, the match was based on an agreement between two prospective fathers stipulating that if one's wife gave birth to a boy and the other's to a girl, the children would be married. Although a gesture of friendship,

Rokhl Kronenberg (Ida Kaminska) meets her fated one, Yankev Mandel (Henryk Tarło), in the study house; a licentious student (Jonas Turkow, standing) watches. At left is Elijah in another of his eight disguises (Zygmunt Turkow, seated) and Rokhl's mother (Esther-Rokhl Kaminska). *Tkies Kaf*.

this *tkies kaf* had the weight of a sacred oath, the violators subject to divine retribution.

Such is the case in Bojm's scenario. Khaym remains in Vilna while Borekh returns west to manage his family's forest. The narrative then jumps ahead some twenty years to the World War and Khaym's sudden death upon hearing that his son has been killed in battle. Because he was unable to show them the secret cache of jewels that, also a Chasidic trope, serves as a material metaphor for the *tkies kaf,* Khaym's widow (Esther-Rokhl Kaminska) and daughter, Rokhl (Ida Kaminska), are left in poverty. However, Elijah, again in disguise, arranges for Borekh's son, Yankev (Henryk Tarło), to go to Vilna

to study. There he boards with his father's friend Shmuel Levine (Lev Mogilov) who, not coincidentally, lives in the house Rokhl and her mother have been forced to sell.[3]

Yankev sees Rokhl—Elijah, appearing as a beggar in the courtyard, has caused their eyes to meet—and falls in love. He encounters the girl again in the *besmedresh* (study house) where she and her mother sell fruit to the students. Buying her entire basket of apples and distributing them to his colleagues, the smitten Yankev imagines Rokhl as her Biblical namesake. (The scene of Yiddish actors in mock Old Testament garb is suggestive of a Goldfadn operetta.) Then, in one of the film's several visions, he suffers the temptations of the flesh. Encouraged by a depraved fellow student who takes the role of an evil angel (Jonas Turkow), Yankev beholds a cabaret filled with transparent showgirls. Sin is depicted as a theatrical performance.

As Yankev and Rokhl discover each other, so the hypocritical Shmuel Levine discovers the hidden jewels (while engaged in his morning prayers!). Now, desiring the maiden himself, he follows the advice of an affably sleazy *shadkhn* and attempts to eliminate his young rival by informing Borekh of Yankev's impious ways: since coming to Vilna, the student has been gradually seduced into secular habits by Levine's son, identified in the film's Polish credits as the "civilizer." Yankev attends a party where boys and girls play blindman's buff, allows the civilizer to cut his *payes,* and is receiving his first dancing lesson when his irate father arrives on the scene. (That Yankev should be corrupted in the city of rabbis and scholars is not as improbable as it sounds. Although known as the "Jerusalem of Lithuania," Vilna was also a cosmopolitan center—populated not just by Jews and Poles, but also Russians and Germans—and a crucible for the modern ideologies that would permeate *Yidishland*'s most remote corners.)

Borekh resolves to marry Yankev off, although suddenly remembering his *tkies kaf,* he initially finds it impossible to sign the contract. Elijah, now a tramp, unsuccessfully tries to keep Borekh from the engagement celebration (which is characterized by horseplay and comic gluttony). Later, the prophet materializes as a beardless woodchopper in Borekh's forest. That night Borekh dreams of his dead comrade Khaym, and the emphatic words *"Tkies Kaf"* are emblazoned over burning trees. In Vilna, Rokhl, who fell ill with Yankev's departure, is about to be

married to Shmuel Levine. Accompanied by her mother, she visits her father's grave to invite him to the wedding. She too is given a dream: the dead, wrapped in *taleysim,* rise from their graves to dance at her marriage. Her partner is Yankev—when he is transformed into old Levine, she wakes with a start.

The chastened Borekh at last realizes that he must fulfill his sacred vow and prevent Rokhl from marrying Levine. Yankev, his engagement broken, arrives at the wedding as well, and he and Rokhl are married, then and there, as they were destined to be. Elijah, who attends the ceremony as a *sheyner balebos* (respectable burgher) and reveals himself by refusing to drink, instead spilling wine on his jacket "to honor my clothes," subsequently appears to the elder Levine as a menacing superimposition and frightens him into returning the jewels to Khaym's widow. The folklore of Elijah was often a vehicle for social protest. In popular tradition, as in *Tkies Kaf,* the prophet rewards the virtuous poor and punishes the greedy rich. And so, having successfully stage-managed the film's narrative, Elijah wanders off.[4]

Although only fragments of *Tkies Kaf* remain—at twelve reels, it was the longest Polish movie made in several years—it is evident from what survives that the filmmakers, no less than the lovers, triumphed over their adversities. Thanks to Steinwurzel's clever lighting, the interiors—Yankev's cavern-like *yeshive,* Rokhl's expressionistic garret—are cramped but detailed. (Eventually, they were shot in Forbert's photography studio under blazing hot incandescent lamps. One bit player, the young critic J. M. Neuman, would later claim that the lighting was so "disastrous" that "for a long while after my appearance, my vision was seriously impaired.")

If *Tkies Kaf* is hampered by a stagy overreliance

on middle shots, it also includes a number of evocative exteriors. Leaving Warsaw, the company went on location to Vilna, where Turkow "mobilized" the local beggars for the wedding scenes and exploited several landmarks—the central marketplace, the entrance to the Jewish quarter, and the old Jewish cemetery, including the tomb of the eighteenth-century spiritual leader known as the Vilna Gaon. Because of this, the director later recalled, "the Rabbinate accused the producers of desecration and attempted, with the help of the government, to have the film destroyed."

Nevertheless, *Tkies Kaf* had its premiere in May 1924 at the Rococo, an elegant Warsaw cinema on the fashionable boulevard Nowy Swiat, where Forbert also had his photography studio, and there, according to Turkow, it "was received with stormy ovations."

The next morning the entire press came out with praise for the director and the participants. After the premiere, several of the producers turned to me with new suggestions, but to suffer such hard labor a second time would have been beyond my strength.[5]

Tkies Kaf, Turkow asserts, was the "most successful" Polish film of its day, and, considering the state of the Polish film industry, he may be right. Andrzej Włast, one of the most respected critics of the period, wrote in the monthly *Ekran i Scena* (Screen and Stage) that, "without publicity, without fireworks . . . the Leo-Forbert company had released a film that I can unhesitatingly call the best movie that has been made so far in this country." Włast praised Turkow's "superb" direction and Bojm's "skillful" use of Jewish folklore. Given the state of Polish society, however,

few public displays of Jewishness could be without controversy. Włast was not a Jew; the critic and screenwriter Leo Belmont, who was (though assimilated), proved less enthusiastic, writing of *Tkies Kaf* in the weekly *Kinema* that while the filmmakers "tried to show the process of emancipation . . . [they] unconsciously idealize superstition."

Infinitely more caustic was the review *Tkies Kaf* received in the influential weekly *Literarishe Bleter*. Invoking the cinema's "limitless possibilities" and the makers of *Tkies Kaf*'s total ignorance of this infinite potential, the anonymous critic scored the movie as *shund* (trash)—a "*mishmash* of real matters and total impossibilities, *Der Dibek* and the Prophet Elijah." The underlying issues were complex. Peretz Markish, who then edited the journal and likely wrote the review, was contemptuous of movies in general, while, as a kind of inside gag, the filmmakers gave

Zygmunt Turkow, left, and Henryk Tarło in the Vilna cemetery. *Tkies Kaf.*

bit parts to a number of young Yiddish writers, including Neuman, who defended movies as a popular art, thus suggesting at least the possibility of a literary feud. (A 1928 essay in *Literarishe Bleter* compares Warsaw's literary cliques to rival Chasidic courts.)

Be this as it may, *Literarishe Bleter* articulates what Belmont only hints at. Not unlike the assimilated Jews of Vienna, the journal's nameless critic seems to have feared the Gentile interpretation of *Tkies Kaf*'s uninhibited ethnicity. Particularly offensive was the film's broad humor: "The people at the wedding don't eat like human beings—even hungry ones. You must remember, this is how anti-Semites perceive Jews [and] this movie will be seen the world over." Although neither *Tkies Kaf*'s slapstick wedding feast nor its parody of a traditional *kheyder* were unknown spectacles on the Yiddish stage, *Literarishe Bleter* was disinclined to offer these images to the Gentile world. Terming the filmmakers irresponsible for not considering the impression such *"vilde bilder"* (wild sights) will make, the critic concluded by asking instead for "serious, truthful, artistic films" about Jewish life.[6]

Like *East and West, Tkies Kaf* bespeaks the Jewish conflict between tradition and modernization. But, less schematic and anxious than the Viennese film, *Tkies Kaf* evokes a wholly Jewish world. It confidently drew on folk tradition—the various misalliances and deceptions resolved through divine intervention—and this supernaturalism was certainly part of its appeal. The filmmakers are generous in their use of special effects while Elijah's presence gives the narrative an expressionist quality.

No less than *The Golem,* although with far greater nuance (and incomparably more humor), *Tkies Kaf* exploited the Gentile sense of Jews as uncanny. Indeed, it is suggestive that Bojm and Forbert at first prepared only Polish intertitles for the film. Not until after the opening engagement were Yiddish titles added.

Tkies Kaf would seem to presuppose a sophisticated Jewish spectator—familiar enough with, yet sufficiently distanced from, Jewish folklore to appreciate its mildly sensational treatment on the screen. Still, whatever the filmmakers' intentions, and despite the support of a critic like Włast, one can confidently assert that the movie's audience was overwhelmingly Jewish. (Polish indifference to Jewish culture was such that, with the exception of a government censor, no interwar Polish writer or scholar seems to have learned Yiddish.)

At the very least, *Tkies Kaf* demonstrated a market for Jewish themes. The Prometheus company's safer *Smierc za Zycie* (Death Instead of Life), a respectably nationalistic tale with no Yiddish performers, opened at the Rococo in November. A more optimistic variant on Arnshteyn's *Der Vilner Balebesl,* the film told the tale of a Jewish innkeeper's son who, thanks to the friendship of a Polish prince, blossomed into a great Polish poet. *Der Lamedvovnik* (One of the Thirty-six), Forbert's own follow-up to *Tkies Kaf,* was both more Jewish and more supernatural—if not without its own evocation of Jewish patriotism.

Bracketed in one history of the Polish cinema with such "sensational movies" of the period as Wiktor Biegański's *Wampiry Warszawy* (Vampires of Warsaw; 1925), *Der Lamedvovnik* appeared in Warsaw on the heels of Arnshteyn's extremely popular Polish-language stage production of *Der Dibek* (itself perhaps stimulated by the success of *Tkies Kaf*). Al-

Cast and crew: Henryk Szaro's *Der Lamedvovnik* (Poland, 1925). Cameraman Seweryn Steinwurzel sits cross-legged on floor, directly behind him is scenarist Henryk Bojm. Producer Leo Forbert is seated left of Bojm; behind Forbert and Bojm is the film's star Jonas Turkow. The director stands by the camera at the extreme right, studying the script.

though *Der Lamedvovnik* was hardly a horror film, screenwriter Bojm again drew upon the uncanny, namely the Chasidic legend of the thirty-six unknown saints who insure the world's continued existence. The Yiddish *"lamedvovnik"* is derived from the Hebrew characters *lamed* and *vov,* which together represent the numerical value thirty-six; the notion of the thirty-six hidden saints required to justify the world to God passed from Cabbalistic tradition into Chasidic lore. Humble by vocation as well as nature, a *lamedvovnik*—who may be unknown even to himself—performs his miracles only at a time of great peril and thereafter disappears.

VYKT stalwarts Jonas Turkow and Moyshe Lip-man headed the cast. As *Tkies Kaf* had gone on location in Vilna, *Der Lamedvovnik's* exteriors were shot in Kazimierz and Sandomierz, towns a hundred miles south of Warsaw on the Vistula. Steinwurzel was the cameraman; Forbert hired twenty-five-year-old Henryk Szaro (born Szapiro) to direct. Variously credited with having studied under Meyerhold and/ or assisted Granovsky, Szaro had arrived in Warsaw the year before with a Russian "literary" theater, and made a youthful reputation when his production of Ossip Dymow's *shtetl* fantasy *Yoshke Muzikant* (Yoshke the Musician)—a major hit for the Vilna Troupe in Bucharest—opened Warsaw's newest Yiddish theater, the Skala. *Tkies Kaf* was his second film; he'd previoulsy collaborated with Steinwurzel on the comedy *Rywale* (The Rivals).

Like *Tkies Kaf, Der Lamedvovnik* refers obliquely to the massive dislocation of Jewish life which Bojm had experienced firsthand during the World War. The setting is a *shtetl* occupied by the Russian army during the 1861–63 Polish uprising. The Russian commandant levies a large tax on the townspeople, which is subsequently embezzled by his adjutant, who happens to be in love with a Jewish girl. As a result, eleven innocent Jews are put on trial. Fortunately, the *shtetl* is home to a *lamedvovnik* (Turkow), a poor woodcutter who sacrifices his own life to save those of his neighbors.

Significantly, in view of Bojm's background, a secular version of this legend appears in Peretz's memoirs. The writer recalls that during the 1861 Russian occupation of his native town, Zamosc, the Jews were blamed for burglarizing the regimental safe. A spurious confession was beaten out of a group of Jewish thieves, already serving time, who were only saved from hanging when an elderly, unlettered, vaguely ridiculous Chasid risked his life to cross the Austrian border and telegraph news of the injustice to influential Jews abroad. (An ugly variation of this occurred again in Zamosc in the fall of 1914, after the Russian army recaptured the town from the Austrians. According to *The Jews in the Eastern War Zone,* a report made by the American Jewish Committee, local Poles denounced their Jewish neighbors as Austrian collaborators. The Russians arrested twelve Jews; after five have been hanged, an Orthodox priest interrupted the execution with proof that the Poles themselves had supported the Austrians.)

Like *Tkies Kaf, Der Lamedvovnik* was well received: Polish critics praised its underlying "human-

istic values" and naturalistic decor. Although this historical tale of Gentile oppression and Jewish martyrdom resembles *Yisker,* the patriotic background (and implied Polish-Jewish anti-Russian solidarity) points toward the historical epic that would be Forbert and Bojm's most ambitious work, their ill-fated 1928 adaptation of Joseph Opatoshu's best-selling novel *In di Poylishe Velder* (In Polish Woods).[7]

Despite the elements of satire in *Tkies Kaf,* Forbert's first two films were characterized by a cautiousness in mapping out generational conflicts and contemporary Polish-Jewish relations. With the possible exception of *Death Instead of Life,* there was nothing produced in Poland comparable to the American melting-pot film (or even Germany's *The Ancient Law*), although one movie of this type was made in Rumania, where the number of Jews had tripled with the postwar settlement.

Rumania, like Poland, was now a multinational state—fully one-third of the population was non-Rumanian. At first, the newly enlarged kingdom made strenuous objections to, and then simply ignored, a special treaty protecting the rights of its national minorities. Although the government severely taxed Yiddish theaters (which, in response, often camouflaged themselves as cabarets) and banned even the posting of notices printed in Yiddish, Bucharest nevertheless became a center for Yiddish culture. Just as ambitious Litvaks and Galicians gravitated to Warsaw, so aspiring writers and actors—including a splinter of the celebrated Vilna Troupe—flocked to the Rumanian metropolis from the *shtetlekh* of Moldavia and Bessarabia.

The stage was then far more important than the

movies; by all accounts, the early Rumanian film industry was a crazy jumble of eccentrics, con men, and would-be moguls. Government agencies produced a few patriotic spectacles, but most motion pictures seem to have been produced by one-shot companies under extremely primitive circumstances. In 1925, the same year that the Foto-Cinematographic Service of the Rumanian army released a paean to "duty and sacrifice," National-Film, an ambitious artists' collective established two years earlier by the young Vienna-trained director Jean Mihail, attempted to elevate the aesthetic level of Rumanian cinema with an expensive adaptation of Moise Roman-Ronetti's celebrated Jewish problem drama *Manasse.*

Born Aharon Blumenfeld in 1847, Roman-Ronetti was a Rumanian Jewish nationalist. *Manasse,* written in 1900, was his most important work; it was translated into Yiddish—in which it was variously known as *Fayndlekhe Veltn* (Hostile Worlds) and *Dray Doyres* (Three Generations)—and also produced in English as *New Lamps and Old.* Dealing with intermarriage, generational conflict, and anti-Semitism, Ronetti's play had been a major scandal in Rumania. The 1902 premiere inspired student riots in Jassy, and similar disturbances forced the closing of a 1908 production staged by the National Theater of Bucharest. Thus, the film adaptation took a certain amount of nerve (and, indeed, although considered an artistic success, its commercial failure and half-million-leu budget effectively ruined National-Film). The screenwriter, left-wing journalist Scarlat Froda, and the twenty-nine-year-old director were both Rumanian Jews; the mixed cast included Josef Kamen, a former member of the Vilna Troupe who later enjoyed a career on the Warsaw and Vienna Yiddish stages.

Not strictly speaking a Yiddish film (although its attempt at authenticity extends to the inclusion of several common Yiddish terms in the titles), *Manasse* regards assimilation as inevitable, while taking a sympathetic view of traditional Jewish life. The major characters include a pious village Jew (the eponymous protagonist, played with Mosaic sternness by non-Jew Ronald Bulfinski), his blandly Europeanized son Nisim, and the comic *luftmentsh* Zelig (overplayed by Kamen). When Manasse's wife dies, the tragic patriarch leaves his Moldavian village of Falticeni for Nisim's home in Bucharest, accompanied by Zelig. Shocked by Nisim's modern life-

Tragic patriarch: Manasse (Ronald Bulfinski) is comforted by his friend Zelig (Josef Kamen) in Jean Mihail's *Manasse* (Rumania, 1925), from the play by Roman-Ronetti; frame enlargement.

style, Manasse tells a cautionary tale about a Jewish daughter of Falticeni who married a Gentile. Meanwhile, unbeknownst to their parents, Manasse's own grandchildren, Leila and Lazar, have fallen in love with non-Jews.

Although the theme of intermarriage links *Manasse* to contemporary American and German films, it is here something of a double-edged sword. Not only were instances of intermarriage and conversion far rarer in Rumania than in Western Europe or the United States, but Rumanian politicians and intellectuals were stridently anti-Semitic in terming Jews an essentially foreign and unassimilable element. In any case, the transformation of Jew into Rumanian is hardly cost-free. The sly and obsequious Zelig manages to broker a more suitable match for Leila but his plans come to naught when she fails to appear for the wedding, having run off with her Gentile lover. As the *khupe* is struck, Manasse collapses and, after the requisite scene of wailing recriminations, dies of grief. The film ends by questioning whether Manasse's children will consent to their children's even more drastic assimilation.

Manasse has been criticized as being "nothing more than 'filmed theater.' " Still, the director transposed as much of the action as possible to exterior settings that range from Bucharest's elegant Calea Victorei to Falticeni's muddy streets and the ancient Jewish cemetery. For those European movies that treated Jewish subjects, the latter site seems to have been almost obligatory. The ominous image of the weed-choked, tumbledown Jewish graveyard occurs in films as otherwise disparate as *The Yellow Passport, The Golem, Judith Trachtenberg, Yisker,* and *Tkies Kaf*; it would subsequently be featured in quite a few more.[8]

NOTES

1. Bojm's difficulty finding backing is often attributed to the timidity of Polish movie moguls. Zalmen Zylberzweig's assertion that "although the entire Polish film industry was in Jewish hands" producers "were not interested in Jewish films, because they feared [such films] would expose their own Jewishness" is typical if not entirely correct. Aleksander Hertz's Sfinks, which produced *Meir Ezofewicz* before the war, was responsible for at least two films of Jewish interest. One documented the Twelfth Zionist Congress, held in Carlsbad in 1921; the other, titled in English *Rachael the Outcast,* suggests *Judith Trachtenberg.* Submitted to the New York State Motion Picture Commission in April 1922, this five-reel feature was referred to Commissioner Levinson on account of its representation of Jewish marriage and burial customs. *Tajemnice Nalewek* (Secrets of the Nalewki), released in Warsaw in late 1921, used the Jewish district as the setting for a high-minded exposé of poverty and superstition and featured Leon Trystan, a future director of Yiddish talkies. There were also several Zionist travelogues, including a six-reel documentary on the opening of the Hebrew University in Jerusalem, made by Seweryn Steinwurzel in 1923, while the Joint Distribution Committee produced a feature-length documentary on Jewish life in Warsaw in 1922.

2. In his history of Jewish film in Poland, Natan Gross speculates that Bojm wanted to adapt *Der Dibek* but was unable to secure the rights. At least one other European writer also dreamed of filming An-sky's poetic drama. In an April 1929 letter to Yvonne Allendy, Antonin Artaud announces plans for a scenario based on *Der Dibek,* "synchronizing the scenes of possession by spirits and exorcism with appropriate shouts and voices." The result, Artaud notes, would be a "film to the credit of the Jews."

3. The surviving print of *Tkies Kaf* is incomplete. Hence, the mystery of where Khaym's son came from is never explained. In any case, Rokhl and Yankev—both fifteen years younger than Khaym's firstborn—are the children who have been pledged in *tkies kaf.*

4. This synopsis is based on the film's shortened and dubbed American version. The original order of events may have been somewhat different. An advertisement for the film in a May 1924 issue of *Literarishe Bleter* gives each of the twelve reels its own title: (1) The Appearance of Elijah; (2) The Rabbi's Festival;

(3) The Vow; (4) The Romance of a Yeshiva Student; (5) Life in the Yeshiva; (6) The Vilna Synagogue; (7) A Night in a Jewish Cemetery; (8) Fire in the Forest; (9) The Dead Friend's Warning; (10) The Vision; (11) The Unfortunate Wedding; (12) The Miraculous Reunion.

5. Still, Turkow was bitten by the film bug. According to Ida Kaminska, in 1930 her "perpetually restless and innovative" husband decided to go to Moscow to study film direction under Sergei Eisenstein. Denied this opportunity, he went instead to Berlin where he succeeded in entering UFA as a voluntary assistant director. In 1937 he codirected a second film, the Yiddish talkie *Freylekhe Kaptsonim (Jolly Paupers)*.

6. Nearly a year later, also in *Literarishe Bleter*, Turkow responded:

"Jewish films!" For quite a few years people have been involved with this matter. . . . Then came a time—after the War—when [Yiddish movies] were a fashionable arti-cle. [*East and West*] was financially quite successful: *Tkies Kaf* was not only financially but also artistically successful. Many people then took up the matter. . . . Notices were published in newspapers. They beat the drum for their great enterprises—they made a big fuss—and nothing came of it.

7. Szaro and Steinwurzel followed *Der Lamedvovnik* with Leofilm's hit cabaret thriller *Czerwony Blazen* (The Red Clown; 1926). Later that year, Forbert lost control of Leofilm; Szaro, however, went on to become one of the leading directors of the Polish silent cinema.

8. Jewish characters figured in at least one other Rumanian silent. In 1929, writer Jean Georgescu and director A. Stefanescu took the title, but not the premise, of the Ion Caragiale story "Lieba Zibal." The Jewish protagonist of their crude melodrama is not the victim of a pogrom but rather of his lifelong obsession with a Christian girl of dubious virtue.

Overleaf: **Menakhem Mendl (Solomon Mikhoels, pointing) and his assistant, Zalmen (Moyshe Goldblatt), supervise the wedding feast in Alexander Granovsky's *Jewish Luck* (U.S.S.R., 1925).**

7

Yiddish Modernism and *Jewish Luck*

HE RUSSIAN CIVIL WAR was the bloodiest tragedy in Jewish history since the mid-seventeenth-century massacres ordered by Cossack chieftain Bogdan Khmielnitsky. Just as these precipitated an apocalyptic climate conducive to the rise of the "false messiah" Shabbtai Zvi, so now many Jews were seized with millennial expectations. For some, the Revolution meant the violent superimposition of one religion upon another. In his story "The Rabbi's Son," Isaac Babel describes a dying revolutionary's "hodgepodge" of belongings.

A directive to a propagandist lay next to the notebooks of a Jewish poet. The portraits of Lenin and Maimonides were neighbors—the gnarled iron of Lenin's skull and the dim silki-ness of Maimonides' picture. A lock of woman's hair marked a page in a bound volume of the Resolutions of the Sixth Party Congress, and crooked lines of Hebrew verse were crowded into the margin of political pamphlets.

No less than the *goldene medine* (golden land) of America, revolutionary Russia promised an extreme form of assimilation. Full citizens at last, Jews imagined they might totally reinvent themselves. The Bolshevik antagonism toward religion, the bourgeoisie, and Zionism seemed an unavoidable price to pay for the end of state anti-Semitism. New secular Jewish institutions supplanted rabbinical courts, weakening traditional authority and helping bind Jews to the revolutionary regime. From 1921 through 1923, the Yevsektsia waged a fierce antireligious campaign in which hundreds of synagogues and over a thousand *khadorim* (religious primary schools) were closed. Meanwhile, as if to compensate for their parents' suffering, a disproportionate number of young Jews joined the Cheka.[1]

"The Communist Jews were not delightful personalities to deal with," Boris Bogen discovered during his 1922 visit to the Soviet Union as the representative of the American Jewish Joint Distribution Committee. Jewish Communists were typically the most ardent pan-nationalists and opponents of religious orthodoxy. Many were former Bundists who continued to play out their rivalry with the Zionists. In this context, the career of Moyshe Litvakov, at once a zealot and an opportunist, seems emblematic. A *yeshive* student until he was seventeen, and then a Labor Zionist (as well as a founding member of Kiev's Kultur Lige), Litvakov joined the Communist Party after the Revolution. As the head of the Jewish writers' section, Lenin's Yiddish translator, and the editor of the Yiddish daily *Der Emes,* he became the dominant ideological *mashgiekh*—which is to say, enforcer—of the new Soviet Yiddish culture. (Indeed, in 1924 Litvakov would criticize his own newspaper as "too Jewish.")

According to Bogen, Jewish Communists rationalized their persecution of Judaism as "good for Jews in the long run," a necessary attitude "in order that it might appear that even among the Jewish Communists there was no special favor for Judaism in this new Russia. . . . Seeing Jews barking at Jews, the dogs of anti-Semitism might be content and seek other objects at which to snap."

But, in reality, the Jewish Communists were moved by inspirations less complicated, and these partly had to do with their own prestige in the party and partly with the nature of the Jew who is forever afraid of what the neighbors may say about him. If in America it is a time for hysterical patriotism he must seem more hysterical than the others, lest it be said that he is not patriotic enough. . . . If in Russia religion had come to be despised, the Jew must be seen tearing down synagogues.

Peace continued the process that war had begun. The devastated Moscow to which Alexander Granovsky relocated his Yiddish theater in late 1920 combined breakdown and exhilaration. *New York Times* correspondent Walter Duranty found the new Soviet capital "a strange hybrid" between a modern metropolis and a mud-choked primitive village. Imposing public buildings stood "side by side with wooden cottages of the seventeenth century, and the latter had suffered least."

Moscow's inhabitants were no less picturesque in their dilapidation. "Everyone was dressed in the most original way," Ilya Ehrenburg recalled of that winter. "Women with pretentions to smartness wore soldiers' faded greatcoats and green hats made of billiard-table cloth. Dresses were made of wine-coloured curtains and livened up with Suprematist squares or triangles cut out of old slipcovers. The painter I. M. Rabinovich strolled about the streets in an emerald-colored sheepskin coat." Not surprisingly, in view of these costumes, the city was also in the grip of a national theater mania.

Whereas the Moscow Art Theater had been the province of the wealthy intelligentsia, the Revolution inspired all manner of mass pageants, street performances, and popular spectacles. Tens of thousands of young people joined dramatic clubs. In Petrograd, Granovsky had conceived of his theater as universal;

in Moscow, where GOSET set up in a ninety-seat auditorium in a liberated "bourgeois townhouse" on Chernyshevsky Street, he realized that, if it were not to be overwhelmed by the other universal theaters, GOSET would need to develop a distinctive repertoire.

Henceforth, Granovsky became the leading impresario of Yiddish modernism. For the next seven years, he used avant-garde stratagems to rework traditional Yiddish sources—Goldfadn, Mendele Mokher Sforim, and especially, Sholom Aleichem. It was the critic Abram Efros who stimulated this development, bringing Granovsky together with Marc Chagall, the *shtetl*-born child of a Chasidic family. Although the two men were temperamentally ill suited for collaboration, the artist had a catalytic effect on the director's subsequent work. "I felt that, at least in the beginning, there would be no accord between us," Chagall wrote in his memoirs.

I, always anxious and worried about the least
thing; he, confident, assured, given to mockery.
    And—this is the essential point—not at all
Chagall.
    I had been asked to paint murals for the auditorium and scenery for the first production:
    Ah! I thought, here is an opportunity to do
away with the old Jewish theater, its psychological naturalism, its false beards. Here on these
walls I shall at least be able to do as I please and
be free to show everything I consider indispensable to the rebirth of the national theater.

Chagall's eight allegorical paintings created a carnival atmosphere: traditional *shtetl* figures represented the various arts—a torah scribe for poetry, a *badkhn* for theater. The largest mural had Efros bearing the artist himself to a waiting Granovsky. The inference was coy but apt, for the new theater's

Solomon Mikhoels in the 1921 GOSET production, *A Sholom Aleichem Evening*. Sets and costumes were designed by Marc Chagall.

first success, a trio of one-act plays that made up the exuberant *Sholom Aleichem Evening,* has been described as a three-dimensional Chagall, with the painter taking it upon himself to redesign actor Solomon Mikhoels's face. "If Granovsky is the mother of GOSET, then I am the father," Chagall proclaimed. But, if Chagall was the father, Vsevolod Meyerhold was the grandfather. As Granovsky followed Meyerhold's lead in incorporating aspects of the circus, music hall, and other popular forms, GOSET took its place beside the other experimental theaters of the period—Nicholas Foregger's Mastfor, the Moscow Proletkult, the Theater of Popular Comedy, and the Factory of the Eccentric Actor.

GOSET's *Sholom Aleichem Evening,* which had its premiere New Year's Day 1921, was followed by a "tragic-grotesque" version of Sholem Asch's *Got fun Nekome* and an austere *Uriel Acosta,* for which Natan Altman built Constructivist sets. Chagall soon moved on, but Altman would later design Granovsky's first film. Through these artists, GOSET found its material; the troupe basked in the warmth of official approval. This new Yiddish theater would be privileged through World War II as a Jewish realm untainted by religion. Raising GOSET's subsidy, the authorities provided a new 500-seat auditorium in a building that included living accommodations, a school, and a museum.

Throughout the early 1920s, peasant rebellions still smoldered in the Ukraine and Belorussia. The summer after GOSET's first Moscow season, famine broke out in the Volga region—eventually five million would starve to death. Lenin responded with a New Economic Policy (NEP). Where "War Communism" had banned commerce and nationalized even small workshops, the NEP reinstituted a state-controlled market and revived foreign trade. Cities depleted by years of civil war swelled with newcomers. In 1891, the tsar had expelled Moscow's tiny Jewish community; by 1923, there were 86,000 Jews living in the city; over the next three years, the heyday of GOSET, their numbers increased by 50 percent.

Natalya Vovsi-Mikhoels maintains that in Moscow, "Jews regarded [GOSET] as their home, their club, their synagogue, a place to forgather and reminisce, a place to meet their friends, above all—a place where they could talk Yiddish freely and without lowering their voices." (The crowds clustered outside GOSET's stage door reminded one visiting American of Chasidim "waiting for the exit of their favorite *tsadek.*") In fact, GOSET's audience was a complex amalgam of often antithetical groups, including displaced traditionalists, *nouveau riche* "NEPmen," and fervent young Communists. These last set the ideological (and emotional) tone. The post-revolutionary Russian vanguard felt itself living out the future. The collapse of old Europe seemed imminent—to be followed by the coming of a classless society and a withering away of the state.

In this heady atmosphere, GOSET's youthful performers might well imagine themselves as revolutionary *Purimshpilers.* Moyshe Litvakov himself contributed to their avant-garde version of Goldfadn's *Koldunye,* which featured twenty-three-year-old Venyamin Zuskin in the plum role of the hideous old witch, and a horde of masked players capering over the double-tiered scaffolding designed by Isaac Rabinovich (of the "emerald-colored sheepskin coat"). *Koldunye* was GOSET's most shocking desecration: the piece parodied religion as well as the old Yiddish theater, mocked the now-banned Jewish Labor Bund along with Habima, GOSET's Hebrew-language rival, which had recently premiered *Hadibuk,* a Hebrew version of *Der Dibek,* with Natan Altman's sets.[2]

Hadibuk depicted a ritual exorcism—the GOSET production *was* one. High-spirited and audacious, Granovsky's theater provided the occasion for a wild Yiddish modernism in which, freed from restraints, young Jews acted out their rejection of the prerevolutionary past. However ambivalent, this sense of liberation made their presentations unusually compelling. Granovsky applied Meyerhold's "biomechanics"–stylized units of movement—to the gestures and expressions of the *shtetl.* Describing the "Cubistic liveliness" of *200,000,* the GOSET's Bolshevized production of Sholom Aleichem's *Dos Groyse Gevins,* in which the impoverished tailor Shimele (Mikhoels) wins the lottery and betrays his class, Berlin critic Alfred Kerr found the performers preternaturally expressive: "The ghetto-figure and ghetto-manner appears in concentrated form—until it almost frightens the Western burgher."

GOSET celebrated Jewishness even as they deconstructed it. "These were Jews of a higher temperature, Jews who were more Jewish," another German critic wrote of the ensemble. "Their passion was by several degrees more passionate, their melancholy even became fierce and savage, their sadness fanatical and their joy rapture." (Not everyone was so enthusiastic. Walter Benjamin visited Moscow in late 1926 and noted in his diaries that Granovsky had "created a farcical, anti-religious, and, from outward appearances, fairly anti-Semitic form of satirical comedy." As for the director, Benjamin thought Granovsky "decidedly Western, he is somewhat skeptical about Bolshevism and the discussion revolves primarily around theater and money matters.")

Hardly restricted to the Yiddish-speaking community, GOSET's popularity had the aspects of a craze. After *200,000,* which would remain the most frequently revived production in GOSET's repertoire for almost twenty-five years, "Comrade" Shimele's songs and sayings, his speech patterns and walk were widely imitated. Muscovites vied with foreign dignitaries to book tickets; two-thirds of the audience required Russian-language synopses. GOSET's heavily musical offerings were especially attractive to foreigners, particularly those who understood German. This fascination of non-Jews with the Yiddish stage suggests the slumming parties that visited Harlem during the Jazz Age: like the

The cover of the June 1924 issue of the Soviet theater journal *Zrelishcha* (Entertainment) is a montage celebrating the GOSET. Director Alexander Granovsky is shown as the locomotive that pulls the train; actor Solomon Mikhoels is the conductor perched atop the engine.

Cotton Club, GOSET was the highly stylized cultural effusion of an exotic race. (One contemporary Russian critic even made this analogy, calling Chagall's murals "Hebrew jazz in paint.") Before the Revolution, as the scholar B. Gorev observed,

authentic Jewish life remained a book behind seven seals for the Russian intelligentsia, which had neither its Livingstones capable and desirous of penetrating this domestic Africa, nor even its Captain Golovnins, who by accident might have dwelt for a substantial time in this alien world.

Jewish reaction to GOSET was, understandably, mixed, and not just because of the theater's hardline anticlericalism. Even more than most vanguards, Yiddish modernists marched ahead of their constituency. The Yiddish audience that had only recently entered the realm of secular art was scarcely prepared to see its naturalistic precepts inverted. Moreover, Granovsky and his troupe were clearly turning the idiom of the *shtetl* against the *shtetl*—most ferociously with a controversial production of I. L. Peretz's poetic drama, *Bay Nakht afn Altn Mark* (Night in the Old Marketplace).

Still, GOSET was a popular theater—"successful when Jewish crowds seethe around it, when Jewish voices resound, when Jewish taste, fashions, and gestures reign supreme," as Osip Mandelstam noted. Each summer GOSET toured the Yiddish heartland of Belorussia and the Ukraine, and it was in that "domestic Africa" where Granovsky set his first film.

Lenin called the cinema "the most important art." But it was not until 1924, the year of his death, that the state film agency Sovkino was established. Only seven features had been completed in 1922; two years later, there were thirty-eight—among them, the stylized, "revolutionary" space-opera *Aelita;* Lev Kuleshov's satiric *Neobychainniye Priklucheniya Mistera Vesta v Stranye Bolshevikov* (The Extraordinary Adventures of Mr. West in the Land of the Bolsheviks); and the "modern" comedy *Papirosnitsa ot Mosselproma* (Cigarette Girl of Mosselprom), which spoofed both the NEP and the nascent movie industry.

In Moscow as in Hollywood, the movies were a magnet for ambitious young performing artists. When, in September 1924, Granovsky wrote to a colleague in New York that he hoped to make "a grandiose Jewish film," he was hardly the only theatrical director drawn to the new medium, although he was one of the few with any prior experience.[3]

Nor was Granovsky's the only Jewish ensemble poised to enter the movies. That spring, newly established Sovkino and the trade-union studio Proletkino invited Habima to appear in an elaborate adaptation of Sholom Aleichem's novel *Der Mabl* (The Deluge). The proposal came at a critical moment for the beleaguered Hebrew-language theater. After nine months of rehearsal, the company had just premiered *Hagolem,* their version of H. Leivick's *Der Goylem,* and first new production since *Hadibuk* began its sensational run three years before. Reviews were mixed; many of the actors were physically exhausted and so declined Sovkino's offer. (Habima had one previous film experience. In 1918, a few months before the ensemble's first public performance, they appeared as extras in *Khleb* (Bread), a three-reel *agitka* codirected by Ryszard Bolesławski for Mos-Kino-Committee.)

Granovsky's *Yevreiskoye Schastye* (Jewish Luck) was also taken from Sholom Aleichem—drawing on the same Menakhem Mendl stories that had inspired *Agentn* (Agents), one of the skits in his epochal Sholom Aleichem "evening." In addition to Mikhoels and Altman, who designed the production and received prominent credit on the film's advertisements, *Jewish Luck* involved other notable Jewish artists. The musical accompaniment was by Lev Pulver, a former violinist with the Bolshoi Ballet, whose modernistic score for *200,000* utilized traditional Jewish melodies, while the idiomatic titles were written by Isaac Babel, an instant literary celebrity for his violent, sardonic stories of the Polish-Soviet War. (So popular was Babel's *Red Cavalry* that two separate Yiddish translations appeared simultaneously—one published in Kharkov, the other in Kiev.) Not until the 1937 Polish production of *Der Dibek* would a film involve a comparable collection of Jewish talent.

As an impoverished dreamer, the archetypal *luft-*

mentsh drifting from one failed get-rich-quick scheme to the next, Menakhem Mendl was a useful emblem for the Jewish plight under the tsars. Although he might just as easily have served as a symbol of the NEP, in *Jewish Luck* this hapless optimist is shown as an instrument of the bourgeoisie and a victim of the *ancien régime*. The scenario—credited to Granovsky's assistant Grigori Gricher-Cherikover, Boris Leonidov (a specialist in action dramas), and the prerevolutionary Odessa director Isaac Teneromo—passes over Menakhem Mendl's misadventures in various stock markets, if not his compulsive insurance selling, to focus on his difficulty eking out a living of any kind. Most of it is taken from the story "It Doesn't Work," describing Menakhem Mendl's characteristically ill-fated attempt at professional matchmaking.

Affectionate but unsentimental, *Jewish Luck* tempers the savage parody of Granovsky's stage work. Despite Mikhoels's delicately exaggerated performance as Menakhem Mendl, the film eschews the grotesque makeup, gymnastic cavorting, and percussive tempo that was GOSET's hallmark. *Aelita,* with sets by *Koldunye*'s designer Isaac Rabinovich, had already brought such expressionistic devices to the Soviet cinema. Granovsky's strategy was precisely the opposite. Turning the camera on an actual *shtetl* would be modernism enough.

Shot mainly in exterior, *Jewish Luck* is almost semidocumentary in its representation of a tumbledown section of Berdichev, the Ukraine's archetypal Jewish town. Where Altman had given *Hadibuk* a stylized Cubo-Futurist flavor, his production design here is virtually ethnographic. Inspired by the An-sky Expedition, Altman had spent the summer of 1913 in Volhynia making rubbings from Jewish tombstones and copying the patterns of synagogue textiles;

although *Jewish Luck* is ostensibly a portrait of pre-October misery, much of it is underscored by a similar preservationist spirit. Religious ritual may be conspicuously absent, but the lengthy open-air wedding that ends the film is a veritable précis of the traditional elements that had inspired Chagall's murals—including a chanting *badkhn,* itinerant *klezmorim,* and ecstatic Chasidic dances.

Jewish Luck had the authority of a folk tradition and the weight of official sanction. No subsequent Soviet movie would cast so sympathetic an eye on the culture of the *shtetl*—or represent it so straightforwardly. The overt emphasis, however, is on Jewish poverty. *Jewish Luck* opens amid the chaos of Menakhem Mendl's large and underfed family. Driven to put bread on the table, the *luftmentsh*

Extras in the Odessa marketplace.
Jewish Luck.

leaves Berdichev for Odessa, where he hopes to sell corsets. Together with his young and equally marginal friend Zalmen, played by the future director Moyshe Goldblatt, he sets out upon "the crooked road of Jewish luck."[4]

After the slapstick failure of even this modest enterprise, Menakhem Mendl stumbles upon a book that contains a list of prospective brides and grooms and decides to become a matchmaker: "Shadkhn—that's a real profession!" In the film's climax, this new career goes spectacularly awry when the would-be "king of the shadkhonim" inadvertently arranges a match between two girls. Although the blunder ultimately brings together the young lovers Zalmen and Beyle (Tamara Adelheim), Menakhem Mendl is betrayed by his wealthy (and ostensibly pious) employer and left to wander off alone.

Granovsky's correspondence suggests that he orig-

Poster designed by Natan Altman for *Jewish Luck.* Solomon Mikhoels is pictured.

inally intended *Jewish Luck* as a means of promoting GOSET's hoped-for American tour. (On January 29, 1925, less than six months before the movie was shot, he wrote that it would have English intertitles and a coda wherein the ensemble would be shown boarding a ship bound for New York.) The film is a marvelous trailer as well as a good deal more. Indeed, *Jewish Luck* begs comparison with 1925's most celebrated film comedy, *The Gold Rush,* with which it shares not only a common theme and time frame, but a similar sense of wistful knockabout and a kindred use of dream sequences. The diminutive Mikhoels gives Menakhem Mendl a Chaplinesque aura of shabby gentility and scurrilous pathos. Obsequious yet irrepressible, he cuts an endearing figure. Unlike Chaplin's Little Tramp, however, Mikhoels's *luftmentsh* is never permitted to triumph —even temporarily—over his social betters.

In the film's marvelous set piece, Menakhem Mendl dreams that he is a *shadkhn* of international proportions. He meets an elegant prospective bride on the steps of the Odessa harbor, presents her with a bouquet, and introduces her to the legendary Jewish philanthropist Baron de Hirsch, who informs him that America is suffering from a shortage of eligible brides. Begged thus to "save America," Menakhem Mendl mobilizes Berdichev. The vision grows increasingly elaborate—its extravagant plenitude of marriage-minded women rivaling the climax of Keaton's *Seven Chances* (another 1925 release)—and, in hindsight, more than a little sinister, as boxcars filled with Jewish maidens, already dressed in their wedding gowns, arrive in Odessa for export overseas. Liveried footmen hold Menakhem Mendl's trademark umbrella and derby as he inspects the brides ("Good enough for Rothschild!") and has them clas-

Menakhem Mendl's dream: a shipment of brides bound for America. *Jewish Luck.*

sified as "special order" or "wholesale" before they are loaded by crane onto waiting steamships.[5]

Bucolic in spite of itself, *Jewish Luck* has marked affinities to the recently introduced American comedies which, along with Hollywood detective thrillers and melodramas, would dominate the Soviet market during the mid-1920s. Briskly paced, skillfully alternating sight gags and character farce, the film is dynamic rather than elegiac. The elaborate treatment of the brides as merchandise has some of the cool, twentieth-century callousness of American slapstick—as does Mikhoels's brilliantly ideogrammatic performance. Whether bathing in the river (still wearing his hat and selling insurance) or simply riding on a train, Mikhoels deploys himself with fan-

tastic, mincing precision, often managing to tilt his body at two opposed angles. More than a master of pantomime, he is the film's most stylized element. As Mandelstam wrote in a Leningrad newspaper, "Mikhoels attains the summit of ethnic Jewish dandyism." Here is "the ghetto-figure in concentrated form." Mikhoels's every movement is a deftly choreographed miniature: accused of smuggling by a tsarist cop, he becomes fawningly coy, offering the official a bribe, with Granovsky lavishing close-ups on his elaborate hand gestures.[6]

Opening in November 1925, less than six weeks before the first public screening of *Potemkin*, Granovsky's "grandiose *kino-film*" (as it was advertised in *Der Emes*) was both a popular and a critical success.

Two *shadkhonim* from
Jewish Luck. Solomon
Mikhoels is at right.

The movie's premiere was treated as a gala event;
Pulver conducted his score with a symphony orchestra at a special preview sponsored by the Society for
the Resettlement of Jewish Workers on the Land
(GEZERD), a quasi-public agency closely associated
with the Yevsektsia.

Surprisingly, *Der Emes* appears not to have reviewed *Jewish Luck,* while *Pravda*'s critic, Boris Gusman, cautiously termed it a "transitional" work,
overly episodic and theatrical, and lacking that "element of propaganda which is essential to the Soviet
film"—but intelligent, lucid, and ingenuous nonetheless. "One can think that something worthwhile
has been contributed to cinema. . . . A good 'theatrical' film is better than a slapdash cinematographic
'original.'" Anything but "theatrical," *Jewish Luck*
was among the first Soviet films made available for
export; within fifteen months of its domestic premiere it was shown in the Baltic states, Hungary, and

China. Nevertheless, it was the only film Granovsky
would make in the Soviet Union.

On paper, at least, a film based on *Der Mabl* promised to be far more sweeping than *Jewish Luck.* First
serialized in 1907, and later published as *In Shturm*
(In the Storm), *Der Mabl* was Sholom Aleichem's
most overtly political work—the story of three families, all with radical children, caught up in the tumult of 1905. Moving back and forth between St.
Petersburg and an unspecified Ukrainian city, the
novel depicted Jews of various social classes and political persuasions, including the revolutionary heroine Masha Bashevitsh, who hangs herself in prison.
There was no shortage of dramatic action: Masha's
memorial service precipitates a riot, and the novel's
other scenes include the "Bloody Sunday" when soldiers fired on a Petersburg crowd petitioning the
tsar, and a climactic pogrom in which the Jews are
aided by revolutionary workers. Still, the original carried some risky political baggage. Not only did Sholom Aleichem use the celebration of Passover as his
ruling metaphor, but his characters included Zionists
as well as Socialists. Moreover, the novel ended with
most of them leaving Russia for America, as had the
author.

The adaptation, when it eventually reached the
screen, kept most of Sholom Aleichem's characters
but "improved" upon his politics: the martyr Masha,
who plays a secondary role in the book, is central to
the film. Imprisoned for "accidentally" shooting a
tsarist officer when police break up a workers' meeting (in the novel she is arrested for participation in a
vague antigovernment conspiracy), she does not
commit suicide but is executed by the authorities,

and it is her death which occasions the movie's grand pogrom—an attack directed only against poor Jews. (With a suggestion of collusion, their wealthy coreligionists are spared.) The film then concludes, not with the immigration of the principals, but with the singing of revolutionary anthems at a mass funeral for the pogrom's Jewish victims.

Originally there was a possibility that Habima might assume some artistic responsibility for the film but, in the end, Sovkino decided against it and the theater accepted the project as a commercial proposition. In his memoirs, Habima member Raikin Ben-Ari explains that "the rights for our participation in the film were purchased from the collective; the money we received went to the group, not to the individual players, and was divided among all of us, whether or not we had taken part in the filming." When their season ended in May, half

the company journeyed to Leningrad. The rest dispersed.

Although the movie's two leading characters, Masha Bashevitsh and her more bourgeois comrade Tamara Shostepol, were played by non-Habima actresses, virtually every other role was taken by a member of the collective. Ben-Ari himself appeared as the proprietor of a Petersburg rooming house inhabited by young radicals; the "reformed" Yiddish actor Yehoshua Bertonov impersonated Masha's working-class father; D. Chechik-Efrati, the prophet Elijah in Habima's recent production of *Hagolem*, here played a roguish police spy while, fresh from his role as the golem, huge Aaron Meskin was comparably cast as the rough-hewn revolutionary Misha Berezniak. Also participating were two prominent Yiddish modernists—Granovsky's brother-in-law, the painter Robert Falk, who had just designed the

Members of Habima in Leningrad for the filming of *Mabl* (U.S.S.R., 1927). Top row, from left: Tmime Yudelevich, Zvi Ben-Chaim, Benno Schneider. Middle: Avraham Baratz, David Itkin, Hanna Rovina, Nahum Zemach, Yehoshua Bertonov. Bottom: D. Chechik-Efrati, Ari Warshawer, Nechama Viniar, Raikin Ben-Ari.

Moscow GOSET's *Bay Nakht afn Altn Mark* in Moscow, and Moshe Milner, musical director at the Ukrainian GOSET (then in Kharkov) and composer of *Hagolem*'s score.

Reports in the American Jewish press suggest that *Mabl,* as the film is known in Russian—a rare but not unique example of a "nationality" film retaining its exotic "foreign" title, albeit with a Russian subtitle that translates as *The Bloody Stream*—was intended to mark the twentieth anniversary of the 1905 revolution. The production seems to have been relatively lavish. "During the filming we lived royally," Ben-Ari recalled. "We stayed at a hotel and were able to treat ourselves to luxuries we had forgotten." The

The rooming-house proprietor Malkin (Raikin Ben-Ari) looks on as police spy Yashke Voroner (D. Chechik-Efrati) implicates the revolutionary Nehemia (Zvi Ben-Chaim) in *Mabl*.

thirty-three-year-old director Yevgeni Ivanov-Barkov (whose last job for Sovkino had been as a set designer), showed an evident concern for Jewish culture. Baruch Chemerinsky, a Habima actor who wrote a production story for *Literarishe Bleter,* reported that Ivanov-Barkov, once he familiarized himself with Russian translations of Sholom Aleichem's work, approached "the great Yiddish humorist with the greatest awe and love and inspiration."[7]

Although Ivanov-Barkov was a neophyte filmmaker, his assistant had once been the owner of a movie studio. Before the Revolution, according to Ben-Ari, this assistant had been a rabid anti-Semite. But now,

a dybbuk . . . entered him and he was all love for Jews and Jewish ways. He beamed with delight over everything that had to do with Jewish customs and was determined to make the film one hundred per cent accurate in its details of Jewish life.

To insure the authenticity of the synagogue scene, Leningrad was ransacked for sacred Torah scrolls. Later, the production went on location to "the Kasrilevkes," as Chemerinsky termed them after Sholom Aleichem's archetypal Jewish town. Sequences were shot in the Jewish quarter of Vinnitsa, Natan Altman's birthplace, as well as the nearby *shtetl* of Litin (site of a 1919 pogrom).

In Litin, Chemerinsky reported, half the town's Jews turned out for a wedding scene, "sitting entire days from early in the morning until night, for half a ruble." Even in Vinnitsa, there was confusion between life and art. Seeing Yehoshua Bertonov "in the tattered clothes of a *balegole* [wagon-driver], Jews scolded him—an elderly Jew—for going about on *shabes* in ragged weekday garb to look for work."

Meanwhile, the local peasants were "astounded" to encounter prerevolutionary police: "They take off their hats . . . make way for them in the streets."

If the picturesque natives showed a naïve appreciation for the film's verisimilitude, Ben-Ari's description of the production suggests that Ivanov-Barkov himself had a fanatical, Stroheim-like concern for naturalism—with a corresponding sadistic tinge. In one shot, Ben-Ari writes, he was required to serve a steaming hot bowl of soup. "What pleased the director most was that the liquid splashed over the brim of the bowl, scalding my fingers. That was 'realism,' he said. I ruefully remarked that it was fortunate we didn't have a scene where we would be beaten or shot. 'Don't worry,' was his rejoinder, 'we have such scenes.' "

For the climactic pogrom, Ivanov-Barkov recruited actual Cossacks, former gendarmes, and a number of neighborhood toughs. "The assistant director 'briefed' them," Ben-Ari recalled. " 'Realism,' he told them—that was the principal thing. The scene must make the audience shudder. . . ."

Bearded actors, in prayer shawls and phylacteries, stood swaying in prayer. The police, hooligans, and Cossacks poised in readiness. The cameraman stood waiting. A whistle from our Gentile director and the attack started. The Cossacks and policemen threw themselves into the part enthusiastically and began to beat the extras whose pure Slavic faces were masked with long beards and earlocks. Too enthusiastically, it seemed, for not all the director's whistling and shouting could stop them. This was "realism" with a vengeance. As it turned out, there were quite a few among the "pogromists" for whom rehearsals were unnecessary.

After this debacle, Ben-Ari reports, the extras not only "categorically refused to take part in any other mass scenes," but would not even wear beards and earlocks.

Despite their obsession with authenticity, Ivanov-Barkov and his nameless assistant proved unable to complete their film. Unlike *Jewish Luck*, *Mabl* was subject to particular political attention. According to Ben-Ari, "the government official whose job it was to pass on the ideological and political complexion of the film brought in another director [Ivan Pyriev, an assistant on Sovkino's successful *Krylya Kholopa*, known in English as *Wings of a Serf*]. He, too, was unable to do a satisfactory job." Finally, Boris Illyitch Vershilov, the assimilated Jew who had directed Habima's *Hagolem,* was pressed into service. Vershilov "brought some sort of order in the chaos, but for all his efforts the film had little artistic achievement to its credit."

The degree of *Mabl*'s chaos became apparent when the Soviet film industry was rocked by a scandal of seemingly epic proportions. In March 1927, *New York Times* correspondent Walter Duranty reported—somewhat hyperbolically—that "fifty or more ex-directors" as well as "prominent members" of Goskino, Proletkino, and Kultkino had been arrested the previous fall and were currently standing trial. According to Duranty, an investigation of the film industry had revealed "a waste of money so outrageous that the Proletkino and Kultkino were immediately suppressed. Persons without the remotest experience in connection with the movie business [were given] responsible posts . . . and the command of hundreds of thousands of rubles." Among the films cited was *Mabl*. The article maintained that the film's script was rewritten four times during production, resulting in an expenditure of $100,000—a third of that going to Moshe Milner's salary—before any usable footage was shot.

Mabl was released—in a state one can only imagine—three weeks after the *Times* piece appeared. By that time, Habima had long since departed the Soviet Union. The troupe left for New York in January 1926 and never returned.

NOTES

1. Indeed, all over Europe, the Russian Revolution fired the imagination of Jewish youth. From the vantage point of Warsaw, where he moved in 1923 to work as a proofreader on *Literarishe Bleter,* Isaac Bashevis Singer had a characteristically sardonic perspective:

Provincial youths—yesterday's yeshiva students who never in their lives had done a lick of work nor had been able to do so—spoke in the name of the workers and peasants and condemned to death all those who wouldn't stand on their side of the barricade. I looked on with alarm and astonishment at how a few pamphlets could transform into potential murderers the sons and daughters of a race that hadn't held a sword in its hand for two thousand years. It had become the fashion among girls to wear the leather jackets worn in Russia by the female members of the Cheka. The mothers and fathers of these murderers were scheduled to become their first victims. . . .

2. The theatrical collective Habima (Hebrew for "the stage") was founded in 1917 by Nahum Zemach and David Vardi and, despite the persecution of Russia's Zionists, performed in Hebrew through the mid-twenties. In 1920, Joseph Stalin, then commissar for national affairs, overruled the Yevsektsia and resumed Habima's subsidy; the theater was attached to the Moscow Art Theater under the direction of Stanislavsky's protégé, Yevgeny Vakhtangov. An Armenian with no knowledge of Hebrew, Vakhtangov staged *Hadibuk* as pure theater—or nearly. The celebrated Beggar's Dance was used to suggest the Revolu-

tion; the bent, contorted creatures who attend Leah's wedding were the oppressed masses siding with the wronged student Khonen against the bride's rich and sinful father.

3. Crossovers were commonplace. The director of Moscow's Zimin Opera Theater broke into movies with the year's major "export" success, *Dvorets i Krepost* (Palace and Fortress); Ukrainian avant-gardist Les Kurbas had already made three features in Odessa; the youngsters of Leningrad's Factory of the Eccentric Actor were preparing their first short film (a comedy in which a Young Pioneer foils Calvin Coolidge's attempt to rob the State Bank), while Sergei Eisenstein (who had incorporated a brief movie in his Proletkult productions) was completing *Statchka* (*Strike*)—which, when it opened, in April 1925, was hailed as the new Soviet cinema's most dazzling tour de force.

4. The Rumanian-born, *kheyder*-educated Goldblatt was praised for his portrayal of Mendele in GOSET's 1927 production of *Masaot Benyamin Hashlishi (The Voyages of Benjamin III),* from the novel by Mendele Mokher Sforim. As a director, he seems to have been something of a troubleshooter. In 1931, Goldblatt became the first head of Moscow's Gypsy Theater; a few years later, he took a sabbatical to direct the Yiddish Theater in Birobidzhan. In late 1933, he assisted Les Kurbas in his abortive GOSET production of *King Lear*. In 1940, according to Joseph Macleod's 1943 *The New Soviet Theater,* he was transferred to Kiev to quell the "feuds and quarrels" of its Yiddish theater. A faithful follower of the party line, Goldblatt told Harold Clurman that his erstwhile mentor Granovsky was "an impressionable fool" (*New Theater*, August 1935). He was eventually named a People's Artist of the Khazar Republic.

5. This sequence, singled out for particular praise by Soviet critics, is nearly a full reel. The scene's location—not to mention the crediting of Sergei Eisenstein's cinematographer Eduard Tissé as one of the film's three cameramen—has fueled speculation that it inspired Eisenstein's own use of the Odessa steps in *Bronenosets Potemkin (The Battleship Potemkin)*, which was shot later that summer. (In his *Five Essays about Eisenstein* Viktor Shklovsky compares "Eisenstein's flight of steps and the steps in Granovsky's film" to show that Eisenstein, and not Tissé, is the visual intelligence behind *Potemkin:* "The flight of steps is the same, and the cameraman is the same. The goods are different.")

Like Tissé, Isaac Babel appears to have been working simultaneously with both Granovsky and Eisenstein; for the latter he was adapting his Benya Krik stories. This script, along with

Jewish Luck, inaugurated Babel's long and ambivalent association with the Soviet film industry. In July 1925, he wrote his family in Paris that he had completed his first scenario and that "according to competent authorities, I did a good job." Babel was offhanded about this feat, observing only that "from the money point of view, it is better than pure literature."

6. When *Jewish Luck* was screened in New York in May 1930, *Daily Worker* critic Harry Alan Potamkin praised it as "one of the few films to have treated the folk-Jew legitimately." Potamkin saw Granovsky's method as analytical, organizing movements in "a design of gestures and body motions. . . . The interplay of the fingers [is] itself a dance!" In Poland during the 1930s, the young dancer Judith Berg was inspired by Mikhoels, using her own characterization of Menakhem Mendl to develop a similar analysis of Jewish folk gestures and body language. Mikhoels himself played Menakhem Mendl once more, in Granovsky's last Soviet stage production, *Der Luftmentsh,* which had its premiere in early 1928.

7. This did not preclude condescension: " 'The devil take it,' [Ivanov-Barkov] once said in Russian style, 'There is an ocean of humor in your Sholom Aleichem for the screen—and why haven't you taken advantage of it until now.' " Why indeed? Ivanov-Barkov went on to become a "nationality" specialist, directing several features in Turkmenistan.

Overleaf: **On location, Broken Hearts (U.S.A., 1926). From left: director Maurice Schwartz, star Lila Lee, and producer Louis N. Jaffe. The shipboard scenes, depicting the journey of a Russian revolutionary (Schwartz) to America, have been lost.**

8

The Prince of Second Avenue

For new york's Yiddish artists, the conflict between tradition and modernity involved several traditions and multiple modernities—as well as a Yiddish stage more vital than stable. In 1918, when the Maurice Schwartz production of *Farvorfn Vinkl* heralded a *"beserer teater"* (better theater), there were eight Yiddish houses in Manhattan, all but one on the Lower East Side. Ten years later, there were half as many.

Despite the erosion of audience and venues, however, the decade between the 1918–19 and 1928–29 seasons was a second Golden Age. Small theaters came and went in Brooklyn, the Bronx, and Newark and virtually every season brought some new high-

minded—if short-lived—company. At the same time, a host of enthusiastic amateur groups, including the Workmen's Circle–sponsored Folksbiene (People's Stage) and its Communist counterpart, the *Morgn Frayhayt*–supported Arbeter Teater Farband (Worker's Theater Group), known as Artef, were performing Yiddish plays and translations throughout the city.

The most resilient showman of the American Yiddish stage, Schwartz announced the dawn and remained into the dusk. Son of a Ukrainian grain merchant turned rag dealer, he was born to survive adversity. At the age of eleven, he had been stranded in Liverpool when his family emigrated to America;

for two years he lived by his wits, until he was located and brought to the Lower East Side. There he found his vocation, acting with a succession of threadbare troupes until he joined David Kessler's company. Like the characters he favored, Schwartz was larger than life—a powerful performer, a charming supplicant, an overbearing director, and a canny producer, jealous of rival talent even as he courted it.

Schwartz had the look of an Oriental potentate, but he understood his public, mixing nationalist spectacles with more elevated productions. His premieres, the Yiddish poet Judd Teller recalled, "brought out a truly elite audience—visiting Zionist eminences, Yiddish poets, the Lower East Side's foremost ideologists, academics and surgeons, and the full Broadway galaxy." Schwartz's 1918 manifesto had called the theater "a sort of holy place," and, as with any religion, there were schisms. At the start of the 1919–20 season, Jacob Ben-Ami broke away to stage Hirschbein's *Grine Felder* (*Green Fields*) at the Madison Square Garden Theater on East Twenty-seventh Street. Schwartz replaced Ben-Ami with the brilliant character actor Muni Weisenfreund, waited until the new troupe disintegrated, and then moved into the Garden to stage *Uriel Acosta* in Hebrew—playing the title role himself, even though he didn't know the language.

For all his hokum, however, Schwartz was a catalytic figure. He opened his 1921–22 season with *Der Dibek,* followed by introducing H. Leivick's *Shmates* (*Rags*), and finished with a Yiddish *Uncle Vanya* (the play's first American performance). Sensitive to European trends, he staged the Warsaw hits *Motke Ganef* (Motke the Thief) and *Yoshke Muzikant,* while his stylized productions of Goldfadn operettas (some designed by Natan Altman's disciple, Boris Aronson) imported—and domesticated—the Yiddish modernism of the Moscow GOSET.

The mid-twenties brought an influx of European talent: Rudolf Schildkraut, Molly Picon, Habima, various factions of the Vilna Troupe. By then, the Lower East Side had itself become a kind of Old Country. During the twenties, 60 percent of its Jewish population would abandon the neighborhood for the greener fields of Brooklyn and the Bronx. Indeed, the 1922–23 season was characterized by several unsuccessful attempts to export Second Avenue—ranging from the Goldwyn studio's *Hungry Hearts,* adapted from Anzia Yezierska's stories of the Lower East Side, to a stage version of *Humoresque,* with Irish-American diva Laurette Taylor playing Jewish mother to Jacob P. Adler's son Luther. Boris Thomashefsky ventured uptown without success, while Schwartz opened an English-language production of Leonid Andreyev's *Anathema* on Broadway—where it, too, flopped.

Mid-season, a week before Christmas 1922, Rudolf Schildkraut and the Yiddish theater made their joint English-language debut at the Provincetown Playhouse in Greenwich Village with *God of Vengeance*; the production received mixed reviews but provoked a major scandal. The theater was briefly closed by the police and extensively investigated by the district attorney, and the *New York Times* refused to accept its advertising. Although Asch's play had been performed in Yiddish without incident, the English version horrified Rabbi Joseph Silverman of Temple Emanu-El, among other uptown Jewish leaders. With Abraham Cahan leading the defense, such luminaries as Eugene O'Neill and the visiting Konstantin Stanislavsky became involved as expert witnesses, the latter pointing out that *God of Vengeance* had even been presented in Russia under the tsar.[1]

East and West, now known as *Mazel Tov,* was to suffer a similar fate. The film arrived in New York in the wake of Picon's triumphant Second Avenue "debut," only to be condemned in its entirety by commissioners Cobb and Levy of the New York State Motion Picture Commission. For the commissioners, *Mazel Tov* was "filled with scenes which tend to bring the religion of the Jew in ridicule and disrepute." The film "is sacrilegious, much of it indecent," the commission informed Kalich and Picon, enumerating the sequences in which the American flapper travesties the Yom Kippur service and the Jewish wedding ceremony, pretends that the mezuzah is a lollypop, "shimmies about on the table [and] appears in her underclothes"—as well as the "several vulgar titles [which suggest that] religion is in the head and brain rather than in the whiskers."

After Kalich filed an appeal, the commission ordered the elimination of three scenes and two intertitles (one reading: "You know as much about the Jewish law as Moses knew about Prohibition"). The movie's distributors, however, were no more reverent than its heroine. Five days after ordering cuts, the commission received a complaint that the unexpurgated *Mazel Tov* was showing at the Prospect Theater in the Bronx. Kalich explained that these were "private" screenings, and the game of cat and mouse continued. *Mazel Tov* was rereleased by one Sam Epstein while, according to reports filed by state inspectors throughout the spring of 1924, the film appeared without the mandated changes at the Lakeland Theater in Brighton Beach and the National on East Houston Street.

Without commenting on this history, the September 3 issue of *Variety* mentioned that *Mazel Tov* recently enjoyed a ten-day run at the Mt. Morris Theater, a sometime Yiddish legitimate house on Fifth Avenue in Harlem. More tolerant than either the Austrian trade papers or the New York State Motion Picture Commission, the show business bible termed the picture "a novelty"—it was shown with Yiddish intertitles—and reported that "the big business drawn has led the producers to arrange for states' right distribution." Two months later, the *Jewish Theatrical News* observed that *Mazel Tov* was still playing in the New York area.

Not until November, when the Picon vehicle was released a third time and shown at the Rutgers Theater, a movie house deep in the Lower East Side, do the commission records show evidence of a revised print. At this point, *Mazel Tov* was evidently cut by 400 feet—although this is by no means certain. When the movie was rereleased with a dubbed Yiddish narration in the spring of 1932, the state of New York again termed the scenes of Molly in synagogue "sacrilegious" and ordered them excised from the print.

In April 1924, Schwartz had brought his Yiddish Art Theater to Europe where, despite (or perhaps because of) their appearance in *Yisker,* the troupe ran out of money and was stranded in Vienna. When Schwartz returned to New York that autumn—thanks to the Hebrew Actors Union, which had taken out a bank loan to wire him cash—word was out in the Jewish press that Sidney Olcott was seeking Yiddish actors for Famous Players–Lasky's *Salome of the Tenements.*

Jetta Goudal (left) plays a Yiddish journalist in the Famous Players-Lasky production *Salome of the Tenements* (U.S.A., 1926), which cost $225,000 to make. Elihu Tenenholz, center, acted with the Yiddish Art Theater and appeared in the 1919 film *Khavah*.

Salome, also adapted from Yezierska, concerned the adventures of one Sonya Mendel (played by Dutch-born Jewish actress Jetta Goudal), the beautiful crusading reporter for a New York Yiddish daily, and, like *Hungry Hearts,* evinced some concern for authenticity. (Indeed, on its release in early 1925, the film was deemed by *Variety* to be of interest only to immigrant Jewish audiences.) This relatively expensive $225,000 production was shot at the Astoria Studio in Queens where Olcott built a set modeled on the corner of Hester and Orchard streets, importing some 500 Lower East Side residents, including 108-year-old Jennie Freeman, to serve as extras. *Sa-*

lome also featured two members of the Schwartz troupe (Lazar Freed and Elihu Tenenholz) together with four other Second Avenue stalwarts—the first time, according to publicity, that Yiddish performers appeared in a studio movie.[2]

Schwartz, however, had *Yisker.* The *Morgn Frayhayt* theater critic Nathaniel Buchwald, who saw the film at a special New York preview in January 1925, found "all the signs of a 'hit.'" Despite mediocre directing and poor set design,

the subject carries you away and produces a melancholy mood. . . . Even the *oysgegrinte* [no longer "green," i.e., Americanized] theater enthusiasts in attendance could not help but shed a secret tear. The film is likely to make an even stronger impression on the Gentiles for, in addition to suspense and human interest, they will find the appeal of the exotic.

Although Buchwald felt that the actors' cinematic *grinkayt* (inexperience) brought freshness to their playing, his opinion was not widely shared. *Yisker* had its American opening in the spring of 1925 at the Premier Theater in Brownsville, Brooklyn, most likely with dual-language (Yiddish and English) intertitles. Unlike *Mazel Tov,* it flopped. While inept distribution may have been one factor, the critics were derisive, the *Jewish Theatrical News* unkindly likening Schwartz to "a ghost playing Hamlet."

The actor was not deterred. For the 1925–26 season he again essayed Broadway (this time in Yiddish), taking up residence two blocks from the Fulton Theater where *The Jazz Singer*—dismissed by the *New York American* as "a garish and tawdry Hebrew play"—had opened its thirty-eight-week run. At the same time, he began a new film project, *Broken Hearts,* which he would both direct and star in. March 2, 1926, the day after Schwartz's final stage premiere of the season, brought the premiere of his first American movie, at the Cameo Theater on Eighth Avenue off Forty-second Street.

Broken Hearts appeared amid a small boomlet of related films. No movies followed *Hungry Hearts* in depicting an immigrant Jewish milieu until 1925 brought *Salome of the Tenements, His People,* the independent *Abie's Imported Bride,* and a pair of films in which Jewish comedian Max Davidson teamed with Jackie Coogan as Lower East Side ragpicker and Irish tyke. Although shot in the Bronx, Schwartz's ambitious eight-reeler was in many ways a throwback to the heroic days of the Lower East Side.

Schwartz adapted a play that, already over twenty years old, was far more old-fashioned than almost everything in his repertoire. The author, Zalmen Libin, was a follower of Jacob Gordin who had worked for years as a cap maker while writing feuilletons that treated the travails of the immigrant Jewish family with a mixture of stark slum naturalism and calculated pathos.

Seizing on Libin as a kind of noble savage, Hutchins Hapgood wrote about him at length in his book *The Spirit of the Ghetto:*

He is a dark, thin, little man, as ragged as a tramp, with plaintive eyes and a deprecatory smile when he speaks. He is uncommonly poor, and at present sells newspapers for a living. . . . A thorough product of the sweatshop, [he is] a man distinguished from the proletarian crowd only by a capacity for feeling and a genuine talent. . . .

A Jewish guardsman in the service of a Polish count: Maurice Schwartz in Sidney Goldin's *Yisker* (Austria, 1924).

Libin, Hapgood discovered, was the author of two plays, *Di Farshpektikt Khupe* (The Belated Wedding) and *Der Umzister Korbm* (A Vain Sacrifice), for which he was paid fifty dollars apiece.

They are each a series of pictures from the miserable Jewish life in the New York ghetto. The latter play is the story of a girl who marries a man she hates in order to get money for her consumptive father. The theme of *The Belated Wedding* is too sordid to relate. Both plays are unrelieved gloom and lack any compensating dramatic quality.

Di Gebrokhene Hertser oder Libe un Flikht (The Broken Hearts, or Love and Duty), in which Jacob P. Adler played an immigrant cantor whose family breaks up under the stress of life in the New World, was first staged in 1903, shortly after Hapgood's profile. Libin's greatest success, it was first filmed, in 1913, by the Warsaw-based Kosmofilm. The new version was produced by Jaffe Art Films, a one-shot company founded by lawyer/realtor Louis N. Jaffe, whose avowed policy was "to present the Jew and he is done in plays, done in an artistic manner."[3]

Characteristically, Schwartz chose to make his film-directing debut with a proven product. The Jaffe credo notwithstanding, *Broken Hearts* was an established, if hokey, crowd-pleaser, certainly not an aesthetic risk. (Indeed, Schwartz had opened his first theater with a dependable Libin melodrama.) Nevertheless the original was altered both to bolster Schwartz's role and to provide a happier, more "modern" ending. Libin's play was adapted for the screen by no less an authority than Frances Taylor Patterson, the serious and erudite author of *Cinema Craftmanship,* an early textbook on "scenario technique," as well as the first "instructor in photoplay composition" ever to teach at Columbia University. (Patterson was nearly as high-minded as Schwartz. In her 1928 *Scenario and Screen,* she predicts that, so far as motion pictures go, "the industry, huge as it is, will one day be outshone by the majesty and magnificence of the art." Patterson modestly avoids mention of her sole screen credit although she does attribute the appeal of Goldwyn's 1923 *Potash and Perlmutter* to titles "which recorded with comic accuracy the garbled grammar of the ghetto.")

In addition to Schwartz, *Broken Hearts* featured a number of players from the Yiddish Art Theater: Wolf Goldfaden, Isidore Cashier, and Anna Appel (all of whom had appeared in *Yisker*), as well as Julius Adler. There was also one genuine movie star: Lila Lee. Formerly under contract to Paramount, the New Jersey–born Lee was a graduate of Gus Edwards's "School Days," the venerable vaudeville act that incubated former child performers George Jessel, Groucho Marx, Walter Winchell, Eddie Cantor, and Mervyn LeRoy. "Cuddles" Lee broke into movies at seventeen (her first major part was as the ingenue in Cecil B. De Mille's 1919 *Male and Female*) and in 1922 scored as Rudolph Valentino's faithful wife in *Blood and Sand.*

Schwartz's biographer, David Denk, present on the *Broken Hearts* set, thought the maestro appeared bewildered by the demands of movie direction. If so, this confusion is not apparent from those segments of the film that survive—having been reedited and dubbed into Yiddish for a 1932 rerelease. *Broken Hearts* is competent, if uninspired, filmmaking. Given the development of Yiddish cinema, the movie's most impressive formal aspect is the lack of staginess—although for this we should perhaps credit Patterson and the experienced cameraman, Frank Zucker.

In his *New York Times* review, Mordaunt Hall commended the film's "sincerity" and "restraint," citing Schwartz's "inexperience" for the problematic pacing. On the other hand, while praising the film's intertitles and Lila Lee's performance, a front-page notice in the *Jewish Theatrical News* found the star *too* restrained: although the anonymous critic deemed *Broken Hearts* an improvement over *Yisker*, Schwartz was still "not given a chance to achieve the dramatic heights he is capable of."

> Everyone said [after *Yisker*] that Schwartz was never intended to appear in the movies. *Broken Hearts* shatters that illusion. . . . Yet, for all that, he is listless, a trifle stunned, a wee bit too careful. This is especially noticeable in the love scenes.

Broken Hearts was cautious and, perhaps in response to the broader strokes of Hollywood's ghetto films, overdignified. "We could almost hear Jaffe and Schwartz behind the camera exclaiming—'We want art—art! Jewish art!'" the *Jewish Theatrical News* joked, adding that "We could have wished for a Tom Mix or a Bill Hart to pep things up." Indeed, the narrative suggests one of Sidney Goldin's prewar two-reelers. The hero, Benjamin Resanov (Schwartz), is not an ordinary immigrant but a political refugee. Bidding farewell to his wife, Esther (the beautiful but untalented Henrietta Schnitzler, married to the owner of the Garden Theater), he flees their Ukrainian village one step ahead of the tsar's henchmen to arrive penniless on the Lower East Side.

Confused and despondent after receiving news of

Handbill advertising a two-day revival of *Di Umgliklikhe Kale*, the dubbed Yiddish version of *Broken Hearts*, at the Windsor Theater on New York's Lower East Side, 1930s.

his wife's death, Resanov boards with the family of Victor Kaplin (Cashier), teaching himself English at night—Schwartz playing his own pensive, refined demeanor off against Cashier's proletarian heartiness. In true tenement symphony fashion, Resanov becomes involved with the girl across the airshaft—Ruth Esterin (Lee), the daughter of Cantor Esterin (Goldfaden). Ruth helps Resanov learn English and inevitably falls in love with the handsome, tragic greenhorn, thus sparking a war of the generations.

Ruth's parents have decided she should marry Milton Kruger, a mustachioed lounge lizard who is the son of the synagogue president. The wealthy Krugers live on Riverside Drive, identified in the titles as "Allrightnik Row." Resanov, though radical, is a model immigrant, at once more traditional in his

Jewish virtues than vulgar Milton and less bound to conventional piety than the hypocritical cantor. He is associated with nature and regeneration, taking Ruth away from the shabby tenements to spend the day in the park. They stay so late that she misses her parents' *shabes* meal, arriving after the Krugers have come to discuss the match, the requisite comic *shadkhn* (Morris Strassberg) in tow. The soirée breaks up in confusion as horrified Ruth, who regards Milton as a "fathead," bolts across the hall to Resanov, followed by the irate cantor.

Esterin demands that Resanov give up his daughter—if he loves her, he will realize that he can never offer her the comforts that a Milton Kruger can. When Resanov announces his determination to marry Ruth, the cantor threatens to disown her. Resanov and Ruth are nonetheless wed and Resanov is enjoying his first success as an American journalist when disaster strikes. While the couple are literally waltzing with happiness, a letter arrives from Esther, who had been imprisoned (and not dead) and has now, thanks to the Revolution, been set free. Having learned of his inadvertant bigamy, Resanov must again leave a tearful bride and return to Russia, "a country which," the title observes, "has seen many changes since the reign of the tsar." Ruth's shame is compounded when, at Milton's raucous wedding, the elder Kruger insults the cantor, who then quits his position.

Persecuted by nosy neighbors, Ruth is now, for the first time, compelled to support herself and finds work in a sweatshop. Here, *Broken Hearts* is closest to Libin's downbeat immigrant milieu, haunted as it is by the spectre of the *agunah,* the abandoned wife who, according to Orthodox tradition, cannot marry for ten years, and then only with the permission of ninety-nine rabbis. (During the period of the Great Immigration, the most troublesome and widely discussed Jewish domestic problem was desertion. Men left their families behind in the Old World or walked out on them in the New. As a regular feature, the *Forverts* offered a "Gallery of Missing Husbands.") After she discovers that she is pregnant, Ruth gives birth alone and leaves New York. All ends happily, however, when she tremblingly visits her parents' home on the eve of Yom Kippur. Resanov reappears —he has returned from the Old Country, where he learned, during the course of his journey, that Esther really has died, and he is thus once again a free man in the New World.

As much as any "melting-pot" film, *Broken Hearts* celebrates success in America. The conflict is not complicated by the bogey of intermarriage. Nevertheless, when the cantor's daughter defies patriarchal authority to wed the revolutionary journalist, she embodies the triumph of the younger, secular generation of American Jews. (Despite this optimistic view of immigrant assimilation, *Broken Hearts* proved scarcely more successful than *Yisker*. The film lasted only a week at the Cameo before it was replaced by a series of Ernst Lubitsch revivals.) Indeed, the degree to which Schwartz's success story broke with the prevailing ethos of the subsequent Yiddish cinema can be seen in the alterations made when the film was reedited and rereleased, with a dubbed Yiddish soundtrack, six years later. In this revised version, Resanov never returns. The *agunah* dies of a broken heart, a warning to those daughters who would flout their parents's wishes.

Mazel Tov, too, was similarly modified: Molly's sacrilegious adventures were framed as a story related by an old woman to a group of children—the revolt against tradition is literally a *bube-mayse* (a grandmother's fairy tale).

NOTES

1. The 1922–23 season was an unusually stimulating one for New York. In addition to the Moscow Art Theater, Broadway saw the premieres of Karel Capek's *R.U.R.* and Luigi Pirandello's *Six Characters in Search of an Author.* John Barrymore played *Hamlet,* sister Ethel appeared as Shakespeare's Juliet, and Jeanne Eagels starred as the fallen heroine of Somerset Maughm's *Rain.*

2. In fact, Vera Gordon and Rosa Rosanova, the Jewish mothers of *Humoresque* and *Hungry Hearts,* respectively, were both veterans of the Yiddish stage. (The producers of *Hungry Hearts* had considered Celia Adler for the central role, auditioning Sarah Adler for, and trying to interest Bessie Thomashefsky in, the part of the mother.)

3. Following the release of *Broken Hearts,* Jaffe provided a permanent home for Schwartz's company in the Folks Theater, at Second Avenue and Twelfth Street. Schwartz moved in for the 1926–27 season, opening with a "futurist" version of Goldfadn's *Dos Tsente Gabot* (The Tenth Commandment) and angered his company by, yet again, committing the sin of *"starism"* (a Yiddish word) in featuring only his own name. Although, according to Celia Adler, Schwartz hoped to protect his theater by becoming "as prominent as Picon or Gabel," persistent financial problems compelled him to abandon this sanctuary after only two seasons.

Overleaf: **Torn between two worlds. Mary Dale (May McAvoy) entreats Jack Robin (Al Jolson) to return to Broadway while Yudelson (Otto Lederer) prepares to hand the singer his father's *talis.* Jack's mother (Eugenie Besserer) looks on. *The Jazz Singer* (U.S.A., 1927).**

9

Making It in America

As IMMIGRATION halted and ties to the Old Country frayed, American-Yiddish culture came increasingly under the spell of American show business. Second Avenue impresario Max Gabel regularly adapted the most sensational Broadway hits and brought them to his Public Theater, where star Jennie Goldstein mixed English with Yiddish in her songs—"When I pretend I'm gay, *es iz mir okh un vey*" (it is, for me, "alas and alack").

Sprightly Molly Picon, herself influenced by the Jewish-American entertainer Fanny Brice, was featured in a series of tremendously popular "literary operettas" whose scores suggested those of the uptown musical theater. Nevertheless, Picon further en-

deared herself to Second Avenue by her stout refusal to abandon the Yiddish stage for Broadway. Not so Ludwig Satz, Picon's only rival as a comic star, who enjoyed an English-language success as Abe Potash in the 1926 Broadway production of *Potash and Perlmutter, Detectives*. The following year, Satz starred in *The Lunatic,* an independent production directed by Harry Garson. Although based on Harry Kalmanowitz's play *Der Meshugener* (The Madman), the movie had no Jewish content.[1]

The prewar lament "A Brivele der Mamen" was superseded by "My Yiddishe Mama," introduced by Sophie Tucker in 1925, the same year the play *The Jazz Singer* had its Broadway premiere. Where "A

Brivele der Mamen" was a tribute to the parent who waits in the Old Country, the forlorn subject of "My Yiddishe Mama" has merely been left behind in the old neighborhood. The song's original 78 rpm recording featured both English and Yiddish renditions. The English words are self-consciously genteel; the less-restrained Yiddish version invokes food, tears, poverty, the Jewish heart, and God. In either language, the song was so totally an American-Jewish anthem that in the spring of 1926, Miss Ethel Walker's rendition preceded the first-run showings of *Broken Hearts*.

In 1924, *World's Work* magazine, which had run a series of articles luridly characterizing Jewish immigrants as the Typhoid Marys of political subversion, published *The Jews in America,* a book whose jacket wondered whether "with their un-American creed, [Jews] will ever be absorbed into the American commonwealth." Jews, of course, were absorbing madly. Far more than Poland and even the Soviet Union, America offered an unprecedented opportunity for assimilation—or mutation. The immigrant Jew had not only the option of exploring secular modes of Jewishness, but of submerging himself alongside other wildly disparate groups in the creation of a new national identity. In *The Jazz Singer*'s extravagant paean to personal reinvention, a cantor's son from Orchard Street, played by cantor's son Al Jolson, becomes nothing less than "The World's Greatest Entertainer"—as Jolson himself was known—by applying burnt cork and singing about his "Mammy from Alabammy."

Mark Slobin, who has written several invaluable accounts of Jewish music in America, points out that, in addition to Jolson, virtually every major Jewish entertainer of the twenties—Sophie Tucker, Eddie Cantor, George Jessel, even Molly Picon—made use

of blackface: "Some of them explicitly state, in memoirs, the comfort they derived from putting on that all-American mask of burnt cork. In blackface, they were no longer the immigrant—they were one with the soul of America as represented by the grotesque co-optation of the slave's persona." (The interest in African-American musical idioms shown by popular composers Irving Berlin, Jerome Kern, George Gershwin, and Harold Arlen is also suggestive.) Meanwhile, the *Dearborn Independent* assailed "Jewish jazz," a.k.a. "the moron music of the Yiddish Trust," comparing its "sly suggestion" and "abandoned sensuous notes" to the insidious corruption of those "Jewish" motion pictures—"reeking of filth" and "slimy with sex."

In fact, American show business was becoming more Yiddish, as well as vice versa. Jolson, Brice, Tucker, Cantor *et al.* represented America's first generation of openly Jewish popular entertainers. In movies and plays, East European Jews came to personify the drama of immigration—particularly after the United States effectively halted the inflow of foreigners in 1924. Following the Broadway success of *The Jazz Singer, We Americans* (a comedy about Jewish adjustment on the Lower East Side, with Yiddish actors Muni Weisenfreund and Morris Strassberg making their English-language debuts) was the surprise hit of the 1926–27 season.

There were other, less obvious ways in which Yiddish popular culture influenced its American counterpart. The movie reviewers of 1920 were impressed by *Humoresque*'s unabashed appeal to raw sentiment and family values. That these, as well as the careful leavening of pathos with pratfalls, were staples of the Yiddish stage was acerbically pointed out by the young Marxist critic Harry Alan Potamkin a decade after the film's release: *Humoresque* was "an impertinent fable written by a sentimental woman, Fannie Hurst, further sentimentalized by the director Frank Borzage, and almost obscenely sentimentalized in the performance of Vera Gordon, a product of the super-sentimental American Yiddish theater." (One wonders if Potamkin might have been any kinder to Gordon had he known that her husband's revolutionary activities required them both to flee Russia after 1905.)

The closing of America's golden door effectively split the Yiddish world into American, Soviet, and Polish centers, each subject to its own centripetal forces. Although the massive pre–World War immigration to America had stimulated the growth of Yiddish press, theater, and social institutions, their continued vitality was dependent upon a constant flow of new immigrants. As the flood became a trickle, spoken Yiddish went into decline and, by the end of the decade, the center of Yiddish culture shifted from New York back to Europe.

America blurred traditional distinctions between religion, worldly success, and popular culture. The late nineteenth-century crowding together of hundreds of *shtetlekh* on the Lower East Side, and the Darwinian struggle thus engendered among their transplanted *shuln*, stimulated liturgical music and promoted a star syndrome already nascent in Europe. In 1885, one American congregation hired a *khazn* for the unprecedented sum of $1,000. This extravagance hardly went unnoticed. A procession of hopeful Russian and Polish cantors arrived in New York, where many learned the art of self-promotion and some turned toward music hall careers.

Forty years later, Jolson and Tucker were frequently referred to as secular cantors, while the

Yosele Rosenblatt, the most celebrated American cantor of the 1920s.

Harlem-based *khazn* Yosele Rosenblatt not only recorded liturgical music but performed it on the vaudeville stage, along with secular items like the ubiquitous "My Yiddishe Mama." The cantorate was a major site for the struggle between the sacred and the secular. Both *Broken Hearts* and the stage version of *The Jazz Singer* end with Yom Kippur reconciliations, having each presented a generational conflict in which an old-fashioned *khazn* disowns his disobedient child.

Although Jolson never appeared in the Yiddish theater, nor sang more than a few Yiddish songs, he

A figure of pathos rather than authority: Rudolf Schildkraut in Edward Sloman's *His People* (U.S.A., 1925).

had, as the foremost Jewish-American celebrity, a special significance for Jewish audiences and performers. In his streetwise apprehension of American popular culture, in his fantastic vitality and gangsterish monomania for success, he was cut from the same cloth as the so-called movie moguls. Brash and egocentric, a compulsive gambler and womanizer, yet insecure and apt to wrap himself in the American flag, Jolson was a flamboyant projection of the mogul persona.

In his preface to the filmed *The Jazz Singer*'s souvenir program, playwright Samson Raphaelson recalled that when, as a college student, he first saw Jolson perform, he was overwhelmed and astonished by the religious fervor of Jolson's ragtime. This epiphany was the genesis of his play. "I hear Jazz," Raphaelson continued, "and I am given a vision of cathedrals and temples collapsing and silhouetted against the setting sun, a solitary figure, a lost soul, dancing grotesquely on the ruins. . . . Thus do I see the jazz singer."

Jazz is prayer. It is too passionate to be anything else. It is prayer distorted, sick, unconscious of its destination. The singer of jazz is what Matthew Arnold wrote of the Jew, "lost between two worlds, one dead, the other powerless to be born." In this my first play I have tried to crystallize the ironic truth that one of the Americas of 1927—that one which packs to overflowing our cabarets, musical revues and dance-halls—is praying with a fervor as intense as that of the church and synagogue. The Jazz American is different from the Negro evangelist, from the Zulu medicine-man, only in that he doesn't know he is praying.

Although the change in the immigration laws effectively halted the flow of East European Jews to America, immigrant Jews remained common figures in American movies through the coming of sound. Indeed, no longer a threatening horde, they were even a source of sentimental nostalgia.

Postwar ghetto films followed the lead of *Humoresque,* which sweetened the melting pot with the promise of upward mobility and the comfort of transcendent maternal love. With *Humoresque,* Patricia Erens notes, a new archetype joined the Stern Patriarch, Prodigal Son, and Rose of the Ghetto in the immigrant family constellation. This was the Long-Suffering Mother. And as the Mother gained in stature, so the Patriarch declined, becoming, in films like *The Jazz Singer* (1927), Edward Sloman's *His People* (Universal, 1925), and Frank Capra's *The Younger Generation* (Columbia, 1929), a figure of pathos rather than authority.

At the same time, in a continuation of the vaude-ville stereotype, Jews continued to appear as comic figures. "Very short and very greasy," N. L. Roth-man described the prevailing stereotype in a 1928 issue of *Jewish Forum,* "a big bulbous nose protruding from between tiny, mournful eyes. . . ."

He waves his hands ludicrously with every word
—he commits the most excruciating faux pas at
any social gathering—if there is anything he
loves better than to cheat at business, with winks
and grimaces, it is to shy bricks at the Grand
Master of the Saint Patrick's Day Parade, with
whom, later, he sheds scalding tears of friendship. This is he, waddling across the silver
screen, to the obscene obligato of roars of
laughter. And the loudest of laughs issues from
our friend, the Jew.

Merging with the ghetto dramas during the mid-twenties, the vaudeville-derived comedies spawned a popular cycle of Jewish-Irish films. While some, like Universal's *The Cohens and the Kellys* (1926) con-cerned business partnerships, most Jewish-Irish films revolved around affairs of the heart. These were doubtless inspired by the enormous success of Anne Nichols's stage play, *Abie's Irish Rose* which, opening on Broadway in 1922, ran for much of the decade, demonstrating that true love transcended religious or ethnic difference. In these films, as in the tragic *Manasse,* assimilation became synonymous with intermarriage.

There were also a number of sentimental dramas that indirectly celebrated the warmth of the Jewish family by having a kindly version of the Stern Patri-arch shelter a Christian waif. In *A Harp in Hock* (De Mille, 1927), no less an eminence than Rudolf Schildkraut plays an irascible old pawnbroker taught love by an adorable Irish orphan boy. (The strength of the Jewish family shown in these films cuts two ways. As Erens points out, "the adoption of Jewish children by Irish families is never treated.") In 1928, at the tail end of the cycle, came Paramount's version of *Abie's Irish Rose*—for the rights to which Jesse Lasky paid an unprecedented half a million dollars —although the Cohens and the Kellys kept right on assimilating into the sound era.

In keeping with the ethos of the melting pot, only a few films showed Jews as they had lived in Europe. Sloman's *Surrender* (Universal, 1927), is one notable example. Based on the 1915 drama *Lea Lyon* by Alexander Brody, the film is set in a Galician village invaded by Cossacks and concerns a love affair be-tween a rabbi's daughter and a Russian prince. Yet even here the generational dynamics are the same as those of the ghetto drama, where the central theme remained the breakdown of authority within the im-migrant family. In the struggle between young as-similators and their tradition-bound elders, the battle was already over. With very few exceptions, most notably Capra's *The Younger Generation,* youth reigned supreme.

As the decade waned, the ghetto film waxed in-creasingly optimistic. Rather than the exotic Other of the German cinema, or the impoverished and persecuted *shtetl*-dweller of the Soviet film, the American movie Jew was a model of successful ad-aptation. Hollywood constructed "Americanism" as an unproblematic process of assimilation—an ideal-ization of the road taken by the movie moguls them-selves. The emphasis shifted from survival to success, from making it to America to making it in America.

This situation was anticipated in the most authentic of German-Jewish films, E. A. Dupont's *The An-cient Law,* which, although set in nineteenth-century Austria, parallels *The Jazz Singer* (and even Mark Arnshteyn's *Der Vilner Balebesl*) as a story of gener-ational conflict and show-biz assimilation. This point was made by Potamkin: Dupont's film shows "the metamorphosis of the young Talmudic Jew into a man-of-the-world. . . . It tells of the battle between two worlds: the testament and the drama." (Po-tamkin rated *The Ancient Law* "far above" *The Jazz Singer:* "There is more scrutiny of the data of folk, and the intensity of the village Jews, passionate of temperament, is rendered." He singled out Avrom Morevsky for particular praise: "This was not slob-bering, though it conveyed the emotionalism in the rigid orthodoxy, the rigid impassioned orthodoxy, of the parent . . .").

To a certain degree, the persistence of the melting-pot films may reflect the interest of the mo-guls themselves. Sam Goldwyn is responsible for both the adaptation of Yezierska's *Hungry Hearts* (1922)—the production of which, studio memos in-dicate, he followed quite closely—and its spiritual sequel, the 1924 comedy *In Hollywood with Potash and Perlmutter.* Edward Sloman, who made several Jewish-theme films for Sigmund Lubin in the teens, maintained that he directed *His People, Surrender,* and *We Americans* (1928) at the behest of Universal boss Carl Laemmle.

And, as the Warner brothers shot *The Jazz Sing-er*'s Lower East Side scenes on location, used the Winter Garden Theater (Jolson's "personal king-dom") for the final number, reconstructed the Orchard Street Synagogue on a Hollywood backlot and included a lengthy interlude of Yosele Rosen-blatt in performance, one cannot but be struck by the surplus of authenticity with which they invested

the film they would advertise as their "Supreme Triumph."[2]

In April 1926, Warner Brothers—a scrappy studio whose major asset was the trained dog Rin-Tin-Tin—had formed a partnership with Western Electric, thus creating the Vitaphone Corporation for which, over the next few years, Sam Warner would produce scores of one- and two-reel "acts" (mainly solo vaudeville performers) with synchronous sound-on-disc accompaniment.

Two months later, on the advice of their then-top contract director Ernst Lubitsch, Warners paid $50,000 for the rights to *The Jazz Singer.* In August, the first Vitaphone program—eight shorts (ranging from a speech by industry *mashgiekh* Will Hays to the overture to *Tannhäuser* to a song by virtuoso guitarist Roy Smeck), plus the feature-length *Don Juan*—had its premiere at the Warners' theater in New York. Sound was in the air, literally. (Newly established radio networks were competing to sign vaudeville stars. In 1926, the *Forverts* began the first Yiddish-language broadcasts on New York's WEVD.) Warners' Vitaphone experiment proved successful: a second program opened in October, a third in February 1927. Now, Warners was ready to produce a feature with music and incidental dia-logue, protecting their investment with the presence of superstar Al Jolson.

Appropriately, the film that would sound the death knell for both silent film and vaudeville opens on a mournful note. To the accompaniment of a pseudo-Semitic melody, a series of titles identifies the Jews as "a race older than civilization" whose culture is threatened by a new urban music which is "perhaps, the misunderstood utterance of prayer." It is *erev* Yom Kippur on the Lower East Side, and thirteen-year-old Jakie, son of Cantor and Sarah Rabinowitz, is to chant *Kol Nidre* in his father's synagogue. Cut to Jakie performing "My Gal Sal" in a local saloon. Jakie is betrayed by Yudelson (Otto Lederer), the film's comic stand-in for the Jewish community, who rushes to report the boy to his father. The cantor (Warner Oland) arrives, drags Jakie by his ear homeward past the pushcarts of Hester Street, and, despite Mama's tearful supplications, administers the strap. Tearful Jakie runs away from home even as his father's *Kol Nidre* wells up on the soundtrack.

A decade or more passes. In a studio reconstruction of Coffee Dan's, a San Francisco show-business hangout of the era, Jolson makes his first appearance as the mature Jakie, now known as Jack Robin. The entire scene is redolent of his liberation from tribal taboo. Jack wolfs down a breakfast of *treyf* with ragtime ebullience, eyes his Gentile patroness with awestruck lust, and puts across "Toot, Toot, Tootsie" with a lascivious self-assurance. That Jack, when called upon to perform, sings "Dirty Hands, Dirty Face," is richly evocative of his conflicted patrimony. The song is a mawkish ballad of paternal love in which, alternately maudlin and mocking, the singer

Jolson sings *Kol Nidre* in *The Jazz Singer*.

revels in the role of father to an incorrigible street urchin who, beneath a grimy exterior, is "an angel of joy." But Jack's inability to sever all connection to his past is made overt in the film's next musical sequence: while on tour, he is drawn to a hall where Yosele Rosenblatt is giving a concert.[3]

This ambivalence is further developed when Jack is called to Broadway and triumphantly returns to New York, heading immediately for the Lower East Side where, as a title informs us, "For those whose faces are turned towards the past, the years roll by unheeded." When he discovers that his mother is indeed alone at home, he springs from her embrace to the parlor piano for strenuous rendition of "Blue Skies." In her only authentic moment in the film, Eugenie Besserer seems utterly flummoxed as Jolson interrupts the song midway to steal a kiss, promise her a new pink dress, offer her a new apartment in the Bronx, and tempt her with a trip to Coney Island, all the while suggestively vamping on the keyboard. (It was this short spoken interlude which effectively destroyed the silent cinema. The Warners had not intended to make "talking" pictures so much as automate the music that accompanied silent ones; only after noting the audience's response to Jolson's spontaneous improvisations did they realize what they had wrought.)

The communion is broken when the cantor appears and, catching his wife and son together at the piano, cries "Stop!"—whereupon the film abruptly reverts to silence. In the ensuing title, the cantor denounces the jazz-singing prodigal for his misuse of divine energy. At first Jack attempts to pacify his father by suggesting that America transcends Jewishness: "If you were born here, you would feel as I do." When the cantor accuses him of apostasy, a startlingly blunt title appears in which Jack makes explicit Raphaelson's point: "My songs mean as much to my audience as yours do to your congregation!"

The Jazz Singer reaches critical mass on the afternoon of Jack's Broadway opening, which is, again, with cosmic inevitability and comic improbability, *erev* Yom Kippur. In the midst of the final rehearsal, his mother comes backstage to inform Jack that only by singing *Kol Nidre* in *shul* that night can he save his dying father (and, by extension, the Jewish community). Refusing his mother's request, Jack rushes madly onstage and hurtles through the chorus line to intone a fevered incantation of mother worship. He is now, for the first time in the film, the full-blown, iconic essence of "Jolson-ness." Finishing the song to tumultuous acclaim, the dazed and tormented jazz singer returns to his dressing room where, gazing into the mirror, he sees not a blackfaced minstrel but a synagogue filled with praying Jews. Jack realizes he must return to the Lower East Side "before the sun is out of the sky." His producer flatly warns him that if he walks out, he will never again play Broadway. Thus caught between conflicting commandments, Jack elects to chant.

It is this prayer which ends the play (as it ran on Broadway and toured the country, as it was performed in the Catskills, and as it was televised in 1959 with Jerry Lewis in the Jolson role). The repentant son replaces his dying father as cantor, who had in turn replaced *his* father (who had in turn . . .), a ritual, sentimentalized affirmation of the eternal burden of Jewishness. For the film, however, the Warner brothers added a dreamlike reversal in which, back in blackface and back on Broadway, Jack goes down on one knee to sing "Mammy" as Mama herself sits beaming in the audience, the fatuously proud Yudelson beside her, and the cantor gone forever from the picture.

If Jolson seemed to the pioneering pop-culture critic Gilbert Seldes to possess a "daemonic" vitality, to his disciple George Jessel he was, in fact, something else. "In 1910," eulogized Jessel at Jolson's West Coast funeral (there were East Coast rites as well),

the Jewish people who immigrated from Europe to come here were a sad lot. Their humor came out of their troubles. Men of thirty-five seemed to take on the attitudes of their fathers and grandfathers, they walked with stooped shoulders. When they sang, they sang with lament in their hearts. . . . And then there came on the scene a young man, vibrantly pulsating with life and courage, who marched on the stage, head held high like a Roman Emperor, with a gaiety that was militant, uninhibited and unafraid. . . . *Jolson is the happiest portrait that can ever be painted about an American of the Jewish faith.* (my emphasis)

Included in *The Jazz Singer*'s souvenir program is the terse declaration that, "the faithful portrayal of Jewish homelife is largely due to the unobtrusive assistance of Mr. Benjamin Warner, father of the producers and ardent admirer of *The Jazz Singer*." This statement, which attempts through paternal approval to legitimize the overthrow of Jewish tradi-

tionalism depicted in their film, suggests that the Warners were uneasily aware that the story of *The Jazz Singer* was not only that of Jolson or many of their employees, but also their own.

Although the ads for *The Jazz Singer* that ran in the *Forverts* gave cantor Yosele Rosenblatt nearly the prominence of Jolson, the movie offered a myth and a self-portrait that would preoccupy American-Yiddish cinema for the next fifteen years. The story *The Jazz Singer* told, no less than the technology it employed, made Yiddish talkies inevitable.

NOTES

1. Ironically, it was given a Yiddish soundtrack and rereleased in 1934 as *Oy di Shviger!* (*What a Mother-in-Law!*).

2. *The Jazz Singer* followed by three months another Jewish triumph: for seven years, Henry Ford's *Dearborn Independent* had been publishing its own version of *The Protocols of the Elders of Zion*. Finally, in 1927, Clarence Darrow filed a $5 million libel suit against the newspaper and Ford, personally. The series ended, and on July 8, the industrialist apologized.

3. Rosenblatt had already made two secular Vitaphone shorts, *Omar Rabbi Elosar* and *Hallelujah;* the piece he sings here is the secular eulogy *Yortsayt*. Thus, it is Rosenblatt's off-screen rendition of *Kol Nidre* that secures *The Jazz Singer*'s claim to be the world's first cantorial, a genre that would come into its own three years later.

Overleaf: Yidishe tokhter, **Russian revolutionary. Tamara Adelheim as the militant heroine of Grigori Roshal's *His Excellency* (U.S.S.R., 1928); frame enlargement.**

10

Once Upon a Time in the Ukraine

THERE WERE NO brash Jolsons in the brave new world of Soviet culture—nor, despite intermittent attempts to render Russian Jews as icons of successful socialist assimilation, were there any transformative epics as optimistic as *The Jazz Singer*. Soviet-Jewish identity was something more schematized, abstract, and fiercely regulated. No less than the Yevsektsia which policed it, Soviet-Yiddish culture labored under a double burden: where Soviet-Russian literature might simply direct Russian workers and peasants across the threshold of the new era, a Soviet-Yiddish literature or cinema would have to first recast the Jewish masses as workers and peasants.

Even as *Mabl* and *Jewish Luck* were completed, the Soviet cinema was accommodating the aspira-tions of various national groups. In April 1923, the Twelfth Party Congress had created a Council of Nationalities and proposed the use of indigenous languages by state agencies serving the national minorities. The next few years saw the creation of numerous such cultural and political institutions. As early as 1924, an amateur filmmaker made the first Azerbaijani movie. The following year brought similar Uzbeki and Chuvashi efforts. In 1926, the Georgian director Amo Bek-Nazarov directed an Armenian feature. By 1927, all of these nationalities —as well as Georgians and Belorussians—had local production facilities.

Unlike Georgians, Armenians, Belorussians, Uzbeks, Chuvash, and Azerbaijanis, however, the Soviet Union's 2.6 million Jews had neither a republic nor

The empty marketplace of a war-devastated *shtetl*, in Abram Room's documentary *Jews on the Land* (U.S.S.R., 1925); frame enlargement.

(until 1934) an autonomous region—and certainly no movie studio. For the most part, the Soviet-Jewish homeland was negatively visualized as the *shtetl* and the Soviet-Jewish cinema was tied to that of another nationality. The Ukraine, where well over half the Jewish population lived, was the largest and most autonomous of non-Russian republics and, for the rest of the silent era, the All-Ukrainian Photo-Cinema Administration, known by its acronym VUFKU, was the major producer of Jewish-interest pictures.[1]

Along with Georgia's Goskinprom, VUFKU (which was organized in 1922 with studios in Odessa and Yalta) was the oldest and most active of the national movie industries. After a 1924–25 cycle of anti-Catholic melodramas, VUFKU grew more artistically ambitious and, by 1926, exhibited a strong experimental bias. Although the avant-garde director Les Kurbas made only three short features, other VUFKU productions drew heavily on personnel from his Berezil theater. The studio employed Vladimir Mayakovsky, Isaac Babel, and the sculptor Ivan Kavaleridze; in addition to supporting Alexander Dovzhenko, it provided a home for Dziga Vertov, producing three of his features, among them *Chelovek s Kinoapparatom (The Man with a Movie Camera)*. *Kino*, the VUFKU journal edited by the futurist poet Mykola Bazhan, was notable for its strong interest in the French and German avant-gardes.

As one of the most visible of Ukrainian cultural institutions, VUFKU was under constant scrutiny. In early 1925, the studio was criticized for insufficient enthusiasm in tackling "Soviet" themes. Still, filmmakers continued to produce Ukrainian historical dramas despite a crackdown on Ukrainian nationalists within the party. The following year, just as a Soviet government commission raised the possibility of resettling half a million Jews on Ukrainian and Crimean collective farms, VUFKU itself explored a number of Jewish projects. Commercial considerations were likely as important as political ones; particularly after the Revolution, Jews outnumbered Ukrainians in the urban areas where most cinemas were located and were consequently an important segment of the movie audience. (There were other reasons as well: "The Ukrainians and Belorussians drive us very hard to publish in Yiddish," wrote Shlomo Yakov Niepomniaschchi, a Hebraist as well as a Communist, to a friend during the summer of 1924. Niepomniaschchi attributed their motives less to "love of Mordecai" than to "hatred of Haman.")

Dovzhenko developed an unrealized (and presumably anti-Zionist) comedy about Jews in Palestine, while Abram Room made *Yevrei na Zemle* (Jews on the Land), a twenty-minute documentary on Jewish settlements in the Yevpatoria district of the Crimea. A native of Vilna, Room had headed an amateur Yiddish art theater there during the World War. The other participants were connected with the Soviet literary avant-garde: Lili Brik supervised the production; Mayakovsky and Viktor Shklovsky collaborated on the script.

Exhibiting a certain amount of "Jewish irony," *Jews on the Land* opens with scenes of a war-devastated *shtetl* (all that's left of the central market is a single pathetic fish stall) and then moves on to an elderly Jew wandering about an even more desolate wilderness. Soon, however, sod-brick settlements rise, and as irrigation ditches crisscross the once-barren plain, the now-productivized Jews are equally transformed. A newborn baby is named "Forget-Your-Sorrows." Tractor drivers and Young Pioneers are given particular pride of place, and the filmmakers emphasize that, among other livestock, these new Jewish farmers are raising pigs.

More substantially, VUFKU inherited a pair of projects developed by Isaac Babel—the first, a script based on his stories of Odessa's Jewish underworld and its "king" Benya Krik, the other taken from Sholom Aleichem's novel *Blondzhende Shtern* (Wandering Stars)—while releasing a one-reel adaptation of Babel's Civil War story "Salt." Babel was then much in demand as a scenarist. In December 1924, the Eisenstein group prepared a script based on *Red Cavalry*. The project was shelved in April but, that summer, while Eisenstein was shooting the film eventually released as *The Battleship Potemkin*, he and Babel worked on adapting *Benya Krik*. After Babel completed the titles for *Jewish Luck*, he was commissioned by Goskino to adapt *Blondzhende*

A devastated *shtetl* in *Jews on the Land;* frame enlargement.

A Jewish kolkhoz in the Crimea: *Jews on the Land;* frame enlargement.

Isaac Babel in the 1920s. Babel wrote the intertitles for *Jewish Luck,* as well as the scenarios for *Benya Krik* and *Wandering Stars.*

Odessa impresario Grigori Gricher-Cherikover, director of two Soviet adaptations from Sholom Aleichem: *Wandering Stars* and *Through Tears.*

Shtern as a follow-up film production for the Moscow GOSET. Granovsky may have initiated the project, but it was ultimately directed by his erstwhile assistant Grigori Gricher-Cherikover, while *Benya Krik* was filmed in Odessa during the summer of 1926 by veteran theater director Vladimir Vilner, a future People's Artist subsequently entrusted with bringing the socialist realist classic *Cement* to the screen.

Gricher-Cherikover had studied art in Kiev; after coscripting and assisting on *Jewish Luck,* he joined VUFKU as a scenarist. His first directorial effort, released in late 1926, was a mildly anti-Western satire: a Soviet tourist in the United States packs a suitcase full of oranges which are mistaken by paranoid American officials for poison-gas containers. Gricher-Cherikover next directed a popular adaptation of Gogol's *Sorochinskaya Yarmarka (Sorochinski Fair),* one of two Gogol films that VUFKU released in 1927, the seventy-fifth anniversary of the Ukrainian writer's death. The only VUFKU director to handle both Jewish and Ukrainian themes, Gricher-Cherikover might have been a character in Sholom Aleichem's satire of the Yiddish stage; in an April 1927 letter to his family, written three months after *Blushdayushtichi Sviosdy* (Wandering Stars) had its world premiere in Kiev, Babel refers to the director sarcastically as "the Odessa impresario" who still owes him a hundred rubles.

Although the "film-novella" *Benya Krik* and "film-script" *Wandering Stars* were published as pamphlets months before either movie reached the screen, Babel's script for *Benya Krik* is said to have been rewritten several times. (Even then, official displeasure with the ending held up its release.) The first two-thirds of the movie were taken from a pair of published stories, "The King" and "How It Was Done in Odessa"; the film's last section, set in 1919, was original—albeit based on the actual demise of Benya's real-life prototype, Mishka Yaponchik ("Mike the Jap") Vinitsky. Here Benya's gang becomes a "revolutionary" regiment. The local military commissar, who has been ordered to disarm them by any means, assigns the gang to "emergency revictualing patrol." Lulled by this plum assignment, Benya falls into the trap and is shot down by Red soldiers. (After coming to terms with the Bolsheviks, Vinitsky had led his men against the Ukrainian nationalist Simon Petliura. The reformed criminals soon wearied of army life, however, and when the Red stationmaster declined their demand for transportation back to Odessa, a struggle broke out during which the gangster king was killed.)

In Eisenstein's hands, *Benya Krik* might have presented Odessa's criminal milieu with the sardonic brio of Brecht's *Threepenny Opera*. But this was Vilner's first film, his inexperience evident from the haphazard mise-en-scène and overly stagy performances. (Although some authentic-seeming Odessa street life shows through the creaky plot contrivances, Vilner used Ukrainian actors without even the most cursory attention to type.) The film hews closely to Babel's script, yet only two scenes suggest its vitality. The wedding of Benya's sister—much of it shot against a black backdrop—has a frantic assemblage of ravenous plug-uglies and reveling floozies serenaded by a single, hyperactive *klezmer* musician. In a related travesty of a traditional ritual, Benya and his men commandeer a funeral ceremony, sending mourners scrambling through the imposing monuments of Odessa's Jewish cemetery.

A less mediocre film might have transcended its political deficiencies. As it was, *Benya Krik* created problems by presenting its swaggering hero as a vic-

Poster for *Benya Krik* (U.S.S.R., 1926). Directed by Vladimir Vilner, the film was adapted by Isaac Babel from his stories of the Odessa underworld.

tim of the Bolshevik regime—as well as evoking the image of the Jew as criminal and profiteer. (In one scene, the "king" receives a bribe concealed in a Torah scroll.) Given its premiere in Kiev on January 18, 1927, *Benya Krik* was almost immediately removed from circulation by the Ukrainian Office for Political Education. The movie was never shown in Moscow—reputedly "so poor a film" that Jay Leyda, who arrived in the Soviet Union in September 1933, could not find anyone to tell him about it.

As the decade closed, Yiddish artists were increasingly vulnerable to charges of nationalism or "petit-bourgeois folkism." One deduces the sensitive nature of *any* Jewish material from Babel's remarkably apologetic introduction to the published scenario of *Wandering Stars*. "Sholom Aleichem's novel was absolutely alien to me, filled with bourgeois motifs," asserts the author (who would later supervise the definitive Russian edition of Sholom Aleichem's writings). Babel adds that it took him two months just to forget the book and begin work on the screenplay. Indeed, the movie bears scant resemblance to Sholom Aleichem's good-naturedly barbed portrait of the "primitive" Yiddish theater.

Babel emphasizes prerevolutionary Jewish persecution, in part by transforming the novel's heroine from an actress into an aspiring doctor and eventual political activist: "One can say of Rachel that her love of science is as great as the love of truth, of Lenin, of Darwin, or of Spinoza." The screenwriter appears to have crossed Sholom Aleichem's novel with elements from the redoubtable *Yellow Passport*. Rachel arrives in Moscow, hoping to study dentistry and, turned away from a "respectable" rooming house because of her Jewish passport, pairs off with a radical student to spend the night in a dive for prostitutes and their johns.

Babel maintains that the script was in continual flux as he reworked it to meet the contradictory requirements of the various actors and directors successively involved with the project. (The one constant, according to the writer, was that the protagonists be forced to flee abroad.) But however it originated, *Wandering Stars* ultimately wound up at VUFKU, where Gricher-Cherikover made his own revisions. The finished film omitted the Yiddish theater troupe altogether, thus erasing "the last traces of Sholom Aleichem," as the drama critic Osip Lubomirsky complained in *Der Emes* when, a year after its Ukrainian release, *Wandering Stars* had its Moscow premiere at two centrally located cinemas—optimistically advertised as "The hit picture of the season!"

Wandering Stars has been lost. In their 1955 account of Soviet cinema, Paul Babitsky and John Rinberg report that, although the film was "an original combination of bitter humor and a melodramatic plot of persecution in a Jewish village," critics regarded it as "ideologically deficient" and "overinvolved with the Jewish past." Many VUFKU treatments of Ukrainian themes were attacked in analogous terms. Although Lubomirsky's review has been cited as a political criticism, in fact his actual thrust is less ideological than aesthetic. Dismissing *Wandering Stars* as an inept, American-style melodrama ("empty and heavy-handed"; "a puzzle whose pieces don't fit together"), the critic—who wrote extensively on the Moscow GOSET during the twenties and would, ten years later, publish an official biography of Mikhoels—blames Gricher-Cherikover for failing to realize Babel's "brilliant, cinematographically rich" scenario.

By the time *Wandering Stars* was released, Trotsky was in exile, and both economic and cultural liberalism were on the wane. As early as 1927, Russians (or Russified Ukrainians) began to assume control of the Ukrainian party apparatus. VUFKU underwent an antinationalist purge during 1927–28; the following year, Ukrainian intellectuals were being arrested for ideological deviations. Although *Wandering Stars* traveled to Paris and Berlin in 1927 as part of an exhibition of recent VUFKU releases, its domestic distribution was further complicated by the "reorganization" of Sovkino in 1928: in May, *Wandering Stars* was among eighteen films withdrawn from circulation because, according to one Moscow journal, "they idealize the pathological and decadent mood of the decaying bourgeoisie [and] popularize covert prostitution and debauchery."

The Moscow GOSET, too, toured Europe. Even before leaving on April 1, 1928, the company had been under political pressure—accused of chauvinism and overconcern with the pathos of prerevolutionary Jewish life. Their final production, *Der Luftmentsh,* another adaptation from the Menakhem Mendl stories, which likely recycled Lev Pulver's score for *Jewish Luck,* received less than enthusiastic reviews. (Lubomirsky, who singled out Pulver's contribution for praise, was a partial exception.) When Soviet authorities canceled GOSET's tour in November, Granovsky remained in Berlin, where his theater had been the major event of the season. The rest of the company returned, and GOSET was entrusted to Mikhoels, who would guide the theater into the radiant future of socialist realism.[2]

"That Yiddish literature has always been a literature of the poor, the untutored, the lowly, inclines the Communists to be respectful to the earliest Jewish authors," a sympathetic American observer wrote in the late twenties. "But although the past is reverenced, there is a strong feeling that literature, together with the other arts, stands on the threshold of a new era." So it was with cinema. The first Soviet nationality films tended to deal with the Civil War and prerevolutionary traditions. After 1927, emphasis shifted to the new life of the present. Sholom Aleichem remained a standard of the state Yiddish stage and a talismanic figure for *Der Emes,* but his writings provided material for only one more film, Gricher-Cherikover's *Skvoz Slezy* (Through Tears).

One of thirty-eight features VUFKU would release in 1928, *Through Tears* opened in April—a few months after the first Ukrainian Party Conference on Cinema declared that Ukrainian film had entered its "second (post-pioneer) stage." More self-contained than either Babel production in elaborating the critique of the pre-1917 *shtetl,* the film has no single protagonist: Sholom Aleichem's "The Enchanted Tailor" is interwoven with tales of the orphaned cantor's son, Motl Peyse, to create an overall view of two imaginary towns, Zlodyevke and Kozodoyevka, whose names can be roughly translated as Thieves' Den and Goat's Milk.

For Sholom Aleichem and his commentators, Motl is a figure with a particular resonance: the Jews were sometimes said to be a *faryosemt folk,* an "orphaned people." For the filmmakers, however, Motl may have offered the most politically expedient of Sholom Aleichem adaptations. In its entry on the author, the *Great Soviet Encyclopedia* singles out the Motl cycle for "posing the question of the fate of the masses under capitalism," taking care to mention Maxim Gorky's contemporary praise for the stories. ("I read, laughed and wept," Gorky wrote, anticipating the film's English title, *Laughter Through Tears.*) As a child of the *shtetl* bound for the Lower East Side, Motl represents a transitional generation. It's scarcely coincidental that he is introduced as his father lies dying.

If the impish Motl is the most resilient of Sholom Aleichem's characters, the protagonist of "The Enchanted Tailor" is among the least, finding himself lost in an absurdist nightmare. The tailor Shimen-Elye buys a she-goat which mysteriously changes gender each time its new owner stops at the inn between Kozodoyevka, where he purchased the creature, and Zlodyevke, where he lives. This prank, perpetrated by the *kretshmer* (innkeeper), ultimately drives him mad. That the story, one of Sholom Aleichem's darkest, intimates the collapse of the traditional worldview (Shimen-Elye can only understand his situation in religious terms) doubtless recommended it to the filmmakers—who raise its class-conflict quotient in having the impoverished tailor further persecuted by the petit-bourgeois inn-

Through Tears (U.S.S.R., 1925); the tailor Shimen-Elye (J. K. Kovenberg), his wife (M. D. Sen-Elnikova), and the demonic goat.

keeper and the superstitious adherents of a rabbinical court.[3]

The filmmakers go on to augment their source with scenes emphasizing Jewish powerlessness and tsarist oppression. Virtually every attempt to find work provokes authority's heavy hand. Meanwhile, the personification of futility, Shimen-Elye tracks back and forth with his demonic goat until, in an ending that echoes Sholom Aleichem's Tevye cycle, he is evicted from his home. This arbitrary punishment is provoked in the first place by a demonstration staged in the tailor's name by a crowd of honest Jewish workers to protest the unfair ruling of the rabbinical court and, in the second, after a tsarist official has his coat dirtied by Shimen-Elye's cat.

(The official's tantrum affords Gricher-Cherikover the occasion for a Gogolian fantasy in which the tailor's mannequins dance, his windows close themselves, and even the mice abandon his shop.)

Scoring political points wherever possible, Gricher-Cherikover and his coscenarist, I. Skvirski, exaggerate Sholom Aleichem's anticlericalism, particularly in the comic scene where the rabbis debate the goat's gender. (In another sequence, a baby amuses himself by making a doll out of a prayer shawl.) For the most part, however, *Through Tears* is faithful to the spirit of the author. Even the chaotic school sequence reflects Sholom Aleichem's satirical view of the traditional *kheyder,* a target of the nineteenth-century Haskalah no less than the twentieth-century Communist Party. Some characterizations are actually softened in the film: Shimen-Elye is hapless rather than boastful. Bruche and Elye, the attractive if dimwitted young couple, are considerably more grotesque in the text—physically mismatched, he is small and vain, she "large and mannish" with "pockmarks and a bass voice." (The young S. J. Silberman, who plays Motl, is as curly-haired and winsome as Shirley Temple.)

Shot, like *Jewish Luck,* with near-documentary verisimilitude and demonstrating an even more pronounced graphic flare, *Through Tears* recapitulates the earlier film's opening by plunging the viewer into domestic disorder and poverty. The Jewish hamlet is hardly a place of nostalgia, but rather, a dusty, ramshackle backwater where young people attempt to better themselves with foredoomed get-rich-quick schemes. Unlike *Jewish Luck,* however, *Through Tears* is more concerned with propaganda than folklore in depicting the bitter marginality of *shtetl* life. The film offers neither community rituals nor fanciful dreams—only the plight of the *luftmentsh* globalized into a universal principal.[4]

The traditional *kheyder,* a target of the nineteenth-century Haskalah no less than of the twentieth-century Communist Party, in *Through Tears.*

Despite his bourgeois origins and Zionist sympathies, Sholom Aleichem was, for Russian Communists, the most important Yiddish writer—his anti-authoritarian humor, his identification with the Jewish masses, and his gift for drawing characters as the product of social forces made him readily adaptable to Marxist readings. (Between 1925 and 1930, no less than thirty different volumes of Sholom Aleichem's work appeared in Russian translation, with another twenty-seven in Ukrainian.)

Leon Dennen, a sympathetic visitor to Moscow in the early thirties reported that, "for good or bad, old

The *shtetl* as the site of foredoomed get-rich-quick schemes. From left: Elye (D. Cantor), Pinye (A. Vabnik), and Beyla (M.D. Gorecheva). *Through Tears.*

values have acquired a new meaning in Revolutionary Russia." Attending a reading at the Hall of the Trade Unions, Dennen discovered that the Sholom Aleichem he knew, "the Sholom Aleichem of the ghetto," was now "a prophet not only of a crumbling order, but also of a new life." After an actor from the Moscow Art Theater read selections (in Russian) from the Tevye stories, Solomon Mikhoels "threw the audience into a frenzy of enthusiasm" with his Yiddish recitation of "The Penknife."

Half the audience did not understand Yiddish. They could only follow his motions and facial expressions. And yet, I saw Ukrainians and Tartars, Russians and Jews applaud violently.

On the other hand, and this is perhaps what the Communists call the dialects of life, I heard Soviet-Yiddish writers who were sitting next to me, chagrined, murmur contemptuously: "Idiots, whom are they applauding, the glorifier of the lumpen-proletariat, the poet of bearded Jews. . . ."

But the audience, particularly the representatives of the Jewish youth, felt differently about it. To them . . . Sholom Aleichem depicted the clash of the patriarchal village order with the capitalist city, thus paving the way for the new order.

The films drawn from Sholom Aleichem would evoke a similar response. When, in March 1928, VUFKU's journal *Kino* featured a special section on "national minority cinema," the Ukrainian critic M. Makotinsky praised *Through Tears, Wandering Stars,* and *Jewish Luck* for their educational value: "Shown to the broad masses, especially the village masses," these films will reveal the "nightmare" of Jewish life under the tsar and "open eyes to the hidden roots of anti-Semitism." *Through Tears,* Makotinsky predicted, "will enjoy great success and not only on the

'Jewish Street.'" Inevitably, however, those who lived on the Jewish street were a good deal more ambivalent.

In the Soviet Union, as in America, the creation of specifically "Jewish" movies jeopardized, even as it enhanced, Jewish insularity. A 1928 letter to *Der Emes,* written by one S. Daytsherman, resembles N. L. Rothman's near simultaneous diatribe against Hollywood stereotypes (quoted above). Daytsherman decries both the paucity of appropriate Jewish films and those few that are made, "especially here in the Ukraine." Witness *Benya Krik,* which suggests that "thieves, prostitutes and speculators created the Revolution, fought for it, defended it and—exploited it. . . . The poison and hatred such a film spreads is obvious to anyone who sees it."

While for Daytsherman, the Sholom Aleichem adaptations *Mabl* and *Wandering Stars* proved that "film companies act like vandals with the work of Yiddish authors," he was more even disturbed by the negative Jewish stereotypes in other VUFKU films, including Gricher-Cherikover's *Sorochinski Fair.* Here, Orthodox-traditional Jews appeared in comic roles as schemers or cowards. "This may be a trifle," Daytsherman concludes, "but . . . it has a bad smell. Especially now, during the struggle against anti-Semitism, one cannot remain indifferent. It is absolutely necessary that the Yiddish press and the Soviet Jewish public use their authority and speak out, so that VUFKU and the like are compelled to consider the Jewish masses." (In fact, Mishka Vinitsky, the prototype for Benya Krik, remained an Odessa folk hero through the twenties because his gang had protected the city's Jews against White pogroms.)

Far more than in America, where anti-Semitism was less a political force than a social fact, every Soviet Jew became responsible for all Jews—not to mention the sum total of Jewish history. Thus, in a pattern that would repeat itself elsewhere, the harshest critics of the new Yiddish culture were invariably Jewish Communists. More self-conscious and less secure than their Russian comrades, Jewish cultural apparatchiks didn't hesitate to attack those Yiddish artists who diverged from official norms. The same issue of *Kino* that published Makotinsky's praise included a blunt critique, offered in Yiddish, by the poet and ideologue Itzik Fefer.

Militantly class-conscious, Fefer was not only hostile to religion but to any literary mode that smacked of elitism. Rather than ambiguous symbols, he demanded "plain, but firm and secure steps." His essay, written in a sort of exhortatory blank verse, begins with the announcement of a Yiddish cultural congress to be held in Kharkov: "This congress will, first of all, evaluate the work that has been done and then, compare the results with the demands of the working masses." As Fefer himself then surveys the realm of Jewish cultural achievement, finding accomplishments in literature, theater, music, and painting, one field seems particularly backward—the cinema.

Fefer scores the "prerevolutionary way of life" dramatized in *Wandering Stars, Through Tears,* and *Benya Krik* ("if we can even consider this to be a Jewish film"). Meanwhile,

The life of the Jewish working man and woman, their struggle against the rich and the "benefactors," their struggle against the Jewish bourgeoisie, and the great part they played in the overall revolutionary movement both before and after October have yet to be embodied in film. . . .[5]

Unlike S. Daytsherman, Fefer formulates the problem in class (rather than national) terms:

Yiddish poet and Stalinist ideologue Itzik Fefer in the 1930s.

More than anyone else, we Yiddish writers are in a position to hear the complaints of workers at literary evenings.

The workers ask: "Why do you only write about *Jewish Luck*? About *Benya Krik* and *Wandering Stars*? Why don't you write about us?"

They ask: "Is Benya Krik more interesting than we?"

The working class wants to see itself, its struggle and life in the new art.

The working class is right . . .

But, even as Fefer advised VUFKU to "involve itself with the Jewish literary community and, with its help, create the film for which the Jewish worker has waited so long," that community was itself divided. The official organ of the Yiddish members of the All-Ukrainian Association of Proletarian Writers attacked a number of prominent Yiddish authors for variously "cutting themselves off from real life," "moving towards individualism," indulging in the "idealization of gradually disappearing classes," exhibiting "lack of self-definition," or demonstrating "a passive attitude towards our reality."[6]

Simultaneously, a similar attack had been directed against the Soviet film industry as a whole. In March 1928, at the first All-Union Party Conference on Film Questions, A. I. Krinitsky, the head of the Central Committee's Department for Agitprop, had praised the well-known movies that celebrated the October Revolution but accused Sovkino of failing to produce even a single worthwhile film on contemporary Soviet life—that is, "the union of workers and peasants, the fight for collective forms of agriculture, our nationalities policy, the work of the trade unions as schools of Communism." The conference concluded that "fictional films must be made in a way that can be appreciated by millions." A year later, the director P. P. Petrov-Bytov launched an ultra-left strike against even those movies that Krinitsky had spared:

When we talk of the Soviet cinema we have a banner on which is written: *Strike, Battleship Potemkin, October, Mother, The End of St. Petersburg,* and we have recently added *New Babylon, Zvenigora, Arsenal.* Do 120 million workers and peasants march beneath this banner? I know very well that they don't.

The first Jewish film to prefigure the new line and adopt a measure of revolutionary militancy was Grigori Roshal's 1928 *Yevo Prevoshoditelstvo* (His Excellency), also variously known as *Hirsh Lekert, Gubernator e Sapozhnik* (The Governor and the Shoemaker), and simply *Yevrei* (The Jew).

Grigori Roshal had studied with Meyerhold and was directing children's shows at the age of twenty in 1919. In the early 1920s, Roshal was associated with the state Theater of Youth (then administered by Ilya Ehrenburg) and Habima; in 1926, he made his first film, *Gospoda Skotininy* (The Skotinin Gentlemen), a caricature of the stupid and depraved gentry, based on a comedy by eighteenth-century satirist Denis Fonvizin. Roshal attracted powerful patrons. *The Skotinin Gentlemen* was edited by no less an eminence than Anatoli Lunacharsky, the Soviet commissar of enlightenment. (In an article entitled "Cinema—the Greatest of All the Arts," published in the Komsomol newspaper in late 1926, Lunacharsky singled out the film for particular praise, along with *The Battleship Potemkin* and V. I. Pudovkin's *Mat [Mother]*.)

His Excellency was shot the following year at Belgoskino's newly established Leningrad studio. The first Belgoskino film had only just been released and, from the perspective of half a century, Roshal recalled working under "primitive conditions." Nevertheless, his cast was distinguished by the presence of Leonid Leonidov, a star of the Moscow Art Theater, and, in a small part, the popular slapstick comedian Nikolai Cherkasov, who would later play the title roles in Eisenstein's *Alexander Nevsky* and *Ivan Grozny (Ivan the Terrible)*.

According to Roshal, his subject matter was so delicate that Lunacharsky oversaw the production personally. The reason, doubtless, was that *His Excellency* took as its protagonist Hirsh Lekert, executed in 1902 for his attempted assassination of the Vilna governor General Victor Von Wahl. An illiterate shoemaker and militant member of the Jewish Labor Bund, the twenty-three-year-old Lekert shot Von

Wahl to avenge the flogging of workers who partici- pated in a May Day rally. Although prominent movement leaders eventually supported Lekert—to whom a monument, no longer standing, had been erected in Minsk in 1922—Lenin dissociated himself from Lekert's act. Moreover, if Lekert was an au- thentic proleterian folk hero, he was also a symbol of the Bund, an organization once regarded by the Communist Party as a deadly rival, identified with Jewish separatism and "petit-bourgeois nationalism." The Bund, formerly a key constituent member of the

Russian Social Democratic Party, had been expelled (by Leon Trotsky, no less) in 1903 for its insistence on organizational—as well as future national- cultural—autonomy. The Bolsheviks suppressed the Bund after the Revolution, and in 1921 most left- wing Bundists joined the Communist Party, con- tributing substantially to the Yevsektsia leadership. (Although many of these former Bundists led the campaign against Zionism and the Jewish bourgeoi- sie, their past "right-wing deviation" would even- tually catch up with them, the Belorussian

The "Jewish fighter" and working-class hero Hirsh Lekert (J. Untershlak) in _His Excellency_ (U.S.S.R., 1928); frame enlargement.

"The law of Israel will be used to crush them": a counterrevolutionary rabbi (Leonid Leonidov) in *His Excellency;* frame enlargement.

Yevsektsia's 1925 purge of "Bundist remnants" offering a foretaste.)

Lekert's martyrdom was the subject of a play by former Bundist (and political prisoner) H. Leivick—written in 1927, the same year as *His Excellency,* albeit in the less hostile climes of New York. In Leivick's *Hirsh Lekert,* a rabbi visits the condemned man and informs him that Von Wahl has agreed to commute his sentence if he will betray his comrades. *His Excellency,* too, involves a Jewish religious leader who is a party to the reactionary status quo. Indeed, to make this totally obvious, Leonidov plays the dual roles of governor and rabbi. The film is further schematized as a generational melodrama: "suffocating" under her father's rule, the rabbi's adopted daughter

(Tamara Adelheim, the ingenue in *Jewish Luck*) joins a clandestine band of youthful Socialists.

His Excellency (which was cowritten by Roshal's sister, Sofya Roshal, and his wife, Vera Stroeva) shifts Lekert's act forward several years, to the period of the 1905 revolution, and sets it in a nonspecific city. There is no mention of the Bund; Lekert, who successfully shoots the governor as he leaves a performance of the circus, is identified only as "the Jewish fighter." Given its touchy premise, *His Excellency* is a surprisingly mannerist film, replete with overdetermined compositions, pretentiously literary intertitles, a convoluted flashback structure, and circus sequences that suggest Leningrad's Factory of the Eccentric Actor. (Eisenstein's *Statchka* [*Strike*] seems the major influence, although the disconcerting mix of expressionistic, theatrically lit interiors and naturalistic location work would be characteristic of Roshal.)

In a 1977 interview with Eric Goldman, Roshal maintained that *His Excellency* was intended as a tract against individualism. (Throughout, the quasi-terrorist Lekert is opposed by his comrades: "Six shots cannot make a revolution.") Still, a greater emphasis is placed on class struggle within the Jewish community. Thus, in finally putting forth a Jewish revolutionary hero, the film carefully stresses the solidarity between Jewish and Russian political prisoners, while making a programmatic comparison between honest Jewish workers and cowardly Jewish reactionaries. (The latter are stigmatized with a number of politically incorrect traits: they are not only bourgeois but seemingly Germanized. They meet beneath a portrait of Theodor Herzl, yet are beholden to a traditional Orthodox rabbi.) As armed police attack the May Day demonstration, Roshal intercuts scenes of wealthy Jews praying in their synagogue. The battle lines are clearly drawn. Not only does the rabbi curse his child for her involvement with a "goy," he excommunicates her Jewish comrades.

Almost in spite of itself, *His Excellency* explicates a Russian Jewish dilemma existing under the rule of the Communist Party no less than that of the tsar. The bourgeois Jews are terrified that they will be blamed for the disturbance created by their proletarian coreligionists—"We're not revolutionaries, we're Zionists," one protests in vain—and send a delegation to the governor to plead for protection from the anticipated pogrom. As they feared, these law-abiding Jewish leaders are held accountable and ordered to punish revolutionaries themselves or else face the consequences. "The law of Israel will be used to crush them," the rabbi promises—more like Fefer than either he or that Communist true believer might ever imagine.[7]

His Excellency was released in March 1928 and was sufficiently correct to be exported, opening at the Cameo in New York as *Seeds of Freedom* in September 1929. (Fourteen years later, the same title was given to a reedited, English-dubbed version of *The Battleship Potemkin* that began with newsreels of the Soviet defense of Odessa, then presented the original film in flashback.) While acknowledging Roshal's modest technique, the *Nation* praised his content in terms that even P. P. Petrov-Bytov might approve:

Be sure that before an audience of plain workers this picture will win out and do so without benefit of arguments about "montage," art, acting, and what not. And all because of the story. . . . There is nothing fancy about the class struggle. . . . In *Seeds of Freedom* it is cold, brutal, painful.

The exigencies of the new climate can also be seen in VUFKU's last three Jewish films. *Zemlya Zovet* (The Land Is Calling) directed by Vladimir Ballyuzek—author of the first Azerbaijani film—and codesigned by Natan Altman, was a postrevolutionary *shtetl* drama, set on one of the new Jewish collectives in the Crimea. Here, a rabbi's daughter spurns the son of a rich landowner for love of the young blacksmith who later organizes an agricultural cooperative to work the kulak's confiscated property. M. Makotinsky, who cited the film favorably in *Kino* several months before its June 1928 release, compared it to the Abram Room short *Jews on the Land* in its "bright picture of determined work."

The Ukrainian critic deemed *Through Tears* and *The Land Is Calling* the first two-thirds of an unfinished trilogy—"How It Was, How It Should Be, How It Is"—and suggested that VUFKU make the final third with a film treating "the life and work of the sons and grandsons of Sholom Aleichem who labor in the factories, the ports, and all other branches of our socialist construction." Gricher-Cherikover's *Nakanunye* (On the Eve), a follow-up to *Through Tears,* did not exactly fit Makotinsky's prescription. Adapted from a well-known story by Alexander Kuprin and set during the period of the 1905 revolution, the film told the pathetic story of a poor Jewish violinist who, having been denied admission to the conservatory, is compelled to eke out his living playing in a tavern by the Odessa harbor; in the end he is beaten to death by the Black Hundreds for his proletarian sympathies.

Whereas *On the Eve* located Jews among the urban poor, Vladimir Vilner's *Glaza Katorye Videli* (Eyes That Saw), released two months later, in December 1928, emphasizes the *shtetl*'s social divisions. While the naïvely patriotic tailor, Motl, enlists in the

tsar's army, his sister Rosa (played by Alexander Dovzhenko's wife, Julia Solntseva) is compelled to wed
the odious son of the factory owner Shkliansky. The
rich Jews live in luxury; when the army expels the
town's Jews for supposed espionage, Shkliansky is
given a military escort to protect his valuables. In a
paroxysm of victimization, Motl is killed at the front
at precisely the same moment that his wife and child
are massacred in a pogrom.[8]

The relative social mobility of Soviet Jews during
the NEP brought a new wave of anti-Semitism, particularly among the declassed bourgeoisie, industrial
workers, and students (including members of the
Komsomol). By 1928, the party was forced to take

**Handbill announcing the American release
of Vladimir Vilner's** *Eyes That Saw*
(U.S.S.R., 1928), known in Yiddish as *Motl
der Shpindler,* **1934. A theater specializing in
Soviet imports, the Acme hoped (in vain) to
equal the earlier success of** *Through Tears.*

steps: citizens who, drunk or sober, voiced anti-
Semitic statements in public were subject to arrest.
The problem was widely discussed in the press and
in Minsk there were several well-publicized trials.
Eugene Lyons, who covered one such affair, wrote
that an ordinary instance of rowdy behavior became
a case of counterrevolution: "Leading journalists
from all over the country attended the trial and my
own presence as the only foreign representative
(aside from correspondents for American Jewish
publications) was played up by the Soviet press as
proof of international interest."

Still, anti-Semitism was far from eradicated. Jews,
Lyons observed, "were hated as NEP-men and as the
liquidators of NEP-men."

> Prejudice had no need for logic. On food queues
> I heard the Jews cursed by simple suffering peo-
> ple, though the Jews were on the queues with
> them. Even within the Communist Party the dis-
> ease was prevalent. . . . To the most ignorant lay-
> ers of the Soviet population, Lenin is still a Jew
> and his regime is still a Jewish regime. Occasion-
> ally one hears Russians assert, without realizing
> the irony of their remark, that they *approve* of the
> Jewish government. The Kremlin is keenly aware
> that anti-Semitism is frequently an indirect
> expression of anti-Communism and must be
> combated as such.

At the same time, anti-Semitism was bracketed with
"Jewish chauvinism" as a right-wing deviation in the
shift from "right" to "left" that characterized the
party as a whole. (Typically, the Yevsektsia spent
more energy pointing out the dangers of "Jewish
chauvinism" than anti-Semitism.)

In May 1928, the Ukrainian Communist Party
held a special conference on anti-Semitism. Among
the resolutions was one that VUFKU should prepare

an "appropriate moving picture" to deal with the problem. Gricher-Cherikover's 1930 *Kvartaly Predmestya* (Suburban Quarters) may well be that film. Directed from a script by *Kino's* youthful editor, Mykola Bazhan, this contemporary *shtetl* story criticized both anti-Semitism and Zionism, while privileging the role of the Komsomol: A young Jewish girl flouts her religious parents to marry a Russian, only to encounter the anti-Semitism of his family. The film ends happily when a public court criticizes the husband's insensitive behavior, his wife defends him, and all recognize the evil of petit-bourgeois religious prejudices.

Simultaneously, Sovkino and its successor, Soyuzkino, produced several anti-anti-Semitic pictures: Petrov-Bytov's *Kain i Artem* (Cain and Artem; 1929) from a story by Maxim Gorky; A. Galai's *Nashi Devushki* (Our Girls; 1930), like *Suburban Quarters,* an account of conflict arising from a mixed marriage; and I. Mutanov's *Zapomnite Ikh Litsa* (Remember Their Faces; 1931). All three emphasized the cooperation between Russian and Jewish workers, the later two films consecrating it under Komsomol auspices.

Roshal followed his evocation of Hirsh Lekert with two films at VUFKU. The first, *Dve Zhenshehiny* (Two Women; 1929), attacked the already defunct NEP; the second, *Chelovek iz Mestechka* (A Man from the Shtetl; 1930) was a another evocation of Jewish revolutionary martyrdom, as well as one of the last films made at VUFKU's Odessa studio. (That year, VUFKU underwent a number of administrative changes—even some non-Ukrainians were purged for their "nationalist tendencies"—and was reorganized as Ukrainfilm.) Venyamin Zuskin, Mi-

khoels's most celebrated colleague at GOSET, played David Gorelik, a poor Jewish youth drafted into the tsar's army in 1914. More nuanced than *Eyes That Saw, A Man from the Shtetl* offered a uniquely Jewish perception of the World War, which was the first occasion in which ordinary Jews faced each other as antagonists in war.

In his report on the Galician front, Sh. An-sky noted many versions of a similar story. In the trenches, two soldiers engage in mortal combat; with his last breath, the dying soldier cries out *"Sh'ma Yisroel!"* To his horror, the killer discovers that the enemy was a fellow Jew. In *A Man from the Shtetl,* Roshal gives this anecdote a particular political meaning. Gorelik struggles against a German soldier, then realizes his adversary is a Galician Jew he had known before the war. Having thus met on the battlefield, the two friends desert their imperial masters and join the Red Army. But friendship and ethnic solidarity go only so far. When the Galician, now a commissar, is convicted of profiteering (a suggestively "NEP-ish" crime as well as a capital one), Gorelik is charged with carrying out the sentence.

As in Roshal's earlier *His Excellency,* the Jewish characters have the responsibility of disciplining their own. For years, the party had successfully channeled the Yevsektsia's antibourgeois antagonism, using the Jewish Section to police the Jewish street. In this sense, however, *A Man from the Shtetl* seems an epitaph to the national policies of the twenties. Stalin's campaign against "rightist deviation" within the party was accompanied by increased centralization and diminishing national autonomy. As early as 1927, Ukrainian "nationalists" were removed from prominent positions; two years later, there were similar purges in Belorussia, Armenia, and Turkestan, while leading Jewish Communists came under fire for "idealizing" the prerevolutionary Jewish labor movement. The beleaguered Yevsektsia made plans for its first conference since 1926. In January 1930, however, the leadership of the republics' Communist parties met and "reorganized," dissolving all national sections. The early thirties brought the arrest of many prominent Jewish Communists and fellow travelers.

A Man from the Shtetl was released in Kiev in December 1930 but did not open in Moscow until August, a few weeks after its New York premiere at the Cameo—released as *A Jew at War,* with English titles by proletarian novelist Mike Gold. Calling the film "a reassuring gesture from Moscow that the Jew has his place in the world brotherhood of man," the *New York Times* termed Roshal "a director with imagination and a good sense of irony." Although he had praise for the "interesting scenes of men at war" and the "sharply etched characters," the critic found them "incidental to a rambling story that is often incoherent [and] pointless—except as a Soviet message to the Jew."

That message was double-edged. After the Soviet victory, Gorelik is made manager of a shoe factory where his fortitude is again tested when laggardly workers demand special privileges. Gorelik refuses to oblige and, betrayed by counterrevolutionary hoodlums, pays the supreme price. "It is the end of David and the end of the picture, but not the end of the revolution," the *Times* noted. "The large audience yesterday got the point and appeared to like it."[9]

NOTES

1. During the brief, bloody interlude of Ukrainian independence, Jews enjoyed a measure of national autonomy and there was even a Ministry of Jewish Affairs. Although the first years of Soviet rule were characterized by a negative attitude toward Ukrainian cultural activities, restraints were briefly relaxed after the Twelfth Party Congress. Use of the Ukrainian language was encouraged in schools and state institutions; there was a Commissariat of Foreign Affairs, permitting the republic to engage in diplomatic relations. This carried over into film production as well. In 1927, VUFKU was second only to the United States in exporting films to Germany.

2. Granovsky directed several productions at the Reinhardt Theater in Berlin (including Habima's *Uriel Acosta*) as well as a few films, both in Europe and the United States. He died in Paris in 1937.

3. Moyshe Goldblatt's first production with the Kiev Yiddish Theater was an adaption of "The Enchanted Tailor" in which he not only directed but played the lead as a "Chaplinesque 'Little Man' [whose] dreams of happiness never come true."

4. Indeed, *Through Tears* proved something of an international success. A shortened version, with Spanish and Yiddish intertitles, was exported to Latin America as *Lágrimas Judías* (Jewish Tears). Later, it appeared in the United States as *Laughter Through Tears* (in Yiddish, *Motl Peyse dem Khazns*), reedited by its distributor to accommodate a dubbed Yiddish soundtrack. This "talking version" opened in November 1933 at the Acme, a 500-seat theater off Union Square where *Variety* reported it doing "exceptional business." Enormously popular, *Motl* was held over at the Acme for an unprecedented six weeks and extensively reviewed in the English-language press.

The *New York Daily News* thought the film propaganda (if "the least objectionable example that this reviewer has ever seen") and the *Daily Worker* found *Laughter Through Tears* "a definite and considerable stride forward of the Soviet film"; but it was the enthusiastic endorsement of George Jessel that made its way into the ads: "I enjoyed every minute. It is a classic, you will rave about it!"

5. While allowing that *Through Tears* was "not the worst film" on the subject, Fefer considered the movie denatured by the loss of those "raisins" which give Sholom Aleichem his special flavor:

We find here none of the lyrical irony which is the essence of Sholom Aleichem's writings. Sholom Aleichem is not a sentimentalist. His works do not simply evoke "tears," he portrays a way of life which provokes laughter —laughter through tears. The screenwriters have consciously or unconsciously killed his humor.

Still, Fefer concedes the film's visual impact ("a profound artistic truth emerges from the *kheyder*, from the crooked, deserted streets"), praises the performances, the production design, and the "talented" director, adding that "it would be desirable to use Gricher as much as possible to strengthen VUFKU's national minority sector."

6. Abraham Abchuk, the Yiddishist who spearheaded this assault, was hardly immune himself. A few years later, his *Hershel Shamay* (a humorous tale in which the Tevye-esque hero, an elderly worker with no understanding of politics, asks deep questions) was attacked by Fefer in *Proletarian Banner* as a "Trotskyite slander" to be "plucked out like a nettle." Meanwhile, the campaign against religion intensified. In a letter written to Joseph Opatoshu in November 1929, Peretz Markish characterized the situation as "very strained." Abchuk's attack was symptomatic. "In general we don't know what world we're in," Markish wrote. "In this atmosphere of trying to be terribly proletarian and one-hundred-percent kosher, much falseness, cowardice, and vacillation have manifested themselves and it is becoming somewhat impossible to work."

7. If Roshal's film attempted to rehabilitate the martyred Lekert for Bolshevism, it apparently succeeded. The year after its release, Fefer's ally Aron Kushnirov wrote a verse drama on Lekert which premiered at the Minsk GOSET. Kushnirov's play was even more anticlerical than Roshal's movie. In his text, it is the rabbi who suggests the floggings. The play is also explicitly anti-Bundist—the Jewish workers must struggle against the cowardly Bund leadership. Still, it did not wholly escape ideological impurity. In the January 1934 issue of *International Theater*, Osip Lubomirsky wrote that "Kushnirov's political orientation is communistic, but by his lending justification to certain opinions expressed by Lekert . . . which bear a strong flavor of anarchism, [he] stumbles into a grave political error."

8. *Eyes That Saw* was first shown in New York in April 1930 as *A Simple Tailor*, the state censor's office having toned down its rhetoric. Four years later, the film appeared under the same title —advertised in Yiddish as *Motl der Shpindler* (Motl the Weaver) —with a dubbed soundtrack. The English-Yiddish advertising flyer invites the public to "Hear! The Badchen—The Wedding —The Old Folk Songs" and "See! How Your People Lived in Old Russia—1918."

A. Solovyev's *Pyat Neyevyest* (Five Brides), released in March 1930, told a similar story of Jewish degradation. When Ukrainian nationalists occupy a *shtetl* in 1919, the rabbi protects the wealthy Jews by persuading their poor coreligionists to placate the Ukrainian officers by offering five Jewish maidens (including Tamara Adelheim) as ransom.

9. Although the *Times* makes no mention of it, *A Jew at War* was released with a musical soundtrack. An advertising flyer heralds the film as "The First Great Movie on Jewish Life, A New Masterpiece of Soviet Film-Art; A Sound Movie with Jewish Music and Songs; Jew Against Jew in War."

Overleaf: **The tormented *Kotsker rebe* (M. B. Sztejn) in Jonas Turkow's *In di Poylishe Velder* (Poland, 1929), adapted from the novel by Joseph Opatoshu.**

11

The Polish Forest

While Warsaw rivaled New York and Moscow as a center of Yiddish modernism, the underdevelopment of the Polish film industry hampered the creation of an indigenous Yiddish cinema. Although *Der Lamedvovnik* had been among the more successful Polish films released during the autumn of 1925, producer Leo Forbert was unable to make an immediate follow-up. Forbert lost control of Leofilm and the company produced no further Jewish films. (The Turkows' art theater was broke as well; two years later, it folded.)

However, the stability (and the dollar loans) that came with Piłsudski's 1927 coup stimulated some recovery—even the tax on movie tickets was re-duced. By the summer of 1928—several months before Michal Waszynski left for Vienna to direct the first Polish-language sound-on-disc talkie *Kult Ciała* (Cult of the Flesh)—Forbert and scriptwriter Henryk Bojm made one more attempt at a Yiddish spectacular, taking as their source Joseph Opatoshu's best-selling *In di Poylishe Velder* (In Polish Woods).[1]

First published in 1921 (and subsequently translated into English, German, Spanish, Hebrew, Russian, Polish, Ukrainian, and Rumanian), Opatoshu's novel provided a panoramic view of mid-nineteenth-century Polish Jewry and its various ideologies. The characters include lusty Jewish foresters and corrupt Cabbalists, otherworldly Chasidim and underground *maskilim,* mystical Polish patriots and followers of the false messiah Shabbtai Zvi. The hero, Mordkhe, grows up in the Lipovets woods, where "plain, wholesome" Jews live in peace with their near-pagan Gentile neighbors, even joining the fisher folk in their annual sacrifice to Wanda, Queen of the Vistula.

Against this colorful backdrop, Mordkhe's soul becomes a Jewish battleground. After a torrid love affair with Rokhl, the dairyman's daughter, he is packed off by his father to Kotsk, site of a degenerate Chasidic court. Although the youth is not without his spiritual side, this attempt at traditional education backfires. The home of the *Kotsker rebe* goes up in flames while, succumbing to the glamorous chimera of universal (or, at least, Polish-Jewish) brotherhood, Mordkhe becomes a legendary agitator—alternately perceived as a Jew and a Catholic—traveling "from village to village, inciting the people to revolt against the landowners and priests."

Although a specifically Jewish epic, it would seem that *In di Poylishe Velder*—which has been lost—was closer to the Polish cinema's mainstream than either *Der Lamedvovnik* or *Tkies Kaf.* The last years of the decade brought a number of artistic and literary features. Shortly before his death in 1928, Aleksander Hertz filmed Nobel laureate Władysław Reymont's *Ziemia Obiecana* (Promised Land), re-

Jews and Poles together: *In di Poylishe Velder.*

made in 1975 by Andrzej Wajda. In 1928 as well, Richard Ordyński brought poet Adam Mickiewicz's epic *Pan Tadeusz* to the screen with Isaac Samberg, (veteran of the Vilna Troupe and three Kosmofilm productions) as Jankiel, the patriotic tavern keeper who was the best-known and most sympathetic Jew in Polish literature. These nationalistic films coincided with others celebrating Poland's revolutionary past, notably Józef Lejtes's *Huragan* (Hurricane), a relative superproduction and rare international success, which evoked the 1863 uprising with compositions based on tableaux by painter Artur Grottger.

In di Poylishe Velder was directed by Jonas Turkow, Zygmunt's younger brother and the star of *Der Lamedvovnik,* as well as a featured performer in *Hurricane.* Silven Rich played Mordkhe, with Dina Blumenfeld (the director's wife) in the expanded role of Rokhl. Opatoshu served as a script adviser and was present on the set. Since the novel ends inconclusively, on the eve of the uprising, Bojm's script incorporated material from the sequel, *1863,* which was published in 1926. Interviewed during production, Bojm spoke enthusiastically of restaging the battles of 1863 as well as a historical flashback depicting the "struggle and heroic death" of Berek Joselewicz, who had been appointed by Kościuszko to lead a Jewish Legion during the revolt of 1794. (An important symbol for Jewish assimilationists, Joselewicz was played by the celebrated Gentile actor Jerzy Leszczyński.) "This will be the first Jewish film that will delight with rich images *and* exciting action," the screenwriter told *Film Velt* (Film World), a new Yiddish-language monthly founded by twenty-one-year-old Shaul Goskind.

Like *Poylishe Velder, Film Velt* (which published its first issue in September 1928) was at once an

Filming *In di Poylishe Velder* on the banks of the Vistula. Jonas Turkow (at right, pointing) directs cameraman Ferdynand Vlassak.

expression of Jewish cultural nationalism *and* the universalist yearnings bound up in the cinema. Today, this "youthful art" is "in full bloom," the journal's first-page editorial announced. Film "is profoundly influencing the lives of broad masses the world over." Goskind's credo is notable, both for its utopian overtones and its religious undercurrents:

In its triumphal march across the continents, the cinema has reached the most remote human settlements, its "naïve muteness" uniting peoples of different languages and colors, thereby blurring the borders of race, nationality, and class.

All of us—admirers of this silent art—are one family, bound together by our love and devotion to film.

First issue of the Yiddish movie journal *Film Velt,* published in Warsaw, September 1928. The cover is a montage of images from *In di Poylishe Velder,* then in production.

Our magazine intends to lead and guide the Jewish reader and moviegoer through this sea of different films. We want to introduce him to the various achievements and successes in international film, while establishing a strict partition between cheap sensations and true art.

In the columns of our magazine, the Jewish reader will find answers to all questions connected with film—this daily spiritual bread of the broad masses.

We hope that those who hold the cinema dear will support us in our work![2]

In addition to Goskind's manifesto and two-page spread on *Poylishe Velder,* the first issue of *Film Velt* included a report from Paris on E. A. Dupont's *Moulin Rouge,* a *"shmues"* (chat) with the American Adolph Menjou, and reviews of several new Polish films (one directed by Henryk Szaro). Pictures of various starlets, assorted industry tidbits, and a piece on how a quartet of film notables (including Ernst

Lubitsch and Pola Negri) began their movie careers, were balanced by a polemical piece on the "secrets of *film-kheyder,*" an essay on film aesthetics by the young literary critic S. L. Shneiderman, and "The Newsboy's Dream," a scenario for a short sound-film fantasy on the life and death of Zishe Breitbart. The last, a nine-scene *"film-shtik,"* taking the strongman from a Lodz smithy to Samson's table in Paradise, was written by cultural journalist J. M. Neuman, who, a half dozen years later, would work with Goskind on Poland's first Yiddish talkie.[3]

Film Velt ran for ten issues, through the summer of 1929. Despite the excitement generated by *Poylishe Velder* and an occasional report on the Yiddish stage, its main emphasis was on the Polish industry and Hollywood. Not surprisingly, the journal paid particular attention to American ghetto melodramas and melting-pot sagas. Edward Sloman's *We Americans* provided the cover image for the second issue; the eighth issue featured an article on the Warner brothers as "Jewish film producers." Nevertheless, *Film Velt* gave *Poylishe Velder* such extensive publicity that it has been suggested by one of Goskind's later associates that the journal was created for that express purpose.

A strip of images from the film graces the cover of the maiden issue, while the lead article, "In the Workshop of *Poylishe Velder,*" details Forbert's Goldfadn-like dedication to the project's realization. The producer is described as having his shirtsleeves rolled up, building sets and personally supervising the film's technical aspects. Forbert doesn't wait for the carpenter, "he himself hammers, saws, cuts" and even "operates the lights during the takes." Though made for relatively little money, *Poylishe Velder* took six months to shoot; in subsequent issues, *Film Velt* updated the production's progress as it moved from Warsaw studio to location in Piaseczno, a village outside the capital. When the movie had its premiere in January 1929 (at the same Warsaw theater which, nine months later, would introduce talkies to Poland by opening Al Jolson in *The Singing Fool),* it was again featured on *Film Velt's* cover.

In making *Poylishe Velder,* Forbert had defied the conventional wisdom of the Polish movie industry. ("Those who believe we have to make artistic films are completely crazy," Henryk Finkelstein, the head of the Sfinks studio, told one journalist later that year. "Those who maintain that we *can* make artistic films in Poland have their heads in the clouds.") No less than Sovkino's ill-fated *Mabl, Poylishe Velder* was what would be termed a "prestige" production—both were ambitious literary adaptations dramatizing revolutionary situations that involved Jewish-Gentile solidarity. The film opened on a patriotic note, its first title acknowledging Polish generosity: "Because the Polish woods are great and wide, they can support the poor people who use them to warm their cold dwellings."

Unfortunately, having essayed the Polish forest, *Poylishe Velder* became lost in it. The film was coolly received and seems never to have been shown abroad. It failed, at least in part, because it was caught between two orthodoxies. *Poylishe Velder* was denounced by the Agudat Israel, a powerful Orthodox-traditionalist political party which included the Jewish community's staunchest Piłsudski supporters. Agudat Israel leaders, among them the heads of several Chasidic dynasties, scarcely appreciated Opatoshu's best-seller and pressured the Polish censor to ban the adaptation.

A special commission, which included govern-

The January 1929 issue of *Film Velt* announces the premiere of Jonas Turkow's *In di Poylishe Velder.*

ment officials, a representative of the Catholic Church, and Rabbi Posner of Warsaw, was established to review the film. "Truly, even in this, Opatoshu is one of the elect—he is the first person in the history of film who had the 'good fortune' to have had his film examined by a Warsaw rabbi," remarked Jonas Turkow sarcastically in *Literarishe Bleter* after *Poylishe Velder* was finally released. This was likely the first motion picture that the rabbi had ever seen. But if Rabbi Posner was

enthralled at the sight of all those "live little people" on the screen, he could not condone the picture of a woman (a granddaughter of the *Kotsker rebe* no less) kissing a man in public, nor the sight of boys and girls mingling socially. . . . This connoisseur saw to it that such offensive scenes were immediately removed.

"Of course, if such riotous behavior caused concern," Turkow explained, then "even more should be cut out of the picture." Most of the scenes at the Chasidic court and even sequences of the uprising were excised. "What remained was a film in tatters, without continuity, having no appeal. Thus was a great piece of work ruined."

The vision of secular heroism and decadent religion offered by *Poylishe Velder* was as offensive to traditional Jews as *Benya Krik*'s portrait of the Jewish lumpen had been for Jewish Communists. (In a sense, both films came under fire from organized religion.) Like *Benya Krik*, *Poylishe Velder* raised the "positive image" question. Now that Jewish movies had entered the public sphere, how were Jews to present themselves to the Gentile world? How should conflicts on the Jewish street be portrayed? Could there be such a thing as Jewish glory on the screen?

With their tales of rebels and lowlifes, both Isaac Babel and Joseph Opatoshu offered a drastic departure in terms of Jewish self-representation. The virile romanticism with which these two writers imbued Jewish criminals paralleled the Zionist, Bundist, and Communist alternatives to the passive, victimized *shtetl* Jew. In his history of Yiddish cinema, Eric Goldman suggests that Grigori Roshal's revolutionary protagonists were the logical successors to Babel's soldiers and gangsters: Jews who are willing to kill to achieve acceptance from the Gentile world. (The difference is in Roshal's political purity. His heroes—Hirsh Lekert and David Gorelik—not only have to kill but also die in order to maintain Gentile approval.)

In both Soviet and American films, traditional Jewishness was necessarily anachronistic; to be a Jewish movie star was, *a priori*, to be an agent of change.

If revolutionary martyrs like Hirsh Lekert or *Mabl*'s Masha Bashevitsh were more physically heroic than that self-invented embodiment of the new Jewish-American, the Jazz Singer, they were no less optimistic. Both types suggest that there is room for the emancipated Jew in the creation of a new, modern, universal culture—be it that of Soviet communism or American show business. There was, however, no such supranationalist ideology in Poland.

Seeking to infuse American-Jewish entertainment with Soviet-Jewish revolutionary ardor, and boldly addressing the romance of 1863 on Jewish terms, *Poylishe Velder* remains the one attempt to effect a synthesis of Polish-Jewish history. Its failure epitomizes the decline of universalist aspirations within the Yiddish cinema. No further Yiddish best-sellers were adapted for the screen. No subsequent Yiddish film would attempt to bridge so many worlds. Forbert and Bojm were unable to realize their planned follow-up, a version of Sholem Asch's play *Motke Ganef*, an underworld picturesque that had been an enormous hit in Warsaw eight years before with Isaac Samberg in the title role. Indeed, not until well into the next decade would anyone attempt to produce another Yiddish feature film in Poland.[4]

Talking pictures, the next stage of Yiddish cinema, were characterized by greater social conservatism. As the Yiddish language remystified Jewish movies and restricted their potential audience, the Gentile world receded from the films. And, as the Gentile world diminished, the youthful cultural and political revolutionaries who acted as emissaries between the two spheres lost their prominence. The new Jewish youth—the activists, flappers, and lapsed *yeshive* students who had populated the silent Yiddish screen—would never again enjoy such prominence, not even in the Soviet cinema.

NOTES

1. The Polish-born Opatoshu immigrated to New York in 1907. His early stories and novels deal with the Jewish underworld, both in Poland and America—one was filmed in 1969 by Abraham Polonsky as *Romance of a Horse Thief*. David Opatoshu, the author's son, began his career on the Yiddish stage and subsequently became an actor in American movies and TV.

2. Goskind edited *Film Velt* in conjunction with Wincenty J. Tenenbaum, who, in the journal's second issue, called upon Jewish filmmakers to throw aside the prejudices between Christians and Jews and debunk the myth of "our supposed exoticism."

3. The Warsaw-born Goskind himself was a political activist as well as a film enthusiast. In 1929, he made a ten-minute 16mm movie on the celebration of the national holiday Lag B'omer by members of his leftist-Zionist youth group Hashomer Hatsair (The Young Guard) and, the following year, produced another short film on the organization's agricultural camp in Czestochowa. (In both cases, the established director Eugeniusz Modzelewski served as cameraman.) Although Hashomer Hatsair was generally hostile to Yiddish, having drawn most of its membership from middle-class students whose first language was Polish and who were influenced by Polish nationalism, the energetic and enterprising Goskind supported all manner of Jewish cinematic expression.

4. One last Polish silent featured a number of secondary Jewish characters. *Szlakiem Hańby* (The Path of Shame), released in November 1929, was shot partially in Kazimierz and included a Jewish wedding.

Overleaf: "You will weep and laugh until you cry." Poster for the first Yiddish partial-talkie, Sidney Goldin's self-proclaimed "$100,000 production," *East Side Sadie* (U.S.A., 1929).

12

The Theater of the Future

THE JAZZ SINGER had its premiere at the Warners Theater on October 6, 1927. Jolson's "persuasive vocal efforts were received with rousing applause," Mordaunt Hall reported in the *New York Times.* "In fact, not since the first presentation of Vitaphone features, more than a year ago at the same playhouse, has anything like the ovation been heard in a motion picture theater."

Throughout 1928, American exhibitors scrambled to wire their theaters for sound as first Paramount and then Warners declared that all future releases would be talkies. New York studios were refurbished for sound production and New York performers were much in demand. Ziegfeld star Fanny Brice,

optimistically touted by Warners as a female Jolson, made a somewhat disappointing debut in *My Man.* Further downtown, D. W. Griffith caught Molly Picon—hailed by the *New Yorker* as "a phenomenon of New York today"—at the Second Avenue Theater in *Hello, Molly* and announced that he would star her in a short talkie, *The Yiddisher Baby.*[1]

Meanwhile, veteran dramatist Abraham Schomer announced plans for a Yiddish sound-film based on his play *Der Griner Milyoner* (The Greenhorn Millionaire), which had been a hit for Boris Thomashefsky thirteen years before. Schomer's movie never materialized, but the first Yiddish talkie was not long in arriving. Advertised as a "$100,000 Production,"

Worldart's *East Side Sadie*—a six-reel silent written and directed by the inevitable Sidney Goldin, with a few synchronous sound sequences and incidental music by Second Avenue luminary Sholom Secunda —opened in New York in May 1929, the same month that the Marx Brothers made their movie debuts in *The Cocoanuts,* and a few days after *The Desert Song,* Vitaphone's first operetta, complete with scenes in primitive Technicolor, had its premiere.

The spring of 1929 saw a glut of "All Talking! All Singing! All Dancing!" musicals as American stars raced to break the sound barrier: Douglas Fairbanks in February, Clara Bow and Mary Pickford in April, Ronald Colman, Paul Muni, and Vilma Banky in

May. Nor was Europe quiet: in London, Alfred Hitchcock was adding sound sequences to *Blackmail,* the first British talkie, while, in Berlin, the German sound consortium Tobis Klangfilm had managed to postpone the premiere of Warners' second, even more successful, Jolson vehicle, *The Singing Fool.* (The first German, French, and Spanish talkies would be produced before the end of the year; Paramount was preparing to open a studio in the Paris suburb of Joinville which would produce talking pictures—and usually the same one—in a dozen different tongues.)

One more novelty among novelties, *East Side Sadie* harked back to Goldin's 1913 *Heart of a Jewess*

Molly Picon on the set of the 1929 Vitaphone short *A Little Girl with Big Ideas.* The actress sang two songs and, although she ordinarily spoke unaccented English, here employed a heavy Yiddish accent, sprinkling her dialogue with Yiddish expressions.

in telling the tale of a Ghetto Rose (played by the director's daughter, Bertina) who toils in a sweatshop to put her boyfriend through college only to see the *shadkhn* match him with a wealthy girl. The talking sequences included a scene of children on a tenement roof singing the New York anthem "East Side, West Side," and the climactic wedding, complete with chanting cantor and one line of shouted Yiddish, translated for the New York Board of Censors as, "Stop the wedding, stop it! Where is that good-for-nothing loafer?"

East Side Sadie contained scarcely more Yiddish than the few words heard in Columbia's *The Younger Generation,* which had opened in March and thus carries the distinction of introducing spoken Yiddish to the screen. For the Yiddish-speaking audience, however, the airwaves set the pace. A few months after *East Side Sadie* opened, the CBS radio network assembled a seventeen-station hookup for a weekly Yiddish-language variety show, produced under the auspices of the New York daily *Der Tog.*

In meeting the challenge of radio, talking pictures revitalized the American movie industry. Business boomed. A hundred million customers bought tickets each week; *The Singing Fool* was the most successful movie ever made (and would remain so up until *Gone With the Wind* surpassed it over a decade later). By the time the New York stock market crashed in October 1929, nearly half the nation's theaters were wired for sound. *Film Daily* had found *East Side Sadie* "amateurish," and "too poor to merit any rating." But, shortly following its release, producer Max Cohen hired Goldin to direct a short all-talkie, *Ad Mosay* (Until When), known in English as *The Eternal Prayer.* Little more than a succession of

Flyer advertising a San Francisco engagement of the short *Ad Mosay* (U.S.A., 1929), "the first Yiddish 'talkie.' "

individual performances—mainly liturgical—punctuated by intervals of blank leader, this thirty-six-minute film was a threadbare analogue to the all-singing "revues" like *The Broadway Melody* and *Movietone Follies* the studios had released en masse the preceding spring.[2]

Harry Alan Potamkin, New York correspondent for the British journal *Close-Up* and perhaps the only critic to comment on *Ad Mosay,* began his first column of 1930 by revealing that he'd just returned from the Bronx where he'd gone to see the Yiddish talkie: "It is about the worst film ever made, indicating absolutely no knowledge of the cinema, even the most elementary, on the part of the makers," Potamkin reported. Nevertheless, "bad as it is," *Ad Mosay*

is of singular importance to any genuinely perspicacious student of the cinema. It signifies the importance of the Jewish physiognomy, like the Negro, an unexploited cinema plastic material, the singularity of the intensive Jewish gestures, and most outstandingly, the Yiddish and Hebrew utterances as the material of the sonal film.

Potamkin's interest in *Ad Mosay* was threefold. First, however poor in execution, the film offered new ideas for the application of sound technology. Second, it exemplified the independent New York production he hoped to encourage. "I urge a New York cinema," the thirty-year-old poet had written in the previous issue of *Close-Up*. Hollywood "is a vested interest community of phlegmatic imaginations and a circle of imitations." (For Potamkin, "New York cinema" included amateur movies, industrial documentaries, and experimental efforts, as well as a commercial film like *Applause*—a New York movie because it was shot at Paramount's Astoria studio.)

Third, *Ad Mosay* provided Potamkin an opportunity to critique the celluloid representation of Jews. His capsule history, one of the first, extends from the pre–World War Sidney Goldin efforts (which Potamkin chivalrously attributes to their star, Irene Wallace) through "Yiddish caption" films and Jewish comedians to *The Jazz Singer*. Potamkin, who spent much of the twenties in Paris and visited Moscow in 1927, is more kindly disposed toward European variants. He praises *The Ancient Law*, invokes Granovsky, and dismisses all previous American efforts—proposing as film material such Yiddish dramas as *Der Dibek*, Harry Seckler's *Dem Tsadeks Nesie* (*Tsadek's Journey*), and H. Leivick's *Shmates* (*Rags*). Scarcely a month after Potamkin's "New York Notes: II" appeared, another Jewish immigrant's son was touting the idea of Yiddish films based on the work

of precisely these three authors—although it is unlikely that Joseph Seiden ever read an essay on "sonal" aesthetics in his life.

The thirty-eight-year-old Seiden, who would be the most resilient of all Yiddish filmmakers, was a Hollywood mogul writ small. As a teenager he had served as projectionist in his father's Brooklyn nickelodeon. Afterward he went to work as a cameraman's assistant for the New York Motion Picture Company, then worked as a full cameraman on several local films, including some produced by Fox and Universal. Seiden started a modest business, producing promotional shorts, until he was caught up in the events of 1919. Accompanying the American Relief Expedition on its mission to the Baltic states as well as helping the new Polish government document Bolshevik "atrocities" along the Ukrainian frontier, he returned in time to serve the United States Army in filming the Pennsylvania steel strike.

After an abortive attempt to found a studio in Binghamton, New York (the first project was to have been an adaptation of Jack London's *Minions of Midas*), Seiden worked for Vitaphone's newsreel unit, specializing in the coverage of prize fights. Simultaneously, in partnership with the veteran producer Ivan Abramson, he made a number of silent Jewish-interest newsreels. In early 1930, not long after Potamkin saw *Ad Mosay*, Seiden, who had branched out into the rental of sound-film equipment, joined forces with Moe Goldman, owner of four Bronx movie houses, to incorporate Judea Pictures. Enlisting Sidney Goldin as their director, the partners entered the Yiddish talkie business. Pragmatism was the watchword: *Variety* noted that Judea was depending upon Goldman to exercise the same "ingenuity" in production as he had in exhibition, having "cheated the electrics by talking for the male screen players and getting his femme cashier to speak for the women."

Judea's first two-reelers were produced in early 1930 at a crudely soundproofed studio on East Thirty-eighth Street: they were *Style and Class* (with comic dancers Marty Baratz and Goldie Eisman re-creating a number currently onstage at Gabel's Public Theater) and *Shuster Libe* (known in English as *The Shoemaker's Romance,* and featuring Joseph Buloff with other members of the Vilna Troupe in what the producers describe as a "modernistic version of a Russian tale"). Conditions were primitive. Because the sound was recorded on disc, each scene was a continuous ten-minute take, and because the budget for both films was $3,000 there were no retakes. Seiden used two cameras, operating one himself; illumination for the hot, cramped set was provided by old-fashioned incandescent stage lights. The films had their world premieres on March 19, 1930, five days after Greta Garbo made her sound debut in *Anna Christie.* Garbo spoke at the Capital on Broadway; Baratz, Eisman *et al.* at the RKO Tilyou in Coney Island. Within a few weeks the shorts were booked by another five Brooklyn theaters, and while not the 250-theater national circuit Judea told *Variety* they anticipated, it was a start. The firm announced that Second Avenue matinee idols Samuel Goldenberg and Jennie Goldstein had signed contracts, with adaptations of *Der Dibek, Der Goylem,* and Seckler's *Ashmidai* in the offing.

Although these ambitious projects seem little more than a publicist's fantasy, Judea did attempt a certain range in its subsequent releases. The next few months brought several cantorials; a performance of Abraham Reisen's plaintive ballad "Mai-Ko-Mashma-

Publicity photo for Judea's first two-reeler, *Style and Class* (U.S.A., 1930). Novelty dancers Marty Baratz and Goldie Eisman (seated center) recreated a number they were currently featuring at the Public Theater on Second Avenue.

Cast and crew of Judea's *Sailor's Sweetheart* (U.S.A., 1930): director Sidney Goldin is seated at center with actress Miriam Kressyn on his knee; her co-star Hymie Jacobson accepts a five-dollar bill from producer Joseph Seiden; composer Sholom Secunda is seated on floor in front of Goldin.

Cast and crew of *Mayn Yidishe Mame* (U.S.A., 1930): star Mae Simon and director Sidney Goldin are seated at center. The young couple behind them (center) are Bernice Simon and Seymour Rechtzeit. Producer Joseph Seiden is seated at far left.

lon" (What Does It Mean?); a film version of *Der Tog's* radio show; *The Jewish Gypsy,* starring eccentric dancer Hymie Jacobson and his wife Miriam Kressyn; Menashe Skulnick as a comic hypochondriac in *Oy Doktor!;* and—the pièce de résistance—an hour-long feature, *Mayn Yidishe Mame* (My Jewish Mother), starring Mae Simon.

Although the film has disappeared, a dialogue translation remains. *Mayn Yidishe Mame* opens with a not altogether appropriate invocation of Abraham and Isaac, considering the plot concerns parents who sacrifice for (rather than simply sacrifice) their children. Mae Rabinowitz (Simon) loses first her husband (run over en route to the toy store to exchange his son's birthday gift) and then her offspring. While Mae slaves in a sweatshop, her daughter learns to smoke and goes astray, the older son becomes a

crapshooter (as played by Seymour Rechtzeit, he is not so degenerate that he fails to sing the title song), and the younger boy simply disappears.

Years pass. The missing son has become a successful lawyer, who, learning of a forsaken mother, prepares to sue her ungrateful children for parent support and is thus reintroduced to his own all-forgiving *yidishe mame.* Having brought to the movies the venerable stage formula of filial blindness and ultimate chastening which Seiden, among others, would faithfully employ for the next dozen years, *Mayn Yidishe Mame* concluded on a note of family reconciliation. Judea made arrangements with a trio of strategically situated movie houses (in Brighton Beach, on Prospect Avenue in the Bronx, and on Second Avenue) to premiere their subsequent releases.

Judea's success did not go unnoticed. In the *Morgn Frayhayt,* their output was ridiculed by drama critic A. Mandelbaum as *"khazeray (pig swill) deluxe."* Here once more, the *Frayhayt* sneered, was that venerable *yidishe mame*—"the same *yente,* not even newly turned out"—warming hearts with her "nationalistic sentiments" and the "familiar Jewish groan." Goldin, the "Yiddish 'talkie' peddler," trafficked in shoddy goods and flattered the audience with cheap chauvinism. His Gypsies were only skin deep: "If need be, the Jewish Gypsy can show the whole world that he has 'kosher' stamped upon his belly-button."[3]

A. Almi, an immigrant poet and New York correspondent for *Literarishe Bleter,* was at once more temperate and more messianic: "We should bless the invention of the sound film, even if this or that epicure turns up his nose." However hackneyed, Almi wrote, Judea's films were no worse than American talkies. What's more, the Yiddish sound-film had an impressive destiny: first, as the "reincarnation" of the dying Yiddish stage; second, as the vehicle for a "universal" Yiddish speech—providing, of course, that filmmakers "make kosher" their Yiddish by eliminating the numerous Anglicisms.

Almi hailed Judea's first few offerings as pointing the way to a Yiddish "theater of the future." For the Yiddish theater of the present, however, the films could scarcely have appeared at a more critical moment. For even as the *Frayhayt* mocked the bogus display of "Jewish unity" that Judea's talkies occasioned, the films were in fact already controversial.

Although the Yiddish theater audience had been in decline for a decade, this loss was partially offset by continued immigration. Now, the end of prosperity strained a steadily eroding base. Even in good times, the Yiddish rialto operated on a narrow profit margin: where Broadway had two unions, the Yiddish theater had seven (actors', stagehands', musicians', ushers', chorus-members', dressers', and doormen's). The Yiddish theater unions were notoriously fierce. Luba Kadison recalls that in the late twenties, a splinter of the Vilna Troupe attempted to play a season with nonunion stagehands in a decrepit old theater on 149th Street in the Bronx. The experiment failed, in part because their performances were picketed and disrupted by stinkbombs.

It would be another year before the effects of the stock market crash would be felt by most Jews; still, the 1929–30 season saw two minor Yiddish theaters fold and two Second Avenue houses put up for sale. The manager of a third theater committed suicide, and even Maurice Schwartz cut short his season for a stint in American vaudeville, playing Shylock in English on a bill with Rin-Tin-Tin and *Captain of the Guard.* Thus, despite its incomparably lower cultural aspirations, and certainly for different reasons, *Mayn Yidishe Mame* stirred scarcely less debate in Yiddish cultural circles than *In di Poylishe Velder* or *Benya Krik.*[4]

The Judea film brought fiery protests from the Hebrew Actors Union. Three years before, the union advised members against appearing on the radio. Now, on June 25, 1930, the leadership adopted a resolution barring the membership from working in Yiddish talking pictures. Reuben Guskin, the ex-barber who had ruled the union since 1922, maintained that Judea had not only used nonunion actors but harmed the reputation of the legitimate Yiddish theater by conning the public into thinking that the films were actually personal appearances. (In fact, Mae Simon was starring in the play *A Yidishe Mame* while *Mayn Yidishe Mame* was in release.)

Production shut down for the summer as Judea and the union exchanged statements and counterstatements in the Yiddish press. At length an agreement guaranteeing compensation for the use of nonunion actors was reached and Goldin completed Judea's second feature, *Eybike Naronim* (Eternal Fools), which, like *Mayn Yidishe Mame* (if in marginally more literary fashion, having been adapted by Harry Kalmanowitz from his Second Avenue melodrama), was a saga of filial ingratitude and parental sacrifice. Indeed, as the title suggests, the film elevated this syndrome to a universal principle: humiliated by his children's selfishness, the workaholic sewing-machine operator Morris Rothstein is about to destroy the fruit of his labors when his elderly father reminds him that the children's behavior is no different than Morris's own.

Eybike Naronim opened at the Bronx Playhouse on Rosh Hashanah—the trailer for a theatrical season so disastrous that, despite reduced ticket prices, only Picon's Second Avenue Theater was even breaking even. Meanwhile, *Mayn Yidishe Mame*'s scandalous career reached new heights. Rivlin and Company of Tel Aviv purchased the film for distribution in Palestine and Syria, where *The Singing Fool* had broken the sound barrier in late 1929. Sold on the novelty of a Jewish talking picture, the exhibitors seemingly forgot that for many Zionists—particularly in the Yishev—Yiddish was anathema, a contemptible holdover of dispersion and exile. Less than four years earlier there had been a well-publicized fracas over a performance of Goldfadn's Biblical operetta *Shulamis,* and it was not unknown for groups like the

Battalion for the Defense of the Hebrew Language to disrupt gatherings where Yiddish was spoken.

When *Mayn Yidishe Mame* had its premiere at Tel Aviv's Mograbi Theater on September 27, 1930 (the first Saturday night after the Jewish New Year), demonstrators splattered the screen with ink and caused such confusion that British troops were called in to restore order. Thus *Mayn Yidishe Mame* suffered an even more drastic fate than *In di Poylishe Velder:* municipal officials ordered the movie banned until all talking sequences had been excised. Not for another twenty years would a Yiddish movie be exhibited in Tel Aviv in its original language.

Back in New York, where, by December's end, two-thirds of the Broadway theaters would close and even the Shuberts be forced into receivership, the Yiddish stage seemed near collapse. Molly Picon left on a European tour; Ludwig Satz switched to American vaudeville. Mid-season, the managers of New York's nine remaining Yiddish venues issued an ultimatum: either wages be reduced by 40 percent or the theaters would close. Led by the stagehands and musicians, the unions threatened to strike, and on December 8, 1930, the theaters went dark. (Two days later, a panic at the Delancey Street headquarters of the Bank of the United States ruined thousands of Jewish small businesses.)

The lockout lasted two weeks, until the unions and theater managers settled on compromise wage reductions of 10 to 25 percent, but the 1931–32 season saw a further dispersion of Second Avenue stars. Schwartz jumped to Broadway. "Around the Café Royal and the Hebrew Actors Union quarters there is much talk about his 'betrayal' of the Yiddish theater," the *New York Times* reported. Even Thomashefsky opened on Forty-second Street with an ill-fated English version of *The Singing Rabbi*. (Legend has it that, after acknowledging the applause greeting his appearance, the star lapsed into Yiddish—his confused supporting cast delivering their lines in a mélange of English, Yiddish, and even Russian. The show ran for four performances.)

By now, the "Depression-proof" movie industry also felt the pinch. Whereas 1930 had been the best year in Hollywood's history, three studios finished 1931 in the red; in 1932, all lost money except MGM. Nevertheless, although capital was as scarce as risks were abundant, the 1931–32 season was bracketed by the most ambitious Yiddish talkies yet.[5]

It must have been with some ambivalence that the Hebrew Actors Union greeted the appearance of two reigning stars in filmed versions of their recent plays. The first to arrive was *Zayn Vaybs Lubovnik* (*His Wife's Lover*). Produced by distributor Nathan Hirsch's short-lived High Art Pictures, this Ludwig Satz vehicle took Yiddish talkies well beyond vaudeville turns and primitive melodrama. *Zayn Vaybs Lubovnik* never transcends its stage origins, but, as tough and racy as it often is, the film compares well to the theatrical adaptations that dominated the major studios' 1930–31 output, and, like many of them (Paramount's enormously successful *Animal Crackers* not the least), is basically a showcase for inspired clowning.[6]

The gifted Satz had been Second Avenue's reigning male comic for much of the twenties. Audiences adored him; his mere appearance on stage would inspire anticipatory laughter. Renowned for his use of makeup, Satz had a large repertoire of stock characters, including a tragicomic saintly fool and a naïve *yeshive-bokher* whose high-pitched voice presages Jerry Lewis's more strident nudnik. For all his on-

stage charm, however, Satz was privately a troubled man, morbidly sensitive, contemptuous of himself and his success. Born in 1891, he had been a prodigy, a child singer who became the principal comedian at the Lemberg (Lvov) Yiddish Theater, as well as an aspiring Yiddish poet.

Leaving Galicia for Budapest and London, Satz arrived in America on the eve of the World War. He appeared both on the Yiddish stage and in motion picture comedies, working with Jacob P. Adler and the Lubin Film Company. Although an original member of Schwartz's Yiddish Art Theater, he beat a lucrative retreat to the popular Yiddish (and then the American) stage after *Forverts* editor Abraham Cahan savaged him with a scathingly negative review. Every season Satz was rumored to be returning to Schwartz, but his thin skin evidently proved stronger than his theatrical ideals.

A measure of this conflict is dramatized and displaced in *Zayn Vaybs Lubovnik* as Satz enacts an elaborate masquerade which, for most of the play, precludes his being loved for himself. The actor appears as Eddie Wien, a worldly Yiddish matinee idol who, while watching the chorus girls rehearse, sings "I Hate All Women" with the impassioned acerbity of a practiced rake. This opening number would hardly seem out of place in a Brecht-Weill *Singspiel*. Wien, however, is merely cynical; his backer, sweatshop owner Oscar Stein, played with ineffable sleaziness by Isidore Cashier, is a true misogynist. He wagers $10,000 that Wien will never find a faithful woman. Golde Blumberg (Lucy Levine), a nubile but virtuous girl who works in Stein's shop, is chosen to stand the test. Eddie and Golde are already attracted to each other, but he will debase them both by courting her in the guise of a rich, repulsive old man. As

Poster for the Ludwig Satz vehicle *Zayn Vaybs Lubovnik* (U.S.A., 1931), an adaptation of a musical that had been a hit at the Folks Theater on Second Avenue during the previous season.

The stars of *Zayn Vaybs Lubovnik:* (from right) Lillian Feinman, Isidore Cashier, Ludwig Satz, and Lucy Levine.

he makes up as the bucktoothed, drooling Herman Weingard, Satz sings another bitter ditty: "How can a *sheyne meydele* marry a monkey like me?"

Stein's workers go on strike and, like the Yiddish theater owners, the unscrupulous boss uses the threat of a lock-out to pressure Golde into this "practical" marriage. Her aunt is also drafted into service, fawning over Weingard despite his idiotic pranks. Nagged to sacrifice herself, Golde at last succumbs and marries Weingard, although on their wedding night she locks herself in her room and sleeps with a picture of Eddie Wien. (This despite a bluntly ideogrammatic three-shot montage: ring placed on finger, foot smashing glass, panties dropping to negligee-sheathed ankles.) Three weeks into their honeymoon, at a beach resort in fashionable Far Rockaway, Golde still refuses to share Weingard's bed. Having lost his wager as well as his heart, not to mention all sense of reason, the actor makes a second bet with Stein, staking $25,000 that, as she has selflessly married the grotesque Weingard, Golde will at least remain faithful to her husband—even though the infatuated Wien will court her as himself.

Zayn Vaybs Lubovnik is a tour de force for Satz, and the irrepressible performer stacks the deck against the "normal" Wien's second wager by playing Weingard with hilarious gusto. He wears an absurd inner tube at the beach and runs coweringly away from the waves; he tries to get Golde to dance, collapses from the exertion, then petulantly demands a kiss. When she responds with irritation, he brays an infantile, obnoxious love song recorded by Satz in 1929 as "Oy Gite Vaybele" (Oh, Good Little Wife). Finally, Eddie appears, takes Golde rowing, and sings to her in the moonlight as she sobs. With Stein gloating over their tryst like the devil in a medieval morality play, Golde announces that although she loves Eddie, she cannot betray her husband. Weingard then reveals his true identity and the couple celebrate a second, consummated wedding night.

A gala event in itself, this "first 100-percent Yiddish singing and talking picture" had its premiere September 25, 1931, at the Clinton Theater, on the Lower East Side. The *Forverts* ran its favorable review above that for *Palmy Days,* the vehicle for another local hero–turned–movie star, Eddie Cantor. Held over a second week at the Clinton, *Zayn Vaybs Lubovnik* opened at no less than three Brownsville theaters in mid-October, and played the Bronx with *Dos Land fun Frayhayt* (The Land of Freedom), a Judea two-reeler starring "wonder child" Seymour Rechtzeit.

The movie even attracted favorable attention in the English-language press. "The occasion is one of interest inasmuch as Mr. Satz has not made many recent stage appearances," the *New York World-Telegram* reported, noting that "only a year or two ago [Satz] was busily engaged in building Broadway bridges. . . . The photography is surprisingly good and the direction, as supervised by Sidney Goldin, is in many instances above the average."

The first few months of 1932 saw a last series of East Side melodramas—Warner Brothers' *The Heart of New York* and RKO's *The Symphony of Six Million* (both featuring Second Avenue veteran Anna Appel) —as well as the most celebrated Yiddish passage in any Hollywood movie. Five minutes into Warners' *Taxi!,* Irish cabdriver Jimmy Cagney is carrying on a rapid-fire conversation in *mame-loshn* with an excit-

Poster advertising the 1932 Warner Brothers release *Taxi!* **Five minutes into the movie, star Jimmy Cagney delighted Jewish audiences by carrying on a conversation in Yiddish.**

able Ellis Island–bound fare. Cagney, who rocketed to fame in the title role of Warners' 1931 *Public Enemy* and would soon be hailed by Lincoln Kirstein as "the first definitely metropolitan figure to become national," learned Yiddish growing up on the streets of New York, and his pleasure in the exchange—in which, among other things, he mocks a noncomprehending police officer for his *"goyisher kop"* (Gentile head)—is palpable.[7]

Even as this sequence, complete with Yiddish dialogue balloons, was used to advertise *Taxi!* in Jewish neighborhoods, another one-shot production company, Yiddish Talking Pictures, commissioned Sidney Goldin to codirect Maurice Schwartz in a film of Schwartz's stage adaptation of Sholem Asch's 1918 novel *Uncle Moses.* No previous Yiddish talkie had nearly so much prestige: if Schwartz was America's foremost Yiddish artiste, Asch was the nation's most popular "serious" Yiddish writer.

Uncle Moses was originally serialized in the *Forverts* and, like editor Cahan's English-language novel *The Rise of David Levinsky,* published the preceding year, it articulates the disillusionment of the half-Americanized *allrightnik.* The titular antihero is a wealthy clothing manufacturer and a distorted image of his Biblical namesake. When poverty and persecution compel his Polish *landsmen* to leave their *shtetl* (the same Kazimierz, or "Kuzmir," where exteriors for the Polish silent *Der Lamedvovnik* were filmed), "Uncle" Moses—the crude and lusty former butcher—welcomes them to the promised land of his Lower East Side clothing factory. A master in the harsh new American system, with its fourteen-hour workday, Moses attempts to reconstruct the lost harmony of Kuzmir's community in the paternalistic order of his sweatshop.

Although written and set during the period of the Great Immigration, Asch's novel readily lent itself to that of the Great Depression. (The March 1932 issue of the militantly mimeographed *Workers Theater* cited no less than eleven Jewish Workers' Clubs in the Bronx, Brooklyn, and Manhattan that were offering political plays in Yiddish.) Indeed, despite certain anachronisms, the film *Uncle Moses* makes no attempt to date its action to an earlier era. Thus, for the first time, a Yiddish talkie engaged directly the progressive currents of the day, political and aesthetic. Young Jews were now a dynamic force in the New York theater—not just as entertainers and the authors of sophisticated musical comedies, but as socially conscious (and self-conscious) artists. Meanwhile, the serious Yiddish stage had coalesced around two poles: Schwartz's Yiddish Art Theater and the Artef. Ever since the Artef's 1929–30 pro-

duction of Sholom Aleichem's *Mentshn* (People), the theater and its director, Benno Schneider, had developed a cult following. "Word spread around Second Avenue, Greenwich Village, and Broadway about this Yiddish theater director who had worked miracles with shopworkers," Judd Teller recalled. "Artef's performances became the 'in' thing."[8]

Too obvious for Schneider, no doubt, *Uncle Moses* was resurrected by Schwartz, who, recognizing the timeliness of its social significance (not to mention a superb part for himself), adapted Asch's novel for the stage. Fittingly, the play was presented during the 1930–31 "strike" season. It was not, however, considered among the Yiddish Art Theater's finest productions. In the *New York Times,* William Schack criticized the play as "scrappy and superficial," "a picture of life which in the course of an evening works the heart like an accordion, crushed close in stark tragedy and expanding in broad comedy."

Though based on "minor literature," *Uncle Moses* raised the artistic ambitions of the American Yiddish cinema, as well as American independent cinema in general. The movie, whose release coincides with that of the first independent "race" talkies (*The Exile,* produced by Oscar Micheaux in Chicago, and *The Black King,* Donald Heywood's fictionalized view of Marcus Garvey) is easily the most polished of such films up until Dudley Murphy's 1933 adaptation of *The Emperor Jones.* Goldin was paired with Aubrey Scotto, whose most recent credit was the English-language *Divorce Racket.* Scotto was hired to improve Goldin's technique, which, thanks to some tentative camera movements, a few shifts in camera angle, and an awkward experiment in overlapping dialogue, is more advanced here than in *Zayn Vaybs Lubovnik.*

Like the earlier film, *Uncle Moses* is basically

canned theater and only marginally less set-bound. The obligatory opening track down Orchard Street aside, it was shot entirely at the Metropolitan Studios in Fort Lee, New Jersey. Still, *Uncle Moses* remains the most confidently urban of all Yiddish talkies, even more sprinkled with English words than contemporary Warners slum dramas were spiced with Yiddishisms; it was also the most American. The film's extensive use of "Yinglish," as well as American slang, might have disconcerted *Literarishe Bleter*'s A. Almi, but its inventive use of sound to record all manner of "Yiddish and Hebrew utterances" would surely have delighted Harry Alan Potamkin.

The first extended talking sequence strikes a complex "sonal"—and appropriately cynical—note. A rabbi from Moses' old *shtetl* visits the great man's shop to solicit a donation. (He has first to cool his heels while the boss deals with the importunities of two paramours—one the wife of a luncheonette owner, the other a *"Poylishe shikse."*) The scene is a ferocious vignette of mutual manipulation. The rabbi entertains Moses by chanting the Yom Kippur prayer *Ovenu Malkenu* ("Father in Heaven, write us into the book of prosperity and sustenance . . ."), pandering to Moses' nostalgia, even as Moses flaunts his power. Here, as throughout, Schwartz dominates, and not just by virtue of his regal profile. *Uncle Moses* is his show: small wonder the *Morgn Frayhayt* criticized the film for *"starism."* Schwartz's Uncle Moses is a Jewish Godfather, vain and sleazy, ruthless yet sentimental—devoid of illusions, if not irony. The subsequent mention of money in his presence will start *him* chanting snatches of *Ovenu Malkenu*.

Moses leaves the management of his affairs to his nephew Sam, a smooth, Americanized flunky. Meanwhile, his old father (coproducer Rubin Goldberg in a role originated onstage by Joseph Buloff)

Wealthy sweatshop owner Uncle Moses (Maurice Schwartz) greets his *landsmen*. **Uncle Moses (U.S.A., 1930) was based on Schwartz's stage adaptation of Sholem Asch's 1918 novel and it was the most prestigious Yiddish talkie to date.**

wanders around the shop, chanting a favorite *nign* (melody) and bitterly joking about their collective lot in this cruel and mercenary New World: "Our *shtetl* Kuzmir will never die. It lives on in America." Calling his son "Tsar Nicholas" and "Pharaoh, King of Egypt," the old man declares himself to be Moses— the weather is hot, so he will lead the Jewish workers out of bondage to bathe in the sea.

In the context of Asch's drama, Moses' father is the fool who speaks the truth. The film's most powerful aspect is its evocation of tenement life, the tensions of generation crammed together, the tensions that break families apart. When lissome Masha (Judith Abarbanel) comes to Moses to beg for her feckless father's job, Moses is smitten and rehires the

man. Meanwhile, Charlie, Masha's sweetheart, vows to organize Moses' factory. (That Charlie, played by Zvee Schooler, is a Marxist is signified by a picture of his namesake Karl on the wall). As the workers struggle to form a union, Moses contemplates one for himself. He woos Masha, dispenses largesse to her neighbors as he climbs the stairs to her fifth-floor walk-up, showers her parents with presents, and even shaves his beard.

Virtually everyone in *Uncle Moses* is caught between two worlds. Even Charlie invokes his idol, Karl Marx, and the notion of a *bashert* (fated one) in the same speech, while using the imagery of the Passover seder to illustrate Moses' desire for Masha (rather than simply to help her parents): "He's not interested in the Haggadah, he's waiting for the soup." Like the heroine of *Zayn Vaybs Lubovnik,*

A half-traditional celebration: the old *allrightnik* marries the young daughter of one of his employees (Judith Abarbanel), in *Uncle Moses.*

Masha gives herself to an inappropriate suitor to please her family and improve their situation. The wedding, held in her parents' apartment, is watched by the impotent Charlie from across the airshaft, as framed through a tenement window. Although we see a traditional celebration (or a half-traditional celebration), complete with *klezmorim,* a *badkhn,* and close-ups of the dancers' feet, its frantic revelry suggests the near-bacchanal of the even more grotesque misalliance in Tod Browning's *Freaks* (released three months later, in July).

If Moses reaches the pinnacle of his authority when, threatened by the union, he vengefully reminds his employees to whom they owe their life in America, he softens when Masha becomes pregnant. In the end, however, Moses is neither able to reinvent himself nor become a true patriarch. On the very day his son is born, his employees strike. In the last of the film's set pieces, a worker takes the floor at a tumultuous union meeting and, continuing the ongoing set of Biblical allusions (while offering an astonishing example of displaced Talmudic disputation), declares Charlie the "new Moses" who will lead the unwilling and fearful Jews out of slavery.

The workers must choose between two evils—the false community of the transposed *shtetl* or the more appropriate, if alienated, community of the union. A transitional figure, Moses ultimately proves irrelevant. Sam calls in hired *shtarkers* (thugs) to break the strike and, sickened by the use of force against his "people," Moses collapses. (Schwartz plays the broken king to the hilt—could this be the end of Uncle Moses?) Leaving a quarter of his estate to his employees, Moses divorces Masha. In a brief epilogue, the aged and lonely empire-builder returns to his shop to visit the workers he called *"mishpokhe"* (family), and tells them a last story.

I was walking past the Great Synagogue. I walked in and heard a preacher delivering a sermon. He was talking about "man." "Man" is this, "man" is that, "man." . . . He spoke for an hour and never said what "man" is all about. So I asked him: "Mister, what is a man? He builds houses, factories, brings his *landslayt* [countrymen] to America, and after all, the grave awaits him. He builds, he makes a commotion, and the grave still waits."[9]

Uncle Moses and *Zayn Vaybs Lubovnik* reprise a theme that most likely received its starkest representation in the 1914 Kosmofilm adaptation of Jacob Gordin's *Di Shkhite*. (There is even an invocation of the word "slaughter" when Masha is led in to meet her wealthy suitor.) Both talkies pivot on the forced —read "arranged"—marriage of a virtuous Ghetto Rose to a gross *allrightnik* old enough to be her father. In selling themselves, Golde and Masha are the Yiddish equivalents of the innocent "fallen women" who populated the pre–Production Code Hollywood movies of the early thirties. They are not gold diggers but victims. A horror of American materialism is blended with a distaste for the traditional economic underpinnings of a *shtetl* match. In each case, American wealth has corrupted the older generation while the promise of American freedom inspires the younger generation—the appropriate suitors are an actor and a labor organizer, respectively.[10]

In both films, the younger generation prevails, or, at least, the older generation declines; but there is no sense of a broader social coherence. America may well be a disaster—"not worth a pinch of salt," according to Moses' father. "A curse on Columbus" is a common phrase in *Zayn Vaybs Lubovnik*. "I would

have married anyone to escape my slavery," Golde unhappily admits. Later, in an intensely melodramatic scene, she confronts the factory boss Stein: "I came alone to these shores in search of happiness, but instead I found your cold machines." Even more than the earlier film, *Uncle Moses* is characterized by Depression despair. The immigrants are weak and easily corrupted. The former shop worker who controls the *shtarkers* is clearly modeled upon the gangster Edward G. Robinson played in the previous year's *Little Caesar*.

Religion is present largely as an absence—it's striking that, even after Moses renounces his worldly goods, he does not turn to God. In the harshest ending of any Yiddish film, Moses asks one of his old workers to sing the *nign* he sang for his father, and the melody is drowned out by the roar of the machines. In the context of the early sound period, and even beyond, *Uncle Moses* exudes a primal ferocity. Dealing as palpably as it does with exploitation and misery, it is the most visceral of Lower East Side movies—the confluence of a number of forceful, if sometimes crude, talents. Fittingly, it had its premiere the same month that Schwartz's erstwhile rival Paul Muni established his film reputation with *Scarface*, opening on April 20, 1932, at three New York theaters—the Clinton, the Stadium in Brownsville, and the Benenson in the Bronx.

Der Tog, the most self-consciously literary of Yiddish dailies (identified on its masthead as "the newspaper of the Jewish intelligentsia"), noted that *Uncle Moses* had changed little from the stage production and hailed it as "the first good Yiddish talkie." In Warsaw, *Literarishe Bleter* carried a generally favorable account of this "first [sic] Jewish talking film." Schwartz would have approved. With some irony, the *Morgn Frayhayt* reported that the actor appeared in person at the movie's premiere to announce the dawning of a "new epoch." In fact, *Uncle Moses* coincided with a new literary awareness, as first-generation Jewish-American writers addressed the pathos of immigration and the circumstances of their childhoods. The film was preceded by Michael Gold's *Jews Without Money* (1930), and followed by Daniel Fuchs's *Summer in Williamsburg* (1934), Henry Roth's *Call It Sleep* (1935), and the first plays of Clifford Odets.

Even as these works appeared, however, the subject of American Jews ceased to be an issue for "literary" Yiddish movies (or for Hollywood). As immigrant drama, *Uncle Moses* had no successors, although in adapting a serious play it did presage a new development for Yiddish talkies. Due to the Depression, however, that era would not arrive for another five years, and thanks to the resurgence of European anti-Semitism, it would concern itself mainly with Jewish life in an idealized Old World.[11]

NOTES

1. Picon made her talkie debut the following autumn, but not for Griffith. Instead, she sang "Temperamental Tillie" and "Yiddisher Blues" in the Vitaphone short *A Little Girl with Big Ideas*. Although the actress ordinarily spoke unaccented English, she employed a heavy Jewish dialect, sprinkled with Yiddish. (*The Yiddisher Baby*, meanwhile, remained unborn.)

2. Samuel Kelemer, who, as the boy cantor Shmulikel, was one of *Ad Mosay*'s featured performers, recalled that the picture involved scant preparation and no retakes. A fragment preserved in the YIVO archive is a home-movie quality recording of Shmulikel chanting the memorial prayer. *El Mole Rakhamim* in the midst of a large (and self-conscious) chorus. According to Eric Goldman, who located this footage and interviewed Kelemer, the film was made in response to the massacre of Jewish settlers in Hebron several months earlier.

3. Mandelbaum's heavy-handed satire also swipes at several prominent literary figures for whom, he maintains, this latest "Yiddish cultural achievement" has occasioned a "joyous" display of national unity. Drama critic A. Mukdoyni, who had evidently praised Judea's *Shuster Libe* in the *Morgn Zhurnal*, "doesn't write criticism—he blows the Jewish *shofar*"; and poet Abraham Reisen is obliged to endorse Yiddish talkies after Judea made such a *"tsimes"* (fuss) over his "disgusting" "Mai-Ko-Mashmalon."

These seemingly gratuitous personal attacks suggest that the *Frayhayt* was still smarting from the events of the previous summer. August 1929 had brought the first Arab assault on Jewish settlers in the Yishev. Initially the *Frayhayt* denounced the massacre; within a few days, however, the paper reversed its position and blamed "Zionist-Fascists" for provoking the Arab uprising. As a result, newsstands refused to carry the *Frayhayt*; the paper lost national advertising, then local ads, and finally even those of the Yiddish theater. Influential writers like Reisen and H. Leivick resigned from the staff, while Mukdoyni and others excoriated the burgeoning Yiddish-Communist culture as a sham.

4. The mildly risqué *Oy Doktor!* also ran afoul of authority. The New York State Motion Picture Division required Judea to eliminate several "indecent" double entendres—as, for example, Skulnick's incredulous reply when a female patient mistakes him for a doctor and requests an examination, "She says she wants to have children and that I should help her."

5. Seiden's Judea Pictures continued to produce short films through 1931, as well as a five-reel version of *Shulamis*, thus bringing the number of items in the Judea catalogue to nineteen, all directed by Goldin. Other companies also tried their hand. In 1931, Jacob Berkowitz hired Goldin to make two shorts, *Khazn afn Probe* (A Cantor on Trial) and *Di Seder Nakht* (The Feast of Passover).

6. Written by Sheyne Rokhl Simkoff, *Zayn Vaybs Lubovnik* seems inspired by Ferenc Molnár's *The Guardsman* even though it uses a situation that, in Yiddish theater, goes back at least to Goldfadn's *Tsvey Kuni Lemls* (Two Kuni Lemls). The stage production played the Folks Theater during the 1929–30 season and, although the movie credits its score to Satz, was the first hit for composer Abraham Ellstein, who, after writing incidental music for the Vilna Troupe, the Artef, and *Ad Mosay*, would become Molly Picon's accompanist and a pillar of the Yiddish "literary" operetta.

7. Sound revived the vaudeville tradition of ethnic humor. Patricia Erens, citing the addition of Jewish-dialect comedian Benny Rubin to the sound version of Cosmopolitan's 1929 *Marianne* and MGM's 1930 remake of the silent *Spring Fever*, observes that comic foreign accents were part of the pleasures afforded by early talkies. A few words of Yiddish, however, also signified New York street smarts. In Columbia's *Virtue*, released in October 1932, a prostitute played by Mayo Methot calls her gangster lover a *mamzer* (bastard) and contemptuously refers to an Atlantic City Elks' convention as a *geshtank* (stench). Warners' *Lawyer Man,* which premiered two months later, has William Powell awkwardly speaking a few lines of pidgin Yiddish. Indeed, until ethnic Jews disappeared from the screen in the mid-thirties, Yiddish phrases continued to pepper a number of Warner movies, including *Employees Entrance* (1933), *The Mayor of Hell* (1933), *Wild Boys of the Road* (1933), *Lady Killer* (1934), and *Wonder Bar* (1934), in which Al Jolson reads the *Forverts* in blackface. (Eddie Cantor's early talkies are similarly filled with Yiddishisms, as are the animated cartoons produced by Max and Dave Fleischer.)

8. The Artef audience, Teller noted, transcended race and religion, including left-wing "zealots," "followers of the avant-garde," "unkempt Greenwich Villagers, and Park Avenue culture-slummers in minks and tuxedos." The Artef influences were nearly as varied. With its emphasis on a dynamic choreographed ensemble and the integration of set and performers, the Artef brought to New York the intensity of the Soviet-Jewish theaters, mixed with the Weimar agitprop of Brecht and Piscator. (Simultaneously, its combination of political and artistic commitment helped build an audience for the Group Theater, which staged its first production in 1931.)

9. Compare the opening of Cahan's *The Rise of David Levinsky:*

the metamorphosis I have gone through strikes me as nothing short of miraculous. I was born and reared in the lowest depths of poverty and I arrived in America—in 1885—with four cents in my pocket. I am now worth more than two million and recognized as one of the two or three leading men in the cloak-and-suit trade in the United States. And yet [my inner identity] impresses me as being precisely the same as it was thirty or forty years ago. My present station, power, the amount of worldly

happiness at my command, and the rest of it, seem to be devoid of significance.

10. For the older generation, the idea of a love-match was itself an exotic fantasy. In *A Walker in the City,* Alfred Kazin's memoirs of a Brownsville childhood, the writer recalls a prevailing belief that "love . . . was something for the movies, which my parents enjoyed, but a little ashamedly. They were the land of the impossible." Kazin remembers that, on those rare occasions when his mother put away her sewing machine and attended a picture show, "she would return, her eyes gleaming with wonder and some distrust at the strangeness of it all, to report on erotic fanatics who were, thank God, like no one we knew."

The Stadium Theater—"the great dark place of all my dream life"—was located next door to the modest wooden *shul* where Kazin received his religious training: "That poor worn synagogue could never in my affections compete with that movie house, whose very lounge looked and smelled to me like an Oriental temple. . . . In the wonderful darkness of the movies there was nothing to remind me of Brownsville." Nothing perhaps until *Zayn Vaybs Lubovnik* and *Uncle Moses* played the Stadium a few years later.

11. In another sense, however, *Uncle Moses* did announce a new epoch for Schwartz. In the fall of 1932, he made a dramatic return to Second Avenue with a spectacular adaptation of I. J. Singer's *Yoshe Kalb.* The novel, a panoramic spectacle of Chasidic degeneration and nineteenth-century Polish-Jewish life, had caused an uproar almost from the moment the *Forverts* began serializing it in early 1932. Eclipsing the modest success of *Uncle Moses, Yoshe Kalb* was the single most celebrated production of the New York Yiddish stage. Several weeks after William Schack hailed Schwartz's "ambitious" production in the *Times,* lead critic Brooks Atkinson's front-page rave in the Sunday drama section insured its crossover success. Schwartz had the theatrical sensation of that dismal winter. Numerous celebrities—Charlie Chaplin, George Gershwin, Albert Einstein—trekked to Twelfth Street to see *Yoshe Kalb,* which played the entire 1932–33 season. Schwartz spent the next few years trying to capitalize on this breakthrough, following up with a similar pair of spectacles (both flops), while fruitlessly negotiating an MGM contract. Finally he took *Yoshe Kalb* on tour and spent two and a half seasons in Europe.

Overleaf: **Somewhere in Belorussia, summer 1932: on location during the filming of *Nosn Beker Fort Aheym,* the only feature-length Yiddish talkie produced in the Soviet Union.**

13

Jews of Steel

FOR A TIME in the early 1930s, the Soviet Union seemed immune to the Depression that had gripped America and Europe. Sometime *Variety* correspondent Eugene Lyons reported that the streets of the Soviet capital, "its shops, street-cars, markets, theaters, movies, museums, [were] everlastingly crowded, pushing, noisy."

The country is in a fever of construction that strains every nerve and muscle. Giants are going up and miracles being accomplished without the aid of the outside world, in the face of opposition from the outside world. . . .

Borya, camera-man, has just returned from "shooting" a talking picture in the Donets basin coal-fields. Dmitri, director, starts today for the Dneprostroi hydro-electric site to do a film. For neither of them is the moving-picture industry a means of acquiring wealth or mansions or sunken bathtubs. It is a glorious weapon in the battle for higher cultural levels, greater industrial production, more rapid laying of the foundation of socialism. . . .

Dmitri's "vehement eloquence," Lyons wrote, was beyond his own capacity for transcription:

Eisenstein and Pudovkin, he thinks, have had their day. Their epoch is past—epochs can be crowded into a few years or a few months in Russia. They are futurists, symbolists, "degenerate Mayakovskys of the screen." New leaders are crowding forward—leaders like himself, of course—to meet film demands of the new epoch, to picture the terrific tussle between the past and the future on the battlefields of the present, these battlefields being the collective farms, new plants, grain-factories, mechanized mines, universal education. . . .

That the first Soviet sound-film, Abram Room's compilation-documentary *Plan Velikikh Rabot* (Plan for Great Works; 1930), would celebrate the Five Year Plan was hardly coincidental. Talking pictures arrived just as the Communist Party began implementing a crash program for industrialization, collectivized, agriculture, and the consolidation of state power. Indeed, after viewing three early sound features in 1931, Stalin himself decided to divert additional resources to the development of this new technology.

As Lyons observed, the "command economy" provided filmmakers with a new propaganda mission that linked their work to the overall task of building Soviet industry. Thus Dziga Vertov's *Enthusiasm* (1931) extolled the miners of the Don basin to fulfill the plan in four years and Alexander Dovzhenko's *Ivan* (1932) was a paean to the Dneprostroi hydroelectric dam. Significantly, *Ivan* was also the first Ukrainian talkie. (Nevertheless, silent films continued to be made through 1936. In April 1934, the *New York Times* reported that only 1 percent of the Soviet Union's 30,000 movie theaters were equipped for sound. Two years later, half the nation's theaters were still silent and there were still many prerevolutionary handcranked projectors, particularly on the collective farms.)

In the Soviet Union, as elsewhere, however, sound threatened the universality of the silent film. The question of national cinemas was bound to arise. Yuli Raizman's *Zemlya Zhazhdyot* (*The Earth Thirsts*) virtually allegorized this dilemma. In this late silent, produced by Vostok-kino (a studio created in 1928 to make films for the Crimea, North Caucasus, and Volga regions, as well as Siberia and Buriat-Mongolia) and rereleased in 1931 with a postsynchronous soundtrack, a group of idealistic young engineers (one Russian, one Turkmen, one Jew, one Ukrainian, one Georgian—all Communists) overcome local superstitions to construct a canal in a remote Turkmenian village.

Less homogeneous in its representation of minority culture, Belgoskino's first sound film, Yuri Tarich's one-reel *Poema Imemi Osvobozhdeniya* (Poem of Liberation; 1931), featured traditional Belorussian, Polish, and Yiddish songs. Unlike the Ukraine, the Belorussian S.S.R. had been organized as a multinational state, with Yiddish one of four official languages. Many non-Jewish Belorussians spoke some Yiddish, which throughout the twenties and into the thirties was extensively used on posters, street signs, and façades. (Nina Sirotina, an actress with the Moscow GOSET who grew up in Gomel, a city with a large Jewish population, recalls seeing silent movies with Yiddish intertitles.) In 1932, Belgoskino went a step further with *Nosn Beker Fort Aheym* (Nathan Becker Goes Home), known in English as *The Return of Nathan Becker,* a feature-length Yiddish talkie starring Solomon Mikhoels.[1]

Released almost simultaneously, *Nosn Beker* and *Ivan* were the ethnic components in a cycle of now-forgotten talkies dealing with social conflict and epic industrialization—most of them released to coincide with the fifteenth anniversary of the October Revolution. Alexander Marchet's *Dela i Lyudi* (Jobs and Men; 1932) pitted a Russian worker against an

American engineer during the construction of the Dneprostroi power station; Friedrich Ermler and Sergei Yutkvich's *Vstrechnyi* (Counterplan; 1932) pictured "bourgeois specialists" sabotaging work targets at a Leningrad factory; Boris Barnet's *Okraina* (Outskirts; 1933) evoked divided national loyalties in a Russian village during the World War.

But, if the party's new emphasis on "socialism in one country" mitigated the significance of foreign revolutionary movements, and hence the propaganda value of Soviet policy toward certain of its own internal nationalities, *Nosn Beker* suggests the importance placed on addressing American Jews. If nothing else, Belgoskino's film gave the idea of Jewish national aspiration a unique twist: After twenty-eight years in America spent "laying bricks for Rockefeller," Nosn leaves the land of breadlines and Depression for his Belorussian hometown and thence, having been reunited with his aged father, on to the new industrial center of Magnitogorsk.[2]

Nosn Beker spoke to the failure of American assimilation while offering a non-Zionist *aliyah* (return to Zion). Moreover, in dramatizing the liquidation of so-called "declassed" and "nonproductive" Jews and their migration out of their primitive *shtetlekh* and into the industrial cauldron of Great Russia, *Nosn Beker* was the first Soviet film to directly address the 150-year-old *"productivizatsia"* debate. (Holding that agriculture was productive and trade was not, Jews and Gentiles, Communists and Zionists had long engaged in both theoretical and practical attempts to transform Jewish middlemen into a "productive" social element.)

Aesthetically as well as ideologically, *Nosn Beker* is a complex artifact. The film was directed by Boris Shpis and Rokhl M. Milman from an original scenario by Peretz Markish, then the most widely pub-

Production still, *Nosn Beker Fort Aheym* (U.S.S.R., 1932). This film's codirector, Rokhl M. Milman, is in the foreground, studying a script.

lished and translated of Soviet-Yiddish writers; it weds a self-conscious Yiddish folk culture to the optimistic methods of the first Five Year Plan, melding the theatrical stylization of Mikhoels's Moscow GOSET to that of Leningrad's avant-garde Factory of the Eccentric Actor (FEKS). Shpis, who was evidently not Jewish, had been assistant director on *Shinel* (The Overcoat) and *S.V.D.*, two 1927 films by FEKS leaders Grigori Kozintsev and Leonid Trauberg. His first feature, *Chuzoi Pidzhak* (Someone Else's Jacket), a satire on the NEP, also released in 1927, was heavily populated by FEKSniks. Milman, married to a prominent economist and related to Osip Brik, served as assistant director on all five of Shpis's features, coscripting *Mstitel* (The Avenger), his 1931 semidocumentary on the modernization of the Tungus tribe in Siberia. David Gutman, who plays Nosn Beker, was also associated with FEKS, having appeared as the department-store owner in

Nosn's American colleague Jim (Kador Ben-Salim, left) and his father, Tsale (Solomon Mikhoels, center). The town cantor is suitably impressed: "This is your Nosn from America? How did he get so blackened . . . like the earth?"

Kozintsev and Trauberg's 1929 *chef d'oeuvre, Novyi Vavilon* (New Babylon).

The "eccentric" elements of *Nosn Beker* are indistinguishable from the propagandist ones. America the decadent is briefly (and pragmatically) represented by stock footage of the Manhattan skyline. A startling *hommage* to the most radical aspects of silent Soviet technique depicts a boat sailing out of New York harbor intercut with a stroboscopic montage of cars, cosmetics, and can-can dancers—the images, culled mainly from German magazines, some held as briefly as two frames. A mock lyrical shot of garbage floating in the harbor provides a segue to Nosn on the ship. Like the hero of the then-popular Soviet novel *Jack Vosmerkin the American*, Nosn is returning to his native village to serve the

Revolution. "Well, Mayke, we are going home," he tells his dubious wife (Elena Kashnitskaya). The couple are traveling with Nosn's black colleague, Jim (Kador Ben-Salim). "You, too, are going home," Nosn adds.

An actor whose mere presence signified American injustice, Ben-Salim had recently appeared in P. Kolomoytsev's *Chernaya Kozha* (Black Skin), a 1931 Ukrainfilm production that favorably compared Soviet racial attitudes to those of the United States; his first and most famous role was as the street acrobat Tom Jackson in the popular Civil War adventure *Krasnye Dyavolyata* (Red Imps) and its four sequels. Although Ben-Salim is used more as a prop than a performer in *Nosn Beker,* his appearance in the Belorussian *shtetl* is a subject for mild vaudeville humor. "Is he a Jew too?" asks Nosn's father, Tsale (Mikhoels). "He is a bricklayer," Nosn replies with consummate political correctness. The town cantor rushes over to Tsale's hovel, shakes Jim's hand and is suitably impressed: "This is Nosn? Your Nosn from America? How did he get so blackened . . . like the earth?"

Unlike Jim, however, the figure of Nosn was not completely exotic. The early thirties saw a small immigration from the United States back to the Soviet Union. In his memoirs, Lyons reports that "the news that Russia had liquidated unemployment and was in dire need of labor power brought hundreds of foreign job hunters to Moscow." Most, however, were disappointed. "Even where they had specific mechanical trades, only one in a hundred managed to cut through the jungles of red-tape around Soviet jobs." According to Lyons, by the year of *Nosn Beker*'s release, "these hordes of stranded Americans became a real problem."

Nosn Beker has received scant attention in Soviet cinema histories although, in a 1935 essay on "Film Art in Soviet White Russia," it was singled out for particular praise by Sergei Dinamov, the youthful editor of the important *Literary Gazette*. A dogged opportunist with the disarming manner of a country schoolteacher, Dinamov had set the tone of the January 1935 All-Union Creative Conference on Cinema Affairs when, as presiding officer, he defined the basis of the new Soviet cinema as "optimism, heroism, and theatricality." Dinamov publicly rebuked Kuleshov, Eisenstein, and Pudovkin, but writing the same year on *Nosn Beker* he displayed far more enthusiasm:

The artist, the producer, and the [camera] operator have shown here with great force the life of a Jewish townlet that preserved its old appearance during the first years after October. Houses that look like dovecots, brick buildings that look worn out by age. The brick does not at all resemble brick, it looks so rotten and chipped. And the people still breathe the pre-October air.

Years go by. Into the life of the townlet there breaks in the fresh wind from far-away Magnitogorsk, where grand industrial construction is in progress. Old Becker and his son Nathan, just returned from America, go out to work there. . . . Magnitogorsk opens up a new world to both the father and the son, but they conceive it differently. The regenerated townlet after the Revolution has re-educated the old man Becker. . . .[3]

"There are beautiful and fascinating passages in this picture," Dinamov concludes. "The language is succulent, the words sinewy and precise. The author of the scenario, the well-known Yiddish writer Peretz Markish has splendidly coped with his task."

Markish, the lone Soviet-Yiddish writer to receive the Lenin Prize (awarded to him in 1939, the year Dinamov was arrested and executed), was born 1895 in the Volhynian *shtetl* of Polonnoye, where he received a traditional *kheyder* education and rebelled against it at an early age. In her memoirs, his wife, Esther, describes him as practically another Jolson.

When Peretz was about seven, he developed a remarkable voice and began to sing in the synagogue. But as time went on he began to feel pent up in his father's ramshackle house with its small opaque windows, and stifled in the *shtetl,* with its hunched-over Jews weaving fantasies of a better life and its omnipresent white goats wandering through the twisting streets. At the age of ten, he ran away from home to the hamlet of Romanov, where he sang in the synagogue and led a free but half-starving existence until he moved on to Berditchev.

A flamboyant, Byronic personality, Markish started writing poetry at fifteen and soon established a precocious reputation as one of the Kiev group. In 1921, he left the Soviet Union for Warsaw, where he remained long enough to collaborate with I. J. Singer on an anthology of avant-garde Yiddish writings and serve as an early editor of *Literarishe Bleter,* before departing on a whirlwind international tour. He had not, however, lost his faith in the Revolution, and after five years abroad returned to the Soviet Union.

Given the political concessions Markish would subsequently make, one wonders whether, as the story of an exile's chastening, *Nosn Beker* conceals a certain amount of veiled autobiography. Still, in Moscow as in Warsaw, Markish was a prime literary model for the new Jewish youth. His two-volume novel *Dor Oys, Dor Ayn* (A Generation Goes, A Generation Arrives), published in 1929, is fiercely antitraditional. A wooden synagogue in a Ukrainian *shtetl* is described as looking "as if it were wearing shingle rags and sinking into the earth." The temple is stooped and hunched, "its crooked back carrying the women's section with the tiny windows the way you carry a paralytic." The atmosphere inside is "stale," smelling of "grease, of wax, of parchment, and of gingerbread and vodka."[4]

As though consigning the misery of the Diaspora to the dustbin of history, *Nosn Beker* gives less authority to tradition—even as an adversary—than any previous Soviet-Yiddish film. The movie opens in a miserable tumbledown *shtetl* populated mainly by old men, stray dogs, and ragged children. Unlike

the Ukrainian settings of Granovsky's *Jewish Luck* and Gricher-Cherikover's *Through Tears,* this dilapidated Belorussian village is eerily underpopulated, halfway toward becoming a ghost town. Although the *shtetl*'s haunting sense of emptiness and abandonment carries inadvertent associations with the catastrophic, manmade famine that even then was decimating the Ukraine, the film is probably an accurate representation of *shtetl* conditions. In his *Where the Ghetto Ends,* a survey of Jewish life in the new Russia that was published in 1934 and takes as its epigram Harry Alan Potamkin's poem "The First Collective, Ukraine," Leon Dennen interviews a lonely old woman in a *shtetl* outside Kiev:

Her daughter is a teacher in Moscow. Her son is somewhere in far off Siberia, Biro-Bidjan. They send her money but she has seen neither of them for many years.

This, without exaggeration, was the story of every inhabitant of the town. The revolution has robbed them of their children. The youth has deserted them. It has gone off to the cities, where new industries are rising, where there is activity and life. The former ghetto youth is today dispersed all over Russia.[5]

Nosn's arrival draws a crowd of urchins, layabouts, and beggars. The rumor has spread that he is "a commission from America bringing dollars." A pathetic *klezmer* plays his clarinet and sings a toneless ballad about poverty and starvation: "With such a song you would become a rich man in America," Nosn tells him, expansively.

Intentionally or not, this opening parodies the 16mm home movies made by successful immigrants of their Old World villages. But even as the returning son is greeted by old Tsale, the town is honored with another distinguished visitor. A pretty *Komsomolka* appears in an official car to recruit workers to help build Magnitogorsk. (As she steps from the automobile, promising "a truckful of work," one urchin steals her shoe.) An enthusiastic mob abruptly materializes, chanting the mysterious name "Magnitogorsk" as though it were a sacred spell, falling over themselves in their desire to leave the *shtetl* for the steel city beyond the Urals.

Constructed in the first frenzy of the Five Year Plan on an empty steppe on the eastern slope of the Urals, Magnitogorsk symbolized Soviet industrial growth: "A quarter of a million souls—Communists, kulaks, foreigners, Tartars, convicted saboteurs and a mass of blue-eyed Russian peasants—making the biggest steel combinat in Europe in the middle of the barren Ural steppe," the American welder John Scott wrote in his firsthand account of the city's rise. "Money was spent like water, men froze, hungered and suffered, but the construction work went on with a disregard for individuals and a mass heroism seldom paralleled in history."[6]

The new arrivals included 40,000 Jews. Indeed, one of the outstanding figures of Five Year Plan literature—David Margulies, the "positive hero" of Valentin Kataev's 1932 celebratory novel of Magnitogorsk, *Time, Forward!*—is nominally Jewish. However, as an engineer, Margulies was distinguished mainly by his profession; most of the workers who flocked to Magnitogorsk were unskilled, with bricklayers in particular demand at the beginning of 1933.

Nosn is assigned to the Central Institute of Labor as an instructor, along with a German specialist who has been imported to teach the workers movements that combine efficiency, artistry, and pleasure. (This unspecified form of Taylorism suggests the theories of the theatrical director Ippolit Sokolov who, dismissing Meyerhold's biomechanics as unscientific, believed actors must be trained like workers to synthesize "physical culture and the labor process.") As Magnitogorsk produces steel, so it also transforms the unproductive. "Are they studying to become actors?" the incredulous American asks. "The worker plays his work as though it were a piano," the instructor explains, and the solicitous, optimistic construction leader Mikulitch adds that "the backs of the workers are as important to us as the building of the wall."[7] Unconvinced, Comrade Becker petulantly overturns the table on which the bricks have been arranged: "Piano they play? Why not hire musicians then? *Meshugoim!*" The American considers his Soviet comrades madmen. Unpacking his trowel, he proposes an "American-style" competition. "I will show them who works better, *Sovetisher klezmer* or American bricklayer."

The *Daily Worker* would observe that "twenty-eight years of intense economic struggle to live have left their mark on Nathan Becker. He has become a machine, an automatic robot. . . . The new type of Soviet worker whom he now meets, a new man with a new outlook on life, is incomprehensible to him." The *Worker,* however, missed the nuance. Nosn is not robotic enough. As Katerina Clark points out in her 1981 study of socialist-realist literature, the industrial utopia envisioned during the Five Year Plan embraced such automation: "It was often claimed, especially in fiction, that human psychology could be changed by putting people to work at machines: inexorably, the machine's regular, controlled, rational rhythms would impress themselves on the 'anarchic' and 'primitive' psyches of those who worked them."

Tsale Beker watches the contest intently, along with the Jewish elders who have also left the *shtetl* for Magnitogorsk. By the seventh hour, their American champion is exhausted. As the unflustered Russian forges ahead, Nosn vainly remembers the movement class he scorned. Humiliated, he decides to return to America: "Any boy here knows how to work better than I do." His wife reminds him of the American unemployed fighting for soup, and his father explains that "these are different times," but Nosn is determined to leave until Mikulitch confronts him: "You're not in America. We're not going to fire you. We're going to learn from you. But you must learn from us, too."

The chief of operations praises Nosn's work—he was working more efficiently, but tired sooner than his rival—and suggests combining the systems. The synthesis of American and Soviet techniques will increase production.[8]

Clearly, *Nosn Beker* was made with at least one eye on the American audience—Yiddish-speaking elders as well as ardent young Communists. Virtually every ad in New York's Yiddish press stresses the spectacle of *"alte Yidn in dem nayem Rusland"* (old Jews in the new Russia). In the end, the know-it-all *Amerikaner* must acknowledge his father's wisdom. ("You keep on quarreling with us, Nosn. You keep on fighting," is Tsale's fond, recurring reprimand.) Structurally, at least, the movie has a conservative bias. In the Yiddish literature of the Five Year Plan, the generational schism is wider and the emphasis more upon the new Soviet youth.[9]

Despite its tendentious narrative, *Nosn Beker* is a surprisingly playful movie. As the advertisement in the *Morgn Frayhayt* proclaimed when the film opened in New York: "Jewish workers, this is your

yontev [holiday]!" (Subsequent ads advised readers to "Share May Day with the First Yiddish Talkie from Soviet Russia.") In fact, *Nosn Beker* did celebrate a relative improvement for many Soviet Jews: the popular anti-Semitism of the NEP receded as the Five Year Plan created tens of thousands of new jobs. (Not only were previously "unproductive" Jews now able to find acceptable "proletarian" occupations but, in the tensions that arose when disparate peoples were brought together in vast work projects, Asians more often bore the brunt of prejudice and violence.)

Nosn Beker is at least as full of comic routines—one of them devoted to the old men of the *shtetl* signing up for the "shock brigade" as it is steeped in Stalinist propaganda. "There's a definite strain of the native Jewish sense of humor," *Variety* would observe. "A Soviet film that has definite laugh situations! That's news in itself." The reviewer added that "a lad named S. M. Mikhoels plays the part of a stuttering old Jew with beautiful perfection." The forty-two-year-old Mikhoels, who uses a mysterious mixture of Russian and Yiddish, is delightful. Indeed, the fractured language he speaks is virtually his own—interspersed with chuckling, clucking, and the continual humming of a *nign*.

As he had in *Jewish Luck,* Mikhoels constructs his persona out of stylized bits of business. It's an overwhelmingly tactile performance—as precise as ballet. (In one comic throwaway, Mikhoels picks up a handy bust of Marx, stares at it, and reflectively strokes his own beard.) While glum David Gutman is a stolid proletarian type with a generic resemblance to William Bendix, looking more like Mikhoels's brother than his son, Elena Kashnitskaya is also something of a comedienne whose constant confusion about the date (she is always asking when it will be *shabes*) is a joke on the Five Year Plan's notorious "continuous-production week" of four workdays followed by one day of rest.

Given the light mood, it seems appropriate that a circus would provide the site for the competition between Nosn and the Soviet bricklayer. (If Shpis and Milman here acknowledge their FEKS background, according to John Scott, the circus was Magnitogorsk's most popular form of entertainment; and although "the performance was of third-rate Barnum and Bailey quality" and "occasional attempts to tie up the program with the construction of socialism in one country or with plan-fulfillment in the plant tended to be ludicrous," seats had to be booked well in advance.) Still, despite the absence of a harsh moral or strong positive hero, *Nosn Beker Fort Aheym* fulfills Andrei Zhdanov's capsule formula for socialist realism—"a combination of the most matter-of-fact, everyday reality with the most heroic prospects."

True to its genre, the movie ends with a hymn to labor. "We must win. We will win," the chorus sings. "Long live the day of victory!" Meanwhile, the camera peers up at happy Nosn perched on the scaffolding beside old Tsale and the ever-beaming Jim. "Here the workers work not only with their hands but also with their hearts," the American rhapsodizes. "And also with their heads," his father adds. In a final gag that recalls the exercises of the Institute while proposing its own sort of folk Taylorism, Tsale instructs Jim in the fine points of his ubiquitous *nign*, complete with appropriate hand gestures.

Nosn Beker Fort Aheym, **final scene: atop a construction site in Magnitogorsk, Tsale (Solomon Mikhoels) instructs Jim (Kador Ben-Salim) in the finer points of his ubiquitous** *nign;* **frame enlargements.**

NOTES

1. *Nosn Beker* exists in both Russian and Yiddish versions. The latter may have been just for export; in any case, it is only the Russian version which, missing its first reel and perhaps other material, survives in Soviet archives. (The policy of dubbing "nationality films" into Russian for exhibition outside their native republic continued into the 1980s.) A few fragments of the Yiddish version have been found. That the two versions may have had other differences is suggested by Wolf Kaufman's *Variety* review of the Yiddish version: "For no good reason, along about the middle of the film, there's an insert from a previous Russian talker, *A Jew at War* [Roshal's *A Man from the Shtetl*]." No such insert exists in the Russian material.

Other early non-Russian talkies include Goskinprom's *Posledni Maskarad* (The Last Masquerade), released in 1934, and Armenkino's *Pepo*, released in 1935.

2. Like *Jobs and Men*, *Nosn Beker* also belongs to a group of early talkies involving foreign visitors to the Stalinist utopia—including *Tommy* (1931), wherein a British soldier is converted to Bolshevism, and Pudovkin's 1933 *Deserter*, which concerns an exiled German Communist. The most ambitious exercise in proletarian internationalism was undoubtedly *Black and White*, an English-language film conceived in early 1932 to dramatize American race problems. The original plan was to use Russians in burnt cork to play the black steel workers of Birmingham, Alabama; it was later decided to import real blacks from America. On June 14, 1932, twenty-two actors (among them Langston Hughes) set sail from New York and wound up in Moscow for a well-publicized debacle. The movie was never completed; it may have been a casualty of improved relations between the Soviet Union and the United States.

3. Reeducated in some respects, that is. As Jay Leyda notes in *Kino*, Mikhoels speaks a markedly purer Yiddish than Gutman, whose command of *mame-loshn* has presumably been corrupted by America.

Of course, this was not necessarily how the movie was perceived in the United States. When *Nosn Beker* opened in New York, the strongly anti-Communist *Forverts* scored the actors' use of a "Moscow Yiddish" that "is certainly pure but not quite Jewish." Because "the Soviet Yiddish stage has dropped the rich, melodious Ukrainian dialect in favor of *Litvish* [Lithuanian] Yiddish, with *echt* Russian pronunciation, one often has the impression that some of the actors in this Soviet talkie are struggling to

speak the language. Each word has to be hammered out." (The writer found Mikhoels mannered but exempted him from this criticism, noting that in the theater where he saw *Nosn Beker* the actor more than once received spontaneous applause.)

4. Despite his progressive anticlerical attitudes, Markish was targeted for criticism in the shifting climate of the Five Year Plan. After his novel was published, he was publicly rebuked as a nationalist by Moyshe Litvakov (himself trying to establish his militant credentials) for exhibiting a "national apologetic point of view" in making his revolutionary protagonists all Jews and ignoring class divisions in the *shtetl*. Markish responded that no one objected to a Russian novel "which has only Russian revolutionaries."

5. The sense of entropy is emphasized by Yevgeni Brusilovski's mournful score and the accompanying montage of crooked roofs and empty, unpaved streets. (Like more than one Soviet-Jewish artist, the twenty-seven-year-old Brusilovski became an ethnic specialist, writing the first Kazakh operas and symphonies.)

6. Magnitogorsk was the crucible of the Five Year Plan. Nineteen thirty-two also brought Joris Iven's fifty-minute documentary paean *Pesn o Geroyakh* (Song of the Heroes), scored by Hanns Eisler, which focused on the building of a blast furnace by members of the Komsomol and the transformation of a nomad into a model worker.

7. Boris Babochkin, who plays Mikulitch with appropriately radiant cheer, became a national hero two years later in the title role of the enormously popular Civil War drama *Chapayev*.

8. This conclusion not only sent a fraternal message to American Communists, it also smacks of applied Eccentrism. In their admiration for the dynamism and unpretentious populism of American mass culture, FEKS theorists declared that the art of the future would be a Russian version of American "vulgarity." Proletarian poets like Alexei Gastev also imagined adding "the pulse of America" to "the hurricane of revolution." In the late twenties, even Stalin spoke of fusing "American efficiency with Russian revolutionary scope."

Two years later, Markish published a novelization of his script titled *Eyns af Eyns* (One Plus One). Again the contrast was made between Soviet and American work habits, lifestyles, and ideologies. In the novel, however, the line is somewhat sterner: Nosn gradually comes to understand that, despite hardships and inefficiency, the new Soviet way of life is, on the whole, superior to that of America.

9. The quintessential Jewish positive heroine is Elke Rudner, freethinking protagonist of *Der Step Ruft* (The Steppe Calls), published in 1931 by twenty-five-year-old Note Luria. A wise and courageous *Komsomolka,* Elke is dispatched to the depths of the Ukraine where she successfully organizes a kolkhoz of "traditional" Jewish farmers. Youth knows best. In H. Orland's 1935 *Aglomerat,* the young people of the Ukrainian *shtetl* form a "shock brigade" to construct a blast furnace; their parents, meanwhile, pray for the factory to fail so that the children will return to them.

In this light, the literature is truer than *Nosn Beker* to the actual situation. In his history of the Yevsektsia, Zvi Gitelman observes that, as Jewish Communists "failed to associate Yiddish with progress, prestige, and modernization," the language—which was now virtually the only acceptable expression of Jewish identity—was fatally linked to Jewish underdevelopment. Thus, during the first Five Year Plan and after, "when the city and the factory throbbed with the excitement of construction and development, Jewish identity was seen as superfluous and stultifying, as something to be cast off as quickly as possible."

Overleaf: **Flyer advertising** *Dem Rebns Koyekh,* **a reissue of the silent** *Tkies Kaf* **with a dubbed Yiddish soundtrack. Joseph Buloff, who provided the narration, is given star billing.**

14

The *Faryidisht* Film

THE HOLLYWOOD of the 1930s may have been the center of world film production, attracting emigré talents from every nation, but New York City was the capital of international film exhibition, populated by substantial immigrant communities from all over the globe. Perhaps no city in the world exhibited so many foreign movies: in 1936, the *New York Times* conservatively estimated the weekly audience for non-English-language films at 100,000 patrons. The number of foreign releases increased spectacularly throughout the decade—in 1937 alone, some 350 opened in New York. Although a number of theaters specialized in foreign films per se, others were devoted to specific languages. With the arrival of sound, virtually every ethnic enclave supported its own specialty house.[1]

In Manhattan, the first feature-length Yiddish talkies appeared at the Acme or the Clinton. The former, located just below Union Square, specialized mainly in Soviet films. The latter, a run-down, cavernous theater on Clinton Street north of Delancey, one of the most congested and clamorous areas of the Lower East Side, had been showcasing Yiddish vaudeville since the World War. A week or two after their East Side premieres, popular films might move over to the Palestine, an even more dilapidated theater off Houston Street, or open at neighborhood movie houses in the Bronx, or in Brownsville and

Williamsburg, the two largest (and poorest) Jewish sections of Brooklyn.

For the general public, as well as the New York State Board of Censors, Yiddish films were considered foreign films, even when they were produced in New Jersey. In this sense, they were part of a larger phenomenon. New York was not simply a distribution nexus for ethnic cinema, but a production center for all-black and foreign-language movies. After abandoning their ambitious, multilingual production facility in Joinville, Paramount shot two Spanish-language Carlos Gardel vehicles at their Astoria studio (where *Bonjour, New York,* a French short with Maurice Chevalier, and *The Golden Kimono,* the first Japanese talkie, were also filmed).

"Race" movies had been produced in New York since the early 1920s, while, on an even more subterranean level, the Dnipro Film Company struggled unsuccessfully for three years to complete a Ukrainian feature. The firm was liquidated in 1927 but the next decade would bring a trio of Ukrainian features and several documentaries, as well as the Armenian-language "Persian operetta" *Arshin Mal Alan* (The Peddler Lover), directed by and starring Setrag Vartian. Indeed, the world's first Serbo-Croatian talkie, *Ljubav i Strast* (*Love and Passion,* also known as *Born to Kiss*) was made in New Jersey by a team of Yugoslav immigrants under the direction of Hollywood veteran Frank Melford. (This hour-long musical, which starred Melford's wife, Raquel Davidovich, opened in Yorkville in late 1932 but was never shown in Yugoslavia.)

Although rigidly defined by audience, the New York ethnic films overlapped in technical facilities and creative personnel: Yiddish actor Louis Weiss coproduced *Uncle Moses* (on which Frank Melford served as assistant director) in 1932 and the all-black

Drums o' Voodoo the following year. Edgar G. Ulmer directed both Yiddish- and Ukrainian-language movies—and also *Moon over Harlem.* Joseph Seiden made films for black as well as for Jewish audiences. Experimental filmmaker Josef Berne "graduated" first to Yiddish movies and then to Spanish-language versions of Hollywood pictures.

Like all independent productions, ethnic films were characterized by low budgets and pragmatic craft. The most radical example of this pragmatism, however, was unique to the Yiddish film industry. This was the transformation of silent films into Yiddish talkies—a practice that testifies to the uncritical nature of the market, the ingenuity of independent producers, and the sheer pleasure audiences derived from hearing Yiddish at the movies.

The reworking of existing films also attests to the degree of access that Jews had to the medium and predates the invention of sound. If the young Lumière agent Francis Doublier was the first to create a Jewish-interest film out of non-Jewish footage, he was scarcely the last. Zygmunt Turkow decried such practices in a 1925 article written for *Literarishe Bleter,* reporting his amazement at finding a Równe movie house announcing a film, *Yidn fun Sibir* (Jews of Siberia), starring Clara Young and Molly Picon. "Anyone who knows anything about our theater world knows that such a match has not yet been made. But so what? Two famous names—they want 'names.' So much for truth in advertising!"

In Zamosc, Turkow continued, the streets were plastered with posters advertising *Fun Yidishn Lebn* (From Jewish Life), a movie supposedly based on the current Yiddish stage hit *Yoshke Muzikant.* Surprised ("*Yoshke Muzikant* filmed? When? What?

Where?"), he went to see for himself and discovered "an old *shmate* made before the war, a story with a musician, a servant, and a bourgeois son, with *a shtikl pogroml* [a bit of a pogrom] thrown in for good measure." *Fun Yidishn Lebn* was not only not *Yoshke Muzikant* but nearly devoid of any Jewish material. "To the crime of slapping a fresh label on shoddy merchandise, let us add the film's special merits," Turkow railed.

There is not a single Jewish face, not one good actor, and not the slightest Jewish content. We cannot forget that the appeal of a Jewish movie is its special atmosphere, the *shtetl* ambience. Here, there are no Jewish images, even a cemetery is tastelessly depicted—crude wooden markers and extras with shampoo'd cat's tails pasted on for *payes*.

Talking pictures presented new possibilities for such exploitation; in general, the rush to sound produced all manner of hybrids. During the winter of 1931, both *The Birth of a Nation* and *Way Down East* were rereleased in New York with added soundtracks. Other spectacles followed: *Maciste in Hell* dubbed a prewar Italian epic; the anti-Bolshevik *Forgotten Commandments* cannibalized footage from Cecil B. De Mille's silent *Ten Commandments*. Almost immediately, Jewish showmen realized that antique silent films, particularly Biblical epics, could be inexpensively recycled as "spectacular" Yiddish talkies.

Even before *Mayn Yidishe Mame* had its premiere, Chicago-based Yiddish actor-impresario Adolph Gartner had ballyhooed something called *Joseph and His Brethren* as "the first Jewish talking picture in the world." There is no record of this movie being shown in New York, but two and a half years later, in the fall of 1932, Gartner and his wife Jennie were barnstorming midwestern cities with another film (in which they starred), *The Sacrifice of Isaac,* the "First Yiddish Biblical Talkie Picture Produced." In addition to the Gartners, the film boasted "a cast of ten thousand, a five-hundred-voice choir, and a one-hundred-person orchestra." Less successfully, Asher Chasin attempted to rework the silent *Destruction of Jerusalem* as a Yiddish-English talkie to publicize the work of the Joint Distribution Committee. (According to Judith Goldberg, Chasin sought to raise money for the project—to be known as *Kaddish*—by charging prospective participants for lessons in acting or filmmaking.)

The leading practitioner of this dubious form was George Roland—not, apparently, Sidney Goldin's onetime assistant, but a New York–based editor employed by Warners to rework their foreign releases. Roland specialized in refurbishing silent films by adding a minimal dramatic frame and a maximal Yiddish voice-over. His first opus, made in 1931 with Abraham Leff, was *Avrom Ovenu* (Our Father Abraham), also known as *The Wandering Jew;* it was fashioned from the silent *Story of the Bible* and augmented by a few synchronous-sound sequences set in a *shul* (as well as some wildly inappropriate music from Grieg's *Peer Gynt*). Later that year, Roland transformed a 1914 Italian film, *Joseph in Egypt,* into a Yiddish talkie, dubbing a narration and filming a small amount of new footage.

Joseph Seiden developed a similar mode. In September 1931, the same month *Zayn Vaybs Lubovnik* opened at the Clinton, Seiden's Judea firm released *Di Shtime fun Yisroel* (The Voice of Israel). This ten-reel, $20,000 "special" was a homemade epic created by splicing together all manner of scenes from silent movies (some dating back to before the World War).

Flyer advertising *Di Umgliklikhe Kale,* a 1932 rerelease with dubbed Yiddish soundtrack of Maurice Schwartz's 1926 silent *Broken Hearts.*

The apocalyptic imagery—ranging from volcanic eruptions to staged pogroms to travelogue shots of Palestine—is knit together by an English voice-over and interpolated with performances by some of the most celebrated cantors of the period. According to Seiden, *Di Shtime fun Yisroel* was a *succès d'estime* but a box office failure: "Alas and alack . . . while we received plenty of praise, we almost went broke with our first classic."

Seiden's partners took this moment to sell their interests in Judea. Before long, however, the resilient mogul hit upon a more profitable form of recycling old films—taking as raw material the silent Yiddish hits of the twenties. Thanks to the "Seiden Sound System," Judea released a talking version of the Molly Picon vehicle *Mazel Tov* in May 1932. The silent footage was accompanied by sound effects and framed by a sequence in which an old woman relates the story of Molly's visit to Galicia. Solomon Krause

and Abraham Armband, the scenarist of *Avrom Ovenu,* are listed as directors. The same month, Gloria Films capitalized on the release of *Uncle Moses* with a dubbed version of Goldin's 1924 *Yisker,* also starring Maurice Schwartz. Outfitted with a new opening and a rendition of Kaddish, the movie credited Roland as director.

As the Depression took its toll on independent film production, 1932 marked the high-water mark of the recycled silent. Quality Films put out *A Yidishe Tokhter* (A Jewish Daughter), known in English as *A Daughter of Her People* and refashioned by Roland out of Henrik Galeen's 1921 German production *Judith Trachtenberg.* As with *Yisker,* the silent footage is framed and punctuated by a sync-sound sequence in which the plot is narrated and discussed —in this case, by a group of young people gathered around "the grave of a Jewish *meydl.*" That year as well, Henry Lynn used Seiden's technology to release a sound version of Schwartz's *Broken Hearts,* opportunistically retitled *Di Umgliklikhe Kale* (The Unfortunate Bride) after a recent, if unrelated, Yiddish stage hit.

If the rereleasing of silent movies with soundtracks was by no means limited to Yiddish producers, Roland, Seiden, and Lynn felt unusually free to rework the original material. *Di Umgliklikhe Kale* is not just *Broken Hearts* as narrated in Yiddish and accompanied by bandleader Art Shryer's blend of Slavic folk songs, Strauss waltzes, and Yiddish laments. The new version reverses the resolution of the original generational drama; what had been a triumph of secular Jewishness becomes a punitive and reactionary tragedy of patriarchal justice. In part, this is accomplished by re-presenting the original as a cautionary tale told by a bearded elder (Yiddish radio personality Michael Rosenberg) to his nubile granddaughter and young grandson. The "text" of *Broken Hearts* is further ruptured with an assortment of cantorial clips and Rosenberg's repeated injunction against violating the fifth commandment. Most drastically, Lynn truncates the original narrative to suggest the death of the rebellious Ruth, and thus eliminate her climactic conjugal reunion and simultaneous reconciliation with her family.

Roland subsequently recycled the 1924 Polish feature *Tkies Kaf* as *Dem Rebns Koyekh* (The Rabbi's Power), known in English as *A Vilna Legend*. Again the narrative was propelled by a group of bearded performers, with Joseph Buloff relating the story to his tavern cronies. As with *A Yidishe Tokhter,* the poet Jacob Mestel was credited with the dialogue, although Buloff appears to have put his own sardonic spin on his lines at least. Finally, in November 1933, Joseph Burstyn's Worldkino—a leading distributor of foreign art films, including *Nosn Beker Fort Aheym* —released the 1928 Soviet silent *Through Tears* as *Motl Peyse dem Khazns* (Motl Peyse the Cantor's Son). Known in English as *Laughter Through Tears,* this sound version had a score by Sholom Secunda and narration by Michael Rosenberg.[2]

Poster advertising *Motl Peyse dem Khazns* as "the newest talking picture from Soviet Russia." This dubbed rerelease of the 1928 silent *Through Tears* was held over for seven weeks after opening at the Acme Theater in November 1933.

As the intermittently visible, but continually and overpoweringly audible stars of *Dem Rebns Koyekh* and *Motl Peyse,* name performers like Buloff and Rosenberg suggest a Yiddish analogue to the Japanese silent-film narrator, or *benshi,* whose function was to instruct the audience by explaining the movie, even to the extent of elaborating the obvious. That the first films to be shown in Japan were by and large foreign *actualités* doubtless stimulated the development of this convention. One suspects that part of the *benshi*'s job was to "naturalize" imported movies and make them more Japanese—and in this, too, his role parallels that of the Yiddish narrator.

Before the film screening, the *benshi* made a ceremonial entrance and took his place on a platform beside the screen. During the course of the movie, he supplied the characters with voices and provided a running commentary—often, according to Noel Burch, "repeating himself in chanting patterns if he ran out of anything new to say." Although producers sometimes distributed a dialogue script with their films, the *benshi* was not compelled to hew to it. Indeed, a strong *benshi* was sufficiently individualized to make a picture his own. Ultimately, the *benshi* became a movie's most important attraction. Protected by cost-conscious producers, a strong union, and twenty years of convention, this institution served to delay the introduction of Japanese talking pictures well into the 1930s.[3]

A cross between a *benshi* and *badkhn,* the Yiddish narrator gives a performance—involving all manner of invented dialogue, humorous commentary, interpolated chants, colorful hyperbole, and highly coded cultural references. Not simply explaining the action, he deepens the allusions in a way that cannot be fully conveyed by the typically sparse subtitles. The Spanish and Yiddish intertitles of *Lágrimas Judías,* the surviving silent version of *Through Tears,* introduce the sturdy and industrious Bruche as her family's "only ray of sunshine"; in Rosenberg's pithier, less sentimental narration, the audience is told that "she would like to hear dishes breaking"—meaning she's anxious to be married. Later he adds an earthy dimension to a meeting between Bruche and the wistfully amorous Elye by announcing he is attracted to her "like a cat to sour cream." And when mail arrives, the narrator speculates gratuitously that "maybe there's a letter from America," reminding the audience of its privileged position vis-à-vis the less fortunate Jews on the screen.

This parallel discourse matches the expressive gestures of the actors which, particularly in the GOSET-inflected *Through Tears,* might be considered a form of Jewish kabuki. The Yiddish narrator stands outside the text and describes the images as they appear, always in the immediacy of the present tense. The film is thus returned to an oral tradition, albeit one mediated by Yiddish radio (a source of work for numerous stage actors). "Now the *khasene* [wedding] starts," Rosenberg announces as a flashback shows Russian police breaking into the printshop where Elye had his last job. And when errant Motl is called to account by the irate *melamed,* the narrator treats the situation as a sporting event: "So begins the big trial of the little orphan. The rabbi is racking his brain—he's wondering what sort of punishment he should award this little *pogromnik.* The best thing to do would be to send him to Siberia."

In *Dem Rebns Koyekh,* Buloff maintains a constant chatter, commenting on the action, supplying motives, dramatizing the characters with various comic voices. Occasionally, his jokes are predicated on foreknowledge of a scene's development: when the provincial hero Yankev arrives at his antagonist Shmuel Levine's impressive Vilna home, he immediately dons a *talis,* wraps himself in *tfilin,* and begins to pray—thus embarrassing the assimilated son of the house. Young Levine is "like a *baleboste* [housewife]," Buloff explains, as the character, perhaps searching for some bit of theatrical business, perfunctorily moves some objects around and hastily makes his exit. "First, he must straighten up—then he'll pray."

More frequently, however, Buloff's comments suggest the spontaneous witticisms of a sarcastic member of the audience. (His presence in the tavern sequences suggests the ironic, sleepy-eyed attitude of a bemused hipster.) In one scene, Yankev surreptitiously removes his *yarmulke* to blend in at a party where other, more secular young people are gathered around the piano to sing "Orchi Chiornia" (undoubtedly a Polonaise in the original). When Yankev is later seen having his *payes* cut, Buloff remarks, "Now he can hear 'Orchi Chiornia' better." Similarly, the narrator spices the engagement banquet (which so offended the reviewer from *Literarishe Bleter*) with his own wisecracks: "This one is attacking the chicken as if it were her husband," he says of a particularly greedy guest.

Rosenberg, too, must fill every second, especially since as the narrator he is specifically identified with author Sholom Aleichem. Indeed, *Motl Peyse* was not only dedicated to the memory of the "beloved folk artist," but manages to evoke the quality of his prose. Mimicking the author's literary ventriloquism, the garrulous Rosenberg plays a virtual Jewish stock company, distinguishing the various comic characters through vocal timbre and phrasing: the tailor Shimen-Elye is high-pitched and querulous, the duplicitous innkeeper is expansive and hearty, the *melamed* is given a deep mumble, the Russian police are hoarse and guttural, speaking a menacing, broken Yiddish.

"From the very first moment" in Sholom Aleichem, the critic Sh. Niger observed, "the reader likes the *narrator* more than he likes the story itself." The same was true of the dubbed *Motl Peyse*. Writing in the *Forverts,* Mendel Osherovits praised extravagantly the "operation" that the American distributor performed upon the Soviet original. On the one hand, the movie seemed so authentic that it might be a documentary; on the other, Rosenberg's vocal characterizations exhibited such charm that "it hardly seems to be the invisible narrator who is speaking, so much as the figure you see on stage [*sic*]." Osherovits called *Motl Peyse* "an amazingly successful combination of sound and picture" observing astutely that had the movie been an actual talkie, it would likely have been less compelling than this hybrid. (Indeed, "The Enchanted Tailor," from which much of the original film was derived, is among Sholom Aleichem's most remarkable performances—a mock-epic that employs Biblical repetitions, distorted quotations, and a complex interplay of Yiddish and Hebrew to underscore the tailor's unjustified pride in his Talmudic knowledge.)

Rosenberg is less detached and ironic than Buloff, and like the *benshi,* he occasionally vamps by repeating certain phrases or tropes (Elye's "empty pockets," Pinye's "quick millions") until the image becomes almost tangible and the film a form of illustrated radio. A performer unafraid of excess, Rosenberg at one point bursts into toneless singing to suggest the clamor of the *shtetl* marketplace and uses other incidents as the occasion for the equivalent of stand-up set pieces: whereas in the intertitles of *Lágrimas Judías* the *melamed*'s wife describes her goat as merely "the best goat in Russia," Rosenberg launches into a full-scale satire of a *shtetl* hard sell, insisting that the animal will bring *"glik un mazl"* (happiness and good fortune) for the next 120 years and extolling the animal's *"yikhes"* (pedigree)—conventionally used to convey the prestige of a distinguished Talmudic scholar. Later, in a corresponding bit of hyperbole, he will have Shimen-Elye's wife, Tsipe-Beyle, refer to the creature as her *"bashert,"* a term for one's true love.

An even more elaborate and multilayered example of Rosenberg's artistry occurs when the Russian policeman drags Motl home for selling tainted cider. "Look at how he's licking his chops," Rosenberg-the-narrator says of the cop before adopting the persona of Tsipe-Beyle to sweet-talk the official—promising him that she will punish Motl ("he will lay in the ground with broken bones"), grandly refusing to stand on ceremony (*"protokol-shmotokol"*) even while she simultaneously curses the cop under her breath ("You should burn!") and encourages him to try a piece of her homemade pastry ("Taste! Taste!"). Once the policeman begins to eat, Rosenberg resumes his identity as narrator without missing a beat: "Look at him stuffing his face."

Although Rosenberg never contradicts the image, his narrative inevitably changes the nature of the film. In this there is a striking precedent, namely the tendency of the nineteenth-century Yiddish press and stage not simply to translate Gentile literature but to render it *faryidisht* (more Jewish). Jacob Gordin's transpositions of Shakespeare to Vilna and Ibsen to the Lower East Side are only the most celebrated examples. His *Jewish King Lear* and *Nora* were preceded by a Yiddish version of Gogol's *The Inspector General* and are contemporary with *Der Yeshive Bokher,* a version of *Hamlet* set in a rabbinical court. Similarly, Yiddish newspapers "borrowed" Maupassant, Flaubert, even Nietzsche—while modifying the originals for their readers.

Motl Peyse is also *faryidisht* in the literal sense that it intensifies the original's Jewish elements. (The *faryidisht Tkies Kaf* does this by simply using the title *Dem Rebns Koyekh,* exaggerating the importance—as well as the strength—of an extremely marginal character.) Expressing the prevailing attitude of Jewish Communists toward the *shtetl,* the original *Through Tears* emphasizes unemployment, starvation, and tsarist oppression, while establishing religious leaders as footpads of the bourgeoisie. *Motl Peyse* does not efface this representation—indeed, Sholom Secunda's score emphasizes a bit of mass action with a few bars of the Marseillaise—but, by its very nature, Rosenberg's homespun narration introduces another set of historical and religious associations.

The cinematic Esperanto of which Soviet film theorists dreamed is here radically particularized. Just as Yiddish words and metaphors continually, effortlessly, and inevitably draw upon the most popular aspects of Jewish observance, so does Rosenberg's description of the action. In his introduction of the characters, he establishes Tsipe-Beyle's bad temper by suggesting that she beats the Yom Kippur scapegoat (usually a chicken) "every Monday and Tuesday." The *melamed*'s arrival is likened to that of the *malekhamoves* (angel of death); when Motl, who has to mind the *melamed*'s baby, watches the other children at play, "his heart feels like it's Tishabov" (a

reference to the gloomy holiday commemorating the destruction of the Second Temple in A.D. 70).

Shimen-Elye, who curses the name of Jew-hating Haman when his goat changes sex, spends the second half of the movie humming "Had Gad-ya," the concluding song of the Passover seder that, despite its childlike structure and appeal, has been traditionally seen as an allegory of Jewish history. Even more dramatic is Rosenberg's use of the Yom Kippur chant *Al T'shlikheyni,* in which the supplicant begs God not to abandon him. Rosenberg chants this prayer as Motl Peyse's father dies, and repeats it at the end of the film when Shimen-Elye and family are driven from the village. Like the other liturgical references, it locates Jewish suffering in the context of the Diaspora rather than the class struggle.[4]

From a formal point of view, *A Yidishe Tokhter* is a somewhat more drastically *faryidisht* film, as it was not taken from a proto-Yiddish silent. The source of the original movie is a novella by the nineteenth-century Austrian author Karl Emil Franzos. Franzos, like his contemporary Leopold Ritter von Sacher-Masoch, wrote a number of stories and feuilletons on the "exotic" customs of Galician Jews—many of them concerning fatal liaisons between Polish or Hungarian nobles and Jewish girls.

In Galeen's version, *Judith Trachtenberg,* the Jewish heroine meets a Polish count at a ball given by the local prefect and becomes his lover. Her family casts her out but the count takes her in; when she becomes pregnant, he arranges a false marriage because local law forbids his marrying a Jewess. Meanwhile, Judith is condemned as an apostate by the Jewish community, which goes so far as to bury her in absentia—

even though it is her father who has died (of humiliation). The count finally travels to the more tolerant state of Sachsen-Weimar to make a legal marriage, but Judith cannot reconcile herself to excommunication and takes her life by drowning.

To make this grim tale more palatable to his audiences, Roland alters the chronology so that Judith first elopes with the count and is then rejected by the community. The original footage is further *faryidisht* through the introduction of Hebrew prayers on the soundtrack and an interpolated, synchronous-sound scene in which Judith is mourned by an entire synagogue. The whole story is placed in a Jewish context —not only by virtue of its Yiddish narration (delivered in a poetic, incantatory fashion by Joseph Green) and the cautionary framing story, but also through the introduction of a new character. The town rabbi appears at regular intervals throughout the film to be apprised of Judith's apostasy, to comment upon her sin, and, finally, to recite Kaddish for her.

A similar Yiddishization is the item that Harry S. Brown released in April 1934 as *Oy di Shviger!* (*What a Mother-in-Law!*) The original footage is taken from *The Lunatic,* a 1927 silent film starring Ludwig Satz; the framing footage features Max Wilner and Paula Klida as a married couple, and an unidentified actor, most likely Jacob Mestel, as Wilner's "Uncle." (As with *A Yidishe Tokhter,* the dialogue is credited to Mestel.) *Oy di Shviger!* has an appropriately vaudevillian frame story. Wilner and Klida quarrel about the radio (he wants to listen to a Yiddish program, she doesn't), then make up and sing a duet. The uncle comes to visit his nephew; Klida leaves the men to sit around the characterless movie set and drink. A discussion of mothers-in-law

Opening title for *Oy di Shviger!,* the 1934 *faryidisht* version of the 1927 silent *The Lunatic;* frame enlargement. The "all-star cast" is not further identified, and except for Ludwig Satz, no credits are given for the original film.

provides the segue into the original film, which is narrated by Wilner.

It is Wilner's task to *faryidish* the original, which is set in a world of flappers and society functions and —save for the presence of Satz and a brief street scene affording a glimpse of one storefront with Hebrew characters—has no Jewish content whatever. Wilner does what he can, calling the crying baby entrusted to Satz a *"khaznte"* (female cantor) and providing Satz with a mock-Talmudic formula to chant after he spills the milk he's heating for the child: "Half for you, half for me, half for the stove." Given the movie's haut-bourgeois setting, however, the narrator's discussion of dowry, marriage contract, and *get* (religious divorce) is totally incongruous. In effect, *Oy di Shviger!* attempts to reverse the process of assimilation.

Movies like *A Yidishe Tokhter* and *Oy di Shviger!* not only approximate the effect of the Japanese *benshi* but invent the strategies later employed in Woody Allen's *What's Up, Tiger Lily?* (1966) and Peter Bogdanovich's *Voyage to the Planet of the Prehistoric Women* (1968), both ingeniously fashioned for American-International Pictures out of "unreleasable" foreign genre-films. Although it is unlikely (but not impossible) that Allen was influenced by *faryidisht* movies, *What's Up, Tiger Lily?* could well be the inspiration for *The Cowboy,* a ten-minute clip from a 1932 Bob Steele western (*Son of Oklahoma*) that was dubbed into Yiddish in 1968 and distributed in 16mm as a novelty item. (The joke of unassimilated Jews on the range is one of the oldest and most resilient tropes of Jewish-American show business, with antecedents in late-nineteenth-century Yiddish vaudeville and in nickelodeon films; Erens finds seven versions released between 1908 and 1915.)

As *The Cowboy* testifies, *faryidisht* material was not always originally silent. *Le Golem,* Julian Duvivier's 1936 remake of the German silent, first released in New York in March 1937, was dubbed into Yiddish for a second run six months later at the Clinton, Ascot, and People's theaters. (The original film which, although shot on location in Prague, was spoken in French, had already impressed American reviewers with its authenticity for presenting sections of Jewish liturgy in Hebrew.) At least one film appears to have been *faryidisht* in Poland. In December 1938, Best Films released a dubbed Yiddish version of the Polish comedy *Pietro Wyzej* (The Apartment Above), directed by Leon Trystan and retitled *Shkheynim* (Neighbors).[5]

In 1939, Henry Lynn *faryidisht* the 1933 British version of *The Wandering Jew,* a Conrad Veidt vehicle directed by Maurice Elvey. This piece of goods required far more radical alterations than *Judith Trachtenberg.* Lynn mitigated the original's anti-Semitic premise—its protagonist is a Jew who spat upon Jesus on the road to Calvary and thus doomed himself to roam the earth until the Savior's return—by cutting over an hour's worth of footage (including all references to Jesus), and dubbing in Ben Adler's impassioned, nationalist Yiddish narrative. The sixty-five-minute result, mainly scenes of Veidt coping with the Roman Empire and Spanish Inquisition, was released as *Dos Eybike Folk;* it was known in English variously as *A People Eternal* and *A People Who Shall Not Die.* Outrageously advertised as "the first million-dollar Yiddish film spectacle," *Dos Eybike Folk* opened at the midtown Miami Theater in late October and played the New York metropolitan area through April 1940, at times on a discordant double bill with *Shkheynim.*[6]

NOTES

1. In Yorkville, the Eighty-sixth Street Casino, Seventy-ninth Street Theater, and Deutsche Lichtspiel presented German productions; a few blocks downtown, the Tobis showed only Hungarian films, and the New Annex was a bastion of Czech imports. Many Harlem movie houses regularly exhibited all-black features, while the Cervantes on 110th Street screened Spanish-language films from Mexico and Argentina. Soviet movies were featured downtown at the Acme and midtown at the Cameo. Two Broadway theaters, the Cine-Roma and the World, were devoted to Italian movies which might later be given second runs in the city's Italian neighborhoods; similarly, Polish features were shown at a number of midtown houses as well as the Chopin and Roosevelt on the Lower East Side.

2. This enormously popular movie opened at the Acme and was held over for an unprecedented six weeks. The Acme followed its success with the sound-effects version of VUFKU's *Eyes That*

Saw, known in Yiddish as *Motl der Shpindler* (Motl the Weaver) and in English as *A Simple Tailor*. Far from repeating the first *Motl*'s success, the second was run out of the neighborhood by *Der Kholem fun Mayn Folk* (*The Dream of My People*), a feature-length cantorial *cum* travelogue with Yosele Rosenblatt, which opened the same day for a limited run at the Yiddish Art Theater, less than five blocks away. *Der Kholem* subsequently displaced *Motl der Shpindler* at the Acme, where it played three weeks before returning to the Yiddish Art Theater for another two. Surpassing even *Motl Peyse*'s success, *Der Kholem* played the Clinton two more weeks, while enjoying hold-overs throughout Brooklyn and the Bronx. (It may not be entirely coincidental that the Acme followed up with the New York premiere of *Sabra*, a Polish feature shot in Palestine by Aleksander Ford using performers from Habima.) In May 1935, Worldkino released a dubbed version of Granovsky's *Jewish Luck*, again narrated by Michael Rosenberg. The film's Yiddish title, in the U.S.A. as in the U.S.S.R., was *Menakhem Mendl*; in English it was called *The Matchmaker*.

3. Although the *benshi* has antecedents in such specifically Japanese forms as *kabuki* and *bunraku*, pre-1910 American nickelodeons sometimes employed the native equivalent of a "lecturer." This practice was never codified and rapidly disappeared, but there is reason to believe that theaters catering to non-English-speaking audiences may have continued to supply live narration. I have been told, but have not been able to verify, that piano players in pre–World War nickelodeons sometimes translated English intertitles into Yiddish.

4. In 1932, Tel Aviv exhibitor Ya'acov Davidon used an American silent, *The Bible* (1920), as the basis for a new movie. Davidon, who often reedited foreign films for local consumption, augmented the Old Testament stories with contemporary images of Zionist settlers. In lieu of a soundtrack, he provided a live narration in English and Hebrew and at one point encouraged the audience to join in song.

Davidon subsequently dubbed several Yiddish talkies into Hebrew. (These include the Polish films *Al Khet* and *Yidl mitn Fidl*, and the American movies *Dem Khazns Zundl* and *Shir Hashirim*.) The most elaborate production was the Soviet *Through Tears*. For this, Davidon recalls in his memoirs, he had to travel to an Italian-owned studio in Alexandria where he spent a month working on the soundtrack. Considering the size of his audience, however, the process proved too expensive. Although Davidon had acquired the rights to *Jewish Luck* and *Uncle Moses*, he put them on the shelf. The former was restricted to ciné-clubs, the latter waited until after 1948, when Yiddish movies could be shown openly.

5. It's telling that, for the most part, New York's English-language dailies were oblivious to the dubbing and regarded the film as a breakthrough. The *Daily News* hailed *Shkheynim* as "one of the few Yiddish films to divorce itself from the traditional appeal of orthodoxy, racial customs and copious scenic views of the old country"; The *World-Telegram* found "sequences and characterizations . . . so delightful in many instances as to remind one of Dickens or that Mark Twain of Jewish literature, Sholom Aleichem"; and the *Journal-American* called *Shkheynim* "highly promising for the future of Yiddish films." Only a few critics noted that the film had a New York run eleven months earlier as a Polish talkie.

6. By this time, *faryidisht* cinema had a sinister counterpart. In December 1938, the *New York Times* reported that "the Swedish film *Petterson and Bendel* has been made over for German use and will be given to all leading movie houses. It ridicules the Jews." Presumably the Nazi regime dubbed and/or recut the original film, which dealt with the relationship between two business partners (one of them a Jew), to accentuate its anti-Semitic elements. Two years later and even more drastically, the Nazis would incorporate footage from the 1938 Polish-Yiddish talkie *Der Purimshpiler* in the notorious pseudodocumentary, *Der Ewige Jude* (The Eternal Jew).

Overleaf: Played by Gertrude Bullman, the heroine of Henry Lynn's *Di Yugnt fun Rusland* (U.S.A., 1934) is a lively *Komsomolka* whose affection for her old-fashioned father (Wolf Goldfaden) cannot dampen her enthusiasm for the new Soviet regime.

15

Between *Rusland* and *Daytshland*

W HEN *Nosn Beker Fort Aheym* opened April 14, 1933, at the Europa Theater on Fifty-fifth Street east of Seventh Avenue, the exultant *Morgn Frayhayt* celebrated with a short review by editor Moissaye Olgin, then the most influential Jewish Communist in America. Olgin offered a few *pro forma* criticisms—"Jewish kolkhoz workers are hardly mentioned," Jewish poverty is "overemphasized," "problematic social conditions are barely touched upon"—but hailed *Nosn Beker*'s triumphant demonstration of "how the Soviet state straightens the back of the Jewish masses and makes yesterday's *luftmentshn* into Builders of Socialism."

It is fresh. It is real—with a reality we can only find in Soviet films. . . . The film is joyous. It sings. It laughs. It is crammed with humor. It is *amkhodik* [suffused with the spirit of the ordinary Jew].

Olgin concluded his piece by noting that a woman in the audience was astonished by the sight of official documents written in Yiddish: "Oh Comrade," he sang, "they write in Yiddish, they organize in Yiddish. . . . [This is] the road to Communism."

Not surprisingly, the more prosaic and analytical review in the *Forverts,* written by city editor Mendel Osherovits, found *Nosn Beker* as predictable in its propaganda as the most mediocre melodrama. This blemish, however, did not blind Osherovits to "some excellent scenes" and "wonderful Jewish humor." The critic deemed *Nosn Beker* inferior to the first

Soviet talkie *Putyovka v Zhizn* (*The Road to Life*), but "more artistic, better photographed, and of greater substance than the average, American-made Yiddish talkie."

Although dismissed by William Troy in the *Nation* ("from beginning to end the picture may be responded to as something either very important or grotesquely funny—according to one's point of view"), *Nosn Beker* seems to have been as popular as *Variety* had predicted it would be. The film ran four weeks at the Europa, then moved downtown to the Acme, a venerable, somewhat seedy movie house specializing in Soviet films and located across from the former headquarters of the American Communist Party, on Fourteenth Street. There, its two-week run included benefits for both the *Daily Worker* and the *Frayhayt*.

Like *Zayn Vaybs Lubovnik* and *Uncle Moses, Nosn Beker* was an event—particularly insofar as a year's worth of *faryidisht* silents had destroyed the reputation of Yiddish talking pictures. But while Osherovits's anticommunism was tempered by the demonstration of Soviet concern for Yiddish culture, the international climate had also changed drastically in the four months between *Nosn Beker*'s Moscow and New York premieres.[1]

The March 5 election that confirmed Nazi power in Germany was followed by a nationwide rampage in which Brownshirt gangs beat and arrested Jews and political opponents. The new regime sponsored a one-day boycott of Jewish businesses on April 1 and promulgated its first anti-Jewish legislation (forcibly retiring non-Aryan civil servants and banning non-Aryans from practicing law) on April 7, a week before *Nosn Beker* opened at the Europa. Indeed, Osherovits began his grudgingly favorable review by noting the significance of the venue: in presenting

this Soviet-Yiddish film, the Europa, hitherto a showcase for German-language talkies, was "apparently joining the protest against Hitler's violence towards the Jews."

The subject of the Nazi consolidation was not long in entering the American-Jewish public sphere. On March 27, the American Jewish Congress and *Der Tog* held a mass anti-Nazi rally at Madison Square Garden, where Senator Robert F. Wagner (a German-born Catholic), former governor Al Smith, Mayor John Patrick O'Brien, and a number of prominent Christian clergymen addressed a crowd of 55,000. Left-wing militants, who had already organized their own protests, considered the rally a pallid affair, but it was broadcast to Europe, as well as throughout the United States.

The first theatrical offering in the United States to address Nazi Germany was *City Without Jews*—the previously proscribed Austrian silent film *Die Stadt ohne Juden,* newly outfitted with a dubbed sound-effects track by distributor Nathan Hirsh (who had produced *Zayn Vaybs Lubovnik*). Promoted as an exposé of "the truth about Hitlerism," this remarkably prescient film opened on April 8 for a week's run at the Fifth Avenue Theater. On April 22, both the *Forverts* and *Der Tog* called for a boycott of stores selling German-made goods. In early May, the Clinton Theater featured a satiric play entitled *Hitlers Mapole* (Hitler's Downfall), while the American Jewish Congress organized a protest march through Manhattan. Police estimates put the crowd at 100,000.

That July, as anti-Nazi organizing gained momentum, one Herman Ross announced the formation of Jewish American Film Arts, which he compared in seriousness to the Yiddish Art Theater. With its first movie, *Der Vanderer Yid* (*The Wandering Jew*), produced later that summer at the Atlas studio on Long Island, JAFA would dramatize the situation of German Jews. The project involved several talents responsible for recycling old silents as Yiddish talkies, particularly director George Roland and screenwriter Jacob Mestel; more prestigiously, the film starred Jacob Ben-Ami, the sometime artistic hope of the Yiddish theater, as a persecuted German-Jewish artist.

The most ambitious American-made Yiddish talkie in the eighteen months since *Uncle Moses, Der Vanderer Yid* was conceived in the wake of the most dramatic American-Jewish response to the Nazi regime, the English-language spectacle "The Romance of a People." This elaborate pageant of Jewish history from the Creation to 1933 was intended to raise money for the resettlement of German Jews in Palestine. "The Romance of a People" had its premiere on July 3 at the Chicago World's Fair, and New York's *Daily News* planned to underwrite an even grander version at the Polo Grounds, home of the New York Giants, on September 14.

In addition to honorary sponsors Governor Herbert H. Lehman, Senator Wagner, and Mayor O'Brien, the pageant involved a cast of over 6,000 performers, mainly students from local Hebrew schools. Ben-Ami, now through with his chores for *Der Vanderer Yid,* was hired to direct them. Though warmed for the rest of the summer in the sun of constant publicity, "The Romance of a People" suffered a setback of Biblical proportions when, on the eve of the announced opening, New York experienced a four-day deluge. The venue was hastily switched from the Harlem stadium to a remote armory in the Bronx, and there the spectacle ran for

German-Jewish painter Arthur Levi (Jacob Ben-Ami) holds a portrait of his Aryan fiancée as his valet (screenwriter Jacob Mestel) awaits his decision. *Der Vanderer Yid* (U.S.A., 1933) was not only the lone Yiddish movie to depict the situation of Jews in Nazi Germany, it was also the first American feature film to do so.

six weeks before traveling on to Philadelphia, Cleveland, and Detroit.

"The Romance of a People" offered a powerful counterritual, an affirmation of Jewish identity in the face of the mass demonstrations that embodied National Socialism's particular synthesis of aggression, discipline, and aesthetics. By the summer of 1933, the Nazis had purged Jews from every aspect of German culture. Mestel, who had been an Austrian officer during the World War, made this the subject of *Der Vanderer Yid.* Although the film's dramatic premise—antagonistic Jewish and Christian artists competing for a woman's love in an environment of

"Shall it be Palestine, Argentina, Canada
. . . or Birobidzhan?": the Eternal Wanderer
(M. B. Samuylow, left) exhorts his son
(Jacob Ben-Ami) to continue the pilgrimage
in *Der Vanderer Yid.*

state-sanctioned anti-Semitism—carries traces of Joseph Lateiner's enormously popular *Dos Yidishe
Herts* (The Jewish Heart), first staged in 1908, *Der
Vanderer Yid* is less melodrama than exposé *cum*
visionary pep talk.

The film remains lost but its plot may be reconstructed from its reviews. Arthur Levi (Ben-Ami), a
great Jewish painter who has "been living in the
dreamland of [his] art," only experiences the new
German anti-Semitism when his masterpiece, a portrait of his Polish-born father entitled "The Eternal
Wanderer," is rejected by the Berlin Academy of
Art, which also asks for his resignation as a professor. Brownshirts are demonstrating in the streets and

a jealous rival takes advantage of the situation to woo
away Levi's Aryan fiancée who, although she loves
Levi, finds herself unable to "stand against an entire
nation."

When the Nazis decree that all Jewish culture
must be obliterated, Levi prefers to destroy his masterpiece himself. But just as he lifts his knife, a miracle occurs—the figure in the painting speaks to
him. The Eternal Wanderer then recounts the tragic
history of the Jewish people as illustrated by stock
footage of the Babylonian Captivity, the sacking of
Jerusalem, the Spanish Inquisition and a Russian pogrom, as well as the more positive images of Soviet
Russia ("a new order—maybe the future order of
the world"), the Spanish Republic, and contemporary
Palestine. Here, as in *Nosn Beker Fort Aheym,* the
generations are reconciled. The film ends with newsreel shots of the March anti-Hitler rally at Madison
Square Garden, as the Eternal Wanderer exhorts his
son to continue the pilgrimage and Levi wonders,
"Shall it be Palestine, Argentina, Canada . . . or Birobidzhan?"[2]

Like "The Romance of a People" *Der Vanderer
Yid* was a historical pageant, albeit a somewhat
cruder one. "Jacob Ben-Ami hurts himself here," *Variety* wrote, "a splendid actor, but in this instance
giving an amateurish performance and considerably
hampered by direction." Ben-Ami evidently agreed.
But, although he would later deny that he ever appeared in the film, *Der Vanderer Yid* originally received something close to a rave from the *New York
Times:* "This graphic account of the tribulations of
the Jewish people from the days of Pharaoh to those
of Adolf Hitler, produced in New York, grips the
spectator from start to finish. It is difficult to imagine
a more crushing indictment of Nazism and all its
works." (It is also difficult to imagine that some re-

viewers failed to recognize Roland's use of stock footage: "They spend money freely if one must judge by the lavish sets and innumerable mob scenes that cover the various historical periods," *Film Daily* remarked tartly.)

The *Forverts*, whose generally favorable notice did point out the source of the historical reconstruction, found this extended montage impressive but inappropriate. The movie's epic context was a distraction which served to "obscure the most powerful drama in Jewish history, the tragedy of the German Jews." Still, the film made a particularly strong statement. For this reason, perhaps, it encountered somewhat more opposition than the oblique spectacle "The Romance of a People." After certifying *Der Vanderer Yid* for exhibition, the New York State Motion Picture Board suddenly balked at the prospect of English subtitles—which effectively de-*faryidisht* the film.

A panicky Motion Picture Board memo dated six days after the original license was granted explains:

As originally presented in Jewish dialogue and titles, [the picture] contained an appeal merely to the Jewish people to maintain their religious ideals and standards through whatever difficulties, as had been their history in the past. *By putting English titles on the picture it became a propaganda picture. . . .* (emphasis added)

This "partisan appeal" to an English-speaking audience, it was speculated, "might create a good deal of friction and trouble, and possibly violence." Accordingly, the Motion Picture Board gave only provisional consent for the use of English subtitles, while reserving the right to demand subsequent cuts in the film, or ban the titled print outright, on the basis of public response. That response proved lukewarm, at least initially. *Der Vanderer Yid* opened at the Cameo on October 21. After a few weeks in midtown and a brief run at a pair of Brooklyn theaters, the film disappeared—an example of premature antifascist agitprop.

The next, made in English, would be *Hitler's Reign of Terror*, an independently produced melange of newsclips and dramatic reconstructions based on Cornelius Vanderbilt's visit to the Reich. The film opened in May 1934, the same month that the Film and Photo League leafleted Fox's New York offices to protest the pro-Nazi bias of the Fox Movietone newsreels and prevented the Broadway opening of the German propaganda epic, *S.A.-Mann Brand*. Nineteen thirty-four also brought two prestigious films that, although less blunt than *Der Vanderer Yid*, made some response to the Nazi regime. Both were historical spectacles dealing with the social construction of German Jewry and both would be "remade" by the Nazis in 1940.

The House of Rothschild, produced by non-Jew Darryl F. Zanuck for Twentieth Century, offered a sympathetic view of the world's most famous Jewish bankers. Praised by *Variety* for handling "the delicate subject of anti-Semitism with fact and restraint," *The House of Rothschild* topped *Film Daily*'s annual critic's poll, handily defeating *It Happened One Night* as the year's best film. *Power*, another tale of finance and oppression which opened at the Radio City Music Hall six months later, was the most expensive British film to date. It adapted Lion Feuchtwanger's best-selling novel *Jude Süss* and starred Conrad Veidt, fresh from his role in the less-sympathetic British production, *The Wandering Jew*.

Although Feuchtwanger, Veidt, and director Lothar Mendes were all German Jews, producer Michael Balcon was afraid that American Jews might boycott the movie. Apparently they did not. *Power* (which had already been staged as a play by the Yiddish Art Theater in October 1929) could still be found in the spring of 1935, playing neighborhood movie houses—including the Clinton—that specialized in Yiddish films. By that time, Jews had quietly disappeared from the American screen.[3]

Initially, anti-Nazi fare did not even have a large Jewish constituency. *Der Vanderer Yid* opened in midtown the same week that Ossip Dymow's contemporary drama *Daytshland Brent* (Germany Aflame) had its premiere at the Second Avenue Theater, as part of Joseph Buloff's attempt to upgrade the commercial Yiddish stage. *Daytshland Brent* was a resounding flop. ("The failure of this play to appeal to the Jewish public at all—it was withdrawn in a week—is more a matter for the psychologist than the dramatic critic," wrote William Schack.)

In view of this, perhaps it should not seem so remarkable that, alone among Yiddish talkies, *Der Vanderer Yid* does not seem to have had an initial theatrical run on the Lower East Side. The film would be revived with increasing success toward the end of the decade. In the autumn of 1933, however, the major hit on the Lower East Side—at least so far as Yiddish movies were concerned—was the *faryidisht* version of VUFKU's 1928 *Through Tears, Motl Peyse dem Khazns.* The problems of Russian Jews were more engaging than those of their German brethren.

Opening in early November, *Motl Peyse* was held over for seven weeks at the Acme (the "Rendezvous of the Intelligentsia"), a venue in front of which, according to a wry description published in the *New York Herald-Tribune,* a barker customarily exhorted passersby to enter and see "the world ablaze," "the whirl of revolution," and "the triumph of the work-

ing class!" Having once been the luxury nickelodeon showcase of D. W. Griffith's early films and later fallen into what the *Herald-Tribune* termed "the most dubious practices that a picture-house can indulge in" (pseudomedical sex hygiene lectures), the Acme now specialized in Soviet films, augmented by Film and Photo League newsreels, and a daily trailer urging diplomatic recognition of the Soviet Union. (Two weeks into *Motl*'s run, the U.S.A. and the U.S.S.R. did establish formal ties.) The Acme is a prominent landmark in Albert Halper's 1933 proletarian novel, *Union Square:*

> It was by careful glancing at the photos displayed in front and also the reading matter tacked onto the billboards that Officer McGuffy had first begun acquiring the extensive knowledge of Russian affairs which made him highly respected by his fellow officers.

Officer McGuffy's expertise also made him a true native of the Lower East Side, where postrevolutionary Russia remained a source of fascination. Given the class origin and national background of much of the Yiddish film audience, it is scarcely surprising that Yiddish film culture would overlap that of the pro-Soviet left. *Soviet Film News,* a free four-page flyer published by the Soviet film distributor Amkino during the early thirties, was printed in Yiddish as well as English and, throughout the decade, even the crassest Yiddish movie distributors made extensive use of the Amkino circuit.[4]

Just as the Acme received successful "'moveovers" from the Cameo, the Clinton occasionally picked up hits from the Acme—mainly sentimental spectacles like Grigori Roshal's *Petersburgskaya Noch* (Petersburg Nights) or the musical "jazz comedy" *Vesyolye Rebyata,* known in English as *Moscow Laughs.* In

November 1934—when even the incidental music for Molly Picon's current operetta, *Di Kale Loyft* (*Here Runs the Bride*), featured themes from the Internationale—the Clinton premiered the year's only original Yiddish talkie, *Di Yugnt fun Rusland* (*The Youth of Russia*). This seven-reel, two-set tragicomic exploitation musical was written and directed by sometime soap manufacturer Henry Lynn and produced by composer Jacob Stillman under the fraternal rubric Sov-Am Film.

As its title suggests, *Di Yugnt fun Rusland* depicts the conflict between Jewish tradition and the Soviet state in generational terms. The veteran Yiddish actor Wolf Goldfaden plays Israel Zlotopolsky, a former lumber dealer whom the Revolution has reduced to mending shoes. The elderly Goldfaden is particularly confused by the new marriage laws. His daughter Kaile (Gertrude Bullman) is a lively *Komsomolka,* whose affection for her old-fashioned father cannot bridle her enthusiasm for the Soviet regime. That this enthusiasm is overtly sexual—Kaile scandalizes Israel by taking five husbands in the course of a single year—is the source of the film's conflict as well as its audience appeal. *I'm No Angel* had been the past year's single biggest box-office attraction, and Bullman's cheerfully promiscuous young Communist is a sort of high-spirited Mae East. (*Di Yugnt* is lost, but existing stills show the buxom actress with her blouse torn, passionately embraced by an actor in Russian peasant garb, or perched upon a narrow bed in a most un-Yiddish state of *déshabillé.*)

Lynn has something for everyone, *Di Yugnt* is part generational melodrama, part political satire (after marrying the ridiculously Russified Comrade Goldberg, Kaile spends her fourth honeymoon watching a Red Army parade), and part pure vaudeville: the heart of the movie, in which a semiclandestine sab-

Poster for Henry Lynn's *Di Yugnt fun Rusland*. Despite the internationalism of its name, the Sov-Am Film Corporation was an American production company.

bath feast is intercut with Kaile's celebration of her fifth wedding, is a twenty-minute mixture of traditional prayers, Russian dances, and folk ballads ranging from "The Chinese Flower Song" to black actor Harry Miller's Yiddish rendition of "Der Rebe Eli-Melekh." The one thing that the movie is not is overtly anticommunist. The traditional Jews express bemusement at the new religion of work, but stoutly condemn the old regime of the tsar.

Released the year the Hollywood Production Code went into effect (and code-enforcer Joseph Breen prevented Lewis Milestone from making *Red Square,* a sympathetic treatment of Soviet life), *Di Yugnt* basically uses the new Russia as a pretext to discuss the sensational "issues" that once preoccupied the popular Yiddish stage. Kaile's fifth husband, significantly named Abrasha (Abraham), is a new synthesis of Jew and Communist who tells Israel not to be so harsh in his judgments ("We live under a new system") and argues against the rigid Jewish divorce law by narrating a cautionary one-reel flashback in which a traditional father's refusal to allow his daughter, an *agunah,* to divorce her long-gone husband results in her marrying a Christian.

Israel finds Abrasha "wise" but misled. Unlike *Nosn Beker,* there is no successful conversion—only the unmercifully sentimental deathbed finale in which Israel gives Kaile his blessing and Kaile wails that "Papa had hoped so much that somebody would be left to say Kaddish for him." This is the last line of dialogue. (According to the script, Abrasha looks at Kaile, then the assembled guests and "nods his head, as if to say, that would be demanding too much.") Somewhat jarringly, the final title takes a positive view of old Israel's passing: "With new

Returning to old Dudino from the Lenin kolkhoz, Venyamin Zuskin has seen the light. *Border* (U.S.S.R., 1935); frame enlargement.

hope, new vigor, the Youth of Russia marches onward." Not a major hit, *Di Yungt fun Rusland* ran two weeks at the Clinton with limited exposure elsewhere.[5]

In *Rusland* itself, *Nosn Beker Fort Aheym* proved an unrepeatable experiment. The film was virtually the last cinematic expression of Soviet-Yiddish culture. In 1933, Ukrainfilm unceremoniously canceled Vladimir Vilner's *Shtetl Ladeniu,* based on a popular comedy by the Ukrainian-Jewish writer Leonid Pervomaisky. Still, a last Soviet *shtetl* film was released in June 1935, two months before the formal proclamation of the Popular Front: Lenfilm's *Granitsa* (Border). One of several movies made during the transitional 1933–35 period emphasizing the hostile regimes (but fraternal workers) bordering the Soviet homeland, *Border* locates the prerevolutionary *shtetl* in contemporary Poland.

Old Dudino may be only a few miles from the Lenin kolkhoz and the Belorussian S.S.R., but clearly it is another world. Here, the worst of the old ways prevail. The oppressed Jews make a religion of their despair. A rich factory owner dominates the town's economic life, using the local rabbi as his front. Meanwhile, the superstitious villagers try to improve conditions by staging a "Black Crown," marrying the *shtetl's* oldest spinster to an eligible widower in the cemetery at midnight. The prospective bridegroom, a poor shoemaker, agrees only because the authorities have duplicitously promised to free his son, a Communist organizer, from jail.

When the wedding is disrupted by Polish soldiers, the bridegroom kills one and must be smuggled across the border into the Soviet Union. This prom-

A wedding canopy is raised in the graveyard in Mikhail Dubson's *Border*; frame enlargement.

ised land is never seen; the film ends with the *shtetl* underground singing a traditional Jewish song with "a new subject" that the shoemaker's would-be son-in-law (Venyamin Zuskin), has brought back from the fabled Lenin kolkhoz. Although Zuskin's sensitive clerk is still mourning the death of his fiancée, a sympathetic Zionist, the movie suggests a more international solution. In the final moments, his Belorussian comrade (Nikolai Cherkasov) joins fraternally in the *nign,* drawing deeply on his hearty baritone, jaunty cigarette, and proletarian smile.

Deliberately paced, shot mainly in close-up, and accompanied by Lev Pulver's spare, eloquent score, *Border* achieves a voluptuous stasis. The stark, misty Black Crown sequence, much of it framed by the Mogen David in the cemetery gate, is a lyrical grotesque worthy of Granovsky. (Also in the manner of GOSET is a synagogue scene wherein the deaf shoemaker and the rabbi converse in gestures, the latter praying all the while.) Writer-director Mikhail Dubson gives *Border* a tone at once comically anticlerical and subversively nostalgic—both attitudes amply evident in the lengthy opening sequence, set in a wooden synagogue. The cantor chants throughout as

A virtuoso cantorial performance opens the last Soviet *shtetl* film, Mikhail Dubson's 1935 *Border;* frame enlargement.

Dubson cuts back and forth between gossiping (or wailing) women and mumbling men. The service is presented as a virtuoso performance. When the *khazn* looks out the window and catches a peasant woman's eye, he flirtatiously redoubles his cantorial efforts. Although ostensibly intended to ridicule, the scene is as powerfully imagined as a child's first memory—the Soviet-Jewish cinema's last look back.[6]

NOTES

1. The same year as *Nosn Beker,* Lev Kuleshov took a similar theme for his first talkie, *Horizon,* and gave it much harsher treatment. Drafted when the World War breaks out and deserting soon after, Leo Horizon (Nikolai Batalov, also the star of *The Road to Life*) makes his way to New York, where he discovers his uncle Isaac and cousin Rose being evicted from their apartment. Horizon and Rose care for the elderly Isaac. When the girl runs away, Isaac commits suicide and Horizon enlists in the American army. His unit is dispatched to Russia to aid the Whites, but, deserting the imperialists once more, Horizon joins the Bolshevik cause. The film ends, some fifteen years later, with a comparison of Horizon, now a distinguished locomotive engineer, and a formerly wealthy man who cannot reconcile himself to the Soviet regime. *Horizon* followed *Nosn Beker* into the Europa and was panned by the *Daily Worker* both as disjointed filmmaking and as "mechanical in its presentation of the Jewish question."

2. In 1928, the undeveloped, sparsely populated region of Birobidzhan, bordering China in the Soviet Far East, was offered to Jewish colonists. Although it was rumored in Moscow that this distant outpost had been selected by Yuri Larin, an assimilated Jew with the dubious distinction of having sold Stalin on the idea of the "continuous work week," the 1930 disbanding of the Yevsektsia and the 1931 Japanese invasion of Manchuria made the prospect of a Jewish settlement in the Far East doubly strategic. By 1934, when the area was declared a Jewish autonomous region, Birobidzhan was an integral part of the Communist program.

3. The Hollywood moguls were notoriously loath to attack Hitler directly. Although the erstwhile head of Universal was agitated to discover that his native Laupheim had changed the name of Laemmlestrasse to Hitlerstrasse, the rulers of the dominant studio, MGM, were less perturbed. Louis Mayer received reassurances from his friend William Randolph Hearst that Hitler's bark was worse that his bite, while, upon returning from a 1934 trip to Germany, Irving Thalberg blandly reported that "a lot of Jews will lose their lives [but] Hitler and Hitlerism will pass." Although the Nazi regime would, by the end of the year, ban all movies with Jewish performers and close down Hollywood's distribution offices in Germany, Thalberg's view was that German Jews should accept their fate; outside pressure was counterproductive. Not until the eve of World War II did Hollywood weigh in, with Warner Brothers' *Confessions of a Nazi Spy.* According to Jack Warner, who reportedly considered a film version of "The Romance of a People" back in 1933, "no picture ever aroused so much bigotry and hatred as this one." The German government filed a diplomatic protest, the German-American Bund threatened Warners with a $5 million lawsuit. The studio hired extra security for the film's New York premiere, and in Milwaukee one theater showing *Confessions* was torched by Nazi sympathizers.

4. The Clinton was augmented as a first- and second-run Yiddish movie house by the Ascot and Radio theaters in the Bronx, and the People's Theater in Brownsville. All also showed Amkino releases. (The last two—as well as the Roosevelt, another Amkino affiliate on Houston Street—were run by former Judea mogul Moe Goldman.) In the late thirties, when a number of Yiddish talkies had premieres on Broadway, several (including such apolitical items as *Der Purimshpiler, Mirele Efros,* and *Der Vilner Shtot Khazn*) opened at the Cameo.

5. Despite the ample cheesecake, ambiguous political content, and lengthy discussion of Kaile's marital escapades, the New York State Motion Picture Commission was most offended by the liaison between an Asian woman and a black man, mandating the elimination of the latter's offhand remark, "Of course, Chong Lee and I are going to be married." (The film was, however, rejected by the British Board of Film Censors in the summer of 1935.) In early 1938, at the height of the Yiddish film boom, it was rereleased in New York as *Der Yidisher Foter* (The Jewish Father).

6. *Border* was praised in the Soviet film journal *Kino* as "an event in our art" and "a lesson in revolutionary vigilance." *Variety*'s Moscow correspondent found it reminiscent of *Humoresque* but "more genuine and less sentimental," predicting this "unpretentious" picture "should enjoy a world-wide Jewish nabe market." (Indeed, there does seem to be a line written particularly for the international audience. When one worker wonders why a Jewish kolkhoz has been named for Lenin, another explains that "for a Jew, he's a Jew. For a Russian, he's Russian. For Americans . . .") Nevertheless, the movie seems never to have had an American commercial release.

Overleaf: **Cast and crew of *Der Yidisher Kenig Lir* (U.S.A., 1935). Producer Joseph Seiden stands in the back row, fourth from the left; beside him, the star Maurice Krohner raises a glass. The movie recorded a long-running Federal Theater production of Jacob Gordin's Yiddish classic.**

16

Shund

WHILE NEW YORK's Yiddish theater enjoyed a final artistic flowering in the mid-thirties, this was hardly reflected in the first Yiddish talkies that were made once regular production was established. On the contrary.

With one dubious exception—Joseph Seiden's recording of the Federal Theater production of Jacob Gordin's *Der Yidisher Kenig Lir* (*The Jewish King Lear*)—the four features released between Passover 1935 and Passover 1936 drew upon the most hackneyed clichés of the Yiddish stage. *Bar Mitsve* (*Bar Mitzvah*), Henry Lynn and Jacob Stillman's 1935 follow-up to their Soviet exposé *Di Yugnt fun Rusland,* was as much an exploitation film as their first effort—this one trading on personality rather than

subject matter. The attraction was Boris Thomashefsky, now sixty-nine, the original superstar of the American Yiddish stage, in his first and only talking picture.

Thomashefsky was all of sixteen when, during the summer of 1882, he participated in New York's first Yiddish performance; within a decade of this hastily organized production of Avrom Goldfadn's *Koldunye,* the plump, curly-haired singer was a certified matinee idol. Less august than Jacob P. Adler, more darkly ethnic—a corpulent precursor of Rudolph Valentino—Thomashefsky billed himself "America's Darling," rode a horse on stage, and, backed by a full orchestra and a trained corps de ballet, pranced about like a professional wrestler, bare-chested in pastel tights. The stories of his excesses, like those of all poor boys who become deities, are legendary; he demanded his pay in gold and kept it in a money belt; he amazed the East Side with his chauffeured limousine and Asian valet; he made love to a different woman between each act of every show. Indeed, the National Theater that Thomashefsky built for himself on Houston Street had a dressing room fit for a pasha—sybaritism was part of the act.[1]

By the thirties, however, America's Darling had, like America itself, fallen on hard times—even before he fell into the hands of Stillman and Lynn. *The Singing Rabbi,* Thomashefsky's disastrous foray onto the English-language stage, ran less than a week in September 1931. Two years later, his International Music Hall, located on Southern Boulevard in the Bronx (where the Jewish population now exceeded Manhattan's), proved another costly failure, and the Great Thomashefsky was reduced to performing at a Rumanian steakhouse on Allen Street.

Thomashefsky's life story is a wondrous epic. *Bar Mitsve* is not. A melange of mismatched reaction shots, it gives the impression of having been shot in someone's apartment and assembled with a trowel. There are problems with focus, sound-blimping, and continuity; the scenario, based on a vehicle the star had written for himself a decade before, is scarcely more sophisticated than the technique. Thomashefsky plays Israel, a widower whose wife Leah was lost at sea ten years earlier en route to America. Now, in the company of his duplicitous fiancée Rosalia (Anita Chayes) and nubile daughter Birdie (Gertrude Bullman), he returns to his unspecified European homeland for the Bar Mitzvah of his son Yudele. Naturally, Leah (played by Thomashefsky's wife, Regina Zuckerberg) is alive, and, regaining her memory

on the very day of Yudele's entry to manhood, she appears, grasps the situation ("I can't live anymore, I'm going back to the ocean"), and then, bursting from her hiding place at the climax of her son's Bar Mitzvah speech (a homage to his dead mother), exposes Rosalia as an unscrupulous gold digger.

Although the drama is enlivened by crude special effects, as when Yudele's soul leaves his sleeping body to sing a duet with Leah's soul, liberated for the occasion from her portrait, Thomashefsky is the major attraction. Treated as a sacred monster throughout—his parents (Morris Strassberg and Leah Noemi) are introduced caressing his childhood *talis* and *tfilin*—Thomashefsky plays to the camera as though it were the second balcony. His scenes with Chayes are particularly outrageous. Vamping like Mae West, she sings to him seductively, while he, no less kabuki in his stylization, lets his mouth gape in a leer of erotic enchantment.

The word to describe *Bar Mitsve* is *shund*—a term of contempt indicating literary or theatrical "trash" and denoting variously an inept mishmash, a vulgar display, a mass-produced trifle, or a piece of sentimental claptrap. *Shund* encompasses the full range of Yiddish kitsch, from the primitive Biblical operettas that followed Goldfadn to the grim domestic melodramas that came to dominate Yiddish theater after the World War.

"*Shund* was the first art form to express the distinctively American Yiddish community." Nahma Sandrow has maintained, and in many respects, this *shund* became Americanized through the immigrant Jewish contribution to Tin Pan Alley, Broadway, and Hollywood—as Harry Alan Potamkin recognized when he linked the "melting-pot" hit *Humoresque* to the tearful Yiddish stage. Of course, Potamkin's withering scorn is no less characteristic. The Jewish intellectual is not amused by *shund*, but morally offended. In part, this is because *shund* can never be only *shund*. As Irving Howe has observed, "Whatever else *shund* may have been, it was not 'escapist' in any obvious sense; it coarsened and corrupted, but it drove right to the center of 'the Jewish heart.'" ("The Jewish heart," of course, is a standard *shund* trope.)

True *shund* must be uplifting, pandering variously to nationalist, family, or religious sentiments. In 1924, Thomashefsky had imperiously informed the *Jewish Theatrical News* that contemporary Yiddish plays "contain nothing about Jewish life and nothing that offers Jewish education. Ask an East Sider what it means to be 'bar mitzvah.' He can not tell you— he does not know. I am preparing a play called *Bar Mitzvah* in which it is all explained to him." Indeed, the play's hit song was an injunction to "Erlekh Zayn" (Be Virtuous). Thus, during the movie's climactic Bar Mitzvah, Yudele is presented with a prayer book that "has lived through persecutions and pogroms" and this injunction: "Study the world's literature. . . . Learn new languages but don't forget your own."[2]

A Jew, Israel explains, is not just a beard and *payes*. "One can be an aristocrat and still remain a Jew." Despite these enlightened sentiments, Thomashefsky's crude and passé vehicle failed to duplicate the excitement that greeted the first talkies by the younger stars Ludwig Satz and Maurice Schwartz. Nor did it approach the earlier films' resiliency. Opening March 15, 1935, at the Clinton, it ran for two weeks and then disappeared. (Neverthe-

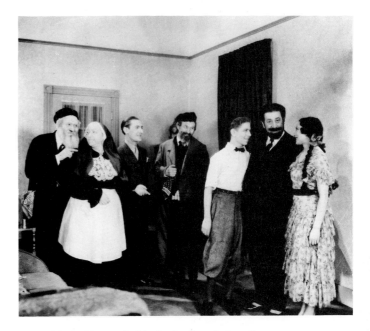

Boris Thomashefsky looks directly into the camera in this production still from Henry Lynn's *Bar Mitsve* (U.S.A., 1935). The original superstar of the American Yiddish stage, Thomashefsky is flanked by his "children" (Benjamin Schechtman and Gertrude Bullman); his "parents" (Morris Strassberg and Leah Noemi) are at far left.

less, *Bar Mitsve* received international exposure. Joseph Green distributed a print in Poland, where Yiddish talkies were still a rarity. Two years later, the film remained in circulation, playing a small Warsaw theater on a double bill with Errol Flynn in *Green Light*.)

After parting ways with Stillman, Lynn directed another aging matinee idol, the craggy-featured actor-singer-pianist Samuel Goldenberg, in an even more venerable vehicle—Joseph Rumshinsky and

Opening title of Henry Lynn's *Hayntige Mames* (U.S.A., 1939); frame enlargement. The star, Esther Field, was a well-known Yiddish radio personality.

Ansel Schorr's once-daring *Shir Hashirim* (*Song of Songs*). An educated man who spoke half a dozen languages and was a graduate of the Warsaw Conservatory, the fifty-three-year-old Goldenberg had once managed his own theater on Irving Place. There, he alternated trashy melodramas with more literary works. As the piano was his specialty, he found ways to work elaborate solos into dramatic scenes. (His most celebrated gimmick concealed a piano behind the pasteboard tombstones of a cemetery set so that he seemed to coax sepulchral notes out of the graves.) In *Shir Hashirim*, music is integral to Goldenberg's persona; he plays a happily married composer led astray by his seductive niece.

The film, which has (perhaps mercifully) been lost, had its premiere in October 1935, "Just for a

change the little Acme Theatre on Union Square is running a home-made Yiddish talkie instead of an importation from the Soviet Union," the *New York Times* noted, adding that "for some esoteric reason, the spoken dialogue is accompanied by English titles." But if the *Times* found *Shir Hashirim* a quaint piece of nonsense, the film provoked an outraged diatribe from *Variety*'s Wolf Kaufman: "In all the world there isn't a language which is as international as Yiddish," Kaufman began. Yiddish literature and Yiddish theater were both world class and yet, "not once has there been a Yiddish film completed which was worthwhile." Take *Shir Hashirim*:

> The director's name is Henry Lynn. Maybe he's a Jew and maybe he isn't. If he isn't he doesn't belong at the helm of a Yiddish film. As a matter of fact, judging from his work here, he doesn't belong at the helm of any kind of film.

What infuriated Kaufman most about *Shir Hashirim*, whose budget he estimated as between ten and fifteen thousand dollars, was its utter desultoriness. The camerawork, he pointed out, is justifiably uncredited and the mise-en-scène virtually nonexistent: "Sets? Who needs it? Put up a cardboard wall, stick a table here and a chair there." All that justified the film was its audience: "Yiddish films have a corner which is enviable and exceptional. They can go places. They can get not only glory, but coin. But they can't do it with junk like *Song of Songs*." According to *Variety*, *Shir Hashirim* was withdrawn from the Acme after only four days.

An entrepreneur about whom little has been recorded, Lynn continued to direct films throughout the thirties. (A decade after founding Sov-Am, he was in Brooklyn, manufacturing fiberglass products and plastic novelties.) In each case save one, the formula was the same: Lynn built a slipshod, old-fashioned vehicle around one certified headliner who had no previous movie experience: Celia Adler starred in *Vu Iz Mayn Kind?* (*Where Is My Child?*), Michael Michaelesco in the 1938 *Di Kraft fun Lebn* (*The Power of Life*), and radio star Esther Field, billed as her on-air persona, *"Di Yidishe Mame,"* was featured in the following year's *Hayntige Mames* (*Mothers of Today*).

Lynn's most unusual project was also made in 1935, this time in collaboration with radio star Herman Yablokoff. Booked into the McKinley Square Theater in the Bronx, Yablokoff had concocted a play named for his current song hit "Papirosn" (Cigarettes). Although the song was the plaintive ballad of a child cigarette peddler, the play concerned the tribulations of an opera-struck *khazn* with a nagging wife. It was scarcely a dozen years since Sergei Eisenstein used a short film in one of his Proletkult stage productions, and as a novelty, Yablokoff planned a fifteen-minute movie to illustrate his song.

This 35mm film was shot by Lynn at the Parkside Hotel in the Catskills, where, according to Yablokoff, it was not only necessary to simulate old Russia but also to create the effect of a torrential rain. As the ragged cigarette vendor, the movie featured Sidney Lumet, the eleven-year-old son of Yiddish actor Baruch Lumet. The film was silent; by way of a soundtrack, Yablokoff played a recording of his own singing voice while he spoke over the theater's public address system.[3]

Papirosn notwithstanding, the 1934–35 and 1935–36 theatrical seasons brought the "social significance"

that would characterize the New York stage through the end of the decade. The Artef, playing their 1934–35 season on Broadway, premiered *Rekrutn* (*Recruits*), a Soviet update of a rediscovered Yiddish satire. In January 1935, the Group Theater scored with Clifford Odets's *Waiting for Lefty* which, six months later, was playing the Public Theater in Yiddish.

The winter of 1935 also marked the first presentations of the Federal Theater Project, including those of its Yiddish Drama Unit, supervised by Harry Thomashefsky, Boris's son and erstwhile manager. The younger Thomashefsky's production of *Der Yidisher Kenig Lir* was performed in New York throughout 1935 at a variety of Jewish community centers, YMHAs, Talmud Torahs, and rest homes. At some point during the year, Joseph Seiden hauled a camera into one of the venues and, in the fashion of Siła recording the Kaminsky troupe in prewar Warsaw, documented the production.

Sheet music for the title song from Herman Yablokoff's 1935 stage play *Papirosn*. The image of future director Sidney Lumet in the upper left corner is taken from a fifteen-minute film projected as part of the performance.

Der Yidisher Kenig Lir had been Gordin's first great success. In transposing Shakespeare to turn-of-the-century Vilna, he crystallized the Lower East Side conflicts between traditional, immigrant parents and their modern, Americanized children. At a family seder, the wealthy merchant David Moshele announces his intention to retire to Jerusalem, leaving his fortune divided between his three daughters and administered by his eldest son-in-law, Kharif. As Moshele's failure to recognize Kharif's cynical schemes compels him to return from Jerusalem and ultimately become a beggar in the street, so he mistakes for rebellion his youngest daughter Taybele's desire to study medicine in St. Petersburg. The patriarch may be blind, but Joffee, Taybele's equally modern sweetheart, isn't; he knows his world literature and dubs Moshele "the Jewish King Lear."

Premiered in 1892, the play gave Jacob P. Adler his most important role and Yiddish theater its most celebrated anecdote. Watching Moshele's eldest daughter begrudge her father a bowl of soup, one spectator supposedly rose and cried: "To hell with your stingy daughter, Yankl! She has a stone, not a heart. Spit on her and come home with me. My *yidene* is a good cook; she'll fix you up!" But while Gordin's play achieved its popularity by dramatizing parental suffering and filial ingratitude, the Federal Theater production is striking for endorsing progressive values. Kharif is a greedy businessman, and Moshele's second son-in-law is a smugly indolent *yeshive-bokher*. Taybele and Joffee are the circumspect 1890s equivalent of *di yugnt fun Rusland*. Their climactic wedding is not just a family reconciliation but (unlike the resolution of Gordin's *Mirele Efros*, *Lir*'s even more popular companion piece) a vindication for the enlightened younger generation.

Seemingly a regression to the prewar Yiddish stage, the Federal Theater's choice of *Der Yidisher Kenig Lir* actually represented a forward-looking ideology. It is a play that endorses modernization for those whom the New World had left behind. Unfortunately, this attitude hardly applied to Seiden's film technique. *Der Yidisher Kenig Lir* is inferior to both *Zayn Vaybs Lubovnik* and *Uncle Moses*, marred by poor sound and a static camera. Although the film was completed by the fall of 1935, its New York opening was delayed until the following February (presumably to avoid conflict with the show's remaining performances).

Rather than stimulating a more *"literarishe"* cinema, *Lir*'s modest success (and low overhead) enabled Seiden to reenter production. In the spring of 1936, while *Lir* was in release, Maxwell Hamilton of the *Brooklyn Daily Eagle* visited the so-called Seiden Studio of the Talking Picture, located just off Columbus Circle at 33 West Sixtieth Street, to report on the shooting of the "gigantic super-production" *Libe un Laydnshaft* (Love and Passion). As the Fire Department had not certified the Seiden Studio of the Talking Film, production was restricted to weekends and evenings. Persuading Seiden's "front-line defense" that he had not come to collect the rent, Hamilton was granted access to a "ramshackle" three-room suite that consisted of a tiny "sound stage," a combination lab and storage space, and an office *cum* dressing room. The telephone, Hamilton noted, was padlocked.

"Sit!" beams Mr. Seiden, after his assistant has been assured that the visitor is O.K. and has dug Mr. Seiden out of the back room—"Sit down and have a laugh. If you can't laugh, there's no story here."

Libe un Laydnshaft, or *Love and Sacrifice* as Seiden translated it, took two weeks to shoot, involved a cast of hundreds, and cost a mere $3,000. Only last month, Seiden explained, he was searching for an appropriate property for a movie to open at Passover, just "three weeks away." Then, one Saturday in an Allen Street bookstore, he discovered a dog-eared copy of Isidore Zolotarefsky's 1926 *Libe un Laydnshaft.* That the book was both "out-of-date" and "printed in Poland" doubtless recommended it to the producer who, investing twenty cents, spent the rest of the weekend reworking the novel for the screen. Monday, he assembled his cast, and by the end of the week, the Seiden Studio was humming. When the star, Rose Greenfield, sprained her ankle, Seiden revised the script to insure that the rest of her scenes could be close-ups, then shot them "on location" in her home. (Seiden was clearly a believer in producer as *auteur.* The credits for *Libe un Laydnshaft* list George Roland as director and A. Armband and M. Kenig as screenwriters.)

Greenfield plays a middle-class matron who shoots the man who compromises her. But *Libe un Laydnshaft* places less emphasis on her crime than on her sacrifice—for the sake of her children's future, she insists upon being treated as dead after being sent to prison. This martyrdom is duly rewarded when her daughter marries the lawyer who frees her, not realizing he is rescuing his future *shviger.* The movie opened at the Clinton on April 7, 1936. Although *Variety* was suitably unimpressed, assuming a "three-day" shoot of a script seemingly "manufactured as the cameras ground," the film was held over three weeks—the most popular Yiddish movie the Clinton had shown to date.

Of course, *Libe un Laydnshaft* trod well-traveled territory. The suffering parent and the redeeming child were *shund* archetypes long before Goldin deployed them in *Mayn Yidishe Mame.* Having deferred their own gratification, Jewish immigrants developed what Howe has termed "a culture utterly devoted to its sons" upon whose backs were freighted all manner of parental "aspirations and delusions." Like a collective Moses, immigrant parents had led their flock to a promised land they could not enter, sacrificing themselves so that their children might attain what they were denied. Although virtually every Yiddish film contains a wedding, the relationship between parents and children is typically more charged than that between men and women.[4]

There is a certain appositeness in the movie *Der Yidisher Kenig Lir*'s revitalizing Seiden's career—the Yiddish generational melodrama, too, had its origins in the work of Jacob Gordin. In both *Lir* and *Mirele Efros* a powerful, traditional, self-made parent is betrayed and humiliated by callow, selfish children. *Mirele Efros,* which was first staged in 1898, is likely the single most widely played piece in the Yiddish theatrical canon. Even more than *Lir,* it justifies the parent, in this case a widowed businesswoman. The play has the logic of a ritual affirmation ("half culture-myth and half tearjerker" Howe called it); it seems no coincidence that the conciliatory ending involves the Bar Mitzvah of Mirele's grandson. *Mirele Efros* was filmed in 1912 and again in 1939. The latter uses wailing choruses to accentuate sacramental suffering, building up to the son and daughter-in-law's fearful confession, "We committed a great sin, you and I."

Vu Iz Mayn Kind? elevates the mother-son relationship to a kind of cosmic delirium. Adapted from a play by Sam Steinberg and William Segal, this extremely successful potboiler—which opened in four movie houses plus the former Yiddish Art Theater in December 1937 and was still playing Jewish neighborhoods five months later—is quintessential *shund.* (Jacob Ben-Ami called Segal "the world's worst playwright," warning his interviewer not to inquire further. "As a writer, you shouldn't even know about him—it might be contagious.") The film begins with the forty-eight-year-old Celia Adler as a young immigrant widowed en route to America. She is prevented from hurling herself and her newborn son off a bridge by a passing doctor (Morris Strassberg) who suggests she bring her child to a Jewish orphanage, which she does. Within minutes of signing the final papers, Adler has a change of heart, but it is too late. After six years of wandering, she tracks down the adoptive parents and demands her child back; Strassberg then has her committed to a mental hospital.

Poster for the American film *Vu Iz Mayn Kind?* Opening in five New York theaters in December 1937 (and still playing Jewish neighborhoods five months later), this extremely successful potboiler elevated the mother-son relationship to cosmic heights.

Two decades later, Adler's son (Mischa Stutchkoff), himself now a doctor, is working at the same mental hospital and is unaccountably fascinated by the near-catatonic old woman who sits by herself, crooning over a doll pathetically fashioned from her bedclothes. If the force of Adler's longing is so powerful as to have vaporized its ostensible object, Stutchkoff's attraction to this unhappy patient is so atavistic that he insists upon inviting her to his parents' house to help celebrate his engagement to Strassberg's daughter. There, Adler recognizes Strassberg who, simultaneously recognizing his own guilt, informs Stutchkoff of his true origins. In a moment of supreme vindication, Stutchkoff resolves to leave his adoptive parents to live with his biological mother. The movie ends with with Adler's triumphant cry, *"Es Iz a Got!* [There Is a God!]"[5]

A similarly redeeming child appears in Seiden's 1939 *Motl der Operator.* Motl (Chaim Tauber), a poor garment worker, is attacked by thugs for leading a strike. While he lies unconscious in the hospital, his wife is compelled to surrender their baby for adoption. Then, crazed with guilt, she turns on the gas and asphyxiates herself. The *Daily News* deemed *Motl* "even more calamitous than some of its predecessors," a film that "delves so deeply and relentlessly into misery that for many it will only be an embarrassing, exaggerated spectacle."

Indeed, like *Vu Iz Mayn Kind?, Motl* evokes a nexus of guilty feelings—anxiety at being unable to care for one's child, rage at the child's lack of appreciation for one's sacrifice, a real or projected shame of origins. When Motl recovers, three years later, he finds no trace of his family—even his tenement is rubble. For the next fifteen years he wanders the pavement, a bearded old *Yid,* selling flowers and singing his sorrows. Meanwhile, his son Jackie has grown into the lawyer who will defend him when he accidentally kills a villainous blackmailer. Jackie, having no idea of Motl's identity, presents him to the court as "a messenger from God," which is essentially what he is—a self-effacing saint whose only concern is for his son's well-being. This includes protecting Jackie from potential embarrassment: Motl will never let him know their true relationship.[6]

If some films present offspring as redeemers, more stress filial ingratitude—building up to the child's climactic appreciation of parental wisdom. (There is even an element of this in *Nosn Beker Fort Aheym*. "In twenty-eight years I learned less there than I learned here in one day," the contrite son tells his triumphant Old World dad.) One of the suffering *Hayntige Mames* goes hysterically blind when her gangster son pushes her aside to elope with the woman of his choice. Her bitter satisfaction comes a few reels later with his heartrending shriek, "Now you'll lead me to the electric chair instead of the *khupe*. Children whose parents are strict with them are lucky."

Shund is filled with this sort of sour, unintentional humor. It also thrives on fabulous coincidences. At the climax of *Ir Tsveyte Mame* (*Her Second Mother*), Surele is brought before a judge who turns out to be her biological father (he lost his memory in a car crash after her mother died in childbirth), thus making possible the line: "I see my daughter for the first time as a criminal!" Or, as a sightless old woman cries, when confronted with *her* errant daughter-in-law in *Mayn Zundele* (*My Sonny*): "Thank God, I'm blind!" Generational *shund* makes a spectacle of outrageous self-sacrifice. The virtuous Surele takes the blame for a crime committed by her adoptive family's natural daughter, grimly announcing, "I am paying you part of my debt." The protagonist of *Di*

An errant mother (Polish singer Fania Rubina) entertains the residents of the Bialystoker Home for the Aged in Joseph Seiden's *Mayn Zundele* (U.S.A., 1937). (Jerry Ross, who, as Jerry Rosenberg, played the film's eponymous "sonny," later cowrote the musicals *The Pajama Game* and *Damn Yankees!*)

Kraft fun Lebn embezzles money to save his daughter's fiancé from prison, to put his ungrateful older son through college, and to provide medical care for his youngest. "We live solely for the children's happiness," he tells a friend, after being sent to Sing Sing. "That's the true power of life—finding our happiness in theirs."

Surele notwithstanding, children rarely understand their parents' obligations. "You're willing to sacrifice everything after the way that I've shamed you?" a daughter arrested on a charge of armed robbery asks in disbelief. "I'm a mother," is the simple reply. The parental vocation is absolute. ("In Second Avenue drama you learn that even a gunman has a mother," William Schack once observed in the *New York Times*.) The protagonist of *Mayn Zundele* is relentlessly punished for putting her own career as an actress on the same level as her role as a mother. In short, parenthood is divine.

Seiden's 1940 *Eli, Eli* (a bargain-basement version of Leo McCarey's 1937 *Make Way for Tomorrow,* in which a devoted old couple are separated by their insensitive offspring) compels a Jewish mother to endure all manner of insults. (Excluded from her grown son's birthday party, she brings her present to his office; he refuses to take it and sends her back home, where her daughter-in-law insults her cooking.) The movie is grotesquely sentimental. At one point, the mother sings a version of the title song which reminds children that:

An angel, to watch over you,
has flown down upon earth.
Children, if you only knew
what a mother is worth—
How holy her wonders!

In the last scene, after a miracle has restored the family fortunes, the barely apologetic son announces that he needs $2,000 or he'll lose his home. The parents look at each other: "I'll go to the bank Wednesday," the old man declares.

However debased, there is an operatic quality to *shund.* "In the Yiddish theater, the stage as spectacle, outburst, expression, was almost always more vital than dramatic text or program," writes Howe. "Vast outpourings of creative energy made the perfor-mance of a Yiddish play an occasion for communal pleasure—the kind of pleasure that audiences took in seeing their experiences (or, more often, their memories) mirrored back to them in heightened form." In the Yiddish popular theater, no one could sing that aria as piercingly as Jennie Goldstein.[7]

In *Tsvey Shvester* (Two Sisters), her single venture into Yiddish cinema, Jennie Goldstein manages to telescope both the ingenue and mature aspects of her stage persona. The film was adapted from a story by the prolific shundist Samuel H. Cohen, the script most likely written by Goldstein herself; it was directed by Ben K. Blake and financed by a New York–based, one-shot company called Graphic Films. Relatively lavish for a Yiddish movie, *Tsvey Shvester* opened at the Broadway area Continental Theater on November 30, 1938, and was extensively panned by the English-language press.

The film wastes no time assaulting the tear ducts. After a brief montage of Lower East Side street scenes, the camera tracks through an anonymous tenement window and into a dying woman's face. She is the mother of two small daughters and her last words instruct the older girl to be both sister and mother to young Sally. Twenty years pass. The girls now live with their uncle, a butcher sufficiently prosperous to have an apartment on the Grand Concourse. Elder sister Betty has grown into Goldstein—a peculiar icon, petite and plump, with a tiny head and an abundance of suppressed hysteria—while Sally is played by svelte Sylvia Dell, who looks barely half her costar's age.

Betty is engaged to marry Dr. Max Feinberg (Muni Serebroff), a handsome profile who works in the same hospital as Sally. Evidently, Betty has driven herself into premature middle age putting Sally through nursing school, as well as subsidizing

Max's medical studies. And inevitably, while Betty is out furnishing an office for Max's practice and a home for their marriage, Sally and Max fall in love. The film then careers through a succession of outrageous handkerchief scenes: Betty confronting Max in his office, pointing and wailing, "Mine! Mine! Mine! Everything in this office belongs to me! You belong to me!"; Betty cornering Sally and shrieking —"I have sacrificed my life for you, and you repay me by taking my Max!"—until the girl tops her by threatening to throw herself from the window.

Max tries to tell Betty that her love for him is somewhat maternal, but what stops her cold is Sally's accusation that she is "too old-fashioned" for Max. Broken, but still the martyr, Betty decides that Sally must marry Max on what was to have been her wedding day, wearing what was to have been her wedding gown. (She even throws in the house as a wedding gift.) Just before the ceremony, Betty and Sally's tubercular father arrives from the sanatorium where Betty has been supporting him. Discovering that Sally is marrying Max, he collapses. Sally, again, proves equal to the situation, eclipsing her father's simulated coronary by inviting him to rip off her dress and drive a stake through her heart. In the confusion, Betty begs Max to dance one last dance with her—a pathetic, erotic, hopeless moment. The wedding over, Betty is left to congratulate the portrait of her dead mother. *"Mazltov, Mame,"* she says, without apparent irony.

The first Yiddish films were predicated upon the victory of youth, but by the 1930s the pendulum had swung back toward the assertion of parental values. *Tsvey Shvester* is fascinating for trying to have it both ways. The film neatly breaks down into antithetical worldviews: arranged marriage versus romantic love, "old-fashioned" versus modern, Yiddish versus American. Central to this dual world is the monstrous figure of Betty, who, in her merging of roles, particularly regarding Max, seems to have forgotten the Yiddish maxim "When a man gets married, he divorces his mother." Betty's tragic flaws are precisely her virtues. Her "selflessness" is identical to her selfishness ("Mine! Mine! Mine!"); her hubris (to be a mother without having given birth) is a factor of her filial goodness.[8]

The dual reading that *Tsvey Shvester* demands mirrors the mindset of its original audience. Eager to assimilate into American society (or more exactly, for their children to be assimilated), yet conscious of their own connection to a dying traditionalism, the Yiddish audience for the movie were part of Howe's "transitional generation," stoically postponing gratification for the sake of their offspring. By presenting the psychic stresses of assimilation as an optimistic tragedy (or a grotesque comedy), *Tsvey Shvester* acknowledged the situation of this transitional generation with a directness that precludes escapism.

Better organized than Lynn, Seiden lasted longer as a purveyor of low-budget Yiddish melodrama. Although he briefly retired from Yiddish talkies after the release of *Ikh Vil Zayn a Mame* (*I Want to Be a Mother*) in 1937—apparently to produce *Human Wreckage,* an "educational" film on venereal disease that was denied a license to open in April 1938—he returned full force two years later, grinding out *Mayn Zundele, Kol Nidre,* and *Motl der Operator,* as well as the all-black *Paradise in Harlem,* between March and December 1939.[9]

Seiden employed only a skeleton crew: a cameraman, a soundman, and a minimum of electricians, grips, and prompters. George Roland had been hired

A sweatshop and a mom-and-pop store: Joseph Seiden, second from left, directs Chaim Tauber, seated behind a sewing machine, in *Motl der Operator* (U.S.A., 1939).

to direct *Libe un Laydnshaft* and *Ikh Vil Zayn a Mame*, but once Seiden left West Sixtieth Street for a converted garage in Fort Lee, New Jersey, he assumed that chore himself (thus saving Roland's $250 fee). The Seiden operation was at once a sweatshop —temperatures rose so high that the crew worked stripped to the waist and cooled themselves on a block of ice—and a mom-and-pop store. A son-in-law served as soundman and sometime editor. On the last few productions, Seiden's son Harold operated the camera. Mrs. Seiden doubled as script girl. (Because her husband had no reading knowledge of Yiddish, the dialogue was written phonetically in Latin characters. Seiden directed in English.) Costumes were supplied by a brother-in-law in the business. The sets were dressed with Seiden's home furnishings.

Libe un Laydnshaft had no exteriors, later films included a few perfunctory shots of Bensonhurst or the Lower East Side. Seiden manufactured his special effects himself, including titles and fades. He made the latter by dipping the original negative in bleach, one frame at a time: "Opticals were five, ten dollars apiece. You had thirty, forty opticals, that's $40. I would spend a couple of days and do it by hand." The Clinton sometimes advanced Seiden money to make his payroll and the actors themselves worked for very little. Seiden populated his characterless sets with a mixture of good actors down on their luck (like Lazar Freed, a veteran of the original Hirschbein and Schwartz troupes), stolid second-raters, and aging ingenues. Rose Greenfield, Esta Salzman, and Muni Serebroff appear in film after film. Dapper, pomaded Cantor Leibele Waldman is a fixture of Seiden's early work, and madcap comedienne Yetta Zwerling is an axiom of his "mature" oeuvre—between 1937 and 1941 she appears in every production save one (and is often the best thing in them).

While Lynn invested in established stars, Seiden exploited foreign talent. He paid the visiting Polish soprano Fania Rubina $150 to star in *Mayn Zundele;* and when the *klaynkunst* (cabaret) troupe Yidishe Bande arrived from Poland in early 1939, he cast a number of the players—including the young principals Lili Liliana and Leon Liebgold, stars of the Polish film *Der Dibek* (who each received only $100)—in *Kol Nidre,* a moralistic tearjerker about a Jewish girl who refuses to marry her rabbi suitor, eloping instead with an actor who makes her pregnant and deserts her. "I get my casts very easily," Seiden confided in the *Brooklyn Eagle.* "I hang around the beaneries on Second Avenue, there's always an actor who wants to get into the movies. I don't pay him nothing. Over a cup of coffee, I give him a smile and a promise and he's willing." In an interview with Judith Goldberg, Leo Fuchs explained how, a year after his arrival from Lvov, while a supporting player in the stage hit *Papirosn,* he became a featured performer in *Ikh Vil Zayn a Mame.*

Approaching Fuchs at the Café Royal, Seiden described his latest project and offered the twenty-six-year-old actor a major role. Fuchs didn't even think to glance at the script: "I was so excited about having my name above the title." Because he was appearing

at the Second Avenue, his scenes were scheduled for one late-night shoot. After the curtain on the appointed evening, however, the aspiring movie star forgot his commitment and returned home. Undeterred, Seiden showed up at Fuch's apartment and rousted him from bed. "We went up there, spoke our lines and set the camera and that's how we did it. I just did what they told me to do. Perhaps, when they were discussing the songs, maybe I made a *mentsh* out of myself."

Yetta Zwerling and Jacob Zanger provide comic relief on the set of Joseph Seiden's *Der Yidisher Nign* (U.S.A., 1940). Brandishing a fish, Zanger is making a travesty of the ritual *shlogn kapores,* by which Zwerling's sins will be passed on to a "scapegoat." (When the film was shown in Baltimore, the Maryland Board of Censors had ruled that a similar scene, involving a live fowl, be eliminated.)

Fuchs is being modest. In addition to supplying Seiden with two comic songs, he provides *Ikh Vil Zayn a Mame* with most of its *raison d'être*. The film is standard *shund*: Esta Salzman plays an illegitimate child adopted at birth by her uncle, a rabbi so vindictive he refuses to let his fallen sister, Amelia, attend the girl's wedding. ("God in heaven, is my sin so great?" she wails.) At the climax, the bridegroom's father arrives form California and recognizes Amelia as the girl he seduced and abandoned in Europe twenty years before. "Your son has married your own daughter!" she gets to scream before all ends happily with the final revelation that the groom is really his stepson. Periodically, Seiden's shameless contrivance is ripped asunder by the demonic quality of Fuchs's clowning with the *"meydl fun ganz Vilna,"* Yetta Zwerling.[10] Playing an elderly family friend, Fuchs steals the movie with his chicken-like moves, triple-jointed fingers, and comic *badkhn* routine.

Seiden was not the first to recognize Fuchs's potential; two months after the dancer-comedian arrived from Poland (and well before he had learned much English), MGM had him screen-tested. The studio showed no further interest, but Seiden's hunch paid off. By the time *Ikh Vil Zayn a Mame* had its premiere (in February 1937, at the Belmont Theater on West Forty-eighth Street), Fuchs—now touted as "the Yiddish Ray Bolger"—was a star attraction at the Second Avenue in *Der Dishvasher,* Yablokoff's latest extravaganza, complete with scenes at Ellis Island and a Havana nightclub.

Still, that *Ikh Vil Zayn a Mame,* alone among Seiden's movies, opened at a Broadway theater is less a matter of quality or even Fuchs, than of the extraordinary success of *Yidl mitn Fidl,* a Yiddish film imported earlier that winter from Poland.

NOTES

1. "The Yiddish theater made the Left Bank of Paris look like a convent," Thomashefsky's son, Ted Thomas, told theater historian Jerome Lawrence. "There was every form of degeneration you can imagine: murder, suicide, drugs, sex deviations of all kinds. These were the emergent Jews, after years of living a Torah-cloistered existence, suddenly free—and drunk with it."

Still, he who once studied to be a cantor aspired to more than trash: Thomashefsky not only introduced "Eli, Eli" and "A Brivele der Mamen," but rewrote Shakespeare. Like Adler, he had supported Gordin and, in the twenties turned impresario, sponsoring Ossip Dymow, importing Rudolf Schildkraut, Samuel Goldenberg, Michael Michaelesco, Aaron Lebedeff, and the Vilna Troupe.

2. A negative example is seemingly provided by Sam, a visiting American lounge lizard who speaks only English, calls the film's clownish *khazn* a *"khazer"* (pig) and makes numerous jokes on the American confusion between show business and religion. The movie's condemnation of Sam's ignorance is complicated, however, by both the ending, in which he saves Israel's life (and gets to marry Birdie), and the sheer *shund* vitality of his performance: asked by Birdie to perform his *"meshugene* American dance," he taps enthusiastically and lures her into the Yiddish-English duet, "New York Is a *Ganeydn* [Paradise]," which constitutes the movie's liveliest number.

3. *Papirosn* proved so successful that it moved to the Second Avenue Theater the following September. The *New York Times* praised the "interpolation of a fine old silent movie for a flashback," adding, however, "with that the novelty ends." *Variety,* Lynn's *bête noire,* was altogether less tolerant: "One scene, in which a piece of motion picture film is used to illustrate the song on which the show's title is based, is about a new low in entertainment, even for Second Avenue." Nevertheless, the film remained an integral part of the play. Yablokoff mentions in his memoirs that he took two prints with him when he played Buenos Aires in February 1939.

4. The titles of *shund* movies attest to the transcendent importance of intergenerational ties: *Mayn Yidishe Mame* (My Jewish Mother) and *Mayn Zundele* (My Sonny), *A Yidishe Tokhter* (A Jewish Daughter) and *Der Yidisher Foter* (The Jewish Father), *Ikh Vil Zayn a Mame* (I Want to Be a Mother) and *Vu Iz Mayn Kind?* (Where Is My Child?), *Ir Tsveyte Mame* (Her Second

Mother) and *Hayntige Mames* (*Mothers of Today*), *A Brivele der Mamen* (*A Little Letter to Mother*) and *Mamele* (*Little Mother*), *Tsvey Shvester* (*Two Sisters*) and *Dray Tekhter* (*Three Daughters*).

5. Twenty years later, the scriptwriters for Cecil B. De Mille's *The Ten Commandments* gave the same line to Moses' mother, Jochebed, when, recognizing that he is a Jew, Moses leaves Pharaoh's palace to stay with her.

6. Although *Motl* seems a grand summa of Yiddish film motifs, drawing elements from *Uncle Moses, Vu Iz Mayn Kind?,* and even the same year's *Mayn Zundele,* it is in fact based on a play written by its star, Chaim Tauber, a radio personality, who first strode the boards as Motl at the Second Avenue Theater in the spring of 1936. The production subsequently toured Brooklyn and was revived at the Lyric in Williamsburg in February 1937. Tauber seems to have been a particular Brooklyn culture hero. Alone among Seiden's later movies, *Motl der Operator* premiered away from the Lower East Side, playing the People's for a month, before opening at the Clinton in late January 1940.

7. Born on the Lower East Side in 1896, Goldstein made her stage debut at age six, and became the highest-paid performer in Yiddish vaudeville while still in her teens. During World War I, she teamed with writer-producer Max Gabel, who for the next dozen years cast her in a series of sensational melodramas. ("Miss Goldstein counts that stage day lost in which she does not spend a little time either in the gutter or in a psychopathic ward," the *New York Times* observed in 1926.) Goldstein's own life took some melodramatic turns in the late 1920s and she spent the next few years touring the hinterlands before returning to Second Avenue to assume the lease of the National and perform more matronly roles.

8. In *The Anatomy of Criticism,* Northrop Frye reduces comedy and tragedy to narratives which either include or exclude the protagonist in or from society, observing that "the figure of a typical or random victim begins to crystallize in domestic tragedy as it deepens in ironic tone." Frye calls this victim the *pharmakos,* or scapegoat. Clearly, Betty is the *pharmakos* of *Tsvey Shvester.* But despite the pathos wrung from the spectacle of her exclusion, *Tsvey Shvester*'s optimistic projection of Jewish upward mobility (from the Lower East Side to the Grand Concourse to Sea Gate; from sewing-machine operator to butcher to surgeon), not to mention its climactic wedding, makes it strongly comedic. (Indeed, from the point of view of Max and Sally, this domestic tragedy is a comedy in which their romance triumphs over Betty's "parental" opposition.)

9. Seiden released *Eli, Eli* and *Der Groyser Eytse-Geber* (*The Great Advisor*) in 1940, *Der Yidisher Nign* (*The Jewish Melody*) and *Ir Tsveyte Mame* in 1941. During World War II, he became involved in defense contracting, but enjoyed a brief comeback in 1949 with a version of Gordin's *Got, Mentsh, un Tayvl* (*God, Man, and Devil*) and *Dray Tekhter* (*Three Daughters*), the last two Yiddish dramatic features produced in America.

10. Indeed, even on the set this seems to be what happened. Fuchs and Zwerling clicked so well that Seiden subsequently released their out-takes as a fifteen-minute short, *Ikh Vil Zayn a "Boarder"* (*I Want to Be a Boarder*). The film is a small classic of Jewish surrealism—a kind of missing link between the Marx Brothers and the Yiddish stage. Fuchs and Zwerling play a married couple: "Divorce me or I'll run away," is his opening gambit. Tired of being Zwerling's husband, Fuchs reinvents himself as her lovesick boarder, and, bringing her flowers, proposes marriage. "How can I?" Zwerling simpers, "I'm married." The jealous Fuchs then reverts to husband and threatens a divorce: "Your boarder will be my best witness." After several more reversals, the routine ends when Fuchs imagines that, for love of her boarder, Zwerling plans to kills her husband: "A dark dream on your head, so that's your plan—to do away with me!"

Overleaf: Released for Passover 1936, *Al Khet* was the first dramatic Yiddish talkie made in Poland. Rokhl Holzer and Avrom Morevsky came from the Yiddish stage. The expressionistic lighting suggests director Aleksander Marten's prior experience in the German film industry.

17

"We're on Our Way"

THE VIRULENT nationalism that infected Europe as the world drifted again toward war left *Yidishland* isolated and exposed. Borders closed, lines were drawn. As the Jewish Question came again to the forefront of European politics, the making of Yiddish talkies—which is to say, the self-dramatization of the Jewish masses—became a form of cultural resistance. Inevitably, this awareness appeared first in Poland, where proximity to the Nazi threat (not to mention the clamor of Polish nationalists) heightened Jewish interdependence and compelled the revitalization of a common culture. Each in its own way, the American and Soviet Jewish communities had been uprooted from tradition and engaged

by a process that transcended previous national identities. In Poland, however, Jews could only become more Jewish.

When the first full Polish talkies appeared in late 1930, Yiddish was still the primary language for the majority of the nation's three million Jews. In the 1931 census, over three-quarters listed Yiddish as their mother tongue. The trend, however, was toward linguistic assimilation, particularly among the urban middle class. If the parents in such families spoke Yiddish to one another, their children were most often educated in Polish. This was no less true of Yiddish intellectuals. In his memoirs, Isaac Bashevis Singer recalls the "unwritten law among the wives of Yiddish writers and of the great number of so-called Yiddishists that their children should be raised to speak the Polish language." According to Singer, only the poor, the *shtetl*-bound, and the Chasidim brought up their children in Yiddish.

Yet, even as Polish Jews moved toward the majority culture, they found themselves more vilified and even more oppressed than at any time in Poland's history. Universities were closed in late 1931 after attacks on Jewish students resulted in several deaths. Such incidents continued throughout the thirties, receiving additional impetus after the Nazis came to power in Germany. Henryk Rolicki's 1933 best-seller *Zmierzch Izraela* (The Twilight of Israel) posited a Jewish conspiracy as the motor of history; Joseph Goebbels's 1934 state visit resulted in a ten-year Polish-German nonaggression pact. Soon afterwards, Poland officially abrogated the Minorities Treaty. The situation deteriorated further with Piłsudski's death in May 1935. One month later, the first pogrom since 1920 took place in Grodno. There were hundreds of violent attacks on Jews during the remainder of the year, particularly during the September elections (which would coincide with the promulgation of the Nuremberg Laws in Nazi Germany). That Poland's new prime minister, Marian Zyndram-Koscialkowski, was married to a woman of Jewish birth was scant comfort.

As the Nazis began to moderate their anti-Semitism in preparation for the 1936 Berlin Olympics, Poland rivaled Germany as the world capital of Jew-baiting. The autumn of 1935 saw ferocious anti-Jewish agitation in the universities, as well as the publication, by a notoriously anti-Semitic priest, Stanislaus Trzeciak, of an influential attack on kosher slaughtering, asserting it was a Jewish plot to monopolize the meat trade. In February 1936, a bill to ban kosher slaughtering was placed before the Sejm, where it would dominate parliamentary debate for the next two years.

Anti-Semitism was scarcely the only problem for Polish Jews. The nation's economy was a shambles. The end of 1931 found half the peasantry near starvation. One-third of the Jewish population was destitute and another third at subsistence level. Rather than stimulate the economy with public works and credits, the regime remained passive until 1933 when virtually all market activity collapsed. This delay prolonged the Depression in Poland. There were few signs of recovery before 1934, and for many the crisis continued into 1936. The Depression decimated Warsaw theaters, causing most of them to close on the eve of the 1931–32 season. The Yiddish stage was even more precarious, deprived of government subsidies and already in a state of permanent crisis. While many Jews patronized Polish theater, the Yiddish stage lacked the allegiance of large segments of the Jewish community: the Orthodox eschewed theater altogether; the well-to-do dismissed the Yiddish stage as a pauper's entertainment; and both assimilated Jews and Zionists had objections to theater in Yiddish.

The movie industry suffered similarly. In 1931, annual production dropped to a mere six features, while three-quarters of the movies shown in Poland were made in the United States. Movie houses were slow to wire for sound within Warsaw (and slow to be built in the countryside). Only in 1934 did the industry stage a modest revival; this comeback was aided the following year by a protectionist tariff on imported films. It was then that Leo Forbert and Henryk Bojm returned to production with a feature documentary, *Swit, Dzien i Noc Palestyny* (Dawn, Day, and Night in Palestine), the title echoing that of a recent experimental "portrait" of Warsaw. The most ambitious of three Zionist travelogues released in 1934, *Dawn, Day, and Night* was made in Polish with narration by Jakob Appenszlak, editor of the Polish-Jewish newspaper *Nasz Przegląd* (Our Review), and shot by Forbert's twenty-year-old son Władysław, later a participant in the brief revival of Yiddish film production in Poland after World War II.

Given the combined problems of the Yiddish stage and Polish cinema, it is scarcely surprising that no Yiddish film had been attempted since *In di Poylishe Velder*. Indeed, it wasn't until the summer of 1933, when Joseph Green barnstormed the country with his dubbed *Yoysef in Mitsraim* (*Joseph in the Land of Egypt*), that a Yiddish sound-film was even shown in Poland. Two years later, Green returned with Thomashefsky's *Bar Mitsve*. In the interim, *Uncle Moses* was released, apparently with Polish subtitles. Still, the intellectuals were not impressed. "The story of the Yiddish sound-film is short and unhappy," wrote Michal Kitai in *Literarishe Bleter*. Polish Jews, he observed, were faithful consumers of American-Yiddish melodramas, operettas, and now, talking pictures: "More than once did the Jewish press protest the 'goods' with which American entrepreneurs exasperate us, but in vain."

Whatever else might be said about them, the Americans have a powerful weapon (the dollar aside). They understand the taste and tastelessness of the Jewish *kleynbirger* [petit-bourgeois] and *luftmentsh*. Whether or not they are contented, whether life is peaceful (Jews are not beaten) or it isn't (Jews are beaten), such people must have their *kugl* [pudding] and, on the *shabes* table, a *tsholnt*. Eaten with joy, or God forbid, tears and a sigh, it doesn't matter. . . . [America]

served up *tsholnt* and they drooled! It was sweet and greasy and already rancid—still, a *tsholnt*! And how! They licked their fingers clean. So gourmets had convulsions, who heard them?

In late 1935, however, several local filmmakers banded together to produce a classier grade of "*tsholnt.*" "When it was heard that a certain group in Warsaw—producers, together with actors and artists—were going to make a Yiddish sound-film, people were so amazed that it wasn't even believed," Kitai recalled. That film was *Al Khet* (For the Sin . . .), which took its powerfully evocative title from the first words of the Yom Kippur prayer of repentance.

Al Khet was written by J. M. Neuman, the forty-two-year-old drama editor of the Yiddish daily *Haynt,* and directed by Aleksander Marten (born Marek Tennenbaum), a native of Lodz who had studied acting with Reinhardt, played on the Viennese stage, and worked in the German film industry. The theatrical composer Henekh Kon, recently relocated from Berlin to Warsaw, provided the score. The celebrated painter Yankl Adler, ousted by the Nazis from Düsseldorf Academy, worked on the sets. The popular cabaret team of Dzigan and Schumacher made their movie debut in supporting roles. The producer was Shaul Goskind, erstwhile editor of the journal *Film Velt* and, with his brother Itzhik, co-owner of the Warsaw film laboratory Sektor. One of five film labs in Warsaw, Sektor's customers included both Polish and foreign producers, as well as the government news agency Polska Agencja Telegraficzna (PAT). In addition, the Goskind brothers owned the only portable sound recorder in Poland.

With the exception of Goskind, virtually all the participants in *Al Khet* were originally from Lodz which, from 1919 through the early twenties, had been the center of an active Yiddish avant-garde. In addition to poetry and painting, the Lodz vanguard embraced puppet theater, cabaret, and, somewhat more theoretically, film. Still, the painter and puppeteer Yitzhak Brauner is said to have produced a short documentary on Lodz Yiddish culture around 1922, while Neuman, who would later publish a brief scenario in *Film Velt,* collaborated with Sholem Asch on a film script and wrote an unproduced screenplay on the life of the nineteenth-century Polish poet Cyprian Norwid (whose work he also translated into Yiddish).

According to Goskind, the impetus for Poland's first Yiddish dramatic feature came not from America but from the anti-Jewish legislation passed in Germany in the autumn of 1935. One evening at the Piccadilly, a gathering place for Yiddish writers and actors, Goskind was approached by Neuman, with an idea for a Yiddish talkie. As Goskind recalled the scene half a century later, Neuman was sitting with Kon, Adler, and a group of Polish nationals more recently arrived from the German Reich, including Marten and the actor Kurt Katch.

We sat and discussed what to do with them, how to help them—they don't want charity, they are not looking for handouts! Neuman had a treatment all ready, Marten agreed to direct, Adler to do the lighting, Kon to write the music—and they asked me to produce.

After some hesitation ("a Yiddish film in these crazy times") and several phone calls Goskind agreed, in part because he had secured an advance of raw stock from Agfa-Film's soon-to-be-fired Jewish branch manager.

I returned to the table—and it was no accident that correspondents from the Yiddish press were sitting there too—and declared: "Gentlemen, you can announce that the Kinor Company (I invented the name on the spot) and Shaul Goskind are starting production on a Yiddish talking picture called *Al Khet.*"

Then the twenty-seven-year-old producer "ordered dinner for everybody."

Produced on a low budget even by Polish standards, Marten's first attempt at directing was more than credible. The sound recording is primitive but the mise-en-scène evinces a knowledge of craft and even some concern for film form. Stronger on atmosphere than continuity, *Al Khet* has the heavy chiaroscuro of a contemporary European art film. Neuman's scenario, though somewhat perfunctory, is certainly less oblivious to historical events than comparable American melodramas, haunted as it is by the wartime destruction of Galicia.

Rokhl Holzer (a young actress with Ida Kaminska's company) plays a village maid who becomes pregnant by a German-Jewish officer stationed in her town. The couple plan to marry, but the lieutenant, having been sent to the front on the eve of Yom Kippur, is killed in battle. The heaviness of Holzer's sin is emphasized by numerous interpolated synagogue sequences. Disowned by her father (Avrom Morevsky), the unhappy young woman abandons her infant daughter and, as the town is evacuated before the Russian advance, flees to America. Dzigan and Schumacher recover the baby and bring her with them to Warsaw, where they deposit her in an orphanage.

Twenty years later—which is to say, in the present day—the entire town is more-or-less relocated in the same Warsaw neighborhood. The orphan (Ida Kaminska's daughter, Ruth Turkow) has been adopted by a music professor (Katch) in whose living room we see a bust of Chopin prominently displayed. In the same building, unknown to her, lives her aged grandfather. She befriends him, as well as a struggling young violinist who complains that the public is only interested in jazz. At this point, Holzer, elegant and sad, returns to recover her lost child.

Although Holzer is not recognized, the arrival of this mysterious American throws the neighborhood into a state of excitement. While her confidants Dzigan and Schumacher scour Warsaw for the "Levin" who adopted her child, Holzer develops an unhealthy interest in her daughter's violinist and offers to bring him back with her to America. Thus, unknown to each other, mother and daughter find themselves locked in an erotic struggle—but not for long. The film ends with the requisite series of confrontations between adoptive father and biological mother, prodigal mother and unwitting daughter, and finally, the reconciliation of long-lost daughter and remorseful father.

Like Joseph Seiden's *Libe un Laydnshaft* in New York, *Al Khet* was set to open for Passover 1936. But, according to Goskind, there were problems booking a cinema: "The large movie houses were afraid of losing their audience. . . . Anti-Semites might attack the theater." Goskind finally rented the Fama, a 500-seat theater in the Nalewki, and even there feared a nationalist assault. "The tension was high. I must admit, I was actually afraid to go to the premiere—who knew what was waiting for me? The violent Endek guards?"[1]

Goskind sent his driver to the theater and told him to telephone if the situation warranted it: "I got a phone call from him shortly: 'Police cavalry are surrounding the cinema! Crowds are descending on the box office, begging for tickets!' " The film was a triumph. Goskind maintains that, in his literary journal *Skamander,* the modernist Polish poet Antoni Słonimski declared the season's hit movies to be *"Hat"* (*Top Hat*) and *"Het"* (*Al Khet*). *Al Khet,* he says, ran in Warsaw "from Pesakh to Rosh Hashanah" (at least four months), and that those grosses alone covered the film's costs.

Al Khet opened in New York the following Rosh Hashanah at a theater on West Forty-eighth Street that had formerly housed the Artef. The American title was *I Have Sinned.* The *New York World-Telegram* called the film "a Jewish *Madame X,"* a characterization which would fit any number of Yiddish talkies. But if *Al Khet* provided everything a popular movie should, including a hit song, "Shpil Mir a Yidishe Tango" (Play Me a Jewish Tango) it was not without its critics.

After hailing the miracle of *Al Khet*'s existence and conceding that, in terms of music, direction, acting, purity of language, and attention to Jewish folklore, the film was "as far from the Americans as East from West," *Literarishe Bleter*'s Michal Kitai lambasted the script as trivial and irrelevant, particularly considering the earthshaking events of the day. "Why again bring forth black-coats, study houses, *botlonim* [idlers], *khadorim* [religious schools], and other claptrap? We already have more than enough of this in the Yiddish theater. . . ."[2]

Clearly, Kitai had a superior model in mind, for in the following week's *Literarishe Bleter* he wrote a passionate account of another Polish-Yiddish talkie,

Mir Kumen On (We're On Our Way), which documented the Vladimir Medem Sanatorium for tubercular children, founded ten years earlier in the Warsaw suburb of Miedzeszyn by the Bund's Central Yiddish School Organization (CYSHO), a network of perhaps a hundred elementary schools and as many kindergartens, evening schools, and secondary institutions.

Mir Kumen On "is not only the art of the film industry, it is much more: it is the art of life, of sincerity, human relationships," Kitai enthused.

The images shatter us, evoke the deepest sorrow. . . . Such a film speaks directly to the heart, to the emotions. It says more than a hundred speeches, articles, and books. It is an *agitka,* but artistic, a higher order which opens our eyes and pierces our senses . . . pulsating, clamorous, genuine: This is how one lives in the cellars for years and this is how one catches his breath at the Medem Sanatorium.

Ironically, this film involved the talents of many of the same individuals who worked on *Al Khet,* including cameraman Stanisław Lipinski, composer Henekh Kon, and the Goskind brothers (who deferred payment on the lab work). Disturbingly, it had not yet cleared the Polish censor's office. Indeed, *Mir Kumen On* proved to be the bitterest cause célèbre of Polish cinema between the world wars.

The film was directed by Aleksander Ford, who, at twenty-seven, was already the doyen of Poland's politically committed cinéastes. In 1932 he had made the popular and critical success, *Legion Ulicy* (The Legion of the Street), a gritty portrait of Warsaw newsboys and street vendors that anticipated Italian neorealism in its use of staged documentary. Born Moyshe Lipshutz in Lodz, Ford came to Warsaw in

the late twenties to study art history. There he was bitten by the film bug, becoming an early member of Stowarzyszenie Miłośników Filmu Artystycznego (Society of the Devotees of Artistic Film), which was known by its acronym START. This exemplary ciné-club aspired to be both the aesthetic and political conscience of the Polish film industry. START's members, many of whom were film journalists, gave lectures and organized exhibitions in addition to producing a number of short films. Ford made his first short, *Nad Ranem* (At Dawn), in 1929 and followed up the next year with two more—*Narodziny Gazety* (Birth of a Paper) and *Tetno Polskiego Manchesteru* (The Pulse of the Polish Manchester). Both were shot in Lodz, the latter documenting the working-class neighborhood in which the director was born.

Although Ford would later maintain that he learned Yiddish in the sanatorium where he spent a month researching the film, *Mir Kumen On* was his second Jewish project. In early 1933, he had been invited to Palestine to make a movie. There was no prepared script; Ford planned to shoot "dramatic reportage," as he had with *Legion of the Street.* Together with his wife, Olga, and a German cinematographer, he spent six months gathering footage, sometimes using a concealed camera to document events ranging from an international Jewish sports competition to Muslim religious celebrations. Much of this was sent back to Poland, where it was edited into newsreels and a short feature.

Ford ultimately decided upon a fictional narrative that would treat the Jewish-Arab conflict. Set in Palestine at the time of the Balfour Declaration, *Sabra* (named for the desert fruit which provides the term for native-born Israelis) starred Hanna Rovina along with other members of Habima, which had settled permanently in Tel Aviv the preceeding year, and concerns a band of Jewish settlers. The pioneers prevail over an avaricious sheik who tricks them into settling an arid tract of land, with the climactic discovery of water. The successful well precludes a jihad by incensed Arabs, who believe the drought to be an indication of divine displeasure. "This is just a little too much like our Wild West themes, when help always arrived at precisely the blackest moment before the dawn," complained New York's *Daily News* when the film opened at the Acme in April 1934. Still, so far as technique went, the *News* critic agreed with the *Times* reviewer who called the film's cinematography "equal to that of the best Soviet films."

Sabra was released in both Polish and Hebrew versions. When the latter opened at Warsaw's Kino Nowy-Splendid in November 1933, the critical response was mixed. The ban on Soviet films having been recently lifted, some reviewers compared it favorably to Yuli Raizman's *The Earth Thirsts*. But while Polish Jews debated the nature of the movie's sympathies, the Yishev received it as unambiguously pro-Zionist. The British authorities censored the film as "propagandist, anti-Arab, leftist, and dangerous." Tel Aviv exhibitor Ya'acov Davidon recalls that he was able to show the movie only after changing the title from *Sabra* to *Khalutzim* (Pioneers), and cutting out the battle sequences.

Ford and Goskind seem to have joined forces only after Ford's return to Poland in 1933. Sektor did the postproduction work on *Sabra,* and as a result wound up owning 15 percent of the film. Goskind was one of START's patrons and in 1934 produced Ford's fourth feature, *Przebudzenie* (Awakening), based on a poem cycle by the Polish-Jewish writer Julian

Aleksander Ford in the mid-1930s. The youthful doyen of Poland's politically committed cinéastes directed *Sabra* and *Mir Kumen On*.

Tuwim. This heavily Symbolist, protofeminist, and implicitly Communist allegory of three schoolgirls who defy social and family pressures to assert their independence in matters of career and lifestyle was booed at its premiere, blasted in the press, and evidently heavily censored. (Poland appears to have had a hair-trigger film censor. In May 1934, all Warners, First National, and Vitaphone productions were banned for "slurring" the nation. The "anti-Polish propaganda" turns out to be the 1933 boxing drama *The Life of Jimmy Dolan,* which included a disreputable character named Pulaski, and *How Many More Knights,* which featured a gangster named Kosciuszko.)

Goskind attempted to recoup his losses by augmenting the film with new sequences shot by the successful director Jan Nowina-Przybylski and the

"The very stones of these buildings seem permeated with misery": child vendors in Warsaw's Jewish slums, from Aleksander Ford's *Mir Kumen On* (Poland, 1935); frame enlargement.

cameraman Seweryn Steinwurzel, rereleasing it in the provinces as *Miłość Maturzystki* (Loves of a Graduate). Ford followed up with a commercial film for Sfinks, codirecting the comedy *Nie Miała Baba Kłopotu* (Granny Had No Worries) with Michal Waszynski from a script by Konrad Tom. Within two years, every one of these men would be involved in the making of Yiddish talkies. Ford was the first. In 1935, the year START dissolved, he directed *Mir Kumen On*.

Like *Legion of the Street*, *Mir Kumen On* was a kind of staged documentary. The film was the brain-child of Medem Sanatorium's cofounder and director Shlomo Gilinski, who, according to a memoir published by his wife, had nursed the idea for many years. Although J. M. Neuman would later intimate that the film's origins lay in an early proposal of his, the script was written by a thirty-year-old Gentile novelist, Wanda Wasilewska, together with a trio of CYSHO teachers. The daughter of a government minister, and herself a militant socialist, Wasilewska had already reported on the life of the Jewish poor in the book *Prawda o Antysemityzmie* (The Truth About Anti-Semitism):

Here fifteen, sixteen people live in one room. Here five people sleep in one bed. . . . It is against such people that the scoundrels in student's attire move. . . . The slogan of economic struggle is raised against the paupers of the Jewish street. Why look for those responsible [for Poland's economic woes] when it is so easy to find them nearby in a street of the Jewish quarters? Why suppress when it is so easy and safe to vent one's anger in a fight with a bowed porter, a Jewish boy selling watches, an old Jewish woman?

Mir Kumen On opens with just such vivid detail—a brief but pungent city symphony depicting the miserable conditions of Warsaw's Jewish poor. The narrow streets are packed with the hopeless and the unemployed, beggars jostle starving children. The cries of the vendors create a Yiddish cacophony. "The very stones of these buildings seem permeated with misery," the narrator remarks.[3]

After pausing to acknowledge "a bright spot in the slum"—a CYSHO school where the children are reading a pamphlet by Mendele Mokher Sforim, *Di Takse (The Tax on Kosher Meat)*—the filmmakers transport us to Medem Sanatorium. Here, in addition to receiving medical attention, Jewish children play in the open air and sing and dance under the sky, in addition to receiving medical attention. The filmmakers emphasize not only the regimen of personal hygiene but also the intellectual stimulation provided here. The communal dinner is accompanied by a daily news report. The "weekly entertainment" ranges from comic songs and puppet shows to violin recitals and recitations of Walt Whitman. (As in his earlier films, Ford is sensitive to the use of sound and music. The farm work is accompanied by constant singing.) In short, the sanatorium is a model society in which the children are shown to participate—a demonstration not only of Bundist socialist but the progressive ideas on children's self-government identified with Janusz Korczak.

Clearly, *Mir Kumen On* was intended as a fundraiser. One young woman makes a radio speech in the film explaining that lung disease afflicts some 75,000 Jewish children. At the end, the inmates ask the viewers for assistance. Such narrative as there is focuses on one new arrival—a timid, undernourished *kheyder* boy named Zalmen. Painfully skinny, Zalmen wolfs down the bread that's given to him and hoards the rest. He has to be taught that he will always be able to have more. Zalmen's "normalization" becomes the film's theme. Soon he is feeding the rabbits, though still wearing his *kapote*. Later we see him watching a volleyball game with mounting interest. When Zalmen finally joins in with the oth-

Three children at the Vladimir Medem Sanatorium, from *Mir Kumen On;* frame enlargement. The once-sickly Zalman is on the left.

ers, he becomes a symbol of Jewish transformation. The sickly ghetto child is now active and healthy. His *yarmulke* falls from his head and lies, unnoticed, on the ground.

The filmmakers were so certain of their project's success that they booked theaters in two Warsaw neighborhoods even before the movie had passed the government censor. Unfortunately, *Mir Kumen On* appeared at a time of political instability and heightened sensitivity. Unemployment was rising. In March and April there were bloody strikes in Krakow, Czestochowa, and Lvov, as well as a pogrom in Przytyk where Jews battled Endeks, with casualties on both sides. The ensuing trial, which freed the pogrom's instigators, was a tremendous shock to Polish Jews. Jewish leaders appealed to the Catholic clergy but were rebuffed with a pastoral letter that,

Jewish children dance under the sky in the last shot of *Mir Kumen On;* frame enlargement.

although taking a stand against anti-Semitic violence, advocated cultural separation and an economic boycott of Jewish businesses.

Among the topics on the Polish censor's proscription list were "class struggle," "revolutionary riots," and "misery" (along with stories employing a "Russian background" or "gangsters"). *Mir Kumin On* not only showed scenes of Jewish poverty, but included a sequence in which the firebrands of the Children's Council express their solidarity with and offer shelter to Gentile children whose fathers are on strike: "You talk about kasha while the miners' children starve! Let's take them in!" Here, Kon's score integrates themes from the Internationale.

By most accounts, it was this sequence, which also expresses support for "the task of joining militant Jewish workers with the masses of the world," that resulted in the film's ban as a vehicle for the "dissemination of Communist propaganda." It is more than likely, however, that the film's connection to the Jewish Labor Bund was sufficient in itself to give the authorities pause. Resolutely secular and unswervingly socialist, the Bund stood for Jewish cultural autonomy in the context of overall working-class solidarity—and for this reason was anathema to anti-Semites.

Although *Mir Kumen On* was kept from Polish movie houses, there were evidently a number of clandestine or private screenings. The film also circulated abroad, with theatrical showings in both Paris and Brussels. In the spring of 1938, Galinski brought *Mir Kumen On* to the United States, where, with the English title *Children Must Laugh,* it had its New York premiere under the auspices of the International Ladies' Garment Workers' Union and Socialist councilman Barney Vladek. It ran for a week at the midtown Continental Theater (where the Polish-

Yiddish feature *Der Dibek* had just completed a two-month engagement), on a bill with the WPA short, *Work Pays America.*[4]

Dubson's 1935 *Border* had been praised in the Soviet film journal *Kino* as "an event in our art" and "a lesson in revolutionary vigilance." Still, so far as Soviet filmmakers were concerned, the *shtetl* was a dead issue—if not that of Jewish resettlement. The Birobidzhan project was a counter-Zionism (and in some cases a crypto-Zionism) as well as a propaganda offensive.

Leon Dennen, who visited the Soviet Union in the early thirties, reported the following exchange on the day of his departure from a Jewish kolkhoz in the southern Ukraine:

As usual, Leah did the talking. "Nu-u," she said, paraphrasing the old Hebrew saying "Next year in Jerusalem," "Next year in Biro-Bidjan."

"Nothing doing," interrupted the secretary of the Komsomol, "next year in Soviet America . . ."

Everybody wished me luck and the girls remarked jestingly that I ought to learn more jazz steps if I ever intended to visit their kolkhoz again.

Despite a concerted propaganda campaign, the remoteness of the region, not to mention its primitive conditions, discouraged immigration. By 1933, a year when more settlers left than arrived, there were only 8,000 Jews in the region; the original timetable called for six times as many. Still, although Jews were less than 20 percent of the total population, in 1934 Birobidzhan was declared a Jewish autonomous oblast, with Yiddish its official language. That year, the distinguished Yiddish novelist David Bergelson published his *Birobizhaner,* an idealized account of Jew-

ish settlers who transform the taiga as well as themselves—former *luftmentshn* chopping down the primeval forest to build schools and homes.

In her memoirs, Lucy Dawidowicz recalls that the idea of Birobidzhan was attractive even to non-Communists: "To me and my Yiddishist friends, Palestine was a far cry from the Yiddish world of Eastern Europe." The prospects for peaceful settlement, the friendliness of the indigenous population, and the existence of government support were favorably contrasted to the difficult lot of the Jewish settlers in Palestine.

In March 1935, the Acme, on Union Square, was offering *Birobidjan,* a Yiddish-language "documentary featurette" written and directed by M. Slunsky for Soyuzkino News, with a musical score by Lev Pulver. Introduced by Charles Kuntz, the chairman of the pro-Soviet Association for Jewish Colonization in Russia (ICOR), this half-hour newsreel ran for two weeks on a bill with another Soviet ethnic item, *Pesnya o Schastye* (*Song of Happiness*), which was made in the Mari Autonomous Region by Mark Donskoi and Vladimir Legoshin for Vostok-kino. (The January 1935 issue of *New Theater* reported that, for a follow-up, Donskoi was "looking for a scenario on Jewish life," but neither he nor Vostok-kino produced any Yiddish films.)

As the Nazis continued to disenfranchise German Jews, the propaganda offensive gathered momentum. In May 1936, the Soviet ambassador told a New York gathering that Birobidzhan was "the symbol of the struggle against anti-Semitism and against the entire medieval darkness." That summer, the Soviet Central Committee announced that "for the first time in the history of the Jewish people its burning desire for the creation of a homeland of its own, for the achievement of its own national statehood,

The incorrigible *luftmentsh* Pinya Kopman (GOSET star Venyamin Zuskin) en route to resettlement in Birobidzhan, in *Seekers of Happiness* (U.S.S.R., 1936).

has found fulfillment. . . ." The celluloid analogue of that fulfillment was Belgoskino's *Iskateli Schastya* (Seekers of Happiness). Its title recalls Granovsky's *Yevreiskoye Schastye,* which translates as "Jewish Happiness" as well as "Jewish Luck." *Seekers of Happiness* was directed by Vladimir Korsh-Sablin (once considered the "Belorussian Dovzhenko") and I. Schapiro, from a script by Johann Seltzer, and well in advance of its appearance was cited by production chief Boris Shumyatsky as one of the best Soviet movies of 1936.[5]

Although made in Russian, *Seekers of Happiness* included several Yiddish songs arranged by the enormously popular director of the Leningrad Musical Hall, Isaac Dunayevsky, and featured GOSET star Venyamin Zuskin. As an appeal to Jewish nationalism and as a criticism of Jewish life in the Diaspora, the film went far beyond *Nosn Beker.* A poor family of foreign—most likely Polish—Jews immigrates to the promised land of Birobidzhan: they are the long-suffering matriarch Dvoira (popular character actress

and People's Artist Maria Blumenthal-Tamarina), her son Leva, her daughters Rosa and Basya, and Basya's husband, the incorrigible *luftmentsh* Pinya Kopman (Zuskin). They plan to join Dvoira's nephew on the Royte Feld (or Red Field) kolkhoz. (Birobidzhan was officially opened to foreign settlers in 1936; by end of the year, according to the *Vilner Tog,* newcomers included Jews from Poland, Latvia, and Lithuania, as well as from America and even Palestine.)

Despite the poster of heroic Jewish peasants that dominates the Leningrad office where the family apply for their permits, Pinya imagines Birobidzhan as a *shtetl* get-rich-quick scheme. Once in the Jewish oblast, he grows increasingly dissolute and, after nearly killing the virtuous Leva in a struggle over what Pinya imagines to be gold, he attempts to cross the border into China. The rest of the family thrive, however, and to complete the happy ending, Rosa overcomes her mother's misgivings to marry the young Cossack who was wrongly accused of attacking her brother. The film ends with a lengthy wedding scene in which individuals representing a variety of nationalities (including Mongolian, Korean, Siberian, Cossack) present the couple with gifts and serenade them—at times, in Yiddish.

Replete with semidocumentary passages of Jewish agricultural life, *Seekers of Happiness* was shot mainly on location. While acknowledging some of Birobidzhan's hardships, specifically the mosquito infestations in the swampy terrain, the film was overwhelmingly positive. When it was released in the United States as *A Greater Promise, New York Post* reviewer Archer Winsten noted that life in the oblast is even "better than the most optimistic zealot could expect." The movie seems to have established the outer limits of an ersatz Soviet-Jewish culture. Still, if none save the true believers might take seriously its amalgam of Stalinist ideals and ethnic Jewishness, *Seekers of Happiness* was occasionally revived in 1960s Moscow, appreciated as a rare example of "Jewish humor."

Mikhoels, who the same year had a cameo in the musical *Tsirk* (Circus), singing a Yiddish lullaby, was cited as *Seeker*'s "acting consultant." It was Korsh-Sablin, however, who took credit for the film's transformations, telling the *Moscow Daily News,* "I have straightened up the stooping Jews, shaved off the beards and cut their hair and have shown them as healthy, good-looking people, full of life and energy." On that hygienic note, Russian Jews vanished from the Soviet screen. The following year, the NKVD became responsible for transportation of Jewish settlers to Birobidzhan, while the oblast's entire leadership was purged in the Great Terror.

NOTES

1. Goskind refers to adherents of the right-wing nationalist Endejca (National Democrat) movement led by the outspoken anti-Semite Roman Dmowski.

2. "Yes, I have sinned. I wrote the scenario for a broad audience," Neuman would subsequently reply, with some irony. "It's typical that the non-Jewish press reacted more positively to the film than did the Yiddish critics." In a dig at Kitai's politics, Neuman pointed out that traditional material was now finding favor in the Soviet Union as well: "Even the Moscow GOSET is playing *Shulamis* and *Bar Kokhba.*"

3. The extent of Jewish poverty, like the degree of Polish anti-Semitism, during the 1930s is a matter of historical debate. While not all Jews were poor, nor all Poles anti-Semitic, there is ample evidence of both. "It is impossible to walk more than a dozen yards in some of the thoroughfares without being accosted for alms," wrote Joint Distribution Committee official Israel Cohen of a visit to Warsaw's Jewish slums. The streets were filled with "the lame, dwarfs, and idiots, offspring of poverty and disease. . . . Nowhere had I seen such dirt and misery, nowhere had I met with such display of abject resignation."

Lucy Dawidowicz describes a comparable scene in Vilna: "As we were walking through the dirty serpentine streets of the old ghetto area, we were accosted by a swarm of beggars. They besieged us on every side. Ragged children chased after us, screaming for a grosz—the Polish equivalent of a penny. . . ." Adult beggars, "unwashed, foul-smelling . . . dressed in layers of tatters that had once been clothing" also traveled in packs: "At first they pleaded, whined, and wheedled. When we didn't readily respond, they became abusive and began to curse volubly in pungent Yiddish idioms."

4. Goskind was involved in one other politically controversial film in 1936, documenting a conference organized in Warsaw by the revisionist Zionist leader Vladimir Jabotinsky. As the Polish government was sympathetic to Jabotinsky's plan to relocate Polish Jews to Palestine, he was received with full military pomp. Polish officials refused Goskind permission to film this ceremony, so he dispatched the young cameraman Władisław Forbert, wearing the armband of the government news agency PAT, to document the event. According to Goskind, the footage included the singing of both the Polish national anthem and the Zionist anthem, Hatikva, Jabotinsky's placing a wreath upon the grave of Poland's unknown soldier, and a speech, in Hebrew, wherein Jabotinsky declared that "Poland lives and Israel will be reborn." Goskind never submitted his hour-long film to the Polish censor but struck three prints. One was sent to Jabotinsky in Riga, another to Palestine, and the last buried near the Sektor lab. All have apparently been lost.

Ford, whose next project was a poetic semidocumentary on boatmen and others who labored on the Vistula, never made a second Yiddish talkie. Not until after World War II would he direct another film with a Jewish theme.

5. Both Korsh-Sablin and Seltzer had previous experience with Jewish material. *Sovershennoletie* (The Age of the Majority; 1933), directed by Boris Schreiber from Seltzer's scenario, is the story of a Bolshevik hero who goes underground as a Jewish factory foreman; Korsh-Sablin's *Pervyi Vzvod* (The First Platoon), another Belgoskino feature released that year, features *Nosn Beker*'s David Gutman as an aged but virtuous Jewish worker.

Overleaf: **Children of the soil. A Jewish farmgirl (Helen Beverly) teases her brother (Saul Levine) in** *Grine Felder* **(U.S.A., 1937); frame enlargement. Adapted from the play by Peretz Hirschbein, this was the first American Yiddish talkie to be shot outside the studio.**

18

The Greening of Yiddish Film

S THOUGH summoned into existence by the same forces that conjured the illusion of Birobidzhan, the Yiddish cinema produced its own verdant promised lands. Working independently, Joseph Green and Edgar G. Ulmer, two artist-businessmen in their mid-thirties, revitalized the industry and gave it truly international status. Their films were celebratory in a way earlier Yiddish talkies had not been. Suffering was not glorified. Neither was political action—yet the images of Jewish fertility, cooperation, and folk resilience suggest a conscious countermythology in opposition to the virulent ideology of Nazi anti-Semitism.

Both critically and commercially, Green's 1936 *Yidl mitn Fidl* (*Yiddle* [little Jew] *with His Fiddle*) and

Ulmer's 1937 *Grine Felder* (*Green Fields*) were the most successful Yiddish talkies ever made. Green and Ulmer combined a romantic nostalgia for *shtetl* life with a far more ambitious and sophisticated approach to filmmaking than that of the American shundists. Theirs were the first sound films to "green" the Yiddish screen with extensive exteriors; the lyrical optimism of their movies stands in marked contrast to the sanctimonious guilt of the American generational melodramas as well as to the morbid fatalism of later Polish films.

Green and Ulmer came to movies from the Central European art theater and, almost exact contemporaries, have much in common. Both were associated at crucial points in their careers with the

Joseph Green in the mid-1920s. Before turning to movies, Green acted with the Vilna Troupe and with Maurice Schwartz's Yiddish Art Theater.

Austrian-Jewish actors Rudolf and Joseph Schildkraut. Both arrived in New York from Berlin in the middle of the 1923–24 theatrical season. It's even possible that their paths crossed in Hollywood on the set of Cecil B. De Mille's 1927 *King of Kings,* for which Ulmer claimed to have made "huge miniatures of the crucifixion" and in which Green maintained he had a bit part—but, then, both share a tendency to mythologize their careers (often at the expense of talented collaborators).

Joseph Green was born Joseph Greenberg in Lodz, in the first year of the twentieth century. His education was liberal: he attended both a *kheyder* and a Polish gymnasium. His father, a real estate broker, was a devotee of the theater and took his son to see Yiddish, Polish, and German productions. Green entered drama school at fifteen, transferred to another in German-occupied Warsaw two years later, then

moved to Berlin for formal training in 1918. There, he joined an offshoot of the celebrated Vilna Troupe that toured Western Europe with the new Yiddish repertoire (*Der Dibek, Grine Felder,* and *Farvorfn Vinkl*).

In early 1924, when the Vilna Troupe came to America, Green left the company to participate in two short-lived experiments in Yiddish art theater in New York. The high-minded Unzer Teater lasted barely one season despite the involvement of playwrights H. Leivick, Peretz Hirschbein, and David Pinski, as well as Habima founder David Vardi and the ubiquitous Jacob Mestel; its successor at the Bronx Art Theater, a troupe organized around Rudolf Schildkraut, was no less prestigious, and equally fugitive. Schildkraut departed for Hollywood at the end of the 1925–26 season, and Green went along. Among other things, he was an extra in *The Jazz Singer,* appearing as one of the congregation in the synagogue scenes. It was here, Green likes to say, that he got the idea for Yiddish talkies—he claims he heard more Yiddish than English spoken on the set.[1]

Returning to New York and the serious Yiddish stage, Green spent several seasons with Maurice Schwartz (at one point working as Schwartz's publicist), and when Schwartz defected to Broadway during the disastrous 1931–32 season, Green performed with the ephemeral Yiddish Ensemble Art Theater. (This was the group that presented the New York premiere of Leivick's *Der Goylem,* in November 1931.) The movies, however, followed him. In 1932, Green was hired to dub the voice of Joseph in *Yoysef in Mitsraim,* the *faryidisht Joseph in the Land of Egypt,* and was paid with a print of the film. Later that year, when Green had an engagement in Canada, he brought *Yoysef* with him and screened it for a Montreal exhibitor. "The picture opened, I think, on Rosh Hashanah," Green recalled. "At that time I was making about $150 a week. It was good money, but from the picture receipts for the first week I got $4,000. Then it played a second week and a third. I decided right then and there that is what I wanted to do."

In the summer of 1933, Green returned to Poland to perform at Gimpel's Theater in Lvov. He again brought his print of *Yoysef in Mitsraim,* and, passing through Warsaw, showed it to a pair of Jewish exhibitors. Once they had seen the film, Green says, they refused to let him leave without signing a contract. Despite a population of nearly three and a half million Jews, Poland had yet to experience a Yiddish talkie—not one of the American films had yet been exported. Although Green maintained that some Jews feared *Yoysef* might attract anti-Semitic attention, there were no difficulties. On the contrary: "It was like Lindbergh coming to Paris. Thousands of people came to the theater. The film ran about thirty weeks in Warsaw and then it toured all over Poland."

For nearly two years, *Yoysef* was Green's meal ticket. "I made so much money, I didn't know what to do with it," he told Patricia Erens. "I wrote to a friend of mine to send me another Yiddish film." His unidentified New York associate provided him with Thomashefsky's *Bar Mitsve.* According to Green, this full-Yiddish talkie was even more enthusiastically received: "A special screening was even arranged for 200 Catholic priests, who lauded the film. The showing was held at midnight; the priests would not attend a Jewish film in the daytime." By now, Green had an ambitious plan. He formed a production company, with offices in New York and Warsaw, and intended to feature Second Avenue stars in Polish-made Yiddish-language films.

In essence, Green revived the strategy Sidney Goldin had employed thirteen years earlier in Vienna. Contemptuous of the Yiddish films produced in New York (and perhaps of the newly released *Al Khet* as well), Green realized that in Poland he could employ first-rate supporting actors and technicians for a fraction of what it might cost him in the United States. As his former director Maurice Schwartz was playing the 1935–36 season in Warsaw, Green approached him. Their initial idea was a revision of Goldfadn's *Koldunye,* a current hit in a new version by Itzik Manger. (The Rumanian-born Manger was known as the "last Yiddish troubadour"; his lyrical, ironic poems are a unique synthesis of folk ballads, German romanticism, and the Old Testament.) Then Schwartz changed his mind and insisted on *Tevye,* a part he had created in 1919. Understandably cautious, Green was unwilling to deal with the potentially explosive issue of intermarriage: "I told him that to make *Tevye* then in Poland, with anti-Semitism, the Church, the Jews, it wouldn't be good. It was not the right place. So we couldn't come to terms." (Three years later, in New York, Schwartz would film *Tevye* himself.)

Fortunately for Green, Molly Picon was in Paris, her career at a turning point. For Picon, the early thirties had been rocky. She began playing English vaudeville during the summer of 1932; late that year and early the following one, she and her husband-manager-costar Jacob Kalich vainly attempted to break back into movies. All manner of projects, both Yiddish and English, were discussed in New York and Hollywood. Meanwhile Picon toured Europe and South America and, in December 1933, made her belated Broadway debut in the English-language comedy *Birdie.* The show flopped and Picon's Second Avenue comeback the following September was just as unimpressive. After a disappointing season, she again abandoned the Yiddish stage and Kalich once more floated talk of a movie role.[2]

Kalich and Picon might have preferred the Warner brothers to Green, but the tyro producer offered the actress a superstar contract of nearly $10,000 (20 percent of his projected budget) plus a share of the film's profits, then began searching for an appropriate vehicle. Konrad Tom, an experienced performer-writer-director, provided Green with the story of a bride who escapes an arranged marriage by running off with the *klezmorim* during the wedding. As Picon was not particularly suited to play the bride, Green made one of the musicians a girl who disguises herself as a boy in order to travel with her father. (This particular drag act was, of course, a staple of Picon's repertoire; she had dressed up as a boy as recently as her last Second Avenue production.)

Abraham Ellstein, Picon's composer and a regular on her radio show, was brought to Warsaw to write the music, and Manger was engaged to provide lyrics. Despite their different traditions, it was a fortuitous collaboration. From the movie's infectious title number, Picon's unrequited-love ballad "Oy Mame, Bin Ikh Farlibt" (Oh Mama, Am I in Love), to the drinking song and various wedding dances, the score is the most charmingly effective of any Yiddish film —almost immediately entering the repertoires of Poland's real-life *klezmorim*.[3]

With the exception of Picon, the rest of the cast was drawn from Warsaw's various Yiddish ensembles. The character actor Max Bozyk (then thirty-six

Central marketplace, Kazimierz, early 1920s. A picturesque, largely Jewish town, Kazimierz was a favored location for Poland's Yiddish filmmakers. (This photograph was taken by Alter Kacyzne, author of two Yiddish screenplays, including *Der Dibek*.)

years old) had been the star of Manger's *Koldunye* (*Yidl* would make him a bigger one); Leon Liebgold (twenty-six), whose mother had played with Picon when she toured Poland in 1922, was a precocious veteran currently associated with the *klaynkunst* troupe Yidishe Bande. Green supervised the performers (except for Picon, who took direction only from Kalich) and hired Jan Nowina-Przybylski to handle the film's technical aspects. Nowina-Przybylski's best-known film was the 1931 *Cham* (Yokel), one of the Polish film industry's few international successes. His presence established *Yidl* as a Polish production, and thus eligible for various tax abatements and other benefits.

Half hardheaded businessman, half defender of literary theater culture, Green was determined to give Yiddish film a measure of artistic respectability. In an interview published in *Literarishe Bleter* shortly after *Yidl*'s release, he outlined his objectives. He planned to produce technically accomplished films on subjects that were authentically Jewish, yet universal in appeal. The successful Jewish movie, Green explained, "must avoid the *goles Yid* [the negative stereotype of the Diaspora Jew]."

Ignoring the fact that, by strict Zionist standards, he too could be considered a *goles Yid,* Green promised something for every secular Jewish ideology:

While [a Yiddish movie] should have folklore
and ethnicity, it must also expose social injustice.
It can do this artistically, without heavyhanded
propaganda. Such a film must also embody cultural values and purity of language. Above all, it
must be entertaining.

Yidl's interiors were shot in a Warsaw film studio, using German sound technology; the production then went on location for ten days in Kazimierz (which had only recently been the subject of a well-

Molly Picon in the streets of Kazimierz in
***Yidl mitn Fidl* (Poland, 1936).**

received documentary, and was the place where, eleven years earlier, Jonas Turkow had shot the exteriors for *Der Lamedvovnik*). A small, predominantly Jewish town on the Vistula by the ruins of King Casimir's castle, Kazimierz was "discovered" by Polish literati in the late nineteenth century. Sholem Asch spent several summers there; his 1905 novel *Dos Shtetl* made the village a favored resort for Jewish artists and writers.[4]

Still, however picturesque Kazimierz appeared to some, for the Americans it seemed shockingly backward: "I had never seen such poverty—outdoor plumbing, rickety wooden houses bent into fantastic shapes, and the people unbelievably threadbare," Picon recalled. "The skeletal children, with their long *payes* and little yarmulkes, wore trousers that were in shreds and shoes tied on their feet with rope. . . . The whole town was on our heels while we filmed the story. We ordered them around and they fol-

Jewish *klezmorim* in the Polish countryside in *Yidl mitn Fidl*. From left: Leon Liebgold, Molly Picon, Simcha Fostel, and Max Bozyk.

lowed us like lambs." Many of the villagers can be seen in the finished film. *Yidl mitn Fidl* opens with a semidocumentary exploration of the central marketplace, a stagelike area enclosed by stone houses. Here the vivacious Yidl (Picon) and her downcast father (Simcha Fostel) are playing for coins.

Having lost their home, the pair wander the countryside, Yidl disguised as a boy to assuage her father's anxiety. In another town, they first compete with and then join forces with two more itinerant *klezmorim,* the garrulous Isaac (Bozyk) and handsome Froim (Liebgold) with whom Yidl inevitably falls in love. The film's set piece has the four musicians hired to provide the music for the wedding of a wealthy, overbearing merchant (Kaminsky troupe veteran Shmuel Landau). The young bride runs off with the *klezmorim* and joins their band, setting the table for a rather perverse, albeit short-lived, romantic triangle. Eventually Yidl's true identity is revealed and her sudden, if unsurprising, success on the Warsaw stage provides a bit of last-minute melodrama.

Essentially a vehicle for Picon, then thirty-seven, *Yidl* offers a still-fresh collection of her characterizations and routines—ranging from the tipsy *yeshive* boy to the overexcited chatterbox to the pert gamine. *Variety* characterized the film as "a conglomeration of everything she's done on the stage, vaude and on the radio." At the climax of the film, Picon blunders onto a stage, falls into the pit, scrambles about, speaks directly to the crowd, sings, soliloquizes and otherwise demonstrates her rapport with an audience. Although *Yidl* could not have been made in America, there's no mistaking the optimistic logic of the film's progression—from itinerant *klezmer* to Warsaw stardom and then on to New York. A deluge of money is superimposed over Picon and company's preparations to leave Poland.

Green's finest moment as a director was the wedding. A veritable production number, it is introduced by a stylized montage, is largely cut to music, and is elaborately choreographed. Even *Variety,* which was surprisingly skeptical about the film in general, termed this "an ace sequence." Green set up the scene as a sort of staged documentary. He rented a hall, hired a kosher caterer, invited the townspeople as guests, and ran the shoot as though it were an actual wedding. The filming began before dawn and lasted through the night—at four o'clock in the morning, Green realized he had no violinist to accompany the *badkhn* and sent his assistants out to search the town and roust one out of bed. Meanwhile, the food had to be continually replenished for successive shots.

According to Picon, "our poverty-stricken guests couldn't figure out what was happening."

They thought they had been invited to a real wedding, and when one woman asked why so much food, we explained to her it wasn't a real wedding, we were just making a film. I don't think she had ever seen a film, but she said, "Why didn't you tell me that before? With so much food, I could have brought my daughter to get married for real. She has a *khosn* [bridegroom], but we have no money . . . to make a proper wedding."

The filmmakers wrapped the scene at seven the next morning after twenty-odd hours of shooting.

Yidl cost approximately $50,000, and Green recouped his investment well before the movie came to New York. Released in Warsaw in September 1936, five months after *Al Khet*, *Yidl* contributed mightily to the boomlet in Yiddish production the following year in Poland. A new Yiddish-language monthly, *Film Nayes* (Film News), began publication in December; it was followed by the Lodz journal *Ekran un Stsene* (Screen and Stage). Indeed, *Yidl's* influence was scarcely limited to Yiddish filmmaking. In 1937, Konrad Tom wrote and codirected *Ksiazatko* (released in America as *The Lottery Prince*), a Polish-language film in which a young girl disguises herself as a boy in order to work as dance instructor in a mountain resort.

The same month *Yidl* opened, Poland's representative to the League of Nations declared Jewish resettlement to be the country's most urgent priority

Cast and crew of *Yidl mitn Fidl*: Molly Picon (center) is flanked by the film's two directors, Joseph Green (in suspenders, left) and Jan Nowina-Przybylski. Max Bozyk stands directly behind Green, Simcha Fostel is next to him (behind Picon and Nowina-Przybylski).

Poster for *Yidl mitn Fidl's* New York release. The film opened on the last day of 1936 at a legitimate house in the heart of the theater district and was excitedly greeted in the Yiddish press—even the Communist *Morgn Frayhayt* found it "not without charm."

and formally requested colonies to be placed under Polish mandate for that very purpose. Despite the exacerbated (and now officially sanctioned) anti-Semitic climate, Green recalls the Polish government as strongly supportive: "I was called to the Ministry of Culture and given a citation. They felt the film was very moral." In general, *Yidl* received favorable notices, although even the most sympathetic Polish reviewers could not help but see Bozyk in a traditional anti-Semitic light (a character who, as one wrote, "could lie ten times in five words") or wonder "why Jewish restaurant owners hired Polish cooks to make a kosher dinner." *Yidl* was also appreciated as exceptional filmmaking. When the movie opened on Broadway, the *New York Times* pronounced it technically "superior to most of the Warsaw productions."

One of the three top-grossing Polish movies of 1936, *Yidl* was the first truly international Yiddish

hit. It was subsequently released throughout Western Europe as well as South Africa, Australia, and (prudently dubbed into Hebrew) Palestine. *Yidl* was even released, after a fashion, in Nazi Germany. "In 1937," according to Green,

a representative of the Jewish community in Berlin came to see me in Warsaw. He told me the conditions the people were living under—no one was allowed outside the ghetto or to mingle with non-Jews; no one could attend films or theater. But they'd heard about *Yidl,* and had applied to the government to allow them to bring in a print. This was okayed, but with one condition: the Minister of Culture—that meant Goebbels—had to first view the film.

I sent a print out, and received it back a week later. The next day, I got word that the permission had been granted. But there was now another condition: the negative of *Yidl* had to be sent to Germany and prints would be made there. I took a chance, and sent the negative. Three weeks later it was returned. I later learned that the film was a highlight of the year for the Berlin Jews.[5]

Opening in New York on the last day of 1936, *Yidl* was booked at the Ambassador, a legitimate house in the heart of the theater district at Broadway and Forty-ninth Street. The film was excitedly greeted by the Yiddish press—even Buchwald in the *Morgn Frayhayt* found it "not without charm. . . . Manger's lyrics and Ellstein's music supply a memorable background for local color—poverty, strikes, and strife." It received only mildly favorable reviews from English-language reviewers, however. The most enthusiastic was Robert Garland's mixed notice in the *New York American* which concluded by observing that "in its muddle-headed way, Hollywood is making a mistake in passing up our Molly for some of its so-called glamor girls."

While Garland opined that *Yidl* "would be grand in English," Broadway itself had never been so Yiddish. The Artef, ensconced at a theater on West Forty-eighth Street, was offering *200,000* (the Soviet version of Sholom Aleichem's *Dos Groyse Gevins*), and H. Leivick's *Keytn* (Chains). A block away, Joseph Buloff was directing an ensemble of actors from the Yiddish Art Theater. When Schwartz returned from Europe, he attempted to book a Broadway theater as well, hoping to produce a new anti-Nazi play, *Der Grenets* (The Frontier). And the day after *Yidl's* New York premiere, Max Reinhardt's spectacular production of Franz Werfel's Biblical pageant *The Eternal Road* opened at the old Manhattan Opera House, on Thirty-fourth Street.

The last Yiddish talkie to open uptown had been the anti-Nazi *Der Vanderer Yid* (*The Wandering Jew*), which three years earlier had managed a run of barely two weeks before vanishing. *Yidl* enjoyed a six-week exclusive engagement at the Ambassador followed by special premieres at three movie houses —the Clinton, the Loews Brooklyn Palace, and the Loews Boston Road, in the Bronx. The first Yiddish talkie exhibited by a major theater chain, it played neighborhood theaters throughout the spring of 1937, sometimes billed with a reissued 1933 comedy, *Don't Bet on Love*—a bit of proletarian romance featuring Lew Ayres as a plumber enamored of manicurist Ginger Rogers.

By 1937, Green was back in Warsaw to produce *Der Purimshpiler* (The Purim Player), known in English as *The Jester*. The title is one of the most suggestive in all of Yiddish cinema, evoking both the carnival holiday of Purim and the origins of Yiddish theater. But the script, which Green cowrote with the leftwing New York journalist Chaver-Paver, and which Manger then polished, is disappointingly timid. To a large degree, *Der Purimshpiler* rehashes *Yidl's* tale of itinerant performers, star-crossed lovers, and village Jews who become stars in the big city.

For the romantic leads, Green brought over two Americans—a then-married couple, Miriam Kressyn and Hymie Jacobson, both of whom had appeared in Judea's earliest two-reelers. Joseph Buloff, originally slated to star, withdrew at the last minute to appear in a play, and Green replaced him with Zygmunt Turkow. The rest of the actors were Polish, including Isaac Samberg, Shmuel Landau, and Max Bozyk. Like *Yidl*, *Der Purimshpiler* was codirected by Jan Nowina-Przybylski, who died not long afterward. Seweryn Steinwurzel, the cameraman on the Forbert films a decade earlier, was director of photography.

Set in a pre–World War I Galician *shtetl*—a set built for the film on a *khalutzim* farm at the outskirts of Warsaw (with additional material shot on location in Kazimierz)—*Der Purimshpiler* has a homemade operetta quality appropriate to a Hapsburg backwater. The melancholy vagabond Getsl (Turkow) is drawn toward the town by the sound of women singing as they harvest apples. A jack-of-all-trades, he takes work as a shoemaker's assistant to be near Esther (Kressyn), the cobbler's romantic, good-natured daughter. But while Getsl amuses the shop with his tricks and pranks—trading barbs with Esther's clownish, disreputable grandfather (Bozyk)—the girl falls for a smooth song-and-dance man from a traveling circus (Jacobson). Like *Yidl*, *Der Purimshpiler* takes the side of young love against arranged mar-

Getsl (Zygmunt Turkow, seated at right against the balustrade) watches Esther (Miriam Kressyn) dance with Dick (Hymie Jacobson). *Der Purimshpiler* (Poland, 1937).

riages. The shoemaker's daughter elopes with the circus performer and luckless Getsl is left to wander off alone.

As the title promises, the film's most memorable scenes are centered on the carnival of Purim. (Indeed, one wonders if *Der Purimshpiler* wasn't originally inspired by Manger's 1936 *Megile Lider* [Megile Songs], a series of dramatic lyrics which recast the Book of Esther as a *Purimshpil* presented in a nineteenth-century *shtetl* by a group of tailor's apprentices.) On the eve of the holiday, Esther's father invites a wealthy couple and their half-witted son to

his home in hope of arranging a match. The dinner has already turned tumultuous when in marches Getsl with his band of Purim *shpilers* in makeshift costumes and masks, spouting doggerel, capering like a crew of goblins from the Jewish id. Energized by this whirligig—a comic counterpart to *Der Dibek*'s expressionistic "dance of death"—Getsl uses the traditional Purim play to insult and drive off Esther's rich suitor. (Three years later, parts of this sequence would be used to "document" Jewish religious rites in the vilest of Nazi documentaries, *Der Ewige Jude*.)

Der Purimshpiler had its Warsaw premiere at the Fama in September 1937, opening in New York three months later at the Cameo, the midtown showcase for Soviet imports. With respect to this suspect venue, the *Daily News* hailed the film as "an uncommon Yiddish picture, deserving a week in any foreign movie house in Manhattan." Still, despite generally favorable notices, *Der Purimshpiler* was far less successful than *Yidl.* If the vaudeville set pieces offer a taste of Yiddish cabaret, the movie is certainly thematically undeveloped (what, for example, is Esther's connection to her Biblical namesake?) and oddly denatured. Green's attempts to make the film more universal were ineffective, at least in Poland where one trade journal observed that although *Der Purimshpiler* "could be to the taste of certain groups and even shown in the United States, [it] is not really for everyone."

The film has none of the social consciousness one would expect from Chaver-Paver and, a few lovely passages aside, little of Manger's lyricism. Indeed, in failing to live up to its material as well as its predecessor's success, *Der Purimshpiler* was doubly disappointing. Green would maintain that Turkow "was not right for the part. He was too tall . . . and he wasn't funny enough." He also regretted hiring the Viennese composer Nicholas Brodsky (later to work at MGM): "He was very famous, but he was not a Jewish composer." In retrospect, Green thought he'd made a mistake in not substituting a troupe of Yiddish actors for the traveling circus. The latter may have been spectacular—but that sort of showmanship wasn't the source of the Yiddish cinema's appeal. From the original audience's point of view, it is unlikely that all the elephants in Poland could compensate for the absence of Molly Picon.

Although scarcely political, *Yidl mitn Fidl* contributed to the upsurge in Yiddish culture and Jewish consciousness that characterized the period of the antifascist Popular Front. In the United States no less than Poland, Green's success fired the ambition of Yiddish filmmakers—including that of a former Reinhardt set builder, Edgar George Ulmer.

Unlike Green, Ulmer is a director with a reputation; the four Yiddish films he directed between 1937 and 1940 were an interlude rather than a career—albeit an interlude in a career that is fascinating for its subterranean aspects. Primarily a director of low-budget and independent productions, Ulmer was canonized by French critics who saw him as a precursor of their own *nouvelle vague.* But less well-known than the "grade-Z" movies he made for Producers Releasing Corporation (PRC) in the forties are the ethnic films he directed a few years earlier in New York.[6]

Ulmer was born around the turn of the century in the Bohemian town of Ulmitz, where his father was a wine merchant with an interest in socialist politics. Not long after Edgar's birth, the family relocated to his mother's native Vienna. The Ulmers were scarcely traditional Jews—their son was even given a Jesuit education. Indeed, Ulmer would later maintain that he had no idea that he was a Jew until he encountered the Austrian quota system in high school: "Then I learned about the *numerus clausus*, there were only 4 percent of all pupils allowed to be Jews."

Nevertheless, Ulmer studied architecture at the Academy of Arts and Sciences in Vienna. Made homeless during the World War, he was taken in by the Schildkraut family (Joseph was a former schoolmate) and through them became acquainted with Max Reinhardt, for whom he began his theatrical career as a set builder in Berlin. The precocious Ulmer also did production design for various German film companies. In the extensive interview he gave Peter Bogdanovich shortly before his death, he claims to have broken into the film industry building sets for the 1920 version of *The Golem*.

Ulmer came to the United States with Reinhardt in late 1923 when the maestro took *The Miracle* on tour. He subsequently worked for the Broadway impresario Martin Beck before heading to the West Coast, where he was employed as a production assistant and art director at Universal, an association that would last into the early thirties. For the remainder of the twenties, however, Ulmer divided his time between Hollywood and Berlin. In Germany he worked on the production design of F. W. Murnau's *Der Letzte Mann* (*The Last Laugh*; 1924) and *Faust* (1926); back in the United States, he served as assistant director on all of Murnau's American films as well as a number of westerns directed by William Wyler. On his last trip to Berlin, Ulmer collaborated with Robert Siodmak, Billy Wilder, Eugene Shuftan, and Fred Zinneman on the experimental documentary *Menschen am Sonntag* (People on Sunday; 1929).

After departing Europe for good, Ulmer directed *Mr. Broadway* (1932), a low-budget musical starring gossip columnist Ed Sullivan, *Damaged Lives* (1933), a melodrama *cum* educational film on venereal disease (which, despite the sponsorship of the American Social Hygiene Association, could not be shown in New York until 1937), and, most notably, *The Black Cat* (1934), an expressionist horror film pairing Universal's two reigning ghouls, Boris Karloff and Bela Lugosi. During this period, Ulmer met his future wife, Shirley Castle Alexander. That she was married at the time to the nephew of Universal boss Carl Laemmle seems to have cast a pall over Ulmer's career.

According to Bill Krohn, Ulmer was "blackballed not for politics, but for love"; he directed only one more film, the western *Thunder over Texas* (1934), before moving east to build a career as an independent. Ulmer's first assignment was *From Nine to Nine* (1936), a thriller made in Montreal. Then, while Shirley worked as a model, he took intermittent assignments as a New York cameraman for the Pathé Newsreel. One break came as a result of a chance meeting, while shooting a story at Coney Island, with the Ukrainian dancer Vasile Avramenko. Having introduced America to Ukrainian folk dance, Avramenko dreamed of producing a Ukrainian-language film. For a fifty-dollar advance, Ulmer was retained to direct *Natalka Poltavka* (*The Girl from Poltavka*), an adaptation of the classic Ukrainian operetta by Ivan Kotliarevsky.

This account is based on information given Bill Krohn by Shirley Ulmer. In his interview with Bogdanovich, Ulmer tells a somewhat different story, explaining that he was called to New York by a friend who was already involved in *The Girl from Poltavka,* which was to be directed by the Russian emigré actor Leo Bolgakov.

I came to New York and was hired as the associate producer and began organizing. After getting the crew together, I looked at the script and said, "This is no script, nobody can break it down." Bolgakov wouldn't have anything to do with it— he was playing the big director—so I sat down and wrote the script with eight men: the dancer, a designer, a window-washer—everybody wanted to put everything they could think of into the script! I was paid the magnificent sum of $35 a week. . . .

Three days into the shoot, Ulmer maintains, Bolgakov was fired and he took over the direction. (Undeterred, Bolgakov went on to direct *Marusia,* another Ukrainian folk opera shot in New Jersey in 1938.)[7]

The Girl from Poltavka, made for less than $20,000, was financed through subscriptions and two year's worth of advance sales (as well as the sponsorship of the mainly Ukrainian window-washers' union). It was shot during the summer of 1936 in a mock Ukrainian village Ulmer built on a farm outside Flemington, New Jersey. The cast was largely Russian and Ukrainian, the singing was prerecorded. For the production numbers, Avramenko used the same network that had helped him finance the film to supply the astonished Ulmer with 200 dancers:

Sunday night when I came back to the farm, there were cars with license plates from all over America and Canada. They had spread hay all over the farm. [Avramenko] never told me that every one of these groups in these cities and villages had a dancing teacher and for years the kids not only learned how to dance these things, but their mothers sewed the costumes! The parents drove these people to the set; from as far away as British Columbia, they came. . . .

The Girl from Poltavka had a gala preview at the Al Jolson Theater on Broadway, Christmas Eve of 1936. (Six weeks later, the film opened at the Belmont, paving the way for Seiden's *Ikh Vil Zayn a Mame.*) Meanwhile, Amkino, the American distributor of Soviet films, rushed its version of the operetta (directed by Ivan Kavaleridze) into a Lower East Side theater so quickly there was no time to provide the print with English titles. "You can imagine what political things happened," Ulmer told Bogdanovich, explaining that Soviet agents subjected him to something more than verbal abuse for his role in making

a Ukrainian national film. "I was beaten up one night going home by the thugs of Mr. Napoli and Mr. Troftenberg. They were the heads of Sovkino [*sic*] in New York."

As it turned out, Ulmer's next film would be produced by Amkino's former head, Roman Rebush, who had helped organize the company in 1926 and ran it at least into 1932. On July 4, 1937 (three weeks after *Damaged Lives* finally opened to respectful reviews) Ulmer, Rebush, and the 16mm film distributor Ludwig Landy announced the formation of Collective Film Producers. Their progressive politics were evident in the new firm's rubric; their first project, already in preproduction, was an adaptation of Peretz Hirschbein's 1916 *Grine Felder,* a play with the status of a modern classic.[8]

Although Ulmer spoke no Yiddish he was familiar with the Yiddish theater. During his first visit to New York, Rudolf Schildkraut had introduced him to Maurice Schwartz: "I was taken down to Second Avenue and suddenly met the Jewish Art Theater which had quite some tremendous actors—Muni Weisenfreund for instance. . . . Schwartz had a stock company of eighty people. It was a second Broadway down there." It's even possible that Ulmer saw the Vilna Troupe's 1924 production of *Grine Felder,* which may have featured Joseph Greenberg. No matter who first suggested the felicitous choice of Hirschbein's play (Rebush and Landy also took individual credit), Ulmer was scarcely oblivious to the commercial implications of *Yidl mitn Fidl,* which opened in New York one week after *The Girl from Poltavka.* In 1937, he told Bogdanovich that he had "met a group of youngsters, one of whom had brought a film made with Molly Picon in Warsaw. That film made a fortune in New York. Unbelievable."

Ulmer, Rebush, and Landy persuaded Hirschbein to let them film the play. Hirschbein's permission was conditional on the casting of Jacob Ben-Ami in the role of the young Talmud scholar, a part he had originated fifteen years earlier. Although Ben-Ami was clearly too old for the role, Ulmer played to his vanity and agreed. Later, the two men worked out a compromise. Rather than star in the picture, Ben-Ami would codirect. Ben-Ami cast the film and also supervised the actors' readings; leads went to the young Artefnik Michael Goldstein and Helen Beverly, an American-born teenager with experience in both Yiddish- and English-language theater.

Although accounts of his involvement in the project vary, Ben-Ami clearly had no love for the medium of film. (When I interviewed him in 1975, he adamantly denied even having heard of *Der Vanderer Yid,* let alone starring in it.) Although he took full credit for *Grine Felder,* it would be more exact to say Ben-Ami served as dramaturge. Ulmer directed the actors for the camera and handled the technical aspects—setting up shots, designing sets, choosing locations. In this sense, Ulmer's work on *Grine Felder,* as well as *The Girl from Poltavka,* was anticipated by his apprenticeship in the German silent cinema; explaining to Bogdanovich his function as a *"Bild-Regisseur,"* Ulmer pointed out that "up to the coming of sound, there were *two* directors in each picture: a director for the dramatic action and for the actors, and then the director for the picture itself who established the camera angles, camera movements, etc."

The professional relationship between Ulmer and Ben-Ami—who, according to Goldstein, never spoke to each other on the set—was the inverse of that between Joseph Green and Jan Nowina-Przbylski. But like Green, Ulmer was determined to make a new kind of Yiddish talkie:

Now I declared war the first moment I went into [the] picture—I'm not going to do what Schwartz does, I'm not going to do the cheap things which Picon does, I'm going to have my own style and I'm going to do it like I see it— dignified, not dirty—not with beards where they look like madmen. The same decision which Sholem Asch made, which Chagall made.

Grine Felder was by far the most prestigious Yiddish property to be filmed in America. According to Ulmer, three Yiddish dailies—the *Forverts, Der Tog,* and the *Morgn Frayhayt*—were vying for the opportunity to back the film. Although the production was desperate for capital, Ulmer refused them all, not wanting to run the risk of alienating the readers of the two other papers. Instead, "every one of us, the producers, hocked the furniture in his home," and they borrowed $8,000 from Household Finance. This improbably low figure seems as much a factor of Ulmer's flair for the dramatic as the announced budget of $30,000 seems inflated in the interest of credibility. In any case, a number of *Grine Felder*'s backers provided services in return for an interest in the film; other investors included Paul Muni and Helen Beverly's father.

Filmed on the same isolated New Jersey farm Ulmer had used for *The Girl from Poltavka, Grine Felder* is almost entirely exteriors. According to Ulmer, the company spent six weeks rehearsing and then, using a blimped news camera, shot the film in five days. Because the company could only afford to purchase 15,000 feet of raw stock, Ulmer claims to have worked on a virtual one-to-one shooting ratio. Although Ulmer seems prone to exaggerate the vicissitudes of any given project ("the assistant and I had to sleep in the same bed in a broken down hotel in Newark"), the conditions under which *Grine Felder* was made were so primitive that his later work on Hollywood's Poverty Row seems De Millian by comparison.

Once the film was in the can, another sort of finagling began. Using his negative as collateral, Ulmer persuaded his film lab to extend him ninety days' credit on a $3,000 bill. Eighty-nine days later, Ulmer was still cutting the negative and the lab owner was prepared to foreclose. At this point, the story becomes a benign version of *The Godfather,* with the desperate Ulmer compelled to seek help from two powerful men of respect in the secular Yiddish community. He first went to Abraham Cahan, who put him in touch with the head of the International Ladies' Garment Workers' Union, David Dubinsky. If he liked the film, Dubinsky told Ulmer, the union would buy 75,000 tickets, netting Ulmer $20,000—$5,000 of it up front.

In essence, Dubinsky offered Ulmer a version of the "benefit" system which had long supported the Yiddish theater. "I am paying you for a ticket forty cents," Ulmer recalled the union leader telling him. "I can sell it for whatever I want to my members— you have no box office Monday, Tuesday, Wednesday, Thursday, Friday." Ulmer arranged a screening of the rough cut, Dubinsky and his associates adored the film, and the lab got paid. Shortly afterward, Ulmer renegotiated his agreement with the union, splitting the Friday night gate with them ("because we have a negative to pay off"). He then found a new lab, and used his remaining $2,000 to finish and publicize the film. Showing no less ingenuity than Joseph Seiden, he even managed to hire a twenty-four-piece orchestra and pay their salaries with box-office chits.

Loews, which had scored well the previous winter with *Yidl,* offered Collective Film Producers $25,000

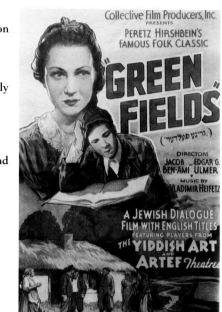

Poster for *Grine Felder* (U.S.A., 1937). Based on a famous play, the film was made without established stars. Although Helen Beverly and Michael Goldstein are pictured, they are identified only by their stage affiliations, the Yiddish Art Theater and the Artef.

outright for *Grine Felder,* but Ulmer turned them down. Instead, as the director told Bogdanovich, he approached the owner of a new theater he spotted west of Times Square and, offering 20 percent of the nonunion gate in exchange for a guaranteed ten-week run, persuaded the owner to inaugurate his theater with *Grine Felder* rather than a move-over of *Mayerling.* (In fact, the Squire was already showing a second run of Joris Iven's partisan documentary, *The Spanish Earth.*) Thus, with Peretz Hirschbein in attendance, *Grine Felder* had its world premiere at the Squire on October 12, 1937. In a speech before the film, Hirschbein recalled that "twenty years ago, the play *Grine Felder* marked the beginning of a better Yiddish theater in America" and expressed the hope that the filmed *Grine Felder* would "mark the beginnings of a better Yiddish film."

It did. "The first weekend we sold out," Ulmer

told Bogdanovich. "Nobody could get into the theater. The Jews came to the theater in the morning and wouldn't get out! We had to turn the light on and plead with them to please leave the theater so other people could see the picture! Impossible. We had to stop the performance and empty the house with the police." Critics were scarcely less enthusiastic. Citing *Yidl mitn Fidl* as *Grine Felder's* only artistic precursor, William Edlin hailed the film in *Der Tog* as one that "can be shown in theaters throughout the world, as are well-made movies from France, Czechoslovakia or Hungary."

It is a joy and a great satisfaction to be able to state that *Grine Felder* is a film we can take pride in; a film which we can point to—the beginning of a new epoch in the experiment of producing American-made Yiddish movies.

That *Grine Felder* should have premiered in a theater that opened with *The Spanish Earth* is hardly inappropriate. The Spanish Civil War, which broke out during the summer of 1936, had no direct or immediate impact on the Jewish Question, but no minority supported the Spanish Republic more ardently than American Jews. The Civil War was the quintessential Popular Front issue; Jews understood that Spain was a test site for the struggle between fascism and Western democracy and identified strongly with the Loyalist forces. (Although by then an anticommunist, Lucy Dawidowicz remembers that, in her mind, "the fate of the Spanish Republic had become coupled with the fate of the Jews. The fall of Spain would presage the fall of the Jews everywhere, once the Nazis and Fascists gained ascendancy throughout Europe.") Indeed, *Grine Felder* played the Squire for eight weeks—neither ten, as guaranteed, nor twenty,

as Ulmer recalled—on a bill with another Popular Front documentary, Frontier Films' *China Strikes Back*.

This unlikely but definitely antifascist pairing underscores the political bias of Collective Film Producers as well as the Squire, which was managed by a former member of the Workers Film and Photo League, Edward Kern. Under the headline EXCELLENT MOVIE BILL AT SQUIRE, the *Daily Worker* not only praised *Grine Felder*, which "carries one back with it into the past of Russia, when Jews lived in a pale and had to fight for knowledge, before the days of liberty and Soviets," but specifically congratulated Kern for this propitious juxtaposition: "Sharing honors with this pastoral poem of youth and love and the traditions of a great people is the epic *China Strikes Back*, wherein we meet the Chinese Red Army and its heroic leaders, Mao Tse-tung and Chu Tehn."[9]

Far more than *Yidl*, *Grine Felder* was incorporated into the culture of the Popular Front. The film's English titles were supplied by no less a fellow traveler than Leon Dennen, and a few weeks after its premiere, several of the participants (including Ben-Ami and Hirschbein) joined together with representatives of Jewish Communist organizations in America for the gala that marked the establishment of the Yidisher Kultur Farband (Jewish Culture Association), or YKUF. That autumn, the ILGWU scored another cultural triumph as well: *Pins and Needles*, a satirical revue performed by members of the union's dramatic clubs, opened at the Labor Stage for a run that ultimately lasted almost three years and over 1,100 performances. In a press release issued for *Grine Felder's* opening, Collective Film Producers compare themselves to the Group Theater and announce subsequent plans for a film adapted from Zola and another with "a decided labor slant."

Grine Felder repeated *Yidl's* success. After the film broke box-office records in New York's Jewish neighborhoods, the Loews chain picked it up and ran a shortened, subtitled version as a B-feature with *Second Honeymoon,* a third-rate screwball comedy from Twentieth Century-Fox starring Loretta Young and Tyrone Power. In *Literarishe Bleter,* Nakhman Mayzel, who had recently left Warsaw for New York, lauded *Grine Felder's* "outstanding artistic and financial success, unparalleled in the history of Yiddish film in America." The film, he reported, had thus far been screened in over seventy different New York theaters; nearly one million people had seen it. As for himself, "a number of scenes moved me to tears."

Ulmer, who received only $300 in salary to make *Grine Felder,* maintained that sometime afterward, Fox production chief Darryl Zanuck offered him the chance to direct two pictures with America's greatest box-office attraction, Shirley Temple. "I said, 'How do you come to me for pictures with Shirley Temple?' So he said, 'You made *Green Fields*—it's a pastoral film.'" (Whether or not this exchange took place as Ulmer recounts, the implications are fascinating: Zanuck, a Gentile, is the only Hollywood mogul ever credited with having seen—or heard of—a Yiddish talkie.) In any case, *Grine Felder* was a pastoral. It could easily have taken its epigraph from the first lines of Eliakum Zunser's "Di Sokhe" (The Plow), a lyric written in 1880 and sung throughout the Yiddish world: "In the plow lies bliss and blessedness, life's true essence. The morning comes, the tiller of the soil goes forth into God's world, full of health and cheer, breathing the clean air of free-dom." It is a plow which supplies the film's final image.

As in Hirschbein's other folk comedies, *Grine Felder's* remarkably unsentimental lyricism is informed by a powerful sense of longing for roots. Totally devoid of pretension, the film evokes a host of Jewish utopian traditions, mixing an inchoate Zionism with a displaced Chasidism, Bundist communalism with childhood nostalgia. Underlying the play is the issue of Jewish "productivization." (Indeed, in 1935, Hirschbein had published a novel, suggestively titled *Royte Felder* [Red Fields], which chronicled the postrevolutionary Jewish farming collectives of the Crimea.) Ostensibly a rustic comedy, the film celebrates an idyllic world of tribal wholeness and innate, stubborn piety, a world where man and nature, work and religion—and even parents and children—can be joyfully reconciled.

Grine Felder offers a multitude of positive, specifically Jewish images, but religious dogma is subsumed in reverence for the *folksmentsh* (man of the people) and the redemptive power of the soil. (Interestingly, this most widely seen of all American Yiddish talkies would be virtually the only one made without "stars.") A key Talmudic citation is offered twice, at strategic moments: "A man without land is not a man." The idea that spirituality is achieved through acceptance, not renunciation, of the material world is made apparent in the film's first scene—one not in the play—wherein the young scholar, Levi Yitskhok (Goldstein), taking leave of his colleagues in a shadowy *bes-medresh,* opens the synagogue door, washing the screen with brilliant light.

Wandering deep into the midsummer countryside, the ascetic student encounters a timeless, verdant world of earthy Jewish farmers and barefoot *sheyne meydlekh.* Planning to stay one night, he re-

Jews on the land: Isidore Cashier and Max Vodnoy cooperate on the harvest, Helen Beverly and Saul Levine work behind them, in *Grine Felder;* frame enlargement.

Yiddish child star Herschel Bernardi, in *Grine Felder;* frame enlargement.

mains to teach the farmers' children (one of them played by the young Herschel Bernardi). In gesture and mannerism, Goldstein's painfully diffident *yeshive-bokher* is as masterful a folk characterization as Mikhoels's Menakhem Mendl.[10]

Drama is provided both by the conflicting ambition of two neighboring families to acquire the unworldly student they call *"rebele"* (little rabbi) as a son-in-law and by the scholar's own recognition that Talmudic learning is secondary to the natural religion of the heart. Levi Yitskhok, who is named for a celebrated *tsadek,* not only falls in love with the beautiful and mischievous Tsine (Beverly) but ultimately comes to realize that among these unlettered *proste Yidn* he has found the "city of pure Jews." The scenario gives this latter point a Popular Front inflection by augmenting Hirschbein's play to include a discussion on "the union of Labor and Torah."

The politics of *Grine Felder* are implicit in its mise-en-scène. The setting not only evokes Hirschbein's lost Lithuania but carries a strong subliminal suggestion of those utopian agricultural colonies founded (and dreamt of) by immigrant Jews in southern New Jersey. *Grine Felder* has a modesty, a poignant economy of means, that shames subsequent representations of the Jewish Pale. Sunlit and air-filled, yet suffused with yearning, the film recalls Renoir and Vigo (and, indeed, according to Ulmer, was awarded a prize in France as the best foreign film of 1938). With its anecdotal narrative heightened by Vladimir Heifetz's soulful score, the film exudes a dreamy pantheism that would never again appear—neither in Ulmer's work, nor in the history of Yiddish cinema.[11]

The power of *Grine Felder*'s open-air photography is such that, despite its New Jersey location, the film seemed to possess an almost verité authenticity.

Forty-five years after its release, Helen Beverly recalled that during the numerous personal appearances she made in the course of the film's run "it was the greatest surprise to the audiences that I came out and spoke English. It baffled them since they were certain I was a little European girl."

By the time *Grine Felder* left the Squire for the neighborhoods, Beverly and Goldstein were both bona fide Yiddish Broadway actors: Beverly was featured in Schwartz's adaptation of *Di Brider Ashkenazi* (*The Brothers Ashkenazi*) at a theater on Seventh Avenue at Fifty-ninth Street; Goldstein had the title role in the Artef's adaptation of *The Good Soldier Svejk*. Ulmer, meanwhile, remained close to Hirschbein, and a Yiddish-theater aficionado, both of which would stand him in good stead in his subsequent Yiddish films.

Nineteen thirty-seven was also the year that Warner Brothers, the most liberal of Hollywood studios, released *The Life of Emile Zola,* a movie that dramatized the Dreyfus case without ever mentioning anti-Semitism. Nevertheless, the 1937–38 season saw an unprecedented number of Yiddish-language films open in New York, many of them at Broadway houses. *Al Khet* arrived in September at the Artef's theater on West Forty-eighth Street; a Yiddish-dubbed version of Julian Duvivier's *Le Golem* appeared that month at the Clinton. In addition to *Grine Felder,* fall 1937 brought a reissue of the 1933 *Der Vanderer Yid,* suggestively retitled *Der Yid in Goles* (Jews in Exile); Henry Lynn's vehicle for Celia Adler, *Vu Iz Mayn Kind?;* and Green's *Der Purimshpiler.* Yiddish was definitely in the air: that same season, the language achieved another sort of apotheosis with the smash success of the Andrews Sisters'

recording of Sholom Secunda's "Bay Mir Bist Du Sheyn."

Dem Khazns Zundl (The Cantor's Son), which starred sometime cantor Moishe Oysher and was another Yiddish talkie shot (at least in part) under the sky, opened at the Squire on Christmas Eve and played neighborhood theaters through April. A more obscure Christmas Eve premiere was Henry Stewart's *Di Heylige Shvue* (The Holy Oath), which opened at the Radio Theater in the Bronx. Although the film soon dropped from sight, its crude polemic makes explicit the sense of isolation and abandonment beneath the idyllic surfaces of Green's films and *Grine Felder.* From its first scene, this forty-two-minute movie is the embodiment of catastrophe. A frivolous young couple prepare to go out to a masquerade ball. The man has no costume, his date is dressed as a Russian peasant. Their leaden repartee—about his fondness for brunettes (she's a blonde)—is interrupted when her father, played by Morris Strassberg, invites them to a Zionist meeting. When they show no interest, the old man, by way of persuasion, recounts the history of the Jews.[12]

Di Heylige Shvue has the tone of an impromptu seder—Strassberg addressing the ignorant young people as those "who know not how to ask" the meaning of the Passover service—as well as being a compilation film in the well-worn tradition of *Theodor Herzl* or *Der Vanderer Yid.* Genesis is illustrated with stock footage of everything from storm clouds and molten lava to Gila monsters and desert nomads; the film goes on to juxtapose fragments of chanted prayers, newsreels of contemporary Palestine, and truncated sequences from earlier Yiddish talkies. (In one of these, a wailing Anna Appel cites "thousands and thousands of years" of oppression, and beseeches "Almighty God" to hear "the prayer of a Jewish mother" as her daughter, played by Lucy Levin, joins in the lament.) Shots of stray bedouins and deserted Jerusalem streets give way to scenes of orange groves and kibbutzim, and then the cultural institutions, hospitals, and beaches of modern Tel Aviv. In the finale, a parade of uniformed Zionist youth is superimposed over the now-chastened American couple.[13]

To judge from the second-hand performances, Stewart appears to have cannibalized the 1929 *Ad Mosay*. Harry Alan Potamkin had termed that glorified cantorial "about the worst film ever made." *Di Heylige Shvue* is perhaps even more technically inept, and yet, the ferocity of its badness gives it a powerful sense of desperation. The film seems to have been acted and assembled in a state of hysteria. Often the action and music are bizarrely skewed: a bit of mild hoochie-koochie, identified as a Palestinian harvest dance, is accompanied by excerpts from Rimsky-Korsakov's *Scheherazade;* a Busby Berkeley–like display of mass calisthenics is scored to the Zionist anthem Hatikvah. (*Di Heylige Shvue* becomes an even headier mishmash for including "Arabian Doina" by the virtuoso *klezmer* clarinetist Dave Tarras.)

Throughout, the father's relentlessly self-righteous presentation is undercut by the desultory montage and indifferent quality of the newsreel footage, and, even more so, by the statuette of a black butler which, in some mad or misguided notion of dressing an otherwise barren set, has been positioned so that it can be seen mindlessly grinning over his shoulder. The brutality of this unintentional alienation effect is exceeded only by *Di Heylige Shvue*'s blunt metaphor of a masquerade for Jewish life in the Diaspora, *der Yid in goles.*

NOTES

1. In one interview, Green elaborated on this remark. The Warner brothers had decided to give their father the honor of directing the synagogue scenes, and as a kind of supportive joke Al Jolson and Yosele Rosenblatt decided to speak only Yiddish: "The whole day, Jolson wouldn't say a word in English. . . . It was hilarious. I remember Harry Warner came down to the set and he said, 'My God, Father, what are you doing?' He wouldn't answer because they had told him not to speak in anything but Yiddish."

2. It was also at this time that Picon firmly established herself as a radio personality with "I Give You My Life," a half-hour evening program sponsored by Maxwell House Coffee and broadcast by WMCA. Although basically English-language, the show was heavily infused with Yiddish and Yiddishisms.

3. The degree to which *Yidl mitn Fidl* achieved folk status may be gauged by the macabre variation of the film's title song sung, in German, by Jewish prisoners in the Sachsenhausen concentration camp:

Yidl mit der Fiedl, Moysche mit dem Bass!
Singt mir mal ein Liedel, müssen wir ins Gas!

[Yiddle with your fiddle, Moyshe with your bass! Sing to me a ditty, we're heading for the gas!]

4. By the mid-1930s, the economy of Kazimierz depended almost entirely on the tourist trade. (Indeed, many of the local Poles spoke fluent Yiddish.) Returning from a visit to America in the late thirties, poet Jacob Glatstein visited the town, and, noting the "many vacationers, women in shorts, men in unbuttoned shirts," thought for a moment that he "was somewhere in the Catskills. Young men carried elaborate shepherds' crooks, as though they were climbing mountains in operettas, with a song on their lips. And some of them were actually singing Jewish songs, in both Polish and Hebrew."

5. Along with Julien Duvivier's *Le Golem, Yidl mitn Fidl* was distributed in Germany by the Palestine Film Office of the Zionist Union of Germany—an organization which, between 1936 and 1938, managed to produce two feature-length and five short documentaries on Jewish life in the Yishev. Censored by the Nazi Ministry of Propaganda and restricted to "members of the Jewish race," these films were screened in Jewish communities throughout the Reich. *Yidl* opened in Berlin in April 1938 and was subsequently shown in other German cities. According

to the historian Jan-Christopher Horak, over 70 percent of the box-office proceeds went to the Tobis Klangfilm Syndicate; *Yidl* had been made with German sound technology, and as Green-Film evidently had not secured the appropriate production license, the Palestine Film Office was compelled to pay for one, as well as for export and exhibition licenses.

6. In *The American Cinema,* Andrew Sarris had some fun with the idea of Ulmer as auteur: "The French call him *un cinéaste maudit,* and directors certainly don't come any more *maudit.* But yes, Virginia, there is an Edgar G. Ulmer, and he is no longer one of the private jokes shared by auteur critics, but one of the minor glories of the cinema. . . . That a personal style could emerge from the lowest depths of Poverty Row is a tribute to a director without alibis."

In addition to four Yiddish and two Ukrainian films, Ulmer directed the all-black *Moon over Harlem* (1939), as well as a series of multiethnic shorts for the National Tuberculosis Association. These include *Let My People Live* (1938), made with an all-black cast in Alabama, the Spanish-language *Cloud in the Sky* (1939), shot in San Antonio, and *Another to Conquer* (1940), filmed on a Navajo reservation in Arizona.

7. *The Girl from Poltavka* has been lost. Some reviews list Avramenko as the director and Ulmer as cameraman; in *Variety* the direction is credited to Ulmer and M. J. Gann, a Ukrainian Jew who had been involved with an abortive Ukrainian feature eight years earlier and who is also listed as a coauthor of the screenplay.

8. Instrumental in the creation of a Yiddish art theater, first in Odessa and later in New York, Hirschbein (1880–1948) drew upon memories of his rural Lithuanian childhood for a series of lyrical pastorals which depicted Jews living "under the sky," as David Lifson put it, with neither sweatshop nor ghetto to remind them of their misery. Through a combination of dramatic understatement and suggestive folk poetry, Hirschbein raised the artistic aspiration of the Yiddish stage; his impact might be compared to that of Chekhov on the Moscow Art Theater, Synge on the Abbey Theater, O'Neill on the Provincetown Players.

9. *China Strikes Back* was as much of a breakthrough in its way as *Grine Felder*. The twenty-three-minute film was by far the most popular of Frontier's reportages. Two years after its premiere, The Museum of Modern Art saluted it as "the first documentary to fight its way into the ordinary, commer-cial theaters purely on its merits as an interpretation of the news."

10. Born to an impoverished Chasidic family in a village near Warsaw in 1907, Goldstein was the youngest of thirteen children, immigrating to the United States as a teenager. A member of the Artef virtually from its beginning, he supported himself as a house painter. Although some would claim that his militant leftism helped advance his career, cognoscenti regarded him as the collective's finest actor. *Grine Felder* featured two other members of the Artef, Dina Drute (Goldstein's wife) and Saul Levine, playing a pair of rustic lovers.

11. Bill Krohn's ingenious, if extravagant, auteur reading turns the film into a personal allegory: Ulmer is "the unworldly scholar" taken in by "an uncultured community of rural Jews" who, just as the Yiddish dailies fought to sponsor the film, compete "for the honor of housing and feeding him." For Krohn, "the utopian dream of *Green Fields* is finally an expression of Ulmer's own feelings of liberation: far from the haunted sound-stages of Bavaria and Hollywood, he created a lyrical fusion of landscape and theatrical artifice where the long takes necessitated by an $8,000 budget evoke an invisible presence brooding over the natural world."

12. Although Strassberg was a veteran of the Yiddish Art Theater, his presence in *Di Heylige Shvue* carries a strong subliminal connection to German Jewry; the previous spring he played the title role in the Federal Theatre's popular production of *Professor Mamlock,* a drama of a German-Jewish doctor's humiliation and murder at the hands of the Nazis. (The Soviet movie version of Friedrich Wolff's play, produced at Lenfilm largely by German-Jewish emigrés, was released in Moscow in September 1938 and opened at the Cameo two months later, just days before Kristallnacht. The film enjoyed a lengthy run, then circulated widely in Jewish neighborhoods, held over four weeks at the Radio during February and March 1939.)

13. Like Aleksander Ford's *Sabra, Di Helige Shvue* identifies Zionism with the modernization of Palestine. But while *Sabra* stresses class solidarity by featuring a Jewish-Arab love affair and showing both Jewish settlers and Arab farmers to be oppressed by the same feudal sheik, *Di Helige Shvue* associates Palestine's underdevelopment less with economic exploitation than with Arab national character traits. In this, the Zionist film it most closely resembles is Juda Leman's hour-long *Land of Promise,* which had its premiere in Berlin in May 1935, opening in New York at the Astor Theater the following November.

Overleaf: The khazn as movie idol. Moishe Oysher (left), with Ben-Zvi Baratoff in Edgar G. Ulmer's Yankl der Shmid (U.S.A., 1938).

19

The Cantor's Sons

For three-quarters of a century in *Yidish-land*, the defenders of tradition had waged a rearguard action against the forces of modernity. With the Nazi threat, and in the light of widespread Gentile indifference, the argument between cultural separatism and cultural adaptation took on a new immediacy. *Yidishland* was polarized between a desire for greater internationalism and the recognition of internationalism's failure, torn between a need to publicize the fate of European Jewry and a revulsion against the spurious universality of the mass media.

The situation in Poland precluded cultural assimilation, that in the Soviet Union assumed it. Only in the United States were Jews sufficiently distanced from Europe—its orthodoxies and its constraints—

to act out their often bitter ambivalence about precisely that freedom. Then, too, the American-Yiddish audience was older than the Polish-Yiddish audience, and inherently more nostalgic. Thus, by the late 1930s, all representation of the struggle between secularism and religion was confined to American films. Indeed, Moishe Oysher—a sometime cantor and the one Yiddish movie star without equivalent stage celebrity—spent much of his career dramatizing that very conflict.

"A cantor is not an actor," Sholom Aleichem explains in *Yosele Solovey,* his 1889 novel about a young *khazn's* rise and fall.

Jews certainly love to hear good singing, admire virtuosity and vocal feats in the synagogue; however, the cantor must never forget he is called *sheliekh tsiber,* a messenger of the congregation, an advocate, a representative, and consequently the congregation demands of him that he be a person of impeccable virtue, a respectable Jew, not a profligate. A house of worship is not a theater.

A cantor is not an actor, a synagogue is not a theater. And yet, the archetypal Yiddish stage performer is a cantor's son or daughter. (Esther-Rokhl Kaminska was the child of a cantor, as is the actress-heroine of Sholom Aleichem's *Blondzhende Shtern.* Boris Thomashefsky, Sigmund Mogulesko, Seymour Rechtzeit, composer Sholom Secunda, and poet Peretz Markish were all either cantors' sons or child cantors, or both.)

In terms of Jewish ritual, the *khazn*'s prominence steadily increased throughout the Diaspora despite a rabbinical disapproval which, as Mark Slobin points out, "parallels outbursts of archbishops and popes against music's preempting of sacred texts for 'sensual' musical purposes in Christendom." By the time Sholom Aleichem wrote *Yosele Solovey,* the *khazn* had become the most important figure in Jewish musical culture. The virtuoso *khazn* was venerated as a star. But, as if in recognition of the Old Testament injunction against idolatry, such veneration carried the seeds of disaster.

The quintessential star *khazn* was Yoel-David Levinshteyn-Strashunsky (1816–1850), already renowned by age eleven, and popularly known as the "Vilner Balebesl" for his marriage at thirteen to the daughter of a wealthy Vilna merchant. (*Balebesl* is the affectionate, and sometimes ironic, diminutive for *balebos,* from the Hebrew for master of the house.) The legend has it that, while on tour, Strashunsky fell in love with a Polish singer and ran off with her to Vienna. This impetuous affair cost the *Balebesl* his voice and his sanity. He returned east a mute penitent, wandering from *shtetl* to *shtetl* before dying, alone, in an insane asylum at the age of thirty-five.

Sholom Aleichem includes a version of Strashunsky's story in *Yosele Solovey,* which echoes the Old Testament tale of Joseph and Potiphar's wife in blaming the jealousy of a wanton Gentile seductress for the *Balebesl*'s destruction. When a Polish count demands to hear the *khazn* sing, the chaste prodigy performs, but with his face to the wall. Nevertheless, the degenerate countess is smitten, and when the *Balebesl* rejects her advances, she turns the count against the Jewish community, then wreaks vengeance on the hapless cantor.

There are to be found, even among Jews, people who for money will do away with a person. Such people were hired by the countess. They gave the *Balebesl* a poisoned drink that robbed him of his voice. As soon as the poor *Balebesl* realized he had lost his voice, he fell into a deep melancholy and went completely mad. He wandered about the world, tattered and torn, not speaking a word to anyone. That was the end of the *Vilner Balebesl*—and all because of her, may her name be cursed.

The most famous literary version of this cautionary tale is Mark Arnshteyn's play *Der Vilner Balebesl.* Here, the *Balebesl* embodies the paradox of the Jewish artist, torn between traditional imperatives and a desire to participate in the culture of the West. That, having gone on the Warsaw stage, Arnshteyn's cantor falls in love with the niece of Polish composer Stanisław Moniuszko is a symptom rather than a cause of his estrangement. The *Balebesl*'s defection, like that of the Jazz Singer, is potential catastrophe for the Jewish community: "They have many singers," his father (a cantor) reproaches him, "we have only you."

Der Vilner Balebesl was first produced in Polish as *Pieśniarze* (Singers) in Lodz in 1902. Four years later, the play was staged in Yiddish, and although controversial, it soon entered the Yiddish repertoire. In 1912, after directing the first films with the Kaminsky troupe in Warsaw, Arnshteyn brought *Der Vilner Balebesl* to London, where, according to theater historian M. J. Landa, it was regarded as "something absolutely new in Yiddish stage-craft—something superior, in fact, to the stage-technique of the West End." The play was performed in Paris during the World War and introduced to New York by the Vilna Troupe in 1924. As *Der Vilner Balebesl* suggests a link between the universalist ethos embodied in *Uriel Acosta* and the assimilationist drama of *The Jazz Singer,* it is scarcely surprising that in 1926 Arnshteyn had been interested in staging a Polish version of the latter.

A spiritual middleman, negotiating the realm between religion and show business as well as God and the congregation, the cantor is a key figure in Jewish modernization. The rise of the star *khazn* coincides both with the Great Immigration and the birth of the Yiddish stage. The Lomzer *khazn,* a minor character in Sholom Aleichem's *Blondzhende Shtern,* comes to America and reinvents himself as the "Lomzer Nightingale," singing *Kol Nidre* "every night in the famous operetta called, by a strange coincidence, *Kol Nidre.*" The rabbi is the congregation's teacher, the *khazn* is its "emissary." In the larger towns of Eastern Europe, study- and prayer-houses were often organized by profession, with shoemakers or tailors sometimes hiring one of their own as *khazn.*[1]

Thus, in the figure of the cantor, the lines between the sacred and the secular blurred—particularly in America, where cantorial music was a staple of the Second Avenue theater and a *khazn* might double as a vaudeville performer, endorse products, make movies, and sing on the radio. The 1919 Boris Thomashefsky production *Tsvey Khazonim* (Two Cantors) put this conflict at center stage. The play concerns the rivalry between a traditional *khazn* and a Westernized, Reform cantor—the latter, significantly, played by Thomashefsky, himself the son and grandson of cantors who, at age five, had created no less a sensation singing an entire service in the Asitnaitchka Synagogue than he would a quarter century later on Second Avenue.

Der Vilner Balebesl makes explicit the commonplace that the adoration accorded a star cantor was akin to that which the Gentile world showered upon a brilliant operatic singer. Indeed, the tales that follow star *khazonim* like New York's Yosele Rosenblatt and Warsaw's Gershon Sirota suggest a desire to engage opera and transcend it. The program of Sirota's American tour included an aria from *Aïda,* which supposedly inspired Caruso to thank God that the *khazn* had chosen "to employ his heavenly gift in a different field"; Rosenblatt, known as "the Jewish Caruso," was known to have spurned a lucrative offer from the Chicago Opera.

Nevertheless, traditionalists remained skeptical of the hoopla surrounding the stars. A youthful cantor in *Hayntige Mames,* the *shund* film most concerned with the erosion of Jewish tradition, is first framed

Judea Film's twenty-thousand-dollar "special," *Di Shtime fun Yisroel* (U.S.A., 1930), featured nine *khazonim* plus the Cantor Meyer Machtenburg Choir.

task for his frequent use of banal and cheap effects and for his sudden outbreaks of unrelated, stunt-like roulades and coloratura acrobatics." The Yiddish poet Judd Teller recalls that during the 1920s the novelty of Yiddish and liturgical recordings created a new form of Lower East Side street theater:

Every evening of the week except Fridays, holidays, and in foul weather, crowds assembled outside the phonograph stores for concerts of records, which were amplified through a horn in the transom. Liturgy and popular music were interspersed. The serious waited patiently for the moment when a cantorial record was put on. Then they exploded into a minor riot of heated polemics, drowning out the voice pouring through the horn. Each coterie of fans acclaimed the records of its favorite cantor, but was divided against itself as to which items in his albums were superior to the others. These disputations involved the pitch of the cantor's voice, the clarity of his diction, the pathos of the sighs, sobs, and exclamations that laced his liturgy.

The rise of Yiddish-language radio in the late twenties, and Yiddish-language movies soon afterwards, created further opportunities for star cantors. The 1929 *Ad Mosay,* only the second Yiddish talkie, was a double novelty for featuring the child *khazn* Shmulikel. Over the next few years, Judea mixed vaudeville shorts with a number of one- and two-reel cantorials. Shmulikel's *Kol Nidre* was released in the autumn of 1930, and Judea put out at least four other cantorials over the next twelve months before releasing their ten-reel, $20,000 "special" *Di Shtime fun Yisroel (The Voice of Israel),* which featured nine *khazonim* plus the Cantor Meyer Machtenburg Choir.

There is no question that these cantors were among the brightest stars of the Yiddish firmament.

by a Jewish gangster and then led astray by the criminal's girl, an aggressively modern girl who wants him to become a pop star. The pious Rosenblatt, who himself was forced to go on the vaudeville stage after he lost all his money in bad investments (an ultra-Orthodox Yiddish daily, a luxury *mikve* on the Lower East Side), was regarded with suspicion. The 1925–26 run of the *Jewish Theatrical News* amply documents that, in leaving the synagogue for show business, Rosenblatt sustained frequent charges of impropriety by Jewish traditionalists.

Similarly, even though Sirota made strenuous attempts to placate his Orthodox critics, the purists, as Slobin reports, were unsatisfied: "He was taken to

The Cantor's Sons   261

The $500 that Judea paid Rosenblatt for his participation in *Di Shtime fun Yisroel* is most likely the highest salary Seiden ever paid any performer. The posthumously released *Der Kholem fun Mayn Folk* (*The Dream of My People*), which presented Rosenblatt praying at the Wailing Wall, among other Holy Land locations, was the most successful of all cantorials. Opening in February 1934 at the Yiddish Art Theater (then struggling through a disastrous season), *Kholem* played there and two other Lower East Side venues for a total of eight weeks, with holdover engagements in Brooklyn and the Bronx as well.

If Rosenblatt was the most celebrated of American *khazonim,* the most filmed was certainly the American-born, baseball-loving Louis "Leibele" Waldman, who began in Rosenblatt's choir and had been a nine-year-old *khazn* on the Lower East Side (as well as a musician on a Hudson River cruise boat). Disparagingly called the "microphone cantor" because he lacked projection, Waldman first recorded in the early twenties. He appeared in at least six shorts released in 1930 and 1931, and was employed by Seiden in another six features over the next decade. (Waldman was "inserted" into, rather than "featured" in, Seiden's potboilers. The cantor was seldom, if ever, given any dialogue; his main function was to provide a suitably thrilling service for a film's climactic wedding.)

Although most of Waldman's performances were straight recordings of various prayers, a few had decided novelty-vaudeville elements. The 1931 one-reeler *Khazn afn Probe (A Cantor on Trial)* is a dramatization of a cantorial audition. The film opens with Waldman in evening clothes, singing against a black backdrop; Waldman subsequently performs as a bearded, old-fashioned *khazn,* and then, made up with goatee and mustache, as a German cantor. (In

Clinton Theater, New York, April 1934. The current attraction is the feature-length cantorial *Der Kholem fun Mayn Folk,* which documented Yosele Rosenblatt's trip to Palestine.

Leibele Waldman in the early 1930s. The American-born, baseball-loving "microphone cantor" was featured by Joseph Seiden in a half-dozen shorts and as many features.

Moishe Oysher (turning toward camera) on location for *Dem Khazns Zundl,* in Easton, Pennsylvania, summer 1937.

each case he faces the camera, away from the congregation which forms his ostensible audience.) The committee members start quarreling among themselves, but a fat fixer solves the problem by bringing on a third, "American" Waldman. Hilariously full of himself, the dapper, clean-shaven cantor struts in and sings a pop song (complete with Helen Kane–style boop-boop-a-doops). Improbably won over, the committee forms a circle around him and begins to dance.

A 1937 press release put out by Waldman's radio sponsor, the World Clothing Exchange, termed him "the only cantor who is under contract to make Jewish talking pictures." In fact, Waldman's hegemony was about to be challenged by a younger and more dynamic figure. Late that year, the thirty-year-old Moishe Oysher would make his film debut in *Dem Khazns Zundl* (*The Cantor's Son*).

In the wake of *Yidl mitn Fidl,* two youthful would-be moguls, Arthur Block and Samuel M. Segal, both with extensive experience in the business end of Yiddish theater, formed Eron Pictures. They immediately signed Oysher and hired the ailing Sidney Goldin (inactive in the five and a half years since *Uncle Moses*) to direct the charismatic singer. Alexander Olshanetsky, a former concert violinist who had previously worked with Oysher at the Second Avenue Theater, composed a score that included his 1932 hit "Mayn Shtetle Belz" (My Little Village Belz). The song, which had been introduced on the stage by Aaron Lebedeff and was full of nostalgia for the old country, was crucial. No less than *Grine Felder,* also in the works during the summer of 1937, *Dem Khazns Zundl* was a post-Green undertaking—an open-air production that looked back toward the tribal wholeness of *shtetl* life.

The film's announced budget was $40,000. Robert Van Rosen, who had worked with Schwartz at the Yiddish Art Theater, built a plywood "Belz" in the Pocono Mountains, near Easton, Pennsylvania. For the first time since the advent of sound, Goldin would have the opportunity to shoot extensive exteriors. However, the director suffered a heart attack in the midst of production and returned to New York, where he died two weeks later at the age of fifty-seven. Goldin was succeeded by the cosmopolitan Ilya Motyleff, who had studied with Reinhardt, assisted Stanislavsky, and directed Pirandello. This last credit seems appropriate to *Dem Khazns Zundl* insofar as it is a movie that self-consciously reflects and comments upon its star's life. Indeed, more than being a pastoral romance or a glorified cantorial, *Dem Khazns Zundl* is an anti–*Jazz Singer*—with Louis Freiman's script designed to dramatize Oysher's return to the fold.[2]

Born not in the Galician town of Belz but in the Bessarabian village of Lipkon around 1908, Oysher was descended from seven generations of cantors and was a vocal prodigy who made his debut at the age of six. Nine years later he joined his (unemployed) father in Canada but, because his voice was changing, could only find work as a dishwasher. Once his voice returned, Oysher sang light opera in dramatic clubs, supplementing his income with freelance cantorial work. The Yiddish actor Ben Galing, who encountered Oysher in the mid-twenties in Minneapolis, recalls that the singer claimed to "make $50 a *shabes*."

In the summer of 1928, Oysher came to New York, hired by Louis Weiss, manager of the Hopkinson Theater in Brownsville and future producer of *Uncle Moses,* to star opposite his wife, Florence. However it may have improved Weiss's box office, the move cost him his marriage. After a hastily arranged South American tour, Oysher and Florence Weiss spent their next season in Newark. Admitted to the Hebrew Actors Union in late 1931, Oysher played one season for Thomashefsky, managed the Amphion Theater in Williamsburg for another, and became a fixture of Yiddish radio as *"Der Mayster-Zinger fun Zayn Folk"* (The Master Singer of His People).

Oysher did not make his Second Avenue debut until the fall of 1935. *Variety,* which caught him in *Der Mazldiker Bokher,* known in English as *Lucky Boy* (the same show that introduced Leo Fuchs), was not impressed: Oysher "has a fine voice [but] his vocal training doesn't alter the fact that he hasn't the vaguest conception of stage acting. He doesn't know what to do with his hands, he doesn't know how to walk, he doesn't know how to make even the slightest speech convincing." This was not *Der Mayster-Zinger*'s only problem. During the High Holy Days, he accepted an offer to serve as cantor at the First Rumanian-American Congregation, on Rivington Street. This return to the pulpit was opposed by a faction of the congregation who were sufficiently impassioned to surround the *shul* with pickets.[3]

The controversy was revived a year later when, after a successful season on Second Avenue, the erstwhile star of *Der Mazldiker Bokher* was engaged as guest cantor at the Yeshivah Hacohen, in East Flatbush. Clearly amused by this "real life parallel" to *The Jazz Singer,* the *New York Evening Journal* reported that Oysher would be "escorted by police to prevent a recurrence of a disturbance which took place in Manhattan a year ago." A disturbance occurred, and *Variety,* too, became intrigued by the tale of the show-biz *khazn* trapped between two worlds:

> AN ACTOR OR A CANTOR,
> YIDDISH THESP'S WORRY
>
> Moishe Oysher is in trouble because he couldn't make up his mind whether he wants to be a Yiddish actor or a cantor. Now he seems to be caught between the two, with no jobs at either.
>
> Oysher started out as a cantor, doing quite well. Radio appearances followed and were clicks, so he went on to legit, making his bow last season as a star at the Second Avenue Theater. But, at the recent high holidays, Oysher, with the Yiddish legit season over, went back to cantoring at a Brooklyn synagogue. That meant probably the first time that an official in a religious ceremony and in a holy house met with critical attention, because a number of Jews objected to an actor, obviously not "a holy man," getting the assignment.

Serious rumpus followed, with a lot of squawking and many cancellations from the synagogue membership, etc., plus a few open catcalls during the services.

Now Oysher is pretty well convinced he is probably through as a cantor unless he forgets all about acting, but he likes acting. At the same time he hasn't been offered a star or feature spot in any of the next season Yiddish legit troupes in New York, because managers feel that perhaps his presence in the cast may bother some prospective customers.

Oysher resolved the issue in 1937. Leaving the stage, he became a certified cantor, employed (often simultaneously) by the Stone Avenue Talmud Torah, in Brownsville, and the Minford Place Synagogue, in the Bronx, as well as by the First Rumanian-American Congregation—which nearly twenty years later he would proudly term "the most Orthodox synagogue in town." But if the theater was now off-limits for Oysher, *Dem Khazns Zundl* might be interpreted as part of his rehabilitation.

The film opens in Belz with the revelation that thirteen-year-old Shloyme is *"tsvishn di komediantn"* (with the actors). As his distraught mother rushes to Felden's Summer Theater (a copy of the outdoor Green Tree Café in Jassy, where Avrom Goldfadn more or less originated Yiddish theater sixty years before), one player is explaining to the boy that he too was a cantor's son, and "so was the great Mogulesko." When Shloyme is recruited for a minor role, his father takes it as near-conversion to Christianity: "He'll beat up Jews yet!" the *khazn* cries. Unheeding, Shloyme runs away with the troop to the Lower East Side.

There he learns that "America is not America."

Fifteen years later, having grown into Moishe Oysher, the starving cantor's son wanders into the Roumanian Garden on Second Avenue and is given a menial job. One day, while the resident chanteuse (Florence Weiss) is rehearsing, the humble floor-washer bursts into song. Overwhelmed, she prevails upon her lover, the nightclub owner, to hire this unknown singer immediately. Success is assured when sultry Weiss and virile Oysher perform a dreamy, subtly syncopated duet of "Mayn Shtetle Belz" in their trademark close harmony.

Back in the *shtetl,* the cantor has been somewhat mollified by a letter from his son that included $25 for a new *talis:* "So our boy didn't forget he was a Jew," he grumbles. Indeed, despite his new celebrity, Oysher remembers little else. A vulgar radio booker (Isidore Cashier) associates Jewish material with "sadness" and pressures the burgeoning star to sing Mozart instead. Oysher, meanwhile, wishes he could drop secular material altogether and chant his father's prayers. Finally, in the midst of a national tour, he decides he must go to Belz for his parent's fiftieth wedding anniversary, and, walking out on his contracts, returns to the Old Country—accompanied not by his consort Weiss but by his manager (a comic role played by Michael Rosenberg).

"America is here! Shloymele has come!" the natives shout. Oysher, in turn, is thunderstruck when he discovers that his childhood sweetheart has become the gorgeous Judith Abarbanel. The New World recedes to but an inexplicable interlude. (As Rosenberg attempts to describe the *goldene medine* to the old maid who is courting him, "America is . . . America is . . . America is . . . America.") In Goldin's two previous features, America was associated with economic exploitation and the failure of community. Here it carries aspects of inauthenticity. "I tried to find my real self but I couldn't," Oysher tells Abarbanel.

Weiss, meanwhile, has had no word from Oysher and, in desperation, sails for Belz, arriving the day before Osyher's wedding. She finds him chanting for the delighted townspeople, and wringing the situation for every tear, congratulates the bride while declining to remain for the ceremony. In the last shot, Oysher watches this manifestation of modernity vanish back across the sea. Then, with a momentous "Yes," he advances toward his untainted Belzer bride. In a sense, American-Yiddish films would do the same: the major features of the next three and a half years would all be set in an idealized Eastern Europe.

Unlike the Jolson of *The Jazz Singer,* Oysher's *Khazns Zundl* comes full circle to willingly endorse traditional Jewish values. Although Oysher's own return to the cantorate was more ambiguous and problematic, the movie was presented as the dramatization of his story. "There is only one slight divergence," the *New York Post* coyly noted. "Florence Weiss, Mr. Oysher's wife in real life, in the film plays the other woman and loses out in the end. That Mr. Oysher regrets very much but he does admit that it would not have been too good box office if the film showed him as a married man of ten years' standing."

Promoted as the most expensive Yiddish talkie to date, *Dem Khazns Zundl* opened on Christmas Eve 1937 at the Squire, the same Broadway-area theater where *Grine Felder* had its premiere ten weeks before. The English-language reviews were mixed, although most praised Oysher's tenor and Olshanetsky's score. If its midtown run was shorter, the Oysher vehicle proved nearly as popular as *Grine Felder* in Jewish neighborhoods, playing some Bronx

movie houses that had never shown a Yiddish talkie before (and some that never would again) for as long as a month as it worked its way up and down Southern Boulevard throughout the winter and spring of 1938.[4]

Flush with the success of *Grine Felder* and mindful of *Dem Khazns Zundl*'s appeal, Collective Film Producers followed with a synthesis of the two. Their source was another Yiddish classic—David Pinski's 1906 drama *Yankl der Shmid* (Yankl the Blacksmith). Reworking *Yankl* as a vehicle for Oysher, with a supporting cast drawn heavily from the Yiddish Art Theater, producer Roman Rebush and director Edgar G. Ulmer engaged Jacob Weinberg to compose a score and playwright Ossip Dymow to work with Pinski on the adaptation.[5]

A naturalistic drama, *Yankl der Shmid* was one of the first Yiddish plays to offer a psychological study of physical passion. Sexual desire is at once a primal drive and a source of ambivalence. Although robust Yankl loves his sickly Tamara, he cannot help but succumb, however guiltily, to the more sensuous charms of his neighbor's wife. In this sense, *Yankl* reflected a part of Oysher's own personality: *Der Mayster-Zinger* had a reputation as a lusty skirt-chaser who drank, smoked, and didn't necessarily keep the sabbath. (It was said that he smoked on *shabes,* even in *shul,* claiming it was necessary for his voice.) Indeed, when Oysher sang in synagogue on Friday nights, he often had witnesses escort him to temple on foot to reassure the congregation that he had not violated the sabbath by taking a taxi.

Religion, however, barely exists in *Yankl der Shmid,* known in English as *The Singing Blacksmith.* Dymow and Pinski modulated the original drama, lightening the tone and opening up the plot with a lengthy prologue and additional (mainly comic) characters. Where the play began with Yankl's engagement to the delicate Tamara, the movie goes back to his childhood. Desiring to leave *kheyder* for the gymnasium, young Yankl (Herschel Bernardi) is instead apprenticed to the hard-drinking blacksmith Bendl (Ben-Zvi Baratoff), from whom he eventually inherits the smithy. Growing up into the dashing Oysher, Yankl is for most of the movie an impetuous roughneck and womanizer—almost as much Cossack as Jew, a *"molodyets"* (a loanword from Russian, meaning a fine youth).

In 1927, A. Mukdoyni elaborated on this development in the Yiddish theater:

In the early days of Jewish operetta the dancing comedian was always a *shlimazl* with *payes* and a long *kapote*. Then a new type of Jewish lad appeared in the Russian-Jewish milieu. He spoke half Russian and half Yiddish. He was a mixture of Russian munificence and good nature with Jewish cleverness and agility. He was a lad with a Russian shock of hair, polished boots, an embroidered shirt and a cap that sat jauntily and cockily on his head.

He had become aware that there are bourgeoisie and proletarians in the world, and he was with the latter. . . .

[The *molodyets*] appeared first in real life, out of the ranks of the Bund and other Jewish socialist parties, who adored these vital, courageous folk children of theirs. . . .

An agile dancer, with a quick tongue, he will beat up anyone who insults him; he will fight for a girl, for the revolution, for a comrade. He is not comical. He is not a *yold* [fool] like the bourgeois sons and daughters. He is full of joy.

He is Yankl.

The movie's plot revolves around the smith's philandering and his eventual marriage to the orphan Tamara (Miriam Riselle). Initially Yankl is resolved to remain free: "Why eat stale bread when I can get fresh rolls?" he jokes. ("Someday you'll choke," warns the freelance *shadkhnte* played by Anna Appel.) Yankl is presently dallying with Rivke, a married woman played by Florence Weiss, but drops her when smitten by the beauteous, lavender-eyed Tamara (scarcely the frail creature of Pinski's play). The pious instinctively dislike Yankl, but Tamara responds to his life-affirming qualities. "I prefer him to that dried-up *yeshive-bokher* who courted me last year," she tells her rich, stingy, disapproving aunt and uncle. Although again tempted by Rivke, Yankl is ultimately transformed. Thanks to Tamara, he becomes a *mentsh*—a conscientious worker, husband, and father (the baby played by Ulmer's infant daughter). Thus, *Yankl* celebrates the *proster Yid* and a *Yidishkayt* (or a *mentshlekhkayt*) far more secular than that of *Grine Felder*.

Visually *Yankl* is closer than *Grine Felder* to the expressionistic noirs and thrillers Ulmer would make in Hollywood during the 1940s. The interiors are dramatically lit and exhibit his characteristic use of odd angles and bold perspective (for example, positioning outsized furniture in the foreground of the frame). The exterior set, with its onion-dome façades and plywood cottages, is far more elaborate than *Grine Felder*'s. The pace, however, is less fluid, although as *Yankl* was first released at nearly two and a half hours and has since lost almost forty minutes (including a scene of the young Yankl's Bar Mitzvah), it is difficult to judge its erratic narrative rhythms. Unlike the principals of *Grine Felder*, Oysher and Weiss had star temperaments—he stub-

Moishe Oysher and Anna Appel in *Yankl der Shmid* (U.S.A., 1938). Note the onion-domed Orthodox church in the background: Edgar G. Ulmer built this *"shtetl"* on a monastery near Newton, New Jersey, and used it for his subsequent Ukrainian talkie, *Cossacks in Exile*.

born, she jealous—and the action tends to grind to a halt for their numbers.

Again, Ulmer had to cut corners. To avoid renting a portable electric generator, he sought a location where he could tap into overhead power lines. The director and his staff—"two boys and four old Jews, in a station wagon we bought for $110"—set out in May 1938 to comb rural New Jersey for an appropriate spot. Following an old dirt road outside of Newton, in Sussex County, they found a perfect site, which turned out to belong to a Catholic monastery, Shrine of the Little Flower. Ulmer and company were initially dubious—after all, 1938 was the year that *Social Justice,* the print organ of the "radio priest" Father Coughlin, began to serialize *The Protocols of the Elders of Zion.* The brothers, however, reminded them that "the Catholic Church has always sponsored the arts," and, as they all had beards, even volunteered to play the parts of the townspeople. Ulmer subsequently discovered that a nudist camp was located on one side of the monastery, while on the other stood Camp Nordland, owned by the pro-Nazi German-American Bund. (This South Jersey sampler of American free speech inspired some useful publicity when the *New York Mirror* ran a color spread on Newton's "Hollywood in Miniature.")

Impressed by the project's ingenuity, the *New York Mirror* ran a production story on *Yankl der Shmid* in its Sunday color supplement (September 18, 1938).

hayt reporter Ber Green rhapsodized over the "homey Russian *shtetl* transplanted bag and baggage to the green fields of New Jersey."

The sun was setting. The technicians, the actors, and the director were all exhausted. . . . I glanced at the nearby lake. It swallowed long shadows from the trees, indifferent to the film that was being born here. Even the field looked tired. It would soon be asleep. Tomorrow it would have another hard day's work. It will have to act in a movie. . . .

According to Ulmer, when *Yankl* had its Broadway premiere in early November, the "entire Catholic clergy of New Jersey arrived in full regalia to see the picture." So, too, did Oysher's *patriotn*. "Not since *Marie Antoinette* opened [at the Astor on August 16] has a night film premiere attracted such an enthusiastic crowd," reported the *Brooklyn Eagle*. "The Continental was packed to capacity. This was Oysher's crowd. It applauded vigorously after he completed each important scene."

Yankl has its share of bravura, chest-baring performances—not to mention a scene in which Oysher demonstrates that he can vocalize while cracking and eating nuts, and another, somewhat anachronistic, number in which he and Weiss scat-sing their current hit "Khasidl in New York," punctuating the harmonized *bim-bom*s of this syncopated *nign* with an occasional *"Oy-vey."* The movie opened less than a week before Kristallnacht, but American Jews, too, were in need of a fearless *molodyets*: that same month, Father Coughlin broadcast a speech explaining that German anti-Semitism, greatly exaggerated by Jews, was just a form of anti-Bolshevism.

With his usual resourcefulness, Ulmer built a trompe-l'oeil *shtetl* that would serve the combined purposes of *Yankl* and his second Ukrainian production, *Zaporezets za Dunayan* (Cossacks Across the Danube; known in English as *Cossacks in Exile*). Having survived a fire that damaged the cast and crew's Newton hotel, Ulmer shot both pictures simultaneously over the course of the summer. *Morgn Fray-*

As an audience film, *Yankl* turned out to be less epochal than either *Grine Felder* or *Dem Khazns Zundl*; it ran a respectable four weeks on Broadway but vanished from the neighborhoods by the end of January. Reviews, however, were almost unanimously favorable. If the Zionist weekly *Der Yidisher Kempfer* (The Jewish Fighter) found *Yankl* a simple-minded vulgarization of Pinski's drama, *Der Tog* and the *Morgn Frayhayt* alike were impressed with the movie's *literarish* qualities. Terming *Yankl* "a splendid picture," William Edlin was gratified to see that "the producers of *Grine Felder* have not lowered their standards"; Ber Green used virtually the same words, while singling out Artef star Michael Goldstein for particular praise in the supporting role of Rivke's hapless husband. (Despite the presence of only one other Artefnik—Luba Riemer, who played Baratoff's wife—*Yankl*'s advertising in left-wing newspapers boasted its "Artef cast.")

The English-language press was similarly positive. The *New York Herald-Tribune* deemed the film a "definite improvement" over *Grine Felder,* some scenes demonstrating the "finesse of [Artef director] Benno Schneider." The movie was a bit exotic as well:

One is not so interested in the gay blacksmith-about-town and his capitulation to a steadying love influence as one is in the manner in which these Russian Jews went about the serious business of getting married. There is a good deal of ritual even in the approach, which takes on a certain charm.

Others were more sensitive to the film's political implications. Finding *Yankl* "a far cry from the usual embarrassing Yiddish films of the type of *I Want to Be A Mother*," the *Daily Worker*'s David Platt praised this "comic-tragic story of life in old Russia, with its splendid people, its back-breaking poverty, its class divisions, its fascinating folk songs, dances and humor."

Indeed, the heartily folkloric and montage-filled *Yankl* resembles the Soviet cinema of the period more than it does any Russian reality: Yankl, who sings an anthem to labor as he sweats in his smithy, is an explicitly working-class hero, the first in American-Yiddish cinema since the Marxist union-organizer Charlie in *Uncle Moses*. Throughout, religion is identified with wealth and snobbery (or, alternately, ignorance and unhappiness). Even Appel's sympathetic *shadkhnte* is given a heroic proletarian dimension: "All week long we struggle for a living," she tells the smith in a bit of class-conscious coffee-klatching.

When Yankl is depressed because Tamara's friends reject him, she comforts him: "Why are they better? Because they are merchants and you are a worker? Great men have written, 'Life depends on the worker.'" A truly progressive girl, Tamara seems familiar with Freud as well as Marx. "A man knows so little of himself," she sighs when, after the designing Rivke leaves her husband, Yankl insists on taking his former mistress in as a boarder, just to prove she has no appeal for him.

After *Yankl*'s premiere, the Collective Film Producers variously announced their next projects as an adaptation of Hirschbein's *Di Puste Kretshme* (The Empty Inn); *The Life of Paul Ehrlich,* a biography of the German physician who developed a cure for syphilis and would be the subject of Warner Brothers' 1940 *Dr. Ehrlich's Magic Bullet*; and *Kol Nidre: Song of the Ghetto,* an anti-Nazi film written by Ber Green on "the oppression of the intellectual Jews and Catholics." None of these came to fruition, and in 1939 the partners went their separate ways. Ulmer produced and directed *Di Klyatshe* (The Old Mare)

while Roman Rebush produced *Mirele Efros,* hiring filmmaker Josef Berne to direct.[6]

Ludwig Landy, also a member of the Collective, went into partnership with Ira Greene to make a third Oysher vehicle. Announced in August, along with an all-black feature and a "documentary on current labor problems," *Der Vilner Shtot Khazn* (The Vilna Town-Cantor), at one point known as *Forsake Me Not,* did not begin production for another three months. Ossip Dymow reworked Mark Arnshteyn's play, *Der Vilner Balebesl* (which is uncredited), the poet Jacob Glatstein polishing the dialogue and Alexander Olshanetsky supplying the music. Sam Rosen, a former associate of Joseph Seiden, manned the camera. To direct, the producers engaged a thirty-eight-year-old German exile, future B-movie director Max Nosseck.[7]

Although Nosseck had not directed a movie in five years (and directed this one illegally, having received a visa restricting his work to the New York World's Fair), his experience is evident: *Der Vilner Shtot Khazn* is characterized by sophisticated chiaroscuro and a reasonably developed film language. The movie's budget was a reported $20,000, and the mise-en-scène is lavish by Yiddish standards, if somewhat mechanical. (Columbia Pictures—where Nosseck's brother Martin worked as Harry Cohen's personal projectionist—was sufficiently impressed with the film to offer its director a contract.) Still, its dramatic power derives mainly from close-ups of Oysher's sensually melancholy face and liquid eyes.

Whereas Arnshteyn's play begins *in medias res* with the *Balebesl* and his family debating whether or not he should accept an offer to appear on the Warsaw stage, for the film, Dymow provides a prologue showing how Strashunsky (Oysher) is gradually seduced by the Gentile world, in the person of the Polish composer Stanisław Moniuszko. The first scene, a veritable production number, has Moniuszko, dressed as if for the opera, attending a Rosh Hashanah service at a Vilna synagogue to hear Strashunsky sing. A cantor and the son of a cantor, Strashunsky is initially as timid as he is pious. In secret, however, he visits the Gentiles to learn about their music. In a scene presided over by a bust of Beethoven, the *Balebesl* succumbs to the *Moonlight Sonata* and eagerly accepts the composer's offer to teach him how to read music.

Subsequently exposed to Chopin, the depressed Strashunsky feels that he is suffocating in Vilna and dreams of visiting Warsaw. His wife (Florence Weiss at last, after two films playing the other woman) is too tenderhearted to discourage him, though his stern father-in-law, Reb Aaron (Maurice Krohner), is less yielding. "So, you took care of their needs? You took your golden voice and made them a present of it?" he cries upon hearing that Strashunsky is considering a trip to Warsaw. "In any language they will hear my Jewish sorrow," the *Balebesl* reasons. Unconvinced, the old man reminds him that "For thousands of years we have called out to a world that is deaf." The rabbi (Lazar Freed) warns Strashunsky that "If you go to them, you'll be left between two worlds." But the *Balebesl* believes that his voice is his own, and, despite a visit to the empty synagogue, where he hears celestial voices and is beset by strange foreboding melodies, he departs for Warsaw to appear in Moniuszko's opera *Halka*.

In the film, some of this ambivalence was displaced onto the realm of language. *Der Vilner Shtot Khazn* was originally announced as a "six-language musical drama, [although] mainly in Yiddish." Three

Der Vilner Shtot Khazn (U.S.A., 1940); frame enlargements. The legendary Vilner Balebesl (Moishe Oysher) chanting the Rosh Hashanah service. Polish composer Stanisław Moniuszko (Jack Mylong Munz) and his conductor (Leonard Elliot) are in the congregation. That night, they introduce the Balebesl to Beethoven; he succumbs. Moniuszko brings the cantor to Warsaw, where he sings opera and captivates a countess's niece (Helen Beverly). Too late, the Balebesl recognizes the price his family and community have paid for his desertion; emotionally exhausted, he returns to Vilna on the eve of Yom Kippur, and, after chanting *Kol Nidre,* dies in the synagogue.

Cast and crew of *Der Vilner Shtot Khazn*: an unhappy-looking Helen Beverly is flanked by her equally somber director, Max Nosseck (left), and costar, Moishe Oysher.

are actually heard: the Gentiles sometimes speak German or *Daytshmerish*; in one scene, a countess, played by Luba Wesoly, starts off in Polish before lapsing into *mame-loshn*. According to film historian Judith Goldberg, Martin Nosseck was still upset nearly forty years after the movie's release that *Der Vilner Shtot Khazn* had been made in Yiddish, thereby limiting its audience. (Nosseck's hindsight may be colored by the failure of the Hollywood Yiddish Film Corporation, which he established in 1939, to produce even a single film.)

The *Balebesl*'s sad, soulful demeanor frightens and excites the Poles, particularly the countess's niece Wanda (Helen Beverly). But enchanting as Wanda is, the cantor never forgets Vilna. As in *The Jazz Singer,* his dressing room mirror allows him to gaze into his past. "I'd give half my life to sing in a syn-

agogue once more," he tells the *shames* (sexton), now his dresser (Max Bozyk). On Passover, Strashunsky misses a performance to go to a synagogue, still wearing his evening clothes, to pray for his mother. ("A cantor is a cantor," his disgusted leading lady remarks.) Strashunsky resolves to return home, but Moniuszko and Wanda join forces to keep him: "You can't and you won't. All Warsaw is at your feet."

Back in Vilna, the *Balebesl*'s little son cries for him in vain. When the child is taken ill and dies, his death scene is intercut with shots of Strashunsky cavorting onstage in some goofy, "goyish" antics. Like an avenging angel, Reb Aaron appears backstage: "The Almighty has punished you," he shouts and rips his clothes as a symbol of mourning. "There is a God!" Strashunsky drifts out in front of the footlights, near-catatonic. Then he disappears. Wanda is bereft; she and the composer visit Vilna, but Strashunsky is not there. "He never stopped loving you and his child," Wanda comforts the cantor's wife. Strashunsky finally returns to Vilna on *erev* Yom Kippur and wanders into the synagogue, stunning the congregation as he suddenly starts chanting *Kol Nidre*. When he is brought up to the Torah, the errant cantor is overcome and falls down dead. The rabbi has the last word: "For them, you sang. For us, you prayed—*Vilner Balebesl*." No cantor's son ever suffered so cruelly. Jewish tradition has lost the battle, but won the war.[8]

Or was it vice versa? In April 1938, when *Yankl* was about to go into production and *Dem Khazns Zundl* was still playing at the Radio, Jacob Glatstein published "Good Night, World":

Good night, wide world,
Big, stinking world.
Not you, but I, slam the gate.

In my long robe,
With my flaming, yellow patch,
With my proud gait,
At my own command—
I return to the ghetto . . .

NOTES

1. The selection of a *khazn* could involve considerable negotiation over everything from salary and job description to personality and style, and these lively debates were often satirized on the Yiddish stage. The song "A Khazndl af Shabes" (A Cantor for the Sabbath), which details the variety of opinions concerning a visiting *khazn*'s performance, was frequently recorded. Both Ludwig Satz and Aaron Lebedeff made comedy recordings comparing the styles of New World and Old Country, or Litvak and Galician *khazonim,* and Al Jolson included a version of "A Khazndl af Shabes" in his 1932 stage production *Wonder Bar* (the only Yiddish song he ever recorded).

2. The forty-two-year-old Motyleff had arrived in the United States three years before, directed the Pasadena Playhouse and spent some time with RKO, before coming east to inherit *Dem Khazns Zundl,* his first and only movie. Three weeks after the premiere, he was directing the first of his two Broadway shows, *Empress of Destiny,* on the life of Catherine the Great.

3. Although Oysher was certainly resented as an apostate, it is not impossible that members of the congregation also opposed paying a high fee for a star *khazn*. The Depression took its toll on New York *khazonim* in general. Concert appearances dwindled and jobs disappeared. By the time *Dem Khazns Zundl* was in release, only 50 of New York's 300 *khazonim* held full-time positions.

4. Even so, the producers seem to have lost money. *Dem Khazns Zundl* had been announced as the first of six "Yiddish operettas," but for Block and Segal it would be the last. Block, not yet forty, died of pneumonia in 1939, and the Mecca Film Laboratory, which likely advanced payment on the lab work, assumed rights to the film (reviving it with some regularity into the 1940s).

5. Along with Peretz Hirschbein, the Russian-born Pinski was among the most highly regarded Yiddish dramatists of the post-Gordin generation. *Der Oytser (The Treasure),* his most celebrated play, was produced in 1910 at the Reinhardt Theater in Berlin. He immigrated to New York in 1899 and was one of the first Yiddish writers to become an active socialist. Dymow, also Russian-born, who had at one time been associated with the Moscow Art Theater, did not begin to write in Yiddish until he immigrated to New York in 1913. One of his first American plays was a satire of the commercial Yiddish stage; he was thereafter associated with various art companies including Rudolf Schildkraut's short-lived theater in the Bronx.

6. Berne's *Dawn to Dawn,* a half-hour farm drama which made use of Soviet-style montage and had some art-house play in 1933, was one of the few nonethnic, nonpolitical examples of independent cinema produced in New York during the Depression. The same year as *Mirele Efros,* Berne directed Gilbert Roland in the Spanish-language *La Vida Bohemia.*

7. Nosseck, who also used the name Alexander M. Norris, was born in the East Prussian (later Polish) town of Nakel. After studies in Berlin, Nosseck broke into the Austrian film industry as a silent movie actor. He is credited with directing four features in Germany during the early thirties. Following the Nazi rise to power, Nosseck moved to Paris, where he directed Buster Keaton in *Le Roi des Champs-Elysées* (The King of the Champs-Elysées). He also made three films in Spain, and the first Portuguese talkie—all released in 1934.

8. Oysher and Nosseck worked together one more time. In 1954, four years before the singer's death (and one year before the filmmaker returned to Germany), Nosseck directed Oysher in the independent production *Singing in the Dark*. In this post-Holocaust variation on *The Jazz Singer,* Oysher plays a German cantor who loses his family and his memory during the war. After the Liberation, he makes his way to America and becomes a hotel clerk at the establishment housing Luli's Gypsy Paradise, "the gayest spot in New York." There, Oysher is befriended by the comedian in residence, Joey Napoleon (Joey Addams). One night the two get tipsy and Oysher bursts into song. Billed as "Leo the Fabulous," Oysher becomes Luli's star—although he can only sing when intoxicated. At length, Leo is knocked unconscious by a gangster trying to collect on Napoleon's gambling debt; when he comes to, he remembers his tragic past and resumes his identity as a cantor and a cantor's son.

Overleaf: **The workings of an implacable fate. A wagon driver (Max Bozyk, left) meets the student Khonen (Leon Liebgold) by a ruined castle outside Kazimierz. Der Dibek (Poland, 1937).**

20

On the Edge of the Abyss

IN NOVEMBER 1936, while *Yidl mitn Fidl* enjoyed its Warsaw run, military hero Edward Rydz-Śmigły accepted the mantle of his former commander, Piłsudski. Rydz-Śmigły's would be the last Polish government before World War II. Although only intermittently authoritarian, the country moved closer to fascism. Hostility toward the Soviets encouraged friendly relations with Germany. At home, Rydz-Śmigły supported the formation of a new movement, the Camp of National Unity, intended to "consolidate" Poland under the auspices of "an organized and singly directed will." The army and the Church were celebrated as the pillars of the Polish nation; the Jews became a national obsession.

For an important segment of the Polish press, the "Jewish Question" was the issue of the day. The public was encouraged to believe that Poland's problems would disappear overnight if the Jews emigrated en masse. The new government followed the Catholic Church in endorsing the nationalists' long-standing anti-Jewish boycott. While politicians played to the grandstands, ordinary Jews were being harassed with restrictions on kosher slaughtering and Yiddish theater, as well as an increasing number of violent demonstrations. Such pressures served to turn the Jewish community inward. While even assimilationists ultimately despaired of either fully identifying with or being accepted by the majority

Polish culture, the generation of Jews that came of age in the thirties was commonly referred to as "a youth without a future."

In March 1930, the *Menorah Journal's* Warsaw correspondent, J. M. Neuman, had closed his examination of Poland's divided and demoralized Jewish population with a pungent account of the pitched battle that broke out between enraged Chasidim and Communist zealots in a Jewish cemetery when the latter attempted to bury one of their comrades beside a venerable *tsadek*. "A revolution in a graveyard! I know of no better symbol for the convulsive struggle in Polish Jewry." Six and a half years closer to the

Klaynkunst team Szymon Dzigan (left) and Yisroel Schumacher in *Freylekhe Kaptsonim* (Poland, 1937); frame enlargement. This unusually bleak *shtetl* comedy was written by Dzigan and Schumacher's "discoverer," Moshe Broderszon.

abyss, Neuman was eerily sanguine in reporting Poland's new "Jewish *kulturdrang*" to his American readers. This cultural breakthrough included "a return of assimilationists to Jewish life" as well as the "passionate pursuit of Jewish cultural values." *Al Khet,* which began as a Neuman brainstorm, was part of the *kulturdrang.* So was the sudden flurry of Yiddish film productions that followed in its wake.

Economic instability and official mismanagement had plagued the Polish film industry since sound arrived with the Depression in 1929. Hollywood dominated the marketplace—so much so that in 1934, with German films under a temporary ban, an astounding 87 percent of the movies shown in Polish theaters were made in the United States (if dubbed in Poland). Exhibitors were also weak. The government levied a tax of 33 percent on box-office receipts while charging movie houses for electricity at higher "nonindustrial" rates. In 1936, however, policies changed. Hoping to encourage production, the ticket tax was reduced on Polish films and increased for foreign ones. As a result, output rose from fourteen features in 1934 to twenty-three in 1937.

This new situation created an opportunity for Yiddish film production—within the industry. After the first three Polish-Yiddish talkies were produced in 1936, three more were released the following year, with a final three in 1938. If, from a technical standpoint, these films were comparable to those of the Polish mainstream, it was because, by and large, they were produced by the same personnel. Indeed, the most successful Yiddish talkies were directed by established industry figures, including Michal Waszynski, Henryk Szaro, Aleksander Ford, Jan Nowina-Przybylski, Leon Trystan, and Konrad Tom (all of whom, save Nowina-Przybylski, were Jews). Two Yiddish talkies, Szaro's *Tkies Kaf* and Waszynski's *Der Dibek,* both 1937, were produced by major studios, Leofilm and Sfinks, and shown with Polish subtitles in the principal Warsaw cinemas.

Freylekhe Kaptsonim (Jolly Paupers), Kinor's follow-up to *Al Khet,* had a somewhat lower profile; it opened at the Fama in April 1937, eleven months after *Al Khet* began its epochal run, and, like the earlier film, featured the young *klaynkunst* stars Szymon Dzigan and Yisroel Schumacher. Inspired by the success of *Yidl mitn Fidl,* Kinor here essayed a lighter tone: a comedy of errors is set in motion when a drunken tramp spills a can of oil in an open field and two friends—Naftali the mechanic (Schumacher) and Kopl the tailor (Dzigan)—imagine that they have discovered petroleum.

Aleksander Marten was originally slated to direct *Freylekhe Kaptsonim,* but after making one Polish feature, he left Warsaw to resume his career in Vienna. Zygmunt Turkow was then drafted to serve as dramaturge with Leon Jeannot, a twenty-nine-year-old former assistant to Henryk Szaro, the technical director. (Jeannot had also made short Yiddish-language documentaries for two Jewish charities, the Association for the Protection of Health [TOZ] and the Association for the Care of Jewish Orphans [CENTOS].) The film's true author, however, was the forty-seven-year-old screenwriter Moshe Broderszon.[1]

Broderszon had discovered Dzigan and Schumacher, and featured them in his *klaynkunst* Ararat until the pair moved on to Warsaw. Thus, *Freylekhe Kaptsonim* reunited the principals of Lodz's Yiddish cabaret. Although designed for a mass audience (and unfortunately lacking topical references), the film is the closest the screen came to a *klaynkunst* sensibility —irreverent, mordant, and consciously theatrical (it opens with a troupe of itinerant actors arriving in the

Production still from *Freylekhe Kaptsonim.* The film includes a tantalizingly abortive sequence of the Yiddish costume drama *Bar Kokhba.*

shtetl of Pinchev and includes a tantalizingly abortive performance of Goldfadn's venerable costume drama *Bar Kokhba*). *Freylekhe Kaptsonim* is also cost-conscious, making extensive use of post-dubbed sound, particularly in the exteriors, shot in Brzeziny, a village northeast of Lodz. Henekh Kon's score playfully telegraphs the action while, as befits a movie produced by a film lab, the barren mise-en-scène is enlivened with numerous optical effects.

More concerned with the pathos of Old World Jewish marginality than with the "dilemma" of New World upward mobility, *Freylekhe Kaptsonim* resembles the Soviet features of the twenties, but lacks their implicit postrevolutionary optimism. Rather, the film is characterized by gallows humor and a sense of economic desperation—it's a virtual *hommage* to the *mekler* (middleman), a kind of free-lance broker who, as William M. Glicksman notes in his study of Yiddish literature in Poland, hypostatized

From the *shtetl* to the stars: Jennie Lovie as Gitl in *Freylekhe Kaptsonim.*

the insecurity of Polish Jews. As a comedy of small-town Jewish life, *Freylekhe Kaptsonim* presages Green's *Der Purimshpiler* which, shot six months later, employs many of the same motifs—the *shtetl* dreamers, the traveling theater, the runaway village maiden. But where *Der Purimshpiler* is romantic, *Freylekhe Kaptsonim* is a satire in the tradition of Mendele Mokher Sforim.

Here, the *shtetl* is synonymous with exploitation: Naftali and Kopl find themselves beset by a horde of nudnik wheeler-dealers who bombard the newly anointed "millionaires" alternately with business offers and demands for handouts. At the same time, the often-feuding partners are wooed by the local *noged* (rich man) and by a visiting American, the president of the Pinchever *landsmanshaft,* who together are scheming to get possession of the oil.

Before long, the inevitable *shadkhn* (Max Bozyk) proposes a match for Naftali's daughter, Gitl (Jennie Lovie). As it turns out, Naftali's wife is after bigger game—she has her eye on the *Amerikaner.* Naftali, meanwhile, decides to further seal his new partnership by hitching Gitl to Kopl's son, Velvl. ("My Gitl should marry that lamebrain Velvl?" Naftali's wife exclaims upon being informed of this permutation.) When Gitl solves the problem herself by running off with one of the actors, she unwittingly wraps her shoes in her father's secret map of the "oil field." As the American and the *noged* scheme to buy up all the land around Pinchev, Naftali and Kopl set off in pursuit of the actors, Gitl, and the map. On their return home—after being detained temporarily in a madhouse—the partners discover that the *Amerikaner* and the *noged* have hired an engineer to survey the field. Eventually it is understood that the land contains no oil, just stones, but Naftali and Kopl remain unfazed. With terrifying prescience they decide to switch businesses: "We'll open a factory for tombstones."

Freylekhe Kaptsonim is the least sentimental of Yiddish talkies and, given the prevailing image of the Jew in Polish folklore, it is a movie which could not help but disturb Jewish audiences even as it amused them. In his 1963 study *The Jews in Polish Culture,* sociologist Aleksander Hertz (no relation to the pioneer film producer) writes that

for the Polish burgher or peasant, the Jew was definitely a *parch,* something worse, lower, laughable. If, for example, a Jew appeared in a minstrel comedy or folk show, it was, as a rule, as a comic figure worthy of derision. His language was ridiculed, as were his dress, customs, and occupation. He was a coward who lived in eternal fear. He was greedy and dishonest and was nearly always punished for it.

Seen through hostile eyes, Broderszon's sardonic and self-deprecating, if essentially good-natured, humor did not illuminate the absurd world in which the Jews found themselves. Rather, it reinforced negative stereotypes of Jewish behavior. For this reason, perhaps, *Freylekhe Kaptsonim* was the least commercially successful of Polish-Yiddish talkies. (Natan Gross also cites the film's relatively short running time as a contributing factor. *Freylekhe Kaptsonim* is barely an hour long, a problematic length for exhibitors, who would have had to rent another movie to fill out the bill.)

Given the failure of Kinor's second release, it was surely the example of Joseph Green—if not an announced movie version of *Der Dibek*—that inspired Leofilm to remake the 1924 silent *Tkies Kaf*. The new sound version was directed by Henryk Szaro, who, since making *Der Lamedvovnik* twelve years earlier, had gone on to a successful career in the Polish film industry with such prestigious hits as the patriotic partial-talkie *Na Sybir* (To Siberia), which marked the twenty-fifth anniversary of the 1905 revolution and ran for three months in Warsaw; the lavish *Pan Twardowski* (1936), which, like *Tkies Kaf*, was based on a supernatural story; and the costume drama *Ordynat Michorowski* (Count Michorowski; 1937).[2]

Racing its original model, *Der Dibek*, to the theaters, the *Tkies Kaf* remake scarcely altered the earlier tale of a marriage pact made (and broken) by two *yeshive* students on behalf of their unborn children. Even the personnel were familiar. J. M. Neuman collaborated on the dialogue with the original scenarist, Henryk Bojm. Zygmunt Turkow again played the prophet Elijah, who intercedes to ensure the fulfillment of the vow (he also helped supervise

the actors); Shmuel Landau recreated his role as the unscrupulous *noged*. The two fathers, Mendl and Khaym, were portrayed by Kurt Katch and Moyshe Lipman (Lipman had Katch's part in the original). Itskhok Grudberg (the youngest Turkow brother) and Dina Halpern played the roles of the fated lovers. The ubiquitous Max Bozyk reprised his role in *Freylekhe Kaptsonim* as a comic *shadkhn*.

The second *Tkies Kaf* is competent filmmaking, but, as is often the case, the remake lacks the freshness of the original, and in this case, its humor as well. In updating the story to the present, the screenwriters drop the underlying tragedy of the World War, but even so, the overall tone is far more solemn. The new *Tkies Kaf* was now doubly nostalgic, both for traditional folkways and for its own earlier, more innocent, version. It's striking that the Jewish custom given pride of place is the *shive* (the week of mourning that follows a death in the family). Differ as they may in subject and tone, both *Freylekhe Kaptsonim* and *Tkies Kaf* share a common fatalism. This sense of predestination would receive its fullest expression in the most celebrated of Polish-Yiddish films, the 1937 version of *Der Dibek*.

Stately, brooding, and deliberate, *Der Dibek* is the most heavily atmospheric and "artistic" of Yiddish talkies. From the opening image of a candlelit synagogue through the nightmarish dances that accompany the unconsummated wedding to the climactic exorcism, the film is steeped in religion and ritual—as well as superstition and supernaturalism.

On the surface, this best-known of Yiddish dramas is a love story. Although betrothed by their fathers at birth, Khonen and Leah grow up unaware of each other's existence. When Khonen, a poor and otherworldly student, appears in the town of Brenits, Leah is drawn to him, as he is to her. Leah's avaricious father, however, prefers a wealthier suitor. The desperate Khonen uses his knowledge of Cabbalah to conjure the aid of occult powers, but dies in the process, and his spirit enters into Leah at the moment when she is to be wed. The venerable *tsadek* of Miropol discovers the source of this possession and attempts to redress the wrong done Khonen and his father—but it is only the threat of excommunication that exorcises the dybbuk. Leah's spirit then joins Khonen's in death.

Der Dibek infuses a specifically Jewish sense of the uncanny with a measure of cultural distance. The power of the past is continually made tangible. The living mingle with the dead, who are manifest as spirits, as hobgoblins, and as monuments. The climax offers the fantastic spectacle of a "lawsuit" in which the plaintiff is a wandering soul and the defen-

Polish poster for *Der Dibek*. The most celebrated of Polish-Yiddish films, *Der Dibek* ran for three months in Warsaw during the fall of 1937 and, unlike previous Yiddish talkies, attracted a Gentile as well as a Jewish audience.

dant a living man. The heroine not only visits the cemetery to ritually invite her mother to her wedding, her village is itself a sort of cemetery—the "holy grave" in the town marketplace memorializes a bride and groom murdered under the *khupe* by Khmielnitsky's Cossacks 200 years before.

Der Dibek is the prime example of the style variously called "Chasidic grotesque" or "Chasidic gothic," which, thanks to the popularity of this play and Leivick's *Der Goylem* (as well as Peretz's *Bay Nakht afn Altn Mark,* the stage version of I. J. Singer's *Yoshe Kalb,* and the writings of Isaac Bashevis Singer), has misleadingly come to seem the mainstream of modern Yiddish literature. For all the emphasis on Jewish mysticism, however, this drama is ultimately less spiritual than tribal. The *tsadek* embodies the authority of the Jewish community—the play emphasizes the fear of that darkness which lies beyond its bounds.

In *shtetl* folklore it is almost invariably young women who are possessed by evil spirits, and, no less than his contemporary Sigmund Freud, An-sky gives this hysteria a sexual content. *Der Dibek* hardly shies away from the link between love and death: "I feel as if I were being dragged to the gallows," whimpers Leah's hapless groom as he joins her under the wedding canopy. In the film, an unusually grim *badkhn* cues the most powerful scene—a grotesque *danse macabre* in which a death-masked figure, shrouded in a prayer shawl, embraces the entranced bride, who, hallucinating Khonen, snuggles in the spectre's embrace.

As the most ambitious Yiddish talking picture to date, *Der Dibek* involved much of literary and theatrical Warsaw. Although the impetus came from Ludwig Prywes, whose uncle had been the financial angel of the original production, the producer Zyg-

The bride, Leah (Lili Liliana), is beset by beggars —some recruited from the streets of Warsaw—in the "Dance of the Poor," choreographed by Judith Berg for *Der Dibek*.

fryd Mayflauer may have been more inspired by the international success of *Le Golem,* a spectacular (and philo-Semitic) Franco-Czech coproduction, also with a Jewish supernatural theme. Prywes engaged Arnshteyn and Alter Kacyzne, An-sky's literary executor, to write the screenplay. The historian Meyer Balaban served as a consultant. Henekh Kon composed the original score ("In my whole life I never approached a work with such devotion," he told *Literarishe Bleter*).

Kon's wife, Judith Berg, who organized Poland's first Jewish school of dance, choreographed the film's half dozen dance sequences. These include the all-male *freylekhs* (circle dance) with which the Chasidim celebrate the betrothal of the unborn Leah and Khonen, and later, the *patshtants* (clapping dance) performed by the wealthy women at Leah's wedding, which is followed by three more expressionistic numbers. Unlike the Chasidic dances, the "Dance of the Poor" involves both men and women, while in the "Dance of the Beggars," the ragged and misshapen mendicants (some evidently recruited from the streets of Warsaw) caper about in a grotesque *danse macabre.* The fanciful *toytntants* (dance of death), led by Berg herself, is based on descriptions she heard from her grandmother.[3]

The cast of *Der Dibek* spans several theatrical generations. In an interview with Patricia Erens, Dina

Halpern (who played Leah's Aunt Freyde) explained that actors were "handpicked" from Warsaw's various Yiddish ensembles: "Many of us were veterans of many different stage productions [and] every person connected with the film production felt privileged, even the extras. . . . It was much more than a choice assignment." Leon Liebgold and Lili Liliana, a striking young couple from the *klaynkunst* company Yidishe Bande, were cast as the ill-fated lovers. (Indeed, Liliana had just performed Leah in Riga with Liebgold as the messenger.) As the *tsadek,* Avrom Morevsky recreated the role he originated in the 1920 Vilna Troupe production. In contrast to Morevsky's intellectual style, the rough-hewn Isaac Samberg—a specialist in proletarian and gangster roles (as well an organizer for the Jewish Artistes' Union) —played the implacable messenger.

Familiar as the material was, the filmmakers felt free to rework it as a series of set pieces. They created a major part for the popular character actor Max Bozyk, while the slender and severe Liliana was given the opportunity to display her surprisingly strong singing voice. (Liliana, who had had to learn Yiddish to appear on the Yiddish stage, starred later that year in a new film version of the Polish national opera, *Halka.*) In addition, Gershon Sirota, the most celebrated cantor in Poland, if not Europe, is heard at length. (Sirota, who toured the United States in 1912, was featured on the first Jewish liturgical recordings, produced in Vienna, Berlin, and St. Petersburg before the World War.)

Der Dibek also had the benefit of a popular showman. Michal Waszynski, the film's flamboyant thirty-three-year-old director, who claimed to have studied under Stanislavsky in Moscow and (like Ulmer) to have assisted Murnau in Berlin, was a reigning wunderkind. Waszynski broke into the Polish film industry as an assistant to Szaro and is credited with making the first sound-on-disc Polish talkie (filmed in Vienna); over the next decade he directed some forty films, virtually all of them money-makers. (No less than eight of these opened in New York between 1934 and 1938.)

Waszynski's speed, range, and impersonality suggest a Polish equivalent of a Hollywood contract director such as Michael Curtiz. He worked in almost every genre, making melodramas, musicals, romantic fantasies, farces, military films, a Polish-Czech coproduction of the Soviet satire *The Twelve Chairs,* even an adventure film shot in Morocco. Polish critics, however, are consistent in declaring *Der Dibek* to be Waszynski's finest work. A Ukrainian Jew whose original name was Wachs, the peripatetic director was born in Volhynia less than a decade before An-sky's ethnographic expedition 'to that region. Waszynski attended gymnasium and studied drama in Kiev under the Polish tragedienne Stanisława Wysocka, before moving on to Moscow and Berlin. (Leon Liebgold recalls that Waszynski spoke no Yiddish, and that he directed *Der Dibek* with a group of "ten or twelve people around him," plus Arnshteyn on hand as translator and *"mashgiekh."*)[4]

Der Dibek was filmed during the late spring in 1937 at the Feniks Studio, using leading designers and technicians (several of them refugees from Nazi Germany). The studio, according to Dina Halpern, was located in one of Warsaw's "most aristocratic" and "most anti-Semitic" neighborhoods:

The old Jews and the young Jewish boys who came to appear in the film as extras had to run the gauntlet of those hoodlums who waited for them on the street corners around the film studio. They were with canes and knives and practically every day during the peak of the filming, the production was held up as we bound their wounds.

(Interestingly, Halpern remembers dubbing a Hebrew soundtrack, presumably for release in the Yishev, in which she spoke for every female character.)

There were also two weeks of location work in Kazimierz, which by now had somewhat the same importance for Yiddish cinema as Monument Valley for John Ford. One summer during the late twenties, the Vilna Troupe had staged an open-air production of *Der Dibek* in Kazimierz under the direction of David Herman. Less old-fashioned than archaic, the movie *Dibek* might almost have been a document of this—its mood has the relaxed, ritualistic pace of a dusk-to-dawn Indian village theatrical. For the most part, Waszynski's *Dibek* is an astute popularization. Where the play opens with the announcement of Leah's engagement, Kacyzne and Arnshteyn's script supplies a lengthy prologue, virtually identical to the first reel of *Tkies Kaf,* in which the two *yeshive* students, Nissen (Gershon Lamberger) and Sender (Moyshe Lipman, yet again), pledge their unborn children in marriage. Finally, in addition to the various interpolated musical numbers, Berg's choreography elaborates on the dances that were features of the Vilna and Habima productions.

Berg's vivid, Brueghelian set pieces are the heart of the film; the haunting music Kon wrote for them is faintly reprised at the end when the dybbuk is exorcised and Leah briefly comes to herself. Indeed, one almost wishes that Berg had directed the entire movie. Waszynski doesn't altogether trust the play's

Michal Waszynski in the 1930s. The Ukrainian-born Waszynski was thirty-three and Polish cinema's reigning wunderkind when he directed *Der Dibek* in 1937.

evocative mood and adds superfluous bits of movie magic: the messenger vanishes and reappears at will; Khonen's superimposed spirit is seen rising from the grave. In the direction of actors, however, Waszynski's instincts are sure. Thus, as the possessed Leah, Liliana speaks with her own voice (albeit deepened and coarsened), and her hysteria is eerily picked up in Morevsky's brilliant portrayal of the sick and dying wonder-rabbi: haunted and trembling, he's an instrument tuned to a frequency that no one else can hear.

Der Dibek opened in Warsaw on September 25, 1937, at the Sfinks, a major cinema (where *Tkies Kaf* had its premiere earlier that summer), and enjoyed a run of nearly three months there. Thanks to the prestige of its source, and unlike previous Yiddish talkies, *Der Dibek* attracted Gentile as well as Jewish audiences. Reviews were similarly mixed. While the trade magazine *Film* hailed *Der Dibek* as "a triumph of national cinematography" that "outclasses much European cinema," the art historian Stefania Zahorska, writing in *Wiadomosości Literackie* (Literary News), found the film "inflated" and "without a single good scene," the "nauseous sediment of pathetic kitsch."

For Zahorska, *Der Dibek* was dominated by a clumsily misappropriated Polish romanticism. The Jewish cemetery mimicked Artur Grottger's paintings, Leah was surely modeled on the virgins of Jan Matejko, the *tsadek* obviously fashioned after the violinist in the poet Adam Mickiewicz's *Forefather's Eve*: "In the turgid pathos of [*Der Dibek*'s] ghosts can be seen all the ghosts of Polish theater." Expressed as it was in the supercharged atmosphere of the late thirties, such criticism suggests the articulation of an antipathy that went beyond an individual Yiddish movie. For whatever its alleged borrowings, *Der Dibek* was certainly the most complexly Jewish of Polish-Yiddish films; in the anxious Poland of Marshal Rydz-Śmigły, it would have been difficult to separate one's feelings about *Der Dibek* from one's feelings about the Jews.

In New York, *Der Dibek* opened on January 27, 1938, at the Continental Theater and remained there for seven weeks, receiving more press than any previous Yiddish (or Polish) film, including coverage by both *Time* and *Newsweek*. The poet Parker Tyler was a particular champion, praising the movie in his book *Magic and Myth of the Movies* and later including it in his 1962 compendium *Fifty Classics of the Foreign Film*. Nevertheless, although most American critics were enthusiastic, or at least respectful, it is not sur-

prising that a film so boldly Jewish as *Der Dibek* would elicit strong reactions, provoking expressions of outright hostility in the United States as well as Poland.

Der Dibek was not yet the popular "classic" it would become; nor were Polish Jews the objects of sentimental remembrance. The *New York Times* critic Frank Nugent, who had a few months earlier written a contemptuous review of *Grine Felder,* found *Der Dibek* an "oppressively tedious" film, "hamstrung (excuse the sacrilege) by a frequently infantile groping after the mystic." *Der Dibek* struck Nugent as an example "of stupidity, silly superstition, outmoded religion."

And, aside from its thematic weaknesses, it is overlong, static in presentation, rather awkwardly contrived [and] as incredible in its way as a documentary film of life among the pygmies or a trip to the Middle Ages.[5]

Coming as it does some four months after Adolf Hitler publicly vowed to protect the "community of European-culture nations" from the conspiracy of "Jewish world Bolshevism," Nugent's rhetoric has an unmistabably sinister undercurrent. Particularly striking is his lack of restraint in venting his distaste. For *Der Dibek* is not just a movie which concerns a tormented individual who has wandered beyond the pale of tribal custom. Like Zahorska's, Nugent's reaction suggests that the film was itself a form of transgression: it is a movie which, in an attempt to plumb the depths of the Jewish soul, risked violating Gentile standards of decorum and taste. Not just Khonen but *Der Dibek* itself was beyond the pale.

NOTES

1. Born in Moscow shortly before the Jewish community was expelled, the exuberant, witty Broderszon grew up in Lodz. Back in Moscow during the World War, he joined the ranks of Yiddish modernism—collaborating with El Lissitzky on *Sikhes Kholin* (Small Talk), a mildly erotic amalgam of Jewish folklore and art nouveau that was printed as a Torah scroll. Returning to Lodz in 1918, he was editor of the avant-garde journal *Yung Yidish* and the soul of the local *klaynkunst* movement—a triple-threat actor-playwright-producer.

2. First filmed by Wiktor Biegański in 1921, *Pan Twardowski* is a Polish *Faust*, set in medieval Krakow. Szaro continued working in the Polish film industry up until the war. He died in 1942, most likely in the Warsaw Ghetto.

3. Berg had begun her career in her teens as a dancer in Broderszon's Ararat cabaret and later toured Poland with Kon. Her most celebrated piece was a version of *Menakhem Mendl*; she also choreographed (and danced in) several productions staged by the Kaminska and Turkow troupes. Like An-sky and the Yiddish modernists, Berg took Chasidic folk forms as the basis for a new Jewish art. In 1986, she told the folklorist Michael Alpert that, having grown up in a Chasidic environment, she saw herself as "choreographing tradition."

4. Waszynski survived World War II and settled in Italy. There he directed two films, *Lo Sconosciuto di San Marino* (1946) and *La Grande Strada* (1948), in collaboration with Vittorio Cottafavi; he was Orson Welles's assistant director on *Othello* (1949–52), and served as art director on several American productions, including *Quo Vadis* (1951) and *Roman Holiday* (1953). In 1960, Waszynski left Italy for Spain where he worked as executive producer on Samuel Bronston's epics. At some point, he began passing himself off as Polish royalty: his 1965 *Variety* obituary lists him as "Prince Michael Waszynski."

5. *Der Dibek* had a similar impact on Joseph Goebbels, who screened it in February 1942 and noted in his diary that although the film was "intended to be a Jewish propaganda picture," its effect was precisely opposite: "One can only be surprised to note how little the Jews know about themselves and how little they realize what is repulsive to a non-Jewish person and what is not."

Overleaf: **Fleeing their town in the midst of World War I, a group of Jews take refuge in a cemetery—Joseph Green's *A Brivele der Mamen* (Poland, 1938). The star, Lucy German, is at right.**

21

Without a Home

I N EARLY 1938, the same week *Der Dibek* opened in New York to unprecedented acclaim, Warsaw's *Literarishe Bleter* published a call by the influential journalist J. M. Neuman for greater planning in the production and distribution of Yiddish films. Last Rosh Hashanah, Neuman complained, three Yiddish talkies appeared in Warsaw at once but none had been prepared for the current season.

Neuman, who had been criticized for scripting the old-fashioned melodrama of *Al Khet*, felt vindicated by the success of *Yidl mitn Fidl, Tkies Kaf,* and *Der Dibek*. Yiddish talkies, he stressed, should be rooted in the traditional Jewish world—secular Jewishness has yet to achieve its aesthetic forms: "European actors know how to wear formal attire. We Jews will never know how to wear anything but the *kapote*. We must show our real faces to the public." For his part, Neuman announced that he was currently developing a historical epic on the origins of Chasidism, to be called *Baal Shem* and filmed on the very sites where the Baal Shem Tov had lived.[1] The project would be lavish. Neuman discussed the idea with both Joseph Green and Maurice Schwartz, but neither felt sufficient money could be raised. The writer had even taken his proposal to New York, although when it was suggested he film *Baal Shem* in America, Neuman refused: "This movie could only be made in Poland."

Molly Picon (center) is the "little mother" who looks after her four siblings (including Gertrude Bullman, right) and feckless father in Joseph Green's *Mamele* (Poland, 1938). Though she had just turned forty, Picon was still playing the teenage gamine.

The Jewish past must have seemed a comforting place. In March, six weeks after Neuman's piece was published, Vienna welcomed the incorporation of Austria into Germany with a burst of anti-Semitic terror and brutality. Polish nationalists too endorsed the *Anschluss*; despite the Polish Corridor dividing East Prussia from the rest of the Reich, there was as yet little fear of war. In any case, Hitler's attention had turned to the Sudetenland and the dismemberment of Czechoslovakia. That summer, as British prime minister Neville Chamberlain made the first of three trips to Germany to discuss the crisis, the Nazis began expelling all Jews who were Polish nationals.

Such was the climate when Joseph Green returned to Warsaw. Rival producers were trying, without success, to float new film versions of Jacob Gordin's *Mirele Efros* and *Khasye di Yesoyme* (Khasye the Orphan); Shaul Goskind had given Itzik Manger a hundred-zloty advance for a never-to-be-produced script on the medieval Jewish jester Hershele Ostropole and was planning another period vehicle on traditional Jewish comedians for Dzigan and Schumacher. For his last two films, however, Green switched from picaresque romance to sentimental family stories.

Originally, Green intended to make only *A Brivele der Mamen* (A Little Letter to Mother). The cannily chosen title was borrowed from Solomon Smulevits's turn-of-the century song, perhaps the best known of Jewish immigrant laments. The screenplay had been written in New York by Mendel Osherovits of the *Forverts,* and the score was composed by Molly Picon's accompanist Abraham Ellstein. As his Polish codirector, Green hired Leon Trystan.[2]

Before the movie went into production, however, Green was approached by Jacob Kalich, who was anxious to follow up on the success of *Yidl mitn Fidl* and wanted Green to make another film with Picon. Kalich proposed adapting *Mamele* (Little Mother), a Meyer Schwartz comedy that had been a hit for Picon over a decade earlier. Although *Yankele* was the vehicle that established Picon in Europe and on Second Avenue, the cozier, more sentimental *Mamele* had always seemed to Kalich to be a potential crossover into the American audience. He had made a point of inviting New York's English-language press when the show first opened, and in 1932 had negotiated, unsuccessfully, with Columbia Pictures on an English version.

Green proved more amenable. Although opposed in principle to the idea of filmed theater, he nevertheless agreed. Perhaps Green felt the increasing instability of the Polish situation and decided to cram two years' work into one. In any case, *Mamele* and *A Brivele* were shot back to back with much of the same personnel—including cameraman Seweryn Steinwurzel, designers Jacek Rotmil and Stefan Norris

(who had worked on *Der Dibek*), the American actors Gertrude Bullman and Edmund Zayenda, as well as Simcha Fostel and Max Bozyk. Neuman and Konrad Tom (who would codirect *Mamele*) adapted Schwartz's play, opening up the action and transposing the setting from the Lower East Side to the slums of Lodz, Green's hometown. Lucy and Misha German, brought to Poland to star in *A Brivele der Mamen,* now cooled their heels for six weeks while Green and Tom filmed *Mamele* in a Warsaw studio, with a few exteriors shot in Lodz and the resort town Ciechocinek.

As in the original, Picon plays Khavtshi Samet, the "little mother" of the title who, like Jennie Goldstein in *Tsvey Shvester,* has promised her dying mother she would look after her four siblings and feckless father, played by Bozyk. (Following *Freylekhe Kaptsonim, Mamele* acknowledges Jewish unemployment. In one scene, pointedly set during the workday, a number of men are shown idly playing dominoes. Although most are bareheaded, their activity is cast as an ironic parallel to traditional study and prayer—they chant a *nign* as they play.) Even more than *Yidl, Mamele* is a vehicle for the vivacious Picon. What's remarkable is that, having just turned forty, she is still playing the gamine: this "miracle" even forms part of the film's subtext. In one of Picon's numbers, lifted from her 1930 show *Dos Meydl fun Amol* (*The Girl of Yesterday*), she ages from adolescent to octogenarian, appearing variously as a little girl, a young woman at her first dance, a stout matron of forty-eight, and a seventy-eight-year-old grandmother.

Khavtshi not only manages the Samet household, keeps a pet kitten, and gives advice to the whole tenement, but is also the guardian of her family's virtue, protecting them from the disorder of the slums. Her nemesis is Max Katz (Yidishe Bande member Menashe Oppenheim), a smooth young gangster who passes himself off as an engineer in order to seduce the beautiful Berta (Bullman) while exploiting the skills of the youngest brother, an apprentice locksmith. Although she saves both siblings, Khavtshi goes unappreciated—until she leaves to find happiness with the young musician who lives across the courtyard (Zayenda).

Picon recalled *Mamele*'s shooting as a "horribly depressing" experience.

The people were all so poor and bewildered. Whenever we would make a call for extras hundreds of people would appear and offer their services for nothing—or, rather, just for a chance to appear in the film in the hopes that some relative abroad might recognize their faces in the picture and send them some money or help them to emigrate.

Still, *Mamele* is essentially a comic melodrama; as a saga of maternal (or Jewish) misery, *A Brivele der Mamen* is far heavier going.

Despite Green's profound contempt for Joseph Seiden (in a 1978 interview, he maintained that Seiden "didn't even use a studio but filmed in his own home" and "not only didn't know Yiddish [but] didn't even know English"), *A Brivele der Mamen* might be considered Seiden's greatest film: the movie is arguably the most artful and shameless of Yiddish weepies.

The stately and sensuous Lucy German stars as the long-suffering Dobrish Berdichevski, another matriarch compelled to support her entire family.

Unlike Khavtshi, however, she must also witness and survive its disintegration. Not until late in the film does Misha German appear, as the providential official from HIAS (the Hebrew Immigrant Aid Society) who reunites Dobrish with her long-lost son. Opening in a Ukrainian city two years before the World War, *A Brivele der Mamen* may convey something of the flavor of Green's childhood—certainly it was his favorite from among his own films.[3]

The Berdichevskis belong to the lower strata of the Jewish middle class. Although Dobrish and her husband David (Aleksander Stein) own a drygoods store, David is at heart a *luftmentsh* who wanders around in a melancholy daze, composing Jewish melodies while Dobrish begs for credit from the wealthy Reb Hersh (Shmuel Landau). Their daughter Miriam (Gertrude Bullman) plays piano in the local dancing school; her brother Meyer (Itskhok Grudberg) is furious because the family has no money to send him to Odessa to study dentistry. Consumed with guilt and stricken by his children's contempt, David leaves for America, setting the stage for a pathetic, fatherless Passover seder in which Arele, the youngest child, a boy of nine or ten, asks a *fifth* question of the father's empty chair: "Why did you leave us?"

In New York, David sits on a park bench sadly humming his version of "Had Gad-ya," while back in the Old Country, his bereft family sings the same *nign*. After Miriam and the dancing master elope, German enjoys her fourth handkerchief scene. Soon David, who is selling ties from a pushcart, sends a few dollars with a steamship ticket for young Arele. ("A man who couldn't skin a cat here—in America he's Rothschild," the neighbors marvel.) Dressing Arele and putting him on the train affords German another virtuoso sequence of withheld tears; she

A moment of happiness: the long-suffering Dobrish (Lucy German, center left) sees her errant daughter (Gertrude Bullman) married in *A Brivele der Mamen* (Poland, 1939).

breaks down only with her final words, asking him to write *"a brivele der mamen,"* as the train pulls out of the station.

By now the movie has become an endurance test to determine the amount of *tsores* one mother can endure. Miriam soon returns home sobbing, having discovered that her lover had a wife and child, but Dobrish manages to marry her to the innocent neighbor boy and send the couple off to Odessa. When the World War finally breaks out, communications with America are disrupted. Meyer is drafted, and Dobrish is forced to flee (through the cemetery) to Warsaw. Living with her former neighbors in a crowded garret, she peels potatoes while the tailor, Shimen (Max Bozyk), sews and complains that "the world is falling apart like a badly made shirt." Even Reb Hersh has to line up for bread; when Dobrish sees him, she gives him half of her loaf. No sooner is peace declared than an armless man shows up with the news that Meyer was killed in battle: "His last word was 'Mother.' He died like a hero."

The next scene finds Dobrish at the HIAS office, waiting in vain for news of her husband. Stricken when no ticket arrives, she soon learns that David is dead and Arele missing. "I'm not crying. I have no tears left to cry," she tells the director, who resolves to take Dobrish to America himself. There, against all odds, she hears the grown Arele (Edmund Zayenda) singing his father's composition, retitled "Memories of My Old Home," at a HIAS-sponsored recital. When he breaks into "A Brivele der Mamen," she rises, transfixed. But Arele is swept away by admirers before she can reach him. As if in a dream, his limo pulls off and Dobrish is run over by another car. Mystically sensing who she is, Arele runs to her side. They are reunited in the hospital: his face comes into focus and she sobs her recognition.

Green needed only three months to shoot both *Mamele* and *A Brivele der Mamen*. While Poland was helping to carve up Czechoslovakia, annexing the border area of Cieszyn on October 1, 1938, Green was editing and mixing the films. Postproduction work was still going on when the Nazi regime orchestrated Kristallnacht, the largest and most savage pogrom against German Jews to date. Convinced that war was imminent, Green arranged for the Polish release of both movies and in December left Warsaw, closing his office and taking his papers with him. Plans for the production of a Polish-language

"The world is falling apart like a badly made shirt": Max Bozyk presses as Lucy German (right) broods in Joseph Green's *A Brivele der Mamen.*

film, a remake of Henryk Szaro's 1928 hit *Dzikuska* (The Wild Girl), were dropped.

Green's negatives were shipped to New York, where *Mamele* opened at the Continental on Christmas Eve. (The night of December 24 was by now a customary one on which to premiere a Yiddish movie and thus create an alternative Jewish gala.) Although it received good notices, this Picon film failed to reproduce *Yidl*'s success. Indeed, as an event, it was largely overshadowed by *A Brivele der Mamen*, which Green held back until September 1939—two weeks after the Nazi invasion of Poland.[4]

The theme of unhappy emigration—or perhaps the impossibility of any escape—came even more grimly to the fore in prewar Poland's last Yiddish talkie, *On a Heym* (Without a Home), produced during the frightening final months of 1938 which saw, among other events, attacks on the office and the forced closing of Warsaw's leading Yiddish daily, *Haynt*.

The director of *Al Khet*, Aleksander Marten, who had returned to Warsaw from Vienna after the *Anschluss*, here tackled a Jacob Gordin play which had been a celebrated vehicle for Sarah Adler thirty years earlier. Produced by Marten and adapted by Alter Kacyzne, *On a Heym* starred Ida Kaminska in her first part since the original *Tkies Kaf*, with Dzigan and Schumacher in supporting roles. Yet despite its powerfully evocative title, not to mention Marten's firsthand knowledge of Nazi anti-Semitism, *On a Heym* was remarkably unpolitical—as though the fate of Polish Jewry were a question that could not be posed directly.

Like *A Brivele der Mamen*, *On a Heym* contrasts the New Land with the Old World. The action be-

Ida Kaminska in Aleksander Marten's *On a Heym* (Poland, 1939). The film was Kaminska's first in the fifteen years since the original *Tkies Kaf*; it was also the last Yiddish talkie produced in Poland before World War II.

gins in Kazimierz. Catastrophe strikes the Rivkins, a family of fishermen, when their eldest son is drowned in a storm. Avreyml Rivkin (played by the director) is so distraught he can no longer bear to remain in Poland. "Since Moyshele is gone, part of my heart has left me," he says as he prepares to leave his wife, Bas Sheve (Kaminska), and their son Khonokh for America where, as we soon discover, the best job he is able to find is washing dishes in a nightclub. In the Gordin original, Avreyml falls in love with a "modern woman," an intellectual; here, his American sweetheart, Bessie, has a more vulgar glamour—she's the singer in the nightclub.

Adam Domb, who played Ida Kaminska's father in the original *Tkies Kaf*, appears as her father-in-law in *On a Heym*.

It's ironic that the only one of Gordin's immigration dramas to be filmed should have been made in Europe. Beyond irony, however, is the movie's attitude: hardly a safe haven, or even a viable alternative to Poland, America is a land of beardless Jews and broken dreams. The overall tone is somber. Even more crudely than in *Al Khet*, Marten underscores the action with a number of sorrowful synagogue sequences, complete with unseen choir. *On a Heym* is as grim a film as its title would suggest—indeed, it is overtly death-haunted. Kaddish, which is chanted in the film's opening moments, is reprised twice, while the action alternates between Avreyml's never-consummated affair (and Bessie's lugubrious

"mother" songs) in New York, and life in Poland, where Bas Sheve and Khonokh are supported by Avreyml's old father (Adam Domb). When two *landsmen,* the letter-writer Fishl (Schumacher) and the *balegule* Motl (Dzigan), show up in New York and tell Avreyml that his family is all but starving, he borrows money from Bessie to bring them over.

Bas Sheve, however, fails to make the adjustment. As in a Soviet film, America is portrayed almost entirely in negative terms: "In America, one is not sentimental," Bessie tells Avreyml. "In America, they have no time for God," his pious father laments. These complaints, some stock footage, and an interpolated image of the George Washington Bridge aside, the film's most visceral evocation of the New World is the use of "colored" characters, played by Poles in blackface. Motl's prosperous uncle has a black maid—"Is this your aunt?" Fishl asks innocently—who announces, in English, that "your cousin from Europe is here." (To complete the round of comic misunderstandings, Motl's aunt embraces Fishl instead of Motl.) Later, when a new batch of greenhorns arrive from Poland, they are startled to see their tenement's black janitor. "He washes in tar," Motl explains.[5]

The family disintegrates under the pressure of poverty and Avreyml's neglect. Bas Sheve becomes increasingly obsessed with the Biblical triangle of Abraham, Sarah, and Hagar, and when it appears that Khonokh, too, has drowned, she suffers a breakdown. Confined to the hospital, she imagines herself back in Poland, rocking an imaginary child. (Kaminska imbues this *shund* cliché with considerable pathos.) Avreyml is brought to his senses by the apparent tragedy—"A fisherman deserts the water, it takes revenge and follows him"—and when it turns out that Khonokh is alive, the family is reunited. In the final scene, Avreyml restores Bas Sheve's sanity by recreating the simple, pious atmosphere of their old house.

Although this perfunctory happy ending did little to mitigate the film's overwhelming pessimism, the conclusion considerably dilutes Gordin's: just as Kacyzne's screenplay stops short of suggesting actual adultery, his denouement arrests the decline into madness which ends the original play. In Gordin's grim text, Bas Sheve is released from a mental hospital to discover that Avreyml has remarried and Khonokh no longer remembers her. The pitiful final scene has her suffer a relapse and decide to return to her village. Neighbors call for an ambulance, and when it arrives to bring her back to the hospital, the broken woman has regressed to her second childhood, capering for joy because she is finally going home.

Shot entirely in the studio by *Yidl mitn Fidl*'s cinematographer, Jakub Joniłowicz, *On a Heym* is the most claustrophobic and threadbare of Polish-Yiddish talkies; Ida Kaminska lends the project its single element of glamour. In an interview given before the film's release, Marten wondered why Kaminska had never been properly "exploited" by Yiddish filmmakers, promising that "this wrong will now be set right." Indeed, it was: during the course of the production, according to Eric Goldman, Kaminska was so conscious of her exploitation—or perhaps so dubious that *On a Heym* would ever be completed—that she stipulated her salary be paid on a daily basis.

Nevertheless, although *On a Heym* was manufactured on the subsistence level of a Joseph Seiden film, it shows far more technical ingenuity than did most American *shund*. Marten and Joniłowicz compensate for their barren set with mirror shots, reverse angles, and expressive lighting; they used models as an alternative to exterior locations, and build tension through dramatic close-ups, which, thanks to the intensity of her performance, are particularly effective in Kaminska's scenes.

The decline in Yiddish film production coincided with the increasingly bellicose nationalism that, encouraged by Poland's military leadership, swept the film industry on the eve of World War II. The late thirties saw a revival of militarist spectacles. (Josef Lejtes's 1938 *Sygnały,* in which Polish partisans are inspired by Chopin's *Revolutionary Etude* to take up arms against the tsar, epitomizes these popular, usually anti-Russian, films.) Despite some talk of a sound version of *In di Poylishe Velder, On a Heym* would be the last Yiddish feature produced in Poland before the war.

None of Shaul Goskind's more ambitious plans came to fruition, but throughout 1938 and into 1939, he and his brother produced a series of short newsreels surveying Jewish life in five then-Polish cities (Krakow, Bialystok, Vilna, Lvov, and Warsaw). According to Goskind, the mandate to document Poland's Jewish communities came from the Zionist leader Vladimir Jabotinsky. Narrated in Yiddish, these artless recordings, with their emphasis on Jewish welfare and cultural institutions, are like snapshots of a civilization about to sink beneath the waves. (The films were shown as short subjects; only one reached New York.)

In January 1939, a bill was introduced in the Sejm that would deprive Polish Jews of the rights to vote, to work in government service, and to teach. In addition, the bill attempted to purge Jews from Polish radio, the press, and the film industry. Soon after, it was reported that Jewish exhibitors in Warsaw would not have their licenses renewed. On January 30, in Berlin, Hitler made a two-hour speech before the Reichstag in which he attacked the anti-Nazi films being planned in America and announced that, should such movies be produced, Germany would respond by producing anti-Semitic films which, he felt sure, "many countries would appreciate." Among other things, he demanded the return of Germany's former colonies (as well as a fair share of the earth's "riches" for Italy and Japan) and prophesied, amid what the *New York Times* reported as "the evening's wildest acclaim":

If the international Jewish financiers in and outside Europe should succeed in plunging the nations once more into a world war, then the result will not be the bolshevization of the earth, and thus the victory of Jewry, but the annihilation of the Jewish race in Europe.

Released in Warsaw in March 1939, *On a Heym* was poorly received. *Literarishe Bleter* was frankly astonished at the film's timing. "What Jew, if he gets a visa to America, will complain he has no home?" the reviewer demanded. *Literarishe Bleter* assumed the film was created for the American market, in which "sentimentality for the *shtetl* is not yet extinguished." When *On A Heym* appeared in New York a month later, however (opening, like a Seiden film, at the Clinton, the Ascot, and the People's), it was casually dismissed. "Were it not for the magic name of Jacob Gordin," the *New York Times* observed, "this sad tale (with a happy ending) doubtless would

be classified as a minor B effort in the foreign film line."

Within a week of *On a Heym*'s Warsaw premiere, Hitler occupied Prague; eight days afterward, Germany took Memel, a district in Lithuania that had formerly been part of East Prussia. The same day, the Polish government began to secretly mobilize its armed forces against a Nazi attack. That July, shortly before she left Vilna, Lucy Dawidowicz remembers seeing the first anti-Nazi film made in Hollywood, Warner Brothers' *Confessions of a Nazi Spy*.

The theater was filled and everyone, Jews and Poles, loved the film, vociferously applauding the Americans and booing the German spies. Just at that time, gas masks went on sale in Vilna. The authorities urged the public to buy them. An adult's gas mask cost seventeen *zlotys*; a child's mask fifteen *zlotys*. If you didn't have the cash, you could buy on the installment plan—two *zlotys* per month.

NOTES

1. Israel Ben Eliezer, known as the Baal Shem Tov (Master of the Divine Name), was born around 1700 in an impoverished Podolian village. Whereas traditional rabbis drew their authority from the Torah and their understanding of Jewish law, the Baal Shem was charismatic both in person and doctrine, valuing spiritual ecstasy over scholarship. He left no writings but, after his death in 1760, accounts of his miraculous deeds were the subject of numerous published legends; his disciples (and their disciples) founded the great Chasidic dynasties.

2. A medical student turned film actor, film critic and, after 1926, film director, Trystan never redeemed the promise of his early films, which were made under the influence of French Impressionism. He remained an active director until 1939 and died two years later in Odessa—most likely killed by the Nazis.

3. Green's affection for the film that would be his last may be gauged in his telling Judith Goldberg that the Academy of Motion Picture Arts and Sciences screened *A Brivele der Mamen* for Oscar consideration (there were no foreign-language Oscars until 1956), and that, although its popularity was less sustained than that of *Grine Felder* or *Yidl mitn Fidl*, it was the highest-grossing Yiddish film of all time.

4. According to Green, the German presence was already apparent when he made *A Brivele der Mamen*. The studio at which the film was shot had recently purchased new sound equipment from Germany.

Being that I was the first one to use it, they brought in two technicians from Germany to supervise this whole production. I had a Polish staff and these two Germans. They behaved nicely with all of them. I had it easy as I speak German fluently. It later turned out that when the War broke out these two men came in uniform and took over the film business in Poland. They were sent at that time to learn everything. They knew where every print was, where every company was. They learned all this while working on my film.

5. Another Schumacher routine left an impression on the American avant-garde filmmaker Ken Jacobs. In program notes for his 1969 film-portrait of his two-year-old daughter, *Nissan Ariana Window*, Jacobs recalls that he and his wife, Flo,

used to go to a theater on Second Avenue that showed old Yiddish films with stage shows in which old Yiddish vaudeville cadavers romped with all the electric energy they once displayed to Kafka. One Polish movie, *Without a Home*, had a subsidiary character, a ne'er-do-well amiable scholar. . . . One scene showed him at his breakfast table in his sunny old-world poverty digs, cracking open his soft-boiled breakfast egg—this said everything—with a tuning fork, to which he then listened.

Overleaf: **The lame Fishke (David Opatoshu) helps the blind Hodl (Helen Beverly) in Edgar G. Ulmer's *Di Klyatshe* (U.S.A., 1939); production still. Adapted from the writings of Mendele Mokher Sforim, *Di Klyatshe* offers the only negative view of the *shtetl* found in an American Yiddish movie.**

22

Phantom Europe

I N AMERICA, the period between the *Anschluss* and the Nazi-Soviet invasion of Poland represented the high-water mark of the Yiddish cinema. Although in New York the Yiddish legitimate stage continued to falter, the 1938–39 season brought more Yiddish talkies than ever before.

The remade *Tkies Kaf* arrived in September, *Yankl der Shmid* in November, *Tsvey Shvester, Mamele*, and *Shkheynim* (*Neighbors*) in December. These appeared in the context of a number of anti-Nazi films, both American independent documentaries and Soviet features. Lenfilm's *Professor Mamlock,* a film about the degradation of German Jewry whose story line was already familiar to New York audiences from the 1937 Federal Theater stage produc-

tion, opened on November 17 at the Cameo, one week after Kristallnacht; it received an extremely wide break for a Soviet feature and could still be found playing Jewish neighborhoods well into the spring. The 1930 *House of Rothschild* was revived in December, while a month later, the 1933 *Der Vanderer Yid* (*The Wandering Jew*)—now known as *Yidn in Goles* (Jews in Exile)—was again rereleased, this time playing RKO theaters all over the New York area.

Hayntige Mames (*Mothers of Today*) had its premiere in February, shortly after the Yidishe Bande arrived from Paris under the auspices of Maurice Schwartz. As Polish nationals, the actors were held up at Ellis Island until Schwartz appealed to Congressman William I. Sirovich to expedite their entry. On April 2, 1939, the same day that the *New York Times* reported the formal capitulation of the Spanish Republic and the "aryanization" of Hungary's theaters, the Yidishe Bande opened on West Forty-eighth Street, at the Belmont (where the last of the Spanish Civil War documentaries, *Will of a People,* had recently completed its run). "Sh! Don't Tell Hitler!" their ad cautioned, making no mention that the show was in Yiddish. "There's 'pins and needles' stuck into the Nazis at every performance of *The World Trembles*—a sensational daring revue—a riot of comedy, satire, music."

On a Heym appeared in April, even as boats filled with desperate Jewish refugees were seeking safe harbor. *Mayn Zundele* opened in mid-May, two days after a tear-gas bomb was detonated at the theater where the Soviet feature *Concentration Camp* was showing and a week after the premiere of *Confessions of a Nazi Spy.* ("Hitler's pledge of non-aggression toward the Americas reached the Warners too late yesterday," began Frank Nugent's review. "They formally declared war on the Nazis at 8:15 A.M. with [the movie's] first showing. . . .")

Late spring brought Grigori Roshal's *The Family Oppenheim,* the second Soviet film to deal specifically with Nazi persecution of the Jews. Like *Professor Mamlock,* it was banned in Chicago. Still, the antifascist coalition continued to build. *Confessions of a Nazi Spy* was playing in some neighborhoods with Edgar Ulmer's all-black *Moon over Harlem.* Meanwhile, Charlie Chaplin had begun *The Great Dictator*; that July, he announced a call for Yiddish-speaking actors to appear in it. With Father Coughlin urging his followers to prepare to defend America "the Franco way," even the Catskills resort Grossinger's was featuring a cycle of class-conscious Clifford Odets plays.

On Second Avenue, the theatrical year was over. An average of one Yiddish talkie a month had been released in New York during the season and there were numerous revivals. As spring turned to summer, the most ambitious Yiddish movies ever to be made in America were in various stages of preproduction: *Di Klyatshe* (The Old Mare), *Mirele Efros, Tevye der Milkhiker,* and *Der Vilner Shtot Khazn.* "Quality" features with solid *literarish* credentials, all four were set in nineteenth-century Eastern Europe. But, while *Mirele Efros* and *Der Vilner Shtot Khazn* looked back to the turn-of-the-century Yiddish stage, *Di Klyatshe* and *Tevye* were absolutely contemporary. They represented the two poles of serious Yiddish theater in New York—the Artef and Maurice Schwartz.

The most stylized of Ulmer's Yiddish films, *Di Klyatshe*—also known as *Fishke der Krumer* (Fishke the Cripple), and given the inspirational English title *The Light Ahead*—has a superficial resemblance to the Chasidic gothic mode popularized by Schwartz's *Yoshe Kalb* and the Polish *Der Dibek.* Its source, however, is older; the script is adapted from the work of Mendele Mokher Sforim, whom Sholom Aleichem had dubbed the Grandfather of Yiddish Literature.

Born Sholom Yakov Abramowitz in the Lithuanian town of Kapulye, Mendele took his pen name (meaning Mendele the Bookseller) when he published his first Yiddish story in 1864. Five years later he published his first version of *Fishke der Krumer,* a picaresque saga of Jewish beggars, as well as *Di Takse* (*The Tax on Kosher Meat*), a corrosive satire that so scandalized the Jewish establishment of his adopted city, Berdichev (to which, in the tract, he had given the name Glubsk, i.e., "fools' town"), that he was ultimately forced to leave. While attending rabbini-cal school in nearby Zhitomir, Mendele wrote *Di Klyatshe*, an elaborate allegory representing the Jew-ish people as a once princely steed now transformed into a broken-down workhorse. At the age of forty-five he finally secured a position as principal of a Jewish school in Odessa and there revised many of his previous works.

An ambitious gloss on Mendele's worldview, in-corporating elements from *Fishke der Krumer* and *Di Takse*, while taking only its title and a certain meta-phoric weight from the *Di Klyatshe*, the film script was written by Chaver-Paver, adapting his own un-produced stage play *Fishke der Krumer*. The writer, born Gershon Einbinder in 1901 in the Bessarabian town of Bershad, had grown up in Mendele's world. (In his memoirs, he notes that Bershad was famous for its *taleysim*, "Mendele Mokher Sforim even men-tioning them.") Arriving in New York in 1924, he became a regular writer for the *Morgn Frayhayt*. As his pseudonym suggests (it comes from a Yiddish nursery rhyme), Chaver-Paver also wrote children's books, and, to supplement his income, taught Yid-dish—but only to the children of Yiddish writers. Besides working on the script for *Der Purimshpiler*, he had enjoyed a long relationship with the Artef, for whom he translated Clifford Odets's *Awake and Sing*, and adapted works ranging from Samuel Or-nitz's Lower East Side novel *Haunch, Paunch, and Jowl* to Sholom Aleichem's *Motl Peyse* and Gogol's *The Overcoat*.

The Artef had first planned to stage Chaver-Paver's *Fishke der Krumer* during their 1936–37 season, but was preempted by Joseph Buloff's pro-duction of a rival adaptation. That August, when Artef and ICOR announced a competition of new Yiddish plays, Chaver-Paver entered *Fishke* and, in

May 1938, won the $700 first prize over 150 other submissions. However, despite the success of *The Good Soldier Svejk* (the only Yiddish production ever given a spread in *Life* magazine), Artef was unable to mount a 1938–39 season. Ulmer then acquired the rights to Chaver-Paver's *Fishke*, and after com-pleting *Moon over Harlem*, began filming during the spring of 1939 at the same Newton, New Jersey, location he had used the previous summer for *Yankl der Shmid* and *Cossacks in Exile*.

Ulmer's cast was headed by Helen Beverly and included David Opatoshu, both of whom had just appeared at a May 28 Town Hall rally in support of Birobidzhan. (Opatoshu, the twenty-one-year-old

Edgar G. Ulmer (standing) studies the *shabes* **scene on the set of** *Di Klyatshe*. **David Opatoshu (fourth from left) smiles as an unidentified visitor to the set spoonfeeds Helen Beverly.**

son of the novelist Joseph Opatoshu and an Artefnik of four years standing, was brought to Ulmer's attention by Chaver-Paver, the actor's childhood Yiddish tutor.) Isidore Cashier, who shared top billing with Beverly (his "daughter" in *Grine Felder*), and who also served as dialogue coach, played Mendele the Bookseller as an enlightened but homespun *folksmentsh* and a jovial champion of the poor.

Given the original material, the script, and the personnel, it's not surprising that *Di Klyatshe* would have more political bite than most Yiddish talkies. Indeed, dealing with exploitation and poverty, *Di Klyatshe* offers the only negative view of the *shtetl* to be found in an American movie. Glubsk is still firmly in the Middle Ages. The life of the town is depicted as miserable and degrading, religion shown to be self-serving and hypocritical—even the dietary laws have been perverted by commerce. "Better a Jew without a beard than a beard without a Jew," one local progressive tells the pious scoundrels of a Chasidic court.[1]

Some 100,000 rubles have been collected in the Glubsk community chest, yet the local *balebatim* refuse to appropriate a penny to build a hospital, insisting that God is their doctor; they will, however, spend to support psalm and prayer societies. (That Chaver-Paver himself was tubercular, and extremely sick during the filming of *Di Klyatshe,* gives these scenes particular piquancy.) Faced with a cholera epidemic, the town fathers ignore the filth that surrounds them and blame the plague on a group of village girls who broke the sabbath by swimming in a nearby stream.

Though it opens with a good-natured Talmudic dispute in a dappled meadow, *Di Klyatshe* takes place mainly at night and plumbs the lower depths, recounting a haunting love story of the blind orphan Hodl (Beverly) and crippled Fishke (Opatoshu). Although they are of the lumpen, Hodl and Fishke are distinguished by their purity—and by the lighting that gives their numerous close-ups a distinctive glow. Neither is mercenary. Hodl refuses to beg, despite her "valuable" assets; Fishke ekes out a living as a bathhouse attendant. Too poor to wed, their humble dream is of a hovel where they can eat potatoes and herring. While Isidore Cashier and virtually every other member of the cast indulge in the overstated supertheatricality that characterized the Yiddish Art Theater (and helped make it so successful), Beverly and Opatoshu give far more naturalistic performances. Whether this reflects a greater sensitivity to movie acting or an exposure to Stanislavsky (or alternately, a sophisticated directorial touch), it has the effect of rendering these outcasts the most normal—and modern—residents of Glubsk.

While cholera continues to spread through the backward village, the superstitious town elders attempt to fight the epidemic by marrying the pair in the cemetery at midnight. Hodl and Fishke's initial resistance at becoming the "cholera bride and groom" gives way when Mendele offers to help them leave Glubsk for Odessa. Cut short in *Di Klyatshe*'s one surviving print, the climactic wedding scene is appropriately hysterical—close-ups of laughing faces are juxtaposed with Hodl's solemn, sightless pirouettes during the handkerchief dance and the wild abandon of a hora amid the graves. (This apotropaic wedding ritual, referred to in numerous *shtetl* memoirs and dramatized in the Soviet film *Border*, also appears as a set piece in *Yoshe Kalb*. Adam Czerniakow noted in his diary that when typhus struck the Warsaw Ghetto during winter of 1942, "the rabbis proposed that a marriage ceremony be performed in a cemetery.")

The cholera wedding: the town's poorest couple, Hodl (Helen Beverly) and Fishke (David Opatoshu), are married in the graveyard at midnight, in *Di Klyatshe*.

Stagier and less supple than *Grine Felder,* whose belated profits enabled Ulmer to produce *Di Klyatshe,* the film is stronger on composition than narrative flow (or camera movement). *Di Klyatshe* is the most expressionistic of Ulmer's Yiddish talkies. The performers tend toward stylized postures, and the frame is complicated by the use of foreground props. With its crazy angles and skewed lampposts, Glubsk suggests the confluence of Marc Chagall and *The Cabinet of Dr. Caligari.* Ulmer's pragmatism extends to the musical score, which is cleverly cobbled together from existing recordings. (The wedding is accompanied by a loop fashioned from 78s of Joseph Cherniavsky's wedding music for Schwartz's 1924 production of *Der Dibek.*)[2]

Particularly striking from an auteurist point of view is the reworking of *Grine Felder*'s central motifs. Whereas the earlier film shows rural Jews as essentially healthy, *Fishke* takes the radical position that *shtetl* Jews have been deformed by their environment. Here it is the countryside that is diseased and the city that offers salvation. Even certain scenes from the earlier movie are echoed. The idyllic *shabes* meal in *Grine Felder* is replayed as a beggars' banquet in which everyone eats with their hands from the same bowl. Just as Tsine wooed the shy *rebele* with apples, here the thief Getsl Gonif offers Hodl an apple and promises her that if he marries him she'll "live like a *rebetsn.*"

The presence of the high-strung and beautiful Helen Beverly further links the films. Her black eyes riveted on some distant point, the winsome gamine of *Grine Felder* has become a creature of tragic intensity. (The music that introduces her is so forebodingly romantic as to be almost Wagnerian.) Beverly and Opatoshu are perhaps the most beautiful couple in the history of Yiddish cinema, and their scenes have a poignant erotic chemistry that helps compensate for the film's overly static mise-en-scène and sometimes shrill polemical tone.

Maurice Schwartz (at left, in costume) directs a scene from *Tevye der Milkhiker* (U.S.A., 1939), filmed during the summer of 1939 near Jericho, Long Island.

Lacking the radiant America of the generational melodramas, *Di Klyatshe* represented a terrifying crisis of authority. Cashier's fatherly speeches—agonized monologues on the dangers faced by the Jews of Eastern Europe delivered in direct address and close up—were scarcely inappropriate to the tense spring and sumer of 1939. With Austria and Czechoslovakia incorporated into the Reich, nearly 800,000 Jews were under Nazi rule, and Hitler was now pressing his claims on Poland.

For the American-Yiddish theater, an era had come to an end. In early July, not long before *Di Klyatshe* wrapped, Boris Thomashefsky died. The *New York Times* estimated 30,000 mourners at the memorial service where Moishe Oysher was one of two cantors and eulogies were delivered by the editors of three Yiddish dailies, as well as by union head Rubin Guskin and Maurice Schwartz. Despite the size of the crowd, the *Times* reported that a "hush reigned on Second Avenue from Tenth to Houston streets while Thomashefsky's funeral was held."

Schwartz, meanwhile, had finally begun work on his long-delayed *Tevye*, the film he first proposed to Joseph Green in 1936 and had publicly announced in January 1938. (Schwartz also acquired from the author's widow the film rights to three other Sholom Aleichem works: *Shver Tsu Zayn a Yid, Dos Groyse Gevins,* and *Stempenyu.*) A $70,000 extravaganza, *Tevye* was produced by Harry Ziskin, co-owner of the largest kosher restaurant in the Times Square area. After three weeks of rehearsal on the stage of the Yiddish Art Theater, shooting began on a 130-acre potato farm near Jericho, Long Island. On August 23, midway through the shoot, Hitler seized Danzig. A Nazi invasion of Poland seemed imminent. The next day, the newspapers carried the mind-boggling news that German foreign minister von Ribbentrop was en route to Moscow to conclude a nonaggression pact.

The late-thirties efflorescence of Yiddish popular culture was, at least in New York, actively supported by Jewish Communists and closely connected to the Communist-dominated culture of the Popular Front. With one stroke, the Hitler-Stalin Pact destroyed whatever confidence most Jews had in their Communist coreligionists. For Yiddish-speaking New York, as former *Morgn Frayhayt* editor Melekh Epstein would recall, "the reaction was volcanic."

Jewish Communists were met by their shopmates with the Nazi salute and a "Heil Hitler!" There were fist fights in the garment center. Many people had their relatives in Poland and the Baltic states threatened by Hitler; they felt Stalin had let them down. Hundreds of Communists again came running to the party offices, on every face a look of shock and simple disbelief. They begged for some explanation, and, not getting any, drifted off like shadows.

The small group of outstanding men of letters, lured by a cause dear to them—Yiddish culture —to collaborate with the Communists in the YKUF, immediately severed relations with that body. For some this was not the first, but the second break with the Communist movement.

Political tensions and the deterioration of the European situation were felt, as well, on the set of *Tevye*. Many of those involved in the production had family in Poland; some were anxious to return. Leon Liebgold booked passage on a boat leaving for Poland on August 31. But *Tevye* had fallen behind schedule—a number of scenes had been ruined due to the location's proximity to Mitchell Airfield. Although his visa had expired, Liebgold was compelled to postpone his departure. The next day, the Nazis invaded Poland.

Three Yiddish movie features were scheduled for Rosh Hashanah. Seiden's *Kol Nidre,* which featured the Yidishe Bande, had its premiere on September 7 at the Clinton. One week later, Green's *A Brivele der Mamen* opened at the Belmont, and was reviewed in the *Forverts* by no less an eminence than editor-in-chief Abraham Cahan. But while *A Brivele der Mamen* played the Belmont for a month, *Di Klyatshe* had no midtown opening. The world premiere was actually in Detroit, at Littman's People's Theater. The film arrived in New York on September 28, with simultaneous engagements at the Clinton and the Ascot in the Bronx.

Di Klyatshe "touches undreamed-of heights," wrote the *New York World-Telegram.* The *New York Times* found the film "remarkably honest and forthright." Opportunistically noting the setting as a Jewish village in "that part of Poland which the Red Army has now liberated from a century of untold suffering," the *Daily Worker* called it "the finest Yiddish film since *Green Fields,*" a "logical answer" to mediocrities like *A Brivele der Mamen. Der Tog* thought *Di Klyatshe* would have particular appeal for Jewish youth; even the Orthodox *Morgn Zhurnal,* which attacked the film both for mimicking Hollywood and for allowing Chaver-Paver to "satisfy his ideology," concluded that it was "not a bad movie."

Despite excellent reviews, however, *Di Klyatshe* performed disappointingly at the box office, at least compared to the other Yiddish talkies released that fall. Although arguably less grim than *A Brivele der Mamen,* the Ulmer film offered little solace, and less catharsis. No miracles are performed, no families reunited. The inspirational English title notwith-standing, Fishke and Hodl face an uncertain future at best. Where Ulmer's film ran three weeks at the Radio and the People's, *A Brivele* lasted five weeks at the former and four weeks at the latter, with an additional Brownsville run shortly after.

Di Klyatshe's lack of commercial success was, of course, relative; the strong competition from other Yiddish releases was surely a factor. Indeed, given the film's disturbingly downbeat romance, continual emphasis on poverty and superstition, and blunt crit-icism of tradition, it could easily have performed even more poorly. In a dispatch from Kansas City, the December 20 issue of the *Hollywood Reporter* noted that

the surprise sensation of the picture business here is the trade being done at the Vogue by *The Light Ahead*, a Yiddish dialogue picture. The show was given rave notices by the local press, which urged Gentiles to enjoy it with their Jew-ish neighbors, resulting in picture fans of all creeds and nationalities buying tickets.

The 1939–40 Yiddish theatrical season was already in place when war broke out. The revived Artef opened with *Mr. Man*, a dramatization of Chaver-Paver's *Clinton Street*, starring David Opatoshu. At-tendance was so poor that ticket prices were reduced —the cheapest seat was now fifty-five cents. More in tune with current political developments, Jacob Ben-Ami and Jacob Mestel had rented the National Theater for a lavish adaptation of I. J. Singer's anti-communist novel *Chaver Nachman*, starring Celia Adler and Ludwig Satz. Schwartz plunged into re-hearsals for his no less spectacular production of Sho-lem Asch's *Der Tilim Yid* (*Salvation*), even before he finished editing *Tevye der Milkhiker*. (The strain was enormous; later that fall, the director would suffer a heart attack and spend the remainder of the season recuperating in Florida.)

Since *Uncle Moses*, Schwartz's career had been marked by the extraordinary commercial success of *Yoshe Kalb*. After a poor 1933–34 season in New York, he went on tour, spending the next two and a half years presenting his *chef d'oeuvre* throughout Eu-rope. On his return to New York, Schwartz took a Broadway theater and, in a comeback of sorts, staged two more *Kalb*-esque epics—*Di Brider Ashkenazi* (*The Brothers Ashkenazi*), adapted from another I. J. Singer novel, in 1937–38, and *Dray Shtet* (*Three Cities*), from Sholem Asch, in 1938–39. *Tevye*, based on a play which Schwartz had first produced twenty years before, was part of this last hurrah. Indeed, in remaking the 1919 silent *Khavah*, Schwartz brack-eted the entire interwar American-Yiddish cinema with Sholom Aleichem's tale.

The most celebrated of Sholom Aleichem's char-acters, Tevye the Dairyman—the pious and home-spun *shtetl* Jew, the father of seven daughters—is the protagonist and narrator of eight monologues published between 1895 and 1914. As with much of Sholom Aleichem, the cycle's underlying subject is the crisis in Jewish tradition, embodied in different ways by Tevye's daughters. His eldest rejects an ar-ranged match and marries an impoverished tailor; his second daughter makes a love match with a Jew-ish revolutionary and follows him to Siberia; the third, Khave, converts and marries a Christian. This is by far the worst betrayal—"the pain is great, but the disgrace is even greater." Nevertheless, when, in the final Tevye story, "Get Thee Out!" the dairyman

About to be married, Tevye's daughter Khave (Miriam Riselle) has second thoughts; her Ukrainian groom (Leon Liebgold) stands behind her on the right. *Tevye der Milkhiker.*

is driven from his village by edict of the tsar, Khave leaves her husband and begs Tevye to let her rejoin him.

Over the years, Tevye has been drafted to serve various ideologies. In an Israeli version of the story, produced by Menachem Golan in 1968, Tevye and the chastened Khave set off for Eretz Yisrael. By contrast, *Fiddler on the Roof,* filmed by Norman Jewison in 1973, emphasizes the generational gap between Tevye and his daughters and ends with Khave

and her Gentile husband leaving for America along with Tevye. A year before Schwartz's *Tevye* was released, the Moscow GOSET staged a version with Mikhoels in the title role. Their reworking limited Tevye to two daughters—Hodl, who refuses the rich prospects her father provides to join her revolutionary sweetheart in Siberia, and Khave. According to the description in Joseph Macleod's 1943 account, *The New Soviet Theater,* Khave "falls in love with a Gentile—a Russian, and an artist at that!"

Tevye's world is breaking up, but he decides that his progressive daughters are right; and there is a strong scene in which he persuades his wife about this. He is evicted by Tsarist officials, but becomes friendly with the Ukrainian peasants and is able to show them that all their troubles are rooted in Tsarist oppression.

On one hand, Schwartz's *Tevye* stands apart from other American-Yiddish talkies in its superior production values. The film is extremely well shot and elaborately orchestrated (the Sholom Secunda score is near continuous). As Tevye, Schwartz gives a bravura performance—a perpetual emotion machine of nonstop singing, humming, and talking. On the other hand, it is distinguished by its theme. Most Yiddish films were set in a completely, and often artificially, Jewish world. Only *Yisker* and *Der Vanderer Yid* had dealt with anti-Semitism or even the uneasy relations between European Jews and their Gentile neighbors. *Tevye* thrives on this tension—Schwartz establishes it in the film's very first scene when, with the harvest in, a group of boisterous young Ukrainians tease the pretty "Jew girl" Khave (played by Schwartz's niece, Miriam Riselle).

Tevye is the only Jew in the town, and hence the more vulnerable. He has a friendship with the local priest (Julius Adler) who considers him "a clever Jew" and wonders what would happen if one of his daughters fell in love with a Gentile. In one of Schwartz's dramatic "improvements" on Sholom Aleichem, Tevye informs the priest that he would rather see his children "perish" than "betray" their faith through intermarriage. Listening to this conversation, Khave swoons—she has fallen in love with the peasant boy Fedya (Leon Liebgold) who woos

her with a gospel of spurious universalism and the books of Maxim Gorky.

Whether or not Fedya must also carry the onus of the Hitler-Stalin Pact, *Tevye* communicates a real hostility. Whereas *Yisker* and *Der Vanderer Yid* made some distinction between good and bad goyim, here the Ukrainian characters, who speak Yiddish with farcically broad accents, are contemptuously referred to as "potato peelers" or "pig breeders" and maliciously represented as boorish brutes. The priest is a sinister figure, and even sensitive Fedya sleeps with his boots on. A town council meeting quickly degenerates into a brawl; a traditional wedding is little more than the occasion for idiotic wrestling bouts and excessive drinking.[3]

When he attends the wedding of Khave and Fedya (which occurs "off-screen" in Sholom Aleichem), Schwartz gets to play the wronged Jew *à la* Shylock. Schwartz's Tevye humiliates himself by pleading with Fedya's parents to restore his daughter; he even prostrates himself before the priest, who responds by ordering him away. (Hidden upstairs, the flower-bedecked Khave moans for her "*tate-mame*.") At the tragic *shabes* meal, Tevye and Golde mourn Khave as though she were dead. She is, in fact, worse than dead, "neither to be mentioned nor remembered" as if she never existed. When Golde takes ill and dies, Khave can only peer in the window of her childhood cottage. Later, in the film's supreme heart-clutcher, she spies her father on the road and piteously attempts to get him to stop. (In Sholom Aleichem, Golde dies much later in the cycle. The film scene between Tevye and Khave is, however, nearly verbatim from the original.)

Like *Di Klyatshe, Tevye* offered the portrait of a *folksmentsh*—more longsuffering than *Di Klyatshe*'s

Mendele, but also more reassuring. The aged Tevye is teaching his grandson a psalm when the villagers arrive to expel him, giving the family twenty-four hours to pack their belongings and sell the rest. ("If the prices weren't low, we'd steal it all," remarks one peasant rummaging through Tevye's belongings.) Khave takes this moment to leave Fedya ("It will never work: we are worlds apart") and return to her father, whom she pleads with to take her back. After letting her grovel and then consulting God, Tevye does so. Shamelessly celebrating the father's absolute rightness, *Tevye* is the ultimate generational film. The final shot of the wagon setting off for Palestine is a triumphant rebuke to the assimilationist *Romance of a Jewess* and all its clones.

In the *Forverts*, L. Fogelman hailed *Tevye* as "one of the best Yiddish films made to date," observing, however, that "merely a shadow of Sholom Aleichem has remained in Tevye's few external characteristics." This position was elaborated in the *Morgn Frayhayt*: "Schwartz himself is even better in the film than he was on the stage," Nathaniel Buchwald wrote; and, he continued, if it were only a question of Schwartz's performance, "*Tevye* should be considered the best Yiddish film ever." Unfortunately, the film "does not at all agree with the spirit and essence of Sholem Aleichem's writings."

Buchwald calls *Tevye* "a steaming of Sholom Aleichem" which preserves only the most melodramatic elements, adding "'stage'-*goyim* from the *shund* theater" and transforming Khave into "the unfortunate heroine of an unhappy '*mame*-drama.'" Although Schwartz's stage production of *Tevye* suffered from similar excesses, "in the film this fault has grown out of all proportion." Far from the spirit of Sholom Aleichem, *Tevye* "reeks of cheap Jewish

Spanish-language poster for the Latin American release of Maurice Schwartz's *Tevye der Milkhiker*, early 1940s.

chauvinism." It goes so far that the English subtitles attempt to soften the actual dialogue. There are

scenes which are obscene, false, bungling, and insulting—not for *goyim* but rather for the dignity of a Yiddish film and of Jewish artists. We should leave the "art" of slandering entire peoples to the Nazis.

Tevye, Buchwald concluded, is "a powerful film [that] will keep you in suspense and move you to tears." It is a film "in which the central role is played with deep understanding" for the character. "But it is not *Tevye der Milkhiker*; it's something else and something worse."

The culture editor of the *Morgn Frayhayt*, and a Communist critic respected even by nonparty intellectuals, Buchwald wrote one of the few substantial contemporary analyses of Yiddish cinema. "Yiddish

Films in America," published in the March 1940 issue of *Yidishe Kultur,* started from the premise that, particularly outside of the large cities, Yiddish talkies had supplanted the Yiddish stage. This, however, was not necessarily a negative development. The audience for Yiddish cinema was larger than the total Yiddish theater audience and also more selective.

Buchwald marshaled statistics to demonstrate that quality films attracted more viewers than *shund* and chastised the intelligentsia for ignoring the potential of the Yiddish cinema.

There is a long-standing tradition of concern with the ailing Yiddish theater. Year after year we reaffirm the sad truth that Yiddish theater is on its last legs, and there is little hope that it will ever get well. This near-obsession has shut our eyes to the burgeoning of the Yiddish film and its potential to become a mighty instrument in the dissemination of the Yiddish word—an eloquent spokesman of Jewish culture even among non-Yiddish-speaking Jews.

Yet despite a potential American audience of a half-million viewers per film, the Yiddish movie industry remained "in the hands of *luftmentshn*—people who have no steady occupation, no capital, and very little practical film experience." This, as well as the financial risk filmmaking entails, discourages the presence of creative artists. "The *luftmentshn* have learned from the Yiddish theater how to avoid payment of salaries and other obligations. They live from film to film, from one vague transaction to another." And no wonder, considering that, according to Buchwald's figures, a "Class A" Yiddish feature cost some $50,000 to produce and, at the very best, could never hope to net more than $75,000.[4]

Yiddish film pioneers, Buchwald pointed out, were at once better off and worse off than those of the Yiddish theater; better off, in that an audience for their work already existed, worse, because this audience had been spoiled by Hollywood. *Shund* merchants tried to beat Hollywood at its own game. Movies like *Vu Iz Mayn Kind?* were "universal *shund.*" The difference was that Hollywood served this material with "refined manners, subtle mastery and remarkable technique, while the Yiddish *shund* films are crude, repulsive, vulgar and—ridiculous!" Although *shund* producers fed off the interest generated by quality Yiddish films, they were more practical and experienced filmmakers. Thus, the danger was that these parasites would "devour their 'host.'" Indeed, *shund* films had already "so poisoned the atmosphere that they have almost discredited Yiddish films in general."

Buchwald's rhetoric is reminiscent of the *beserer teater* manifestos of the 1920s. While praising the technical achievements of *Tevye, Mirele Efros, Der Vilna Shtot Khazn, Tkies Kaf, Dem Khazns Zundl, Di Klyatshe,* and the Green films, he complains that even these are tainted by the "vulgar pranks of the cheap Yiddish theater." This is wholly unnecessary. *Grine Felder*—Buchwald's paradigm, as Hirschbein's plays were for art theater advocates twenty years earlier—proved "an extraordinary drawing card, attracting a larger audience than even *Yidl mitn Fidl.*"

The popularity of *Grine Felder,* which was made without famous actors, reveals the fallacy of the star system. Like Jacob Gordin, Buchwald insists that the vehicle is more important than any one performer: both *Uncle Moses* and *Tevye* were constructed around Maurice Schwartz, yet *Uncle Moses* "was a miserable failure, while *Tevye* is a resounding success." Similarly, *Yidl mitn Fidl* "won the hearts of the audience, while *Mamele* is just an ordinary Yiddish film starring Molly Picon," and *Dem Khazns Zundl* is only "a movie in which Moishe Oysher sings cantorial songs, while *Der Vilner Shtot Khazn* is memorable—with or without a cantor."

Grine Felder is also, for Buchwald, the model photographed play—shot under the sky and liberated from theatrical constraints. However prestigious, other adaptations were unable to transcend their theatrical origins. Although *Der Dibek* "exerted a greater influence on Yiddish theater than *Grine Felder*," Buchwald writes, it "is not the most successful Yiddish film." *Mirele Efros*, too, "created history on the Yiddish stage, but one cannot say the same about the film version."

In 1940, the total circulation of New York's daily Yiddish press was 250,000—less than half what it had been during World War I. Given these figures, Buchwald is astonishingly sanguine. The continued need for young actors remains—"Miriam Riselle, Helen Beverly, and David Opatoshu cannot handle all the youthful roles in future films"—but he saw no dearth of talent. The crisis was not audience shrinkage but rather poor adaptation. Yiddish actors, directors, playwrights, and technicians must find their way from "the declining Yiddish theater" to "the ascendant Yiddish film." The ascendant Yiddish film! If not sabotaged by bungling amateurs or the misconceived "pairing of 'literature' and 'shund,'" Buchwald concludes that Yiddish cinema "has every chance to grow and flourish."

So rosy an assessment was not unique. In *The Story of Yiddish Literature,* published in 1940, A. A. Roback maintained that, having emerged from their initial stage, Yiddish talkies were now "catching on."

Roback cited eight quality films (all literary adaptations), then launched into heady prognostication:

The Yiddish film industry is still in its swaddling clothes; and when some of the larger épopées are shown on the screen, *The Brothers Ashkenazi* for instance, or *Shulamis* properly presented, Jewish, and indeed non-Jewish, theatregoers will think twice before giving precedence to the average Hollywood production. One can even visualize Peretz's *The Old Market Place at Night* as a film; and it might be made into a magnificent spectacle. Sholem Asch's *The Nazarene* will be the first originally Yiddish novel to be filmed on the grand scale of *Gone With the Wind, Wuthering Heights,* or *Les Misérables,* and shown to many millions throughout the world.

In terms of audience support, the fall of 1939 was the most successful period in the history of Yiddish cinema. It was as if Jews found their solidarity at the movies.

The three Rosh Hashanah films (*Kol Nidre, A Brivele der Mamen,* and *Di Klyatshe*) were followed by *Mirele Efros,* which opened in mid-October, ran three weeks at the Cameo—inspiring a revival of the play at the Clinton with Jennie Goldstein—and was playing Jewish neighborhoods three months later. *Kol Nidre* showed more staying power than any previous Seiden opus, still running when the producer released *Motl der Operator,* his third film of the year, in late December. Even more astonishing was the popularity of Henry Lynn's swan song, a cut-and-dubbed *faryidisht* version of the 1933 British feature, *The Wandering Jew.* Opening at the Miami Theater in late October with as *Dos Eybike Folk* (The Eternal People), it ran two weeks on Broadway, then played a succession of week-long engagements in Brooklyn,

The Continental Theater, Seventh Avenue and Fifty-second Street (next to Roseland), where *Tevye der Milkhiker* ran for five weeks during the winter of 1940.

Variety was sufficiently impressed to declare a "Negro and Yiddish film boom," predicting, in their first issue of 1940, "a banner 12 months ahead for the lensing of this type product." One month later, the *New York Herald-Tribune* would greet *Der Vilner Shtot Khazn* as an "artistic triumph for the Yiddish film industry," adding that "one need no longer speculate about the proper place of these films in the many-corridored auditorium of the American theater. Yiddish films have arrived."

NOTES

1. Even so, Chaver-Paver and Ulmer softened Mendele's satire considerably. In *Masaot Benyamin Hashlishi* (The Travels of Benjamin the Third), Mendele describes Glubsk as surrounded by a moat of sewage and swarming with hucksters, beggars, and thieves.

The city's population is split up into clans or castes, not unlike those of the Hindus. There is the Grab-All-You-Can Clan, for instance, who may be considered Brahmins, ruling the town with an iron hand and without any velvet glove nonsense. . . . [Below them are] the Phony Bankrupts; the Rulers of the Market Place; the Holier-Than-Thou Sinecurists, who put their foot down in all matters of religion; those known as the Foolish-Poltroonish-Voiceless Beggars are the pariahs and untouchables, who shiver and shake and quiver and quake before all the other castes.

2. The surviving print of *Fishke der Krumer,* recovered from a European collection in the 1960s, is twenty-five minutes shorter than the film's original running time. To judge from the dialogue translation filed with the New York State Board of Censors, cuts included a discussion of the fraudulent proscription (as unkosher) of chickens raised in a neighboring town, Mendele's agitation for a hospital, and a lengthy scene in the ritual bath, wherein the subject of the proscribed chickens comes up again. In addition, the wedding sequence has been considerably shortened: the original film apparently included several scenes depict-

the Bronx, and on the Lower East Side, lasting into May of 1940.

But the greatest success, by far, was *Tevye*, which opened at the Continental Theater several days before Christmas (and several days after the long-awaited premiere of *Gone With the Wind*, a few blocks away, at Radio City). Indeed, Schwartz's epic may be considered the Yiddish analogue to those fondly remembered archetypes—*Stagecoach, Wuthering Heights, The Wizard of Oz, Mr. Smith Goes to Washington, Ninotchka, Gone With the Wind*—that have led to the canonization of 1939 as the greatest year in Hollywood history. *Tevye* played Broadway for five weeks, was booked by more New York area theaters than any Yiddish talkie since *Grine Felder*, and has since lodged itself in popular memory as the definitive Yiddish film.

ing wedding preparations, and a longer ceremony, with two recitations by a *badkhn*.

3. Sholom Aleichem is scarcely so crude in representing the Ukrainian peasantry, whom he prefers to show as manipulated by the anti-Semitic minions of the tsar. One story concerns a Jew named Shmulik who, like Tevye, lives among the peasants. Because he is literate, the villagers rely on him to explain to them the events of the day—so much so, that when word reaches the town in the wake of the 1905 revolution that the tsar has ordered reprisals against the Jews, the peasants come to Shmulik for instructions, "for how could we have a pogrom against the Jews without Shmulik?" Ironically, 1939 saw a Ukrainian-language production of *Tevye* in Odessa.

4. *Variety* put the average cost of a Yiddish feature at $25,000 —although five-day "cheapies get through at as low as $8,000," and some producers have spent up to $50,000. The journal estimated the profit margin at from "$6,000 for the quickies to $21,000 for the exceptional. Average is about $16,000. . . . In addition to this, foreign exhibition before the war was bringing in an average of about $15,000."

Overleaf: Nat (Leo Fuchs) has had more failed engagements than Judith (Judith Abarbanel) has bridesmaids in this publicity shot from *Amerikaner Shadkhn* (U.S.A., 1940), Edgar G. Ulmer's last Yiddish talkie.

23

Married to America

NOT LONG after *Di Klyatshe*'s release, the Artef leased a small theater on Sixth Avenue at Thirty-ninth Street and premiered its final production, a new Soviet translation of *Uriel Acosta,* from German into Yiddish, with Michael Goldstein in the title role. "If we have to die, let it be in a full dress suit," is how the actor remembered his thinking at the time. In an uncharacteristically commercial ploy, "movie stars" David Opatoshu and Helen Beverly (the Artef's first "guest artist") had prominent supporting roles.

Although the production was well-received, the Artef was finished, a casualty of the Hitler-Stalin Pact. Like all Yiddish theaters, it depended on ad-

vance group sales to secure a run. (At the height of the Popular Front, even the "right-wing" socialists of the Workmen's Circle held benefits at Artef productions.) *Mr. Man* had already gone down in a hail of canceled theater parties; *Uriel Acosta* never got off the ground. Goldstein, who gave a series of newspaper interviews vainly pleading for an audience, was reduced to ending each performance by asking those who came for additional contributions of small change.

The culture of the Popular Front was over. When *Der Vilner Shtot Khazn* opened at the Cameo in early February of 1940 (the last Yiddish talkie for ten years to enjoy a Broadway premiere), the *New York Times* was moved to observe that "the accredited home in New York of Soviet films [has] definitely undergone a 'change of policy.'"

[The] first attraction under the new regime [is] as remote from the fiery red tub-thumpers of old as an antiquated tearjerker, such as this one, is from a modern social drama. Apparently the management felt the oldest broom would sweep the cleanest.[1]

That same month, the *Times* reported that the Artef planned to take *Uriel Acosta* and *Mr. Man* on the road or "appear in motion picture versions of

A pious cantor (Isidore Cashier) is reduced to working in a newsstand in Joseph Seiden's *Der Yidisher Nign* (U.S.A., 1940). The film turned Europe into a fantasy realm; the customer at the extreme left holds a copy of the *Daily News* with the headline "Hitler Terror."

Yiddish plays." Nevertheless, neither Goldstein nor Opatoshu made another Yiddish film. Opatoshu joined the Group Theater; Goldstein was cast in a Broadway play in 1941; Helen Beverly married Lee J. Cobb (the son of a *Forverts* typesetter and himself a former member of the Group) and switched back to the English-language theater, costarring with her husband in the 1941 Broadway production *Clean Beds*.

"Everybody wanted to get into the American theater, you know," one of the younger Artefniks recalled, forty years later. "That's what everybody wanted—except people who knew they couldn't because they didn't speak the language. Everybody in the Yiddish Art Theater really wanted to break into American theater. Schwartz wanted to. . . ." But if the writing was on the wall, Edgar G. Ulmer hadn't yet read it. Even as *Di Klyatshe* wound down its disappointing release, Ulmer was directing one final Yiddish film—the provocatively titled *Amerikaner Shadkhn* (*American Matchmaker*).

Ulmer's ethnic swan song was one of two new Yiddish musicals to open during the spring of 1940, made and released during the "phoney war," while Western Europe awaited the Nazi assault. As if to acknowledge this brief period of unreality, as well as the unbridgeable chasm that had opened between American Jewry and the Yiddish heartland, both films are strikingly denatured. As Eastern Europe is too painful to conceptualize, these movies portray traditional Jewish figures in fantasy realms that suggest Yiddish versions of Italy's so-called white-telephone films—romantic comedies in lavish settings, populated by men and women of leisure for whom love and marriage are life's greatest problems.

Joseph Seiden's enjoyably witless *Der Yidisher Nign* (*The Jewish Melody*) arrived first, opening at the Clinton in late April. The film's protagonist, Morris, played by radio star Chaim Tauber, is a cantor's son, albeit a modern one. His prospective father-in-law, the president of a prominent Brooklyn synagogue, has sent him to Italy to study opera. (One of the most exotic settings in any Yiddish film, this "Venice" is composed of stock footage of the Grand Canal and studio interiors festooned with cheap wall tapestries and littered with plaster busts of Beethoven.) The world of European culture is here an annex of *Yidishland*. That the maestro and his daughter Rosita speak Yiddish (with Italian accents) is only partially explained when Rosita turns out to be a bona fide *yidishe tokhter*. In the final reel, she comes to Brooklyn and foils the various misalliances by revealing herself as the illegitimate daughter of the synagogue president.

Der Yidisher Nign ends with not one but three weddings, though, despite the perceived boom in Yiddish film production, such enthusiasm was scarcely warranted. In early 1940, Mecca Lab foreclosed on *Di Klyatshe*, as it had on *Dem Khazns Zundl*. Ulmer was nevertheless able to persuade Z. H. Rubinstein, managing editor of *Der Tog* and producer of Molly Picon's radio show, to invest in a new Yiddish picture. *Amerikaner Shadkhn*, a low-budget film even by Ulmer's standards, resembled a Seiden production for being shot almost entirely in the studio, as well as for its somnolent camera, flat lighting, and copious use of incidental English. Costs were cut to the bone. Sholom Rubinstein, who wrote the film's English subtitles, remembers that the musicians' union refused to work with Ulmer because he owed members back salary from his previous projects. The main attraction was Leo Fuchs, who

Isidore Cashier, center, in *Der Yidisher Nign.*

had begun the 1939–40 season with the Yiddish Art Theater production of *Salvation* and was substituting for the ailing Schwartz in *Ven Ikh Bin Rotshild* (*If I Were Rothschild*) when Ulmer engaged him to make his first film since Seiden's 1937 *Ikh Vil Zayn a Mame* (*I Want to Be a Mother*).

Fuchs, who was touted as the "Yiddish Fred Astaire" when he arrived on Second Avenue in the mid-thirties, plays a particularly Astaire-esque figure in *Amerikaner Shadkhn*—Nat Silver, a debonair and fabulously wealthy Jewish-American businessman. Nat has clearly made it in America, yet, although he has amassed more than enough money to transcend his origins and retire from the garment trade, he has repeatedly failed to take a wife and thus become fully a *mentsh*. In order to learn how to make a marriage, he reinvents himself as a *shadkhn*. This career move is scarcely a step up in status; the *shadkhn* is almost always a comic, if not a ridiculous, figure. Still, although poor and often obsequious, the *shadkhn* is not without some power: his qualification as a quantifier of individual *yikhes* makes him a kind of a social arbiter. The successful *shadkhn* is also a skilled psychologist who, among other things, mediates between the material facts of an arranged marriage and the Jewish folk-belief that each marriage is divinely preordained. Perhaps the archetypal *shtetl* Jew, the *shadkhn* is at once the instrument of a divine plan and a *luftmentsh*.

The *shadkhn* is also the enemy of romance, and thus a hopeless anachronism in the New World. By 1916, a reporter for the *Forverts* might profess surprise that, although most Lower East Side Jews preferred to wait for love, "hundreds or even thousands still use *shadkhonim*." It was an enduring institution. Twenty-two years later, when the *New Yorker* published Meyer Berger's profile of *shadkhn* Louis Rubin, the marriage broker was sufficiently exotic to be portrayed as a figure of some authority.

One of Rubin's chief assets is the full-length black beard that covers up his collar and reaches down toward the fat-linked gold watch chain looped across his comfortable paunch. He wears a real silk *yarmulke,* too, slaps a wide-brimmed Whitmanesque sombrero over the *yarmulke* and carries a dark stick thick as your wrist. Ever since he went into the marriage-broker line, twenty-five years ago, he has stuck grimly to somber black suitings, a sort of half-frock effect that inspires customers to put confidence in him. Right now the Rubin ledgers show 7,168 weddings. . . .

Amerikaner Shadkhn opens far from Rubin's world, in an Art Deco *cum* arte povera penthouse where Silver is hosting an elegant bachelor party to celebrate his recent engagement (his eighth). Despite this affluence, however, something is awry. The jokes are sour, almost hostile; the ambience is sterile. Even Nat's canary lacks a consort. The next scene has intimations of *Zayn Vaybs Lubovnik* and *Uncle Moses*—movies in which young girls are effectively sold to rich old men. Nat is rousted from a dream of his intended bride when a distraught young man invades his penthouse, pulls a revolver, and demands his sweetheart back, explaining that "her mother loves your bankbooks." The angry lover terms Nat "old" and accuses him of being cynical, but Nat, who does not protest, is neither. Nor is he simply an inappropriate suitor *à la* Schwartz's tragic Uncle Moses or Satz's grotesque Weingard. Beneath his tuxedo, Nat Silver is what his sister calls a "schlemiel," a character a psychoanalyst might describe as a masochist possessed of a strong unconscious will to fail.

In *Jewish Wit,* Theodore Reik terms the schlemiel "the hidden architect of his misfortune." In *Amerikaner Shadkhn,* that misfortune is presented as a matter of heritage as well as character. With the collapse of Nat's eighth engagement, his mother, who regards him as an ideal son, reveals that he resembles an uncle who, back in the Old Country, became a *shadkhn* precisely because he had such bad luck with women. (A flashback shows a bearded Fuchs as a traditional marriage broker with frock coat and umbrella.) "This is America, not Europe," Nat protests. "Family characteristics know no bounds," his mother counters. Nat will later characterize his mother as "the only woman who understands me," and he does his best to embrace this new identity. Under pretense of going to Europe, he orchestrates another sort of return—upgrading his name from Silver to Gold and opening a Human Relations Bureau on the Grand Concourse and 158th Street.[2]

As Nat is a victim of "Jewish luck," the Human Relations Bureau fulfills Menakhem Mendl's fantasy of being a world-famous *shadkhn*. Indeed, here the matchmaker is a regular Baron de Hirsch. Nat dresses like a diplomat, running his business in an ascot and morning coat. Because he refuses to charge for his services, Nat is picketed by a comic gaggle of *shadkhonim*, although these are quickly disarmed when he puts them on the payroll of his "shadkhn trust." A far greater challenge arises when an anxious mother comes to him to find a suitable match for her daughter Judith (Judith Abarbanel), a "sophisticated" girl who goes around with bohemian "crackpots." (These undesirables are described as artists, actors, and dancers; they might equally be political "crackpots," which is to say, Communists.) Although Judith speaks perfect Yiddish, she is even more American than Nat.

In her survey of Yiddish cinema, Judith Goldberg has suggested that Yiddish is the only major element that identifies *Amerikaner Shadkhn* as a Jewish film. Yet the movie (whose very title is practically oxymoronic) bespeaks a specifically Jewish crisis in identity—a search for some "golden" mean of appropriate Jewish behavior. Some of this conflict is displaced onto language itself, as when Nat's ostensibly English butler (Yudel Dubinsky) refuses to speak Yiddish in public. Some is manifest in the satire of traditional Jewish figures—the old-fashioned *shadkhonim* who picket Nat's office, the bearded *shelikhim* (fund-raisers) who speak in unison and whom Nat's assimilated sister ridicules as "cowboys with big hats." Some of it is extratextual, as

when Nat sings a song in praise of alcohol, directly contradicting Mendele's assertion in *Di Klyatshe* that where Gentiles drink to cure their sadness, Jews pray.

These inconsistencies scarcely escaped notice. The *New York Post* began its review by admitting that, after sitting through the entire movie, "we're still not sure whether [*Amerikaner Shadkhn* is] meant to be a serious drama with a solution for a problem (boy meets girl) or a rollicking comedy, spoofing the marriage broker institution even now in vogue amid Jewish family circles." Notes written to accompany the film's 1978 reissue conclude that "it is hard to know whether it is the old-fashioned or the 'up-to-date'

Modern marriage broker Nathan Gold (Leo Fuchs) looks on as irate *shadkhonim* picket his new-fangled Human Relations Bureau, in *Amerikaner Shadkhn*.

that is more out of place." Indeed, Judith Goldberg contradicts herself, observing that *Amerikaner Shadkhn* implies two worlds—"the English-speaking one outside . . . and the closed world of Jews, albeit successful ones, wherein one may speak Yiddish and may relax"—and, hence, maps a specifically Jewish problematic.

As visually bland as *Amerikaner Shadkhn* is, its dialogue is rife with references to dreams; as static as the action seems, the characterizations bespeak instability. Like his butler's British accent, Nat's elegant lifestyle might at any moment melt away. Judith, on the other hand, seems to have lost her Jewish identity altogether. In short, the movie is steeped in ambivalence. "Making fun of me? Making fun of yourself?" Nat's butler asks in exasperation at one point, while Nat wins Judith's affections with a melancholy tango about the "sad joke" of his unworthiness, namely the unhappiness he inherited from his Old World uncle.

Bill Krohn, who calls *Amerikaner Shadkhn* "the most mysterious of [Ulmer's] Yiddish films, a comedy in which we see what became of Fishke and Hodl's descendants in the city," notes that it is "also a very personal work, made around the time the director turned forty." It seems no less significant that this now middle-aged filmmaker was a son of Vienna who would later maintain that he first learned of his Jewishness as a teenager. Thus, *Amerikaner Shadkhn*, the only original script of Ulmer's four Yiddish movies, demands to be seen as a belated follow-up to Sidney Goldin's *East and West,* a film made by an assimilated Central European Jew who has had to work through his own Jewish identity.

Where Ulmer's three previous films were derived from Yiddish classics, the story for *Amerikaner Shadkhn* is credited to Ulmer's cousin Gustav H.

Heimo who, before leaving Vienna in the thirties, had written the libretti for several operettas. (The actual script was written by Ulmer and his wife, Shirley, under the name S. Castle.) If *Amerikaner Shadkhn* resembles its predecessors for being a romance in which a troubled young man is able to reorient his life through the love of a clever and sympathetic woman, it is the only one of Ulmer's films that comes close to making Jewishness a joke. As Sig Altman points out in *The Comic Image of the Jew,* although much East European Jewish humor arises from the disjunction between the ideal and the actual, "the Jewish Comic Image, bearing the notion that being Jewish is absurd, was typical only of Central Europe."

Like much Central European Jewish humor, *Amerikaner Shadkhn* is predicated upon an eruption of the *Ostjude.* Freud's *Jokes and Their Relation to the Unconscious,* published in Vienna when Ulmer was five, is a veritable anthology of such humor, containing no less than seven marriage-broker jokes. These, Freud argues, embody "a disguised aggression" directed against "everyone in the business of arranging a marriage: the bride and bridegroom and their parents"—in short, against the entire culture. Ulmer's film resembles the *shadkhn* jokes analyzed by Freud in deriving humor from mismatched couples and physical defects, as when a deaf old man is paired with an equally hard-of-hearing woman. Nat inquires if the man is pleased with his prospective bride; the comic answer—based on the mistaking of *"tsufridn"* (pleased) for *"Yidn"* (Jews)—goes to the heart of the matter. As the titles translate, Nat asks, "Is she what you would choose?" and the old man answers, "Of course, only among Jews."

The joke reveals an underlying anxiety regarding

intermarriage, linking it to marriage outside one's disability. According to Freud, it is precisely this sort of slip, an inadvertent revelation of some truth (usually made by the *shadkhn*), that renders his "laughable figure" sympathetic and "deserving of pity." Freud suggests that many of the *shadkhn* jokes were based on the marriage broker's "characteristic mixture of mendacious impudence and readiness of repartee." (Reading *Jokes and Their Relation to the Unconscious*, it is not difficult to imagine the barely respectable, verbally agile Groucho Marx in the role of the *shadkhn*.) In this sense, the natty Gold turns out to be the opposite of the traditional *shadkhn*—and thus a refutation of the marriage broker's negative traits. Nat is a stylish and modern *shadkhn*, a "Reform" *shadkhn*, whose receptionist is a psychiatrist. Indeed, at once Menakhem Mendl *and* Baron de Hirsch, he is also a philanthropist who expects nothing for himself.

Although Nat's charity toward old-fashioned (that is, European) Jews suggests the guilt American Jews felt regarding their own privileged position, particularly after war broke out in 1939, his philanthropy is most pathological in his response to Judith, when he seeks to marry her to a suitable man. Clearly in love with the girl, he becomes obsessed with giving her a proper wedding—to someone else. That his candidate, one Milton Gellert, speaks no Yiddish and is thus even more deracinated than the *shadkhn* himself is further evidence of Nat's confusion. This deeper crisis has the logic of a Viennese joke recounted by Reik in *Jewish Wit*:

Every day, in a coffee house, two Jews sit and play cards. One day they quarrel and Moritz furiously shouts at his friend: "What kind of guy can you be if you sit down every evening playing

cards with a fellow who sits down to play cards with a guy like you!"

It is a tautology, Reik observes, in which "self-contempt becomes a weapon." The American corollary is Groucho Marx's famous crack that he would never join any club that would accept him as a member. Neurotic as Nat is, he can only get married behind his own back.

Once the *shadkhn*'s alienation from his feelings reaches the point that he insists on *paying* for Judith's wedding to Gellert (and then paying Gellert to go through with it) while Judith (no less a martyr than the heroine of *Uncle Moses*) agrees to the marriage only to make her benefactor happy, *Amerikaner Shadkhn* grows so convoluted as to resemble an unfunny version of Fuchs's absurdist short, *Ikh Vil Zayn a "Boarder."* In the end, however, Gellert simply vanishes with Nat's payoff, and the mortified *shadkhn*, invested in Judith's marriage above all, has no choice but take his place beside the bride under the *khupe*. In his acceptance of her acceptance, the American *shadkhn* becomes an American *khosn*. Gold is married to America—and so is Jewish cinema. The hero of *Amerikaner Shadkhn* is the bridge between the hapless Menakhem Mendl and the neurotic heroes of Woody Allen.

Amerikaner Shadkhn opened on May 7 in Brownsville at the People's and at two Lower East Side venues, the Clinton and the National theaters; at the National, it played along with eight acts of Yiddish vaudeville. (The combination not only presaged the fate of the National but that of Yiddish cinema exhibition. The following year, Louis Weiss leased the Parkway in Brownsville as a combination Yiddish movie and vaudeville house, and for the next quarter century, revivals of Yiddish talkies were typically paired with live performances by increasingly elderly headliners.) Ten days later, Germany invaded France from the north. That summer, Warners rereleased *Confessions of a Nazi Spy* with a newsreel prologue that detailed the fall of France, Belgium, Holland, Norway, and Denmark. *Amerikaner Shadkhn* played sporadically into September without much success. Not only did producer Rubinstein fail to recoup his investment, the lab bills were still outstanding when he died, in 1943.

After finishing *Amerikaner Shadkhn*, Ulmer shuttled between New York and Detroit, making instructional films for the U.S. Army and the Ford Motor Company. Then, after seven years in the East, he left for California to join the returned emigré Seymour Nebenzal (producer of *People on Sunday* as well as Fritz Lang's last two German films, *M* and *The Testament of Dr. Mabuse*) at Producers Releasing Corporation (PRC), a "poverty row" independent studio that had already employed Max Nosseck.[3]

There was now only Seiden, who, oblivious to the failure of *Amerikaner Shadkhn*, ended his most productive year by shooting three features during the summer of 1940. The generational weepie *Eli, Eli* opened in late September, followed in November by the adopted-child melodrama *Ir Tsveyte Mame* (*Her Second Mother*). (In between, Charlie Chaplin appeared—*sans* Yiddish—in what *New York Times* critic Bosley Crowther thought might be "the most significant film ever produced," *The Great Dictator*.)

Eli, Eli and *Ir Tsveyte Mame* were still playing Jewish neighborhoods when Seiden released *Der Groyser Eytse-Geber* (*The Great Advisor*) in late December, the first attraction at the newly reopened Clinton. *Der Groyser Eytse-Geber*, which revolved around the romantic misadventures of a radio "advice-giver" and a duplicitous *shadkhn*, was more modern than previous Seiden efforts: "The producers feel that the world sorely needs more laughter, and we therefore modeled this feature on the type of film produced by the Marx Bros." This presumed desire for Yiddish light comedy was underscored by the revival of the *faryidisht* Ludwig Satz silent *Oy di Shviger!*, which played the Seiden circuit during the fall of 1940.

Although Seiden's Cinema Service paid fifty dollars to Sheyne Rokhl Simkoff, the author of *Zayn Vaybs Lubovnik,* for the rights to her 1925 play *Far di Khasene* (Before the Wedding), the adaptation was never made. Seiden's last prewar film, the compilation *Mazltov Yidn* (which starred Michael Rosenberg introducing "acts" cannibalized from *Ikh Vil Zayn a Mame* and *Kol Nidre,* among other features), opened at the Clinton in April 1941. By then, the Jews of Nazi-occupied Poland had all been confined to ghettos. On June 21, Hitler turned east, driving through the Soviet zone and into the Ukraine. Within weeks, New York's Yiddish dailies were reporting the wholesale massacre of Jewish civilians in Minsk and Lvov. For the first Rosh Hashanah since 1936, no new Yiddish talkie opened on the Lower East Side.

On September 9, 1941, Charles Lindbergh told a rally of the America First Committee in Des Moines, Iowa, that while the Jews, the British, and the Roosevelt administration were all trying to push the United States into the war, the Jews were "the most dangerous" because of "their large ownership and influence in our motion pictures, our press, our radio, and our government." Less than three months later, the Japanese bombed the American fleet at

Pearl Harbor and the United States entered the war. By this time, it has been estimated, the Nazi *Einsatzgruppen* had already murdered half a million Russian Jews.

In early 1942, *Variety* reported theatrical photographer Alexander Archer's plans to produce a Yiddish-language film, *Family Secrets,* based on an Isidore Zolotarefsky melodrama, as a vehicle for his wife Rosetta Bialis, who played Judith Abarbanel's mother in *Amerikaner Shadkhn.* The film was never made; there would be no further Yiddish talkies produced in America during the war. Henry Lynn and Joseph Seiden both became defense contractors,

while Joseph Green operated the Irving Place Theater as a movie house. In the fall of 1944, Green was briefly reinvolved with the Yiddish stage which, save for Schwartz's 1943 production of *Di Mishpokhe Karnovski* (*The Family Carnovsky*), was by then restricted to vehicles for singer Aaron Lebedeff and comedian Menashe Skulnik. Together with Jacob Ben-Ami, Green leased the old Yiddish Art Theater on Second Avenue at Twelfth Street to premiere two topical plays, H. Leivick's *Der Nes in Geto* (*The Miracle of the Warsaw Ghetto*) and David Bergelson's *Mir Veln Lebn* (*We Will Live*).

After the German invasion of Russia, the Soviets

A rabbi advises his people in Columbia's *None Shall Escape* (U.S.A., 1944). In dubbing the picture, Tel Aviv exhibitor Ya'acov Davidon altered this scene so that the rabbi exhorts the Jews in Yiddish to fight the Germans.

distributed a short entitled *Appeal to the Jews of the World* in which three prominent Russian-Jewish artists (Solomon Mikhoels, Sergei Eisenstein, and Peretz Markish) delivered their message of ethnic solidarity in Russian, English, and Yiddish. Still, what would amount to the only wartime Yiddish talkie—and perhaps the most radical ever—was produced in mid-1944 in the Yishev. There, Tel Aviv exhibitor Ya'acov Davidon not only redubbed Columbia's *None Shall Escape,* but altered it to foreground the film's depiction of Nazi brutality in Poland.

Davidon maintains that the doctored *None Shall Escape* was his biggest hit of the year. Columbia—which had dispatched its local representative, an Egyptian Jew, with a threatened injunction—was sufficiently impressed to distribute his version throughout the Middle East, even requesting a print to circulate in New York. Although the original movie showed German soldiers setting a synagogue aflame and massacring Jewish civilians, only one speaking character was a Jew—a philosophical rabbi who plays chess with the local priest. In dubbing the film, Davidon transformed one Nazi into a Jew and completely rewrote the rabbi's dialogue. Thus, instead of offering religious comfort, the rabbi advises the Jews, in Yiddish, warning them that they are being deceived, exhorting them to rebel and fight the Germans. Here, Davidon writes, he dubbed in additional shouts and gunfire. The audience response was nearly as intense: "It's hard to describe in words what was happening in movie theaters during this scene." Fourteen years after the screening of *Mayn Yidishe Mame* incited a riot, the sound of Yiddish in a Tel Aviv movie house produced an agonized wave of Jewish pride.[4]

NOTES

1. In fact, *Mirele Efros* had opened at the Cameo four months earlier, and two other Yiddish talkies (*Der Purimshpiler* and *Der Vanderer Yid*) had their New York premieres at the "accredited home" of Soviet tub-thumpers. As patriotic insurance, perhaps, Oysher's vehicle was billed with *Sons of Liberty,* a twenty-three-minute Warners short starring Claude Rains in the role of Haym Solomon, Jewish financier of the American Revolution. (According to *Variety,* this Technicolor two-reeler, directed by Michael Curtiz, was originally to have been a feature with its "Jewish angle" subordinated to the story of George Washington.) *Der Vilner Shtot Khazn* remained at the Cameo for a month and enjoyed healthy runs that spring at the Clinton, People's, Radio, and Ascot theaters.

2. It seems appropriate that the publisher of *Der Tog* would invest in a movie on this theme. Alone among the Yiddish dailies, the newspaper featured English-language personals placed by both traditional *shadkhonim* and more newfangled variations, such as the Modern Marriage Broker. (Rubin's Prominent Matrimonial Bureau purchased a display ad in every issue of *Der Tog.*) A more direct reference to Rubinstein's other interests, however, is the plug for Maxwell House coffee—the sponsor for Molly Picon's radio show.

3. Ulmer and Peretz Hirschbein doctored the script for PRC's 1942 *Prisoner of Japan;* they also worked together (Ulmer uncredited) on PRC's most elaborate production, *Hitler's Madmen,* a film about the assassination of Czechoslovakia's Nazi administrator Reinhard Heydrich (as well as the first movie that Douglas Sirk would direct in America).

A few Yiddish actors made their way to Hollywood and were featured in anti-Nazi movies. Billed as Walter Lawrence, Moishe Oysher sang Jerome Kern and E. Y. Harburg's "And Russia Is Her Name" in *Song of Russia,* a 1943 MGM musical based, according to Ulmer, on a script he had developed at PRC. Both Maurice Schwartz and his erstwhile employee Kurt Katch had minor roles in Warners' 1943 paean to our new Soviet ally, *Mission to Moscow.* Although Schwartz is not even credited for his part as a defendant in the Moscow Trials, Katch was able to make a go of it in Hollywood, building a career as an exotic, often shaven-pated heavy in *Ali Baba and the Forty Thieves* (1943), *The Mask of Dimitrios* (1944), and *Abbott and Costello Meet the Mummy* (1955), among other films.

Helen Beverly was featured in *The Master Race,* a 1944 anti-Nazi drama directed by Herbert Biberman and, nine years later, appeared in the Biblical spectacle *The Robe* (1952). After the war, her onetime costar David Opatoshu appeared in two films directed by his Artef colleague Jules Dassin—*The Naked City* (1948) and *Thieves' Highway* (1949). Both men were subsequently blacklisted. Schwartz, however, benefitted from the Cold War taste for historical epics, playing dignified patriarchs in such otherwise lurid productions as *Bird of Paradise* (1951), *Salome,* and *Slaves of Babylon* (both 1953).

4. Screenwriter Lester Cole's memoir, *Hollywood Red,* tells an almost identical story. Assigned to work on *None Shall Escape,* Cole, too, found the Jewish characters disturbingly passive. Thus, he added the rabbi's speech to the original screenplay, going so far as to give the rabbi a line associated with Dolores Ibárruri, the fiery Spanish Communist known as *La Pasionaria*: "Fight for freedom, fight for justice. It is better to die on your feet than live on your knees!" The result, Cole writes, "horrified" Columbia boss Harry Cohen who, he says, maintained that "for Jews to blow their own horn on how they're standing up to the Nazis is chutzpah, absolute chutzpah."

Indeed, a month after *None Shall Escape* was released in America, the New York daily *PM* reported that the movie had become a "target for anti-Semites," with screenings disrupted at theaters in a number of New York neighborhoods, as well as Jersey City and Boston. These anti-Jewish outbursts, it was noted, "occurred chiefly at the point in the film at which a Polish rabbi is shot down by Nazi machine guns with his people as he exhorts them to turn on their tormentors."

Overleaf: **Jewish child hiding from the Nazis, in** *Unzere Kinder* **(Poland, 1948); frame enlargement.**

24

The Living Remnant

LIBERATED IN THE spring of 1945, Poland lay devastated. Warsaw was rubble. The war destroyed a third of Poland's industrial installations, 40 percent of the nation's wealth, half the means of public transportation, 60 percent of the schools, postal facilities, and telephones, 70 percent of the nation's livestock, and 90 percent of its Jews.

Some 75,000 Jews remained on Polish soil, with another 200,000 Polish Jews in the Soviet Union. Isolated survivors returned to their native cities and villages to find that they alone, among their families, friends, or neighbors, managed to live through the war. Often their houses were occupied by new tenants. In extreme cases, returning Jews were subject to assault or even murder. There were also incidents of Jews being pulled from trains and buses leaving Poland and beaten to death. On July 4, 1946, a blood libel triggered a pogrom in Kielce in which forty-one Jews were killed and fifty-nine wounded. By that time perhaps half the Jews in Poland had already left the country for the American-occupied zones of Austria and Germany, hoping to emigrate to the United States or Palestine.

The war also destroyed the Polish motion picture industry. In 1945, there were no cameras, studios, or film labs. The nucleus of the new Polish cinema (like the nucleus of the new Polish regime) would come from the Red Army. In 1943, the Kościuszko Division had formed a film unit composed mainly of former START members. When the unit reached Polish soil, it became the Film Studio of the Polish Army. The initial project (as well as the first documentary of Nazi death camps) was Aleksander Ford's *Majdanek*. Two years later, in Lodz, Film Polski was created under the leadership of Ford, now thirty-seven years old.

Back from the Soviet Union, the Goskind brothers rejoined the Polish movie industry. Itzhik was appointed director of Film Polski's library, while Ford offered Shaul Goskind, his former producer, a production unit. Goskind, who still wished to make Yiddish films, preferred to work under the auspices of the Central Committee of Polish Jews, then funded by the American Joint Distribution Committee (JDC). Along with Leo Forbert's sons, Władysław and Adolph (the latter a member of the Polish United Workers' Party), Goskind formed a film cooperative, Kinor (named for the Hebrew word for "harp"), and made a series of newsreel-style documentaries on postwar Jewish life. One of the earliest records the consecration of a Jewish memorial in Skierniwiece in the fall of 1946. The presiding rabbi wears a Polish army uniform; the text is read by Ida Kaminska's husband, Meir Melman.[1]

The new Kinor cooperative, which enjoyed access to Film Polski facilities, employed twenty-seven-year-old Natan Gross as its resident director. Gross, who had survived the war on Polish soil, hidden by a Gentile family, was the son of a Krakow glass merchant, and an enthusiastic Zionist. He had attended a Hebrew-language gymnasium and belonged to Gordonia, a left-oriented, but non-Marxist, youth organization named for pioneer A. D. Gordon, the Palestine-based ideologue of the "religion of labor."

In 1946, Gross had responded to a newspaper advertisement for a one-year director's workshop at the newly established Polish Film Institute in Lodz and wound up serving as an assistant on Stanisław Wohl's *Dwie Godziny* (Two Hours). A sort of small-town *Grand Hotel* set at the close of the war, the film was framed by a train's arrival and departure: concentration camp survivors mix with collaborators, lovers are reunited, betrayals uncovered. (Although it was the first postwar Polish feature to be completed, *Two Hours* was deemed insufficiently "optimistic," and was withheld from release until 1957.)

According to Gross, who learned his Yiddish in the course of working with Kinor, their short documentaries were the first films made in Poland after the war: "Everything else was paralyzed by politics." Polish authorities, however, were not enthusiastic to see their movie industry reborn as a series of Yiddish newsreels. Hence Kinor's early films were never officially released, but shown in cinemas at special shows attended almost entirely by Jews.

In 1947—the year that Warsaw radio broadcast a Yom Kippur service and the Polish United Workers' Party came to power in contested elections—the first postwar Polish feature, Leonard Buczkowski's *Zakazane Piosenki* (Forbidden Songs), was released. This musical drama of occupied Warsaw was followed in 1948 by Wanda Jakubowska's *Ostatni Etap* (The Last Stage), based on her own experiences in Auschwitz. In 1947 and 1948 as well, Gross and Goskind produced two ambitious features, *Mir Lebn Geblibene* (We Are Still Alive) and *Unzere Kinder* (Our Children). Neither would be released in Poland.

Mir Lebn Geblibene—sometimes translated as *We the Living Remnant* and also known as *Am Yisroel Khay* (The Jewish People Live) after the chant which, in the original version, served as the title music—is a survey of postwar Jewish life that, using a clipped newsreel narration and a number of flashy wipes, most likely recycled material from some of Kinor's short documentaries. One segment, released separately as *Produktivizatsye* (Productivization), is an urgent montage of lathes and machines scored to romantic Polish themes. A sewing cooperative is shown making cloth out of rags, a cobblers' collective hammers shoes in unison. Harking back to the experimental documentaries of the late twenties and early thirties as it celebrates the sacrament of work, the film is almost a *ballet mécanique*. (Although there is no narrative, the lush tango switches to a traditional Jewish melody to show a bread factory baking sabbath loaves.)

Everywhere else, however, *Mir Lebn Geblibene* concerns the range of Jewish culture: Chanukah celebrations, a montage of Polish-Jewish newspapers, a conference of Yiddish writers, a Hebrew choir, a Chasidic dance by Felix Fibich and Judith Berg, Fania Rubina's songs of the Warsaw Ghetto, an exhibit of paintings depicting the ghetto uprising. The privileged form is Yiddish theater. Ida Kaminska appears as Mirele Efros; Moyshe Lipman, who had played Kaminska's father-in-law in the original *Tkies Kaf,* is shown as Tevye; and there are scenes from *Hershele Ostropoler* and *Motl Peyse* as performed by companies in Lodz and Lower Silesia.

Mir Lebn Geblibene also records the creation of a Jewish historical committee but, rather than dwell upon the unhappy past (and in keeping with the tenets of socialist realism), the film prefers to gaze into the future. There is considerable emphasis on children—their schools and summer camps, songs and calisthenics, sports activities and youth organi-

The new Kinor: (from left) producer Shaul Goskind, director Natan Gross, and cameraman Adolph Forbert during the filming of *Mir Lebn Geblibene* (Poland, 1947).

zations. Labor Zionist groups are prominent throughout, as are Hebrew songs. The film ends with a surge of optimism and an ecstatic montage of newspapers, factories, and agricultural settlements. As the choir reprises "Am Yisroel Khay," uniformed children run to join a marching band. For several minutes, Jewish youth groups file past the camera in military formation, holding aloft Polish, Communist, and Zionist banners.

Like three-quarters of those Polish Jews who survived the Holocaust, Dzigan and Schumacher had done so behind Soviet lines. Ida Kaminska encountered their Little Art Theater in Tashkent in 1942. She recalls that after the comics had volunteered for General Władysław Anders's Soviet-based Polish army, they were denounced by Polish comrades and sent to a Soviet labor camp. Released in 1946, they succeeded in repatriating to Poland, and by late 1947 they were in Lodz with a revue entitled *Abi Men Zet Zikh* (Just So Long as We Can See Each Other). When Goskind learned of their return, he was determined to star them in a Kinor film, although, under the circumstances, Gross found it difficult to imagine an appropriate vehicle. The result was a semidocumentary on the model of *Mir Kumen On.*

Unzere Kinder dramatizes *Mir Lebn Geblibene*'s concern for the Jewish children who survived the war, but its mildly didactic tone is consistent with Dzigan and Schumacher's own experience of returning to Poland from the Soviet Union to hear devas-

tating firsthand accounts of the Nazi occupation. A newsreel prologue showing Jews deported to Auschwitz, and then Auschwitz itself, is followed by a *klaynkunst* performance given by Dzigan and Schumacher before a Jewish audience in postwar Lodz. In the concluding skit, the two play street musicians in the Warsaw Ghetto. Schumacher sings sadly of his childhood while Dzigan dances and begs for food. In the audience, a group of children from the nearby Helenowek Orphanage grow increasingly restive, becoming so upset when the pair are given a loaf of challah that they disrupt the performance.[2]

Dzigan and Schumacher, who are essentially playing themselves, are disturbed and confused by this response. The orphans, though still quite diffident,

Kinor on location in Lodz for *Unzere Kinder,* autumn 1947. Director Natan Gross is third from the left.

come backstage to apologize, along with the home's director (Nusia Gold). The director explains that these are children who, one way or another, managed to survive the ghetto. The performance not only stirred up painful memories, but offended them with its sentimentalized view of wartime conditions. Thus, *Unzere Kinder* is not only among the first films about the Holocaust, it is also the first to critique its representation. A few of the children describe their own struggle to live. One was a smuggler, another a pickpocket. Fascinated, the two actors accept the director's invitation to perform at the orphanage and learn more about the Nazi occupation.

After a brief passage in which Dzigan and Schumacher go on the road—offering a glimpse of Poland rebuilding—they arrive in Helenowek, where the children first perform in their honor. Then, in one of the most delightful passages in Yiddish cinema, Dzigan and Schumacher stage a playlet based on Sholom Aleichem's story "Kasrilevke Brent" (Kasrilevke Aflame). In dramatizing the comedy of a fire in the *shtetl,* the two take numerous parts including women's. Given the quick changes in sets and costumes, the entire performance is "impossible," in the same way that Busby Berkeley's dance numbers are supposed to be stage-bound. The performance leads to a discussion of fires in the ghetto; the children tell war stories until it is time for bed.

In some respects, *Unzere Kinder* is a psychodrama, the survivors enacting their own situation, and it's characterized by appropriately expressionist touches. Dzigan, Schumacher, and Gold discuss the children's terrible memories. When Schumacher sings a mournful song, the home's director weeps, remembering her own child who was killed by the Nazis. In the kitchen, two women who are unable to sleep describe the concentration camps. The children cannot rest either and tell their own stories, which are shown as flashbacks. One girl recalls the roundup of Jewish children in her village. She survived because a Polish peasant bought her from the Nazis who then tossed her off the Auschwitz-bound truck. Dzigan and Schumacher overhear this story and others even more awful. The next morning, they watch the orphans play in the sunshine, marveling at their resilience. The children present the actors with bouquets, then see them off singing. The ending evokes that of *Mir Leben Geblibene.*

Unzere Kinder was not the only psychodrama made by and with Holocaust survivors. Another— mixing Yiddish, German, and Polish dialogue—was produced in the displaced persons camps of occupied Germany where the refugee Jewish population had swelled to 225,000. In addition to food, clothing, and other supplies, the American Joint Distribution Committee funded the DP camps' cultural activities. Israel Becker, a thirty-year-old native of Bialystok who headed up a JDC-supported troupe of actors, wrote a quasi-autobiographical screenplay and submitted it to the Jewish Film Organization (YAFO), which was formed by the JDC in 1946 to make Yiddish and Hebrew versions of the U.S. Army documentary *Death Factories.*[3]

YAFO evidently recommended Becker's project to the U.S. Army's Information Control Division, which produced the film. *Lang Iz der Veg (Long Is the Road)* was shot in a Munich studio with performers from the Munich Yiddish Art Theater, including Berta Litwina (who had appeared in the 1937 *Tkies Kaf* and *Der Purimshpiler*), Bertina Moissi (daughter of German-Jewish actor Alexander Moissi), and Alexander Bardini (director of the Yiddish Theater

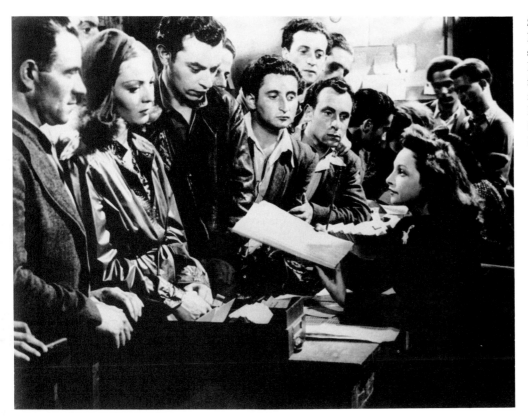

Searching for survivors: Dora (Bettina Moissi, second from left) and David (Israel Becker, third from left) at a Jewish repatriation center in Poland. *Lang Iz der Veg* (U.S.-occupied Germany, 1948).

of the Refugee Remnant). A German filmmaker, Herbert B. Fredersdorf, served as technical director, with Marek Goldstein handling the actors. (Although Becker is only credited with the screenplay, he later told Eric Goldman that there were "difficulties with the cast," and he wound up directing the film himself.)

Following a newsreel prologue, *Lang Iz der Veg* opens in German-occupied Warsaw. As Jacob and Hanna Jelin (Litwina) prepare for *shabes*, their son David (Becker) arrives with the horrible news that the Nazis have ordered all Jews into the ghetto. After the ghetto is liquidated, David jumps off an Auschwitz-bound transport to take his chances in the Polish countryside. Although the first peasant he encounters tries to report him to the Germans, he is saved by a second peasant (Bardini), who not only gives him food and shelter but directs him toward a band of Jewish partisans. In a strikingly ecumenical scene, the peasant kneels before a roadside shrine and prays for David's safety. (*Lang Iz der Veg* is careful to avoid the charge of Jewish chauvinism: later, when sharing a train compartment with a group of ethnic-German Poles being expelled after the war, David will acknowledge that they have suffered as well.)

Like Jakubowska's *The Last Stage* and Alfred Radok's Czech film *Daleka Cesta* (which was released in the United States as *Distant Journey* and advertised in New York's Yiddish press as *Terezin Geto* [Terezin Ghetto]), *Lang Iz der Veg* was one of the first fiction films to attempt to represent Nazi concentration camps from the point of view of the inmates. Becker intercuts David's adventures with scenes of Auschwitz, starkly evoked in the studio through the use of stylization and close-ups. Chanting the *Sh'ma,* Jacob is sent to the gas chamber; Hanna manages to survive until liberation. In the ruins of liberated Poland, David meets Dora (Bettina Moissi). As she is a German Jew, they speak in German. He learns of his father's death and goes in search of his mother, first in Poland, then in the American Zone of occupied Germany. She, at the same time, is hunting for him, until she collapses and is taken to a German hospital. (One wonders if *Vu Iz Mayn Kind?* wasn't among the films shown to DP camp audiences. *Lang Iz der Veg* uses many of the conventions of the Yiddish *shund* film—the montage sequence in which Hanna searches for David could have been lifted from *Motl der Operator*.)

Settled in at Camp Landsberg, the largest all-Jewish DP camp in Bavaria, David gets a job as a mechanic and marries Dora. After a relatively somber wedding, the radiant couple return to their bunk to hear a radio broadcast in which delegates to the World Jewish Congress appeal for the opening of Palestine to Jewish immigration. By chance, David discovers his mother's name in a Yiddish newspaper and rushes to the hospital where she is recuperating. Although she is initially unable to recognize him, the film ends with their tearful reunion. A brief coda shows a young man, possibly David, working the land in Palestine.[4]

In February 1948, the same month Sergei Eisenstein died in Moscow, a Communist coup toppled the coalition government in Czechoslovakia. In June, Marshal Tito was purged from the Cominform—an act with repercussions throughout Eastern Europe, including Poland. By summer's end, the relatively moderate Władisław Gomułka was dismissed as party secretary and, before the year was out, the Polish United Workers' Party had absorbed the Polish Socialist Party and was undergoing its first mass purge. The State of Israel had been proclaimed in May; it became the first nation outside the Soviet orbit to recognize Poland's new western borders.

Working more for history than for Film Polski, Natan Gross commemorated the opening of the Israeli embassy in Warsaw with a short Hebrew-

Dora (Bettina Moissi) and David (Israel Becker) in *Lang Iz der Veg*. Shot in 1947 in U.S.-occupied Germany, this Yiddish-Polish-German-language film was based on Becker's own experiences during the war.

language documentary. (This was his second brief Hebrew-language film. The previous year he had made *Kadima Gordonaim,* in which young Labor Zionists prepare both for the sabbath and their return to Palestine.) Gross's celebration of Israeli sovereignty was shot in late September. One month before, the *New York Times* had announced a Czech-Israeli coproduction called *Melody of the Spinning Wheel,* to be directed by Aleksander Ford. The film was never made.

The creation of modern Israel coincided with the destruction of Soviet-Yiddish culture. So long as Britain held the mandate for Palestine and Zionist militants were the foes of British "imperialism," there was strong Soviet support for a Jewish state. This approval may have been misinterpreted at home, where it was widely rumored that, in acknowledgment of Jewish suffering and heroism during the war, an autonomous Jewish region would be established on the Crimean peninsula. The proposal enjoyed support at the party's highest levels. V. I. Molotov and Lazar Kaganovich summoned the leadership of the Jewish Anti-Fascist Committee—including Solomon Mikhoels, Peretz Markish, and Itzik Fefer—and suggested that they petition Stalin. Mikhoels, in particular, enjoyed access to the Soviet leader; the actor was even thought of as a potential president of this new Birobidzhan. These illusions perished with Mikhoels, whose bloody corpse was found at the Minsk railroad station on the night of January 13, 1948.

Nine months after Mikhoels's murder, the Jewish Anti-Fascist Committee was dissolved. Before the end of the year, the *Emes* publishing house and all Yiddish-language journals were shut down and their linotype machines destroyed. Fefer's arrest on December 24, 1948, began the imprisonment and eventual execution of the regime's leading Yiddish writers. The last Yiddish schools were closed during the summer of 1949, as were all Yiddish theaters.

In Poland, with the consolidation of Communist authority in 1949, all Jewish institutions came under government control. The JDC was expelled while the hitherto small Communist faction of the Central Committee of Polish Jews took charge, breaking off relations with the World Jewish Congress. There was no more money for *Unzere Kinder,* although the enterprising Goskind managed to find a French partner to distribute the film in Europe, shipping a print to Paris via Turkish diplomatic pouch. His ingenuity can be appreciated in light of the bewildering career of *Ulica Graniczna* (*Border Street*), the first postwar feature made by his erstwhile colleague Aleksander Ford.

A Czech-Polish coproduction shot in 1946 and 1947, mainly at the Barrandov Studios outside Prague, *Border Street* detailed the war's impact on one Warsaw neighborhood, dealing frankly with Polish anti-Semitism and the Nazi extermination of the Jews. The film's climax was the Ghetto Uprising. As in *Mir Kumin On,* Ford stressed Polish-Jewish solidarity, and, as *Border Street* was conceived before the 1947 elections, even expressed sympathy for the non-Communist Home Army. According to an interview Ford gave ten years later, the film "immediately ran into trouble." Stalin himself criticized it: "He felt it gave too much credit to the Jews in showing their valiant rising during the destruction of the Ghetto without reflecting enough on the part played by the Communists and the People's Army."

Stalin was not the only one to object. Marek Bitter, an official of the Central Committee of Polish

Jews, told American journalist Richard Yaffe that *Border Street* had been previewed for "top Polish officials" and the Jewish Committee, and that they felt it was premature to show the film to Polish audiences: "Only a little more than two years had elapsed since the liberation of Poland and it was not known how a picture of the Warsaw Ghetto Uprising which puts the Jews in a heroic light would be received." Bitter explained that he too was opposed to releasing the film because he feared it would offend Gentiles—"The audience might leave it muttering 'serves them right.' "[5]

If *Border Street,* which took care to locate Jews in the tradition of Polish heroism, was regarded as dangerously impolitic, what chance had *Unzere Kinder,* which dealt with the suffering of Polish Jews as Jews? Gross had already published an impassioned newspaper article detailing the three years Kinor spent developing a "democratic Jewish film" in the new Poland and describing the collective's "hard work and dedication" in the absence of any support or publicity from the Central Committee of Polish Jews. The final straw, according to Gross, was an official conference on new Jewish art to which the Central Committee had invited Film Polski while snubbing Kinor.

Given this hopeless situation, it is scarcely surprising that Dzigan and Schumacher left Poland for Israel even before *Unzere Kinder* wrapped. With most of the postproduction work completed, Gross departed for Israel on December 31, 1949. (The next day, the Jewish children's homes and schools were nationalized and Yiddish was restricted to religious instruction.) Goskind followed Gross six months later, bringing the movie with him. The two filmed an epilogue documenting the settlement of Polish-Jewish children in Israel, but an inexperienced film laboratory ruined their footage and there was no money to reshoot the final sequence.

Distributed as a Polish film, *Unzere Kinder* had its premiere in 1951 at Tel Aviv's Eden Theater. Accounts of its reception vary. Gross remembers that it ran for three weeks without great success. David Matis, however, reported in the *Forverts* that the Eden was "filled with hysterical shouting and weeping; the owner of the theater stopped showing the film, which later was lost altogether."[6]

The first movies to deal with the Holocaust arrived in New York in the spring of 1947. A Soviet documentary on the Nuremberg Trials opened at the Stanley, the Cameo's successor as New York's "accredited home" of Russian films; a Belgian production, released as *We Lived Through Buchenwald,* appeared at Studio 65. Nineteen forty-seven was also the year of Hollywood's two exercises in anti-anti-Semitism: *Crossfire* and *Gentleman's Agreement,* the latter voted best picture by the New York Film Critics' Circle.

The fall of 1948 brought two European films by and about Jews who had survived the war. *Mir Lebn Do! (We Live Again),* a fifty-minute, Yiddish-language documentary on Jewish war orphans prouced in France and modeled on *Mir Kumin On,* opened in early September at the Stanley on a bill with some horribly anachronistic Yiddish-language Soviet newsreels and *Der Vilner Shtot Khazn. Lang Iz der Veg* had its premiere at the Avenue Theater in mid-November. By that time, the State of Israel was already five months old. Reviews, however, still responded to the film as a political tract. *Variety* called it "honest propaganda" and "a sure bet for the art house circuit," while the *New York Herald-Tribune* pointed out that only 20 percent of Europe's DPs were Jews and scored the film for its special pleading.

Although the JDC declined to endorse *Lang Iz der Veg*, feeling it to be somewhat dated, the film had a second career (shortened by half an hour) as a United Jewish Appeal fund-raiser. Starting in 1950, the UJA distributed another Yiddish-language fund-raiser, the ten-minute short *Dos Getselt* (*The Tent*), also known as *Report on Israel*. This was the first (and for many years, the only) Yiddish-language film made in Israel, where the use of *mame-loshn* was severely discouraged. After a brief tour of the new state, *Dos Getselt* focuses its attention on the refugee transit camp of Pardes Hanna. It is narrated by the camp doctor, who dramatically announces that "In this Israel, yesterday a man tried to kill me." For the next few minutes, the film rivals the greatest emotional excesses of the *shund* cinema, as the doctor rushes to a tent to discover that a young girl has died and then must fend off the child's distraught, knife-wielding father. The uncredited actor is more than equal to the guilt-provoking dialogue: "No room in Israel for a Jewish child!" the bereaved father screams at the doctor. "Even the Germans were more merciful—at least they did it quickly." Told that he will soon be resettled, he sarcastically demurs: "I can live here very well now. I'm used to concentration camps. I'm used to filth and starvation." The drama is over; the doctor addresses us directly: "Do you know how much it costs to operate a new nation?" Still, he himself suffers doubts that can only be assuaged by the climactic montage of documentary footage.

Also in November of 1948, the *New York Herald-Tribune* profiled Joseph Seiden, who had lately built up a 16mm rental library by buying out his competitors, picking up their films at lab auctions, or acquiring the material from their estates. Of the twenty-five Yiddish talkies he now distributed, fewer than half were his own productions. Most, the newspaper reported, were rented by Jewish organizations as fund-raisers: "Occasionally, however, an inclination for these films, born probably of a sudden nostalgia, seizes New Yorkers, and regular movie theaters in outlying Jewish sections show them all at once."

Indeed, even as the *faryidisht* version of the 1924 *Thies Kaf* was revived at the Stanley as *The Vilna Legend*, so Seiden too experienced a sudden nostalgia and with a last burst of energy transformed himself into "Josef Zeiden," making his two most powerful films, both adaptations of stage plays. The first, an all-star version of Jacob Gordin's *Got, Mentsh, un Tayvl* (*God, Man, and Devil*), featuring Michael Michaelesco, Berta Gersten, and Max Bozyk, was likely the costliest production of Seiden's career, and, thanks to his choice of material, also the best.

First staged in 1900 by David Kessler, *Got, Mentsh, un Tayvl* is a grimly atmospheric work that conflates the stories of Job and Faust with an anticapitalist subtext. Having made a wager with God that he can corrupt Hershele Dubrovner, a pious Torah scribe, Satan appears in the guise of a lottery peddler and sells Dubrovner the winning ticket. Following Satan's advice, the scribe uses the lottery money to open a *talis* factory and thus becomes (as Sholem Asch's Uncle Moses will later) the exploiter of his own people. The now corrupt Dubrovner divorces his faithful but childless wife and marries his sexy young niece. When his father protests, he sends him away. Having destroyed his family, Dubrovner becomes an even more avaricious businessman—until a fatal accident at his factory causes him to repent his sins and hang himself. Although Seiden's production is static and declamatory, the performances are robust, with Bozyk bringing tremendous energy to the role of Dubrovner's half-senile old father.

Got, Mentsh, un Tayvl, which opened to indifferent reviews at the Stanley on January 21, 1950—the bill rounded out by the short *Klangen fun Amol* (Sounds from the Past) with Moishe Oysher—was one of the last two Yiddish films to have a Broadway premiere. Remarkably, that same Friday saw the release of the other, several blocks away. Produced by Martin Cohen and written by actor Hy (formerly Hymie) Jacobson, *Catskill Honeymoon* was an insipid series of sketches (*Litvak*-and-*Galitsianer* skits, untalented impressionists) and numbers, ranging from Italian contraltos to "Yiddish folksongs in swing"— all ostensibly performed for an elderly couple celebrating their golden wedding anniversary at Young's Gap Hotel in Parksville, New York.

The film, which is filled with comic stutterers and other jokes on language, has nearly as much English as Yiddish, and the degree of innocent alienation from tradition it embodies is reflected by the acts: Bobby Colt sings "Me and My Concertina" (to a girl named Christina!), while the *khaznte* Bas Sheva switches, mid-performance, from prayers to *Pagliacci.* In a first (and last) for Yiddish talkies, Admiral Records, which paid Jacobson and Cohen $5,000 for the musical rights, released a soundtrack album. If nothing else, *Catskill Honeymoon* (directed by Joseph Berne, who—as Josef Berne—had ten years before made *Mirele Efros*) confirmed that the resorts of upstate New York had supplanted Second Avenue as the capital of Jewish-American entertainment. Such "borscht belt" graduates as Danny Kaye and Milton Berle were already among America's best-known co-

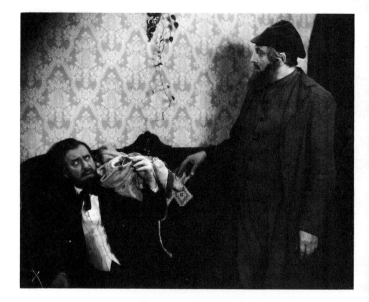

A bereaved father (Leon Schacter) flings a blood-stained *talis* at the exploitative factory owner (Michael Michaelesco) in Joseph Seiden's version of the Jacob Gordin play, *Got, Mentsh, un Tayvl* (U.S.A., 1950).

medians. (They would be followed soon by Sid Caesar and Jerry Lewis.) The summer of 1949 saw the orchestrated "discovery" of Catskills crooner Eddie Fisher, while that fall, bandleader Mickey Katz brought the Catskills to Los Angeles with the first edition of his wildly successful revue, *Borscht Capades.*

Just as *Got, Mentsh, un Tayvl* took Yiddish cinema full circle, back to the filmed Gordin plays of pre–World War I Poland, *Catskill Honeymoon* dissolved Yiddish movies into canned vaudeville. "It is difficult to see why the new film at the Ambassador was brought into a first-run Broadway showcase," the *New York Herald-Tribune* remarked. Nevertheless, this "undistinguished collection of borscht circuit

performers" proved one of the longest-running Yiddish films ever released. Three months after their
Broadway premieres, both *Catskill Honeymoon* and
Got, Mentsh, un Tayvl were still playing Jewish
neighborhoods—while the Stanley, sensing a revival,
booked *Motl Peyse dem Khazns*. Indeed, the High
Holy Days found *Catskill Honeymoon* still playing one
theater in the Bronx and another in Washington
Heights (where, in a most unlikely bill, it was paired
with Edgar Ulmer's 1945 *Detour*).

Never one to miss a trend, Seiden cashed in on
the success of *Catskill Honeymoon* with his *Borscht
Circuit Follies* (a.k.a. *Monticello, Here We Come!*), released in April 1950. This "star-studded Catskill Yiddish American musical revue" was a veritable Seiden
retrospective—freshening his 1941 anthology *Mazltov, Yidn* with clips going back to Judea's earliest two-
reelers. Seiden's final film, *Dray Tekhter* (*Three
Daughters*), was filmed during the winter of 1950 and
seems to have gone directly to the 16mm circuit
without ever having a theatrical premiere. By the
director's standards, the material was reasonably ambitious—an adaptation of a play written by Abraham Blum that had been staged in the fall of 1939
at the Second Avenue Theater.

Dray Tekhter concerns the romantic vicissitudes
of the Gottlieb family. Mr. Gottlieb (coproducer
Leon Schachter), a struggling accountant on the
verge of losing his job, has three daughters: one is
unhappily married to a faithless *luftmentsh*; another
is unmarried and pregnant; Bertha, the eldest and
most responsible, is waiting for the return of her
feckless sweetheart, a musician. Taking a leaf from
Uncle Moses, Gottlieb uses Bertha's charms to secure
his position, parading her before his boss, Abe Zablinsky (Michael Rosenberg, paid Seiden's top fee of
$500 to recreate the role he originated on stage).

The ploy succeeds. A slob so uncouth he makes
Uncle Moses seem like the Baron de Hirsch, Zablinsky is invited to the Gottlieb house for dinner, and
immediately proposes to Bertha. Over the course of
a grotesquely distended evening, Bertha is prevailed
upon to sacrifice her happiness for that of her family
and marry the crude *allrightnik*. Years pass. Miserable Bertha despises her boorish husband and takes to
drink. When, after ten years, her long-lost fiancé
reappears in evening clothes ("*Ikh bin* a composer"),
she gratefully plunges into an affair.

Dray Tekhter is no less set-bound than Seiden's
previous films, and even more claustrophobic. (That
the Soldiers and Sailors Monument in Riverside Park
can be glimpsed from one of the windows lends
credence to Joseph Green's accusation that Seiden
filmed in his own apartment.) Still, shabby as it is,
Dray Tekhter is far more compelling than earlier
shund. The primitive mise-en-scène is paralleled and
justified by Rosenberg's performance. Only recently
returned to the Yiddish theater after a failed attempt
to cross over, Rosenberg plays Zablinsky without the
slightest modulation; his presence ridicules the genteel pretense of the Gottlieb family. Their dutiful
Bertha has married a nightmare. Zablinsky is almost
simian in his mannerisms—shrugging, mumbling,
laughing at his own jokes, babbling away in a guttural English-Yiddish patois. (It's suggestive that, like
Seiden, Zablinsky can only speak pidgin Yiddish.)

Bertha is more or less offered a choice between
glib assimilation on the one hand (the composer,
doubtless the sort of "crackpot" poseur Judith used
to hang out with before she met her "*Amerikaner
Shadkhn*," is a perfect fall guy for Seiden's hatred of
culture), and the coarsest imaginable Jewish stereotype on the other. As she and her musician exchange
their high-flown declarations of love, Zablinsky en-

Abe (Michael Rosenberg) reproaches his errant Bertha (Charlotte Goldstein) in Joseph Seiden's last film, *Dray Tekhter* (U.S.A., 1950).

acts a cruel parody of domesticity. He tortures his wife with guilt, reminds her that everything in their house belongs to him, loudly croons lullabies to their young daughter. For the second half of the movie, Zablinsky alternately sulks and skulks, finally interrupting his wife and her lover with cries of "Mine! Mine!" (an echo of Jennie Goldstein's hopeless lament in *Tsvey Shvester*) as the rest of the Gottliebs troop guiltily on set for the emotional climax.

In her anger at Abe, Bertha has already hinted that their daughter is not his. Now it is dramatically revealed that the child's true *mother* is Bertha's younger sister Lucy. (Some time after her wedding, Bertha took a lengthy Florida vacation with the recently jilted Lucy—soon after which, Bertha presented Abe with a baby.) The family seems destined to break apart, but once the composer has been discredited as a charlatan, Bertha executes an abrupt about-face: "False love blinded me to my sincere, wonderful Abe." (The loudly sniffling Zablinsky obligingly flings himself on his wife's bosom.) A mesmerizing spectacle of free-floating resentment

Twenty years after it was made, *Yidl mitn Fidl* opened on Broadway in a reedited and dubbed English version. The film, Joseph Green's last, was titled *Castles in the Sky* (U.S.A., 1956).

and implicit self-loathing, *Dray Tekhter* telescopes all the conflicts of Yiddish cinema to a struggle between middle-class hypocrisy and cultural despair. It is as if, with Americanization and Zionism as the ascendent ideals, Abe's "sincere" illiteracy was the signifier of a Jewish heart, the last vestige of old-fashioned, Yiddish *Yidishkayt*.

Dray Tekhter remained the most contemporary item in the catalogue of Yiddish films that Seiden distributed until his death in 1972. The only other remaining force in the now-imploded industry was Joseph Green who, after the war, bought a chain of New York movie houses and, under the rubric Globe Pictures, went into film distribution. Although Green entertained notions of producing a musical version

of Hirschbein's *Farvorfn Vinkl* starring Moishe Oysher, his last project was dubbing an English soundtrack onto *Yidl mitn Fidl.* Retitled *Castles in the Sky,* the Anglicized *Yidl* (which also included scenes from *Mamele*) played New York briefly in 1956.

Catskill Honeymoon and *Dray Tekhter* made spoken Yiddish something of a joke. With *Castles in the Sky,* the Yiddish cinema erased even the language and effaced itself out of existence.

NOTES

1. Kinor paid particular attention to the formerly German territories of Lower Silesia, where approximately half of Poland's Jews were resettled and where the Department of Productivization sponsored workshops and vocational training. In addition to short documentaries on subjects ranging from health care and the new Jewish communities to the Kaminska Theater and the Warsaw Ghetto Uprising (the last confiscated by the Polish government), the enterprising Goskind made documentaries for various American-based Jewish welfare organizations, including the JDC and ORT.

2. The Helenowek Orphanage was one of thirty such institutions created after the war, mainly to house those children who had been hidden during the Nazi occupation. The dancers Judith Berg and Felix Fibich were recruited by the Jewish Committee to perform at various orphanages and were briefly in residence at Helenowek. "Every child had a story," Fibich stressed. "Many of them, understandably, resented their Jewishness. We had to win them over with music and dance." Fibich and Berg dramatized the Jewish holidays and, in some measure, these dances were therapeutic. Fibich remembers one particularly disturbed boy who achieved a sense of release while taking part in a Purim pantomime—by playing Haman.

3. The JDC also distributed Yiddish films. The first, shown in May 1946, was Boris Thomashefsky's *Bar Mitsve.* A JDC memo cites the "tremendous demand" for this print; it was followed in August by the circulation of *Tsvey Shvester* and *Mirele Efros,* which barely met the "urgent need." By the summer of 1948, the JDC's Munich office distributed twenty-nine Yiddish-

language features, nine shorts, and a half dozen cantorials. "We have practically cornered the market on Yiddish films in this country," one official wrote another.

4. Becker subsequently resettled in Israel where he joined Habima, ultimately directing fourteen productions including *The Diary of Anne Frank*. Much of Becker's subsequent work in both Yiddish theater and Israeli film was memorable. In 1964 he directed a widely reviewed production of *Got, Mentsh, un Tayvl* at the Folksbiene in New York. Two years later, he directed a Hebrew version of Goldfadn's *Tsvey Kuni Lemls* that would be the second highest grossing Israeli film (behind Ephraim Kishon's *Sallah Shabbati*) up until that point.

5. *Border Street* ultimately had its world premiere in the summer of 1948 at the Venice Film Festival and, having created a stir there, was subsequently released abroad. By the time the film opened domestically on June 23, 1949, Ford was no longer head of Film Polski. According to Richard Yaffe, *Border Street* was so widely distributed during the summer of 1949 that three of the largest cinemas in Warsaw booked the film simultaneously. The movie sold eight million tickets and as late as the 1980s ranked as the fifteenth most popular postwar Polish film.

Before the end of 1949, however, socialist realism became the mandated style and a congress of filmmakers held at Wisla criticized all previous Polish productions, including *Forbidden Songs* and *The Last Stage*. Even after the thaw, in 1957, Polish authorities refused to screen *Border Street* for journalist Gene Moskowitz. Twenty years later, *Border Street* was conspicuously absent from Stanisław Kuszewski's official history *Contemporary Polish Films* (in which *Forbidden Songs* and *The Last Stage* are singled out for praise).

6. According to Natan Gross, the Film Polski representative cut out the "Kasrilevke Brent" sequence and exhibited the clip by itself in kibbutzim and villages. Another print was distributed in Paris—it is this one that was recovered in 1980 and returned to Israel for a second premiere.

Overleaf: **Yiddish language as a means to "see" what is no longer there. Helene Laplower and Boris Lehman stand in for the filmmaker's parents in Samy Szlingerbaum's *Brussels-Transit* (Belgium, 1980).**

A Post-Yiddish Cinema

AFTER WORLD WAR II, the sound of Yiddish in the cinema became the signifier of displacement, nostalgia, and absence. As *Yidishland* dissolved into the American and Soviet mainstreams, rendered obsolete by the creation of an actual Jewish homeland, the survivors of its Polish center were dispersed throughout the world.

Not quite extinct, Yiddish film in Poland ended as it began—a recording of the Yiddish stage. Now, however, it was self-consciously a monument to that which no longer existed. A decade after Shaul Goskind founded Kinor, there was another thaw in Polish cultural life, and one last Yiddish documentary was produced. In April 1957, the forty-two-minute *Jews in Poland* surfaced in New York at the Cameo

on a bill with *Behind the Show Window*, a Soviet comedy about black-market operations in a Moscow department store.

Jews in Poland, also known as *Two Out of a Hundred,* was written by Itskhok Grudberg, directed by Karl Latowicz, and produced by Simon Federman (a writer for the *Morgn Frayhayt*). Made specifically for American Jews, the film retold the story of the Warsaw Ghetto and detailed the postwar reconstruction of Jewish life. The greatest portion of the film, however, was devoted to the E. R. Kaminska State Yiddish Theater, the most visible of Poland's Jewish institutions. In addition to an interview with the theater's director (and the filmmaker's mother-in-law), Ida Kaminska, was a scene from a production of

Mirele Efros. Ironically, *Jews in Poland* coincided with a widespread emigration of Polish Jews that included over a third of the entire community and half the actors of the Kaminska Theater.

Although the so-called Polish Spring that restored Gomułka to power (and permitted the Joint Distribution Committee to reestablish contact with Polish Jews) improved the situation for Yiddish culture, it also saw a revival of politically opportunistic anti-Semitism. As this anti-Semitism was exploited by antireform elements of the Polish Workers' Party, the party's central committee felt obliged to circulate a memo to all provincial, city, district, and local party committees:

> Discerning in occurrences of chauvinism, anti-Semitism, and racism a serious danger threatening the vital interests of our country and our party, the Central Committee appeals to the entire party, and calls for a determined struggle against such occurrences. We emphasize once more with the utmost determination the internationalist character of our party. . . . The Party regards the tendency of the Jewish population to emigrate from Poland as the result of insufficient counteraction by the Party to anti-Semitism. We consider it to be one of the most urgent tasks of the party to wage war against it. At the same time we must persuade the Jewish population to stay in our country.

A far more severe and cynically orchestrated anti-Semitic campaign followed the Six-Day War in the spring of 1967. Although the army was purged of Jewish officers as early as July, it was not until the student demonstrations the following winter that "Zionists" were targeted as an internal enemy. Soon after, *The Protocols of the Elders of Zion* began to circulate. Caught in an intraparty power struggle, Gomułka attempted to defuse the anti-Zionist rhetoric while encouraging those who felt loyalties to another state to emigrate. The apparatus evidently took this to mean every Jew in Poland, for over the next three months, some 8,000 Jews were dismissed from government and party positions. The state Yiddish daily and even the Yiddish theater were suspended. By the end of 1969, virtually all of Poland's 25,000 remaining Jews left the country. This time, Kaminska went with them. She was followed a year later by Aleksander Ford.

In 1973, two years after the Kaminska Theater moved into a new building at Plac Grzybowski under the directorship of Szymon Szurmiej, Polish TV broadcast their *Mirele Efros.* In 1976, the troupe marked the hundredth anniversary of Yiddish theater with a telecast of *Komediantn* (Comedians), which reworked Goldfadn's *Tsvey Kuni Lemls.* Three years later, two more productions—*Der Dibek* and a variety revue, *Shtern afn Dakh* (Stars on the Roof)—were recorded as telefilms.[1]

Alternately maudlin and glitzy, *Shtern afn Dakh* opens with a smooth narrator in a prewar opera cloak reminiscing about the "old Jewish *shtetl*" where he was born. "We'll never forget you—we miss you so much!" he sighs as the members of the company take turns playing such supposed *shtetl* archetypes as the Pickpocket, the Peddler (pleading with his customers to "*Hondl, hondl, hondl*"), and the broken-down Streetwalker who gamely wheezes that as "midnight's long past . . . the old whore will give it free." A *tsadek* sings a song to the Torah as his acolytes dance. Suddenly, they are interrupted by martial music and German commands. A few militants attempt to rouse the dispirited group of Jews imprisoned behind barbed wire. Then the narrator's injunction to "Weep my people, do penance for the six million," gives way to a witless disco paean: "A better generation brings new values . . . building a new world of love and friendship . . . the young flourish, conquer Earth, outer space."

In the end, Jewish history is reduced to the level of an inept Las Vegas floor show. One of the company soubrettes lugubriously sings "Mayn Yidishe Mame." Then a company of male and female dancers gaily cavort—the women styled as imaginary Chasidettes, attired in white satin *kapotes* and *shtraymlekh*. A *tsadek* reprising the Torah song seems only mildly befuddled when joined by a gaggle of shimmying chorines in red sheath skirts.

Only by comparison to this fantastically inappropriate spectacle, can Stephen Szlachtycz's version of *Der Dibek* be considered anything like a serious transposition of An-sky's play. The telefilm, which arrived in New York in lieu of the Kaminska Theater during the summer of 1982, is at once static and sensational, exhibiting a foggy expressionism and a voluptuous sense of decay more redolent of Hammer horror films than Chasidic folklore. A werewolf seems to serenade the overripe ingenue as she collapses in the graveyard; the music that threads through the proceedings could have been lifted from a Sergio Leone western. Even in their absence—perhaps especially in their absence—Jews in Poland remain the subjects of torment and mystery.

One might have expected Yiddish cinema to fare better in Israel, if only as museum pieces. It did not; the new homeland precluded the old *Yidishland*. That Hebrew defeated Yiddish even more resound-

ingly in the Jewish state than Yiddish had bested Hebrew in the Soviet one was a factor of Israel's need to break with its European past. Not surprisingly, Natan Gross's *Hamartef* (The Cellar), the first Israeli feature film to treat the Holocaust, was a commercial failure when released in 1963. (The same year, Zara Shakow's *The Theatre in Israel,* published in the United States by the Theodor Herzl Foundation, relegated the Yiddish stage to a chapter on "foreign-language theater," characterizing its audience as "those who have not yet adjusted to their new environment.")

Still, the new Israeli film industry was not altogether divorced from the old Yiddish popular culture. One can find its influence upon the popular ethnic comedies that characterized three-fourths of Israeli film production during the 1960s and after. Where these once might have been called *shund,* they were now dismissively termed *bourekas,* after a form of Middle Eastern pastry. While Ephraim Kishon's phenomenally successful *Sallah Shabbati* (1964), Menahem Golan's *Fortuna* (1966), and Uri Zohar's *Moishe Vintelator* (1966), took the point of view of Israel's Sephardic immigrants, Israel Becker's 1966 *Kuni Leml*—a hit second only to *Sallah Shabbati*—established a prototype for a form of Ashkenazi *bourekas.* Known as "gefilte fish films," these include Golan's *Tuvya Hakholev* (Tevye the Dairyman; 1968) and *Lupo* (1970), Boaz Davidson's *Lupo BeNew York* (Lupo in New York; 1976), and Yoel Zilberg's *Kuni Leml BeTel Aviv* (Kuni Leml in Tel Aviv; 1976), *Hershele* (1977), *"Millionaire" Betzarot,* (A Millionaire in Trouble; 1978), and *Nisuin Nusakh Tel Aviv* (Marriage Tel Aviv Style; 1980).

At the end of the cycle, in 1982, Roll Films produced an all-Yiddish talkie. This amiable, zoom-happy movie, known as *Az Men Git, Nemt Men* (When They Give, Take) in Yiddish, and as *Give-away* in English, drew heavily on the Kuni Leml formula for its comedy of mistaken identity. Directed by Alfred Shteinhardt from Michael Greenstein's script, this story of two brothers—one a worldly singer who calls himself Mike Stone, the other a *yeshive-bokher* named Mendl Stein—is mainly a vehicle for the comedian Yaakov Bodo. His round face framed by *payes* (but no beard), the pudgy Bodo plays Mendl with the full panoply of stage Yiddish gestures and shrugs, while his brother conforms to the prevailing stereotypes of Israeli macho.

Essentially a situation comedy, *Az Men Git, Nemt Men* is padded with musical numbers, Mendl's fantasies and Mike's rehearsals providing an even more elaborate study in Yiddish yé-yé than *Shtern afn Dakh*. Indeed, it is the sound of modern *mame-loshn* that provides the *deus ex machina*: Adela, a wealthy and *zoftig* blonde from Brooklyn, U.S.A., who is visiting Israel, turns on her radio and falls in love with Mike Stone's voice. An opportunistic *shadkhn* arranges an introduction, suggesting that the pop star protect himself from potential embarrassment by assuming a false identity to meet this *Amerikaner*. Mike first plans to masquerade as a *yeshive-bokher*, then decides to send an actual one instead, namely his brother Mendl. Tipped off by the *shadkhn* that her bashful swain will appear in disguise to test her, Adela marries the happily befuddled Mendl in the belief that she has landed the glamorous singer.

When the truth emerges, Adela bars Mendl from her boudoir, Mike berates himself for allowing this beautiful catch to elude him, and Mendl runs off to consult his *rebe*. Mike, however, not only fails to persuade Mendl to divorce Adela, but alienates his

new sister-in-law when he pursues her to the resort where she has taken refuge. Mendl, on the other hand, woos her successfully by mail. (Before writing, he sings a few bars of "A Brivele der Mamen.") Like the heroine of *Dray Tekhter,* the unhappy wife comes to appreciate her "traditional" husband. A new Adela returns to Tel Aviv and happily gives herself to Mendl. The film ends with a bris—Adela shown wearing a traditional kerchief—and a production number during which the chorus unconvincingly observes that "We sing our song in Yiddish too—in our own land, that's nothing new."

Henryk Broder's 1988 Yiddish-language documentary *Zol Zayn*, which was produced in conjunction with West German television, surveys the remnants of Yiddish culture in Israel, but *Az Men Git, Nemt Men* remains the last attempt at popular Yiddish filmmaking. Of course, in the United States and elsewhere, the Yiddish films of the 1930s are periodically rediscovered and revived for the aging progeny of their original audience.

There have also been several examples of post-Yiddish cinema—movies that use Yiddish to evoke its absence. Ken Jacobs's *Urban Peasants: An Essay in Yiddish Structuralism* (1975) exhibits an ironic detachment worthy of its anthropological title. A key practitioner of the American avant-garde cinema, Jacobs has had a longstanding interest in home movies as folk art. In the early 1960s, he exhibited a found 8mm roll as *Artie and Marty Rosenblatt's Baby Pictures,* accompanying it with a record by Jennie Goldstein. The forty minutes of unedited 16mm rolls he assembled to make *Urban Peasants* was shot by his wife's aunt, Stella Weiss, and records one extended family, mostly in front of their kosher butcher shop in some bleak Brooklyn backwater, during the late thirties and early forties.[2]

The footage is projected in silence: the filmmaker's only overt comment is to sepia-tint—and thus render lyrical—the sequence where the "peasants" visit Prospect Park, and to frame the film with two exercises from *Instant Yiddish,* a Berlitz-style language-instruction record. Even before the first image of *Urban Peasants* appears, we have already had a six-minute lesson in Diaspora history entitled "Situation Three: Getting a Hotel." (The very existence of this record is mindboggling in itself. Where in the world, with the possible exception of Birobidzhan, would one ever have the need to call room service in Yiddish?) A second excerpt, "Situation Eight: When You Are in Trouble," ends the movie with a double-edged punchline: "I am an American . . . everything is all right."

Jacobs's ploy makes it impossible to watch the homely clowning of this petit bourgeois Jewish family without picturing the contemporaneous "situation" of their European counterparts. Indeed, that the filmmaker chose to show this film every day during the summer of 1977 in Kassel, West Germany, as part of the Documenta 6 art show, is a profoundly moving—and enraged—gesture.

Just as *Urban Peasants* stirs up nostalgia only to render it problematic and complex, so does Belgian filmmaker Samy Szlingerbaum's 1980 *Brussels-Transit,* a mainly Yiddish talkie which, like *Urban Peasants,* builds the notion of a "transitional generation" into its very title. A second title identifies the film as *Dakh Brisel* (The Roof of Brussels—or, literally, Roof Brussels—with the sense of Brussels as a refuge) and is identified as *a mayse in di yidishe*

sprakh (a story in the Yiddish language). Szlingerbaum dedicates *Brussels-Transit* to his mother, and it is her Yiddish-language voice-over narration and occasional singing that we hear throughout, linking the filmmaker to a collective past and literalizing the idea of a "lost" *mame-loshn.*

Both Jacobs and Szlingerbaum were raised in Yiddish-speaking environments—the former, born in Brooklyn in 1933, grew up in Williamsburg; the latter was born to Polish-Jewish refugees in Brussels in 1949. Brussels was a center for Yiddish culture in the early 1950s (the poster collection in the YIVO archives attests to numerous showings of Yiddish movies there). Szlingerbaum, who died in 1986 without completing another feature, was closely associated with Chantal Akerman and Boris Lehman, two Brussels-based filmmakers of similar background who have also made films reflecting their parents's displacement.[3]

In *Brussels-Transit,* as in *Urban Peasants* (and also Claude Lanzmann's *Shoah*), the Yiddish language is used as a means to "see" what is no longer there. Even more than *Urban Peasants,* however, *Brussels-Transit* belongs to the tradition of the *faryidisht* film. Against a series of often static, starkly black-and-white compositions—train stations, night streets, empty apartments, shabby quarters of Brussels—the filmmaker's mother relates the story of her family's postwar journey from Poland to Belgium and their subsequent life there. ("The commentary," *Variety* noted, "gives a feeling of people still living between two worlds.")

A complicated act of preservation, memorial-building, and exorcism, *Brussels-Transit* retraces the now-invisible geography of *Yidishland.* One might call this film, which brings the Yiddish cinema full circle, *A Brivele fun Mame,* a letter *from* mother. (In essence, *Brussels-Transit* is the last Yiddish *kino-deklamatsye.*) The subliminal sense of dislocation arising from the film's asynchronous juxtaposition of sound and image is reinforced by the occasional dramatized anecdotes—subtle humiliations suffered at the hands of neighbors, shopkeepers, the police—that flow out of the voice-over narration. For Szlingerbaum, his parents are permanently displaced, their lives reduced to the struggle for survival.

In *Brussels-Transit* as in *Urban Peasants,* the never-mentioned Holocaust is the absence that structures the work. Postscripting the tumultuous history of Yiddish mass culture, Szlingerbaum's austere film has the modesty of the pebble one places atop a Jewish grave. (This book, I put beside it.)

NOTES

1. Supported by Poland's Communist Government, the post-Kaminska Kaminska Theater was an absurd exercise. Jew or Gentile, most of the young actors had to be taught the language, sometimes phonetically, while headsets provided a simultaneous Polish translation for an audience *New York Times* reporter John Darnton described as mainly "diplomats, tourists and Poles drawn by curiosity." In the same article, which appeared in 1979 (the same year as *Der Dibek* and *Shtern afn Dakh*), Szurmiej explained that Jewish values held a fascination for Poles: they came "to get acquainted with a culture that existed for 2,000 years. . . . It raises emotional, irrational questions for them." Darnton observed that the theater raised other questions as well: "Critics say that some of the productions do not present positive aspects of Jewish life, that the characters tend toward stereotypes." As an example, he singled out the current staging of Isaac Babel's *Sunset,* which showed "a Jewish community made up of avaricious, slovenly, scheming degenerates."

2. Jacobs's use of the word "peasant" to describe this half-Americanized, lower-middle-class Jewish family is an interesting slip. *Grine Felder* and *Birobidzhan* notwithstanding, there were virtually no Jewish farmers in Eastern Europe, let alone a peasantry. Indeed, *poyersh,* the Yiddish word for "peasant," can be used insultingly to mean "dullard" (a connotation that seems unmistakable in Jacobs's title).

3. Lehman's 1988 *Gefilte Film* is a fragmented documentary of a family gathered for Rosh Hashanah in which Yiddish is given pride of place (in the context of a half-dozen different languages) and culture is presented as common nourishment. Akerman, who for many years attempted to finance her adaptation of Isaac Bashevis Singer's novel *The Manor,* made *Histoires d'Amérique,* an episodic tribute to immigrant Jewish humor in 1988. The American experimental filmmaker Abraham Ravett is another child of Holocaust survivors whose autobiographical movies are steeped in Yiddish. In *Everything's for You* (1989), the filmmaker uses the language to address his dead father.

Appendix

1 Joseph Burstyn's Documentaries

For the historian of the Yiddish theater, even the worst Yiddish movies have considerable documentary value. The surviving 16mm prints of the Boris Thomashefsky vehicle *Bar Mitsve* are horrendously scratched and dupey, and it is unlikely that there will ever be a campaign to restore the film. And yet, one must be grateful that *Bar Mitsve* was made, for, more than any other performer, its star was the popular Yiddish theater incarnate.

Similarly, Joseph Seiden's inept recording of *Der Yidisher Kenig Lir* is at once an abysmal movie and a singular record of the Yiddish section of the Federal Theater Project. It is unfortunate that more Yiddish stage performances were not so preserved, although,

in the spring of 1935, Joseph Burstyn—the distributor of *Nosn Beker Fort Aheym* (*The Return of Nathan Becker*) and the *faryidisht* versions of *Skvoz Slezy* (Through Tears) and *Yevreiskoye Schastye* (Jewish Luck), among other Soviet and foreign films—produced a pair of extraordinary short documentaries: *Probes fun der Yidisher Aktyorn Union* (Auditions for the Hebrew Actors' Union) and *Kotlers Marionetn* (Cutler's Puppets).

The twenty-minute *Probes* presents itself as a scoop, opening with a written announcement—in Yiddish and English—that for the first time in history the Hebrew Actors' Union has raised the curtain to afford a glimpse at the procedure by which new entrants are selected. A narrator picks up—in Yiddish only—with the excited cadences of a newsreel sportscaster:

Tuesday, April 7, 1935: The entire Yiddish theater family has gathered together to hear the new performers audition! The spirit of the pioneers and builders hovers over the hall—Avrom Goldfadn, Jacob Gordin, Jacob P. Adler. Will these hopefuls bring the Yiddish theater a new Keni Lipzin or Leon Blank? The mood is serious yet festive.

Auditions (or "rehearsals") for membership in the Hebrew Actors' Union were held approximately every two years. Prospective members were required to pay seventy-five dollars and perform two different scenes or songs. Afterwards, the membership would cast secret ballots. The practice had elements of a ritual initation or hazing—more than one Yiddish performer used the term "inquisition" to describe the *probe*. The singer Mordecai Yardeini called the auditions "brutal," while the members who sat in judgment "simply behaved like 'bosses.'" Some of the union's more sensitive members, notably Jacob Mestel and Jacob Ben-Ami, tried to have the practice abolished, but other performers made shameless use of it. Because it was virtually impossible to work in New York's Yiddish theater without a union card, older performers commonly exploited the *probe* to ward off potential rivals.[1]

In part, Burstyn's artless documentary seems to have been a public-relations ploy designed to address precisely such accusations. Before the auditions, Ruben Guskin, who ruled the union with an iron hand, makes a speech denying that the union is closed to new talent. On the contrary, over the past three years the union has accepted forty new members, most of them young performers. With the exception of Victor Packer, a middle-aged radio announcer, who plays a scene in wildly expressionist makeup, the hopefuls are uniformly young, if not altogether unknown. First to appear is Vera Rosanka, reinforcing her radio identity as *"Di Yidishe Shikse"* by performing a Russian peasant song from *Yankl Boyle,* Leon Kobrin's 1912 play about the tragic love of a Jewish boy for a Gentile girl. She's followed by the brothers Sam and Saul Josephson, each performing heavily Americanized routines (in one, a son reproaches his parents for their failure to instruct him in *Yidishkayt*) and the ingenue Esta Salzman, a future staple of the Seiden stable. Salzman trills a number from the operetta *Shir Hashirim,* the static camera carefully repositioned for a shot of her legs as she dances.

The performances are punctuated by a repeated pan over the audience, with the narrator pointing out stars and stoking up suspense: "They are voting. Will she be admitted? Will she be admitted?" The finale has Michael Rosenberg, then the union's most celebrated nonmember, playing a scene from *Yoshe Kalb.* (Rosenberg had made a tremendous impression the previous season in *Yoshe Kalb* as a comic *shames* and consequently encountered problems for performing without a union card. A month before the voting his supporters took out an enormous ad in the *Forverts.*) The film ends with the voting results and the announcement that everyone we've seen has been accepted into the union except Rosanka—who, despite this rejection, was top-billed at the National the following spring.

Probes was first shown in May 1935 at the Folks Theater on Second Avenue along with two other Worldkino presentations—*Menakhem Mendl* (the *faryidisht* version of *Jewish Luck*), and the ten-minute *Kotlers Marionetn,* which preserves a performance by the popular puppet artist Yosl Cutler. Born in a Volhynian *shtetl* in 1896, Cutler attended *kheyder* (where, according to his sister, he got himself in trouble by drawing caricatures of the *melamed*), emigrated to America at fifteen, sold shoelaces from a Hester Street pushcart, took courses at the Cooper Union, and eked out a living as a sign painter. In the twenties, he lived in a studio on Fourteenth Street near the offices of the *Morgn Frayhayt*, for whom he drew political cartoons. Contemporaries remember him as a raw, unharnessed talent, bursting with charm and ideas.

In the mid-twenties, Cutler teamed up with another, slightly older, bohemian, Zuni Maud—the artist most closely connected with the radical poets known as "Di Yunge" (The Young). Together, they designed the sets and costumes for Maurice Schwartz's 1925 production of *Koldunye,* enlivening the marketplace scene with an original puppet show. During the winter of 1925–26 and for several years thereafter, until their East Twelfth Street loft was shut down by the fire department, Maud, Cutler, and painter Jack Tworkov—they called themselves "Modjacot," an acronym of their names—presented Yiddish puppet plays ranging from *Purimshpiln* to political satire. In the late twenties, Modjacot toured the Soviet Union and Poland; they performed a version of *Hirsh Lekert* in Vilna. For a time, they shifted their base to the Maud family's "Summer-Ray," a Catskills resort with an arty clientele, playing union halls and Yiddish camps, and touring the Yiddish theater circuit before breaking up in the early thirties.

Half modernist, half folk artist, Cutler is one of the more intriguing figures associated with the lost world of Communist Yiddish culture. In the summer of 1934, his *marionetn* appeared at the Civic Repertory Theater under the auspices of the Worker' Laboratory Theater. (Lured in by a leaflet emblazoned "Punch Goes Red," a correspondent for the annual *Puppetry* found an audience of "interesting people with foreign accents and wild dark hair. The words 'strike,' 'worker,' and 'New Order' were generously sprinkled in their conversation.") The same year, the International Workers' Organization published a collection of Cutler's writings and drawings called *Muntergang* (a pun conflating *munter* and *untergang*, the Yiddish words for "cheerful" and "downfall").

A straight recording, *Kotlers Marionetn* consists of several skits, all poking fun at Old World Jewish stereotypes. In "Simkhe and His Wife," an immi-

Simkhe and his wife, in *Kotlers Marionetn* (U.S.A., 1935); frame enlargement.

The *mitsve* dance: *Kotlers Marionetn;* frame enlargement.

The peppy little Jews: *Kotlers Marionetn;* frame enlargement.

grant couple are evicted on *shabes.* Simkhe, however, knows enough to go to the Unemployment Council and the bit ends with the pair singing a comic song, using the melody of "Tayere Malke" (Dear Malke), about the vicissitudes of the Depression (and the importance of worker solidarity). After a pair of clownish *yeshive* students cut a few capers, an elderly rabbi appears, complaining, chanting, and finally breaking into a slow, soulful "*mitsve* dance" as another bearded puppet beats time on drum. (The rabbi refers to *shabes* as his "payday"—one is not surprised to find that, along with *Di Yugnt fun Rusland, Kotlers Marionetn* was rejected by the British Board of Film Censors.)

The Yiddish word *marionetn* encompasses hand-puppets and, as such, these creatures are remarkably expressive—their eyes flutter, their legs move. Although the show is a one-man operation (save for the functional, offscreen piano accompaniment), Cutler's specialties include coordinated puppet choreography. Thus the "peppy little Jews" return for a "jazz dance," clapping their hands and butting their heads to "The St. Louis Blues." A brief coda has the puppet-master himself rising to credit his cast—"the first *Yidishe marionetn* in the entire world"—who "take a great part in the amusement of the *Yidishe masn* [Jewish masses] in New York."[2]

Marionetn was made before Cutler left to tour California, where he hoped to raise money for *Der Dibek Krizis* (The Dybbuk Crisis), an extravagant puppet film, using An-sky's play as the basis for a topical satire. A fifteen-minute parody of *Der Dibek* was already part of Cutler's repertoire. (Itche Goldberg, who saw it performed in 1930, remembers that the *tsadek* was a caricature of Maurice Schwartz and that the playlet ended with the puppets chanting

"The Song of the Volga Boatmen" as they attempted to pull the dybbuk from underneath Leah's skirt.) By 1935, however, the piece had become more elaborate and politicized: "Prosperity," visualized as Mae West, is possessed by the dybbuk "Depression"; various holy men, including the "rabbis" Ku Klux Klan, Abraham Cahan, and Franklin D. Roosevelt (waving the NRA Blue Eagle), attempt an exorcism in vain.

"Yes, we're going west," Cutler announces at the end of *Marionetn.* "Maybe we'll see Mae West." He never got farther than Indiana, killed in a highway collision less than a month after *Marionetn* was first shown. There was a memorial service at the Public Theater and a crowd estimated at 10,000 attended his funeral. The following summer, the Yiddish Communist journal *Signal* devoted an entire issue to his work.

2   Partial Yiddish Talkies

Although the Yiddish cinema was insular by definition, there are a few "nationality" films in which Yiddish is employed as a language among languages. In addition to various Soviet films, silent and *faryidisht,* and Henry Lynn's all-Yiddish *Shir Hashirim,* the Acme premiered a few part-Yiddish novelties. *Hell on Earth,* the American-release version of German director Victor Trivas's antiwar *Niemandsland* (No Man's Land; 1931), opened in January 1934 and featured dialogue in German, French, English, and Yiddish, as well as a score by Hanns Eisler. The following September, in time for the High Holy Days, the Acme unveiled *Mass Struggle,* a revolutionary costume drama produced by Ukrainfilm, with dialogue in Ukrainian, Russian, Polish, and Yiddish.

Dramatizing the Ukraine's eighteenth-century uprising against the Polish nobility, *Mass Struggle* employed several Jewish actors, if not a Jewish point of view. Jacob Libert, who plays the count's tax collector, was a former member of the Kaminsky troupe, appearing in no less than four of their pre–World War I filmed productions. His unsympathetic role is balanced by the character of Moshko, described in the film's American promotional material as "a young Jewish worker in revolt against the ancient submissiveness of his race." Another Jewish actor appears as the traditional innkeeper. Despite relatively extensive publicity, *Mass Struggle* was not one of the Acme's bigger hits. *New York Herald-Tribune* critic Richard Watts, who had visited the film's set on a trip to the Soviet Union during the summer of 1933, trekked down to East Fourteenth Street and was disappointed with what he found. The movie seemed incomprehensible—a "torrent of noise of all kinds emanating from the screen and nearly lost in the rapid procession of enormous closeups, reminiscent of the early days of silent film."[3]

Only one European feature, the 1934 Czech production *Marijka Nevěrnice* (Unfaithful Marika), directed by Vladislav Vancura from a story by Ivan Olbracht, shows traditional Jews as an integral part of a peasant community. This least tendentious and most ethnographic of nationality films was shot in the mountains of the Subcarpathian Rus with a mixed cast of Czech actors and local nonprofessionals speaking a variety of languages, mainly Ruthenian-Ukrainian and Yiddish.[4]

The leading literary exponent of Czech expressionism, as well as a pioneer of Czech independent cinema, Vancura made his first film in 1932. (Ten years later he was executed by the Gestapo in their mass reprisal for the assassination of Reinhard Heydrich.) Olbracht was a realist who, during the thirties, devoted all of his attention to the Subcarpathian Rus. In 1937, he published a collection of stories about the region's Jewish poor. *Marijka* was cooperatively produced, in part by a publishing house; and the film's low budget meets its subject of Carpathian poverty at least halfway. "This is a free film, that is clear," Vancura announced before shooting. "Otherwise it would not be poor, but then—it would not be free."

Marijka is a tale of backward development and backwoods passion. Nevertheless, its stark narrative premise is secondary to an evocation of the Carpathian landscape. (That the region is picturesque and "unspoiled" is made clear by the presence of various tourists. One, played by Olbracht himself, asks permission to photograph a group of Jews, who must refuse on account of the sabbath.) The protagonists are all Christian, but most secondary characters are Jews. A number of scenes are set in Jewish inns, and the local folkways include a Jewish wedding and a sabbath meal. In general, Jews are the most voluble but least violent segment of the population in the film—as well as the most educated. When Peter's mother wants to send a letter to her son telling him of his wife's faithlessness while he is in the mountains cutting wood, she finds a Jewish student in the marketplace to compose it; when Peter receives the letter, he takes it to a Jewish tavern to have it read. (Because Ruthenian schools had been banned by the Hungarians, and Hungarian schools were boycotted by the Ruthenians, the peasants were characterized by what one study has termed a "horrifying illiteracy.")

Although Vancura was a Communist, *Marijka,* unlike most Soviet nationality films, has no particular ideological ax to grind. The film makes clear that Jews often suffered as a result of displaced hostility. The unscrupulous lumber boss blames the *kretshmer* for the rotten meat that the boss himself has given his men, leading to a near-pogrom. No less than their peasant neighbors, the Jews are a diverse lot—both traditional Orthodox and explicitly Zionist. While some are sympathetic, the obnoxious Glick is unrelenting in his desire to purchase the luckless Peter's house. (In the end, he gets his way: Peter's home has become a *"turistadum"* with Glick and his son shown welcoming a hiker.)

Marijka was a commercial failure, too raw in subject matter and stylized in montage to appeal to Czech audiences. Released in the United States in 1937 as *Forgotten Land,* it was advertised as "a Carpathian Mountain folk drama" . . . "interesting to the entire Slavonic race, especially to Ukrainians, Russians, Czechoslovakians, and also Jews." (Be that as it may, I have been unable to find any mention of the film, which may not have played New York City until late 1941, in the Yiddish press.) The audience for *Forgotten Land* was most likely the same as for the various Soviet- and American-made Ukrainian talkies. Fully one-third of the Transcarpathian population came to the United States during the Great Immigration—although a significant number subsequently returned.[5]

As in the Warners' early talkies, Yiddish is still occasionally used as a source of authenticity or absurd humor. Bits of Yiddish dialogue flavor two 1974 American movies, Joan Micklin Silver's *Hester Street* and Mel Brooks's *Blazing Saddles*, though to quite different effect. Israeli filmmaker Benjamin Hayeem's quasi-underground *Habanana Hashkora* (*The Black Banana*; 1976), a satire on *Der Dibek* among other things, contains some Yiddish dialogue, as well as English, Arabic, and (mainly) Hebrew. There is also a tradition of oral-history documentaries that contain extensive Yiddish passages, including Steve Fischler and Joel Sucher's *Free Voice of Labor: The Jewish Anarchists* (1980), Aviva Kempner and Josh Waletzky's *Partisans of Vilna* (1986), and, above all, Claude Lanzmann's *Shoah* (1985), which, in its use of Yiddish, Polish, French, and German, reproduces the polylingualism of the Nazi concentration camps.

One quasi-Yiddish production was released in Israel in 1983, the same year as *Az Men Git, Nemt Men. Megile '83,* directed by Ilan Eldad for the West German firm Telefilm, adapts Itzik Manger's retelling of the Book of Esther. Where Manger's *Purimshpil* was performed in a Polish *shtetl* by a group of tailor's apprentices, Telefilm's (which opens in old Jaffa, with subsequent scenes set in the garden of the Astoria Hotel and the Tel Aviv Dolphinarium) adds numerous cute anachronisms: the Persian police wear fedoras and trench coats, King Ahasuerus exercises while listening to rock music through headphones. Less cloying than cartoonish, the film has a childlike quality and includes elements of the rock musical and mime play. A variety of versions of *Megile '83* were made. The one in the Jerusalem Cinémathèque has an English-language introduction, Hebrew dialogue, and Yiddish singing—and may be

Shabes meal in Vladislav Vancura's *Unfaithful Marijka* (Czechoslovakia, 1934). Shot in the Subcarpathian Rus, this is the only European film to show traditional Jews as an integral part of a peasant community.

the only talkie ever released with Yiddish subtitles. In spite of its manifest desire to please, however, the film was a notable failure, performing even more feebly at the box office than *Az Men Git, Nemt Men.*

The 1990 Israeli release *Ahavat Ha'aharon Shel Laura Adler* (*Laura Adler's Last Love Affair*), written and directed by Avram Heffner, is a self-consciously melodramatic story of a threadbare troupe of Yiddish performers. As the troupe tours Israel (and the dramatic action shifts on, off, and backstage), there is considerable switching between Hebrew and Yiddish. Ultimately the troupe's aging diva, played by Rita Zohar, a onetime child star of the Israeli Yiddish theater, dies onstage, a sentimental metaphor for the demise of popular Yiddish culture.

3   Recycled Yiddish Films

That *Laura Adler* would include a clip from the last reel of *Jewish Luck*, misleadingly identified as a Yiddish talkie, is an inadvertent bit of authenticity. Throughout the thirties and later, Yiddish films were frequently revived and rereleased under different titles. At some point, for example, *Yisker* became variously *The Prince and the Pauper* and *The Holy Martyr. Di Yugnt fun Rusland* was transformed into *Der Yidisher Foter* (The Jewish Father), *Shir Hashirim* into *Farbotene Libe* (Forbidden Love), *Mayn Zundele* into *Der Lebediker Yosem* (The Living Orphan). Exhibitors could be shameless. In September 1933, the Parkway Theater in Brownsville advertised a double bill of "two new pictures"—Rudolf Schildkraut in the 1921 *Theodor Herzl,* now titled *Der Vanderer Yid* (*The Wandering Jew*), and Jacob P. Adler in the 1914 *Michael Strogoff.*

Zygmunt Turkow, director and star of the original *Tkies Kaf* **(Poland, 1924).**

Thus, to a certain degree, all the products of Yiddish cinema were subject to a process of continual modification and recirculation. (Today, the material is contested by rival video distributors.) Zygmunt Turkow recalls coming upon the *faryidisht* version of his 1924 *Tkies Kaf* in Paris, Buenos Aires, and even Havana: "It was a strange feeling to sit in some remote place, so very far away and to see myself, my closest friends, even my young daughter looking down at me from the screen."

After World War II, the movie was rereleased yet again as *Dem Rebns Koyekh* (The Rabbi's Power):

In 1950, an advertisement from New York reached me in Brazil with this message: "Come see the great Yiddish talkie, as thrilling as *Yoshe Kalb,* as tragic as *Der Dibuk*: the famous Yiddish actor-star Joseph Buloff in *Dem Rebe's Koyekh* [*sic*]. Jews, Jews, great and small, poor or rich: If you want to amuse yourself then you dare not miss this movie which has interested and enthused the entire Jewish people." . . .

The centerfold of this little leaflet contained four pictures of our movie, *Tkies Kaf* [and] a large picture of Buloff, with the inscription: "The famous Yiddish star actor in the great Yiddish talkie, *Dem Rebe's Koyekh.*" To the right of this picture was another inscription: "Text: Jacob Mestel, Film Director: George Roland"; to their left in small letters was another inscription: "A select cast: Ida Kaminska, Zygmunt Turkow, Jacob Mestel, Louis Kadison, Benjamin Fishbein, Ben Basenko."

"The name of Esther-Rokhl Kaminska wasn't mentioned at all," Turkow remarks crushingly, concluding with the furious observation that both Buloff and Mestel knew that he, the film's director, had "accidentally" survived the war and was living in Brazil. Indeed, Mestel "was in constant correspondence with me and still didn't find it necessary to mention this new transformation of *Tkies Kaf*." Turkow's anger is understandable. Yet that *Tkies Kaf* survives at all is completely due to the *faryidisht* version. This is true of a number of other silent films, including *Yisker, Broken Hearts,* and *Judith Trachtenberg.*

Seiden, of course, recycled himself. In December 1933, his Jewish Talking Pictures released *Gelebt un Gelakht* (Live and Laugh), a compilation of Judea shorts—including pieces of *Oy Doktor!* and *Shuster Libe (The Shoemaker's Romance)*. Max Wilner was credited as director. A revised version of the same (increasingly shopworn) package was released for Passover 1941 as *Mazltov, Yidn.* In 1950, it appeared yet again as *Borsht Belt Follies* and *Monticello, Here We Come!* In the 1970s, one of the inheritors of Seiden's collection produced a homemade assemblage of dramatic scenes, musical numbers, and comic *shtik*s culled from various disintegrating prints and called it *That's Yiddish Entertainment.* The continuing fascination of these scratchy celluloid shards suggests that, for the remaining folk audience, the spectacle of actors speaking Yiddish in the movies retains something of the novelty it had sixty years ago.[6]

NOTES

1. In his memoirs, Pesachke Burstein maintains that when he first auditioned in the late twenties, he was blackballed by a clique of comedians led by Hymie Jacobson and Max Wilner.

Leaving the hall, Burstein was congratulated by no less an eminence than Muni Weisenfreund:

"Let me shake your hand, young man. Do you know what an honor it is *not* to pass into the Union? . . . The great Maurice Schwartz was kept out and I myself was bounced the first time I rehearsed. Yes, my friend, there are a few guys up there who are anti-youth and anti-talent. My own father was never admitted! Do you know that Stella Adler fainted up on that small stage when the old crones up front stared at her murderously."

A number of prominent performers, including Baruch Lumet and the singer Ola Lilit, refused to submit themselves to this ordeal.

2. The latter assertion may be so, but not the former. In 1922, poet Moshe Broderszon, composer Henekh Kon, and painter Yitzhak Brauner staged Yiddish puppet shows in their Lodz cabaret, *Had Gadye.* In Krakow, during the winter of 1919–20, the local Labor Zionists sponsored a Jewish puppet theater which, although originally Polish-language, also used Yiddish.

3. This intriguing movie is almost certainly *Koliivshchina* (The Kolii Rebellion), also known as *By Water and Smoke,* which had been released in the Soviet Union ten months earlier. The film was produced at Ukrainfilm's Odessa studio under the direction of Ivan Kavaleridze. (A known Cubist sculptor before he began directing for VUFKU in the late 1920s, Kavaleridze was the most avant-garde Ukrainian director after Dovzhenko; his anti-naturalistic use of black backdrops, monumental figures, and fragmentary scenarios suggests the influence of stage director Les Kurbas.)

4. The most impoverished region of pre–World War I Hungary, the Subcarpathian Rus became—after a brief federation with the independent Ukraine—the most ethnically diverse part of the newly created Czechoslovakian state. (It was subsequently annexed by the Soviet Union in 1945.) The Ruthenian (West Ukrainian) majority lived amid substantial Magyar and Slovak minorities; Jews, virtually all of them Yiddish-speaking, were 14 percent of the population.

5. Yet another film of Jewish interest may have been made in the Subcarpathian Rus during 1933. The wedding of the daughter of the Chasidic rabbi, Khaym Eliezer Shapira of Mukacevo, was an international event, involving several days of celebration and the opening of Czech borders to Mukacevo Chasidim from

Hungary and Rumania. The subject of a lavish pictorial report in the *Forverts* Arts Section of April 16, the "Mukacevo Wedding" was also documented by either an Austrian news agency or a wealthy American member of the sect. The resulting film —an hour or less in length, possibly with Yiddish narration—is said to have been shown, between vaudeville sets, at the Clinton in late 1939 or early 1940.

6. In a sense, Russ Karel's widely seen documentary *Almonds and Raisins,* made for British television in 1983, is only the most recent of such compilations. Karel uses a number of Yiddish talkies for raw material, mixing them with stock footage and sound bridges to create new sorts of lyrical montages or production numbers. Although ostensibly a serious treatment of its subject, the film fabricates its own world through some bizarrely revisionist geography (the Grand Concourse is located in midtown Manhattan, an immigrant is said to travel "east from Europe to America") as well as a number of egregious and pointless errors in dates, credits, and plot synopses. No less than Seiden, Karel is trafficking in sentiment and old film clips. Indeed, Karel's chutzpah approaches Seiden-like proportions when he allows Herschel Bernardi to twice make the fantastic statement that there were 300 Yiddish talkies produced, or when his documentary blandly presents a clip from the 1969 novelty short *The Cowboy*—"forty years before *Blazing Saddles* there was even a Yiddish western"—as if it were one of them.

Glossary

agunah abandoned wife

allrightnik (American-Yiddish) nouveau riche

badkhn wedding jester

balebos master of the house; a proprietor, landlord, boss, or burgher (fem.: *baleboste*; plur.: *balebatim*; dim.: *balebesl*, ironic term for a newlywed man)

balegule wagon driver

bar mitsve religious confirmation

bashert a fated one; usually one's future mate

batlen impractical, idle person (plur.: *botlonim*)

bobe grandmother

bokher boy; student

bube-mayse old wives' tale; fairy tale

Daytshmerish German-inflected Yiddish

emes truth

faryidisht made more Jewish

folk people

folksmentsh man of the people

foter father

frum pious

get Jewish religious divorce

glik happiness

goldene medine literally "Golden Land," i.e., America

goles Yid Diaspora Jew (generally a disparaging epithet)

goy Gentile (plur.: *goyim*)

goylem golem; creature of stone

heym home

hondl commerce; to bargain

kapote traditional long black coat worn by Chasidic men

khasene   wedding

khazer   pig

khazeray   pig swill; trash

khazn   cantor (fem.: *khaznte*; plur.: *khazonim*)

kheyder   religious primary school (plur.: *khadorim*)

khupe   wedding canopy

kind   child (plur.: *kinder*)

klaynkunst   cabaret performance

klezmer   musician (plur.: *klezmorim*)

kolkhoz   (Russian) cooperative farm

Komsomol   (Russian) 1. Communist youth organization; 2. male member of such an organization

Komsomolka   (Russian) female member of Komsomol

kretshmer   innkeeper

lamedvovnik   one of thirty-six secret saints

landsman   countryman (plur.: *landslayt*)

landsmanshaft   fraternal organization of immigrants originating from the same region or town

libe   love

literarish   literary

luftmentsh   (literally) "air man"; one without regular employment

mame   mother

mame-loshn   (literally) "mother tongue"; the Yiddish language

mashgiekh   supervisor, usually of Jewish dietary laws in an institutional kitchen

maskil   member or supporter of the Jewish Englightenment (plur.: *maskilim*)

mayse   story; tale

mazl   good fortune

mazltov   congratulations

mekler   middleman

melamed   teacher

mentsh   man; person (plur.: *mentshn*)

mentshlekhkayt   human quality; humanity

meshugener   lunatic (plur.: *meshugoim*)

meydl   girl; young woman (plur.: *meydlekh*)

mikve   ritual bath

mishpokhe   family

mitsve   good deed; (literally) commandment

molodyets   (Russian-Yiddish) fine young fellow

nign   melody

noged   rich man

payes   earlocks

probe   trial; audition

prost   common; ordinary

proste Yidn   ordinary Jews

Purimshpil   Purim play

Purimshpiler   Purim player

rebe   rabbi

rebetsn   rabbi's wife

shabes   sabbath

shadkhn   marriage broker (plur.: *shadkhonim*)

shames   sexton

sheyn   beautiful

sheyner balebos   respectable burgher

sheyne Yidn   pious Jews

shikse   Gentile woman

shlimazl   luckless one; fool

shmate   rag

shmues   chat

shtarker   thug

shtetl   Jewish market town (plur.: *shtetlekh*)

shtik   piece (dimin.: *shtikl*)

shtrayml   traditional fur hat worn by Chasidic men (plur.: *shtraymlekh*)

shul   synagogue (plur.: *shuln*)

shund   trash

shver   father-in-law

shviger   mother-in-law

sider   prayer book

talis   prayer shawl (plur.: *taleysim*)

tate-mame   parents

tfilin   phylacteries

tokhter   daughter (plur.: *tekhter*)

treyf   unkosher

tsadek   saint

tsaytbild   (literally) "time-picture"; topical play

tsholnt   traditional sabbath stew

tsores   woes

velt   world (plur.: *veltn*)

yeshive   Jewish boys' secondary school

Yid   Jew (plur.: *Yidn*)

Yidene   Jewish woman

Yidishkayt   Jewishness

yikhes   social pedigree

Yishev   Jewish settlement in Palestine

yontev   holiday

yosem   orphan (fem.: *yesoyme*)

zeyde   grandfather

zoftig   (literally) juicy; fleshy

zun   son (dim.: *zundl*, plur.: *zin*)

Notes on Sources

David Matis's extensive and pioneering bibliographic essay "Tsu der Geshikhte fun Yidishe Film," published in the 1961 *YKUF-Almanak,* is the essential map for all subsequent explorers of Yiddish cinematic terrain. The field was further opened to English readers in 1983 with the publication of two well-researched dissertations, Judith Goldberg's *Laughter Through Tears: The Yiddish Cinema* and Eric A. Goldman's *Visions, Images, and Dreams: Yiddish Film Past and Present.* I am indebted to both, as well as to Patricia Erens's *The Jew in American Cinema.* In all but a few cases, I have tracked their sources back to the original, translating (or retranslating) where needed.

Research for virtually every chapter was done at The National Center for Jewish Film in Waltham, Massachusetts; at the Film Study Center of The Museum of Modern Art, New York; at the Jewish Division, the Slavonic Division, and the Billy Rose Theatre Collection at the Library of the Performing Arts, New York Public Library; at the YIVO Institute in New York; and at the Steven Spielberg Archives (David Matis collection) of the Hebrew University, Jerusalem. I have indicated other archives or special collections where appropriate.

Introduction: *A Brivele der Mamen*

Cine-Phono in Yuri Tsivian, "Some Observations on Early Russian Cinema," *Inside the Film Factory* (New York: Routledge, 1991); Daniel, "Dos Ershte Mal in Kino," *Der Heldisher Brivtreger* (Moscow: Melukhe Farag der Emes, 1940), p. 40; Gross, *Toldot Hakolnoa Hayehudi BePolin,* p. 54; Shneiderman, "Film Hot a Tipern Zin . . . ," *Film Velt,*

September 1928, p. 8; Mukdoyni, *Tsen Yorn Artef* (New York: Artef, 1937), p. 95; Negt and Kluge, "The Public Sphere and Experience," *October,* Fall 1988, p. 61.

For information on Yiddish *kino-deklamatsye,* see David Matis's *"Kiddush Hashem* fun 1914," *Di Tsukunft,* October 1983, and Rashid Iangirov's "Jewish Life on the Screen in Russia, 1908–1919," *Jews and Jewish Topics in the Soviet Union and Eastern Europe,* Spring 1990; for American analogues, "Survivors of a Vanishing Race in the Movie World," *New York Times Magazine* (1/18/20), p. 4. The notion of the Yiddish language as a *"Yidishland"* is put forth, along with many other useful and provocative formations, by Benjamin and Barbara Harshav in the introduction to their *American Yiddish Poetry: A Bilingual Anthology* (Berkeley: University of California Press, 1986).

1 Wandering Stars

Erens, *The Jew in American Cinema,* p. 29; Doublier in Stephen Bottomore, "Dreyfus and Documentary," *Sight and Sound,* Autumn 1984, p. 290; Aleichem, *Wandering Stars,* trans. Frances Butwin (New York, 1952), p. 92; "Dreyfus in Kasrilevke," *The Best of Sholom Aleichem,* ed. Irving Howe and Ruth R. Wisse (Washington, D.C.: New Republic Books, 1979), p. 112; on the Grand Electro, Yudel Flior, *Dvinsk: The Rise and Decline of a Town,* p. 87; *Cine-Phono* on *shtetl* movie houses in Iangirov, "Jewish Life," p. 20; Silverstein in David Rosenbaum, "The First Picture Show," *Film Comment,* March–April 1975, p. 33; *Cine-Phono* on *L'khaym* and Slavinsky's memoirs in Yuri Tsivian *et al.,* eds., *Silent Witnesses,* pp. 102–4, 150; Davidon in Ella Shohat, *Israeli Cinema,* p. 20; Sieracki and Arko in Matis, "Tsu der Geshikhte fun Yidishe Film," *YKUF-Almanak* (New York, 1961); Gordin in Nahma Sandrow's *Vagabond Stars,* p. 132; Lamprecht, *Americana: Reiseeindrücke, Betrachtungen, Geschichtliche Gesamtansicht* (Freiburg im Breisgau, 1906), trans. John J. Appel; Hapgood, *The Spirit of the Ghetto,* p. 145. *The Slaughter* advertised and *Uriel Acosta* announced in *Moving Picture World* (5/23/14), p. 1146; Bush, *Moving Picture World* (6/20/14).

2 Romance in the Ghetto

Patterson, "The Nickelodeons: The Poor Man's Elementary Course in the Drama," *Saturday Evening Post* (11/23/07), pp. 10–11; *Forverts* (5/24/08) in Irving Howe's *The World of Our Fathers,* p. 213; Hansen, *Babel and Babylon: Spectatorship in American Silent Film* (Cambridge: Harvard University Press, 1991); *New York Tribune* (12/26/08) in Lary May, *Screening Out the Past: The Birth of Mass Culture and the Motion Picture Industry* (New York: Oxford, 1980), p. 43; *The Black 107* reviewed as *Mendel Beilis, Variety* (12/5/13), p. 16; *The Terrors of Russia* advertised, *Moving Picture World* (11/29/13), p. 1047; Robinson, *Chaplin: His Life and Art* (New York: McGraw-Hill, 1985), pp. 154–55; Zylberzweig, *Leksikon fun Yidishn Teater,* vol. 1, p. 270; *Universal Weekly* (8/2/13), p. 32; Goldin's cameraman in Kevin Brownlow's *Behind the Mask of Innocence,* pp. 381–82; Terry Ramsaye, *A Million and One Nights: A History of the Motion Picture Through 1925* (New York: Simon & Schuster, 1986), p. 493; *Universal Weekly* (8/9/13), p. 13; Louis Reeves Harrison, *Moving Picture World* (7/19/13), p. 300; "Irene Wallace," *Moving Picture World* (9/20/13); Shmeruke, *The Esterke Story in Yiddish and Polish Literature* (Jerusalem: Magnes Press, 1985), p. 78; *New York Dramatic Mirror* (10/8/13), p. 30; *Universal Weekly* (10/25/13), p. 28; *Teater un Moving Pikshurs* (10/24/13), p. 22; Janet Barry, "Irene Wallace —Star of the Imp Company," *Photo Play,* December 1913; unidentified clippings (2/13/15 and 12/24/15), Irene Wallace file, Billy Rose Theatre Collection; *Teater un Moving Pikshurs* (10/24/13), p. 30; "Films Show Work of Jewish Charities," *New York Times* (4/6/14), p. 18; *New York Dramatic Mirror* (4/1/14), p. 30; *Moving Picture World* (5/2/14), p. 795; Thomashefsky in Stefan Kanfer, *A Summer World: The Attempt to Build a Jewish Eden in the Catskills* (New York: Farrar, Straus, 1989), p. 61; Peter Milne, *Motion Picture News* (2/20/15), p. 53.

For a succinct account of the 1908 campaign against the nickelodeons, see May, *Screening Out the Past*, pp. 43ff; for an overview of Jewish themes in the pre–World War I American cinema, see Erens, *The Jew in American Cinema*, pp. 29ff.

3 "The Face of the Earth Will Change"

Wisse, introduction, *The Best of Sholom Aleichem*, p. x; Berkowitz, "Sholom Aleichem at Work," Melech Grafstein, ed., *Sholom Aleichem Panorama*, p. 196; B. Z. Goldberg (anonymously) in Marie Waife-Goldberg, *My Father, Sholom Aleichem*, pp. 291–92; *The Adventures of Mottel the Cantor's Son*, trans. Tamara Kahana (New York: Harry Schuman, 1953), pp. 329–30; Ruskin, "Sholom Aleichem's Veltel in di Muvis," *Der Tog* (4/12/19), p. 3; Leyda, *Kino*, p. 83, also the source for the descriptions of Russian movie houses, pp. 86–87; Singer, *Love and Exile: An Autobiographical Trilogy* (New York: Doubleday, 1984), p. 33; Kaminska, *My Life, My Theater*, pp. 27–28; Negri, *Memoirs of a Star* (Garden City, N.Y.: Doubleday, 1970), pp. 123–24; *Forverts* headline in Melech Epstein, *The Jew and Communism*, p. 23, see also Zosa Szajkowski's *Jews, Wars, and Communism*, vol. 1, pp. 122–23; advertisement, *Der Tog* (4/11/17), p. 3; Selznick in Ramsaye, *A Million and One Nights*, p. 766; description of *We Are Not Guilty of Their Blood*, *Teatr*, in Tsivian, *Silent Witnesses*, p. 380.

For further discussion of Sholom Aleichem's interest in movies, see David Matis's "Sholom Aleichem fun Film," *Kultur un Lebn*, December 1981. Stephen Aschheim describes the behavior of German-Jewish officers in *Brothers and Strangers*, p. 149. For an account of actions taken against the Yiddish press during World War 1, see Szajkowski's *Jews, Wars, and Communism*, vol. 2.

4 Nineteen-Nineteen

Granovsky in Avram Kampf, "Art and Stage Design: The Jewish Theatres of Moscow in the Early Twenties," Ruth Apter-Gabriel, ed., *Tradition and Revolution*, p. 140; Schwartz in Sandrow, *Vagabond Stars*, p. 262; Don Gussow's description of the Nalewki in Ronald Sanders's *Shores of Refuge*, p. 376; Leyda, *Kino*, p. 136; Jacob Rubin in Brownlow, *Behind the Mask*, p. 369, also the source for information on Arkatov's American career; Reilly, *Moving Picture World* (5/24/19), p. 1237; Ruskin, *Der Tog* (4/12/19), p. 3; description of wartime Warsaw, Boris D. Bogen's *Born a Jew*, p. 133; Babel, *Lyubka the Cossack and Other Stories* (New York: New American Library, 1963), p. 131; Lewin, *Dark Mountains and Blue Valleys* (Cranbury, N.J.: Associated University Presses, 1988), p. 13; Belis, "Peretz Markish," in Joseph Leftwich, ed., *Great Yiddish Writers of the Twentieth Century*, pp. 459–60; Grosbard and Turkow in Michael Steinlauf's "Polish-Jewish Theater: The Case of Mark Arnshteyn" (Ph.D. dissertation, Brandeis University, 1988), pp. 324, 268; Efros in Nicoletta Misler, "The Future in Search of Its Past: Nation, Ethnos, Tradition and the Avant-Garde in Russian Jewish Art Criticism," Apter-Gabriel, ed., *Tradition and Revolution*, p. 149.

Archives: William E. Wiener Oral History Library, American Jewish Committee, New York.

5 Out of Galicia

Kafka's "Report to an Academy," *The Complete Stories* (New York: Schocken, 1983), pp. 250ff., for further discussion see Sander L. Gilman's *Jewish Self-Hatred*, pp. 284–85; Brod, *Franz Kafka: A Biography* (New York: Schocken, 1963), p. 135; Torborg, "Die Budapester," and Roth, "Juden auf Wanderschaft," in Ruth Beckermann, *Die Mazzesinsel*, pp. 86, 24–26; Kaminska, *My Life*, p. 36; Grunwald, *History of Jews in Vienna* (Philadelphia: Jewish Publication Society, 1936), pp. 462–63; Berczeller, "Sodom and Gomorrah," *New Yorker* (10/14/74), p. 50; Landa, *The Jew in Drama*, pp. 264–65; advertisement for *Theodor Herzl* in Beckermann, *Die Mazzesinsel*, p. 105; Maskuf, "A Muving Piktshur fun Rudolf Shildkroyt rirt Viener tsiunisten kiz treren," *Forverts* (4/9/21), p. 19; Picon, *Molly!* p. 36; *Cinémagazine* (1/25/24), p. 142.

Archives: American Jewish Historical Society, Waltham, Mass. (Molly Picon collection).

6 Miracles on the Vistula

Carter, *The New Spirit in the Cinema*, p. 73; Steinwurzel in Eric A. Goldman's *Visions, Images, and Dreams*, p. 18; Turkow, *Di Ibergerisene Tkufe: Fragmentn fun Mayn Lebn* (Buenos Aires: Central Farband, 1961), p. 96 (translation courtesy of the National Center for Jewish Film); see also "Yekhiel Bojm," Zylberzweig, *Leksikon fun Yidishn Teater*, vol. 5, p. 3755; Gross, *Toldot Hakolnoa Hayshudi Bepolin*, pp. 103–4; Artaud's letter to Yvonne Allendy (4/19/29), *Antonin Artaud: Collected Works*, vol. 3 (London: John Calder, 1972), p. 129; *Tkies Kaf* advertised in *Literarishe Bleter* (5/9/24), reviewed in *Literarishe Bleter* (5/16/24), p. 6; Neuman, "Plan-Virtshaft in der Yidisher Film Produksie," *Literarishe Bleter* (2/3/38), p. 91; *Tkies Kaf*'s Polish reviews in Władysław Banaszkiewicz and Witold Witczak's *Historia Filmu Polskiego*, vol. 1, pp. 200, 207; Turkow, "Arum di Yidishe Filmen," *Literarishe Bleter* (10/1/25), pp. 92–93; *The Jews in the Eastern War Zone* in Sanders, *Shores of Refuge*, pp. 285–86; Polish response to *Der Lamedvovnik* in Jerzy Toeplitz's *Historia Sztuki Filmowej* (Warsaw: Filmowa Agencja Wydawnicza, 1956), p. 358; Petre Rado, "Jean Mihail," *Revue Roumaine d'Histoire de l'Art* 15 (1978), p. 104.

7 Yiddish Modernism and *Jewish Luck*

Babel, *Lyubka the Cossack*, p. 131; Singer, *Love and Exile*, p. 50; Bogen, *Born a Jew*, p. 273; Litvakov's characterization of *Der Emes* in Zvi Y. Gitelman, *Jewish Nationality and Soviet Politics*, p. 334n; Duranty, *I Write as I Please*, p. 109; Ehrenburg, *People and Life, 1891–1921* (New York: Knopf, 1962), p. 379; Chagall, *My Life* (New York: Grossman, 1960), p. 162, and Lois Adler's "Alexis Granovsky and the Jewish State Theater of Moscow," *Drama Review* (September 1980), p. 32; Natalya Vovsi-Mikhoels, "The Dark Ages of the Twentieth Century: A Memoir of the Life and Death of My Father" (unpublished précis,

1984), p. 10; Leon Dennen, *Where the Ghetto Ends*, p. 164; Kerr in Adler, "Alexis Granovsky," p. 37; the second German critic, Alfons Goldschmidt, in Kampf's "Art and Stage Design," Apter-Gabriel, ed., *Tradition and Revolution*, p. 140; Benjamin, "Moscow Diary," *October*, Winter 1985, p. 14; characterization of Chagall's murals in Walter Erben, *Marc Chagall* (New York: Praeger, 1957), p. 73; Gorev, "Russian Literature and the Jews," in V. Lvov-Rogachevsky, *A History of Russian Jewish Literature*, p. 16; Mandelstam, *Mandelstam: The Complete Critical Prose and Letters* (Ann Arbor, Mich.: Ardis, 1979), pp. 253, 263.

Granvosky's letters to Mendel Elkin (9/19/24, 1/29/25) in Fania Burko, "The Soviet Yiddish Theatre in the Twenties" (Ph.D. dissertation, Southern Illinois University at Carbondale, 1978), pp. 149–50, 80; Shklovsky in Sergei Eisenstein, *The Battleship Potemkin*, ed. Herbert Marshall (New York: Avon, 1978), p. 252; Babel's letters in Nathalie Babel, ed., *Isaac Babel: The Lonely Years*; *Jewish Luck* reviewed in the *Daily Worker* (5/9/30), advertised in *Der Emes* (11/7/25); *Pravda*'s review in Jean-Loup Passek, ed., *Le Cinéma Russe et Soviétique* (Paris: Centre Georges Pompidou, 1981), pp. 122–23; *Mabl* announced in the *Jewish Theatrical News* (2/16/26); Ben-Ari, *Habima*, pp. 143–45; Chemerinsky, "Vi Mir Haben Afgnefirt Sholom Aleichem's *Mabul* Farn Film," *Literarishe Bleter* (4/30/26), p. 286; Duranty, "Russian Movie Faces Real Tragedy," *New York Times* (3/24/27), p. 7.

8 The Prince of Second Avenue

Teller, *Strangers and Natives*, p. 21; *Variety* (9/3/24), p. 2; *Jewish Theatrical News* (10/1/24); *Salome of the Tenements* in *Jewish Theatrical News*, October 1924; *Yisker* reviewed in *Morgn Frayhayt* (1/30/25), cited in *Jewish Theatrical News* (3/2/26); Hapgood, *Spirit of the Ghetto*, pp. 202, 221; Adler in David S. Lifson, *The Yiddish Theater in America*, p. 327; Patterson, *Scenario and Screen* (New York: Harcourt, Brace, 1928), pp. 191, 210, 61; *Broken Hearts* reviewed in *New York Times* (3/3/26), p. 26, and *Jewish Theatrical News* (3/3/26), p. 1. For the reception of *The*

Jazz Singer see Robert L. Carringer's "Introduction: History of a Popular Culture Classic," *The Jazz Singer*, ed. Tino Balio (Madison: University of Wisconsin Press, 1979), p. 13

Archives: New York State Archives—New York State Education Department, Motion Picture Division Information, Albany, N.Y.

9 Making It in America

Goldstein in William Schack, "Yiddish Theater in Travail," *New York Times* (3/30/30); *World's Work* cited in Teller, *Strangers and Natives*, p. 95; *Dearborn Independent* cited in James Ridgeway's *Blood in the Face: The Ku Klux Klan, Aryan Nations, Nazi Skinheads, and the Rise of a New White Culture* (New York: Thunder's Mouth Press, 1990), pp. 40–41; Potamkin, *The Compound Cinema: The Film Writings of Harry Alan Potamkin*, ed. Lewis Jacobs (New York: Teachers College Press, 1977), pp. 368–70; Rothman, "The Jew on the Screen," *Jewish Forum*, October 1928, p. 527; Sloman in Kevin Brownlow, *The Parade's Gone By*, pp. 185–86; Jessel, *This Way Miss* (New York: Henry Holt, 1955), pp. 193–96.

The most comprehensive discussion of Jewish representation in the films of the 1920s is Erens, *The Jew in American Cinema*. For an excellent analysis of the interplay between American-Yiddish and American popular culture see Mark Slobin, *Tenement Songs*.

10 Once Upon a Time in the Ukraine

Niepomniaschchi in Gitelman, *Jewish Nationality*, p. 335; Babel in *The Lonely Years*; Babitsky and Rinberg, *The Soviet Film Industry*, pp. 134–35; Leyda, *Kino*, p. 230; Babel, *Blushdayushtichi Sviosdy* (Moscow, 1926), p. 3; Lubomirsky, "Teater un Kino: Blondzhende Shtern," *Der Emes* (2/19/28), p. 4; advertisements for *Wandering Stars* in *Der Emes* (2/15/28), p. 4; withdrawal of *Wandering Stars* from distribution reported in *Kino* (Moscow) in Denise J. Youngblood, *Soviet Cinema in the Silent Era*, p. 162; thoughts on the new era in Yiddish literature,

Avrahm Yarmolinsky, *The Jews and Other Minor Nationalities Under the Soviets*, p. 131; "Sholom Aleichem," *The Great Soviet Encyclopedia* (New York: Macmillan, 1973), vol. 29, p. 531a; *Mottel the Cantor's Son*, p. 52; Dennen, *Where the Ghetto Ends*, pp. 137–38.

Makotinsky, *"Skvoz Slezy," Kino* (Kiev), March 1928, pp. 8–9, along with Fefer's article of the same name (also in Ukrainian), p. 3, and Fefer's Yiddish "Vegn Yidishn Film" (an excellent translation of which may be found in Goldman, *Visions, Images*, pp. 44–45), p. 2; Daytsherman, "Vegn Yidishn Films," *Der Emes* (3/15/28), p. 5; *Prolit* in Ch. Shmeruke, "Yiddish Literature in the U.S.S.R.," Lionel Kochan, ed., *The Jews in Soviet Russia Since 1917*, p. 259; Fefer's attack on Abchuk in Judel Mark, "Yiddish Literature in Soviet Russia," Gregor Aronson *et al.*, eds., *Russian Jewry, 1917–1967*, pp. 239–240; Markish's letter to Opatoshu in Gitelman, *Jewish Nationality*, pp. 471–72; Lunacharsky in Richard Taylor and Ian Christie, eds., *The Film Factory*, p. 156; Roshal in Goldman, *Visions, Images*, p. 23; Lubomirsky, "Soviet Jewish Dramaturgy," *International Theatre*, January 1934, p. 44; *Seeds of Freedom* reviewed in the *Nation* (9/11/29); Lyons, *Assignment in Utopia*, p. 188; *A Jew at War* reviewed in *New York Times* (7/25/31), p. 11.

Babel's scenario for *Benya Krik* exists in English, *Benya Krik, a Film-Novel*, trans. Ivor Montagu and S. S. Nolbandov (London: Collet's, 1935); a fragment of *Wandering Stars* is included in *The Forgotten Prose*, ed. and trans. Nicholas Stroud (Ann Arbor, Mich: Ardis, 1978). For information on the first All-Union Party Conference on Film Questions, see Richard Taylor's *The Politics of Soviet Cinema*, pp. 107–8; for the Ukrainian Communist Party conference on anti-Semitism see Solomon Schwarz, *The Jews in the Soviet Union* (1951; reprint ed., Salem, N.H.: Ayer Co. Pubs., 1972), p. 283.

11 The Polish Forest

Opatoshu, *In Polish Woods*, trans, Isaac Goldberg (Philadelphia: Jewish Publication Society, 1930), pp. 4, 372; "In

Varshtat fun di *Poylishe Velder*" by Emil [S. L. Shneiderman] and "Fun der Redaktsie," *Film Velt*, September 1928, pp. 6–7, 1; Tenenbaum, *Film Velt*, October 1928, pp. 2–3; Finkelstein in Banaszkiewicz and Witczak, *Historia Filmu Polskiego*, vol. 1, pp. 210–11; Turkow, "Opatoshu in Film," *Literarishe Bleter* (2/14/30), p. 136; Goldman, *Visions, Images*, p. 48.

Interviews: Natan Gross (Jerusalem, July 1988); S. L. Shneiderman (New York, September 1989).

12 The Theater of the Future

Hall, "Al Jolson and the Vitaphone," *New York Times* (10/7/27); "Molly," *New Yorker* (4/27/29); *East Side Sadie* reviewed, *Film Daily* (6/2/29), p. 3; Potamkin, *Compound Cinema*, pp. 362–67; Goldman, *Visions, Images*, p. 56; "Jewish Films in Own Tongue," *Variety* (1/22/30); Mandelbaum, "Khazeray De-Luks: Felyeton," *Morgn Frayhayt* (7/3/30); Almi, "Di Ershte Yidishe Klang-Filmen," *Literarishe Bleter* (7/18/30), p. 548; Schwartz's "betrayal" reported by William Schack in "Again the Yiddish Stage," *New York Times* (9/6/31); D. Kaplan, "Ludwig Satz in Zayn Ershter Yidisher Talkie, A Lustige Komedye," *Forverts* (9/30/31), p. 6; *New York World-Telegram* (9/26/31); Kirstein, "James Cagney and the American Hero," *Hound and Horn*, April 1932, pp. 466–67; Teller, *Strangers and Natives*, p. 145; Schack's characterization of *Uncle Moses*, "The Yiddish Stage's Year," *New York Times* (5/17/31); *Uncle Moses* reviewed, *Morgn Frayhayt* (4/27/32), p. 2, and *Der Tog* (4/28/32); Cahan, *The Rise of David Levinsky* (New York: Harper, 1917), p. 3; Kazin, *A Walker in the City* (New York: Harcourt Brace Jovanovich, 1951), pp. 57, 39–40.

For a report on the Hebrew Actors Union resolution, see the *Forverts* (7/1/30). The demonstrations against *Mayn Yidishe Mame* are detailed in "Yiddish Film Starts Rioting in Palestine," (unidentified clipping, Seiden papers, National Center for Jewish Film); see also Goldman, *Visions, Images*, pp. 61, 64, and Judith Goldberg's *Laughter Through Tears*, p. 61. For a report on an earlier, similar

incident see *Jewish Theatrical News* (4/6/26); for an overview, see Shohat, *Israeli Cinema*, pp. 53–56.

13 Jews of Steel

Lyons, *Moscow Carousel*, pp. 19–20, 39–40, *Assignment in Utopia*, p. 521; *New York Times* (4/22/34); *The Return of Nathan Becker* reviewed in *Variety* (4/25/33), *Daily Worker* (4/19/33), *Forverts*, (4/16/33), p. 5, *Morgn Frayhayt* (4/14/33), p. 7, briefly described in Leyda, *Kino*, p. 288; Dinamov, "Film Art in Soviet White Russia," A. Arossev, ed., *Soviet Cinema* (Moscow: Voks, 1935), p. 115; Markish, *The Long Return*, p. 38; Markish, *Dor Oys, Dor Ayn* excerpted as "Generations" in Joachim Neugroschel, ed. and trans., *The Shtetl: A Creative Anthology of Jewish Life in Eastern Europe* (New York: Marek, 1979) p. 462; Litvakov in Nora Levin, *The Jews in the Soviet Union Since 1917*, p. 208; Dennen, *Where the Ghetto Ends*, p. 60; Scott, *Behind the Urals*, pp. 91–92, 240; Clark, *The Soviet Novel: History as Ritual* (Chicago: University of Chicago Press, 1981), p. 94; Gitelman, *Jewish Nationality*, p. 371.

For the status of Yiddish in Belorussia, see Levin, *Jews in the Soviet Union*, pp. 173–74; for a reference to the first Belorussian talkie, Pearl Attasheva, "News of the Soviet Cinema," *Close Up*, September 1930, p. 180; for information on Sokolov, Mel Gordon's "Program of the Minor Leftists in the Soviet Theatre, 1919–1924" (Ph.D. dissertation, New York University, 1982), p. 205; for an overview of Yiddish socialist realism, Bernard J. Choseed's "Jews in Soviet Literature," in Ernest J. Simmons, ed., *Through the Glass of Soviet Literature: Views of Russian Society* (New York: Columbia University Press, 1961).

Archives: Film Study Center, The Museum of Modern Art, New York (Tom Brandon papers, Joseph Burstyn papers); New York State Archives; William E. Wiener Oral History Library.

14 The *Faryidisht* Film

New York Times (7/5/36), sec. 9, p. 4, also Sigmund Gottlober, "New York's Polyglotic Silver Screen," *Playbill* (c.

1938); *Film Daily* yearbooks, 1931–1940; Turkow, *Literarishe Bleter* (10/1/25), pp. 92–93; on Gartner and Chasin, Goldberg, *Laughter Through Tears*, pp. 64–65, 68; Seiden, undated press release, Seiden papers, National Center for Jewish Film; Burch, "To the Distant Observer: Towards a Theory of Japanese Film," *October*, Spring 1976, p. 34; Niger, *Sholom Aleichem* (New York: 1928), p. 52; Oscherovits, *Forverts* (11/14/33), p. 6; Erens, *The Jew in American Cinema*, pp. 38–39; *Shkheynim* and *Dos Eybike Folk* reviews, *Neighbors* and *A People Eternal* clippings, Billy Rose Theatre Collection, New York Public Library; on *Petterson and Bendel*, *New York Times* (12/6/38).

For information on Davidon see Shohat, *Israeli Cinema*, p. 25., and Davidon's memoirs, *Fated Love* (Tel Aviv: Zmora-Bitan, 1983), pp. 248–49.

Archives: Film Study Center (Brandon papers).

15 Between *Rusland* and *Daytshland*

Olgin, *Morgn Frayhayt* (4/14/33), p. 7; Osherovits, *Forverts* (4/16/33), p. 5; Troy, "*Marius* and Others," *Nation* (5/3/33), p. 511; Horizon reviewed in the *Daily Worker* (5/16/33); *Der Vanderer Yid* reviewed in *Variety* (11/24/33), *New York Times* (10/21/33), *Film Daily* (10/21/33), p. 4, *Forverts* (10/23/33), p. 6; *The House of Rothschild* reviewed in *Variety* (3/20/34); Thalberg in Neal Gabler, *An Empire of Their Own*, p. 338; Warner in Lester D. Friedman, *Hollywood's Image of the Jew*, p. 81; Schack, "Yiddish Season Ends," *New York Times* (3/11/34); J. C. Furnas, "Dedicated to Workers Exclusively," *New York Herald-Tribune* (8/21/32), sec. 7, p. 3; Halper, *Union Square* (New York, 1933), p. 45; *Kino*, in program notes prepared by Naum Kleiman for "The Unknown Soviet Cinema" (1/26/90), The Museum of Modern Art, New York; *Border* reviewed in *Variety* (10/23/35). For a study of "The Romance of a People," see David Garfield, "The Romance of a People," *Education Theater Journal* 24, no. 72 (1973), pp. 436–42.

Archives: Film Study Center (Brandon papers); New York State Archives.

16 *Shund*

Thomas and Ben-Ami, Lawrence, *Actor,* pp. 40, 104; Sandrow, *Vagabond Stars*, p. 129; Howe, *World of Our Fathers*, pp. 482, 493; Thomashefsky in "Yiddish Theater Must Come to Broadway," *Jewish Theatrical News*, November 1924, p. 25; *Shir Hashirim* reviewed in *New York Times* (10/11/35), p. 31, and *Variety* (10/23/35); *Papirosn* reviewed in *Variety* (9/23/36); Adler anecdote, Howe, *World of Our Fathers*, p. 484; Hamilton, "Movie-Maker Joe Seiden Keeps 3-Room Studio Humming; Script for His Latest Epic Cost 20 Cents—And It's a Wow," *Brooklyn Daily Eagle* (4/7/36); *Libe un Laydnshaft* reviewed *Variety* (4/15/36); Howe, *World of Our Fathers*, p. 251; *Motl der Operator* reviewed *Daily News* (1/16/40); Schack on gunmen and Jennie Goldstein, "The Yiddish Theater in Travail," *New York Times* (3/30/30) and "Bernhardt of the Yiddish Stage," *New York Times* (9/21/26); Frye, *The Anatomy of Criticism* (New York: Atheneum, 1967), pp. 41–44; Seiden on special effects in Morris Freedman, "Contemporary of William Fox Still Making Yiddish Films," *New York Herald-Tribune* (11/14/48), on finding actors in Hamilton, "Movie-Maker Joe Seiden"; Fuchs in Goldberg, *Laughter Through Tears*, pp. 77–78.

Interviews: Leon Liebgold (New York, March 1989); Harold Seiden (telephone, December 1989).

17 "We're on Our Way"

Singer, *Love and Exile*, p. 187, see also Celia Heller, *On the Edge of Destruction*, pp. 215, 238–41; Kitai, "Ershter Yidisher Klang-Film, *Al Khet*," *Literarishe Bleter* (5/8/36), p. 305, and "Vegn Klangfilm *Mir Kumin On*," *Literarishe Bleter* (5/15/36), p. 318; Goskind in Natan Gross, "*Al Khet*," *Al Hamishmar* (12/20/85), translation courtesy The National Center for Jewish Film; Neuman, "Plan-Virtshaft in der Film Produktsye," *Literarishe Bleter* (2/3/38), p. 91; *Khalutzim* reviews, Billy Rose Theatre Collection; Cohen, *Travels in Jewry*, p. 113; Dawidowicz, *From That Place and Time*, pp. 147, 21; Goskind and Jabotinsky, Gross,

Toldot Hakolnoa Hayehudi Bepolin, p. 86; *Kino,* in program notes for "The Unknown Soviet Cinema," The Museum of Modern Art, New York; Dennen, *Where the Ghetto Ends,* p. 111; Soviet Central Committee in Schwarz, *Jews in the Soviet Union,* p. 181; Winsten, *New York Post* (10/8/36); Korsh-Sablin in *Moscow Daily News* (10/11/35).

For further information on *Sabra's* production, exhibition, and reception, see Shohat, *Israeli Cinema,* pp. 39–40, and Barbara Armatys *et al., Historia Filmu Polskiego,* vol. 2, p. 225. Information on the making of *Mir Kumin On* drawn from Armatys *et al., Historia Filmu Polskiego,* vol. 2, pp. 170–171, and Lyuba Kantorovitsh Gilinski, "Der Film *Mir Kumin On,*" in Kh. Sh. Kazdan, ed., *Medem Sanatorye Bukh* (Tel Aviv: Menorah Press, 1971), pp. 174–78.

Interviews: Aleksander Ford (New York, 1979), courtesy YIVO sound archives; Joseph Fryd, Polish film critic (letter, June 1989).

18 The Greening of Yiddish Film

Ulmer in Peter Bogdanovich, "Edgar G. Ulmer, An Interview," *Film Culture,* nos. 58–60 (1974), p. 200; Green on *The Jazz Singer,* Goldman, *Visions, Images,* p. 89; Green's regrets regarding *Der Purimshpiler,* Goldberg, *Laughter Through Tears,* p. 108; Green's subsequent citations, unpublished 1974 interview by Patricia Erens (The National Center for Jewish Film), Rob Edelman, "Shtetls and Samovars on Screen," *Brooklyn,* December 1978, p. 52, unpublished 1979 interview by Dr. Geoffrey Wigoder (Oral History Department, Hebrew University, Jerusalem); Green in *Literarishe Bleter* (9/25/36) from Goldman, *Visions, Images,* p. 90; Glatstein, *Homecoming at Twilight,* p. 247; Picon on *Yidl, Molly!* pp. 67–68 (for a more sanguine account see her "Fiddling in Old Kazimierz," *New York Times* [1/17/37]); *Yidl* reviewed in *Variety* (1/6/37); "Jüdischer Todessang," in ZDF telefilm *Das Jiddishe Kino* (Frankfurt, 1985); Polish reviews of *Yidl* and *Der Purimshpiler* in Armatys *et al., Historia Filmu Polskiego,* pp. 306,

316; New York reviews, including *Variety, New York Times* (1/2/37), *New York American* (1/2/37), Billy Rose Theatre Collection; Horak, "Zionist Film Propaganda in Nazi Germany," *Historical Journal of Film, Radio and Television* 4, no. 1 (1984), p. 55.

Sarris, *The American Cinema: Directors and Directions, 1929–1968* (New York: Dutton, 1968), p. 143; Ulmer, Bogdanovich, "Edgar G. Ulmer," pp. 192, 206–8, 210, 212–13, 217–18, 222, and Bill Krohn, "King of the B's," *Film Comment,* July–August 1983, p. 61; *Natalka Poltavka* reviewed as *The Girl from Poltavka* in *Variety* (2/17/37); Lifson, *Yiddish Theater in America,* p. 100; Hirschbein and Mayzel in David Matis, "When Abe Cahan and David Dubinsky Rescued a Yiddish Film," *Forverts* (12/2/83), translation—as well as Edlin's " 'Green Fields' as a Movie," *Der Tog* (10/37)—courtesy The National Center for Jewish Film; Dawidowicz, *From That Place and Time,* p. 23. (For further analysis of Jews and Spanish Civil War, see Melech Epstein, *The Jew and Communism,* p. 304, also source for Zunser, p. 169.) Charles E. Dexter reviewed *Grine Felder, Daily Worker* (10/13/37) p. 7; Collective Film Producer's plans, "New Yiddish Film Producing Outfit, à la Group Theatre," unidentified clipping, Billy Rose Theatre Collection; Beverly, "The Autobiography of Helen Beverly" (12/6/82), unpublished typescript, The National Center for Jewish Film; Potamkin, *Compound Cinema,* p. 368.

For a production story on *Der Purimshpiler,* see "In 'Shtetl' fun dem Grin-Film," *Literarishe Bleter* (8/13/37), p. 533; for an account of *China Strikes Back,* Russell Campbell, *Cinema Strikes Back: Radical Filmmaking in the United States* (Ann Arbor, Mich.: University Microfilms, 1982), p. 195.

Interviews: Ben Bazyler, Polish *klezmer* (Parksville, N.Y., December 1989); Jacob Ben-Ami (New York, April 1976); Reizl Bozyk (New York, June 1989); Michael Gorrin/Goldstein (New York, May 1976); Joseph Green (New York, September 1977); Shirley Ulmer (telephone, September 1990).

19 The Cantor's Sons

Excerpts from *Yosele Solovey,* Aliza Shevrin's translation, *The Nightingale* (New York: Putnam Publishing Group, 1985), pp. 117, 34; on rabbinical disapproval, Slobin, *Tenement Songs,* p. 19; accounts of *Der Vilner Balebesl,* Steinlauf, "Polish-Jewish Theater," pp. 162, 172–77, and Landa, *The Jew in Drama,* p. 291; accounts of Rosenblatt and Sirota, Mark Slobin, *Chosen Voices,* pp. 21, 59–60; Teller, *Strangers and Natives,* p. 71; *Der Mazldiker Bokher* reviewed *Variety* (11/26/35); Oysher profiled, *New Yorker* (1/14/56), pp. 18–19; Mukdoyni in Irving Howe and Kenneth Bibo, *How We Lived,* pp. 261–62; Bernardi in Eric Goldman, "A World History of Yiddish Cinema" (Ph.D. dissertation, New York University, 1979), p. 153; *Yankl der Shmid* reviewed *Der Yidisher Kemfer* (11/25/38); Ulmer, Bogdanovich, "Edgar G. Ulmer," pp. 214–15; "Hollywood in Miniature,'" *New York Daily Mirror* (9/18/38); Green, *Morgn Frayhayt* (7/11/38); *Yankl* was regularly advertised in the *Daily Worker,* Winter 1939; *Der Vilner Shtot Khazn* announced, *New York Times* (8/12/39; 11/6/39); Martin Nossek in Goldberg, *Laughter Through Tears,* p. 99; Glatstein in Harshav, *American Yiddish Poetry,* p. 305.

For the disturbances occasioned by Oysher see "Stage Star Rabbi to Get Police Guard," *New York Evening Journal* (9/9/36), "An Actor or a Cantor, Yiddish Thesp's Worry," *Variety* (7/22/36), and Slobin, *Chosen Voices,* p. 74.

Interviews: Ben Galing, Yiddish performer (Parksville, N.Y., December 1989); Sholom Rubinstein (New York, June 1988); Shirley Ulmer (telephone, September 1990).

20 On the Edge of the Abyss

Characterization of Polish-Jewish youth, Ezra Mendelsohn, *The Jews of East Central Europe Between the Wars,* p. 59; Neuman, *Menorah Journal,* March 1930 and Autumn 1936; Kon, "In Film-Atelye," *Literarishe Bleter* (7/23/37), p. 485; Berg in Michael Alpert, "*Freylekhs* on Film: The Portrayal of Jewish Traditional Dance in Yiddish Cinema," *Jewish Folklore and Ethnology Newsletter* 8, nos. 3–4 (1986), p. 7; Halpern, unpublished 1974 interview with Patricia Erens (The National Center for Jewish Film); Polish reviews of *Der Dibek* in Armatys et al., *Historia Filmu Polskiego,* pp. 308–9; Nugent, *New York Times* (1/28/38); Goebbels in "Dr. Goebbels at the Cinema: 1) Extracts from the Diaries," *Sight and Sound,* August 1950, p. 235.

For a recent view of Lodz's Yiddish avant-garde see S. L. Shneiderman, "A Yiddish Renaissance on the Eve of the Holocaust," *Midstream,* April 1989. Kon's piece on *Der Dibek* followed by one issue another production story, "Af Landshaft-Afnamen tsum Dibuk-Film," published by the pseudonymous M. Filmikus in *Literarishe Bleter* (7/16/37), p. 469.

Interviews: Judith Berg (May 1989, New York); Reizl Bozyk (New York, June 1989); Joseph Fryd (letter, June 1989); Natan Gross (Jerusalem, July 1988); Bernard Hornung, Polish theater owner (October 1989, telephone); Leon Liebgold (New York, March 1989); S. L. Shneiderman (New York, September 1989).

21 Without a Home

Neuman, "Plan-Virtshaft in der Film Produktsye," *Literarishe Bleter* (2/3/38), p. 91; Picon, "The Piquante Miss Picon," *New York Times* (1/8/39); Green in Edelman, "Shtetls and Samovars," p. 54, Erens unpublished interview, 1974, pp. 12–13; Marten in "A Nayer Yidisher Film: A Shmues mitn Rezshiser Aleksander Marten," *Literarishe Bleter* (12/16/38), p. 752; Kaminska, Goldman, *Visions, Images,* p. 109; Hitler in *New York Times* (1/31/39); *On a Heym* reviewed in *Literarishe Bleter* (3/10/39), p. 145; Dawidowicz, *From That Place and Time,* p. 77.

Interviews: Joseph Green (New York, September 1977).

22 Phantom Europe

Confessions of a Nazi Spy reviewed in *New York Times* (4/29/39); Chaver-Paver, *Clinton Street and Other Stories,* p. 211. Mendele, *The Travels and Adventures of Benjamin the*

Third (New York: Schocken, 1968), pp. 92–93; Thomashefsky funeral, *New York Times* (7/11/39); Epstein, *The
Jew and Communism,* p. 350; *Di Klyatshe* reviewed in *New
York Times* (9/23/39), *World Telegram* (9/23/39), *Der Tog*
(9/28/39), *Film Daily* (10/12/39), *Hollywood Reporter* (12/
20/39), see also David Matis, *Forverts* (7/8/73); *Tevye* reviewed in *Morgn Frayhayt* (12/22/39), *Forverts* (12/25/39),
p. 4; Buchwald, "Yidishe Films in Amerike," *Yidishe Kultur* (March 1940), pp. 21–28; Herb Golden, "Negro and
Yiddish Film Boom," *Variety* (1/30/40); *Der Vilner Shtot
Khazn* reviewed in *New York Herald-Tribune* (2/10/40).

For a memoir of *Di Klyatshe*'s reception, see David
Matis, "Mendele Mokhir Sforim in Film," 1957 typescript,
The National Center for Jewish Film; for Opatoshu's ac-
count of the production, Masha Leon, "Interview with
David Opatoshu," *Jewish Daily Forward* (English supple-
ment, 1/16/83); for the production of *Tevye,* Thomas M.
Pryor, "Outside of Jericho," *New York Times* (7/30/39),
sec. 9, p. 3.

Interviews: Leon Liebgold (New York, March 1989);
David Opatoshu (1981, courtesy Mel Gordon); Shirley
Ulmer, (telephone, September 1990).

23 Married to America

Der Vilner Shtot Khazn reviewed in *New York Times* (2/
10/40); Berger, "Bearded Cupid," *New Yorker* (6/11/38);
Reik, *Jewish Wit* (New York: Gamut Press, 1962), pp. 41,
57–58; *Amerikaner Shadkhn* reviewed in *New York Post*
(5/7/40); Goldberg, *Laughter Through Tears,* p. 93; Krohn,
"King of the B's," p. 64; Altman, *The Comic Image of the
Jew: Explorations of a Pop Culture Phenomenon* (Ruther-
ford, N.J.: Fairleigh Dickinson University Press, 1971), p.
198; Freud, *Jokes and their Relation to the Unconscious,*
trans. James Strachey (New York: Norton, 1963), pp. 106,
55; *The Great Dictator* reviewed in *New York Times* (10/
16/40); Davidon, *Fated Love,* pp. 251–54; Cole, *Hollywood
Red: The Autobiography of Lester Cole* (Palo Alto, Calif.:
Ramparts, 1981), pp. 203–6; John T. McManus, "Speaking of Movies: A Job for the Cops and Christianity," *PM*

(5/2/44); Betty Yetta Forman makes a comparison between Nat Gold and Woody Allen's Alvie Sargent (as well
as Abraham Cahan's David Levinsky) in "From *The
American Shadchan* [sic] to *Annie Hall,*" *National Jewish
Monthly,* November 1977, pp. 12–13.

Interviews: Dina Drute and Michael Gorrin/Goldstein
(1981, courtesy Mel Gordon); Lulla Rosenfeld (1981,
courtesy Mel Gordon); Sholom Rubinstein (New York,
June 1988); Shirley Ulmer (telephone, September 1990).

24 The Living Remnant

Kaminska, *My Life,* p. 200; Goldman, *Visions, Images,* p.
144; Ford in Gene Moskowitz, "The Uneasy East: Aleksander Ford and the Polish Cinema," *Sight and Sound,*
Winter 1957–58, p. 137; Yaffe, "Film Bucked Anti-Semitism," *PM* (4/25/50); Matis, "Dzhigan's Lost Films," *Jewish Daily Forward* (English supplement, 4/19/81); *Lang iz
der Veg* reviewed in *Variety* (11/17/48) and *New York
Herald-Tribune* (10/12/48); Freedman, "Contemporary of
William Fox Still Making Yiddish Films," *New York
Herald-Tribune* (11/12/48); *Catskill Honeymoon* reviewed
in *New York Herald-Tribune* (1/28/50).

Information on the resumption of Yiddish filmmaking
in Poland drawn from Natan Gross's "Haseret Hayehudi
Bepolin Acharei Milchemet Haolam Hashniya" *Kolnoa,*
May 1974, pp. 63–71, and *Toldot Hakolnoa Hayehudi
BePolin,* pp. 90–101. For an account of *Unzerer Kinder*'s
rediscovery, see Abe Kramer, "The Late, Late Show,"
Jerusalem Post (3/6/80), and "The Miraculous Recovery of
a Film," *Pioneer Woman,* September 1980, p. 10.

Archives: American Joint Distribution Committee,
New York.

Interviews: Felix Fibich (New York, May 1989); Natan
Gross (Jerusalem, June 1988); Rita Karpinovich, Yiddish
actress (Parksville, N.Y., December 1987).

Epilogue: A Post-Yiddish Cinema

Polish Workers' Party central committee memo in Joseph
Banas, *The Scapegoats,* pp. 29–30; Shakow, *The Theatre*

in Israel (New York: Herzl Press, 1963), pp. 122–23. For a provocative analysis of Israeli *"bourekas"* see Shohat, *Israeli Cinema,* pp. 121–39.

Archives: Jerusalem Cinémathèque.

Interviews: Michael Burstein (telephone, November 1986); Israel Ringel, Israeli producer (telephone, December 1986).

Appendix

Yardeini, *Words and Music,* trans. and ed. Max Rosenfeld (New York: YKUF, 1986), p. 202; Burstein, *Memoirs of the Yiddish Stage,* ed. Joseph Landis (Flushing, N.Y.: Queens College Press, 1984), pp. 210–11; Donald Cordry, "Punch Goes Red," *Puppetry: A Yearbook of Puppets and Marionettes,* 1934, pp. 9–10; Vancura in Pavel Taussig's "On the Sunny Side of Film," *Czech Modernism: 1900–45* (Houston: Museum of Fine Arts, 1989); *Der Vanderer Yid* and *Michael Strogoff* advertised in the *Forverts* (9/9/33); Turkow, *Di Ibergerisene Tkufe.* Ruthenian illiteracy is analysed in Alexander Baran, "Jewish-Ukrainian Relations in Transcarpathia," Peter J. Potichnyj and Howard Aster, eds., *Ukrainian-Jewish Relations in Historical Perspective* (Edmonton, Alta.: Canadian Institute of Ukrainian Studies, 1988), p. 163.

Archives: Film Study Center (Burstyn papers).

Interviews: Philip Cutler (telephone, June 1989); Rose Cutler Helfand (New Jersey, June 1989); Itche Goldberg (New York, September 1989).

Selected Bibliography

Books

Abramsky, Chimen; Jachimczyk, Maciej; and Polonsky, Antony (eds.). *The Jews in Poland.* Oxford: Basil Blackwell, 1986.

Apter-Gabriel, Ruth (ed.). *Tradition and Revolution: The Jewish Renaissance in Russian Avant-Garde Art, 1912–1928.* Jerusalem: Israel Museum, 1986.

Armatys, Barbara; Armatys, Leszek; and Stradomski, Wiesław. *Historia Filmu Polskiego,* vol. 2, *1930–1939.* Warsaw: Wydawnictwa Artystyczne i Filmowe, 1988.

Aronson, Gregor; Frumkin, Jacob; Goldenweiser, Alexis; and Lewitan, Joseph (eds.). *Russian Jewry, 1917–1967.* New York: Yoseloff, 1969.

Aschheim, Stephen. *Brothers and Strangers: The East European Jew in German and German Jewish Consciousness, 1800–1923.* Madison: University of Wisconsin Press, 1982.

Babel, Nathalie (ed.). *Isaac Babel: The Lonely Years, 1925–1939.* New York: Farrar, Straus, 1964.

Babitsky, Paul, and Rinberg, John. *The Soviet Film Industry.* New York: Praeger, 1955.

Banas, Joseph. *The Scapegoats: The Exodus of the Remnants of Polish Jewry.* London: Weidenfeld & Nicholson, 1979.

Banaszkiewicz, Władysław, and Witczak, Witold. *Historia Filmu Polskiego,* vol. 1, *1895–1929.* Warsaw: Wydawnictwa Artystyczne i Filmowe, 1989.

Baron, Salo W. *The Russian Jew Under the Tsars and Soviets.* New York: Schocken, 1987.

Beckermann, Ruth. *Die Mazzesinsel: Juden in der Wiener Leopoldstadt.* Vienna: Locker Verlag, 1984.

Ben-Ari, Raikin. *Habima.* Translated by A. H. Gross and I. Soref. New York: Yoseloff, 1957.

Ben-Nun, D. *The Jews in Latvia.* Tel Aviv: Association of Latvian and Estonian Jews in Israel, 1971.

Berest, Boris. *History of the Ukrainian Cinema*. New York: Schevchenko Scientific Study, 1962.

Bogen, Boris D. *Born a Jew*. New York: Macmillan, 1930.

Bren, Frank. *World Cinema: Poland*. Champaign: University of Illinois Press, 1988.

Bristow, Edward J. *Prostitution and Prejudice: The Jewish Fight against White Slavery*. New York: Schocken, 1983.

Brownlow, Kevin. *Behind the Mask of Innocence*. New York: Knopf, 1990.

———. *The Parade's Gone By*. New York, Knopf, 1968.

Burko, Faina. "The Soviet Yiddish Theatre in the Twenties." Ph. D. dissertation, Southern Illinois University at Carbondale, 1978.

Butwin, Joseph, and Butwin, Frances. *Sholom Aleichem*. Boston: Twayne, 1977.

Carter, Huntly. *The New Spirit in the Cinema*. New York: Arno, 1970.

Chaver-Paver. *Clinton Street and Other Stories*. Translated by Henry Goodman. New York: YKUF, 1974.

Cohen, Israel. *Travels in Jewry*. New York: Dutton, 1953.

Cohen, Sarah Blancher (ed.). *From Hester Street to Hollywood: The Jewish American Stage and Screen*. Bloomington: Indiana University Press, 1983.

Csato, Edward. *The Polish Theater*. Translated by Christina Cenkalska. Warsaw: Polonia, 1963.

Cypkin, Diane. "Second Avenue: The Yiddish Broadway." Ph.D. dissertation, New York University, 1986.

Dawidowicz, Lucy S. (ed.). *The Golden Tradition: Jewish Life and Thought in Eastern Europe*. New York: Schocken, 1984.

———. *From That Place and Time: A Memoir, 1938–1947*. New York: Norton, 1989.

Dennen, Leon. *Where the Ghetto Ends: Jews in Soviet Russia*. New York: Alfred H. King, 1934.

Dobroszycki, Lucjan, and Kirshenblatt-Gimblett, Barbara. *Image Before My Eyes: A Photographic History of Jewish Life in Poland, 1864–1939*. New York: Schocken/YIVO, 1977.

Dunin-Wasowicz, Krzysztof. *Warszawa, 1914–1918*. Warsaw: Panstwowe Wydawnictwo Navkowe, 1989.

Duranty, Walter. *I Write as I Please*. New York: Simon & Schuster, 1935.

Epstein, Melech. *The Jew and Communism*. New York: Trade Union Sponsoring Committee, 1959.

Erens, Patricia. *The Jew in American Cinema*. Bloomington: Indiana University Press, 1984.

Flior, Yudel. *Dvinsk: The Rise and Decline of a Town*. Translated by Bernard Sachs. Johannesburg: Dial Press, 1956.

Frick, John W. *New York's First Theatrical Center: The Rialto at Union Square*. Ann Arbor, Mich.: UMI Research Press, 1985.

Friedman, Lester D. *Hollywood's Image of the Jew*. New York: Ungar, 1982.

Fritz, Walter. *Kino in Osterreich, 1896–1930*. Vienna: Osterreichischer Bundesverlag, 1981.

Gabler, Neal. *An Empire of Their Own: How the Jews Invented Hollywood*. New York: Crown, 1988.

Geipel, John. *Mame Loshn: The Making of Yiddish*. London: Journeyman, 1982.

Gilboa, Yehoshua. *The Black Years of Soviet Jewry, 1939–1953*. Boston: Little, Brown, 1971.

Gilman, Sander L. *Jewish Self-Hatred: Anti-Semitism and the Hidden Language of the Jews*. Baltimore: Johns Hopkins University Press, 1986.

Gitelman, Zvi Y. *A Century of Ambivalence: The Jews of Russia and the Soviet Union, 1881 to the Present*. New York: Schocken/YIVO, 1988.

———. *Jewish Nationality and Soviet Politics: The Jewish Sections of the CPSU, 1917–1930*. Princeton, N.J.: Princeton University Press, 1972.

Glatstein, Jacob. *Homecoming at Twilight*. New York: Yoseloff, 1962.

Glicksman, William M. *In the Mirror of Literature*. New York: Living Books, 1966.

Goldberg, Judith N. *Laughter Through Tears: The Yiddish Cinema*. East Brunswick, N.J.: Fairleigh Dickinson University Press, 1983.

Goldman, Eric A. *Visions, Images, and Dreams: Yiddish Film Past and Present*. Ann Arbor, Mich.: UMI Research Press, 1983.

———. "A World History of Yiddish Cinema." Ph.D. dissertation, New York University, 1979.

Goldsmith, Emanuel S. *Modern Yiddish Culture: The Story*

of the Yiddish Language Movement. New York: Shapolsky, 1987.

Grafstein, Melech (ed.). *Sholom Aleichem Panorama.* London, Ont.: The Jewish Observer, 1948.

Gross, Natan. *Toldot Hakolnoa Hayehudi Bepolin: 1910–1950.* Jerusalem: Magnes Press, 1990.

Hapgood, Hutchins. *The Spirit of the Ghetto: Studies of the Jewish Quarter of New York.* New York: Schocken, 1966.

Heller, Celia. *On the Edge of Destruction.* New York: Columbia University Press, 1977.

Heller, Mikhail, and Nekrich, Aleksandr M. *Utopia in Power: The History of the Soviet Union from 1917 to the Present.* New York: Summit Books, 1986.

Hertz, Aleksander. *The Jews in Polish Culture.* Translated by Richard Lourie. Evanston, Ill.: Northwestern University Press, 1988.

Howe, Irving, and Libo, Kenneth. *How We Lived: A Documentary History of Immigrant Jews in America, 1880–1930.* New York: Marek, 1979.

———. *World of Our Fathers: The Journey of the East European Jews to America and the Life They Found and Made.* New York: Schocken, 1989.

Hurwic-Nowakowska, Irena. *A Social Analysis of Postwar Polish Jewry.* Jerusalem: Zalman Shazar Center, 1986.

Kahan, Arcadius. *Essays in Jewish Social and Economic History.* Chicago: University of Chicago Press, 1986.

Kaminska, Ida. *My Life, My Theater.* Edited and translated by Curt Leviant. New York: Macmillan, 1973.

Kampf, Avram. *Jewish Experience in the Art of the Twentieth Century.* South Hadley, Mass.: Begin & Garvey, 1984.

Kochan, Lionel (ed.). *The Jews in Soviet Russia Since 1917.* Oxford: Oxford University Press, 1978.

Kugelmass, Jack, and Boyarin, Jonathan. *From a Ruined Garden: The Memorial Books of Polish Jewry.* New York: Schocken, 1983.

Landa, M. J. *The Jew in Drama.* Port Washington, N.Y.: Kennikat Press, 1968.

Landis, Joseph (ed.). *Memoirs of the Yiddish Stage.* Flushing, N.Y.: Queens College Press, 1984.

Lawrence, Jerome. *Actor: The Life and Times of Paul Muni.* New York: Putnam, 1975.

Leftwich, Joseph (ed.). *Great Yiddish Writers of the Twentieth Century.* Northvale, N.J.: Aronson, 1987.

Levin, Nora. *The Jews in the Soviet Union Since 1917: Paradox of Survival.* New York: New York University Press, 1988.

Levine, Ira A. *Left-wing Dramatic Theory in the American Theatre.* Ann Arbor, Mich.: UMI Research Press, 1985.

Leyda, Jay. *Kino: A History of the Russian and Soviet Film.* New York: Collier, 1973.

Leyda, Jay, and Voynow, Zina. *Eisenstein at Work.* New York: Pantheon/The Museum of Modern Art, 1982.

Lifson, David. *The Yiddish Theater in America.* New York: Yoseloff, 1965.

Liptzin, Sol. *The Flowering of Yiddish Literature.* New York: Yoseloff, 1963.

———. *The Maturing of Yiddish Literature.* New York: Jonathan David, 1970.

Lvov-Rogachevsky, V. *A History of Russian Jewish Literature.* Ann Arbor, Mich.: Ardis, 1979.

Lyons, Eugene. *Assignment in Utopia.* New York: Harcourt Brace, 1937.

———. *Moscow Carousel.* New York: Knopf, 1935.

Macleod, Joseph. *The New Soviet Theater.* London: G. Allen & Unwin, 1943.

Madison, Charles. *Yiddish Literature.* New York: Schocken, 1971.

Marcus, Joseph. *Social and Political History of the Jews in Poland, 1919–1939.* New York: Mouton, 1983.

Markish, Esther. *The Long Return.* New York: Ballantine, 1978.

Mendelsohn, Ezra. *Class Struggle in the Pale: The Formative Years of the Jewish Workers' Movement in Tsarist Russia.* Cambridge: Cambridge University Press, 1970.

———. *The Jews of East Central Europe Between the World Wars.* Bloomington: Indiana University Press, 1983.

———. *Zionism in Poland: The Formative Years, 1915–1926.* New Haven: Yale University Press, 1981.

Miller, Jack (ed.). *Jews in Soviet Culture.* London: Institute of Jewish Affairs, 1984.

Miller, James. *The Detroit Yiddish Theater, 1920–37.* Detroit: Wayne State University Press, 1967.

Moore, Deborah Dash. *At Home in America: Second Generation New York Jews.* New York: Columbia University Press, 1981.

Nahsen, Edna. "The Arbeter Teater Farbund (ARTEF): An Artistic and Political History, 1925–1940." Ph.D. dissertation, New York University, 1988.

Petric, Vladimir K. "Soviet Revolutionary Films in America, 1926–1935." Ph.D. dissertation, New York University, 1973.

Picon, Molly. *Molly!* New York: Simon & Schuster, 1980.

Potichnyj, Peter J., and Aster, Howard (eds.). *Ukrainian-Jewish Relations in Historical Perspective.* Edmonton, Alta.: Canadian Institute of Ukrainian Studies, 1988.

Rabinowicz, Harry. *The Legacy of Polish Jewry, 1919–1939.* New York, Yoseloff, 1965.

Rischin, Moses. *The Promised City: New York's Jews, 1870–1914.* New York: Harper & Row, 1970.

Roback, A. A. *The History of Yiddish Literature.* New York: YIVO, 1940.

Rosenfeld, Lulla. *Bright Star of Exile: Jacob Adler and the Yiddish Theater.* New York: Crowell, 1977.

Roskies, David G. *Against the Apocalypse: Responses to Catastrophe in Modern Jewish Culture.* Cambridge: Harvard University Press, 1984.

Roskies, David G., and Roskies, Diane G. *The Shtetl Book.* New York: KTAV, 1975.

Sanders, Ronald. *The Downtown Jews: Portraits of an Immigrant Generation.* New York: Harper & Row, 1969.

———. *Shores of Refuge: A Hundred Years of Jewish Immigration.* New York: Schocken, 1988.

Sandrow, Nahma. *Vagabond Stars: A World History of Yiddish Theater.* New York: Harper & Row, 1979.

Schoenfeld, Joachim. *Shtetl Memoirs: Jewish Life in Galicia under the Austro-Hungarian Empire and in the Reborn Poland, 1898–1939.* Hoboken, N.J.: KTAV, 1985.

Scott, John. *Behind the Urals: An American Worker in Russia's City of Steel.* Cambridge: Houghton Mifflin, 1942.

Secunda, Victoria. *Bei Mir Bist Du Schon: The Life of Sholom Secunda.* Weston, Conn.: MagiCircle Press, 1982.

Seller, Maxine Schwartz (ed.). *Ethnic Theater in the United States.* Westport, Conn.: Greenwood, 1983.

Shneiderman, S. L. *The River Remembers.* New York: Horizon, 1978.

Shohat, Ella. *Israeli Cinema: East/West and the Politics of Representation.* Austin: University of Texas Press, 1989.

Slobin, Mark. *Chosen Voices: The Story of the American Cantorate.* Urbana: University of Illinois Press, 1989.

———. *Tenement Songs: The Popular Music of Jewish Immigrants.* Urbana: University of Illinois Press, 1982.

Steinlauf, M. C. "Polish-Jewish Theater: The Case of Mark Arnshteyn." Ph.D. dissertation, Brandeis University, 1988.

Szajkowski, Zosa. *Jews, Wars, and Communism.* Vol. 1, *The Attitude of American Jews to World War I, the Russian Revolutions of 1917, and Communism (1914–1945).* New York: KTAV, 1972.

———. *Jews, Wars, and Communism.* Vol. 2: *The Impact of the 1919–20 Red Scare on American Jewish Life.* New York: KTAV, 1974.

———. *The Mirage of American Jewish Aid in Soviet Russia, 1917–1939.* New York: Szajko Frydman, 1977.

Taylor, Richard. *The Politics of Soviet Cinema, 1917–1929.* Cambridge: Cambridge University Press, 1979.

Taylor, Richard, and Christie, Ian (eds.). *The Film Factory: Russian and Soviet Cinema in Documents, 1896–1939.* Cambridge: Harvard University Press, 1988.

Teller, Judd L. *Strangers and Natives: The Evolution of the American Jew from 1921 to the Present.* New York: Delacorte, 1968.

Tenenbaum, Joseph. *Underground: Story of a People.* New York: Philosophical Library, 1952.

Tsivian, Yuri, *et al.* (eds.). *Silent Witnesses: Russian Films, 1908–1919.* London: British Film Institute, 1989.

Waife-Goldberg, Marie. *My Father, Sholom Aleichem.* New York: Simon & Schuster, 1968.

Wat, Alexander, *My Century: The Odyssey of a Polish Intellectual.* Edited and translated by Richard Lourie. Berkeley: University of California Press, 1988.

Weinrich, Beatrice Silverman (ed.). *Yiddish Folktales.* Translated by Leonard Wolf. New York: Schocken, 1988.

Weisser, Albert. *The Modern Renaissance of Jewish Music: Events and Figures Eastern Europe and America.* New York: Bloch, 1954.

Wisse, Ruth R. *A Little Love in Big Manhattan.* Cambridge: Harvard University Press, 1988.

Wynot, Edward D., Jr. *Warsaw Between the World Wars: Profile of the Capital City in a Developing Land, 1918–1939.* Boulder, Colo.: East European Monographs, 1983.

Yardeini, Mordecai. *Words and Music.* Translated and edited by Max Rosenfeld. New York: YKUF, 1986.

Yarmolinsky, Avrahm. *The Jews and Other Minor Nationalities Under the Soviets.* New York: Vanguard, 1928.

Youngblood, Denise J. *Soviet Cinema in the Silent Era, 1918–1935.* Ann Arbor, Mich.: UMI Research Press, 1985.

Zborowski, Mark, and Herzog, Elizabeth. *Life Is With People: The Culture of the Shtetl.* New York: Schocken, 1962.

Zylberzweig, Zalmen. *Leksikon fun Yidishn Teater.* 6 vols. New York and Mexico City: Hebrew Actors Union, 1931, 1959, 1961, 1967.

Articles

Adler, Lois. "Alexis Granovsky and the Jewish State Theatre of Moscow." *Drama Review* 24, no. 3 (September 1980).

Alpert, Michael. "*Freylekhs* on Film: The Portrayal of Jewish Traditional Dance in Yiddish Cinema." *Jewish Folklore and Ethnology Newsletter* 8, nos. 3–4 (1986).

Attasheva, Pearl. "News of the Soviet Cinema." *Close Up* 8, no. 3 (September 1930).

Bogdanovich, Peter. "Edgar G. Ulmer, An Interview." *Film Culture,* nos. 58–60 (1974).

Buchwald, Nathaniel. "Yidishe Films in Amerike." *Yidishe Kultur,* March 1940.

Christie, Ian. "Soviet Cinema: Making Sense of Sound." *Screen* 23, no. 2 (July–August 1982).

Edelman, Rob. "Shtetls and Samovars on Screen." *Brooklyn,* December 1978.

Fefer, I. "*Skvoz Slezy.*" *Kino* (Kiev), March 1928.

———. "Vegn Yidishn Film." *Kino* (Kiev), March 1928.

Fishman, Pearl. "Vakhtangov's *The Dybbuk.*" *Drama Review* 24, no. 3 (September 1980).

Garfield, David. "The Romance of a People." *Education Theater Journal* 24, no. 72 (1973).

Goldman, Eric A. "The Soviet Yiddish Film, 1925–1933." *Soviet Jewish Affairs* 10, no. 3 (1980).

Gordon Mel. "Granovsky's Tragic Carnival: *Night in the Old Market.*" *Drama Review* 29, no. 4 (Winter 1985).

Gross, Natan. "*Al Khet.*" *Al Hamishmar* (12/20/85)

———. "Haseret Hayehudi Bepolin Acharei Milchemet Haoloam Hashniya." *Kolnoa,* May 1974.

Horak, Jan-Christopher. "Zionist Propaganda in Nazi Germany." *Historical Journal of Film, Radio and Television* 4, no. 1 (1984).

Iangirov, Rashid. "Jewish Life on the Screen in Russia, 1908–1919." *Jews and Jewish Topics in the Soviet Union and Eastern Europe,* Spring 1990.

Kitai, Michel. "Ershter Yidisher Klangfilm, *Al Khet.*" *Literarishe Bleter* (5/8/36).

———. "Vegn Klangfilm *Mir Kumin On.*" *Literarishe Bleter* (5/15/36).

Krohn, Bill. "King of the B's." *Film Comment,* July–August 1983.

Leyda, Jay. "New Soviet Movies: Films of the National Minorities." *New Theater* 2, no. 1 (January 1935).

Makotinsky, M. "*Skvoz Slezy.*" *Kino* (Kiev), March 1928.

Matis, David. "Sholom Aleichem fun Film." *Kultur un Lebn,* December 1981.

———. "Tsu der Geshikhte fun Yidishe Film." *YKUF-Almanak* (New York, 1961).

Neuman, J. M. "Plan-virtshaft in der Film Produktsye." *Literarishe Bleter* (2/3/38).

Prizel, Zoya. "The Narrator in Sholom Aleichem's 'The Enchanted Tailor.'" *Yiddish* 2, no. 4 (Summer 1977).

Rosenbaum, David. "The First Picture Show." *Film Comment,* March–April 1975.

Rothman, N. L. "The Jew on the Screen." *Jewish Forum,* October 1928.

Shneiderman, S. L. "A Yiddish Renaissance on the Eve of the Holocaust." *Midstream,* April 1989.

Journals and Newspapers

Der Tog (New York, 1919–45)

Der Emes (Moscow, 1925–28)

Film Velt (Warsaw, 1928–29)

Forverts (New York, 1921–50)

Jewish Currents (New York, 1965–77)

Jewish Theatrical News (New York, 1924–26)

Literarishe Bleter (Warsaw, 1924–39)

Menorah Journal (New York, 1923–37)

Morgn Frayhayt (New York, 1926–50)

Motion Picture News (New York, 1915)

Moving Picture World (New York, 1913–19)

Nasz Przeglad (Warsaw, 1937)

New York Dramatic Mirror (New York, 1913–14)

Teater un Moving Pikshurs (New York, 1913)

Universal World (New York, 1913)

Variety (New York, 1913–1980)

Wiener Morgenzeitung (Vienna, 1921)

Photograph Credits

Steven Spielberg Jewish Film Archive, Jerusalem/David Matis Collection: 6, 76, 77, 79, 109, 130, 131 (top), 164, 180, 184, 196, 286, 356

Paolo Cherchi Usai/Gosfilmofond/Le Giornate del Cinema Muto: 15, 16, 19

Western Jewish History Center, Judah L. Magnes Memorial Museum, Berkeley/Bassya Maltzer and Philip Biber Collection: 153

Yivo Institute for Jewish Research, New York: 4, 12, 21, 41, 56, 95, 107, 115, 126 (top), 131 (bottom), 133, 142, 144, 145, 152, 155 (top), 160 (bottom), 207, 209, 220, 238, 240, 242, 260, 261 (bottom), 262, 277

Index

Numbers in italics refer to illustrations or to their captions.